THE SELECTED WORKS OF GORDON TULLOCK

VOLUME 1

Virginia Political Economy

THE SELECTED WORKS OF GORDON TULLOCK

VOLUME 1 *Virginia Political Economy*

VOLUME 2 *The Calculus of Consent: Logical Foundations of Constitutional Democracy* (with James M. Buchanan)

VOLUME 3 *The Organization of Inquiry*

VOLUME 4 *The Economics of Politics*

VOLUME 5 *The Rent-Seeking Society*

VOLUME 6 *Bureaucracy*

VOLUME 7 *The Economics and Politics of Wealth Redistribution*

VOLUME 8 *The Social Dilemma: Of Autocracy, Revolution, Coup d'Etat, and War*

VOLUME 9 *Law and Economics*

VOLUME 10 *Economics without Frontiers* (includes a cumulative index for the series)

Gordon Tullock

THE SELECTED WORKS

OF GORDON TULLOCK

VOLUME 1

Virginia Political Economy

GORDON TULLOCK

Edited and with an Introduction by

CHARLES K. ROWLEY

Liberty Fund

This book is published by Liberty Fund, Inc., a foundation established to encourage study of the ideal of a society of free and responsible individuals.

The cuneiform inscription that serves as our logo and as the design motif for our endpapers is the earliest-known written appearance of the word "freedom" (*amagi*), or "liberty." It is taken from a clay document written about 2300 B.C. in the Sumerian city-state of Lagash.

Printed in the United States of America

Paperback cover photo courtesy of the *American Economic Review*

Frontispiece courtesy of Center for Study of Public Choice, George Mason University, Fairfax, Virginia

11 19 20 21 22 C 6 5 4 3 2
19 20 21 22 23 P 8 7 6 5 4

Library of Congress Cataloging-in-Publication Data
Tullock, Gordon.
Virginia political economy / Gordon Tullock, edited and with an introduction by Charles K. Rowley.
p. cm. — (The selected works of Gordon Tullock ; v. 1)
Includes bibliographical references and index.
ISBN 0-86597-520-5 (alk. paper) — ISBN 0-86597-531-0 (pbk. : alk. paper)
1. Social choice. 2. Economics—Political aspects. 3. Economics—Sociological aspects. 4. Tullock, Gordon. I. Rowley, Charles Kershaw. II. Title.
HB846.8.T837 2004
330—dc22

2003065963

LIBERTY FUND, INC.
11301 North Meridian Street
Carmel, Indiana 46032

CONTENTS

Introduction, *by Charles K. Rowley* xi
Gordon Tullock, *by Mark Blaug* xxv
Gordon Tullock: Distinguished Fellow, 1998 xxvii

1. GENESIS
Economic Imperialism 3
Public Choice 16
Public Choice: What I Hope for the Next Twenty-five Years 27
Casual Recollections of an Editor 36

2. PROBLEMS OF MAJORITY VOTING
Problems of Majority Voting 51
The Irrationality of Intransitivity 62
Entry Barriers in Politics 69
Federalism: Problems of Scale 78
The General Irrelevance of the General Impossibility Theorem 90
Why So Much Stability 105
Is There a Paradox of Voting? 124

3. THE DEMAND-REVEALING PROCESS
A New and Superior Process for Making Social Choices
(*T. Nicolaus Tideman and Gordon Tullock*) 133
The Demand-Revealing Process as a Welfare Indicator 149
Demand-Revealing Process, Coalitions, and Public Goods 164

4. RENT SEEKING
The Welfare Costs of Tariffs, Monopolies, and Theft 169
The Cost of Transfers 180
More on the Welfare Costs of Transfers 194
Competing for Aid 199
The Transitional Gains Trap 212

Efficient Rent Seeking 222

Rent Seeking 237

5. REDISTRIBUTIVE POLITICS

Inheritance Justified 247

Inheritance Rejustified 258

The Charity of the Uncharitable 262

The Rhetoric and Reality of Redistribution 276

6. BUREAUCRACY

Dynamic Hypothesis on Bureaucracy 297

The Expanding Public Sector: Wagner Squared (*James M. Buchanan and Gordon Tullock*) 302

7. THE SOCIAL DILEMMA

The Edge of the Jungle 309

Corruption and Anarchy 323

The Paradox of Revolution 329

Rationality and Revolution 341

8. THE PROBLEM OF SOCIAL COST

Public and Private Interaction under Reciprocal Externality (*James M. Buchanan and Gordon Tullock*) 349

Social Cost and Government Action 378

Public Decisions as Public Goods 388

Information without Profit 394

Polluters' Profits and Political Response: Direct Controls versus Taxes (*James M. Buchanan and Gordon Tullock*) 412

Polluters' Profits and Political Response: Direct Controls versus Taxes: Reply (*James M. Buchanan and Gordon Tullock*) 425

Hawks, Doves, and Free Riders 427

9. LAW AND ECONOMICS

An Economic Approach to Crime 441

The Costs of a Legal System (*Warren F. Schwartz and Gordon Tullock*) 456

On the Efficient Organization of Trials 465

On the Efficient Organization of Trials: Reply to McChesney, and Ordover and Weitzman 480

Judicial Errors and a Proposal for Reform (*I. J. Good and Gordon Tullock*) 484

Court Errors 495

Legal Heresy: Presidential Address to the Western Economic Association Annual Meeting—1995 509

Juries 521

10. BIOECONOMICS

The Coal Tit as a Careful Shopper 537

Biological Externalities 541

Biological Applications of Economics 553

The Economics of (Very) Primitive Societies 558

11. IN THE PUBLIC INTEREST

A (Partial) Rehabilitation of the Public Interest Theory 577

How to Do Well While Doing Good! 589

APPENDIXES

Gordon Tullock: Biographical Note 605

Contents of the Selected Works of Gordon Tullock 611

Index 623

INTRODUCTION

Scope and Method for the Series

Virginia Political Economy is the first volume in a series comprising the Selected Works of Gordon Tullock.[1] The series consists of ten volumes of selections from the major monographs and scholarly papers published by Gordon Tullock between 1954 and 2002. Volumes 2 and 3 were originally published as monographs and are here republished in their entirety, including the original prefaces, introductions, forewords, and any appendixes. Volumes 6 and 9 include works originally published as stand-alone monographs. The remainder of the series consists of collections of chapters in books, papers, and essays by Tullock arranged by theme.

In selecting the papers for this initial volume, I was guided by a few important principles. First, the volume should reflect the full range of Tullock's scholarship. Second, I have favored the early classic statements by Tullock over later restatements. Third, I have favored the more general essays and papers over narrower and more technical contributions.

The series does not purport to be the entire collected works of Gordon Tullock. I have omitted a number of his papers and essays as well as portions of some monographs, in part to avoid an unnecessary degree of overlap, in part to satisfy space constraints. I believe, however, that the intellectual coverage of the series is complete in all essential respects. Only material published before December 31, 2002, was considered for inclusion.

In general I have restricted my editing to ensuring homogeneity of style and reference conventions, and to the correction of typographical errors, conspicuous grammatical errors, and errors of fact. As editor, I have attempted to highlight links between specific contributions and other themes in Tullock's work, to discuss the significance of the relevant monograph or group of papers in Tullock's thought, and to place Tullock's work in the context of other literature. To this end I have written a separate introduction for each volume. An index has been prepared for each volume, and a cumulative index for the series is included in volume 10.

Gordon Tullock has provided relevant materials whenever asked, but oth-

1. Hereafter referred to as the Selected Works or the series.

erwise has played no role in the editorial process. I bear the full responsibility over all matters of inclusion and exclusion, over the titles of each volume, and over the location of books, essays, and papers through the series.

Content for Volume 1

Gordon Tullock is a founding father of the Virginia School of Political Economy. *Virginia Political Economy*, the first volume of the Selected Works of Gordon Tullock, comprises a selection from Tullock's published academic papers and essays designed to introduce the series and to offer a representative picture of his work. Every paper published here reflects an aspect of the traditions of that school both in its normative and positive dimensions.

The volume begins with the only two pieces in the Selected Works that are not written by Tullock himself. The first is the brief assessment of Tullock's contributions Mark Blaug made in 1985 when explaining why he had included Tullock in his list of the one hundred great economists since John Maynard Keynes.[2] The second is the short statement published in the *American Economic Review* in September 1998, recognizing Tullock as a distinguished fellow of the American Economic Association.[3]

Gordon Tullock is an economist by nature rather than by training.[4] He attended a one-semester course in economics for law students given by Henry Simons at the University of Chicago, but is otherwise self-taught. For most budding economists, such a background would be a handicap. In Tullock's case, arguably it has proved to be an enormous advantage, enabling him to deploy his formidable intellect in a truly entrepreneurial manner.[5] The papers included in "Genesis," the introductory part of this volume, reflect various aspects of this facility.

"Economic Imperialism," the first paper, deals with the issue of economic

2. Mark Blaug, "Gordon Tullock," in *Great Economists since Keynes: An Introduction to the Lives and Works of One Hundred Modern Economists*, ed. Mark Blaug (Brighton: Wheatsheaf, 1985), 252–53.

3. "Gordon Tullock, Distinguished Fellow, 1998," *American Economic Review* 88 (September 1998): ii.

4. James M. Buchanan, "The Qualities of a Natural Economist," in *Democracy and Public Choice: Essays in Honor of Gordon Tullock*, ed. Charles K. Rowley (Oxford and New York: Basil Blackwell Publishing, 1987), 9–19.

5. Charles K. Rowley, "Gordon Tullock: Entrepreneur of Public Choice," *Public Choice* 71 (September 1991): 149–70.

imperialism[6] and highlights three important aspects of Tullock's scholarship, namely the importance that he attaches to the rational choice approach as the scientific basis of economic analysis, his resistance to conforming to rigid disciplinary boundaries, and his ingenuity in locating creative solutions to apparently insurmountable obstacles.

The second paper reprints "Public Choice," Tullock's definitional article on public choice,[7] a field he helped to create and develop. In "Public Choice—What I Hope for the Next Twenty-five Years," Tullock outlines a range of topics in public choice that he believes need more attention by scholars if they are to extend their influence over public policy.[8] His suggestions bore fruit as public choice scholars pursued such policy-relevant research in light of his paper.

"Casual Recollections of an Editor," the fourth paper, chronicles Tullock's career as editor of *Public Choice*, which began as an attempt to provide a publishing outlet for papers that would otherwise be spurned by the conventional mainstream journals in economics and political science.[9] His tenure as editor was twenty-five years, a quarter century that carried public choice from its early beginnings to its ultimate recognition as a significant field of study.

Part 2 of this volume brings together seven papers by Tullock that deal with a variety of potential problems of majority voting.

The first, "Problems of Majority Voting,"[10] deals with problems of majority voting as a basis for allocating scarce resources and paves the way for *The Calculus of Consent*.[11] In 1959, most economists and almost all political scientists were strong supporters of the majority vote principle, not because

6. Gordon Tullock, "Economic Imperialism," in *Theory of Public Choice: Political Applications of Economics*, ed. James M. Buchanan and Robert D. Tollison (Ann Arbor: University of Michigan Press, 1972), 317–29.

7. Gordon Tullock, "Public Choice," in *The New Palgrave: A Dictionary of Economics*, vol. 3, ed. John Eatwell, Murray Milgate, and Peter Newman (London: Macmillan, 1987), 1040–44.

8. Gordon Tullock, "Public Choice—What I Hope for the Next Twenty-five Years," *Public Choice* 77 (January 1993): 9–16.

9. Gordon Tullock, "Casual Recollections of an Editor," *Public Choice* 71 (September 1991): 121–39.

10. Gordon Tullock, "Problems of Majority Voting," *Journal of Political Economy* 67 (December 1959): 571–79.

11. James M. Buchanan and Gordon Tullock, *The Calculus of Consent: Logical Foundations of Constitutional Democracy* (Ann Arbor: University of Michigan Press, 1962).

they were acquainted with the median voter theorem, but because they believed that democratic elections enabled simple majorities to dominate policy over an electoral cycle. Tullock challenged the validity of this judgment by noting that democratic voting through the secret ballot failed to allow minorities with strong preferences to enter into welfare-improving bargains with majorities endowed with less intense preferences. If logrolling is feasible, as is always the case in open voting within a representative assembly, the minority voters will strike bargains with the majority as a means of safeguarding their most highly valued programs. If one assumes that all individuals are rational self-seekers, Tullock demonstrates that majority voting may lead to an overallocation of resources through the political process.

The next paper, "The Irrationality of Intransitivity," addresses a concern among certain welfare economists in the 1950s that individuals might be endowed with intransitive preferences when confronted with pair-wise comparisons, preferring, for example, A over B, B over C, and C over A.[12] Tullock points out that such a preference function would imply that the individual would be incoherent when asked to choose among the three alternatives, something that does not happen in reality. This short paper clearly signals the emphasis that Tullock consistently attaches to the rational choice model.

In "Entry Barriers in Politics," Tullock's point of departure is that government possesses a natural monopoly of the use of force, with its scale determined by the majority vote principle.[13] However, the ability to abuse this discretionary power is limited by the constraint of periodic elections when the apparatus of government is put up for auction. It is further limited by the ability of new political parties or party coalitions to form and to enter the political marketplace. Tullock's focus on the importance of entry and exit costs in political markets preceded by many years the application of similar ideas with respect to the importance of contestable markets for regulating the behavior of private natural monopolies.

"Federalism: Problems of Scale" focuses attention on issues concerning the appropriate scale and degree of federalism of government.[14] The conven-

12. Gordon Tullock, "The Irrationality of Intransitivity," *Oxford Economic Papers* 16 (October 1964): 401–6.

13. Gordon Tullock, "Entry Barriers in Politics," *American Economic Review* 55 (May 1965): 458–66.

14. Gordon Tullock, "Federalism: Problems of Scale," *Public Choice* 6 (Spring 1969): 19–29.

tional economic view during the late 1960s was that the existence of externalities (third-party effects not taken into account by private markets) was a major justification for collective action. As Tullock notes, however, collective action never completely eliminates external effects, and indeed creates external effects of its own. In such circumstances, why should government not be encouraged to grow without limit? The explanation is that the ability of individual voters to control government declines as the scale of government increases. In such circumstances, a case can be made for the coexistence of multiple governments, for example, one for defense and another for domestic policy.

There then follow three papers addressing issues of perceived instability in majority vote systems of government. The first of these is "The General Irrelevance of the General Impossibility Theorem," which attempts to show the insubstantiability of "Arrow's General Impossibility Theorem."[15] In 1951, Kenneth Arrow posited the logical impossibility of rationally aggregating preferences.[16] The majority vote rule appeared to be vulnerable to endless cycles. Yet, in reality, democracies tend to be highly stable. Tullock's resolution of this paradox relies, once again, on the importance of institutions. Rules of voting preclude endless pair-wise voting and limit the probability that outcomes will depart significantly from the center of the vote distribution.

The next two papers, "Why So Much Stability" and "Is There a Paradox of Voting?" return to the Arrow paradox.[17] Tullock argues that the Arrow paradox does not arise when either logrolling or strategic voting occurs. Because these are evident in all representative assemblies, the Arrow problem is insignificant, even when procedural voting rules do not impose stability.

Part 3 of this volume brings together three papers that discuss the demand-revealing process, an ingenious mechanism designed to motivate individuals to reveal their true preferences for public goods.

The first paper, "A New and Superior Process for Making Social Choices" (coauthored with Nicolaus Tideman), draws upon a discovery by Edward H.

15. Gordon Tullock, "The General Irrelevance of the General Impossibility Theorem," *Quarterly Journal of Economics* 81 (May 1967): 256–70.

16. Kenneth J. Arrow, *Social Choice and Individual Behavior* (New York and London: John Wiley and Sons, 1951).

17. Gordon Tullock, "Why So Much Stability," *Public Choice* 37 (1981): 189–202; "Is There a Paradox of Voting?" *Journal of Theoretical Politics* 4 (1992): 225–30.

Clarke that a carefully designed tax (the authors label it the Clarke tax) is immune to strategic maneuvering on the part of individual voters (though not in the case of coalitions of voters).[18] The essence of the process is that each individual is offered a chance to change a public good outcome that would occur without his vote, in exchange for paying a special charge equal to the net cost to others that arises from including his vote in the decision. "The Demand-Revealing Process as a Welfare Indicator" and "Demand-Revealing Process, Coalitions, and Public Goods" elaborate on the nature of the process, its relative efficiency in comparison with alternative processes for dealing with the problem of public goods, and its limited vulnerability to voter coalitions.[19]

Part 4 of this volume assembles a set of pathbreaking papers on rent seeking.

The first paper, "The Welfare Costs of Tariffs, Monopolies, and Theft," focuses attention on the welfare costs of tariffs, monopolies, and theft, and suggests that such costs are significantly understated in the conventional economics literature.[20] The standard view during the late 1970s, pioneered by Arnold Harberger, was that the welfare costs involved were insignificant, captured by the deadweight loss triangles first identified by Alfred Marshal, but now referred to as Harberger triangles.[21]

Tullock challenges Harberger's view by asserting the likelihood that the welfare costs are much greater than those identified and measured by Harberger. Government typically imposes a tariff or dispenses a monopoly privilege to designated beneficiaries. It does so in response to lobbying pressures and campaign contributions. The rent seekers (a term coined by Anne Krueger in 1974[22]) competing for such favors will outlay resources in direct relationship to the magnitude of the rents. Much of these outlays constitutes social waste.

18. T. Nicolaus Tideman and Gordon Tullock, "A New and Superior Process for Making Social Choices," *Journal of Political Economy* 84 (October 1976): 1145–59.

19. Gordon Tullock, "The Demand-Revealing Process as a Welfare Indicator," *Public Choice* 29 (Special Supplement to Spring 1977): 51–63; "Demand-Revealing Process, Coalitions, and Public Goods," *Public Choice* 29 (Special Supplement to Spring 1977): 103–5.

20. Gordon Tullock, "The Welfare Costs of Tariffs, Monopolies, and Theft," *Western Economic Journal* 5 (June 1967): 224–32.

21. Arnold Harberger, "Monopoly and Resource Allocation," *American Economic Review* 44 (March 1954): 77–87.

22. Anne O. Krueger, "The Political Economy of the Rent-Seeking Society," *American Economic Review* 64 (June 1974): 291–303.

In "The Cost of Transfers," Tullock extends the rent-seeking theory to income redistribution.[23] Even with respect to charitable giving, Tullock suggests that rent seeking on the part of would-be beneficiaries wastes resources. With respect to transfers mediated through the welfare state, Tullock argues that rent seeking is endemic and that perhaps as much as 95 percent of all such transfers are involuntary, driven by middle-class lobbying.

"More on the Welfare Costs of Transfers" and "Competing for Aid" demonstrate the applicability of rent seeking to the behavior of lower-level governments competing for aid from a higher-level government.[24] Tullock explains that the grants from a higher-level government are always worth less to the local community than is their cost to the central government.

"The Transitional Gains Trap" describes why many government programs do not seem to benefit their targeted beneficiaries.[25] According to Tullock, although the initial beneficiaries frequently do benefit from the provided special privilege, the benefits are quickly capitalized. Subsequent entrants must pay the capitalized value to access the resources and thereafter earn only a normal return on their investments. If the privilege should ever be withdrawn, such later entrants would suffer a capital loss.

The sixth paper, "Efficient Rent Seeking," utilizes game theory to define the circumstances under which competing rent seekers exactly dissipate the rent available (efficient rent seeking), the circumstances in which they underdissipate, and the circumstances in which they overdissipate.[26] The seventh paper provides a summary for *The New Palgrave* of the status of rent-seeking scholarship in 1987.[27]

Part 5 of this volume brings together four of Tullock's best-known papers on redistributive politics.

The first two papers, "Inheritance Justified" and "Inheritance Rejustified," attempt, by dismantling ideologically based arguments, to justify laws that al-

23. Gordon Tullock, "The Cost of Transfers," *Kyklos* 24, fasc. 4 (1971): 629–43.

24. Gordon Tullock, "More on the Welfare Costs of Transfers," *Kyklos* 27, fasc. 2 (1974): 378–81; "Competing for Aid," *Public Choice* 21 (Spring 1975): 41–51.

25. Gordon Tullock, "The Transitional Gains Trap," *Bell Journal of Economics* 6 (Autumn 1975): 671–78.

26. Gordon Tullock, "Efficient Rent Seeking," in *Toward a Theory of the Rent-Seeking Society*, ed. James M. Buchanan, Robert D. Tollison, and Gordon Tullock (College Station: Texas A&M University Press, 1980), 97–112.

27. Gordon Tullock, "Rent Seeking," in *The New Palgrave: A Dictionary of Economics*, vol. 4, ed. John Eatwell, Murray Milgate, and Peter Newman (London: Macmillan, 1987), 147–49.

low testators to bequeath wealth to designated beneficiaries.[28] Opponents of unrestricted inheritance rely in part on envy, as a negative externality, and in part on supposed ideological preferences for an egalitarian distribution of wealth as justifications for placing major restrictions on inheritance.

"The Charity of the Uncharitable" advances the hypothesis that the poor would receive larger transfers from a system of purely private charity than they receive through redistributive politics.[29] Tullock uses the logrolling model deployed in *The Calculus of Consent* to suggest that the dominant political coalition is located among middle-class groups, who disproportionately tax the rich in order to finance government programs that benefit themselves.[30] Although they justify such taxes on grounds of equalizing incomes, the decisive middle-class coalition has no intention of allowing significant redistribution to the poor.

"The Rhetoric and Reality of Redistribution" is Tullock's 1980 presidential address to the Southern Economic Association.[31] In this address, Tullock likens both U.S. policies toward illegal Mexican immigrants and Swedish and Swiss policies toward legal Turkish immigrants to the policies administered by white South Africans to blacks under apartheid. What is the logic, he asks, in restricting redistribution to a nation's citizens? Those Americans who genuinely believe in equality should be willing to sacrifice very large portions of their personal wealth to raise living standards in the Third World.

Part 6 of this volume assembles two papers on bureaucracy, a topic that is taken up in much greater detail in volume 6 in this series.

The first paper, "Dynamic Hypothesis on Bureaucracy," makes the point that, as the size of the government's bureaucracy expands, so does the voting power of its bureaucrats.[32] This increased voting strength may be used either to expand the size of the bureaucracy, or to increase the rents of existing bureaucrats, or some mixture of both. Tullock hints that the only remedy for

28. Gordon Tullock, "Inheritance Justified," *Journal of Law and Economics* 14 (October 1971): 465–74; "Inheritance Rejustified," *Journal of Law and Economics* 16 (October 1973): 425–28.

29. Gordon Tullock, "The Charity of the Uncharitable," *Western Economic Journal* 9 (December 1971): 379–92.

30. Buchanan and Tullock, *The Calculus of Consent*.

31. Gordon Tullock, "The Rhetoric and Reality of Redistribution," *Southern Economic Journal* 47 (April 1981): 895–907.

32. Gordon Tullock, "Dynamic Hypothesis on Bureaucracy," *Public Choice* 19 (Fall 1974): 127–31.

this dynamic tendency for bureaucracy to overexpand is to disenfranchise all government bureaucrats.

The second paper, "The Expanding Public Sector: Wagner Squared" (coauthored with James M. Buchanan), continues the hypothesis of the previous paper, presenting evidence that the real growth of bureaucracy in the United States as a percentage of gross domestic product over the period 1952 to 1972 was significantly less than the official statistics indicated.[33] The discrepancy reflected rents extracted by politically influential bureaucrats in the form of salaries and perquisites well in excess of opportunity cost. The authors categorize this phenomenon as "Wagner squared."

Part 7 of this volume brings together four classic papers by Tullock that deal with the social dilemma posed by anarchy, corruption, and revolution. These issues are taken up in more detail in volume 8 of this series.

"The Edge of the Jungle" demonstrates Tullock's belief that society is built on Hobbesian foundations and that Hobbesian anarchy still beckons to any established society from the edge of the jungle.[34] Tullock explains, in terms of prides of lions, why a weaker member of the pride may irrationally threaten to attack a stronger member when the food supply is insufficient, even though the attack, if implemented, would result in serious injury to the weaker member and the failure to secure food. Such behavior has a basis in rationality since, without it, the weaker lion (together with its genes) would surely die. These arguments are extended to human beings, with the major distinction that man's capacity to reason enables bargaining to take place, something that lions cannot achieve.

"Corruption and Anarchy" uses the Coase theorem to argue an economic case for certain kinds of governmental corruption.[35] However, as Tullock demonstrates, the Coase theorem cannot apply to the situation in which all laws are corrupted, since this would negate the property rights basis on which the Coase theorem is grounded.

"The Paradox of Revolution" and "Rationality and Revolution" identify the nature of the paradox of revolution, namely the reality that the removal of unpopular dictators is rarely achieved through popular uprising and much

33. James M. Buchanan and Gordon Tullock, "The Expanding Public Sector: Wagner Squared," *Public Choice* 31 (Fall 1977): 147–50.

34. Gordon Tullock, "The Edge of the Jungle," in *Explorations in the Theory of Anarchy*, ed. Gordon Tullock (Blacksburg, Va.: Center for Study of Public Choice, 1972), 65–75.

35. Gordon Tullock, "Corruption and Anarchy," in *Further Explorations in the Theory of Anarchy*, ed. Gordon Tullock (Blacksburg, Va.: Center for Study of Public Choice, 1974), 65–70.

more frequently is achieved through the coup d'état.[36] Tullock evaluates, from the rational choice perspective, the rare cases historically where popular dissent has culminated in successful revolution.

Part 8 of this volume consists of seven papers dealing with a range of policy issues that are affected by the presence of Pareto-relevant externalities and by publicness characteristics.

"Public and Private Interaction under Reciprocal Externality" (coauthored with James M. Buchanan) and "Social Cost and Government Action" focus attention on the appropriate role and scale of collective action regarding programs beset by reciprocal externalities (i.e., externalities that differentially affect private markets and government actions).[37] These contributions follow up and further elaborate on the fundamental insights outlined initially in *The Calculus of Consent*.[38] They are important because they reflect the leveling of the intellectual playing field in the ongoing welfare economics debate concerning the appropriate balance between market and state. "Public Decisions as Public Goods" extends this discussion yet further by analyzing public decisions themselves as public goods.[39]

The fourth paper, "Information without Profit," shifts attention from government to the relationship between original donors and the nonprofit charitable organizations that dispense their donations.[40] Tullock argues that donors will be alert to any fraudulent misuse of their donations because such behavior by a charity will adversely affect their reputations. However, donors will choose to be relatively uninformed about the efficiency of the charity, since there is no direct return to investing in such information. This was the first paper to subject the relationship between donors and charitable nonprofit organizations to a rational choice critique.

36. Gordon Tullock, "The Paradox of Revolution," *Public Choice* 11 (Fall 1971): 89–99; "Rationality and Revolution," *Rationality and Society* 7 (January 1995): 116–28.

37. James M. Buchanan and Gordon Tullock, "Public and Private Interaction under Reciprocal Externality," in *The Public Economy of Urban Communities*, ed. Julius Margolis (Washington, D.C.: Resources for the Future, 1965), 52–73; Gordon Tullock, "Social Cost and Government Action," *American Economic Review* 59 (May 1969): 189–97.

38. Buchanan and Tullock, *The Calculus of Consent*.

39. Gordon Tullock, "Public Decisions as Public Goods," *Journal of Political Economy* 79 (July/August 1971): 913–18.

40. Gordon Tullock, "Information without Profit," *Papers on Non-Market Decision Making* 1 (1966): 141–59.

"Polluters' Profits and Political Response: Direct Controls versus Taxes" and the reply to various comments on this paper (both coauthored with James M. Buchanan) address an important paradox in high transaction-cost environmental externalities, namely the clash between economic theory (almost universally in favor of tax solutions) and governmental behavior (almost universally in favor of direct controls).[41] The papers demonstrate that the paradox is reconciled once the interests of the polluters as well as those of the victims are figured into the public choice equation.

"Hawks, Doves, and Free Riders" approaches the problem of free-riding behavior in economic and political markets from the perspective of biology.[42] The hawk-dove equilibrium is one in which the doves benefit when hawks attack, kill, and injure each other. In such circumstances, the doves are able to free ride on the hawks. Tullock applies this theory to individual behavior in both financial markets and corporate bureaucracies.

Part 9 of this volume brings together eight important papers each offering a rational choice approach to law and economics.[43]

The first paper, "An Economic Approach to Crime," is an early contribution to the literature on the economics of crime and punishment.[44] Tullock develops a simple set of computational tools capable of defining an optimal law for two everyday crimes, namely illegal parking and tax evasion.

"The Costs of a Legal System" (coauthored with Warren F. Schwartz) outlines the complexity of assessing the costs of a legal system designed to enhance efficiency with respect both to various assignments of rights and to various enforcement mechanisms.[45] "On the Efficient Organization of Trials" and "On the Efficient Organization of Trials: A Reply to McChesney, and Ordover and Weitzman" focus attention on the relative efficiency of two different trial procedures, one emanating from Roman law and utilized by most

41. James M. Buchanan and Gordon Tullock, "Polluters' Profits and Political Response: Direct Controls versus Taxes," *American Economic Review* 65 (March 1975): 139–47; "Polluters' Profits and Political Response: Direct Controls versus Taxes: Reply," *American Economic Review* 66 (December 1976): 983–84.

42. Gordon Tullock, "Hawks, Doves, and Free Riders," *Kyklos* 45, fasc. 1 (1992): 25–36.

43. Gordon Tullock, *The Logic of the Law* (New York and London: Basic Books, 1971).

44. Gordon Tullock, "An Economic Approach to Crime," *Social Science Quarterly* 50 (June 1969): 59–71.

45. Warren F. Schwartz and Gordon Tullock, "The Costs of a Legal System," *Journal of Legal Studies* 4 (January 1975): 75–82.

countries in continental Europe, the other emanating from various medieval precedents and utilized by Anglo-Saxon countries.[46]

"Judicial Errors and a Proposal for Reform" (coauthored with I. J. Good) develops a measure of judicial error for U.S. Supreme Court decisions, based on the majority-minority split.[47] The authors argue that Supreme Court decisions based on 5 to 4 or 6 to 3 splits should not stand as precedents for lower courts to follow.

"Court Errors" further explores the implications of court errors in criminal and civil cases both for the selection of disputes and for the behavior of the litigants.[48] "Legal Heresy" (Tullock's presidential address to the Western Economic Association) uses experimental evidence on the relative magnitude of common law and civil code court errors to augment his case for shifting the U.S. legal system away from the common law in favor of the civil code procedures.[49] "Juries" critically evaluates the role of juries both in civil and in criminal cases in the U.S. legal system.[50]

Part 10 of this volume is a collection of four papers on bioeconomics.

"The Coal Tit as a Careful Shopper" is Tullock's analysis of the coal tit as a careful shopper.[51] Tullock utilizes data, provided by biologists, on the consumption of the eucosmid moth by coal tits to demonstrate that coal tits maximize the return on their efforts in searching out food supplies.

"Biological Externalities" applies the concepts of Pareto optimality and externalities to ecological problems.[52] If two or more species adversely affect each other in a given geographical area, these effects are classical negative externalities that, if unchecked, lead to suboptimal outcomes. By appropriate

46. Gordon Tullock, "On the Efficient Organization of Trials," *Kyklos* 28, fasc. 4 (1975): 745–62; "On the Efficient Organization of Trials: Reply to McChesney, and Ordover and Weitzman," *Kyklos* 30, fasc. 3 (1977): 517–19.

47. I. J. Good and Gordon Tullock, "Judicial Errors and a Proposal for Reform," *Journal of Legal Studies* 13 (June 1984): 289–98.

48. Gordon Tullock, "Court Errors," *European Journal of Law and Economics* 1 (1992): 9–21.

49. Gordon Tullock, "Legal Heresy," Presidential Address to the Western Economic Association Annual Meeting—1995, *Economic Inquiry* 34 (January 1996): 1–9.

50. Gordon Tullock, "Juries," in *The New Palgrave Dictionary of Economics and the Law*, vol. 2, ed. Peter Newman (London: Macmillan, 1998), 395–400.

51. Gordon Tullock, "The Coal Tit as a Careful Shopper," *American Naturalist* 105 (January–February 1971): 77–80.

52. Gordon Tullock, "Biological Externalities," *Journal of Theoretical Biology* 33 (December 1971): 565–76.

species management, it should be possible to increase the population size of all species in a given area. "Biological Applications of Economics" extends the rational choice approach to primitive societies (wasps, ants, and bees), showing, with the use of game theory, that where cooperation is necessary for survival, noncooperative genes are selected out by the extinction of the entire nest that contains them.[53] "The Economies of (Very) Primitive Societies" outlines the obstacles to cross-disciplinary research that had limited the development of bioeconomics prior to 1987.[54]

The final section of this volume brings together two papers that focus attention on Tullock's commitment to utilitarian moral philosophy. Although much of Tullock's work takes the form of positive economic analysis, nevertheless it is strongly motivated by normative considerations.

The first paper, "A (Partial) Rehabilitation of the Public Interest Theory," argues for a partial rehabilitation of the public interest theory in public choice.[55] Tullock recognizes the force of altruistic preferences in the vote motive even though such motives must compete with the solipsism of the special interest groups. In a sense this paper is a precursor to the later public choice scholarship on expressive voting.

The final paper, "How to Do Well While Doing Good!" explains to the economist that virtue does not have to be its own reward.[56] The economist can benefit his own career while making a contribution to the public welfare by publishing papers arguing the case for simple welfare-enhancing reforms in policy-oriented journals.

I hope that the collection of papers in this first volume of the Selected Works of Gordon Tullock reflects Tullock's invaluable contribution to securing the liberty of the individual, limited government, and the rule of law against the strong tide of intellectual socialism that swept across the academies during the middle years of the twentieth century.

53. Gordon Tullock, "Biological Applications of Economics," in *The New Palgrave: A Dictionary of Economics*, vol. 1, ed. John Eatwell, Murray Milgate, and Peter Newman (London: Macmillan, 1987), 246–47.

54. Gordon Tullock, "The Economics of (Very) Primitive Societies," *Journal of Social and Biological Structures* 13 (1990): 151–62.

55. Gordon Tullock, "A (Partial) Rehabilitation of the Public Interest Theory," *Public Choice* 42 (1984): 89–99.

56. Gordon Tullock, "How to Do Well While Doing Good!" in *Neoclassical Political Economy: The Analysis of Rent-Seeking and DUP Activities*, ed. David C. Colander (Cambridge, Mass.: Ballinger, 1984), 229–40.

Acknowledgments

I should like to place on record my debt to Liberty Fund for initiating and funding this project and for implementing it with their customary full measure of devotion. In particular, T. Alan Russell, chairman, George B. Martin, then president, Emilio J. Pacheco, executive vice president, and most especially, Patricia A. Gallagher, vice president of publishing, and Laura Goetz, senior editor, deserve my thanks for their enthusiasm and active support.

Ironically, even though Gordon Tullock rarely writes explicitly about liberty, it is entirely appropriate that Liberty Fund is publishing this collection. For, if eternal vigilance is the price of liberty, Tullock has paid that price in full measure as he has systematically chipped away at and eroded the fatal conceit of socialism by exposing its fallacies to the cold logic of rational choice.

My thanks are also due to Don Boudreaux, who first suggested the Tullock project to Liberty Fund; to Tyler Cowen, who encouraged me to take on the project; to Robert D. Tollison, who gave generously of his time and experience both to guide me on my editorial path and to provide comments on my introductions; to William F. Shughart II, who helpfully commented on the design of the project as well as providing comments on my introductions; to Janet T. Landa, who kindly steered me through the details of the bioeconomics research program; and to James M. Buchanan and David Fand, who both commented on my introductions.

Most especially, I want to express my deep gratitude to the fine editorial team that has helped to carry the project to completion, namely Jo Ann Burgess, the editorial coordinator of the project, and Anne Rathbone, the editorial assistant. They are the engines that have driven this project. I am the helmsman whose great joy and privilege it has been to steer a safe passage through sometimes rocky and turbulent waters. Finally, I should like to thank Gordon Tullock for his unfailing support.

CHARLES K. ROWLEY

Duncan Black Professor of Economics, George Mason University

Senior Fellow, James M. Buchanan Center for Political Economy, George Mason University

General Director, The Locke Institute

2003

GORDON TULLOCK, *by Mark Blaug*

Gordon Tullock was one of the principal founders of the Public Choice Society, and he has pioneered the application of economic principles to collective decisions, thus invading an area traditionally assigned to political scientists. Co-author with Buchanan of *The Calculus of Consent: Logical Foundations of Constitutional Democracy* (University of Michigan Press, 1962), Tullock's writings have ranged even wider than those of Buchanan, and he has been a central figure in the effort to revitalise old-style political anarchism as a new brand of libertarianism. Books like *The Politics of Bureaucracy* (Public Affairs Press, 1965), *The Social Dilemma: The Economics of War and Revolution* (Center for Study of Public Choice, 1974), *The New World of Economics* (Richard D. Irwin, 1975; 2nd ed., 1978), with R. B. McKenzie, and *Trials on Trial: The Pure Theory of Legal Procedures* (Columbia University Press, 1980) explore the economics of organisation, conflict resolution, voting behaviour, crime and the foundations of the legal system from the standpoint of the theory of public choice joined to the theory of property rights.

It is not always easy to see a common thread in Tullock's works: he is almost too fertile and throws off so many ideas in all directions that the connecting links between them threaten to disappear from view. Any simple summary of his "system," therefore, must wait on some future effort of his own. However, a common thread in his work, as in that of all public choice theorists, is the view that human behaviour must be viewed in all circumstances as a "rational" response to the twin constraints of the physical environment and the prevailing social institutions; people will always strive to maximise their satisfactions in the face of these constraints, taking due account of the costs of alternative choices. What characterises economic analysis, therefore, is not a set of questions called "economic activity" but a particular method of analysing any set of questions. Hence, when people make collective rather than private decisions, public choice theory asks what transaction costs, given the technical and social constraints, can cause individuals to prefer the outcomes of the ballot box to those of a market mechanism, and

Reprinted, with permission, from *Great Economists Since Keynes: An Introduction to the Lives and Works of One Hundred Modern Economists*, ed. Mark Blaug (Brighton: Wheatsheaf, 1985), 252–53.

what are the feasible changes in the prevailing constraints which are capable of altering such preferences? The result is a sometimes startlingly new way of looking at old questions in political science.

Tullock was born in 1922 in Rockford, Illinois. He received a degree in law from the University of Chicago Law School in 1947 and went on to graduate studies at Yale University (1949–51) and Cornell University (1951–52). From 1947 to 1956, he was employed in the Foreign Service of the US State Department. His first teaching post was at the University of South Carolina (1959–62). Subsequently he moved to the University of Virginia (1962–67), Rice University (1967–68), the Virginia Polytechnic Institute and State University (1968–83), and, finally, George Mason University, where he teaches today as Professor of Economics at the Center for Study of Public Choice.

He was President of the Public Choice Society in 1965 and the Southern Economic Association in 1980.

GORDON TULLOCK

DISTINGUISHED FELLOW, 1998

Gordon Tullock came to a scholarly calling through a circuitous route that involved a stint in the foreign service and almost no formal training in economics. Nevertheless, his natural ability as an economist enabled him to make fundamental contributions to economics and political science over a span of some 40 years. Tullock's insistence on the *Homo economicus* approach and his work in expanding the domain of economics have contributed to an environment in the profession in which work in nontraditional areas, such as political science, law, biology, military strategy, and conflict resolution, is taken seriously.

Tullock's scholarly contributions, both in amount and significance, are extensive. His early work on logrolling and his contributions to *The Calculus of Consent* (with James M. Buchanan) establish him as one of the key founders of the public choice paradigm. From 1962 forward, a steady flow of important scholarship has flowed from Tullock's pen. Among his works are basic contributions to the theory of bureaucracy, the theory of rent seeking, externality theory, the theory of demand-revealing processes for public goods, the theory of regulation, voting behavior, and the theory of conflict resolution.

Tullock's seminal paper (1967) on the theory of rent seeking set off a vast theoretical and empirical literature. There are no clearly identifiable precursors to Tullock's insight that the expenditure of scarce resources to capture a pure transfer is a social cost, to be counted on a par with traditional deadweight losses as a social cost of monopolistic, regulatory, and other related institutions and practices in the economy. Indeed, the term "rent seeking" (coined by Anne Krueger) has entered the popular culture as an expression denoting unsavory behavior by political actors.

Moreover, Tullock played a key role in the institutional evolution of the public choice movement. He was founding editor of *Public Choice*, a position which he held for 25 years, and he was instrumental in the formation of the Public Choice Society.

Reprinted, with permission of the American Economic Association, from *American Economic Review* 88 (September 1998): ii.

Tullock's scholarship and entrepreneurship have left an indelible imprint on economics. He is a pioneer who has worked almost exclusively at the frontiers of the discipline. As Gordon is often fond of saying of Duncan Black, it can now be said about Tullock himself—he is a Father of us all.

PART I

GENESIS

ECONOMIC IMPERIALISM[1]

If we define "economics" as "what economists do," then a vast expansion of that field is one of the more interesting intellectual developments of this generation. There is now a sizable literature by economists and use of recognizable economic methods in the field normally described as political science. Since von Neumann and Morgenstern's book was published, economists have been working in the field of military strategy. Recently this interest has expanded to take in problems in the field of diplomacy and international relations. These developments are in addition to economic interest in problems of management and efficiency in all branches of the government. Indeed, although I suppose that applications of economics such as cost-benefit analysis can hardly be regarded as outside the theoretical sphere of traditional economic interests, until recently almost all work on such matters was left to the students of public administration, a branch of political science.

Economists are not only doing research in "public administration," they have also invaded the field of business administration, with the result that a number of leading members of the profession now draw more of their income from consulting contracts than from their academic work. To continue, economists are now producing work on criminology, where, as usual, their approach appears unorthodox to the point of eccentricity to the traditional practitioners. After generations of repeating that economics could say nothing about income distribution, economists are now working on the economics of charity and income redistribution. Here they are, in a way, inventing a new field rather than invading an existing one, although I suspect many Ph.D.'s in social welfare administration would deny it. The recent upsurge of economic interest in the operation of nonprofit organizations, however, is clearly the creation of a new field rather than an imperialistic invasion of an existing one.

Reprinted, with permission, from *Theory of Public Choice: Political Applications of Economics*, ed. James M. Buchanan and Robert D. Tollison (Ann Arbor: University of Michigan Press, 1972), 317–29.

1. The "economic theory of democracy indeed as developed by Anthony Downs and others is a very good example of what I have sometimes called 'economics imperialism,' which is an attempt on the part of economics to take over all the other social sciences," Kenneth Boulding, "Economics as a Moral Science," *American Economic Review*, 59, No. 1, March 1969, 1–12.

But we are not finished. Economists have devoted much time recently to educational problems. Admittedly, their interest has been mainly confined to education as a form of investment, a subject which educationists have normally neglected, but they are showing some interest in teaching techniques, so far mostly in connection with the teaching of economics as a subject. Problems of the organization of science have also attracted some economic interest recently. Here they directly compete only with a few sociologists, but most natural scientists have strong views on the subject and tend to be annoyed by the economists' tendency to calculate instead of emote. The economic historians have recently produced information on such matters as the actual cost to the thirteen colonies of the British restrictions on trade which are of great importance to standard history, although the historians do not seem conscious of this fact. Lastly, at least one economist, myself, is interested in economic applications in the field of biology. So far, the biologists have ignored me, but in view of the impact of Malthus on an earlier generation of biologists, I still have hope.

But all of this intellectual activity, important as I think it is, has attracted remarkably little attention. The readers of this book are certainly more interested in these new fields of economics than the overwhelming majority of the academic community who will not read it, yet I doubt that many of them will have even heard of much of the work I have listed above. The average economist is even less informed. If we consider academic specialists in the fields now being invaded by economists, the overwhelming majority will not have even heard of the movement. Among those few who have become vaguely aware of this threat to their disciplinary sovereignity, only a small proportion will know anything about the actual work done by the economists. In most cases, the number who have actually familiarized themselves with the new approach is still smaller.

Why this lack of attention to what appears to be an important development? One obvious answer would be that the economists engaged in applying their tools to new fields are simply wrong: that their work is wasted and not worth studying. I do not believe that this is so, but I shall not devote any time here to refuting it. If the other essays in this volume have not already convinced the reader that economists are doing important work outside the traditional field of economics, it is unlikely that I could do so in a few pages. There are other explanations than the possible lack of real worth to these studies, and it is to these other explanations I shall now turn.

The fact that only a minority of economists are interested in these forays of economists outside their traditional field arises, I think, mainly from the rapid growth of specialization within economics. Only a minority of economists are interested in almost any given specialty within the general area of economics. Economics has now become such a broad and complex subject that a detailed knowledge of all of its branches would be beyond the intellectual capacity of most, probably all, economists. The human brain, after all, is finite and the steady increase in the total of scientific knowledge carries with it the corollary that any individual human being must reduce the percentage of that total which he learns. Thus disciplines were originally established, and thus specialties and subspecialties are now developing.

It is notable that economists who are specialists in public finance will normally be interested in the new developments, such as those in this volume, which fall in the traditional field of political science simply because they are obviously closely related to problems of public finance. Similarly, economists interested in economic development normally are concerned with the economics of education which is closely related to their subdiscipline, and in fact was largely developed by people interested in the backward countries and their problems. The lack of an active body of economists interested in some of the other new fields is largely the result of the fact that there is no obviously closely related subdiscipline in the existing organization of economics. As these fields develop it is likely that only a fraction of the economics profession will be interested in them simply because only a fraction of the economics profession is interested in any subdiscipline.

The reasons why academic specialists in the fields being invaded by the economists are relatively uninformed about this development are, in my opinion, quite different. In the first place, some of these fields, the social organization of science or nonprofit organizations, are not within the ambit of any well defined discipline. It is true that a few sociologists have done work in these general areas, but they are not major interests for any recognized subdiscipline of sociology. The total number of sociologists interested in either field is small, and most of them have other interests.

In such fields as political science, however, a great many scholars are directly concerned with the problems dealt with in such an "economic" book as *An Economic Theory of Democracy*.[2] The fact that most political scientists have not read it (although the situation is rapidly changing) can be put down to another result of the finite nature of the human brain. Learning a discipline

2. Anthony Downs, *An Economic Theory of Democracy* (New York, 1958).

is a capital investment process in which the individual invests time, energy, and some direct physical resources in acquiring knowledge. If a man has made such an investment and a book is produced which purports to deal with his subject but which requires a totally different set of intellectual capital to understand and evaluate its message, he is understandably reluctant to read it. To an economist, Downs' book is relatively easy to read. To a political scientist who has had the traditional training, it is an extremely difficult book. Not only is reading it hard, he is likely to misunderstand it. This is not because economists are smarter than political scientists; there are books which political scientists regard as easy which would raise great difficulties for economists. It is true, however, that a political scientist who wanted to become familiar with the economic approach to his field would probably find it necessary to devote six months to a year to acquiring the necessary intellectual capital in the form of a good background in economics.

Clearly the political scientist is not going to make this sizable investment unless he feels considerable assurance that it will be worthwhile. Indeed, he may fear that the intellectual capital he has already accumulated will be rendered obsolescent.[3] Under the circumstances, we should not be surprised if political scientists do not rush into this sort of speculative investment. On the contrary, we may be surprised that so many of them have shown serious interest. Most political scientists, however, are working with their traditional methods and ignoring the new developments. With time, this will probably change (the younger members of the profession are much less conservative, probably because they have less accumulated capital in danger of obsolescence) and the example of Vincent Ostrom, William Riker, and L. L. Wade will be followed.

The fact, then, that the new drive to apply economic methods in fields far from traditional economics has so far had relatively little impact on the average scholar is not surprising. Neither is it particularly unfortunate. Almost

3. I cannot forebear giving an example of this sort of Ludditism which affected me personally. I left the University of Virginia in somewhat tense circumstances. Sometime thereafter, there was an exchange of correspondence on the subject in the pages of the student newspaper (*The Virginia Weekly*, Vol. 2, No. 11, January 15, 1968). The editor of the paper, clearly reflecting the views, and probably the language, of at least one member of the Department of Political Science editorialized: "Admittedly Mr. Tullock published a good deal, but the quantity of his writing easily exceeded their quality. Mr. Tullock, who had pretentions to competence as a political scientist as well as an economist, was looked on by professionals in the field very much as George Plimpton was looked on by members of the Detroit Lions."

by definition the scholars now working in these fields have been self-selected for originality and interdisciplinary interests. They are building a solid body of work which will provide a foundation for future expansion. A gradual spread of the new approach, with research solidly backing each new advance, is healthier than a sudden fad based on preliminary findings. We can anticipate that our influence will grow somewhat slower than our knowledge. On the whole this is healthy, if sometimes frustrating.

The restrictions on the development of economic approaches in other fields of the social sciences, however, are clearly temporary. The boundaries between the disciplines are mere traditions and they are automatically eroded by the passage of time. We can confidently expect that twenty years from now the problems of specialization and conserving of intellectual capital which today still restrict the influence of the new methods will no longer constitute serious barriers. What will be (or should be) the shape of the social sciences then? I should like to devote the remainder of this essay to attempting an answer to this question. Since prophecy is notably difficult, I can hardly ask the reader to give much weight to my guesses as to the future, but if he will regard what I have to say as a proposal for the reorganization of the social sciences, I think he will agree that it is at least worth serious consideration. It would not only eliminate some artificial barriers between closely related disciplines, it would provide a framework for specialization which should make cooperation between fields easier and less subject to disciplinary jealousy than at present.

Let me begin my proposal for the future with a brief survey of the past. The Enlightenment was, in my opinion, one of the high points of human intellectual development. In the latter part of those halcyon days, economics was founded by two friends, David Hume and Adam Smith. Although we can clearly see in their work, particularly, of course, Smith's *The Wealth of Nations*, the origins of scientific economics, it does not appear that they felt that the distinction between economics and the rest of the social studies was of any great importance. *The Wealth of Nations*, after all, contains chapters on military affairs, administration of justice, public works, and education.[4] Hume also normally discusses both economics and politics in a manner which we now normally associate with economics.

With Hume and Smith, then, we see an "economic" approach to a very

4. All of these subjects are discussed under the general title "of the expenses of the sovereign of commonwealth," but the text goes much farther afield.

large part of social behavior. They called their discipline "political economy" and certainly thought of it as as much political as economic. It happened, of course, to be easier to analyze economics (in the modern meaning) than politics with these tools, and they made more progress there, but they would probably have been both surprised and disappointed if told that their work would, for nearly 200 years, be regarded as the foundation of economics, but largely ignored by scholars in other areas such as the study of politics. It is probably the influence of David Ricardo which led to the reduction in the scope of the area studied with the methods of Smith and Hume to what we now call economics. Brilliant though Ricardo undoubtedly was, however, there seems no inherent reason why his tastes in the fields he wished to study should mold the present-day structure of the disciplines. The differences between politics and economics are real, but they are readily bridged, as witness the number of economists who have written in political science.

For a more fundamental organizing principle for the social sciences, let us return to a distinction that Hume and Smith thought vital: the difference between "reason and the passions." That Hume thought this distinction important is, I suppose, not in doubt, but it deserves further emphasis. To Hume, the role of reason was simply that of a servant of the passions. Putting the same thought in modern terms, we have a set of preferences, and we use our intellectual capacities for the purpose of achieving as much of the things preferred as possible. Thus the "rational model" dealt with the means men would adopt to achieve goals determined upon by nonrational means. Smith, on the other hand, wrote two books, not one. *The Wealth of Nations*, I think, can be taken as a working out of the slave-reason role in society, particularly in that portion of social action which we call economics; and the other, *The Theory of Moral Sentiments*, an effort to explain why human beings have certain of the "passions." It should not be forgotten that it was *The Theory of Moral Sentiments* which originally made Smith's reputation, and guaranteed that *The Wealth of Nations* would receive serious consideration.

Let me put the distinction between reason and the passions into a more extensive modern form. Any individual has a collection of preferences. We may equate this preference structure to Hume's "passions." The individual, in attempting to achieve his preferences as much as possible, makes use of his rational faculties and makes choices of various sorts between the alternatives available to him. Traditionally, the study of these choices and their interaction with the choices of other individuals within the sphere that we call economics has been the basic field studied by those members of the academic community who are called economists. What has happened in recent years is that the economists have begun to study such choices and their interaction with the choices of other individuals in areas which are not traditionally economics. Fortunately, it turns out to be possible to bring into these areas a very large part of the apparatus already developed in economics, but a good deal of new invention is also necessary. It also turns out, as this book has demonstrated, that much of the work in at least one of these new branches, public choice or the theory of governmental decision, is applicable to areas which, I think, would previously have been called a subsection of economics — public finance.

Economists in general have been relatively little interested in the preferences that individuals have. They assume the preferences and then deduce what the outcome is but do not pay much attention to investigation of these preferences. Traditionally, an economist will tell you that this is a problem for the psychologists rather than for economists. In practice, however, it is not only the problem of the psychologist, it has to a very large extent been the problem of the sociologist and of the behavioralist political scientist. A great deal of the research of the sociologists, behavioralists, and political scientists concerns the type of person who is apt to be involved in some particular activity. This can be thought of as an effort to determine which people have certain sets of tastes and preferences. The economist, for example, if asked about why people are lawyers or garbage collectors, will point out that there is a positive return to these activities and state that people of suitable degree of talent would enter these fields until the returns of labor effort invested in these fields is equivalent to that in other fields for persons with the same amount of talent.[5] He would probably add the statement that individuals may have particular tastes for certain particular activities and are more likely to be found in those activities than in those for which they have a personal dislike. The sociologist, considering the same problem, will turn to the question of what particular type of people are apt to be lawyers or garbage collectors. He may determine, for example, that lawyers are brighter, more likely to come from upper class backgrounds, more likely to be of somewhat studious bent, etc. than garbage collectors.

Traditionally, these two approaches to the same problem have led to a good deal of conflict. This conflict is unfortunate because the two approaches are perfectly consistent. They simply are aimed at different objectives. It has

5. With a large number of modifying factors which need not be discussed here.

turned out that the examination of the outcome of preferences which the economists have undertaken permits much more elaborate, precise, and testable statements about the real world than does the examination of the tastes themselves by the other social scientists. The reasons for this greater advance of economics are probably that it is older and more developed, and also probably because it is dealing with somewhat easier problems. In the present state of knowledge of psychology, determining why people have some particular set of preferences is an extraordinarily difficult problem, and it is even extremely difficult to find out what preferences they have unless they "reveal" their preferences by some type of interaction which the economist would logically study.

As the reader will no doubt already have deduced, my proposal for the future organization of social sciences is that they be divided into two grand domains, the sciences of choice and the sciences of preferences. The sciences of choice would essentially be an outgrowth of economics and would be devoted to determining the likely outcome of the interaction of individuals attempting to maximize their preference functions in a society where it is not possible for everyone to have everything he wants. It would no longer be confined to what is traditionally known as economics, but could deal with any institution. No doubt subdisciplines within this major field would rapidly develop because of the finite nature of the human mind. Still, it would be recognized that these subdisciplines were defined solely by the particular institutional structure they happen to be dealing with and not through any difference of approach or method.

On the other hand, there would be the sciences of preferences, tastes, or passions. They would be devoted to attempting to determine what the preferences of various people in society are, to examining individual preferences, to trying to find out how the preferences in society can be summarized conveniently, and, what is perhaps more important than all these things, the factors which mold preferences.

With this division of labor between two general areas, it would seem that we would have a basis for cooperation, rather than conflict. Presently most economists tend to regard sociologists and the political scientists as among the unwashed. They look down on their methods and point out, quite correctly, that they do not have anything in the way of elaborate theories and that their empirical research is usually an effort to find specific fact instead of an effort to validate a general theory.

This feeling on the part of economists is, to put the matter mildly, fully reciprocated by the sociologists, political scientists, etc. One of the major points that they will make again and again and again is that man is not rational, and hence the economists' assumption that he is, is false. In discussion with people of this persuasion, I've always found that they define rational in a way which is not characteristic of the economist. They have as their idea of a rational man a person who is perfectly informed, cold-blooded, takes very long views, gives a great deal of consideration for all decisions, and invariably aims at direct, selfish aims. Needless to say, with this view of the word rational, it is easy to demonstrate that men are not rational. Still, the fact that people I have talked to who propose this view are, generally speaking, unwilling to accept my assurance that because I do not think that people are rational in their meaning of the term is indicative of deeper drives. When I attempt to present the economist's meaning of rationality and point out that it is reasonably immune to the criticism that men are not rational, I normally find an unwillingness on their part to admit that such use of the word rational is legitimate or that it is possible for me to justify the "rational models" of economics by alleging that the word rational means something different from what it means to the sociologist, etc.

It seems to me that much of this clash comes from the fact that the borders of the two disciplines are not so located that cooperative activity is easy. In general, if an economist and a sociologist, say, deal with the same problem, each will find that the other's research is of very little value to him, and they regard each other as opponents. Coming from different intellectual backgrounds, they also find a good deal of difficulty understanding each other. An explicit division of labor in which the economists consider the consequences of people making choices in efforts to maximize their preferences, and the psychologist-sociologist-behavioralist study of those preferences themselves, would permit a relaxation of the current tension in the social sciences.

This division of labor would not be radically different from the actual present organization of the social sciences. There are some differences, of course. The economists have, of necessity, some rather primitive ideas as to the preferences people have because this is necessary to test their theories. The political scientist and sociologist on the other hand have some rather primitive theories of the effect of differing individual choices in social interaction. Nevertheless, it seems to me that an explicit division of the field in these terms would be an improvement on the present situation. It will require relatively little change in the things that are actually being done by people in different parts of the social sciences.

Speaking as a man who has gradually over the years tended to become an economist, I should like here to suggest certain mild reorientations in the research now undertaken by the social scientists who are not economists. Since the principal point of this mild reorientation, other than improving the nature of that research itself, is to make it more usable by economists in the division of labor which I have suggested, it may be that noneconomists will resent my advice. Nevertheless, as will be seen, it does not reduce the scope or importance of the work of noneconomists.

Let me begin by pointing briefly to a sort of general theory which underlines much of noneconomic work in the social sciences. I can do no better than quote John Harsanyi, "The implicit assumption usually has been that 'all good things come together,' all desirable factors have positive correlation with one another. Greater popular participation can only make the political system 'more democratic' in all respects; greater democracy can only increase the rate of economic development; more freedom and more permissiveness for the child can only improve its academic progress, etc.

"We shall call this implicit assumption the positive correlation fallacy; it has been one of the main obstacles to clear thinking among social scientists and is probably responsible for a high proportion of the bad policy recommendations we have made."[6]

That this criticism is, at least in part, well founded, I think would be hard to deny. But, it seems to me that the political scientists, sociologists, and psychologists are not really totally wrong in taking this attitude if we assume that they are attempting to reconstruct people's preference structures. If we look at the typical "behavioralist" article in a political science journal or a sociology journal, we will find that it involves some such question as what type of people are apt to be in some occupation or what preferences do people in some occupations apparently have. In both cases, this is a matter which economists would call taste, although I'm not at all certain the political scientist and sociologist would recognize it under that title. It happens to be so that, to the best of our current knowledge, there is no intrinsic reason why an individual who has a taste for one "good" thing under the specification of some particular value system may not have a taste for other "good" things as specified by the same value system. In many ways, the purpose of education *is* to produce people all of whose values are "good" in the terms of the appropriate general value system.

6. "Rational Choice Models of Political Behavior vs. Functionalist and Conformist Theories," *World Politics*, July 1969, 537–38.

Thus, it is very commonly so that if we look at individuals who have been trained in any particular society, "all good things come together." They will be indoctrinated in the values of that society. Hence, there will be a distinct correlation between the degree to which they accept the values into which they have been indoctrinated in one field, and the degree to which they accept them in another. Further, much activity of politically interested people is directed towards attempting to indoctrinate particular value sets in people, and, in general, this is done in a way which once again produces this type of correlation.

Looking at it from the standpoint of the economist, we might say that there is no particular conflict, at least as far as our present knowledge exists, between a person having a "good" set of preferences in one area and his having a "good" set of preferences in another. The education of an individual produces a set of preferences, and giving a preference for A in one field and B in another field is, on the whole, as easy as giving a set of preferences for A in one field and A in another field.

Thus, the behavioralist "positive correlation fallacy" is not, if we are thinking about preferences only, necessarily a fallacy. It is only when we look to policy and interaction that we find this a fallacy. In certain areas it isn't even a fallacy there. In general, if we have something or other which is desirable in all ways, i.e., meets all the requirements of all individuals, we will rapidly carry it out. It is only the fact that we've already normally exhausted all *easy* possibilities for such quasi-Paretian moves, that leads to the "scarcity" of resources which economics studies. No economist would deny that if a positive correlation between all good things *did* exist, we should move out along the ray indicated. What we, in fact, say is that we have already reached the end of the possible changes which have this favorable outcome, and must now pick and choose among possible courses of action which have both advantages and disadvantages. To put the matter differently, we must now choose between policies which some people favor and other people do not.

Thus, a theoretical "positive correlation" among preferences and tastes may well exist. It is among the interactions of the real world that the assumption of this positive correlation leads to fallacious outcomes. "Greater democracy" *may* "increase the rate of economic development," but the fact that both of these things are, in certain value systems, desirable is irrelevant in discussing whether it will or will not. If it turns out that these two desirable characteristics are not interrelated in such a way that one can increase the rate of growth by increasing the rate of democracy, then we must make choices between things that we desire. This is a characteristic situation for economic investigation. A great deal of the noneconomic discussion of these problems has, in essence, foreclosed this type of problem by carrying over the "positive correlation" assumption from the area of taste to the area of interaction.

Having criticized the noneconomists, it is perhaps only sensible that I close this essay by offering a somewhat similar criticism of the economists themselves. There are pure theories of human interaction which will fit any possible set of human tastes. These theories are, of course, not testable by operational means, since any conceivable outcome in the real world could be explained by some particular taste. In order to make their theories testable, economists implicitly, not always explicitly, *do* make assumptions about the tastes that people do have. These assumptions, which I call the 90 per cent selfish hypothesis, normally take the form of assuming that the people under study have a set of desires for their own personal well-being which are rather similar to those of the economist himself, although not identical. Further, they are rarely specified in any detail.

This set of rather primitive assumptions about human behavior, which is implicit in empirical testing of economic theory, works out rather well in practice because it is not thought by the economist who is *implying* the theory that he can exactly specify the tastes of the group of people under test. He assumes that his assumption is, at best, a reasonable approximation of their tastes. Thus, the deviation between the tastes of the individuals and the tastes which the economist is ascribing to them becomes a random variable in the statistical testing routine and is dealt with in the normal manner in which noise is cut out in statistics.

The end product is to provide a mechanism for testing economic theory which works out rather well. It should be realized, however, that it works very much less well than a more specific and exacting view of human preferences would. Economists have always ignored this problem, and it seems to me this is a real defect in current economics. I do not propose that economists begin to investigate human preferences, but that they recognize that it is a problem for people in another field of the social sciences and pay attention to discoveries in these fields. It does not seem to be likely that great progress will be made in the "science of taste" in the near future simply because it seems to me these are extremely difficult areas; but they are also areas which will repay extensive research.

The reader may not regard my proposal for reorganization of the social sciences as desirable. Certainly he is unlikely to regard the prophecy that this may happen in the next twenty years as having a high degree of probability. I think he will have to admit, however, that my proposed reorientation would make only a small difference in the actual research being undertaken by people in the two different grand divisions which I have specified. There would be minor changes in what they study and their methods of study, and there would be a possibility of cooperation and understanding between them to replace the present antagonism and interdisciplinary warfare. In a sense, my proposal is that the other social sciences accept the recent sharp expansion of economics—that they recognize that the objectives of the economic research are basically different from the objectives of the researchers now in these fields. In return, I suggest that the economists welcome sociologists, psychologists, etc. who are attempting to determine the nature of human preferences in the economic or political area. Whether the net effect of this is an expansion of the economic profession or an expansion of the noneconomic disciplines I cannot now say. Further, although this is important in terms of our personal ambitions to be members of rapidly growing disciplines, it has no significance for the progress of science.

PUBLIC CHOICE

In the 18th and 19th centuries a number of mathematicians (Condorcet, Borda, Laplace and Lewis Carroll) became interested in the mathematics of the voting process; their work was forgotten until Duncan Black rediscovered it.[1] Black can be called the father of modern Public Choice, which is in essence the use of economic tools to deal with the traditional problems of political science. Historically, economics (political economy) dealt to a very large extent with the choice of government policies with respect to economic matters. Whether protective tariffs were or were not good things would be a characteristic topic of traditional economics, and in examining the question, it was assumed, of course, that the government was attempting essentially to maximize some kind of welfare function for society.

We do not expect businessmen to devote a great deal of time and attention to maximizing the public interest. We assume that, although they will of course make some sacrifices to help the poor and advance the public welfare, basically they are concerned with benefiting themselves. Traditionally economists did not take the same attitude towards government officials, but Public Choice theory does. To simplify the matter, the voter is thought of as a customer and the politician as a businessman/entrepreneur. The bureaucracy of General Motors is thought to be attempting to design and sell reasonably good cars because that is how promotions and pay rises are secured. Similarly, we assume that the government bureaucracy will be attempting mainly to produce policies which in the views of their superiors are good because that is how their promotions and pay rises are secured.

In all these cases, of course, the individual probably has at least some willingness to sacrifice for the public good. Businessmen contribute both time and money to worthy causes, and politicians on occasion vote for things that they think are right rather than things which will help them get re-elected. In both cases, however, this is a relatively minor activity compared to maximizing one's own well-being.

Reprinted, with permission of Palgrave Macmillan, from *The New Palgrave: A Dictionary of Economics*, vol. 3, ed. John Eatwell, Murray Milgate, and Peter Newman (London: Macmillan, 1987), 1040–44.

1. See, e.g., D. Black, *The Theory of Committees and Elections* (Cambridge: Cambridge University Press, 1958).

The only surprising thing about the above propositions is that they have not traditionally been orthodox either in economics or political science. Writers who did hold them, like Machiavelli in parts of *The Prince*, were regarded as morally suspect and tended to be held up as bad examples rather than as profound analysts.

Public Choice changes this, but even more important, by using a model in which voters, politicians and bureaucrats are assumed to be mainly self-interested, it became possible to employ tools of analysis that are derived from economic methodology.

As a result, fairly rigorous models have been developed which can be tested with the same kind of statistical procedures that are used in economics, although their data are drawn from the political sphere. The result is a new theory of politics which is more rigorous, more realistic and better tested than the older orthodoxy.

While the basic thrust of the Public Choice work has been positive (directed towards understanding politics), from the very beginning it has also had a strong normative component. Students of Public Choice might modify Marx to read that "the problem is to understand the world so that we can improve it." Thus the design of improved governmental methods based on the positive information about how governments actually function has been an important part of Public Choice work, and is usually referred to as the theory of constitutions.

Before discussing this, it is necessary to briefly outline related discoveries in four general areas, viz: voters, politicians, the voting process which relates voters to politicians, and the theory of bureaucracy.

We begin with voters. One of the earliest discoveries of the new Public Choice[2] was that a rational voter would not bother to be very well informed about the votes that he cast. The reason is simply that the effect of his vote on his well-being is trivially small.[3] Apparently voters have always known this, since empirical studies of voter knowledge show them extremely ignorant, but it was something of a revelation to traditional professors of Political Science. Further, this general ignorance of the voter is not symmetrical. The voter is likely to know a good deal about any special interest which he has.

2. See A. Downs, *An Economic Analysis of Democracy* (New York: Harper & Row, 1957), 207–78.

3. See G. Tullock, *Toward a Mathematics of Politics* (Ann Arbor: University of Michigan Press, 1967), 100–114.

Further, organized special interest groups will put effort into propagandizing the voter in such areas. Thus the voter is not only badly informed, but what information he has tends to be biased very heavily in the direction of his own occupation or avocation. The farmer is much more likely to know the views of the candidates on farm programmes than their views on nuclear war. It could be said that even on the farm programme he is probably not very well informed, just better informed.

One should not exaggerate of course. The voter, simply by living and following current events in newspapers and on television, does acquire a certain amount of general information about politics. Not much of it seems to stick, however, and in any event it is very heavily affected by temporary fads. It should also be emphasized that some kinds of special interests of the voter are not in any real sense selfish. For example, in the USA many people are influenced in their vote by such institutions as Common Cause and Liberty Lobby and make voluntary cash contributions to them. Clearly, this is an expression by those people of their interest in good government, even though the two groups define this in a radically different way. There is no doubt, however, that a well-organized special interest is apt to have more impact on any specific issue than either the general media or so-called public interest groups like Common Cause or Liberty Lobby, even though in the very long run, considering what one might call the "general mystique" of government, the media are very important.

Consider next the politician. A politician is a person who makes a living by being elected by voters of the kind described above. Further, many politicians are themselves voters as, let us say, members of the House of Representatives. While in the latter capacity, although it is not true that politicians' information is as bad as that of the voter, a similar effect is still at work. An individual member of the House of Representatives or the House of Commons who switches one hour a week from general study of the issues on which he must vote to constituency service will normally reduce only trivially the quality of the legislation as it affects his constituency. On the other hand, by so re-allocating his time, he may materially improve his relations with his electors. Thus we would expect that politicians will be less well informed on general matters than we would like.

This is simply one example of a large number of cases in which politicians' behaviour is not necessarily that which maximizes the public welfare: they vote in Congress and seek public positions in terms of what they think the voters *will* reward, not in terms of what they think the voters *should* reward.

Since a politician knows that his constituents are badly informed, these two positions can be radically different. Nevertheless, if we are believers in democracy, which literally means popular rule, then the government should do what the people want and not what some wiser person feels that they should want. In any event, "in order to be a great Senator, one must first of all be a Senator."

Obviously the cost to the public of this kind of behaviour is quite considerable. It is particularly so when we think of the investment of resources and influence in the government which are, to a considerable extent, wasted. However, if we contrast functioning democracies with the other types of government which we observe, we are not likely to feel that democracies are markedly less efficient.

We now turn to the voting process, which connects the public to the politicians and the latter to the actual policy outcomes. Uninformed people think that this is basically a trivial problem, you simply count the votes. Unfortunately, this does not follow, even though the author of this essay is one of the few Public Choice theorists who regards the problems to be discussed next as being possibly illusory.

Condorcet, Borda, Laplace and Lewis Carroll and, in the 20th century, mathematical economists like Black and Kenneth Arrow discovered a set of mathematical problems sufficiently difficult to be taken as proof that democracy is either an illusion or a fraud. Basically, if we assume that all individuals can order various policy proposals, producing a personal ranking from top to bottom (indifference between alternatives being permitted), and that these orderings differ from person to person (and do not fall into a set of narrowly specified and rather unlikely patterns), then one of the following three phenomena can occur under any conceivable system of voting:

1. Endless cycling with A beating B and B beating C then C beating A.
2. An outcome which is dependent on the order in which the various proposals are voted on. (It should be pointed out in this connection that if this is so, and the people are well informed, voting on the order of voting reproduces the same problem.)
3. A situation in which the choice between alternative A and alternative B depends on whether alternative C (which in itself has no chance of winning) is or is not entered into the voting process. Most legislatures follow procedures which fall under the second of these possibilities.

If there is a possibility of arranging all of the alternatives in a single dimension with individuals having an optimal point and their preferences falling away monotonically as one moves away from that optimal point in either direction (single peakedness), then the problem is avoided. Unfortunately, most choices involve policies that differ from each other in more than one dimension and so cannot be arrayed in such a one-dimensional continuum. Furthermore, voting on them one aspect at a time reintroduces the second of the problems above. Nevertheless, the assumption of single peaks (whose validity is probably due to voter ignorance) has been successfully used in much empirical work.

While there is no doubt about the mathematical accuracy of the proofs of the above propositions, the real problem is whether they are of great practical significance in voting. Unfortunately, this turns out to be an extremely difficult question whose solution is unlikely to be found in the near future. In essence there are two possibilities when we observe such voting bodies as the House of Representatives and look at the outcome. The first is that the outcome is essentially random, that is, matters are taken up in some order, that order determines the voting outcome and the members of the House do not realize that they could then change that outcome by changing the order in which the propositions are voted on. This possibility would imply that luck plays an immense role in democracy.

The alternative is to say that the outcome is manipulated by somebody who understands the situation and who has control over the agenda. The House majority leader, or the chairman of the Rules committee, is sometimes suggested as that person. This implies that we really have a dictatorship, one that is well concealed.

In my opinion, the indeterminacy thrown into the outcome by these propositions of social choice theory is actually quite small in practical terms. Thus the Chairman of the House Rules Committee may be able to change an appropriation bill by, say, one hundred thousand dollars, but not by an amount which (given the size of these appropriations) is particularly relevant.[4] Among Public Choice theorists mine is a minority point of view. The majority, although it is deeply concerned about these problems, tends to ignore the implications of its point of view on the desirability of democracy as a form of government.

4. See G. Tullock, "The General Irrelevance of the General Impossibility Theorem," *Quarterly Journal of Economics* 81 (May 1967): 256–70.

Empirical evidence has clearly demonstrated that agenda control can to some extent affect the outcome. This of course is going to surprise nobody. One does not need the complex mathematics of voting in order to realize that those members of any assembly who are in a position to control the order upon which things are voted have power. Similarly the control of what propositions are actually put before the voters can have considerable impact on the outcome. The demonstration of the empirical impact from agenda control, however, does not really support the theorems given above. Of course, we cannot say that the failure to find clearcut proofs that the outcome in a democracy is essentially either random or fraudulent (as would be implied by the mathematical work on voting) proves that it is not. The problem is difficult and subtle and in the present state of our knowledge must be left for further research. Meanwhile, we all go on with faith that the voting process produces an acceptable outcome even though mathematical investigation raises grave doubts.

Turning now to the theory of bureaucracy, once again Public Choice thought has worked a revolution. The traditional view was either that bureaucrats followed the orders of their political superiors or alternatively that they simply did what was right. Public Choice theorists, following the work of Tullock,[5] Downs[6] and Niskanen,[7] believe that these are not proper statements about the bureaucrats' motives, although to some extent the bureaucrats do attempt to do what is right—including obedience to the views of their superiors. However, in modern societies where civil service legislation makes it all but impossible for the superiors either to dismiss them or even to reduce their salaries, the degree to which the bureaucrats are so compelled is moderate. Furthermore, in most civil service situations the power of a political appointee to reward his inferiors by promotion is very much restricted. Promotion decisions are to a considerable extent controlled by both legal and public-relations considerations which may compel a superior to promote someone whom he actually thinks has been sabotaging his policy.

While this is a characteristic of most modern civil service structures, there is no law of nature which says that government should be organized in this way. Traditionally, higher officials have been free to promote, demote or dis-

5. G. Tullock, *The Politics of Bureaucracy* (Washington, D.C.: Public Affairs Press, 1965).

6. A. Downs, *Inside Bureaucracy* (Boston: Little, Brown, 1967).

7. W. Niskanen, *Bureaucracy and Representative Government* (Chicago: Aldine-Atherton, 1971).

miss their subordinates. Even here, however, the fact that the higher official cannot possibly know everything that is going on at the lower ranks means that his control gradually diminishes as one moves away from his position down the pyramid of ranks.

For example, in the USA it was recently discovered that it is not possible for the Secretary of Defense to know the specifications which a civil servant, located at a vast distance down the pyramid, produced for a new coffee pot for military aircraft. In this case, the civil servant who specified a coffee pot capable of withstanding a crash that would kill the entire crew of the plane was neither dismissed nor even reprimanded. Indeed the newspapers that reported the story did not even mention his name, but instead concentrated on the Secretary of Defense. In 1870 a military procurement agent who made a mistake like this (and which got into the newspapers) would have found it necessary to hunt for a new job within an hour or so.

Basically the average employee in a bureaucracy is interested in retaining his job and gaining promotion and for this purpose wants to please his superiors. Under the old-fashioned system where he had little job security, and where promotion was determined strictly by his superiors, there was considerable pressure on him. In present circumstances, where to all intents and purposes he cannot be dismissed and where even his promotion is to some extent protected from political intervention by his superiors, this pressure is less important. However, even in a different case, in which he did indeed want to please his superiors, this would not necessarily lead to activity which is in the public interest. That would depend on the political situation of the party or individual who at that time was in control of his branch of the government.

This attenuation of control, in which much of what is done by lower-ranking officials is simply unknown to those of higher rank, is characteristic of all bureaucracies. There are however various ways by which the higher ranks can become, to some extent, aware of what is being done by the lower ranks. Undoubtedly the most efficient of these is simply an accounting system. In the case of a private company, whose motive is making money, the accounts do a reasonably good job (no more) of signalling what the various lower-ranking officials are contributing to that goal. When we turn to government, however, we have the combination of a set of objectives that are either vague or not clearly specified and a situation where there is no accurate way of measuring the contribution of each person to those objectives. Under such circumstances, control is much more severely attenuated.

When we have a civil service structure which separates the individual from much of the control power of his superiors, the problem is even more severe. Whether an individual bureaucrat works hard or not, prepares himself or herself well or not, is largely a matter of individual choice. As a rough rule of thumb, those people who do work hard and prepare themselves well are those people who have their own idea of what government should do in their particular division and work hard at that. In a way they are hobbyists. It should be said however, that their hobby is normally motivated by a desire on their part to maximize what they think is the public good. In other words, they are usually well-intentioned individuals who can be criticized only in that their idea of the public good may or may not coincide with that of their superiors. If it does not coincide, this does not prove that they are wrong and the superiors right, but it does mean that the government is not apt to follow a coordinated policy. In times past, it used to be normal to refer to the US Department of State as "a loose confederation of tribal chieftains." The phrase is not used any more, but as far as I can see this is only because the confederation itself has broken down.

Bureaucrats normally have several private motives. One is, of course, simply not to work too hard — a motive which does not seriously affect the hobbyist described above. Another is to expand the size of one's own department and, in the process of so doing, being willing to go along with the expansion of all the rest. A third is to improve the "perks" that accompany the particular position.[8]

Note that this is not intended as criticism of the bureaucrat. We would expect anyone who is given the kind of opportunities that are given to bureaucrats to do more or less what they do. However, the consequence is that large bureaucracies tend to grow larger, tend as they grow larger to follow less in the way of integrated policies and more in the way of policies that develop in the lower reaches of the pyramid and tend in fact not to work terribly hard.[9]

The problem is multiplied when bureaucracies become very large, because the members of the bureaucracy can vote. Furthermore, empirical evidence[10] shows they vote more frequently than non-bureaucrats. Thus their percent-

8. See J. L. Migué and G. Balageur, "Towards a General Theory of Managerial Discretion," *Public Choice* 17 (Spring 1974): 27–43.

9. See J. T. Bennett and W. P. Orzechowski, "The Voting Behavior of Bureaucrats: Some Empirical Evidence," *Public Choice* 41(2) (1983): 271–84.

10. See note 9 above.

age in the voting population is somewhat larger than their percentage in the actual population.[11] Thus, the political superior must consider the people working for him as in part his employers rather than his employees. He may not be able to fire them, but in the mass they can fire him. Altogether, the system is not well designed and does not work very well.

So far we have been talking about Public Choice and what has been learned, but not of the lessons of a normative nature that have been drawn, i.e., the theory of constitutions. It is to this that I now turn.

Not all students of Public Choice favour the same reforms in each area. Further, some have not specifically said what reforms they would prefer because they believe that not enough is yet known about the process to be able to suggest improvements. Nevertheless, there are several rather general propositions which most students would agree upon as ways of improving the functioning of government. In a discussion as brief as this, it is not possible to include all the differences of opinion and all the modifying clauses which would be appended to each suggestion for reform. Thus the reader should not assume that everyone studying Public Choice agrees with all the propositions which follow.

To begin with the voter, no student of the subject has any idea of how to improve the voters' information. With respect to voting itself there have been some proposals for improved voting methods, but no widespread support exists for any particular improvement. In spite of this, I think it can be said fairly that most students would like to see voters vote more than they do now, favouring more direct voting on issues, and legislatures with larger membership (so that the connection of an individual voter and his representative is closer).

The basic desire to give voters more control of the mechanism is not based on any false idea of how well the voters are informed. It is simply that the voters are the only people in the whole process who do not have an element of systematic bias in their decision process. They may be badly informed, but what they want is their own well-being. The well-being of its citizens should be the objective of the state. When we turn to other parts of the government invariably we find at least some conflict between the interests of the officials and the interests of the average man. Thus increasing the average man's control is not particularly likely to improve the efficiency of the government using some abstract definition of efficiency. But it is likely to make the govern-

11. See B. S. Frey and W. W. Pommerehne, "How Powerful Are Public Bureaucrats as Voters?" *Public Choice* 38(3) (1982): 253–62.

ment more in accord with the preferences of the common man; i.e., it brings us a little closer to the objective of popular rule which is supposed to be what democracy is about. Those who do not favour popular rule would not regard this as desirable, but there are few elitists among the students of Public Choice.

The actual decision-making procedures used in the legislatures have been widely discussed and some proposed improvements command wide acceptance. First, many would like to have at least one house of the legislature elected by proportional representation. Secondly, Buchanan and Tullock's arguments in *The Calculus of Consent*[12] for bicameral legislatures have generally been accepted. The further suggestion there that more than a simple majority is desirable for most legislation is seldom directly criticized, but is not so widely approved. The argument that this higher-than-majority requirement would change the structure of the log-rolling process in a favourable way has seldom been directly criticized, but the asymmetrical effect of such a rule (i.e., the status quo is retained unless a reinforced majority can be obtained to change it) offends some people.

Turning to the bureaucracy, there is much more agreement on reform. First, that a bureaucracy should be brought more firmly under the control of the political leaders is, I think, uniformly accepted. The dangers of this are recognized — but there are various ways in which the higher officials could be given the right to discipline civil servants while still reducing their power to fill the government with their cousins.

Apart from such straightforward proposals for changes in the personnel structure, there are other ways of putting pressure on the government. The first is to work some competition into the system. Currently, not only do most government departments have a monopoly over whatever function they perform, but almost every proposal to increase the efficiency of government takes the form of eliminating what little competition has popped up. Competition between government departments should be encouraged rather than discouraged.

Finally, it may be possible to "contract out" government activities or literally transfer them wholely to the market. The mere threat of this will frequently lower the cost of government activity. Having several private companies bidding for a government service, however, is better.

It can be seen that at the concrete level, those who study Public Choice

12. J. Buchanan and G. Tullock, *The Calculus of Consent: Logical Foundations of Constitutional Democracy* (Ann Arbor: University of Michigan Press, 1962).

have been able to provide more in the way of suggestions for reform within the bureaucratic structure than in the higher-level parts of democracy where the voters control the legislature, and the legislature and executive then control the bureaucracy. This is unfortunate but not surprising. Nevertheless, there are suggestions for improving the whole structure of government and with time, it is hoped, there will be both more ways of making improvements and better scientific evidence that the "improvements" are indeed improvements.

Public Choice is a new and radical approach to government, but its firm foundations in economic methodology mean that we have more confidence in its accuracy than with most new ideas. Further, it has by now been empirically tested very thoroughly. Government is the solution to some problems and the source of others. Public Choice shows strong promise of being able to reduce significantly the difficulties we now have with democratic government.

PUBLIC CHOICE

WHAT I HOPE FOR THE NEXT TWENTY-FIVE YEARS

Samuel Goldwyn is reported to have said: "Prediction is very hard, particularly for the future." If I look back on my previous predictions of the future for public choice, I find that they were normally wrong. I do not expect my future estimates to be much better. Nevertheless, the editors have asked me to make some guesses, and I am willing to oblige. The reader should keep in mind, however, that that is what they are: guesses.

Indeed, they may be even less than guesses. I have put "Hope" in the title of this essay to indicate that I am not really trying to guess the future. I am saying what I would like it to look like. There are various things I would like to have happen, but whether they will or not is an open question.

First, public choice started as a revolutionary science and with time became a normal science. Although it is now a normal science progressing somewhat slowly, I believe that it is progressing a good deal faster than either standard economics or standard political science. These latter disciplines are what one might even call subnormal sciences in their rates of growth. I sometimes think that economics is moving backwards.

Let me turn to my wish list. The first is that public choice pays more attention to non-democratic forms of government. We are, at the moment, in an historic high for democracy, but, frankly, I do not think that this is going to be a permanent phenomenon. Even now, the non–democratically controlled part of the world is still a very large part, though less than half. Traditionally, non-democratic governments have been common and democratic governments scarce. We may go back to that, although I would think it more likely we will go back to the point where both democratic and non-democratic governments are common, but the non-democratic are the more prevalent of the two.

In any event, I feel we need further study of non-democratic systems. Today, most discussion of non-democratic systems consists simply of pointing out that they are not very nice. This is true enough, but not very helpful. We need studies of why they are not very nice, why different kinds of non-democratic government exist, and what their effects are — all of these are subjects to which we should, I think, give attention.

Reprinted, with kind permission of Kluwer Academic Publishers, from *Public Choice* 77 (January 1993): 9–16.

A second area which I think should be looked into is the internal arrangements of bureaucracy. A good deal of work has been done indicating that bureaucracies are to a considerable extent motivated by the individual benefits of the bureaucrats. It is hard to read about the functioning of bureaucracies, however, and not to feel that that is merely a first step.

We should of course keep in mind that bureaucrats like everybody else will attempt to maximize their own well being, but anyone who pays careful attention to the behavior of bureaucrats realizes that that is by no means all there is to it. Bureaucrats clearly engage in some activity when they could remain completely idle. This may, of course, be because of the fact that they are easily bored, but it seems to me that we should have some better explanation. Further, they clearly have ideas as to what their part of the government should be doing and attempt to do it, even if that is not what their superiors want. Once again, we should have a better explanation of such behavior than we have.

To continue, the information conditions within the bureaucracy should be examined. Since Downs' first book, we have realized that the voter is rationally ignorant of many things. The bureaucrat is also rationally ignorant, but he rationally has certain types of information and certain types of misinformation. Both these categories have great effects on his behavior, and we know very little about them. I think that is a situation which should be remedied.

The above are areas where, I think, improvements should be made. I would now like to turn to some areas where, as far as I know, we simply have no ideas at all.

The first of these is what I call the growth paradox. Rather by accident, I stumbled on some long-term data on the size of government and the size of GNP for the United States and discovered that, except for wartime, from 1790 to 1930 the federal government was 2–3 percent of GNP. After the end of the disturbances of the Depression and World War II, the federal government began growing as a percentage of GNP in an almost straight-line way. A fairly steep straight line, in fact, fits the data since the end of the Korean war about as well as a horizontal line did before. The period between 1929 and 1953 is a disturbed period.

Inspired by this, I looked up some other countries and found that Denmark and Sweden showed the same phenomena except that their basic rate of central government growth was higher and had reached higher levels. In their case the break was clearly in the 1930s. England, where the data goes back to 1640, is a little more difficult. The most warlike country in Europe, the English were almost continuously at war, with the result that the early period of this data is very disturbed. Nevertheless, it looks as if they had a stable level of government, possibly a declining level of government, up to about 1905–1910, when their government began straight-line growth.

Italy, whose data are particularly difficult because during the Fascist period they seem to have been largely imaginary, showed a stable level (excluding the Fascist period) until 1960 and then a very steep rise.

I know of no theory of government which explains both the long period of stability and then the almost straight-line growth. There are theories that explain the straight-line growth, but they unfortunately depend on characteristics of democracy which democracies share in the period before and after the growth began. They cannot explain both.

There has been a theory of government growth put forward by Buchanan that it is a result of Keynesianism. I do not want to swear that this is not true, but the data certainly do not fit this theory very well. England, Denmark, and Sweden all began their growth before Keynes wrote his famous book. For the United States it is difficult to say when it began, but it looks as if it began before the book had much influence, and Italy, of course, did not begin government growth until 1960.

It seems to me that we should have a theory of this growth. I should also say that, although there are not any good data, I believe that the same pattern of a long period of basically level expenditures and then sharp growth would be found true of the dictatorships as well as the democracies. The problem is that there are just not enough data to test it in any countries except the five I have mentioned above. This is clearly a public choice problem, and one to which we have no answer.

There is another choice problem of considerable importance which is not well explained. Beginning in the early 1960s countries began running large peacetime deficits. The United States was a late entrant into this field and has never had a deficit which, as a share of GNP, was at the same level with, let us say, Belgium. Nevertheless, it is a big enough country so that the deficit is quite conspicuous.

Once again, theories are available which explain why democratic governments would run large deficits, but they do not explain why they did not do so up to 1960. Further, as a matter of fact, dictatorships do about as much in the way of running deficits as democracies. All of this is a sharp change from the nineteenth century when one of the arguments for democracy was that it tended to be fiscally conservative whereas royal governments were not.

As the reader may know, I have a theoretical explanation for all of this, but it is a very poor one. Accepting it for the time being, it assumes that most politicians thought that it was literally impossible to run large deficits in peacetime. Whether they meant by that that the voters would throw them out, or they thought there was some kind of scientific rule that made it impossible, I do not know.

If my theory is correct, the politicians in one country accidentally ran a deficit in peacetime and discovered there were no consequences, so they did it again the following year. This is rather like the developments in the United States in the 1970s and '80s. Of course, it occurred much earlier elsewhere.

Other politicians in other countries noticing this development began doing the same thing (dictatorships and democracies at about the same rate). I do not claim this is a good theory, but I do claim that no one has offered anything else which fits the available data. It is necessary to produce a theory which fits both dictatorships and democracies and which explains both the long period in which they did not run peacetime deficits and then very large deficits year after year. Of course, not all countries have run such deficits and some of those that did have stopped. This is a further problem for research.

Another mystery to me, in any event, is why Europe and its overseas extensions like the United States and Australia have become such a dominant part of the world. Hume talks about the flourishing nature of the Chinese monarchy in 1775. Indeed, in those days no one seemed to think the Chinese were behind the Europeans. It was not just the Chinese. India was at that time in the process of being conquered by England, but nobody thought that it was a backward part of the world. Indeed, one of the reasons for concern about gold flow among those "economists" who were worried about it was the steady flow of gold to the Far East by way of foreign trade. It was not possible for Europe to produce enough goods to pay for the imports from India and China. Even Turkey was in a powerful and advanced state in 1700. The last Turkish attempt to take Vienna occurred during the reign of Louis XIV. The Arab states at this point were mainly dominated by Turkey, but there were other places in the Far East which were thought to be reasonably progressive. No one thought of Thailand, Persia, Burma, or Japan as backward.

All of this changed suddenly. Europe shot up and surpassed all of these other countries and became overwhelmingly the dominant part of the world. Since it is a rather small continent and since the parts of the rest of the world which it not only conquered but settled are products of this expansion, I find this mysterious and would like to have an explanation.

We will now turn to a completely different problem and one which is essentially technical. When we look at the world, we observe that not only are there undemocratic governments, but there is a great deal of variance among democratic governments as well. Most of the non-English-speaking world uses some form of proportional representation. Parts of the English-speaking world, Ireland and Australia, use proportional representation, but in their case it is the Hare method which is quite different from the type of proportional representation used by other countries.

We would immediately assume that this makes a considerable difference, but if you look at the data, it is rather hard to differentiate the performance of a country like Germany from that of the United States. It is true that the United States has a smaller government than most of these proportional representation countries, but it is larger than Switzerland, and Switzerland is the purest proportional representation country in the world.

It seems to me that careful investigation of these different forms of government is desirable. In this connection, the widespread use of direct voting by various forms of the referendum on government policies which is so common in Switzerland and California should be included among the subjects studied. With the exception of some rather general statements of my own, there has been no investigation of these different forms of government or efforts to make comparative analyses. I think this is a major problem and would like to have people investigate it.

Of course, I favor the demand-revealing process. Politically, it does not seem likely that it will be adopted any time in the near future, but I think it is highly desirable that examination of it be included in any comparative study of different voting methods. This will at least keep the idea alive, and will improve our knowledge in an area which I, at least, think is important.

I favor the two-chamber legislature, one of which is elected by proportional representation and the other by a single-member or constituency system. It should be admitted, however, that the basic reason I am in favor of this is not a careful study of either of these, but a desire simply to have two houses which are elected in radically different ways. A single house voting by a 60% majority was suggested in a proposed amendment to the Constitution for some fiscal measures. It just barely missed being passed by Congress. I think it would be about equally effective.

In practice, there are not just these two different methods of voting. As a matter of fact, when one looks at these things in detail, the methods of voting vary immensely. Proportional representation means different things in the Netherlands than in Switzerland.

Further, single-member constituency voting means different things in different parts of the world. England, for example, has a scheme under which all Scotsmen have heavier weight in the elections than do Englishmen. For a long time Northern Ireland had its own autonomous government and, as a sort of payment for that, had a lower weight in Parliament than its population would normally have given it. This is by no means all the peculiarities for England. For a long time there were representatives from various colleges sitting in the House of Commons. This was abolished at the end of World War II, but as far as I know, no one has looked into the question of whether these representatives had a favorable or unfavorable effect on the outcome.

This is merely a start. There is a radical difference in the population needed to elect a senator in Nevada and California. Does this have major effects on the outcome of the bills respecting those two states? As far as I know, there are no actually careful studies of this issue.

Another extremely interesting case would be Greece and France. The reason Greece and France are interesting is because the governments of these two countries frequently change their election methods before an election, with the idea of scuppering the opposition. Since they are not very skillful, they have so far not been very successful in this objective, but they still, one would think, provide a great deal of data for comparative analysis. So far as I know no one has studied these cases.

To return to the chambers of the legislature, most democracies have more than one. Nebraska is almost unique in its unicameral, single-member legislature, although it shares that with Israel. I think many places, however, have two chambers, one of which is markedly weaker than the other. Is this better or worse than having two chambers which are of equal power or even a single chamber or for that matter three? In a way, giving the president the veto power means that our legislature has something equivalent to a three-chamber legislature.

In Iran, Khomeini introduced an interesting system in which there is a supreme court (the Council of Guardians), which depends upon a much more ancient constitution than our supreme courts, specifically the Koran and the Hadith. Does this make a difference? I should pause here to say that on the whole the government of Iran since 1900 has had strong elected elements. It has rarely been what we would call a perfect democracy, but it nevertheless has had a good deal of democratic influence, as it does today.

There is a strong tendency among Americans to assume that any country with which we have had very bad relations is probably a dictatorship. This, for example, leads people to allege that Germany was a dictatorship in 1914 and Japan in 1940. Khomeini was undoubtedly a nasty man, so the allegation he was a dictator is almost automatic.

This rule of antagonism works the other way. Our southern neighbor, Mexico, roughly from the 1930s when the parties of the left came into complete control until the present, is an odd rotating dictatorship in which the president is in very nearly complete control but is required to retire after 6 years. In compensation he is permitted to appoint his successor. I expect most of my readers do not know these facts because we rather like the leftist government of our next-door neighbor and hence assume that it is democratic.

These are all subjects which I think would merit investigation, but I should repeat that a comparison of dictatorial and democratic governments is important. Some of South America has had a very long tradition of alternating democratic and dictatorial governments. Whether this tradition is going to be revived, I do not know. At the moment they have only three genuine dictatorships, Cuba, Peru, and Mexico, and the present dictator of Mexico, Mr. Salinas, is showing signs of attempting to switch to democratic techniques.

Regardless of the future, the past should provide a strong study area in which to compare democracies to dictators. Was there a great change in policy when dictatorships were replaced by democracies and vice-versa? Paldam has investigated this with respect to their monetary and deficit problems, but this is a very narrow investigation.

Another problem is who should vote? At the moment, most democratic countries have adult suffrage, although usually there are some classes — felons — that are not permitted to vote. Universal adult suffrage, however, is a relatively new idea, and as far as I know, there were no cases of it before World War I. England did not even have universal male suffrage during World War I, and only adopted it shortly after the end of the war. Before that time you had to have a certain, admittedly quite low, amount of money to vote if you lived in the countryside. It did not achieve universal adult suffrage until the 1930s.

Does any of this make any difference? By looking at the comparative votes in different states in the United States as the states gradually permitted women to vote, we could find out if there were changes in their legislation. I am sure we can expect them for those bills that reflect women only — such as rights of marriage partners. But I am not sure that anything else would show up as different. International comparisons would also be very helpful here.

Making international comparisons and considering England, you must remember they have a two-house legislature, the upper house of which is inherited and appointed. Now it is true that the upper house has steadily had its power reduced since about 1904, and there are now a number of members of it who are not hereditary peers. Does this make any great difference? Does the bizarre appointed upper house of Canada make any great difference in outcomes there?

The last constitutional crisis in Australia came when the upper house refused to pass the budget and the governor-general took this as a reason for dissolving parliament. The fact that this led to a crisis is fairly good evidence that the upper house was not thought to have very much power. Does this make any difference? Once again, we should try to find out. An examination of whether their constitutional structure makes any difference should begin by careful comparative analysis of existing constitutions.

I have made a good many theoretical statements about different constitutional structures, but I would like to have the empirical data available to test them. Except for a long series of studies on American states by Tollison and his co-authors, this is largely lacking. Unfortunately, Tollison et al. were forced by data limitations to deal with mainly minor rather than major problems.

That these constitutional measures are believed to be important can be seen from the fact that there are lengthy debates about them. At the moment the Israelis think that their extreme proportional representation rule is not working well and are talking about moving toward the English system, a system which they apparently do not fully understand. At the same time, the English, feeling that their system is not working very well, are talking about moving toward a proportional representation system, once again without very much evidence that they fully understand it. In both cases there is a great deal of excitement about potential change. I mentioned above that the Greeks and the French tend to change the election rules almost every election in hopes of sustaining the currently dominant party in power and normally fail. This indicates both bad motives and ignorance.

But any discussion of such constitutional questions automatically raises another fundamental problem which involves the defense of the Constitution. One can say the Constitution prevents certain types of legislation or requires a two-house legislature or something of that sort, but what prevents the Constitution itself from changing either violently and quickly or slowly and gradually? What we need is a self-enforcing constitution, and as far as I know, there is no real theory of how we can design such a thing.

When I was a boy, I would have said it was very simple — the Supreme Court upheld the Constitution against the executive branch and the Congress. Today, of course, I know better. Since the 1930s, the Court has been probably the major source of changes in the Constitution — certainly far more important than Congress and the executive branch.

Further, looking back at the past, it is obvious that this always was, to some extent, true. It might not have been so that the Court was the major source of such changes, but it was always a source. The famous constitutional cases that you read in courses in constitutional law in law schools are almost exclusively cases in which the Supreme Court laid down a rule that was not in the Constitution. In many cases the rule seems to be rather inconsistent with the rest of the Constitution although, of course, in other cases it simply extends them.

To repeat what I said above, we have no theory or practical rule for a self-enforcing constitution. How can a constitution be designed so that it defends itself? This is in many ways the most important question which public choice faces, and certainly a very important question for applied politics in general and unfortunately, we have no answer.

I was asked to predict the next 25 years in public choice. I have not predicted; I have expressed hopes. If I am lucky, my hopes will be accepted as research plans by various scholars with the result that, in fact, they will become successful predictions.

CASUAL RECOLLECTIONS OF AN EDITOR

Introduction

The first issue of *Papers on Non-Market Decision-Making* is dated 1966 but I actually began work on it some time before publication. I should, perhaps, confess that it wasn't much work, but the little work that was involved did get spread over some time. I have resigned as editor and been formally installed in a state of great prestige and little power as Founding Editor as of the first of May 1990. My influence, however, by way of a backlog of accepted articles, will extend into 1991. I think, therefore, I can claim 25 years as editor. I can't say that it's been a hard grind — on the whole, I enjoyed it. It's perhaps been a hard grind for people who wanted to publish articles in my journal and found that I was obstructive.

I don't think that I had better advise people on editing since, in the first place, my editing methods are radically different than those used for other journals. Secondly, I tried two other journals, one of which, *Frontiers in Economics*, had to be closed down after three issues, and the other, *The Journal of Economic Criticism*, only made one. I have one hit out of three tries. Aspiring editors or founders of new journals would be better advised to follow the routine rather than my deviant procedures. Nonetheless, I propose to devote this article to recollections of my editorship.

A Gap in the Intellectual Market

In 1965 and 1966 there were not very many people writing articles in the brand new field now called "public choice," but those few articles that were being produced were very hard to get published. I knew of several which were circulating in the invisible college but had not been published and probably never would be if there were no changes made.

As a further problem, I had written an article called "Information without Profit" which was not in what we now call "public choice." It was hard to get published. It dealt with some aspects of the private charity market. As a

Reprinted, with kind permission of Kluwer Academic Publishers, from *Public Choice* 71 (September 1991): 121–39.

matter of fact, the article seems to be by standard measures quite a superior one. It has been incorporated in two anthologies.

The actual origin of *Public Choice*, however, was a casual conversation with the University printer over coffee at the Colonnade Club. I asked him how much it would cost to produce a small booklet, and he gave me a price which was so low that I realized that I could pay it out of my own pocket. If my recollection is right, it was $700.00 although the dollar was worth more then than it is now. In any event, I decided to produce a little book of readings. At the time, that's what I was planning on — a book, not a journal.

Since I wanted to include my own paper, which clearly had not much to do with politics, I chose the title *Papers on Non-Market Decision-Making*. On the whole, this decision was probably fortunate. At that time we were canvassing a number of possible names for the new field, and I would probably have ended up with "synergistics" or "polenomics" if I had just taken one of the words then being suggested. The obvious title "Political Economy" was barred partly by the fact that it was the old name of economics and partly by the fact that the Marxists were already beginning to claim that title as their own.

The actual editorial work was fairly simple and straightforward. I wrote letters to people who I knew had papers circulating in the invisible academy that I thought would be suitable. As a result of hearing about these letters, Otto Davis volunteered his long paper with Dempster and Wildavsky, and I was ready to go.

Economizing

It turned out that my own money was not necessary. The Virginia economics department had received a small research grant which could be allocated as the chairman wished, and I had been working on my book on the social organization of science.[1] In the first draft of the book I advocated having research money distributed by the actual scientists instead of by a central authority. I argued that research grants should be divided among scientists and that they then would voluntarily donate portions to people who they thought had more expensive and important research projects.

The reason why this is relevant is simply that Ronald Coase was vigorously lobbying to get the entire amount of money for himself. He came around to

1. *The Organization of Inquiry*, Duke University Press.

everybody, including me, and pointed out how important it was. Buchanan, however, had been at least partially convinced by my arguments and decided to experiment. He divided the money evenly among the full professors with a somewhat smaller amount to each of the associate professors. I was an associate at that time, and my money turned out to be just about enough to pay for the journal.

It's interesting that although Coase had vigorously argued that we should all agree that the whole amount should be given to him, when this allocation system was announced he dropped all further efforts. Apparently he was convinced that no one would in fact give up their money and no one did. Even those professors who were not really doing research held on to it. Thus, the experiment, small as it was, was conclusive. My suggested method of allocating funds was not a good one.

The procedure for putting *Papers on Non-Market Decision-Making* out was very simple indeed. It was simply typed and then photo-reproduced by the printer. The world's most efficient secretary, Betty Tillman, did the actual typing although later, of course, we had to change that routine.

At the suggestion of the printer, we put up our small number of copies in three forms. Some were bound in paperback, some in hardback, and 100 were not bound. These were sold at quite different prices. The idea was that the hardbacks could probably be unloaded to libraries. I should say that on the whole this project over time was not very successful, but we did get at least some money this way. The 100 unbound copies we cut into the individual articles and sold them to the authors at what was more or less the standard reprint price. At the time I thought this was probably the principal benefit to the authors from the publication because I suspected that not very many copies would be sold, which at first was true.

The high standard price for reprints, however, meant rather to my surprise that I could cover my printing costs even though sales of the actual book were rather small. But the price of the 100 reprints posed one difficulty here. Toby Davis pointed out that granted the length of his article with Dempster and Wildavsky it would be cheaper for him to buy 100 copies of the journal than 100 reprints. This made it necessary for me to make some reductions in rates. It was, nevertheless, true that for this issue and for a number of years thereafter the sale of the 100 reprints provided a major source of income for the journal. With time, of course, and the development of Xeroxing, we had to give it up. Since by then we had a reasonable number of subscribers, this was no great pain.

One of the results of publishing this book was that I began receiving a lot more papers in the mail. I don't think these were papers that had already been circulating in the invisible academy—I think they were papers that people had in mind, but had not written. Once they realized they could be published, they wrote them up and sent them to me. In any event, flush with the payments from the reprint fees, I decided that I could afford to bring out a second volume and put out *Papers on Non-Market Decision-Making II*. If you look at this issue you'll see that there is no date on the cover. At that time, I was not planning on a journal, but simply occasional collections of papers.

Sales and reprint fees more or less compensated me for all the costs. I also got more papers sent to me, and I decided that I could probably produce a regular journal. Thus I brought out Volume III which was labeled on the cover "Fall 1967." The idea was to produce two a year from then on.

Actually, the journal was basically a personal project of my own with payments originally out of my own pocket and then out of a small research grant.

I should say, however, that I succeeded in one way or another in getting a good deal of university support. As I mentioned, the papers were typed up without any charge to me, first by Betty Tillman and later by other secretaries in the Thomas Jefferson Center. Of course, nobody charged me for my use of office space while editing. Further, and this was for a long time a mainstay of my cost-structure, I mailed copies of the journal out by the simple expedient of putting them into the interuniversity mail basket at the department office. It wasn't until my third year at VPI that the department head, Wilson Schmidt, realized what I was doing and began charging me.

The kindly attitude of the university printer was also helpful financially. If you look back to the early paperback versions of the journal, you'll notice that different issues have differently colored covers. This was because I was printing up only a few hundred, and he give me a special price on odd bits of paper stock that he had left over from other projects. As I picked up subscriptions, of course, this became less and less feasible.

Refereeing

It was at this time, also, that I experimented a little bit with conventional refereeing. Obviously, I had always been selective, only publishing some of the papers sent in, but it had been easy to get good papers. The field was a new one and attracted only unusual people dealing with topics that had never been dealt with before, so the supply of good papers exceeded my printing capacity.

Nevertheless, I decided that if I was building a journal, I should follow the usual pattern and send articles out to referees for their opinions. My experience here was unpleasant, although I gather completely normal. It turns out to be far more trouble to negotiate with referees about whether they are willing to read papers, how long they will take, what to do if the two referees disagree, will they either referee or send the paper back if they have done nothing for six months, etc., than it is to make up your own mind. Consequently, I switched over to the scheme which I used throughout the rest of my period as an editor in which I did most of the refereeing myself. Occasionally, for various special reasons, I would have a paper refereed by someone else, but in over 90 percent of the papers, I did it myself.

Although, to be quite frank, I adopted this procedure because it was less trouble than bickering with referees, I think it actually is better than the standard method. As far as I can see, the only argument for the standard method is the reduction of emotional tension and interpersonal irritation that it provides. The referees are anonymous and hence it is not possible to write them nasty letters or snub them vigorously the next time you meet them. Further, they are not motivated in their refereeing decisions by worrying about such things.

What is required here is a certain amount of toughness on the part of the people who make the publication decision. Then you can let their names be known. It seems to be fairly certain that refereeing should be done by people whose names are known who probably would have to one way or another be compensated for the social inconvenience they would suffer. I see no reason why academics should be not held responsible for their decisions if those decisions are made in the capacity of a referee. Nevertheless, anonymous referees is a custom which has been long established and which will be very difficult to shake.

In any event, this direct refereeing gave me the shortest turnaround time in the business. As a result, people not infrequently sent me articles even ahead of journals of much greater prestige simply because they knew they'd get an answer quickly, whereas the greater prestige journal might spend many months.

Although my motive was essentially to reduce my own labor time, my decision was right in other respects, too. I was able to withstand social pressure and although there have been quite justified criticisms of some of my decisions, I think the system works better.

The publication decision should be made either by the editor or one of a short list of permanent referees. It is, however, essential that whoever makes these decisions have an idea of the general quality of the articles now being submitted and the length of the queue. After all, it is necessary to get the journal out and only a certain number of articles can be included in it. The quality of the articles accepted, of necessity, depends on the quality and number of the articles submitted. Thus, for example, the top quarter of the submitted articles, which is roughly the level that I maintained in *Public Choice*, actually represented a different level of quality at different times, depending on the articles that happened to come in in any given 6-month period.

If there was a dearth of good articles it was necessary to accept somewhat more and if there was a surplus of articles it was necessary to reject somewhat more. The amount of articles published, after all, does not fluctuate with these factors. Fortunately, the law of large numbers comes to our rescue here and fluctuations are not large, but they do occur.

The practice of sending articles to referees is one of the reasons, I believe, that most of the regular journals are so hard to read. The referee is normally a narrow specialist in the field in which the author has chosen to write his article. If it contributes to that narrow speciality (and also if it is not too negative about the previous work of the referee) it will be accepted. Whether the article will be readable by somebody who is not specialized in that particular narrow niche is not something that bothers the referee. It should also be said that frequently this will lead to a deluge of articles on basically unimportant areas where it just happens to be easy to do the research.[2]

I should perhaps mention here one of the several editorial policies (I did have editorial policies) which I adopted. This was to send all comments on any given article to the author before I made up my mind whether I would accept or reject them. I made it clear both to the author of the comment and the victim of the comment that although I thought the author of the article was a suitable person to advise, I did not undertake to follow his advice. The author is both expert and biased.

I assumed at the beginning that almost all the authors would recommend the publication of the comment on their paper because publication of the comment, by giving them a chance to reply, guaranteed them a further publication. I expected this to be particularly significant for young assistant pro-

2. For further discussion, see *The Organization of Inquiry*, Duke University and American University Press, pp. 139–146, and also "What's Wrong with Editing," *Speculations in Science and Technology* 3.5 (1980): 6–16.

fessors en route to tenure. To my surprise this has not been, on the whole, true. Insofar as there is bias, the recommendations are against publication. Articles that make silly comments about my work are, I think, an opportunity for me to knock somebody down and to get an additional item on my bibliography. Apparently there are a great many young assistant professors who don't make that calculation.

Growth

It was about this time, at a meeting held in Chicago, that what was being referred to as the "no-name society" formally adopted the name Public Choice Society and the journal was named *Public Choice*. At this time, of course, the current distinction between public choice and social choice was unheard of. We ran the articles indiscriminately in *Public Choice*. It is still true that the two groups are very closely connected and social choice people attend public choice meetings, etc. Nevertheless, there now are separate journals.

In any event, the experiment was successful and the journal was published with a spring and fall issue through 1972. The principal technical change here was the acquisition of a new typewriter in 1969 with the result that the articles had the right ends adjusted.

In 1973 we went to three issues a year. I should say that I don't think that this expansion in any sense involved reduction in quality, although of course as we moved to a more routine approach we did get less originality. It was simply that more people were coming into the field and I think that this, in a real sense, reflects the success of the journal. One of my objectives was to provide a way in which people interested in public choice could get articles published and hence get promoted. Previously, people interested in public choice could write articles but had only a tiny possibility of getting accepted in the regular literature. This wouldn't help much on promotions.

I think that the journal, by making it possible for the ambitious academic to write in the field and still get promoted, led to a considerable expansion of the total output. Certainly by now we have a sizeable community of scholars who are publishing in a number of journals and, in fact, have made major penetrations into the standard journals in both political science and economics.

To return to financial matters, I received a small three-year grant from the

National Science Foundation to cover expansion of the journal, which, needless to say, was quite convenient, particularly as contributors were beginning to make difficulties about buying the reprints.

The University of Virginia for the third time refused to promote me to full professor. I moved to Rice University and took *Public Choice* with me. While I was at Rice, the journal continued to be printed (and mainly typed) in Virginia.

I had become a full professor on arrival at Rice — in fact, it was a full professorship in economics and political science — I was the only full professor in the brand new political science department. Nevertheless they weren't willing to meet Virginia Polytechnic Institute's offer so I then moved to Virginia and to Blacksburg, taking the journal with me.

This led to one of the more unpleasant bits of confusion. The particular issue of the journal that was being printed in Virginia and edited at Rice when I moved to Blacksburg, through accident was never proofread. I thought it was being proofed in Virginia and the people in Virginia thought I was proofing it.

In consequence, an equation-rich article by James Coleman got printed without any of the pluses and minuses that were supposed to be there. Since Coleman is a former professional heavyweight boxer, I was, needless to say, disturbed by this but I'm happy to say that I was able to keep out of his way until his temper cooled. In any event, as those of you who know him are aware, he is an equitable man and he did not get terribly angry. I, of course, distributed lengthy corrigenda immediately.

There was another minor difficulty more amusing than anything else. When the National Science Foundation grant ran out, we were supposed to report our expenditure of funds including any money we had left over. Needless to say, we, like all other NSF recipients, had arranged not to have any more money but we did have a number of unsold copies of the journal sitting around. An insane accountant in the research support organization of the university insisted on reporting these to NSF at their nominal retail value.

I am happy to say that Howard Hines and James Blackman were understanding about all of this. I did offer to send them all the copies if they wanted them but they rejected that proposal with great vigor. At this time, I was still receiving a good many grants from the NSF, but the other grants had nothing to do with the journal.

In 1974 we went to 4 issues, which we stuck with until the arrangements at Martinus Nijhoff to take over publication were complete. I think I was getting more people promoted, but once again I do not think there was any decline in the average quality of the journal even though there were more articles being printed. It was, however, becoming somewhat more routine as the field itself became more routine.

This was a disappointment to me. We started out with a revolution. I was in favor, like Jefferson, of more revolutions at a fairly rapid rate. It did not happen. There's been no further paradigm change. We are now "normal science," although I think we can honestly say that we are making progress faster than most aspects of economics and certainly more than political science. This is not because we are any brighter or harder working, but because it's easier to find interesting topics of research in a relatively unexplored field.

At VPI I got another small grant from a private foundation to help with the production of the journal. The purpose of the grant was to make us self-supporting in the future. When we did become self-supporting by transferring the journal to Martinus Nijhoff in 1978, I offered to return the surplus funds to the foundation. They not only rejected the money, but suggested that I set up a little school to teach other editors how to actually become self-supporting. Apparently they had made a number of grants to journals for the purpose of getting the journal self-supporting and, in all cases, found that this had simply led to further requests for grants.

During the period that I was working on this grant, we hired Barry Keating to act as an assistant professor of economics and do the hard work in connection with the journal. He was extremely efficient in all ways, to say nothing of the fact that both he and his wife were very pleasant people. From my standpoint, the largest single advantage of having him was he insulated me from the university printer at VPI. Because I was at VPI it was necessary to shift the printing from Charlottesville to Blacksburg. The printer at VPI, although like all printers a relatively artistic type who was a great help on design problems, was a hard person to get along with. Barry saved me from a stomach ulcer.

I mentioned that we were publishing the journal in hardback in hopes that libraries would buy it, but unfortunately most of them didn't. What they would do would be to get the paperback and then at the end of the year bind it, rather than taking the hardback. This was more expensive for them than buying the hardback but it was also in accordance with their routine. In 1976 I gave up on this but attempted to help the libraries by providing them with a bound volume, either hardback or paperback, for the entire year. Although it was cheaper and more convenient for them to do this than to rebind their paperback of quarterly issues, very few libraries were interested and after having tried the experiment again for another year, I dropped it.

I had been trying to interest various publishers such as Sage in the journal but without any real success. Introspectively, I think the reason was simply a lack of much real sales effort on my part. I rather naively thought that if I could point out that I had a journal with the kind of circulation I had even without their facilities, they would realize that we would be profitable. Apparently they were used to being given very very long sales pitches, and my modest pointing out that they would make money didn't seem to impress them.

Nevertheless, in late 1977 a man came into my office and informed me he was an editor at Martinus Nijhoff and he would like to take over the journal. I naturally agreed, and our relations with Martinus Nijhoff have been friendly and efficient ever since.

I had only two complaints about Martinus Nijhoff: I had not anticipated being paid as editor by them since I hadn't been before, but from time to time they would decide to pay me a small amount of money and do so and then decide not to and stop. The amount, in any event, was small and it was more of a minor irritation than anything else.

The second problem had to do with their continuous desire to expand the journal. As the readers will know, it's now 12 issues although with the new editors it's going back down to 8. Fortunately, I was able to get an input of good articles. This was a matter of some work but nothing more. Indeed, during this period I was able to somewhat raise my cutting level for the average article. The sudden upsurge of competitive journals which occurred just as I was leaving, may have a temporary effect on this matter.

What I anticipate is simply that more people will write articles because there are more outlets. Since it takes time for scholars, even assistant professors aiming at tenure, to adjust, there may be a temporary difficulty in getting sufficient quality articles. It shouldn't be a serious or permanent problem—all that will happen in the long run is that there will be more opportunities to publish and hence there will be more people writing in the field.

This brings the main structure of the story up to my recent resignation as editor. I assure the readers that this was completely voluntary—I am now 67 and it was obvious that we should make preparations for the future. The adjustment in other editors' positions is not quite so voluntary but nevertheless has caused no great difficulty. Normally, journal editors expect only a rather limited tenure and I presume that *Public Choice* will become a normal journal in this respect in the future. Bill Mitchell is thinking of retiring as book review editor and I sincerely hope we can talk him into staying. He has been markedly better in that role than anyone we ever had before and I'm sure better than anyone we could get to replace him.

Entrepreneurship in Ideas

From the account so far, the reader has probably received the impression that I simply looked at my mail and published the best articles. As a matter of fact, this is not true and I am rather proud of actually having editorial policies. From time to time I have decided that some particular subject should be encouraged; hence, I have lowered my standards for that particular subject with the idea of making it obvious to bright young assistant professors that this is a particularly easy place to do research which will be published. And then, as I get more articles, I raise my cutting level again but have meanwhile changed the total structure of the discipline.

My first venture of this sort was (Bob Tollison, one of our new editors, may resent this) to cut the quality level for acceptance of empirical articles. I had encountered a number of people, particularly political scientists, who had said that *Public Choice* was purely theoretical and not empirical. I knew that various people, including Tollison, were beginning to do work in this area and I decided it should be encouraged. I'm not of course saying that Tollison was a direct beneficiary of this policy, but surely at least some of his students were.

Another, and much more recent, case has been my interest in dictatorships. Even with the developments in Eastern Europe and the completely unprecedented level of democracy in Latin America, it is still true that a very large part of the population in the world live under dictatorships or some other form of despotism.

Historically, this has indeed been the normal form of government and my own personal guess is that the current rise in democracies is a temporary phenomenon. Regardless of whether that guess is right or wrong, in any event we should pay attention to the other form of government and I have been attempting to encourage articles in that area.

I don't know whether the new editors will be interested in this, and I suspect they won't be interested in another bit of editorial policy which is quasi-charitable. I occasionally receive articles which I think are out of scope for *Public Choice*, but where I think that the standard refereeing process in the regular journals is apt to be very unfair. I applied what I called my "safety net procedure" for the better of these articles. I agree that if they submit it to three regular journals, and get it rejected, I will publish it.

Now this means that we do occasionally print articles that are fairly radically out of scope in *Public Choice*. Clarence Morrison's article on the second best is an example. It is a fairly simple mathematical article which offers quite strong evidence that the second best is unimportant. It was, of course, sent to experts on second best by other journals and, needless to say, they didn't like this point of view. In consequence, it ended up in *Public Choice*. But, to repeat, I don't know whether the new editors will be willing to engage in this quasi-charitable activity.

In addition to publishing the journal and making the effort to start two more, I have a small book-publishing organization called Public Choice Monographs.

On the whole, it is commercially successful if you assume that the overhead, such as it is, is handled by various universities, which it always has been. I still have copies of these books around and would be delighted to sell them to any reader of this article. Readers will no doubt notice that a good many of these are either written or edited by me. In fact, some people have claimed that it's my "vanity press." In any event, some titles are still in stock:

Public Choice in New Orleans
Economic Theory of Learning
Toward a Science of Politics
Simons' Syllabus
Social Dilemma
Explorations in the Theory of Anarchy
Further Explorations in the Theory of Anarchy

There are also the public choice ties which can be purchased either from me or from the center at George Mason.

Envoi

To finish off, it has been for me an intellectually stimulating and pleasant 25 years. I hope that it has also been a valuable one from the standpoint of the society and that my editorial policies will not be regarded by other people as simply exhibits of bias.

PART 2

PROBLEMS OF MAJORITY VOTING

PROBLEMS OF MAJORITY VOTING

Economists have devoted a great deal of thought to problems of governmental policy and, in particular, to the question of proper allocation of resources between the public and private sectors.[1] On the other hand, little attention has been given to the actual process of decision-making or to the type of policy likely to come out of the process.[2] It is the purpose of this article to discuss one particular method of making governmental decisions—majority voting—and to attempt to derive conclusions about its implications for resource allocation and government policy. It is hoped that the conclusions will be more realistic than current doctrine, which is based on an essentially economic view of what "ought" to happen.

Since it is impossible to talk about everything at once, the demonstration will be confined to certain features of the majority process. A number of other serious problems raised by the voting system will be disregarded. The most important of these concerns a series of difficulties and paradoxes in the voting process itself.[3] I will also disregard the fact that voters are frequently very poorly informed or even deceived in voting, the great oversimplification of issues necessary in order to reduce them to a form such that they can be determined by vote, and innumerable other possible limitations on the functional efficiency of the democratic process.

I shall consider the operation of majority rule under two different restrictions: logrolling (i.e., vote-trading) permitted and logrolling not permitted, starting with the latter. Since logrolling is the norm, discussion of the non-logrolling case must start with consideration of the institutional structure which eliminates logrolling. The standard referendum on a simple issue is the best example. The voter cannot trade his vote on one issue for votes on oth-

Reprinted, with permission of the University of Chicago Press, from *Journal of Political Economy* 67 (December 1959): 571–79.

1. See Julius Margolis, "The Economic Evaluation of Federal Water Resource Development," *American Economic Review*, 49 (March, 1959), 69–111, for a review of some of the recent literature on the subject.

2. Pioneers have begun to appear. See Anthony Downs, *An Economic Theory of Democracy* (New York: Harper & Bros., 1957), and Duncan Black, *The Theory of Committees and Elections* (Cambridge: Cambridge University Press, 1958).

3. See Black (*op. cit.*) for a comprehensive view of the difficulties discovered to date.

ers because he and his acquaintances represent too small a part of the total electorate for this to be worth the effort involved. Further, the use of the secret ballot makes it impossible to tell whether voting promises are carried out. In these circumstances the voter will simply vote in accord with his preferences on each individual issue.

The contrary case, logrolling permitted, occurs under two circumstances. First, it occurs where a rather small body of voters vote openly on each measure; this is normally to be found in representative assemblies, but it may also be found in very small "direct democracy" units. Under these circumstances trades of votes are easy to arrange and observe and significantly affect the outcome. It is probable that this fact is one of the major reasons for the widespread use of representative democracy. The second type of logrolling, which may be called implicit logrolling, occurs when large bodies of voters are called on to decide complex issues, such as which party shall rule, or a complex set of issues presented as a unit for a referendum vote. Here there is no formal trading of votes, but an analogous process goes on. The "entrepreneurs" who offer candidates or programs to the voter make up a complex mix of policies to attract support.[4] In doing so, they keep firmly in mind the fact that the voter may be so interested in the outcome of some issue that he will vote for the party which supports it, although the party opposes him on other issues. This implicit logrolling will not be discussed further.

In the system in which logrolling is not permitted, every voter simply indicates his preference, and the preference of the majority of the voters is carried out. The defect, and it is a serious one, of this procedure is that it ignores the various intensities of the desires of the voters. A man who is passionately opposed to a given measure and a man who does not much care but is slightly in favor of it are weighted equally. Obviously, both could very easily be made better off if the man who felt strongly were permitted to give a present to the man who had little preference in return for a reversal of his decision. The satisfaction of both would be improved, and the resulting situation would, on strictly Paretian grounds, be superior to the outcome of voting that weighed their votes equally. By way of illustration it is conceivable that a proposal to send all Negroes to Africa (or all Jews to Israel) would be passed by referendum. It would have not the slightest chance of passing Congress because the

4. This problem is discussed in a paper presented by Julius Margolis at Public Finances: Needs, Sources, and Utilization: A Conference of the Universities—National Bureau Committee for Economic Research, held April 10 and 11, 1959, at Charlottesville, Virginia.

supporters of these two minorities would be willing to promise to support almost any other measure in return for votes against such a bill. In the absence of vote-trading, the support for it might reach 51 per cent, but it would not be intense, at least in the marginal cases, and hence the trading process would insure its defeat.

Even voters who are more or less indifferent to a given issue may find their votes on it counting as much as those of the most highly concerned individuals. The fact that a voter votes normally proves that he is not completely indifferent, but many voters are motivated to vote on referendum issues more by a sense of duty to vote than by any real concern with the matter at hand. Under these circumstances even the tiniest preference for one side or the other may determine the issue. Permitting the citizens who feel very strongly about an issue to compensate those whose opinion is only feebly held can result in a great increase of the well-being of both groups, and prohibiting such transactions is to prohibit a movement toward the optimum surface.

Note that the result under logrolling and under non-logrolling differs only if the minority feels more intensely about the issue than the majority; if the feeling of the majority is equal to or more intense than the minority, then the majority would prevail both with and without logrolling. It is only when the intensity of feeling of the minority is enough greater than that of the majority so that they are willing to make sacrifices in other areas sufficient to detach the marginal voters from the majority (intense members of the majority might make counteroffers if they wished) that the logrolling process will change the outcome.

As an introduction to logrolling, let us consider a simple model. A township inhabited by one hundred farmers who have more or less similar farms is cut by a number of main roads maintained by the state. However, these roads are limited-access roads, and the farmers are permitted to enter the primary network only at points where local roads intersect it. The local roads are built and maintained by the township. Maintenance is simple. Any farmer who wishes to have a specific road repaired puts the issue up to vote. If the repairing is approved, the cost is assessed to the farmers as part of the real property tax. The principal use of the local roads by the farmers is to get to and from the major state roads. Since these major roads cut through the district, generally there are only four or five farmers dependent on any particular bit of local road to reach the major roads.

Under these circumstances the referendum system would result in no lo-

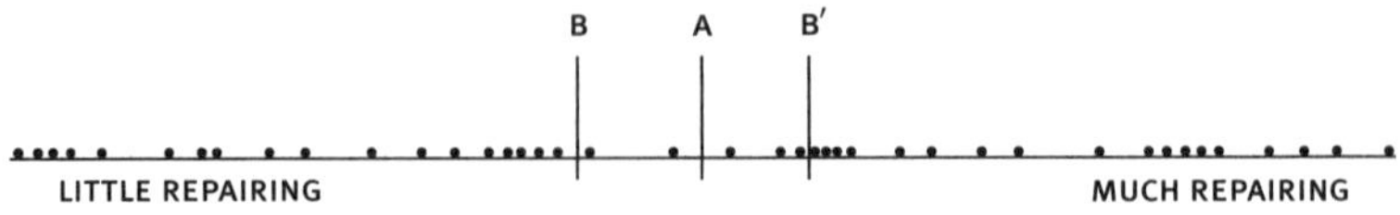

FIGURE 1

cal roads being repaired, since an overwhelming majority would vote against repairing any given road. The logrolling system, however, permits the roads to be kept in repair through bargains among voters. The bargaining might take a number of forms, but most of these would be unstable, and the "equilibrium" involves overinvestment of resources.

One form that the implicit bargain among the farmers might take is this: each individual might decide, in his own mind, the general standard that should be maintained. That is, he would balance, according to his own schedule of preferences, the costs of maintaining his own road at various levels of repair with the benefits to be received from it and reach a decision as to the point where the margins were equal. He could then generalize this decision: he could vote on each proposal to repair a given road in the same way as he would vote for repairs on his own road. If every voter followed this rule, we would find a schedule of voting behavior such as that illustrated in Figure 1. Each mark on the horizontal line represents the standard of one voter for maintenance of all roads. If a proposal for repairing a given road falls to the left of his position, he would vote for it; if it falls to his right, against. If each road has at least one farmer whose preference for road repairs falls to the right of the median (*A* in Fig. 1), then a proposal for repairs would be made as soon as a given road fell below his preferred degree of repair, and successive further such proposals as the road gradually deteriorated. When it reached the median level, a repair proposal would pass; hence all roads would be repaired at the median preference.

Although this result would not be a Paretian optimum, it would be possible to argue for it in ethical terms. In fact, I believe that this is the result that most proponents of democracy in such situations have in the back of their minds. In any event, I intend to use this result, which I shall call "Kantian," as the "correct" result with which I shall contrast what actually happens. Since my Kantian result differs from the "equal marginal cost and marginal benefit" system used by most economists in this field, it is incumbent on me to explain why I use it. The reason is simple—it is the best I can do. I have been unable to find any system of voting which would lead to a social matching of costs and benefits at the margin.

If the farmers generally followed this policy in voting, then any individual farmer could benefit himself simply by voting against all proposals to repair roads other than his own and voting for proposals to repair his road at every opportunity. This would shift the median of the schedules slightly so that his taxes would be reduced or his road kept in better-than-average repair. If the other farmers on his road followed his example (we shall call farmers who follow this rule "maximizers"), they would be able to shift the standards of repair so that the roads on which they lived would be repaired at level B' while reducing the standard of repair on other roads to B. Since the largest share of the cost of keeping their road up falls on other taxpayers, while the largest share of their taxes goes for the repair of other roads, this change would be greatly to the advantage of the maximizers and greatly to the disadvantage of the Kantians.

If the farmers along another road also switched to a maximizing pattern, this would bring the level of road-repairing on the two maximizing roads down toward about that which would prevail under the Kantian system, while still further lowering the standards on the Kantian roads. However, it is likely that the two groups of maximizers could benefit by forming a coalition in order to raise the standards of road maintenance on their own roads.

Let us consider the situation of an individual maximizer debating whether or not to enter such a coalition. Since he will pay only about 1/100th of the cost, practically any proposal to repair his own road is to his benefit. If, however, in order to obtain support for some repair project on his own road, he must also vote for the repair of another road, then he must also count the cost to him of this other repair project as part of the cost of his own road. In weighing the costs and benefits, he must consider not only the tax cost to himself of the repair of his own road but the tax cost of the other repair job which he must vote for in order to get his road done. In the particular case we are now discussing, when the farmers on all the roads except two are still Kantian, this would put few restraints on feasible projects, but it would still have to be considered. However, as more and more Kantians become tired of being exploited by the maximizers and switch to a maximizing pattern of behavior, this consideration would become more and more important.

Let us now examine a rather unlikely, but theoretically important, special case. Suppose that exactly 51 of our 100 farmers were maximizers, while 49 were Kantians. Further suppose that all the maximizers lived on certain roads while all the Kantians lived on others. Under these circumstances the Kantians clearly would never get their roads repaired, but the level of repair on the maximizers' roads presents a more difficult problem. In order to simplify it, let us assume (plausibly) that they are maintained on a high enough level so that all the Kantians vote against any project for further repair. Under these circumstances it would be necessary to obtain the votes of all the maximizers for each repair project. A farmer considering whether he wants to have his road repaired must consider the whole cost, including the taxes he must pay in order to repair the roads of the other parties to the bargain. He can, however, simply compare his own marginal benefits and costs, and this requires no knowledge of anyone else's utility. He need only decide whether the total bargain is to his advantage or not.[5]

Note, however, that, while no roads leading to the Kantian farmers' houses will be repaired, they are required to contribute to the repair of the roads leading to the houses of the maximizers. Thus part of the cost of the road-repair projects will be paid by persons not party to the bargain, and, since the maximizers only count the costs to themselves of their votes, the general standard of road maintenance on the roads on which they live should be higher than if they had to count also the cost of maintaining the roads on which the Kantians lived. Under such conditions, where virtue so conspicuously is not paying, it seems likely that at least some of the Kantian farmers would decide to switch to a minimizing policy. For simplicity, let us assume that all of them do this at once. Since they would still be in a minority, their change of policy would not immediately benefit them, but surely they could find two of the original maximizers who would, in return for very good maintenance, desert their former colleagues. It is again obvious that the new majority would be susceptible to similar desertions; a permanent coalition of 51 farmers for the purpose of exploiting the remaining 49 could thus not be maintained. In terms of game theory any combination of 51 voters dominates any other size of combination, but no combination of 51 dominates all other combinations of 51.[6]

5. In practice the problem of getting the unanimous agreement of 51 persons might be insoluble. Since we are now only discussing a rather unlikely special case, we can ignore the point. Alternatively, the reader can assume that there are 53 or 54 maximizers, and those who set their terms too high can simply be left out.

6. In the "Theory of the Reluctant Duelist" (*American Economic Review*, 46 [December, 1956], 909–23), Daniel Ellsberg contends that game theory really only applies to "reluctant"

The outcome is clear. Each farmer would enter into bilateral agreements with enough farmers on other roads to insure that his own was repaired. He would then be forced to count as part of the cost of getting his road repaired the cost (to him) of repairing the roads of the other 50 farmers. These bilateral agreements, however, would overlap. Farmer A (more precisely the farmers on road A) would bargain with Farmers B, . . . , M. Farmer M, on the other hand, might make up his majority from Farmer A and Farmers N, . . . , Z.

Counting the cost to himself of the maintenance of his road in terms of support for other road-repair projects, each farmer would consider only those projects for which he voted. Thus his expenditure pattern would count the tax payments of 49 voters as a free gift. The natural result would be that each road would be maintained at a level considerably higher and at greater expense than is rational from the standpoint of the farmers living along it. Each individual behaves rationally, but the outcome is irrational. This apparent paradox may be explained as follows: each voter pays enough in support for repair of other roads to equalize the benefit he receives from the repair of his own road. But his payments counted under this system include only part of the road-repair jobs undertaken.[7] There are others which are the result of bargains to which he is not a party. Taken as a group, the road-repair projects for which he votes represent a good bargain for him, but other *ad hoc* bargains to repair other roads will also take place. He will vote against these, but, as he will be in the minority, he will have to pay for them. The result is a sizable loss to him.

Any farmer following any other course of action will be even worse off. A Kantian farmer, for example, would never have his own road repaired but would pay heavy taxes for the support of repair jobs on other roads. The whole process will proceed through elaborate negotiations; the man who is the most effective bargainer will have a considerable advantage, but the general pattern will be less than optimal for all parties.

This seems a rather unsatisfactory result, and we should consider whether there are not ways of improving it. First, however, I should like to discuss

---

players. Our case is a particularly pure example. The voter must "play the game" by entering into bargains with 50 of his fellows, even though this leads to rather unsatisfactory results, simply because any other course of action is even worse.

7. The fact that he is taxed for other roads not part of his bargain reduces his real income and hence, to some extent, reduces the amount of road-repairing he would wish to consume.

certain possible objections to my reasoning.[8] It may be said that the maximizers are behaving wickedly and that ethical considerations will prevent the majority of the population from following such a course. Ethical systems vary greatly from culture to culture, and I do not wish to rule out the possible existence somewhere of an ethical system which could bar logrolling, but surely the American system does not. Under our system logrolling is normally publicly characterized as "bad," but no real stigma attaches to those who practice it. The press describes such deals without any apparent disapproval, and, in fact, all our political organizations bargain in this fashion.

A second argument asserts that each farmer in our community would realize that, if he adopted a maximizing policy, this would lead all other farmers to do the same. Since the "maximizing equilibrium" is worse for all[9] the farmers than the "Kantian median," each farmer would, on the basis of cold selfish calculation, follow the Kantian system. This argument is similar to the view that no union will force its wage rate up because each union realizes that such action will lead other unions to do the same, the eventual outcome being higher prices and wage rates but no increase in real income. There seems to be overwhelming empirical evidence that men do not act this way. In addition, the argument contains a logical flaw: this is the observation that, in any series of actions by a number of men, there must be a first one. If this can be prevented, then the whole series can be prevented. This is true, of course, but there also must be a second, a third, etc. If any one of these is prevented, then the whole series cannot be carried out. If all our 100 farmers would refrain from a maximizing course of action because each one felt that his personal adoption of such a course would lead to a switch to the "maximizing equilibrium," then, if one of them had done so, we could construct an exactly similar argument "proving" that no 1 of the 99 remaining farmers would follow his example. But if this second argument is true, then the first is false; and hence the chain of reasoning contains an inconsistency.

I turn now to possible methods of improving the results. Could the members of a community somehow enter into an enforceable bargain under which they act according to the Kantian model? In the very narrow special case of

8. James Buchanan kindly permitted me to present this paper before his graduate seminar in public finance, and the objections made by some of the students tended to follow these lines.

9. Not necessarily for all. There might well be one or more farmers whose personal preference schedules called for a large enough investment in roads so that the "maximizing equilibrium" was preferable to the "Kantian median."

our model, it is at least conceivable that they could. It is possible that a clear, unambiguous formula for telling when a road needed repair might be agreed upon, and then the exact figures to be inserted in the formula determined by general voting. Probably even in our case this would not be practical, but the theoretical possibility must be admitted.

In the more general and realistic case where governmental units deal with a continuing stream of radically different projects, no such agreed formula would be possible. A formula which would permit weighing such diverse programs as building giant irrigation projects in the West to increase farm production, paying large sums of money to farmers in the Midwest to reduce farm production, giving increased aid to Israel, and dredging Baltimore's harbor is inconceivable. There could not, therefore, be any agreement on an automatic system of allocating resources, and this throws us back to making individual decisions with the use of logrolling.

This is by no means a tragedy. If it were possible to set up some system by present voting to determine future resource allocation, it is more likely that this determination would take a form favored by a simple majority of the voters than a form favored by the whole group unanimously. This is likely to result in a worse decision than that resulting from logrolling. The problem of intensity must also be considered. The Kantian system makes no allowance for the differential intensities of the voters' preferences. If the voters who wanted more resources spent on road-repairing felt more intensely about it than the voters who wanted less, then the Kantian system would not result in an optimum distribution of resources. Permitting logrolling would take care of this problem.

Requiring more than a simple majority would reduce the resources spent on roads, since more people would have to be included in each bargain, and the cost to each voter of repair to this road would consequently be increased. The larger the majority required, the more closely would the result approach a Pareto optimum. Practically, however, the difficulty of negotiating a bargain would increase exponentially as the number of required parties increased, and this might make such a solution impossible. The provision in so many constitutions for a two-house legislature, each house elected according to a different system, raises much the same issues.

Our next problem is to inquire to what extent the results obtained in our simple model can be generalized. It would appear that any governmental activity which benefits a given individual or group of voters and which is paid for from general taxation could be fitted into our model. It is not necessary that the revenues used to pay for the projects be collected equally from all voters. All that is necessary is that the benefits be significantly more concentrated than the costs. This is a very weak restraint, and a very large number of budgetary patterns would fit it. If the taxes were collected by some indirect method so that individuals could not tell just how much they were paying for any given project, then this fact would accentuate the process. In the marginal case the individual might be indifferent about projects benefiting other people whose cost to him was slight and difficult to calculate.

One requirement of the process has not yet been emphasized. It is necessary that the voting on the various projects be a continuing process. A number of different projects or groups of projects must be voted on at different times. If all projects were inserted in a single bill to be accepted or rejected for all time, then 51 per cent of the voters could fix the bill permanently to exploit the remainder. In fact, of course, since government is a continuing process, our condition is fulfilled.

The process which we have been discussing can be generalized to cover other types of government activity. We shall start by generalizing it to cover other types of taxation-expenditure problems and then turn to other types of governmental problems. First, let us suppose that we have some governmental activity of general benefit, police work, for example, which is paid for by some general type of taxation. By reasoning paralleling that which we have done so far, we can demonstrate that special tax exemptions to special groups at the expense of the general efficiency of the police force would be carried on to a degree which would far exceed the Kantian median. Similarly, if a given sum of money is to be spent on two different types of governmental activity, one of which is of general benefit and one of which benefits a series of special groups, too much will be spent on the latter. Defense, for example, will be slighted in favor of river and harbor work.

The same reasoning can be applied to the tax structure. If a given amount of money had to be raised, we would expect it to be raised by general taxes that were "too heavy" but riddled by special exemptions for all sorts of groups. This would greatly reduce the effect of any general tax policy, such as progression, that had been adopted. This pattern appears to be very realistic. On the basis of our theory, we would predict general and diffuse taxes, riddled with special exceptions, and governmental functions of general benefit sacrificed in favor of the interests of particular groups. I see no great conflict between the prediction and reality.

To apply our theory generally to all types of governmental activity, however, we must radically generalize it. For any individual voter all possible measures can be arranged according to the intensity of his feeling. His welfare can be improved if he accepts a decision against his desire in an area where his feelings are comparatively weak in return for a decision in his favor in an area where his feelings are strong. Bargains between voters, therefore, can be mutually beneficial. Logically, the voter should enter into such bargains until the marginal "cost" of voting for something he disapproves of but about which his feelings are weak exactly matches the marginal benefit of the vote on something else which he receives in return. Thus he will benefit from the total complex of issues which enter into the set of bargains which he makes with other people. In making these bargains, however, he must gain the assent of a majority of the voters only, not of all of them. On any given issue he can safely ignore the desires of 49 per cent. This means that he can afford to "pay" more to people for voting for his measures because part of the inconvenience imposed by the measure will fall on parties not members of the bargains.

Unfortunately, the converse also applies. Bargains will be entered into in which our voter does not participate but part of the cost of which he will have to bear. As a result, the whole effect of the measures which result from his bargains and on which he votes on the winning side will be beneficial to him. But this will be only slightly more than half of all the "bargained" measures passed, and the remainder will be definitely contrary to his interest. The same would be true for the *average* voter under a pure referendum system. In fact, the whole problem discussed in this paper arises from the system of compelling the minority to accept the will of the majority.

Although this paper so far has been an exercise in "positive politics," the analysis does raise important policy problems, and at least some comment on them seems desirable. It seems clear that the system of majority voting is not by any means an optimal method of allocating resources. This fact should be taken into account in considering whether some aspect of our economy would be better handled by governmental or market techniques. On the other hand, these problems and difficulties do not materially reduce the advantage which voting procedures have over despotism as a system of government. The primary lesson would appear to be the need for further research. Majority voting plays the major role in the governments of all the nations in which the social sciences are comparatively advanced. It seems likely that careful analysis of the process would lead to the discovery of improved techniques and a possible increase in governmental efficiency.

THE IRRATIONALITY OF INTRANSITIVITY

A recent discussion of welfare economics "summarizes the question of transitivity as follows. There is not now conclusive reason to believe that the assumption of transitivity of preference in individual choice is deeply suspect. There are, however, grounds for being willing to make deep empirical investigations into the validity of the assumption."[1] At another point the same author says: "My conclusions indicate that we currently possess no strong evidence to warrant *dropping* (the assumption of transitivity)."[2] Given the role that transitivity plays in much of the modern literature, and in Rothenberg's book, his attitude towards it seems very defensive. We do not have *strong* evidence against it; there is no *conclusive* reason to suspect *deeply* the assumption. In sum, the evidence against transitivity is not sufficient to condemn it, but Rothenberg is clearly doubtful. In this he is more or less in accord with the bulk of current opinion on the matter.

It is the purpose of this article to present a contrary view. It will be argued that the assumption of transitivity is not particularly doubtful or dubious. In view of the apparent suspicion of the assumption by the bulk of modern welfare economists this might seem to be a revolutionary position, but the practice of the same economists has indicated relatively little real doubt of the transitive nature of preference orderings. Article after article has appeared in which this assumption is made, something which would seem to indicate that the writers have at least some confidence in its reliability. Further, the chains of reasoning based upon this assumption do not appear to have led to demonstrably false conclusions about the real world. This fact, in itself, is powerful although not conclusive evidence for the truth of the transitivity assumption.

The debate about the assumption of transitivity turns upon the interpretation of certain real world experiences. If an individual is asked to take his choice among a large number of pairs of alternatives, with each alternative appearing as one member of quite a number of the pairs,[3] or a large number of

Reprinted, with permission of Oxford University Press, from *Oxford Economic Papers* 16 (October 1964): 401–6.

1. *The Measurement of Social Welfare*, Jerome Rothenberg (Prentice-Hall, Inc., Englewood Cliffs, N.J.) 1961, p. 231.

2. Ibid., p. 19.

3. See Arnold M. Rose, "A study of irrational judgements," *Journal of Political Economy*, Oct. 1957, pp. 394–402, for an example. In this case the choice among the alternatives in-

people are asked to judge between three alternatives grouped in a set of pairs,[4] it is highly likely that in at least one case where an individual has chosen A over B, and B over C, then C over A will appear.

There are two possible explanations for this phenomenon. The first, offered by May,[5] is that the preference schedules are actually intransitive. The individual at one and the same time does prefer A to B, B to C, and C to A. The second, offered by Rose,[6] holds that the effect is an artifact arising in the course of the experiment. This latter explanation is rather complicated, since many things can go wrong. In the first place, the experiment necessarily will take time, and the subject may change his mind. When he was asked to compare A and B, he not only preferred A to B, he also preferred A to C. The questions, however, forced him to think about the general subject, and by the time the experimenter got around to asking him to compare A with C, he had changed his mind; he now prefers C to A and to B. The apparent intransitivity merely reflects the change.

Another problem which may arise involves the fact that in many experiments of this sort the subject is required to choose between the alternatives even though he may be actually indifferent. This could easily lead to apparent intransitivities. The subject may also be bored and simply fill in the blanks on the experiment form helter-skelter without really consulting his preferences.[7] They may also make a number of other "errors" in recording their judgements. The result of all of these factors is that it is quite possible for an experimental subject who has completely transitive preferences to select A over B, B over C, and C over A.

Thus we have a well-established empirical phenomenon and two possible theoretical explanations for it. Rose in his article produced considerable evidence that the second explanation was the true one, but the doubt on the point expressed by Rothenberg would appear to justify another attempt to demonstrate that intransitivity is not the explanation. For this purpose we

---

volved judgements of the severity of a crime rather than preference, but the transitivity problem is the same.

4. See Kenneth O. May, "Intransitivity, utility, and the aggregation of preference patterns," *Econometrica*, Jan. 1954, pp. 1–13.

5. Op. cit. pp. 7–13.

6. Op. cit. pp. 395–96.

7. Rose found that the number of apparent intransitivities in the judgements of each of his subjects was inversely correlated with the time they took to complete the form (p. 399).

need only consider three-element intransitive loops since any larger order loop will necessarily contain at least one three-element loop within it. A demonstration that three-element loops do not occur will also serve to eliminate the possibility of larger intransitive cycles.

As a first step I should like to present a basic statement about the real world: A man confronted with a small (say 5) collection of alternatives will either (*a*) prefer one of them, (*b*) be indifferent among a subset of two or more of the collection but prefer any member of that subset to the remainder of the collection, or (*c*) be indifferent among all the alternatives. It seems unlikely that anyone will seriously question this proposition,[8] but if someone does, it is easily tested empirically. Simple observation of a cafeteria line would probably be the easiest "experiment." Anyone who accepts this statement must, if he is rational, agree that preferences are transitive.

The proof of transitivity is somewhat easier if we initially confine ourselves to a world in which indifference is impossible. In this restricted world our basic statement shrinks to the simple formula that a man will prefer one of a small group of alternatives. The proof of transitivity is a simple example of *reductio ad absurdum*. If the individual is alleged to prefer *A* to *B*, *B* to *C*, and *C* to *A*, we can inquire which he would prefer from the collection of *A*, *B*, and *C*. Ex-hypothesi he must prefer one, say he prefers *A* to *B* or *C*. This, however, contradicts the statement that he prefers *C* to *A*, and hence the alleged intransitivity must be false.

There does not seem to have been any discussion of what a man with intransitive preferences would do if presented with a choice among all elements of the intransitive loop simultaneously. He clearly would not be able to choose, and he equally clearly could not be called indifferent among the alternatives. The only pattern of behaviour consistent with intransitive preferences would be a closed loop in which the subject rapidly went round and round his preferential cycle. Kenneth O. May's article, "Intransitivity, utility, and aggregation in preference patterns,"[9] is surely the *locus classicus* for the intransitivity hypothesis. In the course of the experiment reported there he first found apparent intransitivities in the preference ordering of 17 college stu-

8. An ingenuous colleague has offered the criticism that the individual in question might be totally ignorant of the alternatives and hence neither have preferences nor be truly indifferent. This, of course, involves the question of exactly what we mean by "indifference." Fortunately this semantic problem can be skipped. If the man in question has no preferences with regard to the alternatives, it is at least clear that he does not have intransitive preferences.

9. *Econometrica*, Jan. 1954, pp. 1–13.

dents by paired comparisons. He then presented them with all three alternatives simultaneously and asked them to rank them. They had no difficulty in doing so.[10] This result is, of course, completely inconsistent with the hypothesis that they had intransitive preference schedules.

May, however, did not point out that the ability of his experimental subjects to rank the alternatives proved that they had, at least at the period within the experiment at which they made the ranking, transitive preference schedules. He does not even discuss the point, but merely goes on to present a mechanism to explain the intransitivity which he believes his experiments showed. The simple explanation for May's results, of course, is that the subjects changed their minds during the course of the experiment and that the "intransitivity" merely reflects such changes. In order to accept the intransitivity explanation of the phenomenon it is necessary to assume quite complex patterns. One would be that the subjects did not change their minds during the period in which they were asked the first three questions, comparing *A* with *B*, *B* with *C*, and *C* with *A*, but that they then all changed their minds when they were asked the fourth question which called for ranking all three alternatives.

There is an alternative explanation for May's experimental result which preserves intransitivity as conceivable. If we assume that his subjects' preferences were not only transitive but also depended upon irrelevant alternatives, then his results are explicable. Theoretically it would be possible for a man to prefer *A* to *B*, *B* to *C*, and *C* to *A* while at the same time preferring *A* if presented with a collection of *A*, *B*, and *C*, if his preferences with respect to *A* and *C* were dependent upon whether or not *B* was present. If he prefers *C* to *A* when *B* is not present but prefers *A* to *C* when *B* is present, then May's experimental results could be explained without assuming that his subjects changed their minds during the course of the experiment. Since the time of Occam, however, we have normally chosen the simpler theory, and surely in this case the hypothesis that the subjects had transitive preference schedules but changed their minds is the simpler one.

So far, however, we have been discussing a simplified world in which indifference is absent. If we admit indifference, the situation is more complicated, although the same basic result will follow. Let us consider the situation where it is alleged that a man prefers *A* to *B*, *B* to *C*, and *C* to *A*, and that indifference is possible. If confronted with the collection of *A*, *B*, and *C*, then

10. *Econometrica*, Jan. 1954, pp. 6–7.

the individual might, in keeping with our basic statement, be indifferent between *A* and *B* but prefer both to *C*. This would contradict two links in the alleged intransitivity chain, the preference of *A* to *B* and the preference of *C* to *A*. Hence, once again, the allegation of intransitivity must be untrue if our basic statement is true. Finally, the individual might be indifferent among the three alternatives. Spelled out, this would involve not preferring *A* to *B* or *C*, not preferring *B* to *A* or *C*, and not preferring *C* to *A* or *B*. Clearly this contradicts all three links in the alleged intransitivity loop.

If indifference is permitted, however, more complicated types of intransitivity are possible. An individual might be alleged to prefer *A* to *B* and *B* to *C* but to be indifferent between *A* and *C*. It would be tedious to go through the various possibilities, but this would also be inconsistent with our basic statement. A more interesting case would involve an individual who was indifferent between *A* and *B* and also between *B* and *C* but who preferred *A* to *C*. This is, of course, perfectly possible.[11] When confronted with the choice between *A*, *B*, and *C*, the individual will select *A*. Since this would appear to contradict his indifference between *A* and *B*, some discussion seems in order.

Assume an individual who prefers blue to green and will always choose the "bluest" colour when given an opportunity.[12] He is, however, unable to make infinitely fine judgements. The minimum change of colour which he is able to perceive is some small amount which we will denominate *Y*. We present him with three colours, *A*, *B*, and *C*, in which *A* is the most blue and *C* the most green, but with the difference between *A* and *B* less than *Y*. The difference between *B* and *C* is also less than *Y*, but the difference between *A* and *C* is greater than *Y*. If asked to choose which he prefers when confronted by these alternatives in pairs, our subject should choose *A* to *C*, but be indifferent between *A* and *B* and *B* and *C*. If he is presented with a choice between *A*, *B*, and *C*, he should have no difficulty in selecting *A* because the presence of *C* makes it possible for him to distinguish between *A* and *B*. He can see that *A* is bluer than *C*, but cannot distinguish between *B* and either *A* or *C*. The realization that *B* must lie between *A* and *C* easily follows. The same general process could operate in all cases where indifference is found to be intransitive. The addition of the third alternative, by changing the information

11. The intransitivity of the indifference relation has been analysed by W. E. Armstrong in a long series of articles beginning with "The determinateness of the utility function," *Economic Journal*, Sept. 1939, pp. 453–67.

12. Dr. James M. Buchanan suggested the following analysis. I am also indebted to him for many other helpful comments.

available to the chooser, increases the fineness of his discriminatory powers. Hence his expressed order is, in a sense, actually changed.

So far we have been very largely discussing the logic of the situation. Can we design experiments which would serve to confirm or refute our conclusions? The answer to this question is yes, and hence our conclusions are fully "operational." Speaking for myself, however, the results to be expected from the experiments discussed below have been so obvious that they have remained *Gedanken* experiments instead of experiments to be actually performed. Perhaps one of the readers will be rather more sceptical of my logic.

The first step in any experiment would be to give transitivity tests of the sort developed by May and Rose to a number of subjects in order to find apparent intransitivity loops. When such loops were found it would be easy to distinguish true intransitivity from apparent intransitivity arising from experimental difficulties by simply confronting the subject with all three of the alternatives on the loop. If he is able to rank them, as May's subjects were, it should be clear that the "intransitivity" is only an experimental artifact. This procedure would only be repeating May's experiment, but his sample was rather small (only 17 subjects with intransitive loops), and it might be argued that with a larger sample a case of genuine intransitivity might have turned up.

May's experiment, however, did not cover another possibility. His subjects were required to choose between the alternatives and could not simply say that they were indifferent. It is possible that with less restrictive conditions a different result might have turned up. Perhaps some of his subjects who had chosen *A* over *B*, *B* over *C*, and *C* over *A*[13] might have expressed indifference when confronted with all three alternatives as a group. This result could be explained either in terms of experimental problems, particularly the fact that the subject may have changed his mind, or by a complicated combination of true intransitivity and a most peculiar form of interdependence among the alternatives. Experimental determination of which of these was the correct explanation would be easy. There are a number of routines, but the simplest would be to reduce the choice once again. The subject could be told that since he was indifferent, the experimenter would make the choice. The experimenter could then say that personally he disliked *C* and was indifferent between *A* and *B* and hence would flip a coin to decide between them. The subject, if he has the postulated intransitive loop, should object and sug-

13. Or chosen *A* over *B*, *B* over *C*, but been indifferent between *A* and *C*, if indifference were permitted.

gest that *A* be marked as the preferred alternative. If he does not, he clearly no longer prefers *A* to *B*, and hence the apparent intransitivity must be put down to a change of mind rather than true intransitivity. This procedure can be further elaborated to obtain even greater assurance.

Note that the discussion has involved no direct assumption of rationality on the part of the persons who have preference schedules, only on the part of the student considering them. If our basic statement about the real world is accepted, then any intransitive preference ordering must involve the simultaneous holding of directly contrary preferences. The subject must prefer *A* to *B* and *B* to *A*. Even a schizoid must split these two preferences between his two personalities. Our proof does not involve the basic question of human rationality, but only bars one particular type of irrationality.

ENTRY BARRIERS IN POLITICS

The question, "What is the difference between a political party and a department store?" sounds like a riddle, but I suggest it as a serious subject for inquiry. The two types of organization clearly are very different, and specifying the differences is a good exercise for an economist who is interested in applying the tools of his trade to the study of politics. The subject of this paper came to me while I was engaged in just this exercise (which may or may not be regarded as a recommendation). One of the conspicuous differences is that the department store will normally own its own plant, while the political party does not. The political party may, of course, own some office furniture, but this is only a tiny part of the capital that it will use to serve its customers if it is successful in the competitive struggle. This difference between the political party and the department store is such an obvious one that, like the purloined letter, it is almost invisible. We are also so accustomed to it that a question as to why it should exist may seem eccentric, but, as I hope to demonstrate, it has an economically interesting answer. This is one field where an essentially political problem can be treated entirely as an economic problem, specifically as an example of the problem of controlling natural monopolies. Looking at it in this way, we will see that there is a method of controlling natural monopolies which has not been much discussed by economists but which has been in use by practical men for many years.

Three techniques are normally suggested for dealing with natural monopolies: we can leave them alone, letting their managers do as they wish, we can subject them to regulation, or they can be publicly owned and operated. If you will bear with me in considering the government itself as a natural monopoly, it will be obvious that none of these techniques are suitable for dealing with it. Leaving the monopoly alone, which if we are talking about government means a despotic state, is not at all impossible. In fact, this has been by far the commonest way of handling the problem if we consider the whole of man's history. I suspect, however, that there is no one in this room, no matter how devoted to laissez faire, who will advocate this solution for this type of natural monopoly. In a sense the whole point of democracy is to prevent this sort of "free enterprise."

Reprinted, with permission of the American Economic Association, from *American Economic Review* 55 (May 1965): 458–66.

If the extreme libertarians will not favor free enterprise, it is also an area where devotees of *dirigisme* will not favor controls. It is, of course, a little hard to see who would do the controlling in this case, and who would control the (presumed) monopoly of controlling would be even harder, but I doubt that any democrat, no matter how devoted to planning and controls, would favor controls even if these technical problems could be solved. This is one area where we all favor unrestrained consumer sovereignty. The preoccupation which economists have had since Bentham with improving the information of the parties to a transaction would not be out of place in this area. Efforts to prevent direct fraud would also seem to be sensible, although experience seems to indicate that little can be done on these lines. But these are the same sort of things which we hope for in purely competitive industries, not measures to control a monopoly. The third alternative—public ownership and operation—raises difficult problems of definition. It is not at all clear what a proposal to subject a successful political party to public ownership and operation would mean. The government surely is publicly owned already, and whether it is publicly operated depends upon the definition of public in this particular usage. I am inclined to think that our present set of institutions could best be described as public ownership with private operation.

One of the handy definitions of government is "the monopoly of force." Those of us who have been engaged in what we call synergetics—or the present invasion of political theory by economists—have begun to wonder whether the force really must be monopolized. There seem to be a surprising number of private policemen in New York, and a good deal of our national defense establishment is handled by private companies under contract. It may be that some governmental activities are not so necessarily monopolistic as has been generally thought. Leaving this problem aside, however, clearly a good many of the activities undertaken by governments are natural monopolies. Further, under democratic procedures, the elected members of the government always exercise a sort of monopoly due to the simple fact that there is only one set of them elected. Judge Smith has a monopoly representing Charlottesville, Virginia, in the House of Representatives; a small group of rather estimable gentlemen have a monopoly of governing the city of Charlottesville; and Mr. Johnson has a monopoly of a whole set of governmental activities. The situation is, perhaps, clearer in a parliamentary government where a single party or coalition has complete control over all governmental activities. The natural monopoly here comes from a technological consideration which amounts to a very strong economy of scale: only one majority can exist at a time.

Let us now consider this problem simply as one in economics.[1] Suppose we have an industry, say cement manufacturing, in a small, isolated country in which economies of scale are strong enough so that a company having more than half of the market could operate on a lower cost level than any smaller competitor. Further, to make our analogy complete, assume that the cost advantage would continue up to full market control by one company. If the industry is a vital one where we fear the results of simply leaving it alone, if regulation is ruled out, and if public control is impossible, what can we do?

The problem, of course, is simply an extreme entry barrier. Presumably a competitor could come in and drive the present occupant of the market into bankruptcy by violent competition, but it would be an expensive and risky thing to do. The competitor would have to build a new plant and invest a good deal of funds in staying alive through the cutthroat competition phase, and he would have no assurance of winning out, let alone making enough from the ensuing monopoly to pay him back for his expenditure. Clearly the company in occupation of the natural monopoly would not be completely free from restraints, but equally clearly only really monumental inefficiency would really much endanger its position.[2]

Looked at from the standpoint of the public of the small island country, this situation would clearly be unsatisfactory, but we have barred them from the traditional remedies. There remains an alternative. They could build or buy a cement plant and periodically put its operation up to auction. In its simplest form this auction could require as a bid simply the price which the

1. Given the title of my paper and the nature of this panel, it would have been impossible for me to conceal the political basis of the problem. In private conversations with several economists, I have presented the problem in much the same terms as the next few pages but without giving them any idea of the "industry" under consideration. They have normally accepted the argument and the solution I propose on purely economic grounds. Thus it is experimentally established that the problem can be solved in economic terms even though it arises in political systems.

2. The analogous problem in economics has received considerable attention recently. Perhaps the best discussion is in Joe S. Bain, *Barriers to New Competition* (Harvard, 1959). More recent work has included William H. Martin, "Potential Competition and the United States Chlorine-Alkali Industry," *Journal of Industrial Economics*, July, 1961; Elizabeth Brunner, "A Note on Potential Competition," *Journal of Industrial Economics*, July, 1961; Franco Modigliani, "New Developments on the Oligopoly Front," *Journal of Population Economics*, June, 1958.

entrepreneurial company would charge for cement during the coming year. The lowest bidder would get the right to operate the plant. This, of course, would leave open to the operator letting the plant run down through undermaintenance. We might deal with this problem by having the small country specify the amount and type of maintenance which would have to be undertaken during the year before the bidding. This, however, would involve partial management of the plant by the country, and in any event it is not much like what goes on in the political sphere. Another procedure would be to have the bid include not only the price at which the cement was to be sold but also statements about maintenance, introduction of improvements, etc. The entrepreneurial group who would be permitted to operate the plant would be selected on the basis of a judgment as to which of these rather involved bids was, in all-around terms, the best. Naturally this complicated type of "bidding" raises difficult problems of judgment, but in the governmental case it is hard to see any alternative which is superior. This is, in fact, the type of complex judgment which we normally make in market transactions. In buying a car I cannot simply choose the cheapest; I must balance one package of attributes including a price against another. The choice of the best "bidder" would be similar. The principal difference would be the unenforceable nature of the promises made by the political "entrepreneurs."

Putting the whole transaction in strictly economic terms, we have an industry with an extremely high entry barrier. Public provision of the capital plant artificially reduces that barrier. With the new lower barrier, competition and potential competition will enter much more strongly into the calculations of the present management than it would without this reduction. The small island community could depend upon the cost of its cement being considerably lower than under laissez faire. The problems that would arise would be, essentially, problems of consumer judgment for a complex product and problems of aggregating preferences. The situation would be one of monopoly only insofar as there was a remaining entry barrier even when the plant was provided. Ignoring the latter class of problems for the moment, decisions as to which of the "bids" was best would be similar to ordinary consumer choice in principle, but more complex in practice. A genuine technical judgment on the desirability of the replacement of some given machine in this period or the next would be necessary in some cases. Whether replacement of present equipment by new would be worthwhile would unfortunately be a decision that the "consumer" would have to make. In the recent campaign the desirability of certain capital investments for our military machine was an issue. Further, these decisions have to be made prospectively, not retrospectively. If I am considering buying a Chrysler with a turbine engine, I can at least look at and try an existing car just like the one I would buy. This would not be so with our cement plant if new equipment were proposed. Thus we could and should anticipate less successful judgment of the bids than we find in more normal market situations. This is, of course, realistic. It is true that most people's judgment on whether the Republicans or the Democrats will serve them best is less accurate than their judgment on the same question about a car they are thinking of buying.

The problems of aggregating preferences simply complicate the situation further. They make the judgment of the consumers even less skillful. The fact that this judgment is a relatively poor one raises some special problems. It is sensible for the entrepreneurs who are bidding for the use of the plant to take the relatively uninformed state of the people who will judge the bids into account. Deception and distortion will be easier under these circumstances than in the marketplace. As one example, let us consider the so-called "going concern" value of the plant. If a new group takes over the plant, it will normally be more efficient for them to retain most of the labor force and lower management rather than hire and train new personnel. If the bids were submitted to highly qualified personnel for judgment, no doubt they would be able to require performance which could only be reached by highly efficient operations, and hence the workers and lower management would be taken over by the new group of entrepreneurs. If, however, the people making the judgment as to which bid was best were not highly qualified—and the voters certainly are not—then various rather inefficient provisions might be inserted into the bid. The successful entrepreneurs might, for example, specify that they would work for a fixed fee instead of for a residual.

This procedure might seem silly, but it is a fact that most elected officials do work for fixed fees. This may be simply due to the difficulty of computing anything comparable to a profit on the government's operations, but it may also be because the voters somehow feel that this is a better system. In many types of government contracts where profit as a residual would seem the obvious choice, a fixed fee or contract renegotiation has in fact been adopted, apparently to please the voters. But regardless of the reasons for it, this fixed fee system together with a system of judging bids which is not highly skilled gives the political entrepreneur a motive for behavior which, on the surface, would appear to be simply inefficient. Putting people on the payroll not in terms of their contribution to the enterprise but in terms of their contribution to the entrepreneur would be a quite sensible way of capturing profits not available under the fixed fee system.

The obvious answer to this problem is simply improving the standards by which the bids are judged. If the various entrepreneurs must submit their bids to the scrutiny of real experts (although whether experts are actually ever this good is questionable), they would have to plan on the most efficient methods of management in order to beat out their competitors. Ruling this method out as impractical in a democracy,[3] the only two expedients that seem to remain are simply to let the entrepreneurs do this if it pays them or give the workers and lower management some sort of civil service status. Both expedients have severe drawbacks. Since the disadvantages of a civil service system are, for some reason, normally not discussed, a few words on them might be helpful. The higher management, being unable to discharge the workers without some sort of elaborate procedure, will be less effective. If the civil service system amounts to permanent tenure, as it does in the United States, then the real control that the higher management has over the lower is apt to be much less than optimum. It may, of course, still be better than simply ignoring the problem. The purchase of goods for government use raises somewhat the same problem, although simply requiring bidding may provide a suitable solution.

But to return to the subject of entry barriers and the economics of monopoly, the company now operating the cement plant would have one advantage over any group of entrepreneurs contemplating bidding against them for the next period. They already have a management in existence which has some "going concern" value of its own. The potential competitors will have to establish such an organization simply for the purpose of making their bid. Thus the potential competitor will need to invest some resources into preparing for the competition which will not be required of the present operators. Although the entry barrier has been lowered by the public ownership of the plant, it has not been reduced to zero. This means that the existing management—and the competitors, for that matter—can afford to put their bid somewhat above the "pure competition" level because of this impediment to competition. Indeed, if the profits from managing the enterprise are small, which would be so either if the bid system worked very well or if payment

3. It is not, of course, necessarily impractical for small parts of the government. The government itself must be chosen by the voters, but it might contract for the performance of various services by the method we are here discussing and obtain qualified experts to judge the bids.

was by a relatively small fixed fee and side-payments were prohibited, then even a very low entry barrier might be sufficient to keep the effective level of potential competition low. In most modern democracies the legally available rewards of office are fairly low, considering the size of the enterprise. This prevents large monopoly profits but also eliminates the normal incentives for efficiency. Under these circumstances competition is needed, not to prevent exploitation, but to keep the management on its toes. Thus we might find these entry barriers still too high and look for an expedient to lower them still further.

Perhaps, however, it might be wise to remind ourselves of the exact problem we are examining. Many governmental services are natural monopolies, and economists are naturally apt to think of them when we discuss problems in this general area. Our monopoly, however, is the government itself, not its constituent services. It is a monopoly simply because we can have only one cabinet, governor, mayor, president, or majority in a legislature. The scale advantage which acts as a barrier to entry is the majority voting rule[4] which provides that the "entrepreneurial group" which obtains half the customers can drive the other entrepreneurial group or groups out of the market. This is the basic reason we must depend upon potential competition rather than upon real competition. This is also the reason why there may well be only two competitors—the present occupant and a potential replacement—instead of many competing "firms." The problem of public policy we are discussing in this essay is insuring that the entry barrier is low enough so that this potential competition is a real restriction on the activities of the present occupant of the monopoly.

The problem is that there may not be any significant potential competition. This fact is not very obvious because we normally think of national politics, and during our lifetime there has always been an active opposition party.[5] If we turn to local politics, however, we will frequently observe a complete absence of organized opposition. Charlottesville, for example, has normally only one serious set of candidates for the city council. The job of city councilman, of course, is unsalaried; so the only attractions are the non-

4. If another voting rule is actually used, then analogous problems arise.

5. The United States has had one of the parties disintegrate, with a temporary cessation of organized potential competition, three times: the "era of good feeling," the period just before the foundation of the Republican Party, and 1872 when the Democrats did not nominate an independent presidential candidate.

pecuniary rewards of office. I suspect that the pecuniary and nonpecuniary pains of running for office and being beaten are, in net, much greater than the nonpecuniary gains of being a councilman. It is also quite hard for a potential opposition individual or slate to even get his name and platform before the voters, let alone persuading them that it is sensible to vote for him or them.[6] Under the circumstances it is not surprising that there are few opposition candidates.

The obvious way of insuring potential competition in an organized form would be to raise the rewards of office to a level where they would be worth more than the organizational costs of an opposition group properly discounted by the risks involved. This might be quite expensive, and democracies have characteristically not followed this course of action. Compensation for electoral success—legal compensation, anyway—has normally been quite modest. Another technique would be to pay a potential opposition group. In the very direct form of the official salary for the leader of the opposition in Britain, this procedure has been rare, but in a more indirect way it is the common system. If quite a number of offices are put up for vote, it is fairly certain, human nature being what it is, that one organized group will not get all of them. The occupants of the other offices will receive compensation[7] and will also be in positions where they can fairly easily make their counterproposals to the government's policies known to the voters. Their actual existence and the practice of public debates in legislative bodies makes it unlikely that the present occupants of the monopoly will behave as though they had a highly secure position. Whether this is a cheaper way of getting a given quality of entrepreneurial ability than offering higher rewards to those in power I cannot say, but it certainly works.

Looked at from this standpoint, the purpose of providing offices for the opposition is to effectively lower the entry barrier by paying part of the organization costs of the potential entrant. Parliamentary debates have the function of simply keeping the existence of a well-organized potential competitor continually before the mind of the government and of providing publicity for

6. It might be argued that the communities—and there are many of them—which are governed by such a system are not really democratic. The council is not really subject to any check unless it does something really awful. The councilmen's principal satisfaction comes from "doing their duty." If this theory is true, they would be compelled to give good government, according to their own lights, in order to get the satisfaction for which they hold the office. The system would really be aristocratic government with *noblesse oblige* as the operative motive.

7. In Switzerland and a few other places this compensation is purely nonpecuniary.

the offers of the opposition and government for the next decision period. The system is neat in that no device need be introduced to select the potential competitors who will be supported as opposed to those who will not. The elections select both the government and the opposition. People who do not get elected at all are not supported. Further, the opposition is not motivated to simply settle down to professional opposition because the rewards of office are greater than those of opposition while the costs of trying to replace the present occupants of the monopoly are not significantly greater than the costs of simply holding on.

It is possible to argue that this system would be more efficient if there were more than two competitors. The European systems with many parties give the government to a coalition of parties, and each present member of the coalition competes with each party out of office because it is always possible to make up a new coalition. Whether this really leads to more effective competition, given the fact that the coalitions themselves are the governments while the voters vote for the parties, is not at all certain. In any event, the various systems all do provide for public support for the organizational costs of a potential competitor and hence keep the entry barrier low. Here is one place where potential competition is obviously highly effective, but only because of intelligent public policy.

This paper has, in a sense, been an exercise in applying economic analysis to a completely noneconomic area. In our universities as they are now organized, the subject matter of my paper, political organization, is taught in one department and the techniques of analysis I have employed are taught in another. It is probably for this reason that the rather simple and straightforward line of reasoning I have presented has never before been brought out. In this area, as in so many others, practical men have solved problems that the theorists have not even thought of. It seems to me that this paper is a simple but plain demonstration of the need of some change of our present ways of organizing knowledge. Economists who are interested in politics and political theorists who have a command of economic tools can perform research which is impossible for the more traditionally trained man. This thesis will not be new to the members of this panel, nor, I think, to many of the listeners in this room. I am, in a sense, preaching to the converted, but I am asking you to go out and preach the gospel to all the nations.

FEDERALISM

PROBLEMS OF SCALE

The modern explanation of Democratic government is based firmly on the theory of economic externalities. Individual choices in a situation in which externalities are important may lead to highly inefficient resource use. Government is one way, and frequently the most convenient way, to deal with this problem. This approach also gives an idea of the optimal size of the government or governments. It may be said that the governmental unit chosen to deal with any given activity should be large enough to "internalize" all of the externalities which that activity generates. It would appear that most students do not really aim at totally internalizing all external effects of the given action, but merely internalizing most of them, say 90 per cent. The reason that I am confident that this is so is that they almost never discuss local border effects. Any geographically delimited governmental unit must have a border, and if its function is to deal with an externality producing activity, then its actions just inside the border will normally produce an externality just outside the boundary. Thus total internalization would normally require boundaries which run along some very impressive natural barrier. Such a minor matter as street-cleaning might require a continental or even world-wide governmental unit to totally internalize its effects.

If we assume, however, that it is not (for some reason) desirable to internalize all externalities, only most of them, then the existence of externalities, even when handled in this very crude way, does give a guide for governmental size. National defense would require larger units to internalize 90 per cent of the externalities than would garbage removal. The exact percentage of externalities which are to be internalized, however, is not normally discussed. A policy of internalizing 99 per cent of the externalities would produce much larger governmental units than would a policy of internalizing 80 per cent. We will later see that this is not an insoluable problem.

A second factor traditionally considered in discussion of the size of governmental units is the optimal scale of production for the governmental service. Economies of scale, of course, can be regarded as externalities, but let us discuss them either as a special kind of externality or as a separate phenome-

Reprinted, with kind permission of Kluwer Academic Publishers, from *Public Choice* 6 (Spring 1969): 19–29.

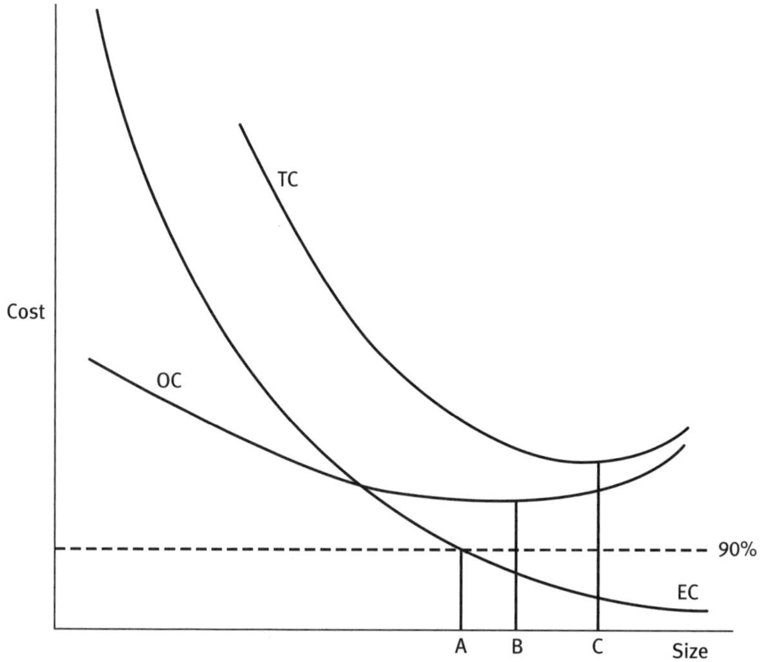

FIGURE 1

non. There is, in fact, a good deal of literature dealing with local government which simply seeks the most efficient operating unit in terms of scale economies. If costs of providing governmental services do vary as the size of the operating unit is changed, this should somehow be taken into account in designing an optimal system of governmental units. Assuming that the governmental unit is to provide its own facilities, then there would be arguments for choosing the governmental unit in such a way as to give the most efficient production unit. This might or might not be the same size as would be chosen on straight externality grounds. The two considerations, however, can be easily combined. In Figure 1, I have put the cost of choice of some governmental unit on the vertical axis, and the absolute size on the other. The external cost (EC) line shows the cost inflicted by the continued existence of noninternalized externalities, and it slopes down to the right throughout its range. If we arbitrarily aim at an internalization of 90 per cent of the externalities, then the optimal governmental size would be A. If, on the other hand, we were only interested in efficiency in producing the governmental service, then we would choose a governmental unit which minimized the operating cost (OC), and this would be at B. Geometrically summing these two cost lines (TC) gives us C as the optimal size of the governmental unit. Note that the optimum size in terms of total cost must always lie to the right of the optimum from the point of view of economies of scale. This is a simple consequence of the fact that the external cost line is continuously downsloped to the right while the "scale" cost comes down and then goes up.

But although I have drawn a correct conclusion from assumptions which a short time ago had been accepted as the modern tradition, the work of our host, Dr. Ostrom, has fairly conclusively demonstrated that there is a hidden, and untrue, assumption in the reasoning. The economies of scale are relevant to the choice if a governmental unit itself must produce the particular governmental service. If it can purchase it from a specialized producer, then the economies of scale cease to have relevance to the decision as to the size of the governmental unit. I need not repeat here the work of Dr. Ostrom, but I take it that we can agree that only conservatism and organizational rigidities prevent widespread purchase of services by governmental units of any size from organizations large enough to obtain the full benefit of any economies of scale which may exist. Thus the "optimal size" of the government as a producer of services can be dropped from the rest of this paper even though it has played a notable role in the recent literature about local governments.

But this leaves us only with the externality criteria, which provide no maximum size for the governmental unit at all. I have introduced an ad hoc assumption that we only try to internalize something like 95 per cent of the externalities from each activity, but this is clearly arbitrary. Not only is it arbitrary, but I have been unable to find[1] any previous example of its use. My only excuse for introducing it is that externality arguments are used in a way which implies that something like this is at the back of the mind of their authors. Clearly, however, it is an inadequate criterion. If there is not a counterbalancing factor, the more of the externality that is internalized the better. That there are other factors, I presume we all agree. Clearly continental or even world governmental agencies for street-cleaning or fire protection are not desirable.

There are, in fact, factors which lead to the optimal size of the governmental unit normally being smaller than is necessary to internalize *all* externalities. The first of these is simply that the smaller the governmental unit the

1. In an admittedly rather cursory survey of the literature.

more influence any one of its citizens may expect to exert; consequently, the smaller the unit, the closer it will come to fitting the preference patterns of its citizens. This is true of all forms of government, although it is easier to analyze the matter formally when we consider democratic governments.

That the average level of adjustment of government to its citizens' desires must increase as the size of the government is reduced can be very readily proved by a technique invented by Pennock.[2] Suppose some governmental unit makes its decisions by majority rule. A majority of its citizens prefer policy A to $\bar{A}$. The government therefore carries out policy A which pleases the majority and displeases the minority. Suppose the area is now divided into two units, and each of these units votes on the issue. There may be a majority for A in both of the new, smaller units, and there certainly will be such a majority in at least one of them. If both new units have majorities for A, then A will be applied in both areas and there is no change in satisfaction. If, however, one of the new units has a majority for $\bar{A}$, then the total number of people in the society who are getting their wish in the matter must go up.[3]

Although Pennock developed this argument for simple majority voting, it may readily be extended to any voting rule. This principle is perfectly general and clearly indicates that the individual will suffer less cost from governmental activities of which he disapproves the smaller the government. This cost would probably take the form shown on Figure 2. Surely this cost is a strong offset to gains which can be made by expansion of the governmental unit. We could add this line on to those of Figure 1 to get an improved optimum size, but there are other costs of governmental expansion.

Suppose you normally eat in restaurants and that there are a considerable number of competitive restaurants to choose among. For the first stage of our model assume that all of these restaurants have a la carte menus. The customer thus chooses each item separately. Let us now assume that all of the restaurants, perhaps as the result of an unwise law, shift to a system under which they list a number of complete meals on their menus, and you must choose from among these without any substitution being permitted. Let us

2. "Federal and Unitary Government—Disharmony and Frustration," *Behavioural Science*, 4 (April, 1959), 147–57.

3. A numerical example may be helpful. Suppose the original unit had a voting population of 10,000, of whom 6,000 favored A and 4,000 favored $\bar{A}$. It is broken into two units of 5,000 voters, and in one of these we find a majority, say 3,000 to 2,000, for $\bar{A}$. The other small unit would have 4,000 for A and 1,000 for $\bar{A}$. Before the division, 6,000 voters got what they wanted; under the new arrangement, 7,000 do.

FIGURE 2

carry this procedure further and assume that the restaurants begin requiring their customers to purchase meals for a full day as a bloc. The restaurants publish daily menus in which you can choose among a dozen or so full menus for the day. Menu A, for example, would consist of toast and coffee for breakfast, vegetable soup and cottage cheese salad for lunch, and roast beef, spinach, and carrots for dinner—one cup of coffee being served with each meal. Menu B, on the other hand, might be less obviously aimed at people who intend to reduce, and so on through menus C . . . N. The individual is still exercising freedom of choice in a competitive market, but I think it would be agreed that his satisfaction would have declined. We can extend the example by assuming fixed weekly menus among which choice is to be made, monthly, or even yearly menus.

The declining degree of satisfaction as the unit of choice is raised comes from two interrelated factors. In the first place it is harder to provide as wide a total range of choice if the unit of choice is large. Consider the breakfast menus of a typical restaurant, for example. If they offered nothing but fixed breakfasts, and simply presented all of the possible combinations which could be made from their present menu, they would have a book instead of a page

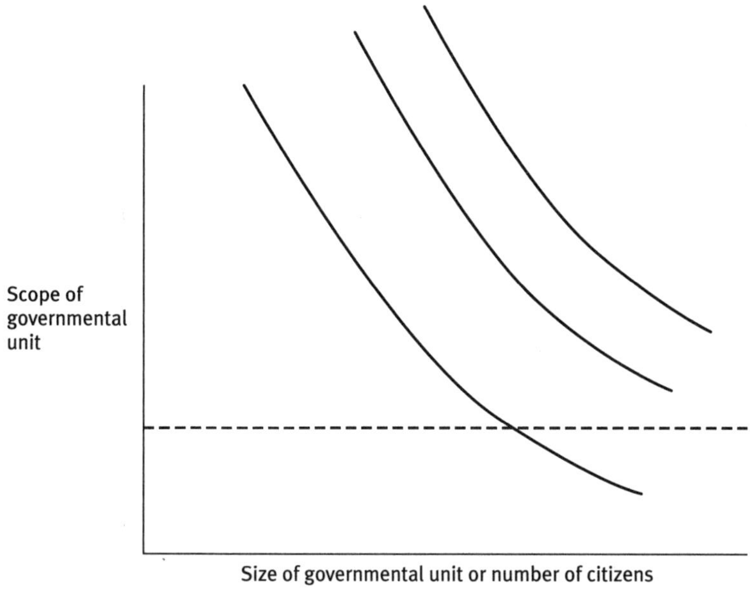

FIGURE 3

or two. Further, the customer obviously would not wade through the innumerable combinations in search of his optimum. He would look at the first page or so and make his choice from this restricted set of choices.

The second problem is related to communication theory. When you choose an item to buy, among other things, you give the restaurant owner information about your tastes which will permit him to adjust his offerings so as to please you and get a competitive advantage over the other restaurants. By restricting the number of choices you can make, the information content of the total "communication" between you and the restaurant manager is reduced. As a consequence, it is less likely that the choices with which you will be presented in subsequent periods will be as desirable as they would be if the solution process were more highly segmented. People who have unusual combinations of tastes would be particularly disadvantaged by the procedure of grouping decisions into large bundles.

The relevance of all of this to the scale of government may not be obvious, but the selection of a governmental unit involves a decision on the size of the bundles of alternatives which will be chosen among in future elections. The situation is depicted in Figure 3.

On the vertical axis the scope of the governmental unit is shown. This means, quite simply, the number of activities that it carries out with respect to any citizen or group of citizens. On the horizontal axis is shown the number of citizens for which it performs these activities. The total number of activities thus increases as you move up and to the right. Since the governmental unit will be elected to deal with all of the activities covered, the farther to the right and up on the figure, the higher the cost imposed by the necessity of making choices in large bundles. If the scope of governmental activities is held constant and the size of it is increased, as along the dotted line, then the cost of the increase would be shown by a cross-section of Figure 3 which would look like Figure 2.

There is a final cost associated with enlarging government units which is extremely popular these days; this is the cost of bureaucracy. The New Left and other groups which we may loosely call "Libertarian" are deeply distressed at the amount of bureaucracy in our society. It is certainly true that the longer the chain of officials that runs between the voter making the choice and the actual provision of the product, the more noise is introduced into the process by the individual bureaucrats who have their own preference functions and by the problems of information transmission.[4] This cost, like the others, steadily increases as the size of bureaucracy grows; in fact it might well increase at an increasing rate—i.e. it might be an exponential function of the size of the government unit. Here again, this function could be represented by a figure like 3. Figure 3 could also represent the sum of all of the costs we have been discussing.

Note that the figure says nothing at all about the total size of "government," taking that term to mean the sum of all governmental organizations. Many American cities and states have numerous different elected officials dealing with different governmental functions. If people actually made independent choices instead of voting a party ticket, then the scope of each governmental agency chosen by the voter might be quite small while the total scope of "government" was very large.

Now, having three costs which vary with the governmental unit dealing with any particular activity, we might simply add them and find the minimum total cost point and choose that as the optimum size for the governmental unit dealing with that particular problem. It should be noted that if

4. See Oliver E. Williamson, "Hierarchical Control and Optimum Firm Size," *Journal of Political Economy* (April, 1967), 123–38.

you have a large number of government activities being carried on by different governmental units, presumably there will be externalities generated by the individual government activities which affect the others. As a simple example, the fire department in many ways makes traffic control difficult. These externalities, external effects of one government agency on another, would themselves be dealt with by other government agencies which would have the specific purpose of providing through taxes and subsidies for internalizing these externalities in the actual operating units.

The end product of our reasoning, if we stop now, would be a genuinely Rube Goldberg arrangement in which the individual citizen would be a member of a vast collection of governmental units, each of these governmental units being in some respect of a different geographical coverage than the others and each one dealing with a separate activity. The reason for this would be simply that each type of government activity has slightly different externality from the others, and as a consequence each one requires a different size. Some of these governmental agencies would be engaged in providing services for the citizen and others would be engaged in internalizing the externalities generated by the individual agencies on each other.

It is, I presume, reasonably clear that this system would not be an optimum government organization. With each individual a member of 5,000 or perhaps 50,000 different governmental units, it would be quite impossible for him to engage in the most rudimentary supervision of his servants. It is, indeed, unlikely that the average citizen would even know the names of the people who are running for office in many of these "governments." If we contemplate an actual voter attempting to deal with this multitude of governmental units, it is fairly certain that he would not even bother to participate in the elections which controlled very many of them. The bulk of them then would be, from this standpoint, quite uncontrolled. It is clear that this pattern would be very, very far from optimum.

In actual economic life we also deal with situations in which the individual cannot hope to make rational decisions for himself. I do not make even the slightest effort to decide the detailed specifications of the automobile that I buy; I leave that to other people and choose among the alternative packages of characteristics that are presented to me. In some cases I hire the services of a specialized consultant, a doctor for example, who will give me advice on what type of unit I should consume. Clearly the same method would be suitable when purchasing government services.

So far we have not specified how individuals choose the government service which is performed. It might, for example, be arranged so that each of our multitudinous governmental units submits all its detailed administrative decisions to a public plebiscite. Clearly, this is not what we normally observe, and we would be surprised if it would be optimum. What we normally do is simply appoint an agent to deal with government activities. Here again, the resemblance to the private economy is considerable. The difference is largely that we appoint our agents in a different manner—through elections instead of through contract. If, then, we assume that the government agencies which we have set up to deal with these specific problems will be controlled by some kind of a special agent or board of agents and the voter selects these agents or boards of agents, let us say at the end of the year, we have greatly simplified the task the voter has in making decisions about these services. Similarly the private economy greatly simplifies its purchasing decisions by grouping the characteristics of automobiles and letting individuals choose among baskets of such characteristics. But though this greatly simplifies matters we still find ourselves with some five to ten thousand decisions for the voter to make. Clearly the grouping of the process should be carried further. We must appoint agents to deal not with the individual government activities but with whole clusters of such activities.

How, then, would we determine the optimum size of such clusters? There is a fairly simple analytical answer to this question; unfortunately actually applying it may be extremely difficult. On Figure 4 the horizontal axis represents the degree of dispersion of governmental activities. It is assumed that as you move to the right, the government is first halved and then each of the halves cut in half etc. Somehow this process is assumed to be continuous in order to give us smooth curves. Curve C represents the cost inflicted on the voter through poor control as the scale of government organizations is shifted. At the left where he faces a single choice, let us say once a year a package of policies covering all government policies in the whole of the country, his costs are quite high. As the government is broken into smaller fragments, his costs go downward. After a while, however, it begins to be difficult for him to make individual choices for each of the fragments, and at this point his cost begins to go up again. Eventually in the Rube Goldberg model of a few paragraphs back they might well be much higher in this highly differentiated government than they are in a monolithic government.

Line E is the cost that will be imposed through grouping governmental units in nonoptimum ways, the optimum way being defined in the way we have done before. We assume that, as you move from left to right, not only is

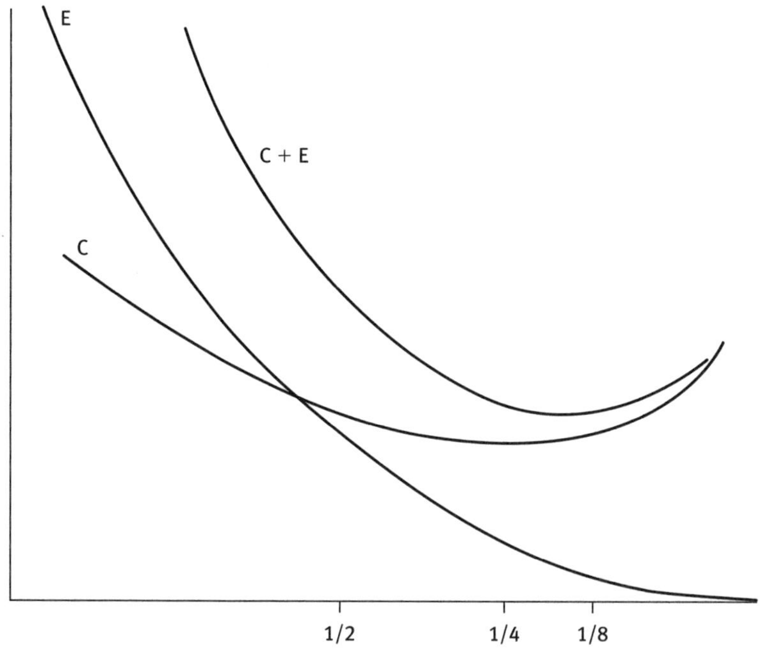

FIGURE 4

the government split into smaller and smaller pieces, but that all of the splitting of the government is done in such a way as to be the "most efficient" arrangement for that particular degree of differentiation in government.[5]

This curve falls monotonically from the left to the right and eventually reaches a point of zero when the differentiation of the government functions has exhausted the full possibilities of the economies by this method—that is when every government function is at its most efficient size. The total costs then of having any particular degree of division of governmental functions can be shown by summing costs C and E as on the diagram. The low point on this curve would be the optimum degree of differentiation of the government. It will always lie to the right of the low point on the C curve simply because E is monotonically decreasing. It might not lie very much to the right.

5. In practice of course, splitting the government evenly into two parts or evenly into four parts or evenly into eight parts would be unlikely to be the efficient arrangement. You might find 65 per cent in one group and 35 per cent in another.

The division of the functions of the government, if it is to be efficient, will take a good deal of care. You can't just randomly allocate several functions to one bureau; there are efficiency considerations here too. In general we need not concern ourselves with the details of these efficiency considerations here, but one point should be made. It is not necessarily true that all functions in a given geographic area should be run by the same unit. One can well imagine, let us say, the voters of the state of Indiana, instead of voting for the state of Indiana government and a city government, voting for two governments for the Indiana area, each of which dealt with a different aspect of affairs.

We have now what appears to be a theoretical structure for deciding the degree to which the government should be federalized. A society actually applying our solution would require a good deal of empirical research which has not yet been written down. If I may be permitted to offer a guess, I would imagine that it would end up with each individual being a member of somewhere between five and eight separate government units. These government units would not necessarily bear any particular resemblance to our present governments. It is, for example, quite possible theoretically that we would have two "national" governments, one of which, let us say, dealt with national defense and the other with all other activities which required nationwide organization.

We should, of course, make every effort to make the voting itself an efficient choice process. As to one example, we could use what used to be called the Soviet system. Voters can elect small governments which themselves elect the next higher unit(s) of government. A scheme in which small government units create larger government units is far more efficient than one in which large government units subdivide their control. The city of Chicago, for example, would be better off controlling its own destiny and participating in electing a government of Illinois, than if the government of Illinois had two subdivisions, one of which dealt with the city of Chicago and one of which dealt with the rest of the state. The reason is simply that the down state voters would have less influence on the city of Chicago under the former system.

Another rather simple method of improving efficiency of the voting process is to arrange that people defeated in the election process, but who nevertheless do reasonably well, are given an opportunity to act as sort of public auditors over the behavior of the people who win. As is rather well known, I am a proponent of proportional representation. If we have proportional representation, and if, let us say, five members were elected to duty on a governing board, whatever that board is, making the sixth-highest-ranking candidate auditor and giving him full access to all records would provide an excellent control without much burden on the voters. Today we have auditors but we usually elect them separately, thus requiring an additional vote and complicating the election process.

In sum, many students seem to think that a highly centralized government is the most efficient government. It would be more accurate to say that centralized government is the most orderly government. If we want the voters' wishes to be served by the government, then a system under which the voters are able to communicate those wishes to the government through the voting process in a more detailed and particular way is more efficient. We cannot carry this detailed voting, however, to its logical extreme because the information costs put on the voter are too great. Still it is probable that we could rearrange things in the United States so that the voter had to know less in order to cast an intelligent vote than he now does—i.e., we could get rid of the long ballot. At the same time we could give the voter considerably more control over his future and his fortunes. The most efficient government is not the most orderly looking government but the government that comes closest to carrying out the wishes of its masters.

THE GENERAL IRRELEVANCE OF THE GENERAL IMPOSSIBILITY THEOREM

A phantom has stalked the classrooms and seminars of economics and political science for nearly fifteen years. This phantom, Arrow's General Impossibility Theorem, has been generally interpreted as proving that no sensible method of aggregating preferences exists.[1] The purpose of this essay is to exorcise the phantom, not by disproving the theorem in its strict mathematical form, but by showing that it is insubstantial. I shall show that when a rather simple and probable type of interdependence is assumed among the preference functions of the choosing individuals, the problem becomes trivial if the number of voters is large.[2] Since most cases which require aggregation of preferences involve large numbers of people, "Arrow problems" will seldom be of much importance.

In *Social Choice and Individual Values*[3] Arrow included a chapter on "Similarity as the Basis of Social Welfare Judgments"[4] in which he discussed possible lines of research which might lead to a method of avoiding the implications of his proof. In this chapter, he pointed to Black's single-peaked preference curves as particularly promising.[5] The generalization of Black's single-peaked curves to more than one dimension will give the fundamental model upon which this article is based. It may, therefore, fairly be said that the present work follows the path indicated by Arrow.

The development of single-peaked preferences for two dimensions was first undertaken by Newing and Black in *Committee Decisions with Comple-*

Reprinted, with permission, from *Quarterly Journal of Economics* 81 (May 1967): 256–70.

1. I regret to say that the phantom has stalked my classrooms with particular vigor. I hereby apologize to my students for inflicting it upon them.

2. The situation with complete independence of preferences is discussed in "A Measure of the Importance of Cyclical Majorities," C. D. Campbell and G. Tullock, *Economic Journal*, 75 (Dec. 1965), pp. 853–57.

3. Rev. ed. (New York: Wiley, 1963).

4. Pp. 74–91.

5. See: "On the Rationale of Group Decision-Making," Duncan Black, *Journal of Political Economy*, 56 (Feb. 1948), pp. 23–24, and *The Theory of Committees and Elections* (Cambridge: Cambridge University Press, 1958), for fuller discussion of single-peaked curves.

mentary Valuation,[6] which was published at about the same time as *Social Choice and Individual Values* and presumably was not known to Arrow. Newing and Black, however, did not give much consideration to cases in which there were large numbers of voters. The model to be used here will involve many voters and will be used to examine the general impossibility theorem.

The proof of Arrow's theorem requires, as one of its steps, the cyclical majority or paradox of voting.[7] In addition to the mathematical reasons, the emphasis on the paradox is appropriate since the method of "aggregating preferences" which immediately occurs to the average citizen of a democracy is majority voting. This article is intended to demonstrate that majority voting will, indeed, always be subject to the paradox of voting, but that this is of very little importance. Majority voting will not produce a "perfect" answer, but the answer it does produce will not be significantly "worse" than if the paradox of voting did not exist. Any choice process involving large numbers of people will surely be subject to innumerable minor defects with the result that the outcome, if considered in sufficient detail, will always deviate from Arrow's conditions. The deviation may, however, be so small that it makes no practical difference.

Most majority voting procedures have arrangements which bring the voting to an end before every tiny detail of the proposal has been subject to a vote. These rules (frequently informal rather than part of the rules of order) mean that when the voting is brought to a stop there almost certainly remain minor changes in the result which a majority would approve if it were possible to bring them to a vote. Thus the outcome will be, in Arrow's terms, imposed, but it will be very close to a perfect result. As an example, suppose a body of men is voting on the amount of money to be spent on something, with the range under consideration running from zero to $10,000,000. The preferences of these men are single-peaked. Majority voting will eventually lead to the selection of the optimum of the median voter as the outcome. If, however, the procedure is such that proposals to change the amount of money by $100 or less cannot be entertained,[8] then the outcome will normally not be at the optimum, but it will be within $100 of it. This result does not meet Arrow's conditions, but there is no reason to be disturbed by this fact.

6. (London: William Hodge, 1951.)

7. Pp. 51–59.

8. Usually the limitation on the introduction of trivial amendments is not this formal, but it normally will be impossible to make very small changes in money bills.

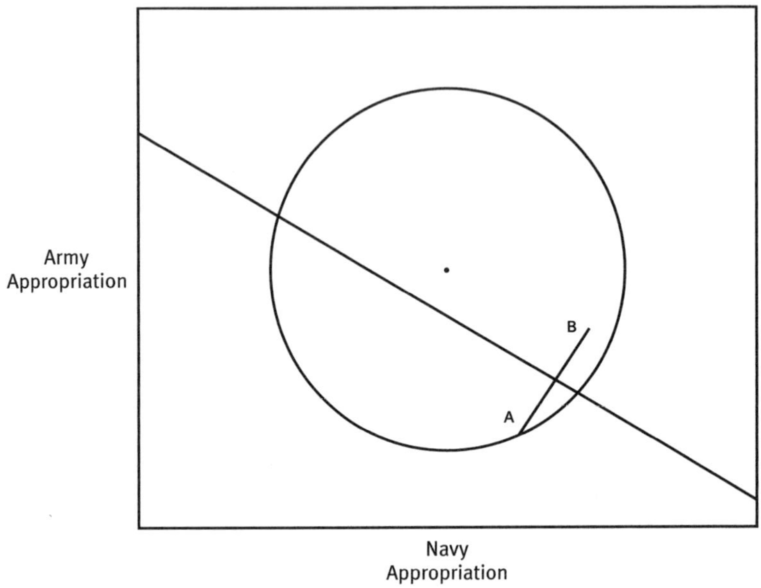

FIGURE I

In order to demonstrate that the cyclical majority is equally unimportant in real world "preference aggregation," let us consider a group of voters deciding two matters, say appropriations for the Army and the Navy by majority voting. In Figure I the vertical dimension is the appropriation for the Army and the horizontal for the Navy. The individual voters each have an optimum combination and a preference mountain which has the usual characteristics. For simplicity let us further assume that the voters' optima are evenly distributed over the space, and that their indifference curves are all perfect circles centering on their optima. The last two assumptions do not correspond with reality and will be eliminated at a later stage. Let us further assume that the number of voters is great enough so that the space can serve as a proxy for the voters. Putting it differently, of two areas in the issue space of Figure I, the larger will contain the optima of more voters than will the smaller. This makes it possible to use simple Euclidian geometry as an analytical tool.

Suppose we wish to determine whether motion *B* on Figure I can defeat the status quo, represented by *A*, by a simple majority vote. Since we are assuming that all indifference curves are perfect circles around the individuals' optima, each voter will simply vote for the alternative which is closest to his optimum. If we connect *A* and *B* with a straight line and erect a perpendicular bisector on this line, then *B* will be closer to the optima of all individuals whose optima lie on the same side of the bisector as *B*, and *A* will similarly be closest to all optima which lie on *A*'s side of the bisector. We can compare the votes for each alternative by simply noting the area of the rectangle on each side of the bisector. As a shorthand method, if the perpendicular bisector runs through the center of the rectangle, there will be an equal number of votes for *A* and *B*. If it does not, then the alternative on the same side of the perpendicular bisector as the center will win. The locus of all points which will tie with *A* is a circle around the center running through *A*, and *A* can beat any point outside the circle but will be beaten by any point inside. Clearly no cycles are possible. The process will lead into the center eventually, since, of any pair of alternatives, the one closer to the center will always win.

This might be called the perfect geometrical model, in which the number of voters whose optima fall in a given area is exactly proportional to its area. Given that the voters are finite in number, small discontinuities would appear. Two areas that differ little in size might have the same number of voters; indeed, the smaller might even have more. Cycles are, therefore, possible, but they would become less and less important as the number of choosing individuals increases. In Figure II we have a point, *A*, in our standard type of issue space, and I have drawn a circle around it. For convenience I shall assume 999,999 voters. Whether any given point on this circle can beat *A* depends upon how the perpendicular bisector of the line connecting it with *A* partitions the voters' optima. We can conceive ourselves as moving around the circle, trying each point on it against *A*. *B* would beat *A*, but *C* would not. With a finite number of voters, the changes between motions would be discontinuous. *B*, for example, might get 602,371 votes to *A*'s 397,628. As we moved around the circle towards *C*, there would be a small space in which this vote would stay unchanged; then it would suddenly shift to 602,370 against 397,629, which would also persist for a short segment of the circle. Needless to say, the segment in which the vote did not change would be extremely small, but it would exist.

If we consider a point which gets only a bare majority over *A*, 500,000 votes to 499,999, and move along the circle towards *B*, there will be a finite gap during which the vote does not change, and then it will shift to 500,000

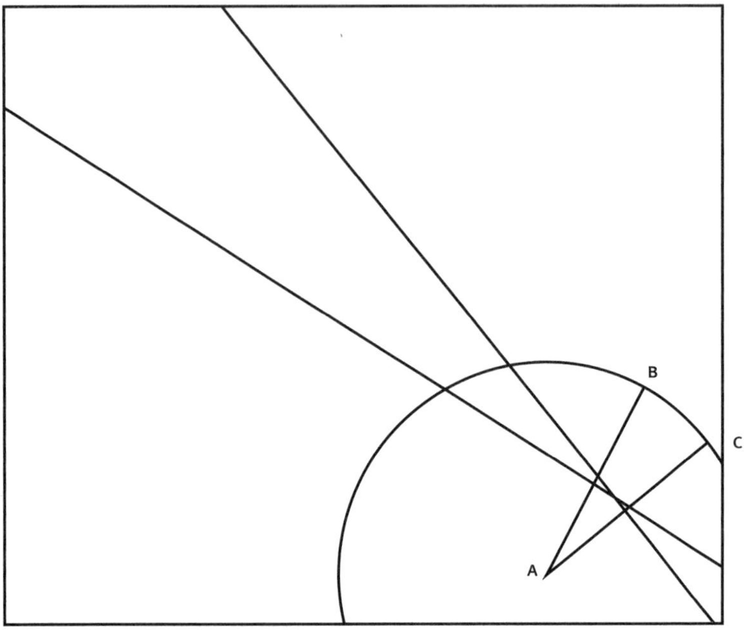

FIGURE II

for *A* and 499,999 for the alternative.[9] Given this finite distance, however, it is sure that at least occasionally a point can be beaten by another point which is more distant from the center than it is. In other words, it will be possible for majority voting to move away from the center as well as to move towards it. This phenomenon makes cycles possible.[10]

Granting these discontinuities, however, we could still draw a line separating those points which could get a majority over any given point from those that could not. With our 999,999 voters this line would no doubt ap-

9. Strictly speaking there would be an indifference point when the perpendicular bisector ran directly through the point of maximum preference for one voter. At this point the vote would stand: for *A*, 499,999, for the alternative, 499,999, indifferent, 1.

10. The referee suggested that the last two paragraphs be replaced by the following passage: "Suppose that two points, *A* and *B*, are equi-distant from the center but that *no one's optimum lies exactly on [his] perpendicular bisector*. Therefore one, say *A*, is preferred to the other. All points within a small neighborhood of *A* are preferred to *B*, and some among these will be further from the center than *B* is." A little experimentation on the understandability of both my version and his seems to show that some people find one easier to follow and some the other. Including both, therefore, seems sensible.

pear to be the circle of Figure I to the naked eye. Examining it through a microscope, however, we should find that it was not exactly circular and that there would be small areas which could get a majority over the original point, but which lay farther from the center than that point. Note, however, that these areas would be very small. If our original point is far from the center (as is *A* in either Figure I or Figure II), then the area which could get a majority over *A* but which lies farther from the center would be tiny compared with the area which could get a majority and which lay closer to the center.

Under these circumstances, unless proposals for changes are introduced in a very carefully controlled and planned manner, the voting process would in all probability lead to rapid movement towards the center.[11] Unfortunately the convergence need not continue until the absolute center is reached.[12] For close to the center, the area which is preferred to *A* and is closer to the center is much smaller than initially. It is therefore more probable than at first that the preferred alternative to *A* would be farther from the center than *A*. Cycling becomes more probable. When we get very close to the center, a point randomly selected from among those which could get a majority over the given point would have a good chance of being farther from the center than it is. At this point, however, most voters would feel that new proposals are splitting hairs, and the motion to adjourn would carry.

Discussion of the point is simplified by the use of a particular type of line which we will call a "median line." A median line is a line passing through two individuals' optima and dividing the remaining optima either into two equal "halves" or, if the number of optimum is odd, into two groups, one of which has one more optimum than the other. Figure III shows one such line and a point, *A*, which is not on the line. If, from point *A*, we drop a perpendicular to the median line, then the point at the base of the perpendicular, *A′*, will be closer to all the points on the other side of the line and the two points on the line than is *A*. It can, therefore, get a majority over *A*. Actually there

11. If there were some body or person who had control of the order in which proposals are offered for vote, and if that body or person had perfect knowledge of the preferences of the voters, then by proper choice of alternatives it would be possible for the "Rules Committee" to arrange the vote in such a way as to lead to substantially any outcome it wished. See: "Majority Rule and Allocation," Benjamin Ward, *Journal of Conflict Resolution* (1961), pp. 379–89.

12. For a proof of the normal absence of a majority motion under assumptions like those we are here using see: *Committee Decisions with Complementary Valuation*, Duncan Black and R. A. Newing (London: William Hodge, 1951), pp. 21–23.

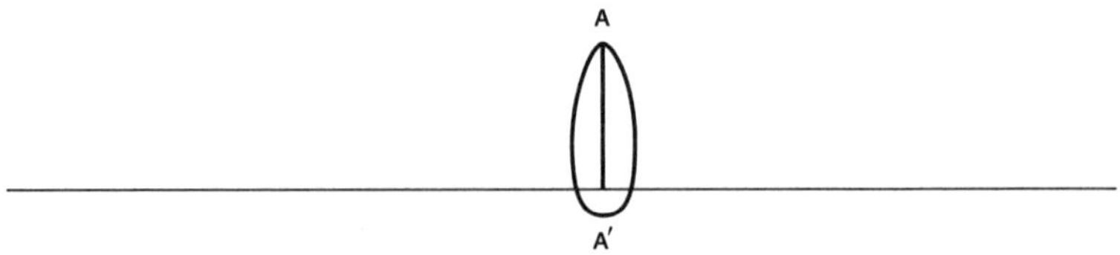

FIGURE III

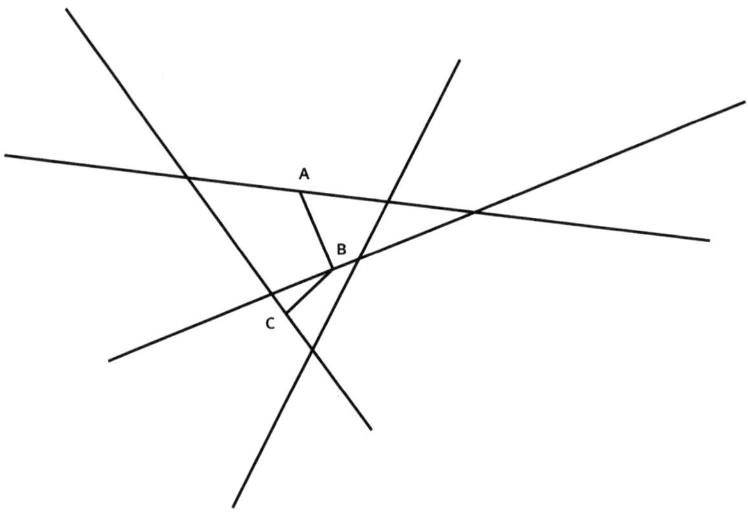

FIGURE IV

would be a small lozenge, as in Figure III, outlining points which could get a majority over *A*. The geometry of this lozenge, however, will vary somewhat depending upon the exact location of the individual optima, so we will confine ourselves to the simple perpendicular relationship.

Most of these median lines would intersect in a tiny area in the center of the issue space. If we greatly magnified this area and drew in only a few of the median lines, we would get something which looked like Figure IV. If we start with point *A*, then our theorem indicates that *B* can get a majority over it. *C*, on the other hand, can get a majority over *B*. Similarly it is obvious that there would be other points which can get majorities over *C*. Starting with any point in this general area, it will be possible to select points which will

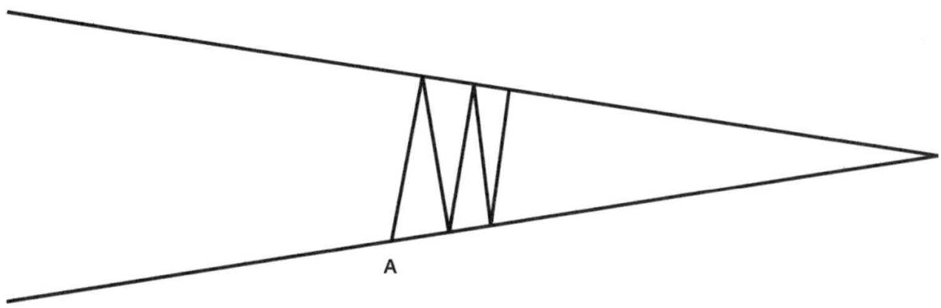

FIGURE V

obtain a majority over it. Thus, there is no point which can get a majority over all other points.

The area in which the bulk of the bisectors intersect is, of course, very small, but in some cases the point of intersection might be far away from the center of the issue space. Suppose that there are an odd number of points and we select one which is near the extreme outer edge of the issue space. It may be possible to draw through this point two lines each of which passes through another point, and each of which divides the optima so that there is only one more on one side of the line than on the other. The angle between these two lines would be extremely small, but by exaggerating this angle we get the situation shown in Figure V. Above this pair of lines there would be 499,999 optima and below the same number. The three points lying on the lines make up our total of 999,999. If we start at any point on either of these lines, such as *A*, we can drop a perpendicular to the other and thus obtain a point which can get a majority over the first point. From this second point, we can then drop a perpendicular to the first line and obtain a point which can get a majority over it. By continuing this process we can eventually approach the intersection point which, by assumption, lies at the outer edge of our space. Thus it is possible, by simple majority voting, to reach points at almost any portion of the issue space. Needless to say, this sort of series of votes is highly unlikely. It can be easily recognized because it would involve a long series of votes in each of which there was only a one-vote difference between the majority and the minority. Since we never see this in the real world, we can feel reasonably confident that this type of movement away from the center does not occur.

Since standard voting procedures do not permit infinitely fine adjustment, the fact that majority voting would not lead to a unique solution seems of very little importance. Black defines a "majority motion" as a proposition "which is able to obtain a simple majority over all of the other motions concerned."[13] The rules of procedure make it unlikely that such a motion will be selected by majority voting. The outcome should be a motion which could not get a simple majority over *all* other motions, but only over those other motions which differ enough so that they can be put against it under the procedural rules. The result is an approximation, but a reasonably satisfactory one. Thus if there is no true majority motion, if endless cycling were the predicted outcome of efforts to obtain perfect adjustment, this would not change the outcome at all if the cycles would only involve motions proposing such small changes that they could be ruled out of order. Even if the cycles slightly enlarged the area in which the voting system was indeterminate, this would be a trivial defect. Only if the cycles would involve "moves" substantially larger than the minimum permitted by the procedural system would they be a significant problem.

The investigation of the likely size of cycles in the real world can proceed by making assumptions about the distribution of voters and the rules of order and then calculating the likelihood of cycles among motions which differ enough so that they could be voted on, or by observing the real world.[14] There would seem to be two possible explanations for this paucity of examples of the phenomenon. Either it does not occur very commonly, which would be in accord with the theoretical considerations given above, or it is hard to detect the presence of cycles even when they are present.

In order to examine the possibility that the shortage of real world examples of cycles is explained not by their rarity, but by the difficulty of detecting them, let us consider the actual methods of voting used in most representative bodies. Under Robert's Rules, or the innumerable variants which exist, the procedure is quite complicated. We need not examine these rules in detail; a simplified generalization of them will suffice. Let us, therefore, examine the following system. A motion is made to move from the status quo. An amendment to this motion may then be proposed and various subamendments to the amendment. All of the amendments and subamendments can be

13. *The Theory of Committees and Elections, op. cit.*

14. Occasional cases which appear to involve cycles have been discovered. See: "Arrow's Theorem and Some Examples of the Paradox of Voting," William Riker, in *Mathematical Applications in Political Science*, S. Sidney Ulmer, Harold Guetzkow, and William Riker (Dallas, Texas: Arnold Foundation, Southern Methodist University, 1965), pp. 41–60.

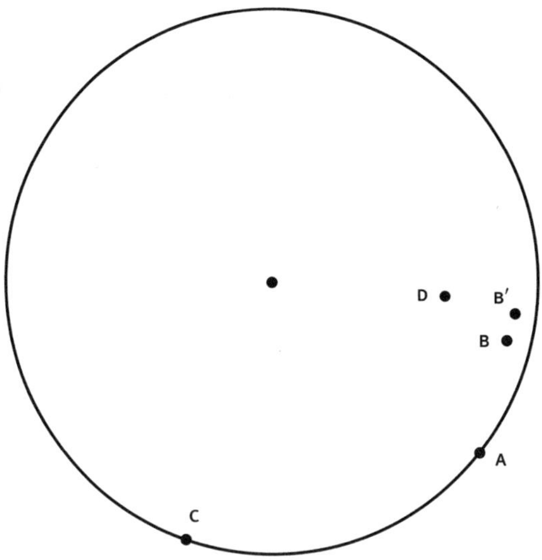

FIGURE VI

regarded as separate proposals. The distinguishing characteristic of this system is that a whole set of proposals is made before any of them are voted upon, and then that they are voted upon in a fixed order which is known in advance.

Suppose that the status quo is *A*. *B* is offered as a motion. *C* would be offered only if its sponsor thought it could beat both *A* and *B*. (Or, in special circumstances, if it might lead to a blocking cycle. This will be discussed below.) But people do make mistakes. Let us suppose, then, that someone in error offers amendment *C*. This is followed by subamendment *D*, which has been correctly calculated and can beat *A*, *B*, and *C*. For our purposes, we may use a simple set of rules providing that motions, amendments, and subamendments are voted upon in reverse order from that in which they are proposed. Thus *D* would be put against *C*, and would win; would be put against *B*, and would win; and then would be put against the status quo, *A*, and win again. Note that *C*, the miscalculation, has no effect on the voting except to delay it slightly. Such mistakes will certainly be made; hope springs eternal in the human breast, but they have no effect on the outcome. We can, therefore, ignore them.

Let us now consider the possibility of cycles. In Figure VI, we start with the status quo at *A*. Suppose that a motion, *B*, were introduced which could beat *A*. Either by accident, or by calculation, another motion, *C*, might be introduced which could beat *B*, but would be beaten by *A*. Deliberate contrivance of such a cycle by people who prefer *A* to *B*, but who realize that *B* would win in a direct confrontation would be rational. The existence of a cycle, of course, does not prevent other amendments from being offered. *D*, for example, could beat any member of the cycle.

If, however, *D* were not offered, the voting on *C*, *B*, and *A* would not immediately lead to an apparent cycle because *A* would be chosen if they were voted on in the order specified. This type of concealed cycle, however, should not lead to a stable result. Once the voting has led to a return to the status quo, further proposals for change would be strongly urged. If there were strict rules forbidding the reintroduction of a measure which had been voted down,[15] then some other proposal, say B', would be offered. We could expect to see essentially the same series of proposals and amendments retraced again and again. The absence of this kind of repetition in actual legislative practice is evidence that there are few concealed cycles in real world legislative activity.

So far we have been mostly concerned with the situation when there are only two variables and they are continuous. The generalization of the conclusions to many-dimensional issue space is obvious, but the effect of shifting to a noncontinuous variable may not be. In Figure VII we show a situation where the two variables are both discontinuous, and hence only certain points in the issue space are possible. The principal difference which this restriction makes is that there are now far fewer points which can get a majority over some given point. Point *A*, for example, is dominated only by the six points marked with *x*'s. The likelihood that one of the points that dominate *A* is equally or farther distant from the center than *A* is reduced when the total number of points is small, and the likelihood that there will be a set of points which are in a cycle is small. The tiny central area where every point is dominated by some other is apt to be nonexistent simply because there are too few points in this region. On the other hand, cycles are only unlikely, not impossible. If a cycle does occur, it is likely to be of more than trivial significance if the distances between the points are sizable and the cycle must, there-

15. Most rules of procedure have such provisions, but they are usually easy to avoid if a majority favors the measure which is reintroduced.

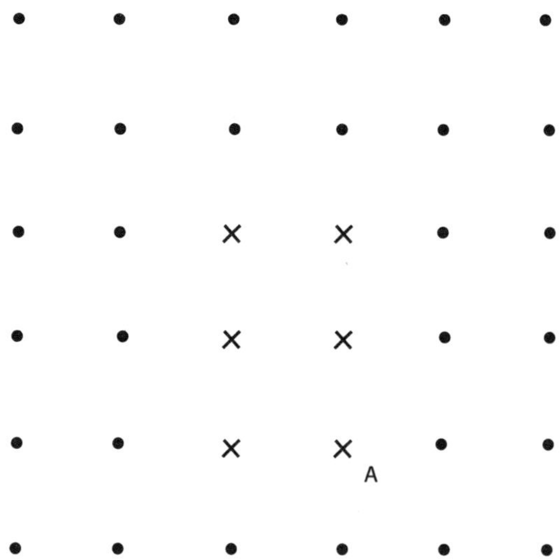

FIGURE VII

fore, involve sizable differences of policy. In sum, with discontinuous issue space, cycles must be rare but are apt to be important when they occur.

Our discussion so far has been based upon a special type of interdependence of the preference structures of individuals. It is assumed that social states, products, and laws differ in a number of characteristics.[16] Each of these characteristics may be arranged along an axis, either as a continuous variable or as a series of points. Each individual is assumed to have some optimum point in the resulting dimensional space, and it is assumed that the individual's degree of satisfaction falls off as we move away from his optimum in any direction. This later assumption, in the form of perfectly circular indifference curves,[17] is too strong, and we shall shortly demonstrate that a weaker assumption will do as well. Similarly, our assumption of even distribution of the optima over the issue space is a simplifying assumption which will shortly

16. If they differ in only one characteristic, then the work of Duncan Black indicates that the cyclical majority is most unlikely.

17. Circles in two dimensional issue space. When more than two variables are considered, the issue space would have more than two dimensions and the indifference hypersurfaces would be hyperspheres.

be dropped. Leaving these two issues aside, however, the general picture should raise few objections from economists. Special cases in which these conditions do not hold can be invented, but most choice problems will arise in environments which lead to this sort of preference system. The fact that each person has a preference structure of this sort, together with the fact that they are all in the same hyperspace gives them a rather probable type of interdependence, and our conclusions are essentially derived from this interdependence. Note, however, the rather special form of this interdependence. My preferences do not in any way affect yours. The interdependence comes solely from the fact that we are choosing from among the same set of alternatives and these alternatives are such that they restrict the form of our preference structures in a way which leads to our conclusion.

So far we have used two unrealistic assumptions, that the indifference curves are all perfect circles and that the individual optima are evenly distributed over the issue space. The elimination of these assumptions will make the model much more realistic. Let us begin by considering more realistic distributions of the optima.[18] Presumably the common distribution is to have the optima arranged in a bell-shaped distribution with its peak somewhere in the issue space. This distribution raises no particular problem for our demonstration. The "median lines" could still be constructed, and they would still mostly intersect near the peak of the distribution. This would mean that the same tendency to move to a small area in the center would exist. Similarly, a skewed normal distribution would raise no particular difficulties, although the point where most median lines intersected would not necessarily be at the peak of the distribution.

Multi-peaked distributions raise more difficulties, although the only clear cases leading to significant cycles which I have been able to produce involve extreme degrees of multi-peakedness. As an example, if the optima are arranged in three discrete groups arranged in a triangle, as in Figure VIII, and roughly a third of them are in each group, then cycling would occur over an area of significant size. The general difficulty of finding such phenomena

18. In a very kind letter Professor Arrow generally agreed with the argument presented in this paper. However, he pointed out that the following portion is not mathematically strict. He expressed a desire for "a stronger and stricter statement." I also would like to convert what is now a strong argument into a mathematical proof, but have been unable to do so. Perhaps some reader with greater facility in the use of mathematical tools will be able to repair the deficiency.

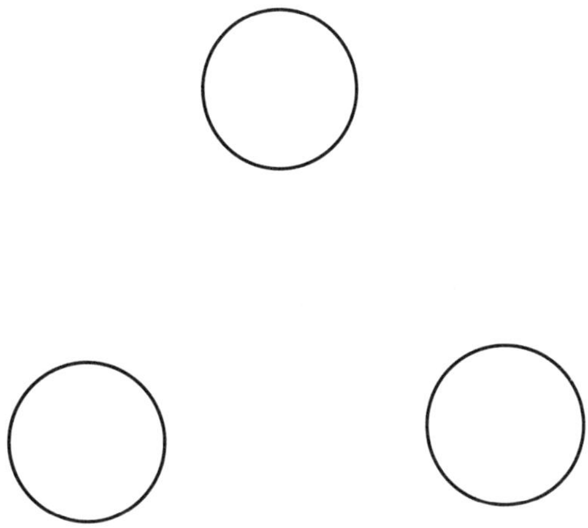

FIGURE VIII

can, perhaps, be illustrated by the fact that division of the optima into four roughly equal groups does not lead to significant cycles.

The elimination of the assumption that the indifference curves are perfect circles raises no particular difficulties if large numbers of people are involved in the decision process. Arrow wrote his book about the problem of selecting a "social welfare function" and this clearly would involve many millions of individuals. In the more general problems of collective choice, there also normally are enough individual preferences to be "aggregated" so that the law of large numbers can be applied. Granted large numbers of individuals,[19] any reasonable preference structure will aggregate in more or less the same way as our perfect circles. On the average—and with large numbers of voters, the average is what counts—majority voting will choose the alternative which

19. Even with large numbers of individuals, a combination of certain strong symmetry relations between their preference curves and special arrangements of their optima will lead to significant cycles. The only cases I have been able to develop involve very unrealistic shapes for the indifference curves, and there seems no point in presenting them here.

is closest to the optima of the majority of the voters. Suppose, for example, that we have two groups of 1,000,000 voters, *A* and *B*. Assume that of two alternatives *X* and *Y*, *X* lies closer to the optima of all members of Group *A*, and *Y* closer to the optima of all members of group *B*. We would expect about 1,000,000 votes for *X* and about 1,000,000 for *Y* if that choice were put to the 2,000,000 voters even if 100,000 voters in group *A* had preference mountains which were so shaped that they preferred *Y* to *X*. This would be so because the law of large numbers would indicate, lacking some special phenomenon, that there would also be about 100,000 voters in group *B* who preferred *X* to *Y*.

Note, however, that we only get an approximate result here. With the voters evenly divided, the small random variation which we would expect would decide the election. If the numbers in the two groups differed by more than the likely random variation, however, the outcome would not be affected. Thus the introduction of what amounts to a stochastic variable by considering indifference curves which are not perfect circles blurs our conclusions a little, and expands the small area in the center of the distribution in which cycles can occur by a small amount, but does not basically alter our conclusions.

That the majority voting process normally leads to a determinate outcome and that this outcome is apt to be reasonably satisfactory will surprise no practical man. Clearly this is what does happen. One of the real problems raised by Arrow's book was why the real world democracies seemed to function fairly well in spite of the logical impossibility of rationally aggregating preferences. The solution I have offered, that no decision process will meet Arrow's criteria perfectly, but that a very common decision process meets them to a very high degree of approximation, permits us to reconcile the theoretical impossibility with the practical success of democracy.

WHY SO MUCH STABILITY

One of Duncan Black's more important contributions was a classically simple proof that with complex issues and majority voting a stable outcome is unlikely.[1] This very simple proof that there would normally be no motion which can get a majority against all others, and hence that any possible outcome is dominated by another, has been elaborated and made more precise by later work. Without most improbable conditions, endless cycling would be expected. This is particularly true when logrolling is present as it normally is.

If we look at the real world, however, we observe not only is there no endless cycling, but acts are passed with reasonable dispatch and then remain unchanged for very long periods of time. Thus, theory and reality seem to be not only out of contact, but actually in sharp conflict. It is the purpose of this article to demonstrate that our existing theory, when properly looked at, does indeed imply a relatively stable outcome to voting. In some cases, however, this stability will not be a true equilibrium because a random member of a large set will be chosen and then that random outcome will be left unchanged for long periods of time. It does not dominate all other outcomes, but is retained merely because of its particular history.

There are already several possible explanations for the observed stability in the literature. We will take them up as they become relevant to the general line of reasoning. I should, however, warn the reader that my own previous work, including joint work with Buchanan, will play a major role here. This may simply reflect egotism, but I think that some of the early work which is now partially forgotten can provide solutions for more modern problems.

Much recent Public Choice work has involved spatial models and these models frequently ignore logrolling. The reason, presumably, is that it is very hard to put logrolling in a two-dimensional diagram. We shall begin considering such special models and assume that the issues are the sort that do not lead to logrolling, and then turn to more complex logrolling problems.

Reprinted, with kind permission of Kluwer Academic Publishers, from *Public Choice* 37 (1981): 189–202.

This article was much improved by comments from T. Nicolaus Tideman.

1. D. Black, *The Theory of Committees and Elections* (Cambridge: Cambridge University Press, 1958), 137–39.

With respect to the first situation in which logrolling does not occur, there is already one possible explanation for the observed stability in the literature, my own "General Irrelevance of the General Impossibility Theorem."[2] I there argued that endless cycling is theoretically possible, but unlikely in practice if the number of voters is large. In oral discussion with various people, I have heard that my proof is not regarded as very reliable any more because McKelvey[3] has proved that majority voting can reach any part of the issue space. I cannot regard this as a disproof of my argument. After all, I said "we should note that it is at least theoretically possible for the majority voting process to get outside the Pareto optimal area."[4]

To somewhat modernize the conclusions of my argument in the "General Irrelevance of the General Impossibility Theorem,"[5] if there is someone with strict control of the agenda and perfect knowledge of everyone else's preferences, and all people always vote their preferences, i.e., the agenda controller is the only strategist among the group, then the agenda controller can achieve his optimum regardless of where it is.[6]

If there are many voters then, unless the agenda controller's personal preference is near the middle of the cloud of optima in the issue space, his maneuvers will be readily detectable by simply examining the record. There will be a very long series of votes in each one of which the outcome is very close. As a general rule, one cannot move away from the general area at the cen-

2. G. Tullock, "The General Irrelevance of the General Impossibility Theorem," *Quarterly Journal of Economics* 81 (May 1967): 256–70. Also in Tullock, *Toward a Mathematics of Politics* (Ann Arbor: University of Michigan Press, 1967; Ann Arbor: Ann Arbor Paperbacks, 1972); subsequent page citations are to the book (1972).

3. R. McKelvey, *General Conditions for Global Informal Voting Models: Some Implications for Agenda Control* (Pittsburgh: School of Urban and Public Affairs, Carnegie-Mellon University, 1977). Mimeo.

4. Tullock, *Toward a Mathematics of Politics* (1972), 31. Also see page 34, "there are numerous positions outside the Pareto optimal area which can get majority over areas within it"; page 43, "Thus it is possible, by a simple majority vote, to reach points at almost any portion of the issue space."

5. I don't propose to run over the argument itself because it is fairly lengthy and already available in print in two different places.

6. Some careless discussion of this point implies that this process could lead to a point outside the Paretian area. The agenda controller has no motive to go anywhere except his own optimum, and his own optimum is by definition in the Pareto optimal area. Only through accident can the outcome be outside the Paretian area.

TABLE 1

$$L_A^2 = 5(A - 10)^2 + B^2 + C^2 + D^2 + E^2$$
$$L_B^2 = A^2 + 5(B - 10)^2 + C^2 + D^2 + E^2$$
$$L_C^2 = A^2 + B^2 + 5(C - 10)^2 + D^2 + E^2$$
$$L_D^2 = A^2 + B^2 + C^2 + 5(D - 10)^2 + E^2$$
$$L_E^2 = A^2 + B^2 + C^2 + D^2 + 5(E - 10)^2$$

ter of the cloud of issue points except by tiny steps in which the majority is also tiny.

If there is no person in control of the agenda, i.e., we are following Robert's Rules of Order in its pure form, or some other procedure which permits anyone who wishes to make a motion, the procedure will move into the center of the cloud of issue points fairly quickly. The exact point at which it will come to rest is indeterminate because within the center endless cycling is possible. If we simply assume that small moves are ruled out, the process will in fact terminate, not because there are no other points that dominate the terminating point, but because all the points that dominate it are so close that they are not permitted to be voted on.[7]

There is another mechanism which can, of course, lead to the middle of the cloud of optimal points in this kind of a system, namely two-party voting. If there are two parties, both will choose policies near the center of distribution; hence the outcome, regardless of which party wins, will be near the center.

The above seems to me fairly simple and straightforward and also not terribly important; hence I have given it a rather brief treatment. The empirically important problem is the case in which logrolling is possible. Most government actions have the characteristic of giving a rather intense benefit to a small group at a small cost to each member of a large group. Simple majority voting would seem to indicate that such bills cannot be passed, but if several small groups get together and logroll they can. Unfortunately, this is very difficult to present in a simple two-dimensional diagram and we need algebra.

Table 1[8] shows a situation with a five-member legislature, each member of

7. There is, of course, some probability, roughly equivalent to the probability that all the molecules of air in the room in which you are sitting will accumulate in one corner, that by sheer accident the motions offered will be such as to lead to a conclusion well away from the center.

8. G. Tullock, "A Simple Algebraic Logrolling Model," *American Economic Review* 60(3) (1970): 419–26.

which (A, B, C, D, and E) has a project which will benefit his district but injure all of the others. A, for example, would like Project A to be implemented at a level of 10 and the others at a level of 0. The equations are loss equations; i.e., they demonstrate the injuries one will suffer at any point other than his optimum as compared to the optimum. The indifference hypersurfaces are, in essence, five-dimensional ellipsoids shortened in one dimension, with each center at 10 units on the axis favored by that member.

With this particular mathematical representation, unanimous consent can be obtained for a joint project in which all five of the projects are implemented to some rather small amount. This is probably unrealistic if we are thinking of such logrolling activities as rivers and harbors legislation. But if we look at the government as a whole it seems reasonable that this would be so.

Note that it is by no means necessary that a project have a positive payoff as projects of Table 1 do. One can imagine a situation in which the individual congressman will be led into very severely damaging his constituents. In Figure 1, we have a 25-member legislature which is considering a set of 25 bills, each one of which will give $15 to a given constituency, at a cost of $25 in the form of $1 tax on each of the 25 constituencies. The individual congressman can decide either to join in the logrolling or refuse to do so. Figure 1 shows the situation which he would face granted that various numbers from 1 to 24 of his fellow congressmen are engaged in logrolling. It will be observed that if only a few members of the legislature are willing to logroll, it makes no difference which policy he undertakes. If, however, 12 or more of his fellow congressmen are willing to logroll, he is always better off if he logrolls than if he does not. This is true even though the ultimate outcome if everybody logrolls is a loss of $10 per constituency.

In Table 1 the injury inflicted on each member of the group from doing nothing is 22.2.[9] The injury inflicted if they engaged in the optimal quantity of the projects is 15. Obviously, they should, if they could reach agreement, adopt the optimal production. A simple majority of voting legislature, however, would be unlikely to meet that goal. Logrolling is called for.

Following *The Calculus of Consent*[10] and my own *Entrepreneurial Politics*,[11] there are two forms that logrolling can take—formal coalitions and individ-

9. Calculation methods for these numbers are contained in the original article.

10. J. M. Buchanan and G. Tullock, *The Calculus of Consent: Logical Foundations of Constitutional Democracy* (Ann Arbor: University of Michigan Press, 1962).

11. G. Tullock, *Entrepreneurial Politics*, Research Monograph 5 (Charlottesville: Thomas Jefferson Center for Political Economy, University of Virginia, February 1962).

	Don't logroll	Logroll
1	0	0
2	0	0
3	0	0
4	0	0
5	0	0
6	0	0
7	0	0
8	0	0
9	0	0
10	0	0
11	0	0
12	0	2
13	− 13	1
14	− 14	0
15	− 15	− 1
16	− 16	− 2
17	− 17	− 3
18	− 18	− 4
19	− 19	− 5
20	− 20	− 6
21	− 21	− 7
22	− 22	− 8
23	− 23	− 9
24	− 24	− 10

FIGURE 1
Each bill will pay $15 to a given constituency at cost of $25 in the form of $1 tax on each constituency.

ual bargains. In formal coalitions, three of the members get together and form a "platform" which calls for production of 7$\frac{1}{7}$ units for A, B, and C, and 0 for D and E. This gives a loss of 12 to the members of the winning coalition and a loss of 25.6 to the two representatives who are not members. *Ex ante* individuals would not know whether they were going to be members or not of the coalition, and hence we can calculate an *ex ante* value which gives a weighting of $\frac{3}{5}$ to the 12$\frac{2}{5}$ to 25.6. This value is 17.4.

The other logrolling technique, and the one to which *The Calculus of Consent* was primarily devoted, involves individual bargains. Thus, Mr. A makes a bargain with Mr. B and Mr. C under which they both agree to vote for his project and he agrees to vote for theirs. Mr. B then, now having two votes, his own and Mr. A's, makes a bargain with Mr. D under which Mr. B's project is passed. Mr. C who also has two votes already, A's and his own, makes a bargain with Mr. E and gets his project passed. Mr. D and Mr. E then close the circle, the result that all five projects are implemented. In this particular case, the loss function for all is 17.2 which is slightly better than the *ex ante* payoff under implicit logrolling. A discussion of the general conditions under which one or the other form of logrolling would give the best results, by Geoffrey Brennan, is attached as an appendix.

Let us begin our discussion with individual bargain logrolling and then go on to formal coalitions. Firstly, individual bargains are likely to involve everyone, as it does in this case, because any individual who is being left out of the bargains can always offer lower prices for his vote and hence get back in. There is likely to be an equilibrium price for votes although in the real world things would not be as symmetrical as in our simple example. The outcome will not be Pareto optimal and the exact outcome is to some extent path dependent, but basically something rather similar to our 7 1/7 all around will come out. This is a stable equilibrium but unfortunately a pretty inferior equilibrium. Too many of these projects are being provided by the voting system. It may, of course, as it is in this case, be better than nothing at all, but still we would like to do something better if there were some way of doing so. In *The Calculus of Consent*, Prof. Buchanan and I implicitly recommended raising the majority, which improves the structure of the equilibrium but also makes it harder to reach. Currently, I would probably recommend the demand revealing process.[12]

So far we seem to have had no difficulty at all in explaining stability. In fact, all of our models have been more or less stable. The real problem in explaining stability, however, comes up when we turn to formal coalitions. Although *ex ante* the congressman would presumably be more or less indifferent between individual bargains and a formal coalition, it is always true that for the members of the majority coalition a formal coalition dominates the individual bargaining form of logrolling. Thus, if A, B, and C can form a permanent coalition among themselves, they will be better off than they would be in a system of individual bargaining. Of course, this is paid for by D and E who are worse off.

12. T. N. Tideman and G. Tullock, "A New and Superior Process for Making Social Choices," *Journal of Political Economy* (October 1976): 1145–59.

The problem here is that this coalition is unstable. D and E can offer C a coalition in which he gets 8 and they each take 6. He will then have 9.6 which is better than under the previous coalition, and D and E will have 13.4 which is also an improvement. But this new coalition is similarly dominated by, let us say, returning to the original distribution for A and B, but leaving C out and substituting either D or E. The cycle is endless. The problem has been the subject of a great many quite sophisticated mathematical analyses but perhaps the simpliest explanation is found in *The Calculus of Consent*.[13] The discussion there assumes a constant sum game. What we have here, of course, is a variable sum game, but the variation, if anything, strengthens the argument.

There is a possible solution to this cycle, first suggested by von Neumann and Morgenstern[14] and then elaborated in *The Calculus of Consent*.[15] Essentially, this explanation assumes that individuals would not like to be in the situation of C in the above second coalition because they realized that his payoff, which is much higher than that of the other members of the coalition, puts him in a particularly dangerous position in further negotiations. It is quite likely that A and B can buy off either D or E. Further, the cost to A and B would, in this case, be substantially nil since they would be in the same situation they were before C defected.

We can divide coalitions into two categories which we shall call egalitarian and aristocratic. Individuals who are members of an egalitarian coalition would be reluctant to join an aristocratic coalition. They would be reluctant for two reasons. One reason is that the serfs in the aristocratic coalition do not make as much as members of the egalitarian coalition. If they are offered the position of an aristocrat, however, they will fear that the coalition is radically unstable and that they are going to lose in the next round. If this suggestion of von Neumann and Morgenstern is correct then egalitarian coalitions would be quite stable. We could not predict in advance which of the innumerable egalitarian coalitions would be formed, but we could predict that one would come into existence if logrolling with formal coalitions were the rule.

It should perhaps here be said that for both types of logrolling, the individual participants are well advised to sell out permanently rather than to

13. Buchanan and Tullock, *The Calculus of Consent*, 148–50.

14. J. von Neumann and O. Morgenstern, *Theory of Games and Economic Behavior*, 3rd ed. (Princeton: Princeton University Press, 1953).

15. Buchanan and Tullock, *The Calculus of Consent*, 149.

simply renting their vote. If they make a practice of voting for some project and then after they have been paid off voting for its repeal, they will shortly find that their vote is valued at very little by potential partners. Thus, we would anticipate logrolling bargains would tend to be fairly stable with respect to the particular things that were in fact voted through. They would not necessarily be stable with respect to future bills.

Note that once again, assuming that there is implicit logrolling and that the particular solution to the permanent cycle discussed above is correct, we reach a situation which is rather spectacularly non-Pareto optimal.[16] We do not know which particular coalition will form, but we do know that there will be overinvestment in projects of the members of the coalition and underinvestment in the projects of the minority.

So far then, we find that logrolling leads to two situations which are stable (in the sense of being unlikely to change) but non-Pareto optimal. Note, however, that the fact that these solutions are non-Pareto optimal does not mean that the world is not better off than it would be without logrolling. Indeed, in this particular example, the *ex ante* value of either kind of logrolling is greater than the *ex ante* value of prohibition of logrolling. We have here illustrated the general stand of *The Calculus of Consent* with respect to logrolling.

So far I have said nothing about the information conditions. There has been a sort of implicit assumption that everybody is perfectly informed. In the real world, of course, this is far from true, but, in general, the information conditions we expect of the real world will, if anything, reinforce all of our conclusions.[17] I propose to continue with what we may refer to as a more or less perfect information assumption throughout the rest of this article, not because I think it is true but because introduction of realistic information restrictions would lengthen this article without really improving it.

It has been pointed out by innumerable mathematicians that formal coalitions, from the standpoint of the members of the winning coalition, clearly dominate logrolling with individual bargaining. If we look at the real world, however, we find no apparent examples of this kind of logrolling. Let us confine ourselves to the American situation. I will discuss only the Congress of

16. If cash side payments were permitted, this situation would not be stable. Cash side payments are, however, prohibited by almost all voting systems. I feel this prohibition is wise but will not go into the subject here.

17. Tullock, *Toward a Mathematics of Politics* (1972), 100–143.

the United States, but I think most people will agree that the state legislatures—and for that matter city councils—will follow much the same pattern. The first thing we see is that almost everybody gets their share, i.e., congressional boodle is passed around more or less equally. That this is so is surely the conventional wisdom among political scientists, but there are, in addition, at least some reasonably formal demonstrations of the point. Butler[18] looked at expenditures by congressional districts and in a quite sophisticated study was unable to find any evidence of discrimination against any individual or class. It is, of course, true that he was not able to totally rule out such discriminations, particularly since expenditures are only one of many variables which congressmen would regard as of value, but he tried all of the more reasonable patterns and found no result. Bennett and Mayberry[19] found roughly the same situation, with benefits and taxes being distributed more or less in accordance with the number of congressmen and senators by states.

It should be said that there is at least some empirical evidence which, it might be argued, cuts the other way. Beginning with Charles Plott,[20] a number of scholars found that allocations and other benefits under the control of a given committee tend to be distributed disproportionately among the districts of the members of that committee and that the chairman, in particular, may do very well. This is not inconsistent with the findings of Butler and Bennett and Mayberry, however. Since all congressmen are on committees, there is every reason to believe that this distortion by committee cancels out.[21]

Nevertheless, it cannot be said that exact equality is maintained, only that there are no groups who seem to be very decidedly left out. So far as I know, the only cases in which we have had groups literally left out occurred in the American South in two periods, the first period during the late Reconstruc-

18. H. Butler, *An Analysis of the Distribution of Federal Expenditures by Congressional Districts* (Coral Gables, Fla.: Center for Law and Economics, University of Miami, 1980). Unpublished manuscript.

19. J. T. Bennett and E. R. Mayberry, *Federal Tax Burdens and Grant Benefits to States: The Impact of Imperfect Representation* (Fairfax, Va.: Department of Economics, George Mason University). Unpublished paper.

20. C. R. Plott, "Some Organizational Influences on Urban Renewal Decisions," *American Economic Review* 58 (May 1968): 306–21.

21. See B. A. Ray, "Federal Spending and the Selection of Committee Assignments in the U.S. House of Representatives," *American Journal of Political Science* 24(3) (1980): 494–510, for the most recent work in this field.

tion when the Republican party was being exterminated by various state Democratic parties and in which the small Republican minorities in the legislature were given nothing, with the result that they tended to become smaller after the next election. The second case, also in the South, concerns the recent revival of the Republicans in that area. For a period, Democratic majorities in the legislatures once again prevented the tiny Republican minorities from getting anything. As the minorities became a little less tiny they were, however, admitted to the club. These are special cases; note that the dominant group in this case was not a mere 51 percent but usually something like 90 percent of the legislature. What happened was that individual bargaining logrolling proceeded but with a small group of people cut out. The implicit logrolling model was not adopted.

This tendency of the legislature to spread the benefits around throughout its entire membership has, generally speaking, not aroused much interest in traditional political scientists, probably because they do not know enough game theory to realize that it is, at least theoretically, unlikely. There are two basic explanations. The first, by David Klingaman,[22] points out that most people are risk averse and hence an even division of the spoils, which is less risky, might dominate a formal coalition. The second explanation, which has been proposed by a number of political scientists, was put in its clearest form by Ferejohn.[23] It says rather little about risk aversion but argues the existence of a sort of ethic of universalism which leads everyone to feel that everyone else should get his share.

It will be noted that both of the above suggestions would point in the direction not of explicit logrolling, but of some kind of essentially Pareto optimal structure. It might, of course, be politically impossible to get a Pareto optimal scheme, but if the various members of Congress are actually interested, consciously, in a universal solution, surely they would not choose the inferior universal solution which comes out of logrolling with individual bargaining.

Here we have to turn to more general evidence, but I think no one who is even remotely familiar with the American Congress or other legislative bodies will doubt that what goes on is individual bargaining logrolling although, as I shall point out below, in some cases this leads to passage of portfolio bills which receive very nearly unanimous consent. Deals are made, however, and

22. D. Klingaman, "A Note on a Cyclical Majority Problem," *Public Choice* 6 (Spring 1969): 99–101.

23. J. A. Ferejohn, *Pork Barrel Politics* (Stanford: Stanford University Press, 1974).

bills produced are very hard to explain in terms of cost-benefit ratios for the country as a whole, although they are frequently beneficial for the particular constituency involved. This does not, of course, mean that the constituency benefits from the entire collection of bills in the logrolling package but only from the individual one that affects the constituency. It loses on the others.[24]

Why are the formal logrolling coalitions so rare? Assuming that all of the coalitions will be roughly egalitarian in shape,[25] it is obvious that there are a great many possible coalitions, any one of which could have a majority. In general, however, none of these coalitions, which equally divide the spoils among varying 51 percent combinations of voters, dominates the others. That being so, if such a coalition can be successfully put together, it will hold.

What then is the process of building such coalitions? Suppose that the entrepreneurs begin building competing proto-coalitions. The individual member of this collective group would be interested in both his payoff, if the coalition which he is contemplating at the moment is successful, and the probability of its success. This would lead to a complex bargaining procedure, but in this bargaining it will always be true that any coalition which looks like it has a good prospect of winning will immediately be attractive to further potential entrants, because the product of their payoff and the probability of success would rise with the probability that the proto-coalition would become a simple majority. This situation is rather similar to that discussed by Brams and Riker[26] at presidential nominating conventions.

One would anticipate a slow bargaining procedure in which various individuals surveyed different proto-coalitions and then, as it became clear that only a few or eventually only one had a chance to win, there would be a rush of people to join. The organizers of the coalition would, of course, not need more than 51 percent and hence would pay nothing for anybody who joined after they had achieved 51 percent, but it would be risky on their part to cut back on payments for the last few people needed for the 51 percent because

24. For an argument on the other side see K. A. Shepsle and B. R. Weingast, *Political Preferences for the Pork Barrel: A Generalization*, Center for the Study of American Business Working Paper 57 (St. Louis: Washington University, June 1980).

25. With a purely redistributive context one would expect to be purely egalitarian, but granted the kind of acts that Congress actually passes, rough egalitarianism is all that can be expected.

26. S. J. Brams and W. Riker, "Models of Coalition Formation in Voting Bodies," in *Mathematical Applications in Political Science*, vol. 6 (Charlottesville: University Press of Virginia, 1972), 79–124.

of the prospect that this would lead to the very quick formation of a counter-coalition.

The individual, in bargaining to enter these coalitions, would face a tricky strategic problem together with, probably, the necessity of making decisions with information which is far from complete. He would know his potential payoff from entering the various proto-coalitions, but his information as to which one was actually going to win would not be very accurate during the period in which it would be of greatest value to him. Under the circumstances the outcome might well be quite random. We would anticipate that egalitarian coalitions would be formed, but we would not be able to tell in advance which egalitarian coalition would attain a winning majority.

Consider, then, a continuing body which will, let us say, meet every year to deal with a bundle of governmental issues, with the bundle being at least to some extent different each year. Under these circumstances what kind of situation would we expect? Leaving aside the possibility of an agreed equal division among all, there are two clear-cut possibilities, although we might expect various intermediate combinations in the real world. The first of these possibilities is that a single coalition would be formed at the beginning, again an egalitarian coalition, and that it would remain permanently in existence. If this occurred, once again we could not predict in advance what the coalition would be, but we could predict it would be egalitarian. The other possibility is that there would be no such coalition.

(The prospect for the third logical possibility, the formation of a new egalitarian coalition each time that the body meets for all measures to be brought up at that time, is, I think, substantially zero. There certainly are at least some gains to be made through bargains that extend from one meeting to the next.)

In real-world legislative assemblies, the membership is not constant from year to year. Members die, retire, and are beaten in elections. A coalition of 51 percent would have to have some arrangement for admitting new members at each session and this would be difficult, albeit not impossible because presumably at each election the number of seats which had changed would be larger than the difference between the previous winning coalition and the minority in the previous session. Of course, it would be possible to maintain the coalition at a size large enough, let us say 60 percent of the votes, that it would still have a majority after the ordinary election losses. This would be particularly easy because members of the coalition would be less likely to lose elections than its opponents in view of the fact that they would do a good job for their constituency.

It does appear, however, that the bargaining problem faced by such a long-term coalition would be extremely difficult and very likely impossible. Consider an individual member or a small clique in such a coalition. In both cases, assume that their defection would convert the majority coalition into a minority coalition. For this individual or clique, there is no great advantage in either being members of the existing coalition or switching over and becoming a member, presumably a favored member, of a new coalition composed of the former minority. If this is so, they would be in a position to bargain very hard with the entrepreneurs of the majority coalition for good treatment.

Of course they would not want to become the aristocrat in an aristocratic coalition, but as we have said above, in the real world perfect egalitarianism is not possible because of the complex bundles of different kinds of measures which are passed by Congress. All of these measures have differential payoffs at different districts and, therefore, by definition some members of the coalition do better than others. The desire to be among the group that does better would presumably be universal in the coalition. Thus, hard bargaining for mildly special positions could be expected.

As part of this bargaining, they would periodically have to make realistic threats of departing. The counter-threats on the part of the management of the coalition, of course, would be to let them go and replace them with other people from the minority. This again, if the bargaining is efficient, must be realistic. Thus, the management of the coalition should practically continuously be seen to be engaging in negotiations with non-members of the coalition in order to keep the members in line.

Of course, it would not be one clique, but practically all members of the winning coalition, including for that matter the entrepreneurs themselves. All of them would be continuously threatening to leave if they didn't get better treatment. Since this is a permanent coalition and since it is clearly possible for the benefits of the coalition to switch in a way adverse to any given member, such maneuvering is more or less necessary.

This kind of bargaining, however, is in the long run unstable. It is rather like the bargaining that went on between China and Russia before 1958. Each year the two parties would enter negotiations for the various aids of an economic nature which the Russians were offering to China, together with the political reciprocation that China was giving. Each year both would threaten to break off negotiations unless the other side offered more, but each year at the end, they would reach agreement. In the following year, however, each party would realize that last year they had finally given in and fear that the other party would assume they were going to do it this time, so they would find it necessary to engage in even more strongly threatening behavior.[27] Thus, each year the threats and other maneuvers intended to indicate to the other party that a break-off was indeed likely were increased. Each year, however, the evidence available to each party that the other party didn't really mean its threats increased. Thus, it became even more important to use stronger techniques next time. Eventually, some kind of mistake is apt to be made and an actual break occurs.

These, however, are two-party arrangements. With multi-party bargaining inside the dominant coalition, together with the good terms that can be offered from outside the dominant coalition, it is likely that the break will come fairly early. The new winning coalition, of course, would be equally unstable. The end product is apt to be the individually bargained logrolling model, with each congressman making a series of individual bargains with others because bargaining problems of attempting to maintain coalitions for a long period of time are too great. In any event, that is what we see in American legislatures.

The situation that we sometimes observe in European legislatures and, in particular, in the English legislature since 1900—in which there is a majority party or a coalition made up of several parties, and the membership of the parties is permanent from election to election but different parties in the government after elections—is not clear. If we look at the actual performance of this type of government, we do not find that they attempt to confine the boodle to districts of the MPs in the winning coalition. The constituencies that apparently do best are the marginal constituencies, with the highly loyal constituencies on either side not doing as well.[28] Why this is true is not clear. Indeed, R. H. Crossman in his memoirs several times discusses the allocation of various funds, specifically housing funds, in such a way that safe labor districts will do particularly well. It would appear, however, there is no great shift in the geographical location of government expenditure when labor is replaced by conservatives or vice versa. The same seems to be true with the various coalition governments on the Continent. Why this is so, I don't know, and I suggest that someone do research on the point.

27. I was mildly involved myself in rather similar negotiations between the American government and President Rhee of Korea.

28. This does not seem to be true in the United States. Butler (see note 18 above) shows that marginal constituencies get no more in government projects than safe ones. Apparently, in the American Congress a vote is a vote is a vote.

Congressmen are busy men and find themselves in need of timesaving devices. One simple procedure is to have the relevant committee which will, of course, contain representatives from both parties, canvass the House and decide which particular rivers and harbors bills would, in fact, pass if implicit logrolling were used on votes on each individual bill. This collection of specific projects can then be put together in one very large bill and presented to Congress as a unit. This saves congressmen time, but it has certain bizarre effects.

The first thing to be said is that the overall bill is contrary to the interest of all constituencies in the United States. This is because it is simply a summation of all the bills that would be passed by explicit logrolling, and the bills that are passed by explicit logrolling normally contain many in which the cost is around twice as great as the total benefit.[29] The congressmen nevertheless will vote for them simply because they know that most of these individual bills will get through anyway and it is quite possible that if this rivers and harbors appropriation is turned down, the press of time will mean that some will not go through and the congressmen who vote against the major general bill are particularly likely to have the projects in their districts among those that are lost when the session adjourns.[30]

But here, once again, we have an equilibrium rather than an unstable outcome. The result is the same as that under explicit logrolling. The only difference is that a timesaving device is used.

Recently, an even more radical timesaving device has been introduced in the formula allocation of funds. There is always a good deal of debate as to the exact techniques of the formula, and apparently pocket calculators are carried onto the floor and quick calculations are made as to how each constituency does. Still, this is a way of distributing the spoils which is even less time consuming than simply combining a whole set of special projects into one bill. Indeed, it saves the time of the committee as well as the time of the congressmen on the floor. Looked at from the standpoint of the individual congressman, it has the unfortunate characteristic that he must anticipate that in some of the bills he will do badly on the formula and well on the others. But the logrolling in this case tends to run across bills, and a congress-

29. Here, of course, I am assuming fairly good information. Assuming realistic information conditions, cost can be a very large multiple of the benefit rather than the simple two-to-one level which I have described here.

30. Since the election of President Carter the rivers and harbors bill, as a whole, has had considerable difficulty, and it is possible that eventually this particular bit of pork will disappear.

man who is willing to accept a particular formula on, let us say the allocation of food stamp money in return for another formula on the housing allocations, will still do reasonably well.

With respect to these formula grants, however, it is possible that the legislature is moving towards the situation which we described in connection with our first example in which each bill is passed by a majority and benefits that majority, but in which there are many other possible majorities (with, of course, different details of the formula) which could just as well have formed and passed their own bills. The result under such arrangements would depend on the kind of coalition building we described in our first model with the various members of Congress anxious to be part of the winning coalition but, in general, unwilling to accept disproportional bids to move from one coalition to another because they realize this jeopardizes their position. Further, once the vote has gone through, the individuals would want to maintain their reputations for keeping their word and hence would be unwilling to vote for repealing or modifying it for at least a number of years. In this case, we would anticipate that the outcome would be one of the various possible egalitarian coalitions winning and that this outcome, although essentially random within that category, would tend to be stable over time.

I began by raising the question why we see as much stability as we do. I believe I have provided a theoretical explanation although, of course, it may not be either the only explanation or one which will withstand empirical examination. But my suggestion is that the stable outcomes that are observed and sometimes selected by procedures with a substantial random component are generally inefficient. They represent equilibria because the conditions needed to produce motion from some initial or intermediate position appear to be more severe than has been generally assumed.

Appendix

The crucial difference between "implicit" and "explicit" logrolling in the Tullock formulation is that in the former case only a minimal majority receives special-benefit legislation in its favor, whereas in the latter case everyone does. Hence, whether losses are larger (or benefits smaller) in the implicit rather than in the explicit case depends on whether the special-benefit legislation has positive net social benefits or not. If it does, then extending that special-benefit legislation to a larger number of voters must increase total social benefit: explicit logrolling is to be preferred.

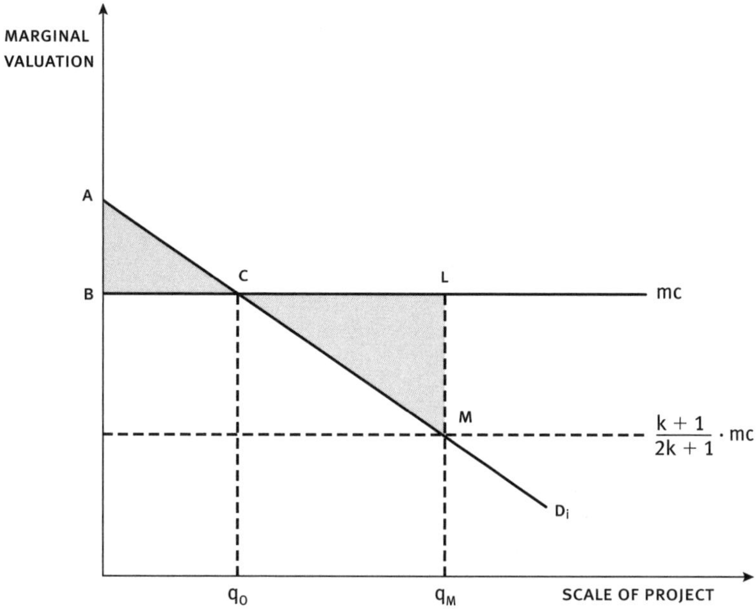

FIGURE A1

A simple diagrammatic example may help elucidate. Suppose there are $2k + 1$ identical voters, each of which desires some project of purely private value. The demand curve of each voter for project size is shown as D_i in Figure A1. If each voter paid for his own project, the size would be q_0, where D_i cuts the marginal cost curve of increasing project size, *MC*. This would be optimal. With collective provision under majority rule and general uniform taxes, the individual will aim to join a majority coalition which provides $(k + 1)$ of the projects, at a marginal cost for each of $\frac{k+1}{2k+1} \cdot MC$. The resultant project size will be q_M, which is inefficiently large.

Under implicit logrolling there will only be one such coalition, and the number of projects undertaken will be $(k + 1)$. Under explicit logrolling, there will be $(2k + 1)$ majority vote-trades and $(2k + 1)$ projects undertaken. Whether we should have $(2k + 1)$ projects or only $(k + 1)$ depends on whether each project of size q_M has positive net benefits. Consider the expected net benefit for any individual under explicit logrolling: this is the total benefit to him of his own project of size q_M, minus his share of the total cost of providing $(2k + 1)$ such projects. If we approximate the first term by the area under the demand curve over the range from zero to q_M (i.e.,

$$\int_0^{q_M} D_i(q)dq)$$

then in the explicit logrolling case, expected net benefit is simply:

$$E(B_i)^E = \int_0^{q_M} D_i(q)dq - \frac{1}{2k+1}(q_M \cdot MC)2k + 1 \tag{i}$$

$$= \int_0^{q_M} D_i(q)dq - q_M \cdot MC \tag{ii}$$

In the implicit logrolling case, the expected net benefit is:

$$E(B_i)^I = P_M\left[\int_0^{q_M} D_i(q)dq - \frac{k+1}{2k+1}(q_M MC)\right] - P_N \cdot \frac{k+1}{2k+1}(q_n \cdot MC) \tag{iii}$$

where P_M is the probability of being in the majority, $\frac{k+1}{2k+1}$; P_N is the probability of being in the minority; and $\frac{k+1}{2k+1}(q_M \cdot MC)$ is the cost to each individual of financing the $(k + 1)$ projects of majority members.
Hence:

$$E(B_i)^I = P_M\int_0^{q_M} D_i(q)dq - (P_M + P_N)\frac{k+1}{2k+1}(q_M \cdot MC) \tag{iv}$$

$$= \frac{k+1}{2k+1}\left[\int_0^{q_N} D_i(q)dq - q_M \cdot MC\right] \tag{v}$$

(since $P_M + P_N = 1$)

so
$$E(B_i)^I = \frac{k+1}{2k+1}E(B_i)^E \tag{vi}$$

Hence, if $E(B_i)^E > 0$, then $E(B_i)^E > E(B_i)^I$.

But, if $E(B_i)^E < 0$, then $E(B_i)^I > E(B_i)^E$.

Diagrammatically, if the area ABC in Figure A1 exceeds the area CLM, then the project, pursued at scale q_M, has positive total benefits, and explicit logrolling is preferable. Clearly, this need not be the case. In that event, implicit logrolling is preferable.

Editorial Note

The Editor [and author] feels that the general subject matter of this discussion is important for Public Choice. In private circulation, the article has already attracted at least one comment (to be published in an early issue) and I should like to encourage other people to join the debate. As Editor, I extend to the author the usual privilege of writing the last comment in the series, but I hope that a number of people will contribute before the discussion ends.

IS THERE A PARADOX OF VOTING?

The purpose of this note is to argue that Arrow's proof does not apply to regular existing democracy because there is a hidden assumption. When I say the assumption is hidden I do not mean that Arrow himself hid it, although he may not have appreciated its importance. In the elaborate literature which has developed based on his theorem, however, it has been ignored. Institutional rules limit many choices to two alternatives. Where they don't, logrolling or strategic voting is normal. His theorem only applies where none of these apply, and hence must be of little practical importance for democracy as we know it.

This forgotten assumption is that people in democracies do or should vote in accordance with their elementary preferences. Arrow specifically makes this assumption in two paragraphs of his introduction. These two paragraphs are not entirely clear, and I reproduce the whole of them rather than a couple of sentences. The parts that are most important for my argument are italicized.

> SOME LIMITATIONS OF THE ANALYSIS
> It has been stated above that the present study confines itself to the formal aspects of collective social choice. *The aspects not discussed may be conveniently described as the game aspects, especially since that term has acquired a double meaning*. In the first place, no consideration is given to the enjoyment of the decision process as a form of play. There is no need to stress the obvious importance of the desire to play and win the game as such in both economic behavior and political. That such considerations are real and should be considered in determining the mechanics of social choice is not to be doubted; but this is beyond the scope of the present study.
>
> The other meaning of the term "game" is that which has been brought to the attention of economists by Professors von Neumann and Morgenstern. *The point here, broadly speaking, is that, once a machinery for making social choices from individual tastes is established, individuals will find it profitable, from a rational point of view, to misrepresent their tastes by their actions, either because such misrepresentation is somehow directly profitable or, more usually, because some other individual will be made so much better off by the first in-*

Reprinted, by permission of Sage Publications, Inc., from *Journal of Theoretical Politics* 4 (1992): 225–30.

> *dividual's misrepresentation that he could compensate the first individual in such a way that both are better off than if everyone really acted in direct accordance with his tastes*. Thus, in an electoral system based on plurality voting, it is notorious that an individual who really favors a minor party candidate will frequently vote for the less undesirable of the major party candidates rather than "throw away his vote." Even in a case where it is possible to construct a procedure showing how to aggregate individual tastes into a consistent social preference pattern, there still remains the problem of devising rules of the game so that individuals will actually express their true tastes even when they are acting rationally. This problem is allied to the problem of constructing games of fair division, in which the rules are to be such that each individual, by playing rationally, will succeed in getting a preassigned fair share; in the case of two people and equal division, the game is the very familiar one in which one player divides the total stock of goods into two parts, and the second player chooses which part he likes.[1]

We note that Arrow specifically rules out log-rolling and restricts his proof to cases where everyone votes according to his tastes. It is obvious to anyone paying much attention to the functioning of any legislative body that most measures obtain their majorities, not because the average person in the legislature is in favor of it, but because they have been purchased. The farm programs in the United States, in England, on the Continent or in Japan are perfectly wonderful examples of this since they are surely favored by only a small minority of the representatives. The others have been bought.[2]

As co-author of *The Calculus of Consent*[3] I naturally tend to think that this kind of log-rolling is a good thing. There are others who disagree. Jim and I, however, would not claim that the outcome is perfect. There are a number of difficulties which I have dealt with elsewhere. This kind of log-rolling is the fundamental support of the bulk of the bills passed through any legislature.

1. Kenneth J. Arrow, *Social Choice and Individual Values* (New York: John Wiley, 1963), 6–7, 11.

2. Congressman Richard Armey, discussing the defeat of his amendment to the agricultural bill which would have prevented the wealthiest farmers from receiving direct subsidies, said: "There are no weak sisters on the Agriculture Committee. They are very good at doing what committees do. They spend five years filling their silos with political chits, and when the time comes, they call them in" (*Washington Post*, 9 August 1990: A4).

3. James M. Buchanan and Gordon Tullock, *The Calculus of Consent: Logical Foundations of Constitutional Democracy* (Ann Arbor: University of Michigan Press, 1962).

1	2	3
A	B	C
B	C	A
C	A	B

1	2	3
B + 100	B	C
A	B − 100	A
B	C	B
C	A	

FIGURE 1

Note that I say the bulk, and not all, a point to which we shall return shortly. The discussion of elections also will be deferred for a few pages.

The point is, however, a little complicated. The upper panel of Figure 1 shows the standard intransitivity diagram which has appeared in so many elementary textbooks. These are the preferences of our three voters. The lower panel shows a situation which will occur when Mr. 2 pays Mr. 1 $100 to vote for *B*. We assume that $B - 100$ is indeed preferred to *C* and *A* by Mr. 2, and that $B + 100$ is preferred to *A* and *C* by Mr. 1. They are not, in Arrow's terms, voting for their preferences.

Some early readers of this article said that as a matter of fact they are voting for their preferences here. Clearly, that is a perfectly good use of English, but it is not Arrow's usage. These people have suggested that the initial "*B*" in the first and second columns be deleted so that the matrix is no longer one which shows the cycle.

To repeat, this is not the way Arrow uses the term. In any event, it does not affect the reasoning. Using their language, the statement would have to be changed to say not that these people are voting against their preferences as a result of a bargain, but that the bargain changes their preferences in such a way as to eliminate the cycle. But granted the frequency of such bargains in real world legislatures, this would also imply that there are almost no legislative cycles.

Another standard textbook diagram is used for an example of the Borda method, which, in turn, is used to illustrate dependence upon irrelevant alternatives. It is reproduced as the top panel of Figure 2. In the bottom panel we once again show the log-rolling outcome with one voter collecting a bribe. The lower panel does not show dependence upon an irrelevant al-

1	2	3	4	5
A	A	A	B	B
B	B	B	C	C
C	C	C	A	A

1	2	3	4	5
		B + 100	B	B
A	A	A	B − 50	B − 50
B	B	B	C	C
C	C	C	A	A

FIGURE 2

ternative. Note that this in a way is a little illegitimate. The Borda voting method asks you to write down your entire preference schedule and here I have changed only one point on a preference schedule. Nevertheless, I don't think we need to complicate the model further.

Once again, if the reader prefers he can abandon Arrow's use of the word "preference" and put in another equally legitimate meaning. He can say that they are now voting in accordance with their preference and *B* in columns 3, 4 and 5 should be eliminated. Once again, this makes only a linguistic difference. The bargain converts a matrix which shows dependence upon irrelevant alternatives to one that does not. Once again, Arrow's theorem does not apply to such cases.

This raises the issue of whether Arrow unduly limits his own proof. It could be argued that the preferences in the lower panels are the relevant preferences. Conceivably they could be arranged in such a way as to lead to intransitivity or dependence upon irrelevant alternatives. As we will see below, this involves unlikely assumptions about the comparability of preferences.

It should be said, however, that in a number of circumstances the voters do indeed vote in accordance with their preferences. For a considerable period of time, in a number of sessions of Congress, the appropriation process miscarried with the result that after the end of the formal fiscal year Congress passed a gigantic deficiency appropriation covering the entire budget. It was a simple yes/no vote and I presume most of the Congress in fact did prefer this entire budget to nothing and hence they would be meeting Arrow's definition of voting their preference.

In this case, however, there were only two alternatives; hence, they fall outside the proof. The same can be said about most bond issue referenda, indeed for most referenda of any sort, and those elections in which there are only two candidates or only two significant candidates.[4]

For example, a road building bond issue failed in Tucson, and the reason that it was thought to have failed was a failure to give voters in the southeastern part of the city anything. The council is now redoing it with roads in the southeastern part of the city and a series of local meetings with citizens all over the city to make sure that everyone is happy. Thus the business of building up a coalition is being done by nonvoting methods. There will be a yes/no vote on the whole road project. This avoids, strictly speaking, Arrow's theorem because there will be only two alternatives.

It could be argued, however, that these real world cases actually involve more than two alternatives. The "no" vote, whether by Congress or the voters of Tucson, is cast with knowledge that it will lead to a new bargain being made up which will then be submitted for a further vote. If so, then the vote is strategic and does not meet Arrow's conditions quoted above.

When there are more than two alternatives, then the outcome may depend upon irrelevant alternatives. In 1912, the Republican party split and both Taft and Roosevelt ran against Wilson. It seems fairly certain that either Taft or Roosevelt running alone could have beaten him. Lincoln's election in 1860 is another case. The Democrats split and he ran against three candidates. It is likely that two of them, possibly all three, could have beaten Lincoln, running alone. In both cases the outcome would have been changed if the vote had not been divided by three or four candidates. The choice between Wilson and Roosevelt was dependent upon the decision by Taft (the poor third) on whether or not to run. Of course, presidential candidates present platforms which are elaborate log-rolls.

As long as there are only two alternatives, there is no problem in the Arrow theorem. The problem then is whether Arrow may have unduly restricted his proof—that is, whether it does indeed appear in log-rolling or strategic voting cases. In other words, does it apply, as Arrow says, only to

4. In European proportional representation elections where there are a number of candidates and where a number of people will be elected, the situation is more or less the same and the Arrow theorem does not rule them out. These systems, however, have minor mathematical problems analogous to rounding error. A mathematically similar problem in allocating congressional seats once led Congress to ask the assistance of the National Academy of Science. They got a dusty answer. After the election in most European systems, it is normally necessary to create a coalition cabinet. As in the budget example, this normally involves a long series of negotiations followed by a simple yes/no vote.

the real preferences which have not been altered by offers of bribes, trades or strategic maneuvering, or does it apply more widely?

The point is significant because, although there are indeed many votes between only two alternatives, in almost all cases there has been an elaborate political process to winnow the alternatives down to those two. After all, the various parliamentary rules are designed to winnow the alternatives down to only two in the final vote. The entire process must be considered, not just the final vote.

The use of simple cash bribes (as in Figures 1 and 2) is not very realistic,[5] but simplifies the reasoning. The "most valuable" outcome would be selected fairly easily as the result of an auction process. In the real world legislature, trades should reach much the same result. Since the calculations are harder, errors on the part of congressmen and other politicians must be expected. Of course the market may be imperfect and hence the bargains may not be optimal. We are all accustomed to imperfections in the market process and surely the political market is much less perfect than even a rather bad economic market. This is quite a different problem from the one raised by Arrow.

It is true that in a zero-sum game, if there are several alternatives all of which have the same "value,"[6] then the choice among them might fall into the Arrow-type problem, but surely that is an extremely rare condition. Thus it would appear that the Arrow problem will be relevant to only very rare special conditions. It is intellectually fascinating but, like the trisection of an angle upon which the Greeks spent so much time, it has no practical importance.

Note that this is not an argument that democracy works perfectly. Anyone who has read much of my work knows that I do not believe that. What I do argue is that the complex theorem invented by Professor Arrow is not directly relevant to democracy as we see it in the world. Real world democracy has difficulties, but not those dealt with by the general impossibility theorem.

5. The Arizona legislature is currently somewhat short-handed as the result of the discovery that such cash bribes were in fact acceptable to at least seven legislators.

6. Buchanan and Tullock, *The Calculus of Consent*, 148–62.

PART 3

THE DEMAND-REVEALING PROCESS

A NEW AND SUPERIOR PROCESS FOR MAKING SOCIAL CHOICES

T. Nicolaus Tideman and Gordon Tullock

This paper describes a new process for making social choices, one that is superior to other processes that have been suggested. The method is immune to strategic maneuvering on the part of individual voters. It avoids the conditions of the Arrow theorem by using more information than the rank orders of preferences, and selects a unique point on or "almost on" the Pareto-optimal frontier, one that maximizes or "almost maximizes" the consumer surplus of society. Subject to any given distribution of wealth, the process may be used to approximate the Lindahl equilibrium for all public goods.[1]

These are strong claims, and it is therefore only sensible to begin this paper by pointing out that the process will not cure cancer, stop the tides, or, indeed, deal successfully with many other problems. As far as we know, all existing social-choice processes are subject to exploitation by suitably designed coalitions. This process is no exception. In addition, as in all democratic voting processes, voters are undermotivated to invest time and effort in a comparative evaluation of alternatives. The motives they are given for making sensible decisions are somewhat stronger than those for persons engaging in voting under majority rule, but voters will be asked to do more in the way of expressing their preferences than simply saying yes or no. Therefore, it is not clear whether the lack of an incentive to vote is more or less of a handicap for this process than it is for ordinary voting processes.

The process may be described most generally as a demand-revealing process. It relies on what might be called an incomplete compensation mechanism that appears to have been first described by Vickrey[2] in the context of

Reprinted, with permission of the University of Chicago Press, from *Journal of Political Economy* 84 (October 1976): 1145–59.

1. The method is also applicable to decisions about income and wealth redistribution. Instead of leaving that issue aside in the conventional manner, it can be used to ensure the competitiveness of markets, and it provides a welfare criterion superior, in our opinion, to Pareto optimality. All of these matters must be deferred for later publication.

2. W. Vickrey, "Counterspeculation, Auctions, and Competitive Sealed Tenders," *Journal of Finance* 16 (May 1961): 8–37.

optimum counterspeculation policy for a socialist economy. The essence of the mechanism is that each person is paid for the benefits (or pays the costs) of his actions, but no one is charged (or credited) as required for budget balance. Vickrey showed that it would be possible to motivate individuals to reveal their true supply and demand schedules for a private good by paying each person the net increase in the sum of the producer and consumer surpluses of other persons in the market that resulted from the supply or demand schedule that the one person reported. Vickrey noted that there would be a problem of financing such a system, since it would generate a deficit. He did not discuss the potential application of such a system to public goods.

Two persons who were unaware of each other's work or Vickrey's discovered the applicability of a similar compensation mechanism to the problem of motivating individuals to reveal their true demands for public goods. The first to publish was Edward Clarke,[3] whose papers until now have made very little impact on the economics profession. The lack of impact can be attributed partly to the nature of the idea that Clarke put forward, which is counterintuitive to almost any welfare economist, and partly to Clarke's difficult writing style. The second person was Theodore Groves; in one paper[4] he offered a mathematically rigorous treatment of a procedure like Vickrey's for allocating scarce private goods within an organization. More recently Groves and Loeb[5] published a procedure isomorphic to Clarke's for selecting the optimal quantities of public goods. Our objectives in this paper are to provide a clear explanation of the demand-revealing process as it applies to public goods and to extend the understanding of the process on several fronts.

While, as Bowen[6] showed, majority rule is efficient if the intensity of voters' preferences is distributed symmetrically, the demand-revealing process does not require for its efficiency any restriction on the distribution of intensities of voters' preferences. Unlike the voting processes proposed by Thomp-

3. E. H. Clarke, "Multipart Pricing of Public Goods," *Public Choice* 11 (Fall 1971): 17–33, and "Multipart Pricing of Public Goods: An Example," in S. Mishkin, ed., *Public Prices for Public Products* (Washington, D.C.: Urban Institute, 1972).

4. T. Groves, "Incentives in Teams," *Econometrica* 41 (July 1973): 617–33.

5. T. Groves and M. Loeb, "Incentives and Public Inputs," *Journal of Public Economy* 4 (August 1975): 211–26.

6. H. R. Bowen, "The Interpretation of Voting in the Allocation of Economic Resources," *Quarterly Journal of Economics* 58 (November 1943): 32–42.

son,[7] Dreze and de la Vallee Poussin,[8] and Tideman,[9] the demand-revealing process requires no special beliefs on the part of voters. Basically, it provides an environment in which each voter is motivated to reveal his preferences correctly. This is accomplished by the use of a special—indeed, bizarre—tax mechanism which rewards truthful presentation of preferences and penalizes concealment or falsification.

In order to explain the process, we start not with the problem with which Clarke's first paper dealt, the choices of the optimal amount of a single-dimensional public good, but with the simpler case of a choice among discrete options, which Clarke's second paper discussed cryptically. For simplicity, we shall start with two alternatives, which may be conceived of as two policies or two candidates. We shall then show how the process can be extended to more than two options. Having introduced the subject with these simple examples, we shall then turn to the choice of the optimal amount of a public good.

Choice between Two Options

Suppose that a collective choice must be made between two options, designated A and B. The rule we describe involves asking each individual to state which option he prefers and the amount of money he is willing to pay to secure his preferred option instead of the other. We shall show shortly why he would have an incentive to respond truthfully. In table 1, we show the "votes" of each of three voters for the two options. Option A is worth a total of $70 to the persons who prefer it and is chosen by the rule because B is worth less to its proponent.

We now turn to why the voter is motivated to correctly state his preferences. There is a "Clarke tax" to be levied, and, as we said before, it is a bizarre tax. We inquire with respect to each voter what the outcome would have been if he had not voted. For example, if voter 1 had not voted, then the outcome

7. E. Thompson, "A Pareto Optimal Group Decision Process," *Papers on Non-Market Decision Making* 1 (1965): 133–40.

8. J. H. Dreze and D. de la Vallee Poussin, "A Tâtonnement Process for Public Goods," *Review of Economic Studies* 38 (April 1971): 133–50.

9. T. N. Tideman, "The Efficient Provision of Public Goods," in Mishkin, ed., *Public Prices for Public Products*.

TABLE 1. ***Aggregating Preferences for Two Options (in Dollars)***

	DIFFERENTIAL VALUES OF OPTIONS	
VOTER	A	B
1	30	0
2	0	60
3	40	0
Total	70	60

would have been that option A would have received $40 total and option B, $60; hence, option B would have won. We charge voter 1 $20, the amount necessary to bring the "votes" for A up to equality with the "votes" for B. By the same line of reasoning, voter 3 pays a tax of $30. Voter 2 pays no tax because his vote did not change the outcome. Note that, had voter 1 understated his preference for A by an amount less than $10, he would have paid exactly the same tax as he did. If he had understated his preference for A by more than $10, B would have been selected. And voter 1 would prefer having A at the price of $20 to having B. Similarly, if a voter overstates his preferences, either the overstatement makes no difference in what is selected or what he pays or else (e.g., if voter 2 said B was worth $100 to him) he changes the result by his action and pays more for his choice than it is worth to him.

To describe the decision rule generally, define S_A as the sum over all voters who state a preference for A over B of the amounts they offer to pay to have A instead of B. Define S_B similarly. The collective-choice rule will be to choose A if $S_A > S_B$, to choose B if $S_B > S_A$, and to flip a coin if $S_A = S_B$. The incentive to respond truthfully is generated by a "Clarke tax," a rule that a voter must pay a portion of his offer if and only if his vote changes the outcome. Any voter who changes the outcome must pay $|S_A - S_B|$, calculated without his vote. In the case of a tie that is decided by a coin toss, every voter on the side that wins the toss is regarded as having changed the outcome. If the result without a person's vote is a tie, he pays nothing.

In effect, this rule gives each voter the choice of (1) leaving the outcome where it would be without his vote or (2) changing it at a price of the reported net loss to other voters. If the value to a voter of his preferred outcome is less than the net value of the alternative to others, then he prefers (1), which occurs if he responds truthfully. If his value is greater than the aggregate net value to others, then he prefers (2), which again is what occurs upon a truthful response. If his value exactly balances the net value reported by others, then he is indifferent between the two possibilities, and we flip a coin if he responds truthfully. A nontruthful response cannot benefit the respondent, and it carries a risk of making him worse off than he would have been with the truth. If he understates his value, he may pass up an opportunity to obtain the result he desires at an attractive price. If he overstates his value, he may wind up paying more than it is worth to him to have his choice.

To characterize the rule in terms of property rights, one might call it "entitlement to the consequence of one's abstention," since the result that occurs if a voter abstains costs him nothing; while if his vote changes the collective choice, he must pay. This has a certain family resemblance to majority rule, where the voter's only entitlement is to what a majority of persons other than himself want, except that, if all others tie, he can decide the issue.

Any money collected from voters in this system must be wasted or given to nonvoters to keep the incentives correct. If voters received the money collected, the possibility of increasing their shares would distort their incentives. However, if the revenue were simply divided equally among all voters, the effective distortion would be minimal if there were more than 100 or so voters; with a large number of voters, it is most likely that no one vote will change the outcome, so that in most cases no taxes for voting will be collected. We will discuss the significance of the lack of budget balance in more detail in the context of decisions about continuous variables.

A serious problem in all voting systems is the weakness of the incentive to vote. The demand-revealing process is no exception. The only wholly instrumental reason for a person to vote is the possibility that his vote will be decisive. Failure to vote carries a risk of passing up a chance to alter the outcome at a favorable price, but the probability of being decisive is usually small enough so that people might still reasonably conclude that voting is not worth the effort. Even if people do decide to vote, they are normally not motivated to give any serious study to their vote in collective decision processes, because the probable gain from acquiring further information or simply reflecting on the information already at hand is usually less than the cost. Thus, ill-informed voting is to be expected. The demand-revealing process is no exception to this general rule put forward by Downs.[10]

It may seem that a person who sustains a large loss when his preference is not followed deserves compensation, but this cannot be given without motivating an excessive statement of differential value. If a voter expected to lose,

10. A. Downs, *An Economic Theory of Democracy* (New York: Harper & Row, 1957).

an offer to compensate his loss would motivate a statement from him of a larger loss. In regard to the uncompensated losses that are produced, the demand-revealing process is similar to majority rule. In the latter, every voter must live with the choice of the majority. His only opportunity to be decisive on the issue is if there is an equal number of other voters on each side. Similarly, in the demand-revealing process, every voter must live with a finding that the aggregate value placed by others on the alternatives is opposed to his own interest, provided that he is not willing to pay enough to give his preference the higher aggregate value.

It might be objected that the demand-revealing process would permit confiscatory action. If there is a proposal to tear down one person's house and make the site a park, and if others report a greater gain from the park than the occupant's loss, then the latter loses his property. The demand-revealing process would indeed have this confiscatory characteristic if there were no constitutional limits on the proposals that could be considered. In this respect, the system is again like majority rule, which has a similar confiscatory potential. It is reasonable to expect that people making collective choices by the demand-revealing process would desire constitutional restrictions that would limit the potential for overt redistribution. For instance, a proposal that a person's property be taken for a public purpose might be admissible only if he would be given reasonable compensation.

Choices among Several Discrete Options

We now show how a demand-revealing process operates when there are more than two discrete options. In table 2 there are three voters, indicated by numbers, and three options, indicated by letters. The numbers in table 2 have been obtained by simply adding a third option, C, to the two shown in table 1, while leaving the differential the voter is willing to pay for a choice between A and B the same as it was in table 1. The difference between the numbers associated with any two options is interpreted as the amount of money the voter is willing to pay to have the one option with the higher number instead of the other. Whether or not this is a legitimate interpretation will be discussed below.

It may be noted that the rank-order preferences generate cyclic choices when majority rule is used. To determine the collective choice by the demand-revealing process, we simply sum the columns and select the option with the

TABLE 2. ***Aggregating Preferences for Three Options (in Dollars)***

VOTER	DIFFERENTIAL VALUES OF OPTIONS A	B	C	TAX	NET BENEFIT OF VOTING
1	50	20	0	30	20
2	0	60	20	0	0
3	40	0	50	30	10
Total	90	80	70	...	...
	TOTAL WITHOUT INDICATED VOTES				
For 1: 2 + 3	40	60	70	...	...
For 2: 1 + 3	90	20	50	...	...
For 3: 1 + 2	50	80	20	...	...

highest total, which in this case is A. There is no cycle, nor could there be, although a tie would be possible.

The tax for each voter is calculated from the lower portion of table 2. For the tax on voter 1, add up the sum of the other individuals' votes. Option C would have been chosen with $70. The tax on voter 1 would be $70 minus $40, or $30, and voter 1 is better off by $20 ($50 − $30) than he would have been by abstaining. Note that if he had understated his preferences enough to avoid being taxed, for instance, if he had reported that A only benefited him $25, C would have been selected and voter 1 would have been worse off than he was by correctly presenting his preferences. In the case of voter 2, there is no tax because his vote does not change the outcome; and in the case of voter 3, there is a tax of $30 ($80 − $50), and he obtains a net benefit of $10 ($40 − $30). These taxes are fairly substantial, but that is because we have only a small number of voters. With many voters, the probability is high that the total tax would be relatively miniscule if not zero.

We next inquire whether the proposed method produces results that are "independent of irrelevant alternatives." If option C is dropped from the example in table 2, what difference would it make? Consider voter 1 first. He reports a differential value of $30 for A over B in table 2. If C were dropped from consideration, voter 1 would no longer have to offer $50 for A instead of C. He would be richer, and he might spend some of his additional wealth to increase his offer with respect to A instead of B, say, from $30 to $32. Such wealth effects could conceivably change the result.

We do not, however, think that this is what is normally meant by a dependence on irrelevant alternatives. Option C is relevant because its presence

TABLE 3. *The Possible Cycle in Three Options (in Dollars)*

	A AGAINST B		B AGAINST C		A AGAINST C	
1	32	0	22	0	50	0
2	0	31	0	21	0	51

or absence affects the wealth of voter 1. If A owns a pizza den and is negotiating with B for its sale and C builds another pizza restaurant directly across the street, this will clearly affect the bargain between A and B. However, we do not think that it would be proper to say that this was a situation which "lacked independence of irrelevant alternatives." In view of the general controversies surrounding this particular criterion of the Arrow theorem, however, we should like to simply discuss the wealth effect in the demand-revealing process rather than attempt to clear up the linguistic problem.

To put the matter another way, when we insist that each voter arrange the options on a linear scale, so that the difference between the numbers on the scale for any pair of options represents what he is willing to pay to have one option instead of the other, we leave no room for wealth effects. It may be that voter 1's true willingness to pay is $22 for B instead of C and $32 for A instead of B, but only $50 (rather than $54) for A instead of C, because if he has to pay $22 to get from C to B, he is poorer than if he starts at B. With his lower wealth, it is not irrational for him to be willing to spend only $28 rather than $32 at that point, to get from B to A. The linear scale does not permit voter 1 to report these wealth effects, so he compromises by reporting the values in table 2.

It might be proposed that voters be asked to report their preferences among all pairs so that wealth effects could be taken into account in the decision process. However, to do that would be to reintroduce a possibility of cycles. Consider the two voters shown in table 3.

Voter 1 has the preferences described earlier. Voter 2 has preferences in the opposite order, of approximately the same magnitude but with less nonlinearity from wealth effects. When the preferences are summed, we find a collective choice for A over B and B over C, but also for C over A. This problem of intransitivity might be resolved by applying some analytic device such as the "tournament matrix" described by Moon and Pullman,[11] but it is not clear how the Clarke tax would then be calculated. Furthermore, as long

11. J. W. Moon and N. J. Pullman, "On Generalized Tournament Matrices," *Society for Industrial and Applied Mathematics Review* 12 (July 1970): 389–94.

as there were cycles, there would be incentives for strategic misstatements. Therefore, it may be best to require each voter to submit a linearized statement of his preferences, letting him make the necessary approximations there. Then if he can guess which option would be selected without his vote, it will be in his interest to present comparisons with respect to that option truthfully.

A Simple Continuous Application

We now proceed with the specific case Clarke presented in his *Public Choice* article.[12] Assume there is some public good which can be purchased in any desired quantity. For the purpose of graphic ease, we assume that it is sold in units which cost $1, no matter how many are purchased, so that the line at $1/unit on figure 1 represents the social-cost schedule for purchasing different quantities. The first stage in Clarke's process is to assign to each voter his share of the total cost. Let us temporarily assume this share is assigned arbitrarily, and for the *i*th voter the share is the line shown at P_i. (Later we will discuss how it is possible to approximate the Lindahl condition in the allocation of these shares.) The voters are now asked to state their demand curves for the public good (voter *i*'s curve is shown as D_i). These curves are then summed vertically to get the aggregate demand (aggregate willingness to pay) curve *AD*. The point where the sum crosses the cost curve, that is, the $1/unit line, is the efficient quantity of public good to purchase. This is, of course, the Samuelson equilibrium and has many fine properties, although not as many as the Lindahl equilibrium, toward which we shall move shortly.

How do we motivate voter *i*, and indeed all of the other voters, to correctly reveal their true demand curves? The answer is by telling each voter he will be subject to a Clarke tax, calculated as follows. When all the ballots are received, the tax for voter *i* will be calculated by summing (vertically) the demand curves of all of the voters other than *i*, generating the curve $AD - D_i$, and finding the intersection between that curve and the line $\$1 - P_i$, which is the share of the tax cost that all voters other than *i* will pay. The intersection in figure 1 occurs at quantity *A*. This is the quantity of the public good that would be purchased if *i* reported a perfectly elastic (i.e., horizontal) de-

12. Clarke, "Multipart Pricing of Public Goods."

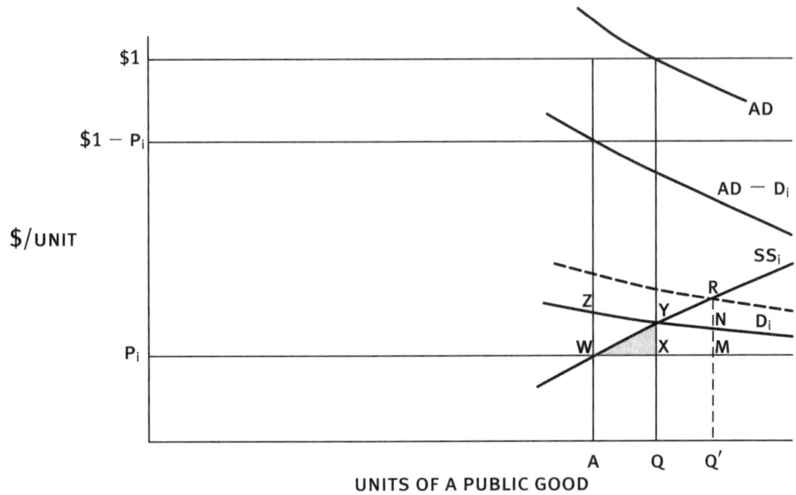

FIGURE 1
The tax on a person whose benefit exceeds his assigned tax share

mand schedule, identical to his cost share. Such a vote, offering to pay one's assigned share of whatever quantity others desire to purchase, is the analogue for continuous choices of abstaining in discrete choices. With voter i "abstaining," the revealed demand (of others) would intersect their share of cost at A, and i's payment would be the rectangle to the left of A and below P_i. In order to compute i's tax when he does not "abstain," we determine from the curve $AD - D_i$ the amount of compensation that voter i would have to pay to keep all other voters indifferent to any change from quantity A. The required compensation per unit at any quantity is the difference at that quantity between the total cost and the aggregate willingness of others to pay. We call the schedule of such amounts, calculated as $\$1 - (AD - D_i)$, a synthetic supply schedule. It can be thought of as the net marginal social cost of supplying i with additional units of the public good after allowing a credit against the gross cost for the value of the good to others. This schedule is shown as line SS_i in figure 1. The schedule SS_i is a mirror image of $AD - D_i$. In this example, we assume that i has a higher willingness to pay than his cost share at A. This implies that the effect of including his demand is to increase the quantity. The intersection of the synthetic supply curve and i's demand is at the quantity Q, and that is the optimal amount of the public good, because that is also the quantity where AD intersects the $1 line.

The amount that would have to be paid to individuals other than i in order to make them indifferent to the move from A to Q is represented by the area under SS_i, while the gain to voter i is the area under his demand curve. Voter i pays a composite tax which is the standard payment if he abstained plus the Clarke tax area under SS_i from A to Q. The total tax is equivalent to his assigned share of the cost of Q units of the public good (the rectangle to the left of line Q and below P_i) plus the shaded triangle WXY. The sum of such rectangles for all voters is enough to pay the total cost of the public good; the shaded triangle and corresponding amounts for other voters must be wasted or given to nonvoters to keep all the incentives correct.[13]

Suppose that voter i had misstated his demand curve in an effort to increase his net benefit. The benefit he has obtained from voting is the triangle WYZ. Clearly, stating his demand as less than it actually is would reduce the size of his triangle. On the other hand, if he stated his demand schedule as higher than it actually is, so that the quantity chosen would be, say, Q', his additional taxes would be $QQ'RY$ while his additional benefits would be only $QQ'NY$. He is best off correctly presenting his demand curve.

It must be mentioned that there is a very slight conceptual problem in the specification of these demand curves. Quantity demanded depends on income as well as price, and one determinant of a person's income is the Clarke tax he must pay. Since one person's Clarke tax depends on the demand curves specified by others, each person could logically say that he could not specify his demand curve until all others had done so. This is not a practical problem, however, because the Clarke tax, as we show below, is very small, and in most cases the uncertainty in the Clarke tax is very small, since it depends only on the elasticity of the aggregate willingness to pay off other voters, and in any event people can simply be directed to report demand curves that reflect their best guesses about their incomes.

In figure 2, we assume that j, given his tax share, wants less than that amount of the public good which the other voters would choose. As in figure 1, D_j represents his true demand for the public good, and quantity A represents the amount which would be purchased if he chose to abstain, that is, the point where the sum of the demand curves of all the other voters intersects the sum of their shares of the tax price. Line SS_j in this case, as in figure 1, represents the rate of compensation per unit which it would be nec-

13. One possibility for avoiding waste would be for pairs of communities to agree to exchange their collections of these excess revenues.

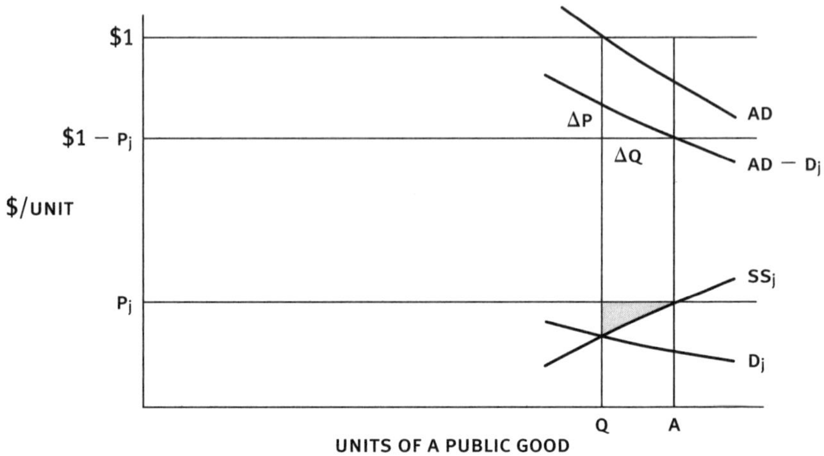

FIGURE 2
The tax on a person whose benefit is less than his assigned tax share

essary to pay the other voters to compensate them for any change from point *A* in the amount of the public good. To the left of point *A*, SS_j may be interpreted as the rate of reduction in taxes for *j* that can be granted while reducing the quantity of the public good and reducing taxes for others by the full amount of the loss of income that they experience. As in figure 1, this compensation is not actually going to be paid, but voter *j* will be taxed this amount.

Once again, the point of intersection between *j*'s demand curve and the synthetic supply curve represents the optimal quantity of the public good, *Q*, which is also the quantity at which *AD* intersects the $1/unit line. In this case, *Q* is less than would be chosen if voter *j* abstained. Voter *j* then pays a tax which is equal to the rectangle to the left of line *Q* and below his tax share, plus the shaded triangle. The rectangle is enough to pay his share of the cost of provision of the public good; the shaded triangle, once again, is wasted or given to nonvoters. We will leave to the reader the demonstration that the correct presentation of his demand curve will maximize his welfare under these circumstances. It is essentially the same as the demonstration for figure 1.

What is true for voters *i* and *j* is true for all voters. They are motivated by this peculiar tax procedure to present accurately their true demand curves.

The motivation, however, represented by triangle WYZ in figure 1, would normally be very small, about the same as the area of the shaded triangle.

To see how small the Clarke taxes would be, note that the shaded triangle in figure 2 is a mirror image of the one with sides labeled ΔP and ΔQ. If the elasticity of $AD - D_j$ is η, then $\Delta Q = \eta Q \Delta P/(1 - P_j)$, so that the area of the triangle is $1/2\eta Q(\Delta P)^2/(1 - P_j)$. The denominator approaches 1 as the number of voters increases, so that if η is on the order of magnitude of 2, then each voter's Clarke tax is roughly $Q(\Delta P)^2$. The values of ΔP would be related to the number of voters (N); it would be implausible for the average value of $(\Delta P)^2$ to be greater than $1/N^2$. Thus, the typical voter, whose share of the resource cost is Q/N, has a Clarke tax on the order of magnitude of $1/N$ times his resource cost, and the sum of all Clarke taxes is on the order of magnitude of one voter's taxes. Thus, if the citizens of the United States were voting on the annual federal budget, the grand total of all the Clarke taxes charged would be in the neighborhood of $2,000, or about one-thousandth of a penny per person.

As the triangles go to zero, the motivation for taking the trouble to present one's demand curve goes to zero. The method is cheat-proof and generates the socially optimal quantity of the public good when every voter maximizes his self-interest, but when N is large, the Downs paradox is present: voters have almost no incentive to vote.

Since the excess revenues generated by the process are so very small, and certainly less than the administrative cost for any situation with more than a very small number of persons, the excess revenues deserve to be ignored. This may be rather untidy, but it is normal in welfare economics to ignore the cost of reaching a decision. If the Clarke tax is considered as part of the cost of making the decision, then it should be ignored. Contrarily, if it is not ignored, the cost of the process of reaching decision rules by other processes should also be included. We feel that our suggestion of simply wasting the extra revenue rather than searching for some complex budget-balancing process which might or might not achieve the same result is an important contribution. It is also one of the reasons why it is so hard for welfare economists (ourselves included) to feel at home with the process.

So far, we have generated the Samuelson equilibrium; we now indicate how the Lindahl equilibrium may be approximated. To this point, we have simply assigned the base share of the total expenditure for the individual in an arbitrary manner. Suppose that, instead of assigning it arbitrarily, we appoint someone to do this, with the stipulation that from his pay we are go-

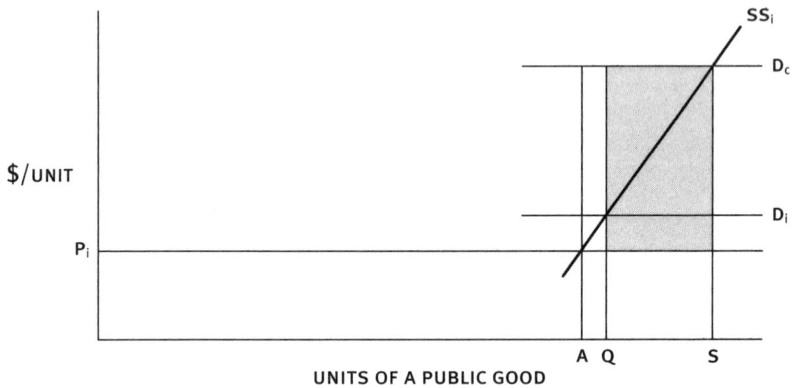

FIGURE 3
The strategic calculation of a coalition

ing to subtract some multiple of the sum of the triangles for all of the voters.[14] The person assigning the fixed shares would be motivated to try to minimize the triangles. In the limit, if he were able to perfectly achieve his goal, there would be no triangles and no loss; we would have a perfect Lindahl equilibrium, with each voter paying for public goods according to his marginal evaluation.

It is unlikely that the official allocating the shares could do this perfectly, but he might be able to do quite well with advanced econometric methods. It should be emphasized, however, that there is one piece of information he cannot use in assigning the tax share of any individual: that individual's performance on previous choices. The voter, in making his choices on each individual decision, must not be able to offset against the optimality conditions for that particular choice the prospect of changing his base tax share in the future, because this would motivate him to misstate his demand curve.

As in all voting methods, there is a possibility for coalitions to distort the result. In particular, consider the strategy for a coalition of N persons whose equal benefits are greater than their equal tax shares. In figure 3, the demand schedule of voter i, D_i, is shown as a horizontal line because changes in the height would generally be negligible over the range of potential effects he and

14. Probably the best way of selecting the "tax setter" would be to solicit bids. Precautions against bribery would, of course, be necessary.

his coalition could have. The higher line, D_c, represents the demand that i would express taking account of the benefit of $D_i - P_i$ that each member of his coalition would receive for each unit increase in the quantity chosen. The distance from A to S is N times as far as the distance from A to Q, where the outcome would have been moved by an honest vote. With N persons in the coalition voting this way, the effect is to move the choice $N(N - 1)$ times the distance from A to Q, compared with honest voting. The gross benefit of the coalition activity to each member, in terms of benefits not paid for by his standard tax share, is $N(N - 1)(D_i - P_i)(Q - A)$, which is the area of the shaded rectangle. Each member's extra tax from coalition activity, apart from his standard tax share, is that portion of the shaded rectangle that is below the synthetic supply schedule. Thus, the net benefit of coalition activity to each member is a triangle like that in the upper left corner of the shaded rectangle, the area of which is proportional to $(N - 1)^2$ and to $(D_i - P_i)^2$. Thus, the benefit of forming coalitions varies with the square of the errors in tax shares and with the square of the number of members minus one. Voters whose tax shares overstate their benefits have a similar opportunity to form coalitions that multiply the understatements of their demands.

In this example, we have assumed that the only thing chosen is the unidimensional quantity of one public good. One of the convenient characteristics of the demand-revealing process is that it is not necessary to restrain voting to one issue at a time. A multidimensional public good or several public goods or public goods *plus* candidates can all be dealt with simultaneously. In general, it is much harder to organize coalitions in cases where the choice is not unidimensional. This is not to say that it is impossible. Still, we suspect that the demand-revealing process is rather less susceptible to coalition distortion than most voting methods.

The extension of the voting method to choices for more than one good is straightforward if the chosen quantity of one public good has no impact on demands for other public goods. However, if the chosen quantity of some goods affects the demands for other goods, a simultaneous solution is needed. One could ignore the interactions in the choice procedure and rely on individuals to make estimates of the quantities of other goods that would be chosen in reporting their demand schedules, but any misestimates by voters would lead to unnecessary inefficiencies.

At a conceptual level, one could ask all voters to report their marginal valuation schedules for each good at every combination of quantities of other public goods, although the data problem if this were really attempted would be unmanageable. If it were not impossible to obtain and operate on the data, the identification of an equilibrium where the appropriate marginal conditions were all satisfied simultaneously would be essentially no different from calculating a competitive equilibrium for private goods. Groves and Ledyard[15] developed the theoretical foundations of such a system in detail.

In later publications,[16] we propose to apply the process to a number of other problems such as income redistribution and badly behaved demand curves, as well as use as a welfare indicator. We will also discuss its practical application in realistic government structure. The purpose of this paper, however, has been to explain the system and to demonstrate that it solves a number of problems previously thought to be unsolvable. The process does not violate the Arrow theorem, but it avoids the problems of the Arrow theorem by not meeting Arrow's assumptions. However, it seems to us that, if the Arrow theorem is considered as a result that suggests that a good voting process cannot be devised, then the real problem raised by Arrow is solved by this process.

15. T. Groves and J. Ledyard, "Optimal Allocation of Public Goods: A Solution to the 'Free Rider Problem.'" Discussion Paper 144 (Evanston, Ill.: Center for Mathematical Studies in Economics & Management Science, Northwestern University, May 1975).

16. Mimeographed preliminary drafts are available on request.

THE DEMAND-REVEALING PROCESS AS A WELFARE INDICATOR

For quite a long time now, welfare economics has been in the rather unsatisfying position of having as its ultimate criterion for policy choice a rule that does not lead to any specific decision. The traditional diagram is shown on Figure 1. When the two-person society (composed of x and y) is at point O, then all points in quadrant A are superior to point O and all points in quadrant C are inferior to point O. With respect to quadrants D and B, nothing can be said except that compensation might produce a move from portions of those two quadrants into quadrant A.[1] If there is some physical constraint (such as the bold line shown) on total consumption so that only the points on or below that constraint are physically possible, then obviously for any point within the constraint, such as O, there is at least a portion of the constraint which lies in the A quadrant. From any point within the constraint line, it is possible to make an unambiguous improvement by moving to such a point on the constraint.

Any movement into quadrant A is a Pareto improvement, and a series of such moves of some minimum size would eventually hit some portion of the constraint. Unfortunately, there are an infinite number of points on the constraint, and traditional analysis does not tell us anything about which point should be selected. Further, characteristically when we come to the question of how we get from point A to some specific point on the constraint, traditional welfare economics throws up its hands in despair.

The first (but admittedly very minor) advantage of the demand-revealing process is that it would select a specific point on the constraint, though not necessarily in quadrant A. Since there are many other procedures which also would select a specific point—such as leaving the decision to Tullock, generating a random number, etc.—this is weak praise, but it is at least an advantage, even if not a great one.

What we would like is to select the best point that lies on the constraint

Reprinted, with kind permission of Kluwer Academic Publishers, from *Public Choice* 29 (Special Supplement to Spring 1977): 51–63.

1. Gordon Tullock, "The Cost of Transfers," *Kyklos* 24, fasc. 4 (1971): 629–43.

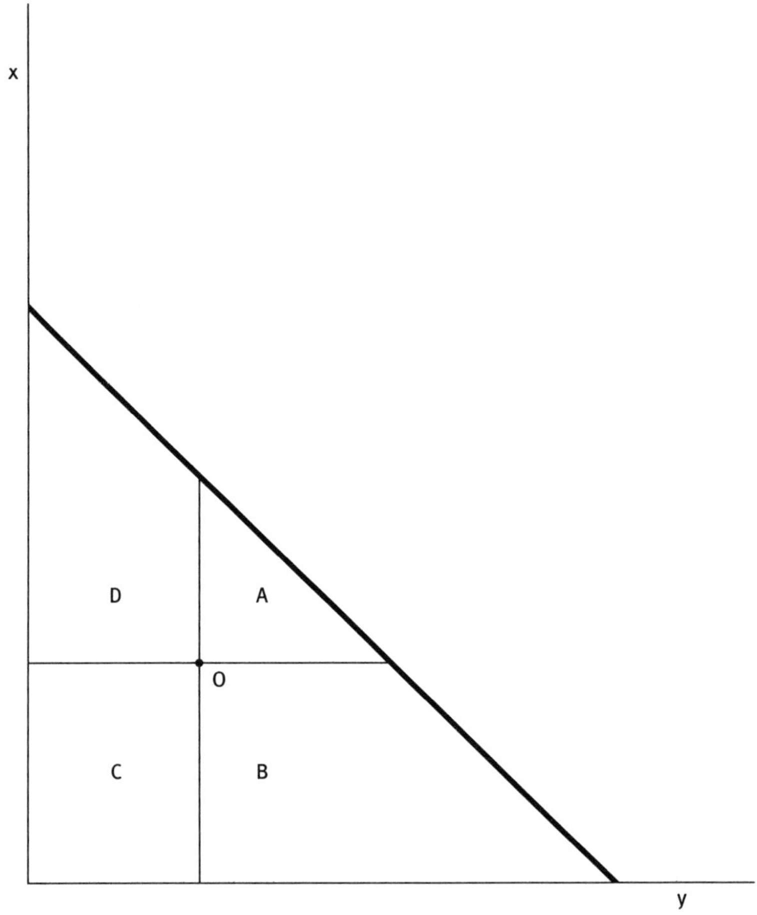

FIGURE 1

line. The purpose of this essay is to argue that the demand-revealing process fills this requirement. I will begin by talking about the problem of getting to the constraint with the demand-revealing process, where it will turn out that it is all a matter of definition, but that in the real world (as opposed to mathematics) this objective is achieved. Secondly, I will turn to the question of whether the point reached is superior to other possible points. Discussion of this must be deferred until the first matter has been dealt with.

To discuss the problem of moving to the constraint, turn to Figure 2.

Once again, we have persons *x* and *y*, currently at point O, and a constraint. Some points such as point A are Pareto optimal in the sense that no further Pareto improvements can be made. However, how do we get from O to A? If some deus ex machina can simply issue an order, that is that. However, even under these circumstances, the deus ex machina would certainly have to devote at least some resources to making up his mind which of the points would be selected.

On the other hand, one or the other parties could be given complete control. If *x*, for example, is dictator, he presumably will take substantially no time (and therefore will invest no resources) in deciding to move to the point where the constraint line meets the *x* axis. If *y*'s well-being happens to figure in *x*'s preference function, then he would choose some other point on the

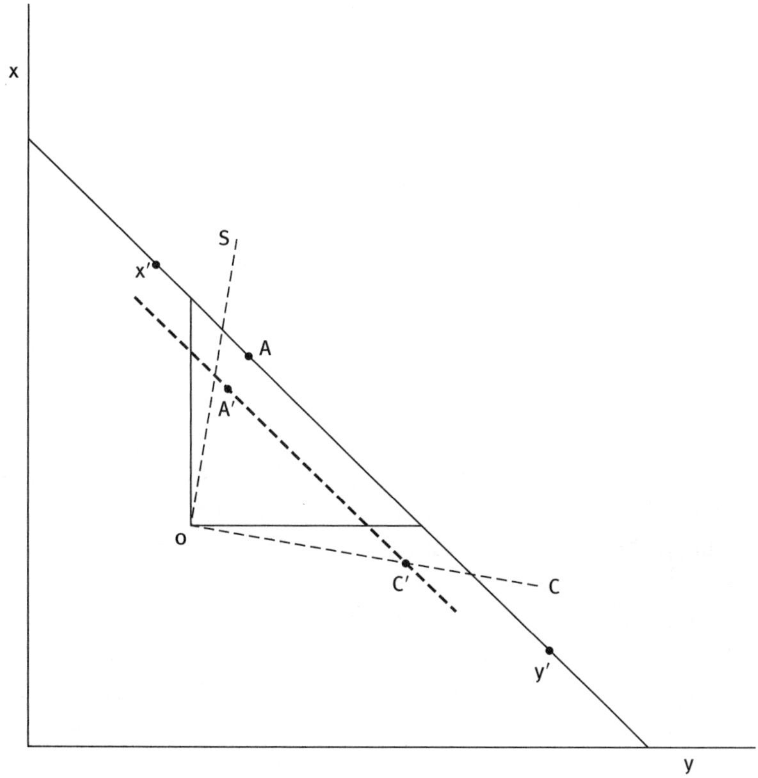

FIGURE 2

constraint such as x'. Perhaps this point might turn out to be within the usual Paretian quadrant, but more likely it will be outside as it is in this case.

Similarly, if y were dictator, the intercept of the constraint with the y axis or some such point as y' might be selected. Granted that neither of these two conditions is likely to lead to Pareto improvements, some method of integrating the preferences of x and y is necessary if we want changes to be Pareto improvements. That method will, of necessity, involve resources, and a new constraint—shown here by the line through A′ and C′ — indicates this.

It is not clear in reading the literature on Pareto optimality whether the Paretian frontier as usually drawn is intended to take into account the costs of decision making and movement to the frontier or not. If it is, then the original constraint line would be beneath the physical possibility line which could be obtained by having some outsider simply order a move. For our purposes, we will assume that the traditional production constraint does not include the costs of bargaining or whatever method of preference aggregation is used.

Once we have decided to integrate the decision costs into our model, however, the particular method used to make decisions becomes important. There are some methods that are very costly and some that have relatively low costs. Bargaining, for example, is normally thought to be very costly, particularly if the number of people involved is high. Indeed, it is so costly that very commonly no effort to get unanimous consent is made in large-number cases. Even when there are only two parties, as on our Figure 2, the process can be costly, particularly since the optimal bargaining technique involves misrepresenting one's preferences, and with both parties misrepresenting their preferences, the probability that a desirable agreement will be missed because of the gaming of the two parties can be large.

We could, in essence, have a whole portfolio of production constraints, each one reflecting the same state of nature but a different technique for aggregating preferences. Presumably, that constraint which is farthest out and up from O is the true Pareto optimum constraint, and the others would represent mistaken choices of technique in the agreement process.

All of this discussion, which is not common in welfare economics, is necessary because, as it happens, the demand-revealing process puts negotiation costs, or agreement cost, in a particularly obvious and straightforward way, while other methods of reaching a social decision frequently conceal their costs. In the case of the demand-revealing process, there is in fact an identifiable value of resources that must be thrown away. If we were dealing with two parties, as in Figure 2, this amount might be quite large, although with many parties it is, as is demonstrated by Tideman and Tullock,[2] trivial.

In fact, I suspect that in most cases where the number of parties is of any size, the demand-revealing process is by all odds the cheapest method of making a move that increases efficiency. Hence, the dotted line would be closer to the constraint line if we used the demand-revealing process than if we used any other method; thus, it would be superior in this sense.

Compare it, for example, with ordinary bargaining. There is no reason why either party in the demand-revealing process need do anything except correctly present his preferences, and if there is a suitable bargain, it will be made. Elaborate investment in strategy, maneuver, and delay, which is so important in ordinary bargaining, is completely eliminated. On the other hand, there is the direct waste of the Clarke tax. Thus, what I am now doing is making a guess on the respective size of the two quantities, neither of which has yet been measured, and one of which—the traditional bargaining costs—would tend to be very large. Nevertheless, granted the trivial size of the Clarke tax for large numbers of individuals, I think that this empirical guess will be joined by most of the readers. If it is so, then the demand-revealing process is the only way of making decisions that is truly Pareto optimal in the sense that there is no way of bettering it without divine intervention.

In the real world when we deal with many people, we customarily choose methods that do not guarantee Pareto improvements. Majority voting, for example, can severely injure a considerable number of voters. A redistribution of resources away from a minority is unlikely to be a Pareto improvement, even if the final result is Pareto optimal in the sense that it cannot be improved upon.

Men, however, are not entirely egotistical and, to some extent, do take into consideration the well-being of other people. This well-being may be taken into account positively, when we refer to it as altruism, or negatively, in which case I shall follow the biologists and call it "spite." For example, suppose that *x* feels that he gets at least some benefit from any improvement in *y*'s well-being. Under these circumstances, his "indifference line" on Figure 2 would not be the horizontal line beginning at O but the dotted line OC; and point OC′ would be acceptable to him as a movement away from O. On the other hand, if *y* positively disliked *x* and felt that any improvement in *x*'s well-

2. T. Nicolaus Tideman and Gordon Tullock, "A New and Superior Process for Making Social Choices," *Journal of Political Economy* 84 (December 1976): 1145–60.

being was an injury to him, then his line of indifference might be OS instead of the solid vertical line.

The demand-revealing process can take this kind of interpersonal comparison into account. Thus, some such point as C′ would be a possible outcome under the demand-revealing process, although some point near the center of the desirable quadrant is more likely.[3]

The demand-revealing process has the intriguing characteristic that it permits a more exacting measure of almost anything, including the gains to be obtained by wealth transfers. Unfortunately, in this particular area the objectives sought through income redistribution have not been specified in enough detail so that it is possible to make use of this additional capacity of the system *and* to know that one is achieving the goals normally favored by the advocates of transfer.[4] Consider Figure 3 which represents a two-person society, one member of which, C, feels charitable toward the other, I (or indigent). The cost of transferring dollars from C to I is shown by the $1 line, and we assume that is also I's demand for such transfers, i.e., the amount he would be willing to pay for them. C, on the other hand, has a demand for transfers to I of the usual form, shown by line CC.

In a Paretian world, C would transfer to I the amount P or out to the point where his return is equal to his cost. Note, however, that from the standpoint of total society, there is an opportunity cost here. If we sum the demands of the two parties, we get the line B, and the quantity which maximizes the social satisfaction is not P, but M. In essence, the shaded triangle is an opportunity cost which is lost under the Paretian system.

The demand-revealing process can be adjusted so that it achieves either P or M. If it is set to reach M, however, then the resources wasted are of the same order of magnitude as the shaded triangle. Thus, in each system there is a net waste of the quantity. Under the Paretian system, it is an opportunity

3. Note that when two parties are taking each other's preferences into account, it is not obvious that the area of Pareto optimal moves will in fact be a quadrant. If the two parties each liked the other and were benefited by improvements in the other's well-being, then the area from which Paretian moves can be made would be greater than a right angle; if they disliked each other, less than a right angle, and if one liked the other and the other reciprocated with hatred (as shown by the dotted lines OS and OC in Figure 2), it could be either greater or less than a right angle.

4. The problem is discussed in considerable detail by Gordon Tullock, "Revealing the Demand for Transfers," in Richard D. Auster and B. Sears, eds., *American Re-evolution, Papers and Proceedings* (forthcoming, 1977).

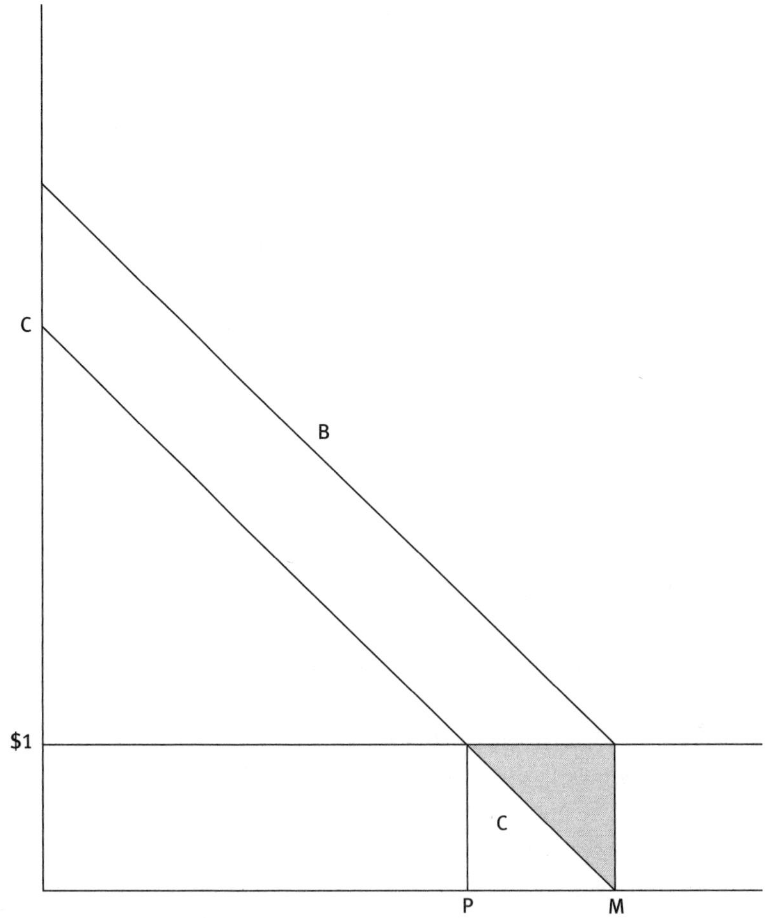

FIGURE 3

which is not taken advantage of, and under the demand-revealing process, it is a direct waste. So far as we know, there is absolutely nothing in the existing literature which would tell us which alternative to choose.[5]

But this discussion of possible interdependence of utilities has been introduced mainly to point out their relevance to the traditional Paretian procedure. Assuming that by now the reader is agreed that the demand-revealing

5. Once again, Tullock, "Revealing the Demand for Transfers," has a more detailed discussion of these issues.

process is itself Pareto optimal in a real-world definition in which transactions costs are taken into account,[6] I now turn to the question of whether the point on the Paretian frontier selected by the demand-revealing process is indeed superior to other points. For the time being, we will assume that the well-being of each individual is a matter of total indifference to all other individuals in the society. Only after we have fully covered this subject will we discuss interdependent utility functions.

Before going further with the demand-revealing process as a welfare indicator, I must frankly make one confession: it cannot in general provide a total welfare solution. It reveals the demand for various public or private goods. This demand, however, must be expressed by actual willingness to pay. Thus, there must be at least something under the complete control of the individual which can be used to make these payments. The point is of theoretical, but not much practical, significance. It does mean that many mathematical proofs and propositions now in existence cannot be fitted to the demand-revealing process. On the other hand, if we look at economics as it is practiced by economists, we find that it is only very rarely concerned with efforts to obtain a total optimum.

Normally the kind of question discussed is whether a tariff should be reduced, is a graduated income tax a superior alternative, or is the construction of a given rapid transit system desirable. The demand-revealing process is suitable for all of these questions. It would even seem to be suitable for some such procedure as the total economic plan, which Communists frequently claim they have. Since most Communists do not in practice propose to control the details of the expenditures of citizens working under the plan, it would be possible for the citizens to use whatever pittance they are given for personal consumption partly to vote on various plans under the demand-revealing process. Really comprehensive planning of consumption, which is intermittently hinted at in Chinese Communist literature,[7] would be impossible, however. Thus, it would appear that this limitation on the demand-revealing process, although no doubt of great importance to mathematical economists, is not likely to be of much importance to anyone else. Further,

6. Actually we need empirical research as to the cost of various procedures for carrying out "transactions." My argument could, in this particular area, always be invalidated by suitable empirical evidence.

7. Strictly speaking, they do not say that it is to be planned, but they discuss at great length what a good Communist would spend his time and energy on.

the demand-revealing process should enter positively in the utility function of mathematical economists because it immediately provides them with an immense area in which they can redo existing theorems with a massive generation of doctoral dissertations, journal articles, etc.

The second limitation also arises from the fact that the process is a "demand"-revealing one. It is clear that the outcome is affected by the initial distribution of resources, because the person who has a lot of them, whether this is in the form of wealth or some other resource, will strongly affect the outcome.

Perhaps it is wise to stop here and explain what I mean by some other resource. It would be possible to run a dictatorship or an oligarchy by the demand-revealing process, provided only that we do not define the dictatorship as one in which the dictator literally is all-powerful and unconcerned with other people's preferences. No such dictator has ever existed in history. Dictatorship is a form of government in which one man has very much more than anyone else, but his power is less than total. As an obvious example, suppose that the dictator decided to instruct his personal guard to shoot each other.

Suppose that we conceptualize the power of the dictator by assuming that he is 1,000 times as powerful as the average citizen, that ministers are each 100 times as powerful as the average citizen, and that members of the secret police are individually 10 times as powerful as the average citizen. We could then use the demand-revealing process, giving to the dictator 1 million votes, each of his officials 100,000, each of the guards 10,000, and each individual citizen 1,000. These points could be used in demand-revealing process operations to determine government policies. Since they would be scarce, they would have a value, and outcomes would be generated in which the dictator would have as much additional say as he would under ordinary dictatorial circumstances. Indeed, it would be an efficient way to run a dictatorship.

Note that this system could be used for any other distribution of resources we wished. For example, if we want to be egalitarian, we could distribute to each citizen 10,000 points and have them use those in the demand-revealing process. However, it does have the disadvantage that, although it would obtain an optimal selection of government policies, the margin between the government and private sector would be inefficient. Further, it would be impossible to assess true Lindahl taxes with this system. We could have an efficient public sector and an efficient private sector, but we would have no idea as to whether the two sectors were of the right size. Of course, if we permitted the individuals to sell their points for cash, we would move to a total equilibrium with the initial equal distribution of points being simply a wealth redistribution procedure.

For the time being, let us assume that we deal with government as we do with private goods, i.e., we permit people who have larger resources to spend them on the purchase of government policy just as they can spend them on the purchase of Cadillacs; distributional problems are being put aside until later. Under these circumstances, the demand-revealing process would always select that point on the Paretian frontier which maximized the sum of consumer surpluses across society. This is what the market itself does; but when we come to public goods or goods that have some degree of externality, the market no longer performs this function efficiently.

The argument for choosing that particular point on the Pareto optimal frontier which maximizes the consumer surplus of the citizens (measuring their consumer surplus in whatever *valuata* are used) is essentially one of individual maximization. Looking forward over a very large number of decisions in the future and trying to assess my likely income from them, under various methods of making those decisions, I should choose the one that gives the highest present discounted value to me. Normally, unless I have extraordinary information, this would mean the one that gives the highest discounted value to a randomly selected individual.[8] That is the result of the demand-revealing process. If one has a nonindividualistic approach to these matters and wants to talk about the well-being of the collectivity, the demand-revealing process can be argued for, also, on the grounds that it maximizes the total sum of the consumer surpluses.

This is the main and, in my opinion, overwhelmingly strong argument for the use of the demand-revealing process as a welfare criterion, but there are several minor arguments leading to the same conclusion. First, if you are risk averse, the demand-revealing process has distinct advantages over voting. In general, the individual who feels intensely about one particular issue will have more weight than those who feel less intensely, which tends to reduce risk. Further, and probably more importantly, the declining marginal utility for any individual of any particular commodity or service will tend to mean that almost everyone will get at least something of everything. Since the value that I put on the first unit of some particular service which will benefit me is greater than the value put on the hundredth unit of some inconsistent service by someone else, the odds are that I will get my first unit, whereas under ma-

8. Note, once again, we are leaving problems of wealth and income distribution aside.

jority voting I might not. In a way, the demand-revealing process tends to move out along the 45° line in the Paretian quadrant, although this tendency is not particularly strong.

However, there is a difficulty with the demand-revealing process which has to do with what we may call compensated moves. Suppose that there is a change from the status quo that will benefit Tideman by $5 while injuring Tullock by $1. In the traditional Paretian apparatus, he and I could bargain and, if we did reach an agreement on the matter, he would pay me some number between $1 and $5 in compensation for my permission to move to the new point. This converts a movement which is not within the Paretian quadrant into a movement which is. Under the demand-revealing process, we would move straightforwardly to that position, and compensation is not essential. I have recommended the use of Lindahl taxes, and, in this particular case, the Lindahl tax would turn out to be a negative quantity for Tullock and a positive quantity for Tideman, with the result that we would once again be in the traditional Paretian quadrant. But suppose we use the demand-revealing process without the Lindahl taxes or suppose (which seems not particularly unlikely) that the calculation of the Lindahl taxes is imperfect enough so that the individual does not get fully compensated: would we favor a system which can make this kind of move?

Looking at the matter ex ante, it seems likely that we *would* favor this type of system. We cannot tell in advance whether we are going to be the winners or the losers, and the gamble is a favorable one. Further, the risk aversion characteristics mentioned above would apply in this case; i.e., the gambles would not normally impose really extreme costs on the loser.

In all of the above cases, I have been assuming that the individuals have no information or very little information about the likely outcomes in future applications of whatever decision-making procedure has been chosen. This seems realistic if we leave aside the individual's knowledge of his own power and wealth in society. That is, a wealthy and powerful man and a poor man living in the same society could reasonably guess that the wealthy and powerful man would do better in future decisions than the poor man. Granted we are not changing the ratios of wealth and power, which is the distributional problem to be dealt with below, this is simply a fact of nature.

The wealthy man would not know in which particular cases he would gain, and he would gain more under the demand-revealing process than under any other system which equally took into account these differential resource endowments of the two parties. Similarly, the poor man would know that he would not do as well as the wealthy man, but would know that he would do better than under any other system. The normal discussion of this problem is made difficult because the implicit alternative, majority voting with each person having one vote, is in and of itself a system which sharply reduces the power of the wealthy as opposed to the poor.[9] If we start from the status quo, in which individuals are relatively egalitarian in dealing with the public sector and have great differences of wealth in the private sector, this should be taken into account in the initial count of resources.

Certainly everyone can have their well-being improved by rearranging the resource allocation system in such a way that the individual can use his "political" resources in the private sector or his "private" resources in the political sector. Presumably when such trades are not possible, he is out of adjustment on the resource commitment between these two sectors, even if (as is not very likely) he is in perfect adjustment both in the government sector and in the private sector.

So far, however, we have only peripherally discussed the problem of wealth and income distribution. This turns out to be an extremely difficult problem to which I have elsewhere devoted an entire article.[10] The reason it is difficult, however, is not that the demand-revealing process does not fit this kind of problem, but that the problem itself has not been properly specified. Although there is a large literature discussing the desirability or undesirability of relatively egalitarian policies, the discussion implicitly assumes that this policy will be rather a crude one. The demand-revealing process makes it possible to massively improve the structural detail of any redistributional system. Unfortunately, the result is to raise a whole series of problems as to what exactly we want in income redistribution. A rather careful investigation of the literature seems to indicate that the problems have not previously been dealt with. Hence, the details of the use of the demand-revealing process are up in the air, not for technical reasons having to do with the demand-revealing process, but for valuational reasons having to do with the desirability of various patterns of redistribution.

We may begin with a fairly easy problem. Almost every government act has as a byproduct some redistribution of wealth in society. Such minor mat-

9. See James M. Buchanan, "The Political Economy of Franchise in the Welfare State," in R. T. Seldon, ed., *Capitalism and Freedom: Problems and Prospects* (Charlottesville: University Press of Virginia, 1975), 52–77. Note that in practice, the democracy is not all that egalitarian.

10. Tullock, *Revealing the Demand for Transfers*.

ters as decisions to repair roads, change the Nuisance Act, or build a new post office in fact change the wealth of the citizens. Traditionally, unless these changes are of a particularly radical nature *and* fall within certain restricted legal categories, no compensation is paid to people who are injured, nor is any special tax assessed on those who gain. The presumed reason is administrative complications. We simply would not be able to compute the appropriate individual taxes and compensation payments.

The demand-revealing process permits the use of (approximate) Lindahl taxes, and Lindahl taxes would in many cases be negative. Thus, we can at least approximately make these assessments and compensations. This is a completely new area of government policymaking, but it seems to me to be an area where most people would be in favor of implementing the program. Temporarily assuming that we could assess Lindahl taxes quite accurately, we could greatly improve the functioning of our society by putting special taxes on the beneficiaries of various government policy changes and using these taxes to compensate those injured. For one thing, it would eliminate all cases in which the policy in net causes more injury than benefit. Further, presumably most of us are risk averse, and therefore the elimination of one rather major type of risk would be desirable.

All of this is based on the assumption that the Lindahl taxes can be assessed with reasonable accuracy. We believe that it is so, but it might well be that in special cases—such as repaving a given street—we would not be able to assess them accurately, in which event the above opportunity would not exist. In any event, the whole problem of the assessment of Lindahl taxes with the aid of the demand-revealing process is dealt with elsewhere in this issue. It is clearly an area for a great deal of detailed empirical investigation.

Much more importantly, the demand-revealing process can, without any great difficulty, be used to assess the degree to which individuals' preference functions are interdependent, that is, the degree to which A has positive or negative feelings about B, and then take them into account. This assessment is measured in terms of demand, which means that it is measured in terms of the resources that A and B possess at the beginning of the process. Radical egalitarians, I presume, would suggest that everything be equally divided before we begin using the demand-revealing process; but unless they are arguing that this should be done regardless of what people's preferences are, there seems no reason to believe that this is indeed the appropriate policy. Still, there are people who feel this way, and granted they do, we would simply point out that once you had made the equal distribution of resources, the demand-revealing process would be an optimal way of making further distribution of resources.

The basic problem, I feel, is a different one: the definition of those who can make the decision. Under present circumstances, we sometimes permit the people who are to receive the redistribution to vote on it and sometimes do not. The obvious case of this is when we are dealing with foreigners. Substantially no American is as poor as several million Banghladeshi. When a decision is made to distribute American government funds to the American citizens, we let the recipients vote. When the decision is made as to how much shall be transmitted to the much poorer citizens of Banghladesh, we do not permit them to vote.

This decision makes very great differences in the amount redistributed under any voting procedure. I have been unable, in a rather careful investigation of the literature, to find any argument beyond simple tradition for the distinction between those who are permitted to vote and those who are not.[11] As a matter of historic fact, many democracies have not permitted recipients of transfers to vote on the size of the transfer. This was part of the law in England throughout almost the entire nineteenth century, and it has rather informally been enforced in various American communities until very recently. I have no opinion on this matter, but I should say that once this preliminary problem has been solved, then the demand-revealing process can be used for either version.

In income redistribution, however, most people have another confusion in their minds, essentially because they are thinking of relatively imperfect decision procedures. They normally are in favor of income redistribution, but have some implicit limits on it. They do not really want all human beings to be treated equally; they do not characteristically even really want all citizens of their own country to be treated equally.

Thus, limits on the amount of redistribution seem to be part of the preference function of most people with whom I have discussed the matter. In general, these limits are not very accurately specified, and indeed they do not even turn up in conversation until you begin pointing out how radical a really egalitarian policy would be. Under the circumstances, we can say very little about implementing these limits, but we do feel that it would certainly be no harder with the demand-revealing process, and it might be much easier.

11. There are certain arguments which are what we may call "derived" traditions; i.e., because we have been American for a long time, we feel more strongly about other Americans than we do about foreigners.

Welfare economists have become so accustomed to seeking Pareto optimality in their calculations that a suggestion that it be thrown away and something substituted for it is likely to strike them as literally insane. Our particular system in one definition is Pareto optimal; and, if you do not want to use that definition, I will argue it is better than Pareto optimal. It selects a single point rather than a zone, and that point maximizes the sum of the consumer surpluses over society. It seems to me clear that this is better than Pareto optimality, although I do not wish to argue that it is the ultimate welfare indicator.

DEMAND-REVEALING PROCESS, COALITIONS, AND PUBLIC GOODS

Although the demand-revealing process is not immune to coalition formation in the pure mathematical sense, for all practical purposes it would be immune when used for any significant number of voters. The problem of forming a coalition in the demand-revealing process is very similar to the standard economic problems of providing public goods or organizing a cartel. It is manageable with few participants, but with many it is impossible.

To see this, consider a simple presidential election between two candidates. As a matter of fact, this two-option situation is one for which coalitions would be relatively easy to organize; so if they are improbable here, in more complex cases—presidential elections with more than two candidates or choices of quantities of public goods along one or many axes—they are even more improbable.

Consider, then, an individual who favors Wallace in an election between Wallace and Reagan and feels that the advantage he would gain if Wallace wins is $100. He is considering forming a coalition with a number of other like-minded voters in order to control the outcome. Suppose, just for simplicity, that a million voters who feel this way all agree to evaluate their preferences not at $100 but at $200, because this will increase the likelihood of Wallace winning, and their gain from increasing the ex ante probability that Wallace will win is less than the ex ante probability for each one of them that they will be "caught" and have to pay some amount between $100 and $200 as a Clarke tax. Clearly, this is not an impossible situation for individual Wallace partisans to find themselves in. Under these circumstances, the first thing to be said is that having entered into the coalition, a Wallace partisan would be wise to vote only $100 instead of $200. His action in this direction would only reduce the probability of Wallace winning by some very small amount, and it would eliminate the prospect of his having to pay between $100 and $200 to obtain Wallace's election.

To look at the matter a little more carefully, the individual, in choosing

Reprinted, with kind permission of Kluwer Academic Publishers, from *Public Choice* 29 (Special Supplement to Spring 1977): 103–5.

to vote $200 when his actual level of preference for Wallace is only $100, will either have no effect on the vote as opposed to voting his $100 or he will have to pay a tax in excess of $100. Thus, he is always better off voting the $100, and he is always better off if other people organize the coalition and he does not participate. It will be seen that this is a characteristic public good problem, and hence we might anticipate many such defections from a large coalition.

The basic problem, however, is even worse. Why should a Wallace voter actually enter into the coalition at all? He could just tell the potential organizers that he really did not favor Wallace, that he was indifferent in the election, or that, although he did indeed favor Wallace's election, the amount by which he favored it was very slight, perhaps 50¢ or $1's worth. Under the circumstances, he might argue that if he offered to vote $100 for Wallace, he would be making the same contribution to the coalition as those who favored Wallace for $100 and were voting $200. Indeed, he could argue that he was making a large contribution since his bid would be 100 times his actual gain.

Once again, it will be seen that this is a public good problem. The voter has a motive to conceal his preferences and negotiate hard, and our experience with private provision of public goods indicates that this type of bargaining problem is generally impossible to solve. Since it is very easy for the voter to conceal his preferences (after all, there is absolutely no objective measure), he should be able to avoid participating in the coalition, even if he does get maneuvered into a situation in which he has to formally agree that he is in.

We do observe two cases in private life in which political coalitions are successfully organized. One of these is the average political party in ordinary democratic politics, and the other is the corporate take-over bid. The reason that these two types of political coalitions can be organized, however, is that each one has a special characteristic which makes it easy. Let us begin with the political party. The individual cannot bargain as to his contribution to the party. He has exactly one vote, and he can either give it or not. He cannot argue that he should be given a lower price for participation than others because his preferences are weaker. Indeed, he is normally not even asked formally to participate. The political party makes up a package of policies and then presents it to the voters. The coalition is constructed by party in a rather entrepreneurial spirit by selecting various policies, with the idea that enough voters will regard it as better than that of the opposition party to get a majority or whatever it needed in the particular election. The individual voter is given no opportunity to negotiate at all. There would be no reason why a voter presented with such a coalition under the demand-revealing process would not simply vote his true preferences. Any other vote could cost him money and could not benefit him.

The take-over bid is somewhat similar. It used to be that when some corporation or wealthy man or group wished to take over a corporation, they proceeded by secrecy and stealth, buying up stock until they had a majority. This was obviously difficult, and the take-over bid was substituted. With it, they simply announce that they will buy the stock at some stated price, if a certain amount (say, 90 percent) is offered to them. Once again, the individuals whose ballots are obtained by this method are given no opportunity to bargain. Indeed, that is one important reason that this particular method is used. Except for minimizing transactions and bargaining costs, it is clearly inefficient. The bargaining costs which it avoids would make the matter normally impossible, without a take-over bid technique.

Thus, although it cannot be demonstrated mathematically that coalitions will not be formed under the demand-revealing process, the theory of public goods indicates that they would only be formed when there were relatively few voters or, in any event, only a few voters who were members of the particular coalition. Coalitions that required many voters (and that, after all, would be the normal case in most democratic elections) would be impossible to organize because of the bargaining problems involved in establishing them.

PART 4

RENT SEEKING

THE WELFARE COSTS OF TARIFFS, MONOPOLIES, AND THEFT

In recent years a considerable number of studies have been published that purport to measure the welfare costs of monopolies and tariffs.[1] The results have uniformly shown very small costs for practices that economists normally deplore. This led Mundell to comment in 1962 that "Unless there is a thorough theoretical re-examination of the validity of the tools upon which these studies are founded . . . someone will inevitably draw the conclusion that economics has ceased to be important."[2] Judging from conversations with graduate students, a number of younger economists are in fact drawing the conclusion that tariffs and monopolies are not of much importance. This view is now beginning to appear in the literature. On the basis of these measurements Professor Harvey Leibenstein has argued "Microeconomic theory focuses on allocative efficiency to the exclusion of other types of efficiencies that, in fact, are much more significant in many instances."[3]

It is my purpose to take the other route suggested by Mundell and demonstrate that the "tools on which these studies are founded" produce an underestimation of the welfare costs of tariffs and monopolies. The classical economists were not concerning themselves with trifles when they argued against tariffs, and the Department of Justice is not dealing with a miniscule problem in its attacks on monopoly.

Statics

The present method for measuring these costs was pioneered by Professor Harberger.[4] Let us, therefore, begin with a very simple use of his diagram to

Reprinted, with permission of Oxford University Press, from *Western Economic Journal* 5 (June 1967): 224–32.

1. These studies are conveniently listed with a useful table of the welfare losses computed in each in Harvey Leibenstein, "Allocative Efficiency vs. 'X-Efficiency'," *American Economic Review*, June 1966, 56, 392–415.

2. R. A. Mundell, Review of L. H. Janssen, *Free Trade, Protection and Customs Union*, *American Economic Review*, June 1962, 52, 622.

3. Leibenstein, *op. cit.*, p. 392. In this article Leibenstein consistently uses the phrase "allocative efficiency" to refer solely to the absence of tariffs and monopolies.

4. A. C. Harberger, "Using the Resources at Hand More Effectively," *American Economic Review*, May 1959, 49, 134–46. It should be noted that Harberger suggested the method for

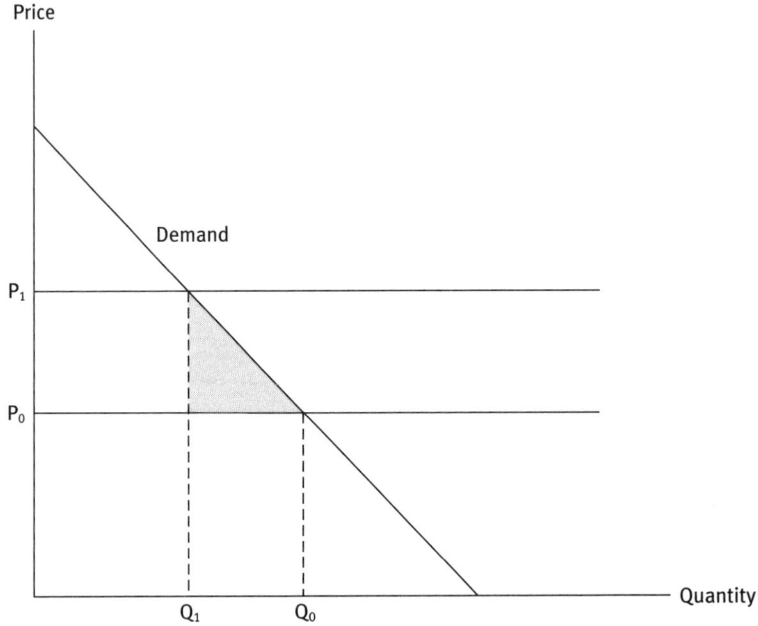

FIGURE 1

analyze a tariff. Figure 1 shows a commodity that can be produced domestically at the constant cost of P_1 and imported at P_0. With the given demand and no tariff, Q_0 units will be purchased at a price of P_0. If a prohibitive tariff is imposed, Q_1 units will be bought at a price of P_1. The increase in price, it is argued, is merely a transfer from some members of the community to others, and the only welfare loss is consequently the shaded triangle. The studies purporting to measure the welfare costs of tariffs have simply computed the value of this triangle. From the geometry it is fairly obvious that the amount would normally be small.

There are a considerable number of costs that are ignored by this proce-

---

the measurement of the welfare costs of monopoly, but its extension to cover tariffs was the work of other scholars. The more careful scholars who have measured the welfare costs of tariffs have not all used this very simple application of Harberger's method, but a method such as illustrated in Figure 2. I have chosen to begin with this method of measurement partly because it simplifies the exposition and partly because this procedure is the "conventional wisdom" on the matter. *(Cf.* Leibenstein, *op. cit.)*

dure. As a starter, collection of a tariff involves expenditure on customs inspectors, etc., who do the actual collection and coast guards who prevent smuggling. Further, customs brokers are normally hired by the shipper to expedite the movement of their goods through customs.[5] Normally we pay little attention to collections costs because they are small, but in this case they may well be larger than the welfare triangle which is also small. Thus by simply adding in collections costs, we significantly increase the "social cost" of the tariff.

For a more significant criticism of this method of measuring the welfare cost let us apply the procedure to a standard excise tax instead of a tariff. Assume that Figure 1 shows a constant supply cost and a declining demand for some commodity in some country. Q_0 units are bought at a price P_0. Now suppose that a tax is imposed, raising the price to P_1, and reducing sales to Q_1. The welfare cost of this tax is measured by the shaded triangle. But suppose further that the revenues raised by this tax are completely wasted, building tunnels, for example, which go nowhere. Now the social cost of the total package of tax and wasteful expenditure is the welfare triangle plus the total tax revenue, or the trapezoid bounded by the lines showing cost, the cost-plus-tax, and the demand function. The people buying the product pay more than the cost, but no one benefits from the expenditure.[6] The funds are not transferred because no one benefits from the existence of the tax. The whole economy is poorer not just by the triangle, but by the whole amount of wasted resources.

The tariff involves a similar waste of resources and consequently its social cost cannot be measured simply by the welfare triangle. Figure 1 can also be used to show the foreign and domestic costs of some type of good and the national demand for it. Since domestic cost is higher than the (delivered) cost of the foreign good, none would be produced domestically in the absence of a tariff. Q_0 units would be imported and consumed at a price shown by P_0. The country now puts on a prohibitive tariff and the higher cost domestic production takes over the complete market. Q_1 units are sold at P_1. The welfare triangle has been used to measure the welfare cost of this operation.[7] The

5. Strictly speaking, the customs brokerage should be added on to the tax thus producing a larger welfare triangle.

6. The government action might slightly increase the rents on the resources used to build the tunnel, and thus the owners of specialized resources might benefit slightly, but clearly this is a very trivial effect.

7. Tibor Scitovsky, *Economic Theory and Western European Integration*, Stanford, 1958.

argument for this procedure is, essentially, that the higher prices paid by the consumers represent a transfer payment, not a real loss to the economy. But who receives this transfer? The owners of the resources now engaged in inefficiently producing the commodity receive no more than they would have received had the tariff never been introduced and they had been employed in other industries.[8] These resources, however, are being inefficiently utilized, and the rectangle between P_1 and P_0 and bounded by the vertical axis and Q_1 measures the social cost of this waste. Thus the total welfare cost of the tariff is the triangle plus the much larger rectangle to its left.

The situation is identical to that which would arise if the government required an established domestic industry to abandon an efficient method of production and adopt an inefficient one. This could be graphed on the same diagram, and it would be generally agreed that the welfare loss would not be just the welfare triangle, but would also include the inefficient use of resources required by the governmental regulation shown in the rectangle to the left of the triangle. Since a tariff shifting production from the production of export goods to import-replacement goods where the country has a comparative disadvantage is, in fact, a governmental requirement that the goods be obtained in an inefficient manner, the cases are identical. The cost of a protective tariff is the triangle plus the difference between domestic cost of production and the price at which the goods could be purchased abroad.

Let us, however, consider the situation in which there is some domestic production before the imposition of a tariff. Figure 2 shows a commodity, part of which is imported and part of which is produced domestically. The supply elasticity of the commodity from foreign sources is assumed infinite, but domestic production is carried on in conditions of increasing costs. Without the tariff, the price is P_0, domestic producers turn out D_0 units, and $Q_0 - D_0$ units are imported to make up the total consumption of Q_0. Suppose now, that Mr. Gladstone is prime minister and imposes a tariff on imports and an excise tax of the same amount on domestic production. With the new price, P_1, consumers will want only Q_1 units, and the shaded triangle measures the excess burden. Domestic production will remain D_0, but imports will shrink from $Q_0 - D_0$ to $Q_1 - D_0$. The government will receive a tax revenue equivalent to the entire rectangle bounded by the two price lines, the vertical axis and Q_1.

8. There might be sizable but temporary rents to the firstcomers when the industry was first established.

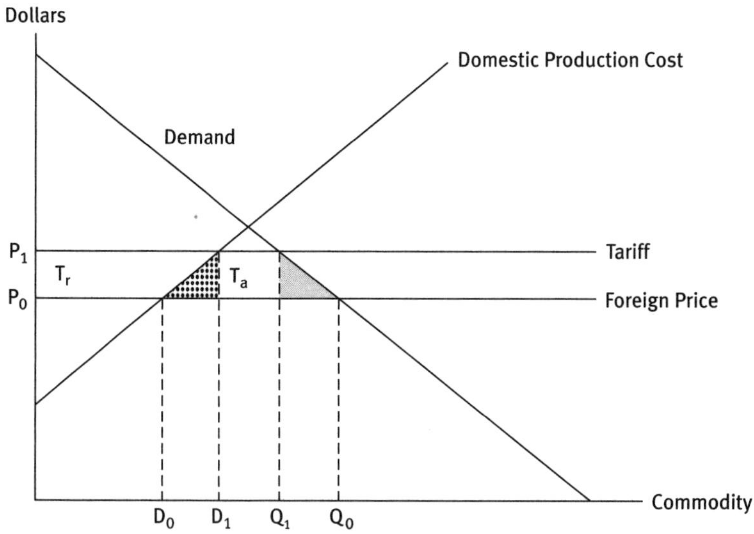

FIGURE 2

Let us now change our example by assuming that the domestic excise tax is repealed, so that we have only a protective tariff. Domestic consumption and price would remain the same, but domestic production would expand to D_1, and imports would shrink accordingly. There would be an inefficient use of resources in producing things which would be better imported, represented by the dotted triangle. Governmental revenues would shrink to the rectangle marked T_a and the owners of the resources in the domestic industry would receive an amount of resources equal to the area of the trapezoid T_r.[9] Clearly the social cost of the tariff is not just the shaded triangle, but also the dotted triangle which shows a net waste of resources in inefficient production.

Dynamics: The Cost of Transfers

The trapezoid T_r, however, would appear to be a pure transfer, and hence not to be included in the computation of the cost of the tariff. Strictly speak-

9. See J. Wemelsfelder, "The Short Term Effect of the Lowering of Import Duties in Germany," *Economic Journal*, March 1960, 70, 94–104.

ing this is so, but looking at the matter dynamically, there is another social cost involved, and its magnitude is a function of the size of this transfer trapezoid. Generally governments do not impose protective tariffs on their own. They have to be lobbied or pressured into doing so by the expenditure of resources in political activity. One would anticipate that the domestic producers would invest resources in lobbying for the tariff until the marginal return on the last dollar so spent was equal to its likely return producing the transfer. There might also be other interests trying to prevent the transfer and putting resources into influencing the government in the other direction. These expenditures, which may simply offset each other to some extent, are purely wasteful from the standpoint of society as a whole; they are spent not in increasing wealth, but in attempts to transfer or resist transfer of wealth. I can suggest no way of measuring these expenditures, but the potential returns are large, and it would be quite surprising if the investment was not also sizable.

Monopolies involve costs of a somewhat similar nature, and it follows that I will not be able to produce a method to measure their social costs. I will, however, be able to demonstrate that the welfare triangle method greatly underestimates these costs. The argument is customarily explained with the aid of a figure like Figure 1. The monopolist charges the monopoly price P_1 instead of the cost P_0 for the commodity, and consumption is reduced from Q_0 to Q_1. The welfare triangle is a clear loss to the community, but the rectangle to its left is merely a transfer from the consumers to the owners of the monopoly. We may object to the monopolist getting rich at the expense of the rest of us, but this is not a reduction in the national product.

In order to demonstrate that this line of reasoning ignores important costs, I should like to take a detour through the economics of theft.[10] Theft, of course, is a pure transfer, and therefore might be assumed to have no welfare effects at all. Like a lump sum tax, it produces no welfare triangle at all, and hence would show a zero social cost if measured by the Harberger

10. The economics of illegal activities is an underdeveloped area, but Harold Demsetz discusses the subject briefly in "The Exchange and Enforcement of Property Rights," *Journal of Law and Economics*, October 1964, 7, 11–26. J. Randolph Norsworthy's Doctoral Dissertation, *A Theory of Tax Evasion and Collection*, Virginia, 1966, is a more comprehensive examination of one type of illegal activity. Two unpublished items have been circulated among a few scholars: Gary Becker's "A Theory of Government Punishments and Rewards," and my own *Law and Morals*, the unfinished manuscript of a book which I began four years ago and which has languished in draft form for almost all of those four years.

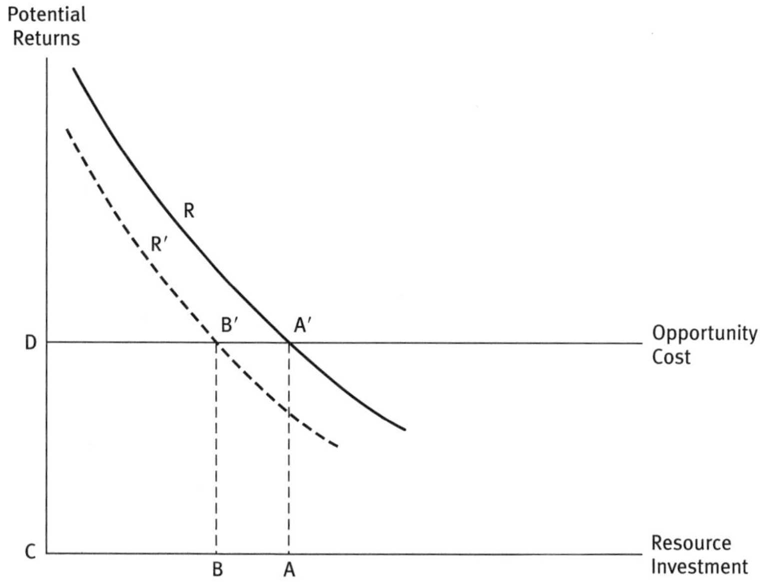

FIGURE 3

method. This would, of course, be incorrect. In spite of the fact that it involves only transfers, the existence of theft has very substantial welfare costs. Our laws against theft do not deal with a trivial and/or unimportant problem any more than our laws against monopoly do.

Figure 3 shows the situation confronting the potential thief. On the horizontal axis is shown the quantity of effort and capital (burglars' tools, etc.) he might invest in a career of crime. On the vertical axis are shown potential returns. The "opportunity cost" line shows the returns he could get for the same investment of work and material in other occupations. It is assumed to be constant. Let us begin by assuming that taking another's property is not illegal. Under these circumstances the returns on various amounts of investment in the activity are shown by line *R*. The potential thieves would invest the quantity of resources shown at *A* in theft, the cost to him would be the rectangle AA′DC, and his net return on the investment would be the triangular area above A′D.

The situation of a person who wished to guard his own assets, who might, of course, be the thief hoping to hold onto his loot, may also be shown on

Figure 3. On the horizontal axis are shown the resources invested in loss-minimizing activities.[11] The cost of each unit of resources put to this use is shown by the horizontal opportunity line, and the savings are on the vertical axis. The line *R* now shows the returns in the form of savings for each unit of "theft prevention." The total amount of resources invested would again be *A*.

The two situations are interrelated by more than the fact that they can be shown on the same diagram. The height of the *R* curve for the thief would depend upon the amount of resources invested by other members of the community in locks and other protections. Similarly, the individual in considering how many locks to buy would find that his *R* curve depended upon the resources being invested in attempts at theft by the rest of the population. When a potential thief invests money, say, in an improved lock pick, the *R* curve for people trying to protect their property moves downward. Similarly, hiring an armed guard to watch your valuables moves the *R* curve for potential thieves down. Putting a new lock on my door reduces the chance that I will be robbed, but whether the gain will be worth the cost will depend upon the effort the thieves are willing to put into getting in. Over time the interaction between the investment in locks, the payoff on lock picks, and the investment in nitroglycerine and safes would come to equilibrium.

This equilibrium, however, would be extremely costly to the society in spite of the fact that the activity of theft only involves transfers. The cost to society would be the investments of capital and labor in the activity of theft and in protection against theft. If we consider Figure 3 as representing the entire society instead of individuals, then the social costs would be the area covered by the rectangle AA′DC. Transfers themselves cost society nothing, but for the people engaging in them they are just like any other activity, and this means that large resources may be invested in attempting to make or prevent transfers. These largely offsetting commitments of resources are totally wasted from the standpoint of society as a whole.

This lesson has been learned by almost all societies that have adopted a collective method of reducing this sort of income transfer. This collective procedure, laws against theft and police and courts to enforce them, can also be shown on Figure 3. On the horizontal axis we now have resources invested by police and courts, with their opportunity cost shown as a horizontal line.

11. The word "activities" may be misleading. One way of minimizing loss by theft is to have little or nothing to steal. In a world in which theft was legal we could expect this fact to lead to a reduction in productive activities and a great expansion in leisure.

The "protection" given by each unit of resources invested in these activities is shown by the *R* line. The society would purchase *A* amount of protective services, and the total cost would be the usual rectangle. The effect of this would be to reduce the expected returns on theft and the savings to be made by private investment in locks, etc. The new returns are shown by R' on Figure 3, and there is a corresponding reduction in the resources invested in each of these fields to B'. Whether the establishment of a police force is wise or not depends upon an essentially technological question. If police activities are, for a range, more efficient than private provision of protection, then the *R* line will have the shape shown, and the police and court rectangle will have an area smaller than the sum of the two "savings" rectangles for theft and locks.[12] This is, of course, what we normally find in the real world.

Note, however, that we do not carry investment in police protection to the extent that it totally replaces private protective expenditures. Clearly it is more efficient to have some protective expenditures by the owners of property. Automobiles are equipped with locks and keys, presumably because the expansion of the police force which could be paid for from the cost of leaving them off would be less effective in preventing theft than they are.[13] The total social cost of theft is the sum of the efforts invested in the activity of theft, private protection against theft and the public investment in police protection. The theft itself is a pure transfer, and has no welfare cost, but the existence of theft as a potential activity results in very substantial diversion of resources to fields where they essentially offset each other and produce no positive product. The problem with income transfers is not that they directly inflict welfare losses, but that they lead people to employ resources in attempting to obtain or prevent such transfers. A successful bank robbery will inspire potential thieves to greater efforts, lead to the installation of improved protective equipment in other banks, and perhaps result in the hiring of additional policemen. These are its social costs, and they can be very sizable.

But this has been a detour through the criminal law, our major subject is

12. It may be suggested that society should not be interested in the saving of the resources of thieves, and hence that the value of the protection afforded by the police should be measured by the lock rectangle only. This, however, would be correct only to the extent that the resources would not be reallocated to socially acceptable production.

13. James Buchanan and Gordon Tullock, "Public and Private Interaction under Reciprocal Externality," in *The Public Economy of Urban Communities*, Julius Margolis, Ed., Washington, D.C., 1965, 52–73.

monopoly. To return to Figure 1, the rectangle to the left of the welfare triangle is the income transfer that a successful monopolist can extort from the customers. Surely we should expect that with a prize of this size dangling before our eyes, potential monopolists would be willing to invest large resources in the activity of monopolizing. In fact the investment that could be profitably made in forming a monopoly would be larger than this rectangle, since it represents merely the income transfer. The capital value, properly discounted for risk, would be worth much more. Entrepreneurs should be willing to invest resources in attempts to form a monopoly until the marginal cost equals the properly discounted return.[14] The potential customers would also be interested in preventing the transfer and should be willing to make large investments to that end. Once the monopoly is formed, continual efforts to either break the monopoly or muscle into it would be predictable. Here again considerable resources might be invested. The holders of the monopoly, on the other hand, would be willing to put quite sizable sums into the defense of their power to receive these transfers.

As a successful theft will stimulate other thieves to greater industry and require greater investment in protective measures, so each successful establishment of a monopoly or creation of a tariff will stimulate greater diversion of resources to attempts to organize further transfers of income. In Gladstone's England few resources were put into attempts to get favorable tariff treatment. In present-day United States large and well-financed lobbies exist for this purpose. The welfare cost in the first case was very low, in the second it must be quite sizable. An efficient police force reduces the resources put into the activity of theft, and free trade or an active antitrust policy will reduce the resources invested in lobbying or attempting to organize monopolies.

The problem of identifying and measuring these resources is a difficult one, partly because the activity of monopolizing is illegal. The budget of the antitrust division and the large legal staffs maintained by companies in danger of prosecution would be clear examples of the social cost of monopoly, but presumably they are only a small part of the total. That very scarce resource, skilled management, may be invested to a considerable extent in attempting to build, break, or muscle into a monopoly. Lengthy negotiations may be in real terms very expensive, but we have no measure of their cost.

14. The margin here is a rather unusual one. Additional units of resources invested in attempting to get a monopoly do not increase the value of the potential monopoly, but the likelihood of getting it. Thus they change the discount rate rather than the payoff.

Similarly, a physical plant may be designed not for maximum efficiency in direct production, but for its threat potential. Again, no measure is possible. As a further problem, probably much of the cost of monopoly is spread through companies that do not have a monopoly, but have gambled resources on the hopes of one. The cost of a football pool is not measured by the cost of the winner's ticket, but by the cost of all tickets.[15] Similarly the total costs of monopoly should be measured in terms of the efforts to get a monopoly by the unsuccessful as well as the successful. Surely most American businessmen know that the odds are against their establishing a paying monopoly, and they therefore discount the potential gain when investing resources in attempting to get one. The successful monopolist finds that his gamble has paid off, and the unsuccessful "bettor" in this particular lottery will lose, but the resources put into the "pool" would be hard to find by economic techniques. But regardless of the measurement problem, it is clear that the resources put into monopolization and defense against monopolization would be a function of the size of the prospective transfer. Since this would be normally large, we can expect that this particular socially wasteful type of "investment" would also be large. The welfare triangle method of measurement ignores this important cost, and hence greatly understates the welfare loss of monopoly.

15. This helpful analogy was suggested to me by Dr. William Niskanen.

THE COST OF TRANSFERS

Most discussions of transfers have assumed that they are costless. They are movements from one point to another on the same Pareto optimal production frontier. In utility terms they may actually move the Pareto optimal frontier out because, with interdependence of utility functions, everyone may feel better off after they are completed. The point of this essay is to demonstrate that transfers may well involve significant costs. Further, we shall demonstrate that the mere possibility of transfers imposes certain costs on society. We are thrown into a game which we cannot avoid playing and which is, unfortunately, negative sum. This game, moreover, applies to a number of situations in addition to those that we have traditionally denominated "transfers." Specifically, bargaining, voluntary charity, government-sponsored income redistribution, theft, and war all produce somewhat the same structural problems. As we shall see, our analysis will fit all of them. It should not be taken, however, as a proof that government income redistribution is theft. It is perfectly possible to be in favor of one and not the other. It will remain possible for those readers who favor income redistribution but who are firm pacifists to keep that pair of beliefs, and those readers who believe we should really hit the Communists hard but that government income redistribution is undesirable will be able to retain those beliefs also.

Let us begin with a simple bargaining example. Suppose that we have a two-person society with *K* and *J* the citizens. Currently, they are at point *O* on Figure 1. Most economists would agree that movement into the area above and to the right of *O* (to such a point as *A*) is unambiguously desirable because it benefits at least one person and, in most cases, both. Movement to point *B*, however, is normally regarded as ambiguous. It clearly benefits Mr. *K*, but it also injures Mr. *J*. The Paretian solution is compensation. Since compensation involves simply a transfer of resources from one party to the other without any change in their quantity, it can be represented by a forty-five degree angle drawn through *B*. This line passes to the right and above *O* and, hence, there is some point such as *C* which could be reached by Mr. *K* and Mr. *J* through agreement, and which would have the same resource input as point *B*.

Reprinted, with permission of Blackwell Publishing, from *Kyklos* 24, fasc. 4 (1971): 629–43.

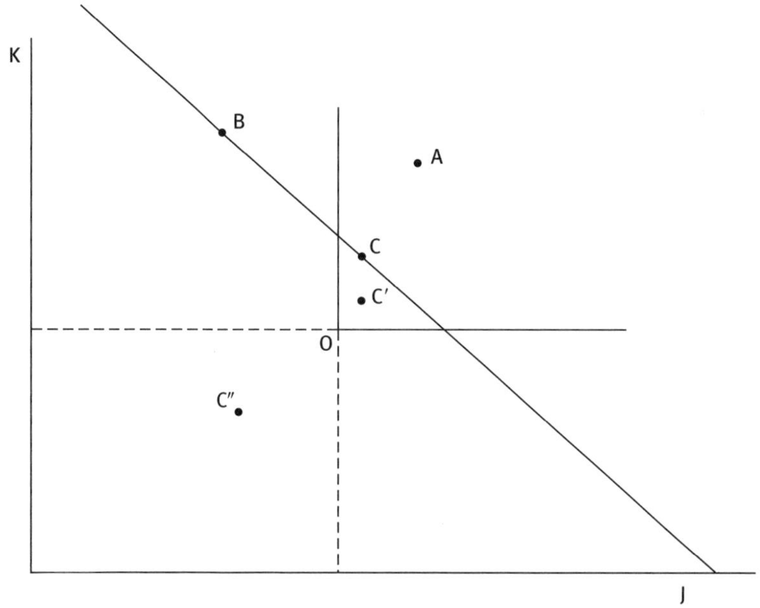

FIGURE 1

This argument as conventionally presented, however, does not really fit the real world. If some technological possibility exists which would permit the "society" to move to point *B* and *J* has a veto over the movement, then movement to point *C* will probably require a good deal of negotiation between *K* and *J*. Since this negotiation absorbs resources, the actual point achieved would not be *C*, but some point within the line upon which *B* lies, such as *C′*. We can indeed imagine a situation in which the investment of resources in bargaining was so great that the end product was at *C″*, which is below and to the left of the original position. As movement up and to the right is unambiguously desirable, movement down and to the left is unambiguously undesirable. Movement into the dotted rectangle is movement to an area where at least one person is injured and no one is benefited. It is only a movement into the areas above and to the left or below and to the right of the starting point which raises doubts about desirability or undesirability of a change.

Granted that some technological change occurred which made it possible to move to *B*, it would be expected that the bargaining between the two par-

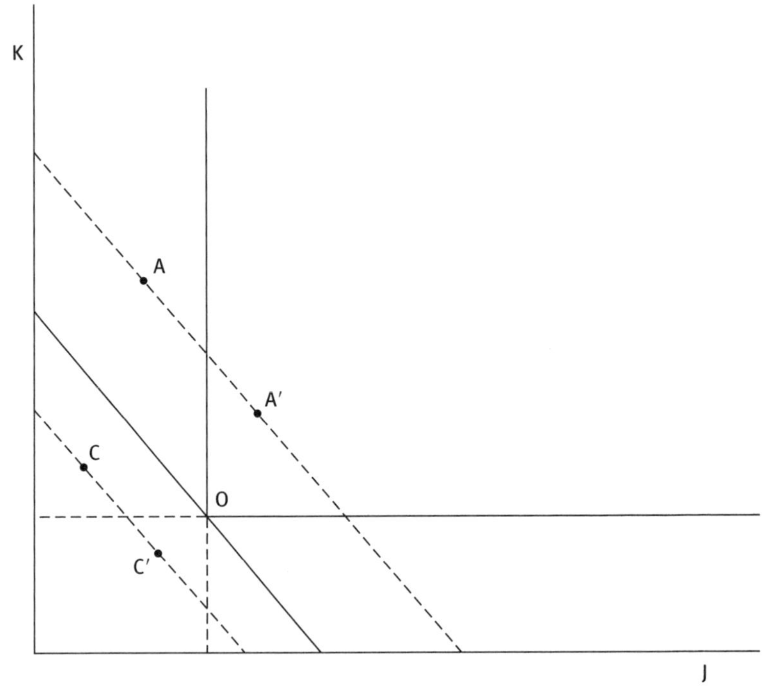

FIGURE 2

ties would lead to some point such as C', rather than a point such as C'', simply because both of the parties must enter into the bargaining voluntarily, and it is unlikely (although surely not impossible) that they will miscalculate to the point where they actually suffer a loss. If they both make estimates of the likely outcome before beginning bargaining, then each must foresee a positive gain. On the whole, one would anticipate that over time these prebargaining estimates would turn out to be correct and, hence, that voluntary bargaining would not lead to such points as C''.

As we shall see, voluntary charity shares this feature with voluntary bargaining, while government income transfers, theft, and war are, in this respect, different. Before going on to these issues, however, let us briefly pause and consider some special aspects of the Paretian criteria using Figure 2. Suppose once again that we are at point O. Some technological change occurs which makes it possible for society to move to point A, which lies on the forty-five degree angle line running through *A′*. We know from the location of point *A* that it is possible for society, by compensation, to reach some such point as *A′*. Further, if *J* is given a veto on movement from *O* to *A*, unless he is compensated, both *J* and *K* will have incentives to reach a bargain which will fall somewhere in the Paretian area. Unfortunately, they each also have an incentive to try to gain the bulk of the profit for themselves, and this means that they will most assuredly use resources in bargaining against each other.

If, however, a proposal is made to move to point *C*, we know, first, that compensation could not lead to some point above and to the right of *O*; there is, in fact, a genuine reduction in the total resources available to society at point *C*. Further, there is no incentive for either *K* or *J* to engage in bargaining since, from the standpoint of at least one of them, any location in the resource area available from point *C* will be a reduction in welfare. We can, mentally perhaps, say that *A* is in a location equivalent to something like *A′*, and *C* equivalent to something like *C′*; hence, in the first case everyone can conceivably be benefited, and in the second, of necessity, there will be injury.

It would be possible to argue that social changes which lie above the forty-five degree line running through *O* should be adopted on the grounds that society in some sense will have its resources enlarged by such a move. The counterpart argument, of course, would be that changes such as *C* should never be adopted for the same reason. This, as stated, violates the Paretian taboo on the comparison of utilities. It is possible, however, to argue for something like it on strictly individualistic and Paretian terms. Suppose that we anticipate that in the future there will be a large number of opportunities open, some of which will be like *A* in that they would lead society to a new point above the forty-five degree line running through *O* and some like *C* in the sense that they would lead to a point below. Assume further that we do not anticipate that these changes, as a whole, will favor one person or one group in society. Under these circumstances, both *K* and *J* might agree on a general rule that all changes which lead to movement of the frontier out and to the right will be accepted, regardless of their distributional characteristics, simply because the present discounted value of such a rule would, for each one of them, be an improvement in welfare. Note that the production frontier would presumably not have the straight line characteristic of the line passing through *A* on our figure. The line represents the transfer possibilities, not the production frontier.

This, of course, involves the assumption that the progress will be at least

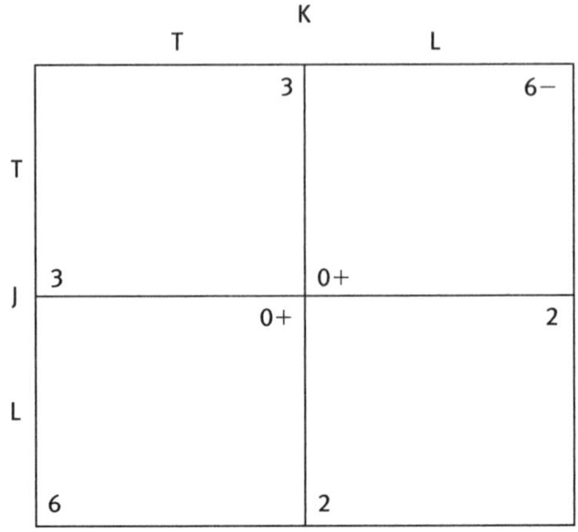

FIGURE 3

evenly enough divided so that each party would anticipate that his particular position would be improved by a large number of such technological improvements, and that no party has too much risk aversion. By parity of reasoning, and much less controversial, movement to points which move the frontier back (such as point *C*) would be undesirable. It seems likely that most people would agree that changes which lie above the forty-five degree angle line lying through *O* have at least something to be said for them, and changes which lie below it are undesirable, although this rule will offend the Paretian orthodoxy.

The investment of resources in bargaining is always a negative sum game. As a handy example, suppose that *J* wishes to purchase a house from *K* and would be benefited by obtaining the house for any price under $18,000. *K*, on the other hand, is willing to sell it at any price over $12,000. If both truthfully stated their reservation price, they could split the difference. Each, however, is motivated to attempt to get the entire bargaining cost himself and, therefore, to lie about his own reservation price. Figure 3 shows the game matrix; *T* stands for truthful statement and *L* for lie. If both speak the truth, the expected outcome is shown in the upper left hand corner; if *J* speaks the truth and *K* lies, then *K* should be able to get almost the entire bargaining range and *J* only a tiny part of it; if both lie, the investment in resources involved in sorting out the false statements, together with the cost of the possibility of the bargain being missed, leads to the result in the lower right cor-

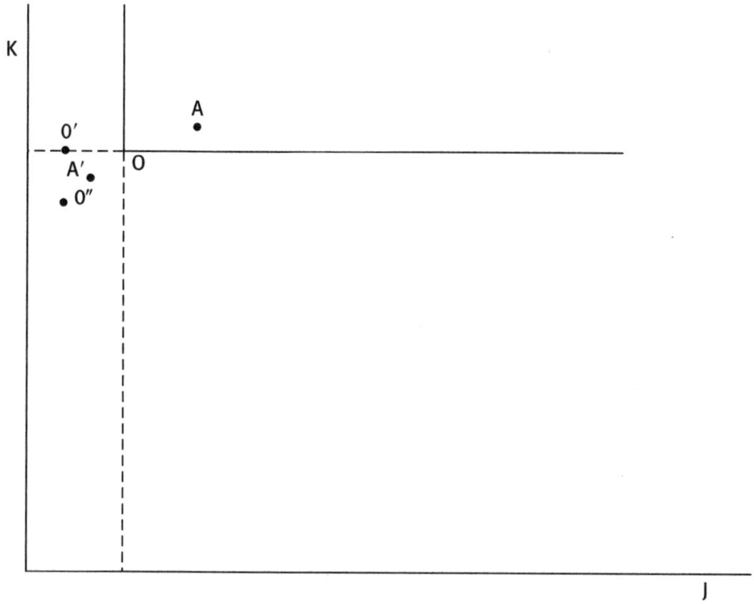

FIGURE 4

ner. It can be seen, of course, that this is a prisoner's dilemma game, and that the parties will (as in fact they do in real life) attempt to mislead each other with the result that there is a social loss. If either of the two parties chose to behave in the socially optimum manner, he would suffer considerable loss himself and the other party would make very large gains. Prisoner's dilemma matrices of this general sort will be characteristic of all the situations with which we will deal in this essay.

So much for bargaining; now let us turn to voluntary charity. In order to do this, we must redesign the standard diagram which we have used so far and put not physical values or dollar values, but utility on the two axes.[1] Thus, suppose that once again *K* and *J* are a two-man society and society is at *O* on Figure 4. If *K* is oppressed by *J*'s poverty, he may wish voluntarily to

1. More elegant but complex methods would retain the physical value measure on the chart, but design the indifference curves of the two parties appropriately. For an introduction to complexities involved in such voluntary charity, see Thomas R. Ireland and David B. Johnson, *The Economics of Charity*, ed. Gordon Tullock (Blacksburg, Va.: Center for Study of Public Choice, 1970).

make a gift to *J* and such a gift would increase his utility. If nothing more happened, then the gift from *K* to *J* might move the society to point *A* which is equivalent to a movement outward into the Pareto optimal region. Thus, a movement which would appear to be simply a movement along the forty-five degree line, if we drew Figure 4 in terms of physical product, is a Pareto optimal move in utility terms. The fact that such moves are possible presumably accounts for voluntary charity.

Unfortunately, the situation is not that simple. Suppose that *J* perceives that *K* may make a charitable gift. Under these circumstances, he would be well-advised to invest resources in becoming a more suitable object of *K*'s charity. This moves the system to O'. Indeed, in the particular cases with which I am most familiar—Chinese beggars—it may move it to a lower level of utility for both *J* and *K*. When I was in China, I used to occasionally see beggars who had deliberately and usually quite horribly mutilated themselves in order to increase their charitable take, and I always found the mutilations inflicted a considerable negative utility on me.

In the Western world, of course, these drastic measures are not normal, but anyone who is at all familiar with people who are objects of charity must realize that they do engage in a certain amount of resource expenditure to improve their receipts. Granted, however, that the potential object of charity may behave in this way, the potential giver is apt to invest resources in attempting to control such activity. This moves the system to O''. Once again turning to a traditional area, the hiring of an almsmonger by medieval princes was an effort to reduce the use of resources in becoming objects of charity by potential beneficiaries of the royal largesse. In modern times, such protection is one of the major objectives of professional administration of charitable programs.

So far, we have moved into the Pareto-dominated area. It should be noted, however, that there is no need for us to remain there. The gift from *K* to *J* might still move us to *A*. It is, of course, possible that it might lead only to A' and, hence, that the society would be worse off, even in utility terms, after the charitable transaction than it would have been had no one thought of the possibility of such charity. Once again, however, the operation is voluntary on both sides, and it thus seems likely that the end product will be a Pareto improvement rather than Pareto dominated.

The problem, as was the case in bargaining and as will be the case in the other matters to which we will shortly turn, is that, although the actual operation of charitable giving is profitable to both parties, its mere possibility sets off behavior on the part of each party which is aimed at improving his own utility and which uses resources. This behavior is mutually offsetting and, taken in and of itself and ignoring the eventual gift, moves the society into the Pareto-dominated area. The movement from O'' to either A or A' is Pareto optimal. The movement from O to O'' is Pareto dominated. If it were possible to see to it that the Pareto-dominated moves never occurred, clearly society would make net gains out of all charitable transactions. There is no way, however, of providing such assurance. Thus, it is almost certain that at least occasionally charitable actions, like bargains, will go wrong, and the net effect will be that society is injured. We may find this unfortunate, but there is no evidence that the world was designed for our convenience.

So far, however, we have been discussing transactions which are voluntary on both sides. There is a sense in which any transaction is voluntary. For example, when the gunman says, "your money or your life," you make a deal with him which benefits both of you. The involuntary part of this transaction, from your standpoint, is the arrival of the gunman, not the trade you make with him once he has put in an appearance and threatens your life. Indeed, the minor paradox which is sometimes used in teaching—the question of whether this is or is not a voluntary transaction—is very easily answered. There is a trade of the victim's life provided by the gunman against the victim's money, which makes both parties better off; the only thing the victim can complain about is that the gunman, without his consent, placed him in a situation where he faced a decision on such a trade. The appearance of the gunman very sharply reduced his utility. The trade which he later made with the gunman improved both his and the gunman's utility. Thus the transaction can be divided into two acts, the first of which was not Pareto optimal and the second of which was.

Returning, however, to our main theme, theft, war, and governmental income redistribution all involve transfers which are not voluntarily entered into by both parties, in the sense that both parties are satisfied with the entire transaction. Note that with respect to government income redistribution, this is only in part involuntary. Presumably, the taxpayer-citizens are interested in making charitable gifts to other persons and may choose to use the state as a cooperative instrumentality for that end. Insofar as this is true, the redistribution of income is voluntary and should be analyzed as such. It seems likely, however, that government income redistribution is carried well beyond the point where those who are paying for the redistribution benefit in utility. The argument which appears below, then, applies only to that component of government income redistribution which is not simply a special way of organizing a voluntary gift. As a subjective judgment, I would think that something on the order of ninety percent of the income transfers by governmental process are of this nature, but I could be very far wrong in this guess. We can, I think, all agree that such major redistributions as the farm subsidy program, the very extensive facilities provided at the expense of the general taxpayer to make private airplane flying cheap and easy, or the transfers to owners of steel mills through restrictions on the import of steel are not the result of deliberate desires on the part of the "donors" to make these gifts. They are the result of activities on the part of the recipients combined, perhaps, with indifference or, more likely, ignorance and political weakness on the part of the people who actually pay for them.

Let us then consider such redistribution. Note that there is no increase in the total product measured in physical terms or in general utility. Thus, the physical transfer falls on a straightforward forty-five degree angle line. No improvement in efficiency in society is expected from such a transfer. The victim will be injured as much as the beneficiary gains.[2] Assume then that we are now at point *O* on Figure 5. Some pressure group—let us say the citizens of Tulsa, who would like their city to be a deep-water harbor—invest a certain amount of resources in lobbying in Congress. This moves society to point *O′*. The amount of resources they would invest would in part be a function of the counter-investment of resources they expect, but let us defer that discussion for the moment.

People who would rather not have their tax dollars spent dredging the river to make Tulsa a deep-water port—*K* in our diagram—now invest resources in lobbying against the measure, with the result that society moves to *O″*. Congress then acts. If the measure to dredge the river to Tulsa is defeated, we would remain at *O″*. Unfortunately, in the real world, the measure carried. There was, thus, a transfer of resources from *K* to *J*. Since the lobbying activity had lowered the total number of resources, this was a forty-five degree movement from *O″*.[3] If the citizens of Tulsa—represented by *J* in our

2. This strictly speaking is not a necessary condition for the analysis which follows. It could be that, although the "donor" would rather not give this particular amount, he nevertheless acquires some utility from the gift, albeit less than its cost to him. This would lead to more elaborate analysis, but no fundamental change in our conclusion.

3. This particular transfer might be a movement which, in and of itself, impoverished society. That is, the dredging might have been worth much less to the citizens of Tulsa than its cost to other people. Under these circumstances, the movement would be along a line at a steeper angle than forty-five degrees. It would be an inefficient transfer. Although in the real

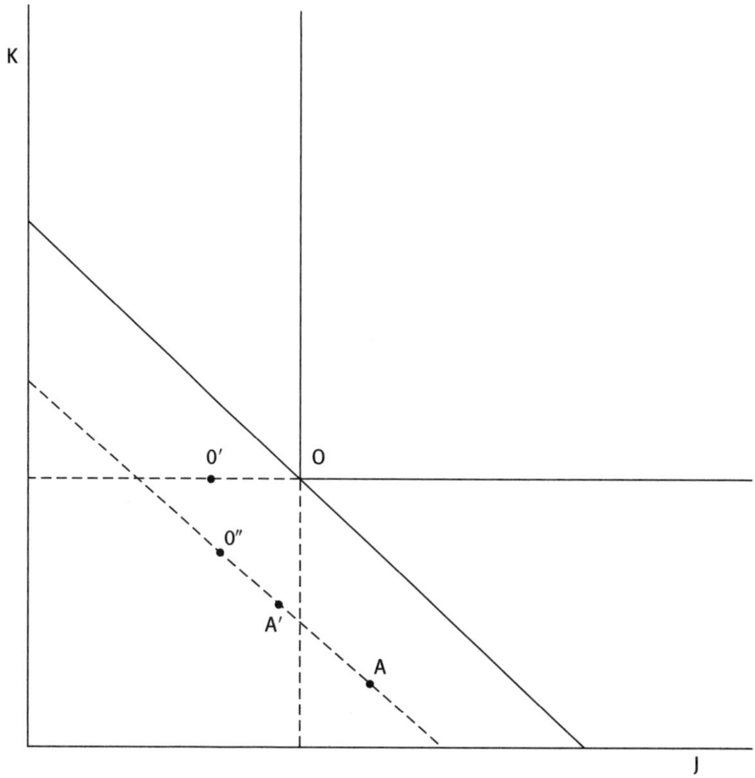

FIGURE 5

diagram—had calculated appropriately, the transfer of resources would be such that they would be benefited as a result of the entire transaction, i.e., they would reach some such point as *A*. If they had calculated inappropriately, the transfer might be less than the loss of resources invested in the effort to obtain the dredging operation; hence, they might end up at *A′*.

We could, I think, assume—looking at the matter solely from the standpoint of those persons engaged in lobbying to cause such transfers—that when the transfer was successful, it would turn out that they had made a net profit on the operation. When the transfer was unsuccessful, of course they would lose. What the present discounted value of the stream of several such

world individual transfers may have this type of inefficiency attached to them, it seems sensible to confine our discussion to the simple case where the transfer does not in and of itself involve inefficiency.

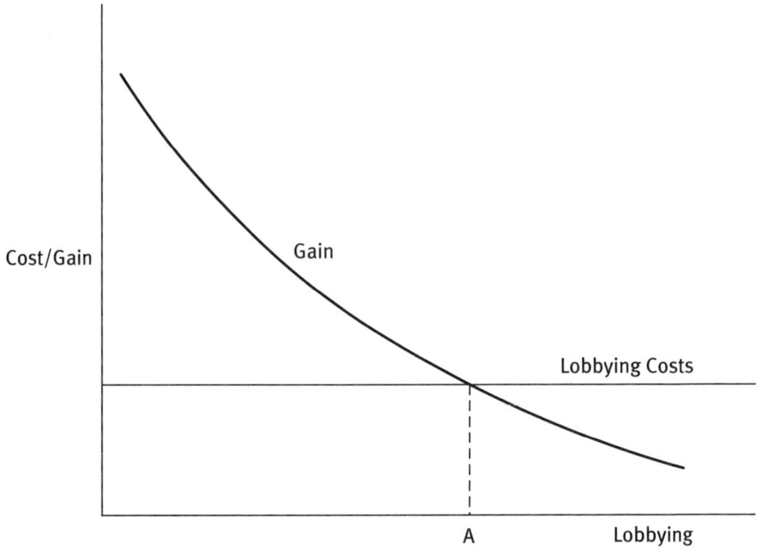

FIGURE 6

operations would be, we cannot say. It might well be some such point as A'. If we assume, however, that everyone is engaged in attempting to get such transfers and that there is a tendency for them to cancel out among different members of society, then clearly we end up in the Pareto-dominated area. In any event, it is clear that the action as a whole has not benefited "society," and that if asked whether we would like such transactions to occur in the future, not knowing whether we would be the beneficiary or victims of them, we would be opposed. The ex ante value of a stream of such redistributions is negative for the average person.

Let us consider briefly the calculation undertaken by some party who finds himself either interested in obtaining a transfer from someone else by lobbying or interested in avoiding a transfer from himself. Under these circumstances, he invests resources in lobbying as shown in Figure 6. Lobbying costs are measured by their costs, and the potential benefits from lobbying (assuming that his opponent is undertaking some fixed amount of counter-lobbying) are shown by the curved line. He would choose to invest amount *A* in lobbying activity and would purchase some particular probability of success. Looked at from his standpoint, this is ex ante a sensible investment of his resources. Ex post, he may win or he may lose, but over time a policy of always making this kind of calculation and investing an appropriate amount in lobbying would maximize his income stream.

Note, however, that we have assumed that the other party's lobbying activities are fixed. In the real world, each of the two parties would adjust lobbying activities to that of his opponent, and the end result would be a standard reaction diagram with—assuming everything is normal—the two curves intersecting at an equilibrium point. Since the resources used in lobbying are self-canceling—*J*'s resources in part simply offset *K*'s—they represent net social loss. If we could predict the outcome in advance, both parties could benefit by accepting that outcome without the investment of resources. Nevertheless, in the real world the individuals would be irrational *not* to make the investment in lobbying, and we can anticipate that this type of prisoner's dilemma will lead to large-scale investment in lobbying in those situations in which transfers are possible.

This article has been entitled "The Cost of Transfers." As can be seen from the diagram, it could also have been called, "The Cost of Resistance to Transfers." The problem is that the possibility of a transfer leads people to invest resources in either obtaining the transfer or preventing it. People who hope to receive the transfer will invest resources until the return in probability of receiving the transfer on the last dollar is worth one dollar. Those against whom the transfer would work will invest similarly. One side or the other will win, but from the social standpoint the resources invested in the conflict between the two groups are entirely wasted.

There is, of course, no a priori argument for one side or the other being favored in elimination of this conflict. If we return to the customs of Gladstone's England in which the government engaged in substantially no transfers, and it was known to all parties that the lobbying costs of introducing a change in this custom for their own benefit would almost certainly be much in excess of the benefit received, we would find very little such resource investment. If, on the other hand, the converse situation existed—it was widely believed that any proposal for a transfer would automatically go through and, hence, it was a waste of resources to resist the transfer—once again, few resources would be wasted in conflict. The reason being, of course, that with little resistance to transfers, there would also be very little resources invested in obtaining the transfers.[4] One might choose between these two social situ-

4. There might be large investments in attempts to determine which particular transfers were to take place.

ations in terms of a general attitude toward transfers, but this would be outside the scope of this essay.

So much for government imposed redistribution of income or wealth. As can readily be seen, war and theft can be analyzed by the same apparatus and, indeed, shown on the same diagrams if we change the labeling a little bit.[5] In each case, resources can be invested to obtain transfers, and in each case if the other side invests very little resources, this will be a profitable operation. The Mexicans, for example, are a very poor people living next to the wealthiest nation in the world. Further, as far as I can see, they rather dislike the citizens of the United States. Under the circumstances, conquest of the United States would clearly be highly desirable for Mexico. The reason they do not do it, of course, is that with our present armament, it would be a militarily impossible operation. If, however, we unilaterally disarmed and, hence, made conquest of the United States cheap, they would be fools not to undertake the action. Needless to say, our military forces right now are not aimed against the Mexicans. They are aimed at other enemies who are so powerful that it is necessary to maintain forces that are vastly superior to those maintained by Mexico. Under the circumstances, we are probably suffering nothing from the enmity of Mexico, and the Mexicans have nothing to fear from our attack upon them.

If, however, we have two major powers, both of which are heavily armed, it is likely that the conflict between them will cost more than the benefit; hence, one would anticipate that on the whole they would choose not to engage in the conflict—although the competitive armament itself is a form of conflict. It should be noted, however, that this is simply because the armament level is high enough so that the costs of conflict are very great. If the armament level by either or both were permitted to slip back to the point where the costs of conflicts would be low, the probable profits of the war would reappear. Consider, for example, the North Vietnamese government's first attempt to overthrow the government of Cambodia. Granted the military preparations which Cambodia had, it seems to me that the decision to make this attempt was a rational one ex ante, regardless of its results ex post.

To summarize, it is customary to say that transfers are costless economically and raise essentially noneconomic problems. I do not wish to quarrel with the statement that transfers normally raise noneconomic problems; the point of this essay has been simply to point out that they also do involve

5. This also applies to revolutions.

purely economic costs. The transfer itself may be costless, but the prospect of the transfer leads individuals and groups to invest resources in either attempting to obtain a transfer or to resist a transfer away from themselves. These resources represent net social waste. Transfers lead to conflict, and conflict is always an example of social waste from the standpoint of society as a whole. Unfortunately, it is very commonly rational for the individuals engaged in it.

MORE ON THE WELFARE COSTS OF TRANSFERS

That lobbying for income transfers in many cases generates public goods or bads cannot, I think, be denied. If this is so, then the investment in obtaining such a transfer would be less than the total present discounted value of the transfer. As I shall argue below, this offers an explanation for the fact that in democracies we see a very large amount of self-cancelling transfers of income back and forth within the middle income groups.

Before turning to this matter, however, I should like to discuss the political costs of transfer mechanism. Browning is, of course, quite correct in his final remark about cost of "legislators spending so much time designing a multitude of redistributive programs" with the result "that they are less well informed about other government programs."[1] What we actually have for many of these programs is what we might call Wagner-type lobbying.[2] The congressmen consider that the voters in their district are more interested in getting projects in the district than in almost anything else, and hence spend much of their time in attempting to get transfers to their districts. Some congressmen also specialize in obtaining transfers to special groups in society who are represented in their district but are also of wider scope: the elderly, farmers, *etc.*[3] Surely this cost in terms of that very scarce resource, legislator's time, must be immense. Further, it must have exactly the offsetting characteristics which I discussed in the original article.

We can go further, however. Another group of people who engage in active lobbying are the bureaucrats in each government bureau. These bureaucrats are essentially interested in transfers to themselves by way of expanding

Reprinted, with permission of Blackwell Publishing, from *Kyklos* 27, fasc. 2 (1974): 378–81.

1. Edgar K. Browning. "On the Welfare Cost of Transfers," *Kyklos*, Vol. 27 (1974), p. 377.

2. Richard E. Wagner, "Pressure Groups and Political Entrepreneurs: A Review Article," *Papers on Non-Market Decision Making*, 1, 1966, pp. 161–70.

3. Although this article and Browning's article are based primarily on American data, as far as I can see these phenomena are universal in democracies. Since one of the editors of this journal once explained to me the method by which the Swiss government decides where to place *Nationalstrassen*, I would gather that my view is not particularly controversial, at least in *Kyklos*.

their particular bureau, but the social costs must be immense.[4] Once again, competition between the bureaux would set off the kind of phenomena that I described in my original article.

Note that in both of these cases, however, the actual effect of this kind of lobbying is much greater than the direct resource cost because a great many people who are not involved in lobbying find themselves affected by the outcome. A dispute between the Department of Interior and the Army Corps of Engineers for appropriations would lead to an investment of resources by those two bureaux which probably fairly well discounted the value to the two bureaux of the switch in appropriations between them which they were fighting for. The effect of that appropriation on the economy as a whole may be vastly greater. But since these are the only people involved in the actual conflict for or against the appropriation, we would anticipate that the effect on the economy as a whole would tend to be relatively random. If so, we would expect that the transfer effect of the outcome of this dispute on the economy as a whole would only by coincidence fit some idea of social policy. Basically, it would simply be a random transfer.

In my original article, I talked mainly about transfers of this sort, *i.e.*, decisions on appropriations or programs which had a fairly concrete and narrow direct effect for some limited group of people. Browning refers to "tax reform" as a typical example and says, "The salient feature, . . . , as (of) most other government programs which redistribute income, is that it transfers income from one group of millions of people to another group of similarly large size." His example is "the degree of progressivity of the income tax structure." He argues that "no voluntary contribution to lobbying" was made on this issue.[5]

Clearly we are talking about different types of programs and I am willing to argue that the type Browning describes is relatively rare. First, turning to facts, the new Musgrave and Musgrave text summarizes the situation fairly well.[6] The total tax burden on Americans is approximately proportional to their income for a long range from about $5,700 a year to about $35,000 a year.[7] Taxes below $5,700 are lower and they rise above $35,000, although

4. See David L. Shapiro, "Can Public Investment Have a Positive Rate of Return?" *Journal of Political Economy*, Vol. 81 (1973), March/April, pp. 401–13.

5. Browning, "On the Welfare Cost of Transfers," p. 374.

6. Richard A. Musgrave and Peggy B. Musgrave, *Public Finance and Theory in Practice*, New York, McGraw-Hill, 1973.

7. *Ibid.*, p. 369.

not very steeply. If one turns to the net result of government action,[8] somewhat the same picture emerges. In other words, the net effect of our tax and government activity is not particularly progressive.[9]

In practice it seems to be necessary for most governments to have a nominally progressive tax system and the fact that it must be nominally progressive no doubt does indeed have some real effects. In the United States, for example, all basic changes in the tax structure apparently require some increase in the nominal degree of progressivity. However, in practice this progressivity is more illusion than reality. Thus, on this matter for which Browning says there is very little lobbying, it is also true that it is not obvious that the government has any particular policy. The actual "degree of progressivity of the income tax structure" is, however, the result of very intense lobbying on a myriad of detailed provisions.

If one looks at the American income tax in detail, one finds an immense body of law and regulation. Buried in this mass of literature is a gigantic number of special provisions which benefit various small special groups. I believe, and I do not expect that Browning will contest it, that these provisions have all been put in by active lobbying by those particular groups. In many cases the lobbyist is, of course, a congressman rather than a professional, but private lobbyists make major contributions, also.

Since such provisions are normally public goods (or bads), albeit for normally quite a small group of people—perhaps 10,000, the theoretical objection raised by Browning would appear to apply here, also. Indeed, I think it does. However, we do observe these lobbies; let us consider how that happens.

If we consider some action of the government that will affect a number of people, it is normally true that it will affect different people differently. There

8. *Ibid.*, p. 376.

9. Indeed, in my opinion it may be sharply regressive. The services which are given by the government are normally evaluated on their resource cost. It seems likely that many of these services, such as elementary education, in fact are of considerably less value to the poor than to the well-off. If this is so and the value of benefits given by the various governments was adjusted accordingly, we might find in the middle ranges (which, after all, include almost the entire population) the net effect of the government is to make the income distribution markedly less equal than it would be without government activity. Once again, although I am using American data, I regard this as characteristic of most democracies. See, Adrian L. Webb and Jack E. B. Sieve, *Income Redistribution and the Welfare State*, London, Social Administration Research Trust, 1971, for data on the situation in England.

may be some for whom the effect is quite large and a number for whom the effect is small. If there are some for whom the effect is quite large, it may be wise for them to invest resources in attempting to get a change in government policy.

In general, the desirability of such an investment from their standpoint will depend on how much the return to them would be from the change in government policy, and, secondarily, the likelihood that there will be opposition. If there is going to be no opposition—*i.e.*, there are no people on the other side for whom there would be a concentrated harm imposed, then the cost of generating the change will be much lower; indeed, it will simply be the cost of overcoming the inertia of the government system. On the other hand, there may be similar concentrated interests on the other side, and hence we may have a conflict. In any event, there surely are very many cases in which it is sensible for at least some people to invest at least some resources in lobbying for or against the change.

Insofar as these people do invest resources in attempting to make such a change, then the argument that I offered in my original article would tend to be true, although of course its strength is diluted. For those people who are affected by the redistributional change but for whom the effect is small enough so that it is not worth their time to invest any resources in it, the outcome is apt to be random. For some of these changes they will benefit, for some they will lose. We would anticipate that, over the population as a whole, individuals who are not involved in active lobbying would tend to gain about as much as they lose. Browning gives $150 billion as the total of transfers in the United States. I see no reason to doubt this, but it should be pointed out that the transfer from the wealthy and to the poor is only a very small part of that amount.[10]

The bulk of transfers, however, are back and forth within that massive group of people who make up the bulk of society and pay the bulk of the taxes. Although individual members of this group may suffer very pronounced negative transfers or receive very pronounced positive benefits as a result of what amounts to participating in a lottery, surely most of them end up with about the same income that they would have to begin with except,

10. There are allegations occasionally found in the literature that the wealthy do not in fact suffer any negative transfers from the tax system. With careful reading, it will usually be found that the author's actual feeling is that the wealthy should have larger transfers of income away from them than they now have, not that they now have no loss through the transfer system.

of course, insofar as the excess burden reduces their total income. The people who are interested in obtaining or preventing transfers on the other hand do invest resources and have a cost which is related to whatever transfer they receive or prevent. Thus, the population either invests resources in lobbying or participates in a lottery. For the first group, which is probably small, my original description is more or less correct. For the second, and much larger group, there is an excess burden but on the average, no net transfer.

COMPETING FOR AID

Economists have known for a very long time that most social states have more than one equilibrium. In particular, there is the agreement equilibrium that corresponds to some point on the Pareto optimal frontier, and that represents cooperation among the members of the society. There is a second, well-known equilibrium—the independent adjustment equilibrium—which occurs when, for one reason or another, agreement is not possible. The independent adjustment equilibrium is normally less satisfactory to the parties than the cooperative equilibrium. Ideally, the role of the state is to affect this independent adjustment equilibrium in ways that lead to superior outcomes. Economists, although occasionally dealing with the independent adjustment equilibrium, have normally confined their research to the cooperative equilibrium.

The independent adjustment equilibrium can be used to analyze a number of very unpleasant situations that have been relatively little considered by economists. In this article, however, I shall deal with a special application in the field of politics. The point is to indicate that the independent equilibrium analysis *has* value and to encourage other scholars to apply it.

Let me begin with an incident that occurred in Blacksburg, Virginia, some time ago. The local paper ran an article explaining the town's plan for road repair and construction. About two weeks later, the same paper reported the letting of a large number of contracts for road repair. It was notable that none of the roads in the road repair "plan" were included among those for which bids had been let. At first, I was puzzled by this phenomenon, but with a little thought I realized that the roads covered by the plan were on the whole important enough so that there was a fair chance of getting the Commonwealth of Virginia to pay all (or a good part) of the cost. The town, therefore, had set up a plan which it was now negotiating with the Commonwealth. On those roads where it was crystal clear the Commonwealth would *not* make any contribution, the city was going ahead on its own.

Note the phenomenon. A "plan" had been constructed not for the purpose of guiding the city's action, but for the purpose of persuading the Commonwealth to act. Further, the repair of the more important roads was

Reprinted, with kind permission of Kluwer Academic Publishers, from *Public Choice* 21 (Spring 1975): 41–51.

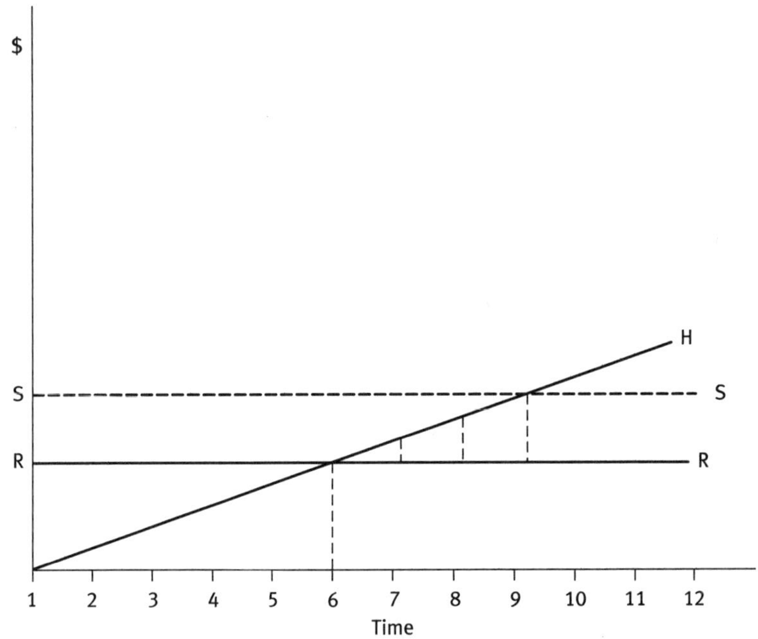

FIGURE 1

actually being delayed, while that of the less important roads was to be undertaken immediately. It is, of course, possible that the unimportant roads had been permitted to deteriorate to a poorer state than the important roads before the bids were let. But there are good reasons why the most important roads might be left unrepaired, even if they were in very bad shape. Repairing the important roads immediately would have cost the town the full amount. With some delay, they stood a finite chance of getting someone else to pay all or part of the cost; hence, it was wise to take the delay. With respect to the less important roads, the opposite situation existed.

Let us, however, look at this matter a little more formally. On figure 1 the vertical axis represents simply dollars, either cost or gain; the horizontal axis is time shown as years from some arbitrary starting point. In our particular case, we assume that some road was completely resurfaced in year one. The cost of resurfacing the road again in any given year is shown by line R. The cost is somewhat simplified. I assume that the actual physical cost of repairing the road is not affected by wear and tear on the road, nor is it expected to change in the future. Further, I assume that the road is eventually to be repaired, i.e., it is not to be permitted to simply deteriorate. The more general (and complicated) model, in which these two restrictions were not included, could be constructed without any great difference in the conclusions. Nevertheless, with these two assumptions, the cost of repairing the road in any given year becomes simply the interest on the money which is foregone by not waiting until the following year. If the cost of resurfacing would be $100,000 and the current interest rate is 10 percent, it cost the county $10,000 to do it this year instead of next year. If the county contemplates a delay of several years, then of course the interest would be compounded. Unfortunately, it is not possible to represent this on a simple diagram; but, once again, introducing this complication would not make any significant difference in the line of reasoning or in the conclusion.

Line H shows the cost to the community (wear and tear on vehicles, delay, etc.) of leaving the road unrepaired for one more year. It should be noted that in Blacksburg, repairs must be made during the summer, and this breaks the time stream down into a series of discontinuous one-year periods. Line H continuously slants upward. In the early period, the inconvenience, discomfort, and possible physical damage to the cars from holes and other defects in the pavement is very small. With time, it grows. If we assume that the community is left entirely to itself, and that the local town council perfectly represents the interests of its citizens, then the road would be resurfaced at the end of the sixth year. At this point, the cost of waiting one year to resurface the road rises above the cost of repairing it. The assumption that the town council perfectly expresses the preferences of its citizens is, of course, an improbable one; but the town council is more likely to represent the preferences of the citizens of Blacksburg than is any higher level government agency.

Assume, however, that there is a state program for rebuilding roads. Assume, further, that the amount of money appropriated by the state for road repair is not sufficient to actually satiate demand for road repairs (a not unlikely assumption), and that the road commission spends this money on those roads where the need for repairs is greatest. Once again, this is a not unlikely assumption, although political considerations would be important, of course. Under these circumstances, the town council must make some calculations. If the amount of road repair funds and the degree of repair of other roads in the Commonwealth is such that the Commonwealth will repair the road during year six, then there is no problem. The town is able to pass the entire burden onto the shoulders of the Commonwealth. This is, however, on the whole a rather unlikely coincidence. Normally one would assume that the road funds would be either in shortage or in excess.

Let us begin by assuming that the total road funds are now supplied in shortage; hence the community realizes that the repair of its roads will not be undertaken by the Commonwealth in year six because there will be other roads that are already more deteriorated. Under these circumstances, the community must make an estimate of the likely delay which will follow if they decide to depend upon the Commonwealth. Assume that the Commonwealth road funds are available in a quantity that makes it possible for the Commonwealth to see to it that all roads are repaired when the cost of further use of them for one more year is at line S, rather than at line R. Under these circumstances, the community would anticipate that the road would be repaired in year nine. This means a wait for the Commonwealth through three more years of gradually deteriorating roads and, in this particular case, I have drawn the diagram in such a way that the cost to the community of these three additional years of delay for the town is approximately the same as the cost to the community of repairing the road itself now.[1]

Thus, the community would choose to repair the road itself at the end of the sixth year if it thought the Commonwealth standard for repairing roads was higher than S, i.e., the delay would be more than three years; but it would depend upon the Commonwealth if it thought the delay would be less than three years. From the local community standpoint, this would be a profit-maximizing decision. Note, however, that the town might have made a misestimate. Perhaps the funds available for road building will not be great enough, so that three years after year six (in year nine) roads deteriorated to the extent to which this particular road will then have deteriorated will be repaired. If the road funds are very restricted, they may be confined to roads that are in even poorer condition. Under these circumstances, in year nine the town would once again have to make an estimate. The cost it has already incurred from not repairing its road is, of course, a sunk cost and it would have to decide whether it is likely that further delay of a year or two would lead the state to repair the road. With my particular diagram, a year's delay from year nine would still be sensible for the town; but if prospective delay expected in

1. Note that I ignore compounding on both sides of the equation. In the real world, a decision for three years would presumably have to take a compounding effect into account, and hence would be more complicated.

year nine was greater than a year, then it would be better for the town to repair the road itself. If this contingency occurred, even if the road was repaired in year ten the town would end up in a worse situation than it would be had it repaired the road in year six. Further, if in year nine the town came to the conclusion that a year's delay would not lead to enough deterioration of the road so that the state would repair it, then it would undertake the repair itself and the losses incurred from leaving the road unrepaired for three years would be a net loss to the community.

This problem does not occur only on the local level. In the early years of the Eisenhower administration, there was a vast expansion of divided center, limited access highways paid for by tolls. The development of these roads was extremely rapid and appeared likely to continue at a similar rate. This is particularly remarkable because the gasoline taxes, which pay for a good part of road building, were collected on gas used on these roads and not used to finance them. The individual using these roads had to pay the usual taxes to support the highway system, *plus* the toll. The speed with which these roads would have developed had the federal and state governments decided to rebate the taxes on gasoline consumed upon them to the toll authorities is hard to overestimate.

Unfortunately, this development did not occur. President Eisenhower got the idea that the federal government should introduce the interstate system at the cost of *all* drivers by way of a special tax on gasoline. When this new program was announced, all the local projects for building toll highways were dropped. As a result, development of divided center, limited access highways was markedly retarded, since the federal government adopted a schedule rather like the one I have specified for the higher authority dealing with Blacksburg, and long delays in construction of such highways resulted. To keep the matter on a local note, Blacksburg itself only achieved full integration into the nationwide interstate system in 1972.

Blacksburg has had another striking example. Fifteen years ago Blacksburg was a very small town which depended for hospital facilities on the county seat, about ten miles away. With the rapid expansion of Virginia Polytechnic Institute and State University, Blacksburg has grown to the point where it is now much the largest town in the county. The establishment of a hospital in Blacksburg seemed desirable, particularly since the hospital in the county seat was becoming obsolete. The town attempted to obtain federal government funds for a new hospital and spent several years in the effort. Eventually, it was decided that the prospects for federal financing were poor, and the town put up a hospital which it partially financed by a bond issue, but which is basically a private, profit-making hospital. The delay of several years was clearly the cost of the effort to obtain federal funds. It was an attempt to obtain a transfer and this attempt had costs.

Nevertheless, the individual city is rational in making its decision to delay provision of some facility because there is a finite chance of a higher authority providing the facility free (or, of course, providing a subsidy). The only question is the present discounted value of the two income streams, and it will frequently be higher if costs are absorbed in the immediate future in order to receive a grant from higher authority later. It should be noted, of course, that a desire to "help" the local city is not by any means the only motive that may inspire a higher level government to make such payments. Highway construction, for example, has very distinct externalities. The Commonwealth of Virginia does have a legitimate interest in seeing to it that the Town of Blacksburg provides somewhat more in the way of street repair than it would on its own. This is because the Town of Blacksburg will not take into account those noncitizens of Blacksburg who use its streets.

The ideal situation with respect to street repair, of course, would be Vickrey's scheme in which each person driving over a street is charged—by way of an elaborate electronic device—for his use of that particular segment of the street at an appropriate fee. Toll roads approximate this ideal. When this is not possible, payments from higher level authorities to lower level organizations may be a rational way of internalizing the externality. Normally, it is not possible to arrange these payments in such a way that the local government cannot partially distort its behavior pattern in order to increase its payments, but the problem is not a desperate one. The basic transfer problem arises when the motive inspiring higher level payments to local governments is a desire to "help" these local governments. Under these circumstances, the local governments are thrown into competition to receive the transfers and problems of the sort that we discussed in connection with figure 1 will arise.

Note that, provided only the amount of money supplied by the central government for street repair pulls the line S low enough to make it profitable for the community to delay repair, the community itself gains from the receipt of this transfer. If, however, we realize that the average community must be paying out as much in taxes to support the gifts as it is receiving in payments, and that the result of competition among the communities to receive such payments is a general delay in road repair, then the net effect of this central government provision of subsidies is actually to injure the citizens of the separate communities. They end up in a worse situation than they were in before the program was begun.

One solution for this problem would, of course, be to appropriate enough money to satiate the demand for whatever public service is being subsidized. As a step in this direction, if the amount of money provided by the state were exactly the amount needed to lower line S to line R, then our particular community would end up with the same road repairs it would have if there were no state program. Assuming it is an average community, it would be paying the same amount of taxes, also. Unfortunately, this solution is unlikely because different communities have different demands for road services, and hence would normally aim at different levels. At the very least, the central program will provide an equal level of service throughout its jurisdiction, which is inefficient.

The central government funds may be more than enough to fully replace the local expenditures. Suppose, for example, that the central government appropriated enough money so that line S was lowered to the point where it intersected line H at 4. Under these circumstances, the community would resurface its roads every four years. Clearly the community would be better off under this arrangement than it would be if it were resurfacing the road every six years, provided one disregards the tax cost. The community, however, would be still better off if the state simply gave it the entire cost of the road resurfacing every four years, and then the community in fact resurfaced the roads every six years. This overrepair of the roads leads to social waste just as does the underrepair discussed before.

So far, however, we have assumed that the state, in deciding to help a given community, simply observes how great the "need" for the particular type of service in that community is. Under these circumstances, the communities are well-advised to create "need," and hence produce a lower level of satisfaction. The desire on the part of the state to help communities which "have inadequate hospital facilities" actually generates inadequate hospital facilities. That community which has the worst hospital facilities will receive the aid.

In passing, I may note an amusing plaque which, at least some years ago, was set in the cement at the entrance to the Toledo, Ohio, airport. This plaque was a letter from President Eisenhower to the City of Toledo in which he congratulated the city on having built their airport entirely on their own without federal funds. He made it clear that he thought this was a highly meritorious, and even noble, act. In order not to raise any misunderstanding in other parts of the country, however, he then went on to say that, of course, those communities which could not provide their own airport must receive federal aid. I take it that the citizens of Toledo never again found it possible to build their own airport.

The alternative, providing enough resources so that communities are able to provide the service before they would themselves regard it as worthwhile, must also lead to net social loss, albeit of a different nature. The result, then, of this type of program is always loss, and this loss comes from the competition among the potential recipients of the benefit for its receipt. The community that lets its hospital run down because it feels that the federal government will replace it is in the same situation as the Chinese beggar who mutilates himself to obtain funds from passersby. In both cases, the individual action is rational, and in both cases the net effect is to lower welfare.

So far our analysis has proceeded in terms of one possible technique which higher authority might use in making transfers among local communities. There are, of course, other methods. Basically, however, I think these methods can be classified into three general categories. The first of these, which we have already discussed, is distribution of the manna according to need. As we have pointed out, this leads to a competition among the potential recipients in generating need. The second is simply to make direct income transfers on some arbitrary basis. This, together with the third method, to attempt to second-guess the local communities, will be discussed below.

To begin with simple income transfers, they have somewhat the same attractions as negative income tax. Suppose, for example, that a higher level government allocates to local governments a fund of so much per head, which can be used in any way the local government wishes. Clearly the effect of this allocation is simply to permit the local government to reduce its taxes. Since the average local government will be paying as much in taxes as it is receiving in its allocation, there will be no income effect, and hence it will purchase about the same services and goods it would purchase without this transfer. Those communities which receive more income than they pay in taxes will have a wealth increase, and hence they will spend more; while those who pay more than they get will have a wealth decrease and will spend less. Basically, however, this leaves the decision as to what should actually be done with the money to local authorities, and has only modest tendencies toward inefficiency.

There is one significant disadvantage of this system, however, which is that it makes it impossible for communities to experiment with the combination of very low taxes and a very low bundle of services. Perhaps these experiments are undesirable, but we must at least note that this procedure makes them impossible. In any event, there is no competition among communities to get funds under this procedure, and hence this type of conflict we have been describing above does not occur.[2] Note that it is not necessary that the subsidy be distributed on a per-head basis, only that it be distributed in such a way that the individual communities cannot obtain increased subsidies by changing their behavior. There may, of course, be a good deal of investment in lobbying, etc., in order to get the higher level government to adopt a particular method of distributing the subsidy which is of advantage to a particular local community.

The third method, and at the moment the most widely used method, consists of a variety of efforts to prevent the local government from either spending the money exactly as it wishes, which it would do under the second method, or deliberately generating needs, as it would do under the first method. These methods are complex and not terribly efficient. Basically, they involve either some kind of incentive payments which are intended to lead the local government in what the central government regards as the correct direction, or direct administrative controls over the way the local government spends the central government's money.

The problem is rather similar to that which has led most major corporations to decentralize managements. It is simply impossible for the central government to know as much about the situation in any local community as the local government does. Thus, if the central government attempts to set up specific regulations or detailed administration, it simply leads to local government activities aimed at taking advantage of this central administration. Indeed, it is probable that it is far less efficient than local administration of the money, because the central government bureaucracy of controllers is offset by a massive local government bureaucracy of planners, city engineers, assistant superintendents, all of whom in fact exist almost solely for the purpose of obtaining as much central government money as can be obtained, granted the restrictions.

The proliferation of local officials that has occurred in areas where central

2. In special circumstances, this is not entirely true. The Town of Blacksburg is expanding and quite deliberately taking in the university campus on the grounds that a certain amount is paid to local governments on a per-head basis by the Commonwealth of Virginia, while the students in fact consume relatively little in the way of government services. The county government, which may lose this asset, is naturally angry.

government grants are available is normally discussed in terms of desirability of "planning." This is a misunderstanding. These officials are there for the purpose of assisting the community in obtaining central government funds, partly by preparing plans which are not intended for local use, but for the central government inspection. As an example that will impress almost all academics, VPI, like most universities, now has a "Dean of Research." According to the table of organization, he is in charge of research in the university. His actual duties are to assist the university in obtaining research grants from Washington and from the foundations. As part of these duties, he does, indeed, exercise some influence on research actually carried on at the university. He makes efforts to push it in directions that will lead to increased funds. He also makes judgments as to whether a particular possible area of research would cost more in terms of university research allocations than it is worth in terms of funds likely to come in. His presence has little or nothing to do with actual research on campus and a great deal to do with raising money.

Not only are such specialized officials as planners and deans of research basically engaged in attempting to get money from higher authorities, but many standard administrators have become specialists in this field. The present-day school superintendent of a large system is apt to be more concerned with attempting to raise money from Washington, or perhaps from the state or private foundations, than with actually running the school system. Surely this must, over time, lead to less efficient supervision of the local activity, together with a higher administrative cost. The local community that hires at high price a very competent school superintendent, in the sense that he is good at getting money from Washington, does well in its competition with other local communities. The existence of this competition, however, means that a great deal of resources are devoted by various local communities to essentially offsetting sales efforts in Washington.

The situation can be illustrated by figure 2. On the vertical axis we have a dollar amount, and on the horizontal axis we have probable receipts in grants from Washington. Note that a certainty of $100 would be shown at the same location on the horizontal axis as a fifty-fifty chance of $200, a one-in-three chance of $300, etc. In other words, no risk factor is shown. In the real world, the community would also have risk aversion, and hence this simple diagram would have to be complicated. A community investing resources in efforts to obtain grants from Washington is assumed in this diagram to make simple, straightforward cash payments, perhaps for additional members of its "planning" bureaucracy. The cost is shown as line C.

As a beginning, we represent the receipts as constant in value; that is, each

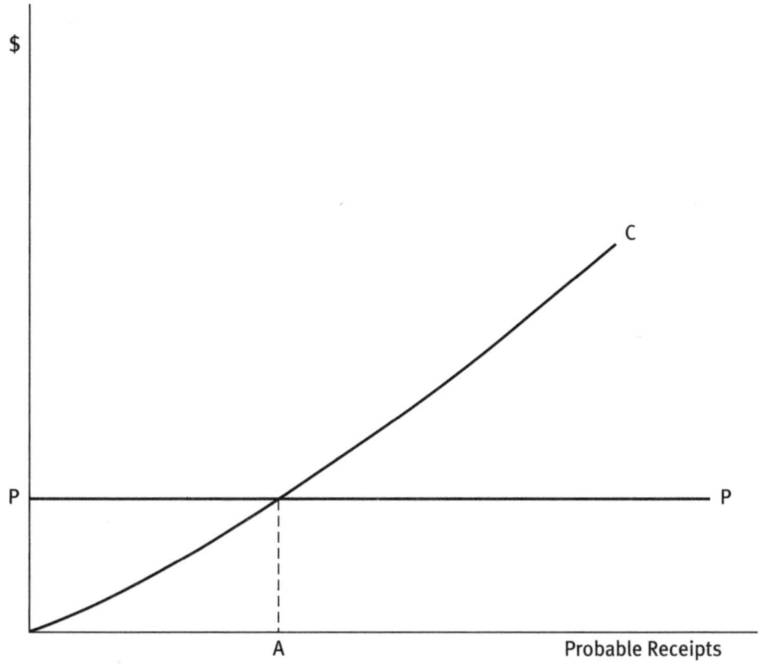

FIGURE 2

unit of receipts on the horizontal axis is shown as a certain number of dollars by the horizontal line PP. The community faces declining returns on its investment in efforts to get transfers, and the cost and return lines cross at A. Thus, the community would invest the total amount shown by the rough triangle under line C and to the left of A, and receive a gross return equivalent to the rectangle to the left of A. The operation would be profitable from the standpoint of the community. If we consider that the national government has some bureaucracy to supervise the distribution of funds, it may or may not be profitable from the standpoint of this one local community plus the national government. Surely, however, from the standpoint of society as a whole, it would be desirable that the funds used to generate this grant and the funds used by the national government to supervise such generation be dropped. It is the competition between this local community and other communities, together with the national government's role as referee over this competition, that causes the waste.

Frequently, however, the national government does not simply make straightforward payments to the local government. The funds delivered must be spent in particular ways or the local government must take certain types of activity in order to receive them. I recall hearing the president of the University of South Carolina explain a project to tear down a neighboring black slum and build some playing fields for the university as part of a federal government urban renewal project. He remarked on the amount of money we would receive for this purpose, but then said this was not all "clear." It would be necessary to spend approximately 25 percent of the grant to develop plans, etc. These plans were not necessary for the development of the playing field, they were entirely part of the federal government's program. The university had hired an expert at getting this kind of money, and the expert had said that it would be necessary for the university to spend a fairly large amount of money on some planning and research documents which were of no interest to it. They were probably not of much interest to the federal government, either. The reasons why the federal government required them will be discussed below.

When the federal government does not make the gift free and clear, then line PP on figure 2 has a somewhat different form. Suppose the federal government has a program that provides some opportunity for the Town of Blacksburg to receive some money. This money, however, must be spent on something which the Town of Blacksburg does not regard as of first priority. If the federal government simply gave them the cash, they would spend it, let us say, on street improvements; but the grant can only be spent on improved recreational facilities. Under these circumstances, the grant is worth less to us than its dollar cost to the federal government, and the line PP would thus be lower than if they were simply making cash payments.[3]

Not only does the tying of the grant lower its value to the local government, it is probable that the line PP should be downward slanting to indicate that the local government will first attempt to get money under those programs that are of greatest value to it, and then under programs of a lower value, etc. This is not sure, however. The local government should be uninterested in the actual dollar cost of the funds to the federal government, and only interested in the benefit to themselves and the cost of generating it. Thus, suppose that there are two government programs, one of which will

3. It is possible for the value of the grant to be higher for the federal government or for the rest of the nation, even though it is lower from the standpoint of the local government. This point will be discussed further below.

cost the federal government $500,000 and provide a benefit which the local authorities believe is worth only $50,000, and another which will cost the federal government $50,000 and provide the local government with a benefit which they think is worth only $40,000. If, in the town's estimate, the cost of obtaining these two grants is the same, the city fathers would prefer the first.

The fact that the government grants to a local community are normally accompanied by special requirements, and that the community's behavior is to a considerable extent adjusted to the desirability of obtaining these grants, means that the grants are always worth less to the community than their cost to the central government. Once again, competition among communities for these grants may lead to very large costs to the community and the nation. Note, however, that the fact that the grant is of lower value to the community than cash does not necessarily indicate that the community should be permitted to disperse the money in an unhampered way. If the objective of the central government is not to aid the local community but simply to internalize certain externalities which would otherwise be ignored by the community, then, although the grant will be worth less than its dollar value to the community, restrictions may be sensible.

If the grant to the local community, however, is motivated by a desire to simply benefit the local community, then the costs which we have been describing are net offsets against the benefits to be obtained from the grant and there is clear social waste. This is particularly true since in many cases the restrictions put on the expenditure of the grant do not represent any general consensus as to values. The central government bureaucrats, allocating funds among a number of competing clients, are likely to develop standards for delivery of these funds which in part are an expression of their own tastes, and in part are designed to reduce their decision problem. Bureaucrats in general, although they like power, normally do not like the business of finally turning down applicants. Thus, the introduction of essentially arbitrary requirements in the review process by reducing the number of applicants is an improvement in the well-being of the bureaucrats. This is particularly so since the imposition of these requirements is as good an expression of their power as the individual decisions would be. Many of the restrictions put on local communities who wish central funds are arbitrary and complying with them is pure social waste, except insofar as individual bureaucrats are benefited by them by reduction in their subjective decision costs.

THE TRANSITIONAL GAINS TRAP

1. Introduction

One of the major activities of modern governments is the granting of special privileges to various groups of politically influential people. Air transportation, for example, has been cartelized by the CAB, surface transportation by the ICC, and we are prevented from receiving "too-high" interest rates on our bank accounts by the Federal Reserve Board and various other government agencies. On the whole, however, the profit record of these protected industries does not seem to differ systematically from the nonprotected. This raises questions of why these special privileges do not seem to do much good.[1]

2. General Argument

The purpose of this article is to discuss this apparent long-run unprofitability of government aid programs. To give a preview of the general plot, it will be my thesis that there are only transitional gains to be made when the government establishes special privileges for a group of people. The successors to the original beneficiaries will not normally make exceptional profits; but, unfortunately, they usually will be injured by cancellation of the original gift.[2] Indeed, we shall be on what, paradoxically, seems to be an inefficient portion of the Paretian frontier.

Although some government restrictions are clearly designed to benefit specific groups of people, this is by no means the only way in which such spe-

Reprinted by permission of RAND, from *Bell Journal of Economics* 6 (Autumn 1975): 671–78. Copyright 1975.

1. All of this has led David Friedman to propound what he calls "Friedman's Second Law," and what others call "Friedman II's Law," which is "the government can't even give anything away."

2. See J. M. Buchanan and G. Tullock, "The 'Dead Hand' of Monopoly," *Antitrust Law and Economics Review* 1 (Summer 1968): 85–96, for a similar analysis of private monopoly. For an earlier analysis in somewhat the same spirit, see G. J. Stigler, "Capitalism and Monopolistic Competition: I. The Theory of Oligopoly—Monopoly and Oligopoly by Merger," *American Economic Review* 40(2) (May 1950): 23–37.

cial privileges can arise. The pharmaceuticals industry, for example, fought hard against the 1962 legislation. Since it has come into effect, they have become, on the whole, satisfied with it, because it turns out that it has reduced the vigor of competition, with the result that their profits are about as big as they were before, without the risk involved in the introduction of new and improved drugs.[3] Even in those cases where the government regulation was fairly clearly motivated by a desire to help some particular group, it usually turns out that at least some features are not to the advantage of the benefited group. Apparently government moves in mysterious ways its wonders to perform, and is not completely controlled even by the best organized pressure group.

3. *Taxi Medallions*

Let us consider a very simple example of government monopoly creation. This example will be the taxi medallion system, although my simplified description will not correspond exactly to that in New York. In Figure 1 we show the demand for taxicab services with the usual downward-slanting line, labeled *D*, and their cost as a horizontal line, labeled *P*. In a competitive environment, the price charged would also be at cost, and *C* units of taxi service would be purchased at a price, *P*. With supply of taxis restricted, the price rises to P' and, of course, there is now a significant monopoly profit, shown by the usual rectangle. We shall, for the moment, ignore the question of what happens to the taxis which are idled by this change and simply concern ourselves with the taxi owners and drivers who have the right to drive under the new dispensation, i.e., who have the taxi medallions. It is clear that they have gained a great deal.

Suppose, however, we wait for a number of years. By now, the capital value of the monopoly profit has been fully taken into account in the industry. New entrants enter only by purchasing the medallion, with the result that they get only normal profits.[4] Further, the surviving original owners have op-

3. See S. Peltzman, "An Evaluation of Consumer Protection Legislation: The 1962 Drug Amendments," *Journal of Political Economy* 81 (September/October 1973): 1049–91; see especially 1086–89.

4. See R. D. Auster, "The GPITPC and Institutional Entropy," *Public Choice* 19 (Fall 1974): 77–83.

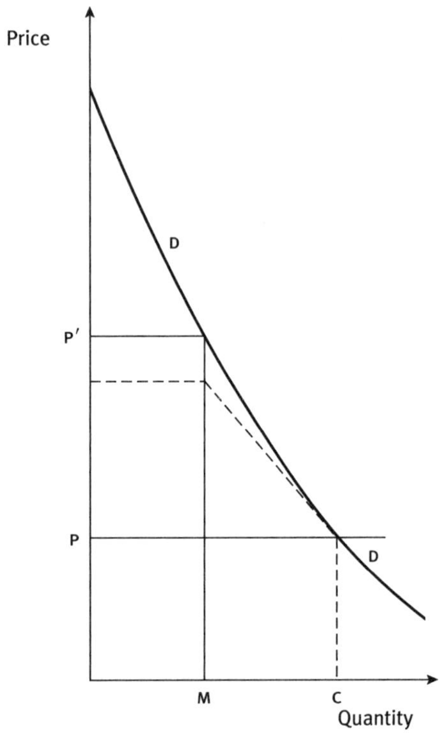

FIGURE 1
Taxi Medallion Monopoly

portunity costs equivalent to the value of the medallions upon which they receive normal returns. The customers, of course, are worse off.

Can we suggest a compensation scheme which would get us out of the mess? Normally, the answer to this question is "no," because the implied transaction costs are excessive. If we could somehow identify those people who are now not using a cab but who would at a slightly lower price and tax *them* so that the distribution of the burden followed the dotted line in Figure 1, it would be possible to gradually buy back the monopoly from its current owners, and hence benefit everyone. Unfortunately, we have no way of doing it, and hence my reference to the situation as being an "inefficient point on the Paretian frontier."

There is a possible way in which we might get out of the trap. It may be that the monopolistic organization of the industry is not efficient for one reason or another. The number of taxicab medallions in New York has remained unchanged for very long periods of time. It seems unlikely that the demand and cost of taxicabs during that period of time have continuously been such that the unchanged number of cabs maximized the monopoly gains. A brief examination of the other regulated industries or specially privileged areas will usually lead to the same conclusion. The owners of the monopoly are not efficiently exploiting the consumer, not because they are stupid, but because the political problems involved in manipulating government are great. Any change in the number of cabs other than doubling or tripling them would require that the medallions be given fractional value, unless it were intended to change the proportionate ownership of different medallions. The problems of having the individual owner of a medallion suddenly find that he had the right to operate 1.07 cabs (or 0.93 cabs) would probably preclude any possibility of political success for such a move. Certainly the transaction costs for getting such a proposal approved by all the cab owners would be immense.

Note that frequently the gains obtained by the organizers or beneficiaries of this kind of a cartel arrangement, even in the transitional period, are quite small. On Figure 1 when the cartel was introduced, there was a sharp reduction in the total number of units produced. Clearly, the cost of reducing capacity in this way could be quite considerable and must be borne by someone. In the particular case of the New York medallions, they were actually provided for all existing cabs and, in the short run, had very little effect. Later, when the demand for cabs went up, they restricted the growth of the cab business. In order to achieve immediate profits, it would have been necessary to dispose of some producing assets in order to get the monopoly gains. This is, of course, not a special characteristic of this type of monopoly.

4. *Blue Laws*

To take an example of the way this kind of thing works, let me offer my own explanation for the reason that Blue Laws are frequently supported by the mercantile community. They are not, of course, the main force behind the Blue Laws. Suppose a community has a certain number of supermarkets which are open seven days a week. It is proposed that they be required by law to close all day Sunday. Merely having the store open imposes certain costs that cannot be totally eliminated. There have to be a certain number of people on duty, the lights have to be turned up to a certain level, heating and air conditioning have to be handled a little differently than when the store is closed, etc. Thus, a reduction in the number of hours the store is open does reduce the total cost. In essence, each sale is accomplished with somewhat less in the way of cost because the customers are compelled to come more closely grouped, and various economies can be derived from that. In a way, requiring that the stores close down on Sunday is somewhat similar in its effect to destroying one-seventh of the stores.

If a private business acquired all of the stores in order to extract monopoly rents, it would find it necessary to reduce its capacity. Presumably, it would do this in part by closing down stores and, to some extent, by reducing the time they are open. The private business could seek the most profitable combination of these two methods of reducing capacity. But this is not really a political opportunity available to the mercantile supporters of Blue Laws; hence, their monopoly will be less efficient than a private monopoly.

The result, then, of forcing the stores to close on Sunday should be, temporarily, a rise in profits. If they are in a highly competitive environment, this profit will be completely competed away; but many retail stores are in monopolistic competitive environments and this will partially protect them from that contingency. Still, a good deal of the cost-saving will inevitably pass on to the consumers, who presumably would prefer to pay a little more and have the greater convenience of having the stores open all week.

Once the Blue Laws have been enacted, however, the stores are operating at somewhat above normal return on their assets, and the customers find themselves a little more crowded in their shopping than they really want to be. Under the circumstances, the construction of new stores is highly likely. Eventually, then, we will have the situation in which there are more stores than there were before and the return on all stores is, once again, normal. The customers are not being served quite so well, so we have a social cost; but it is not practically possible to put a tax on the customers and use that tax to buy the stores back to their original position. On the other hand, although the store owners are now making normal profits, the repeal of the Blue Laws would be quite inconvenient for them. With the Blue Laws repealed, some of them would surely start opening on Sunday and the costs saved by going to a six-day week would be reimposed upon them. They would suffer a considerable transitional loss.

5. Related Phenomena

For Blue Laws the transitional gain was extremely small. In other cases, there may be quite large initial gains. The organization of a new labor union, which raises wages by 15 percent for its current employees,[5] does bring a very large improvement in the well-being of the current laborers who remain employed. Essentially, however, this is simply a capital gift to the existing laborers; it does not significantly benefit the new laborers who will, in the long run, replace them in the industry. With wages in this industry averaging 15 percent above wages elsewhere, the number of people who want to become employees immediately becomes much larger than can be employed. Under the circumstances, some method of rationing jobs is necessary. If this method is a straight hereditary method, i.e., in order to get in, you have to be children of the previous members of the union, then the gain is retained permanently within these families.

More normally, however, the method of rationing these high wage jobs is through the seniority clause. Senior employees have a prescriptive right to their jobs.[6] Granted the work force is not entirely stable; this means that the entire burden of unemployment falls on the new workers. Since in the early years, in any event, the employer will be restricting employment and investing in labor-saving devices (because of the higher wages he is paying), this phenomenon may mean that the new entrant to the union spends a good deal of time as a very low seniority worker with only intermittent employment.

Presumably, the situation is brought into equilibrium with the discounted lifetime income stream for becoming a union member (which means a long period of intermittent employment at first and then high wage employment later) equal to the return on taking a nonunionized job. When this equilibrium has been reached (and it surely has been for all of the older unions), once again we are in a situation where no one is better off as a result of the existence of the union than he would be had the union never been organized. Unfortunately, there is a deadweight social loss and there are a number of

5. Normally, of course, with some reduction in the total number of employees, so some people get hurt even at that time.

6. In some of the lower paid occupations, the opposite phenomenon is currently occurring. Unemployment insurance rates are now high enough so that there is a desire on the part of the senior employees to take paid vacations periodically, with the result of what is called "reverse seniority."

people, the members of the union, who will lose very considerably from the ending of the union. The transitional gain has been completely "sunk," but the possibility of large transitional losses remains.

A somewhat similar situation exists with respect to agriculture. The very large gains in value of farm products, as a result of the Agricultural Adjustment Administration's initial work, were quickly capitalized into the value of land. Whoever owned farm land at the time the program was instituted made immense gains, but these gains were fully capitalized. We are now stuck with the situation in which there are significant social losses, but a powerful political group would suffer transitional losses by the termination of the program. No one is gaining now in the sense that his income is higher than it would be had the institution never been established, except, of course, those people who have received larger inheritances from their parents than they otherwise would.

The higher-than-competitive wages that are now paid in much of the government sector are another example. They depend essentially on the fact that families of government employees now make up something on the order of one-third of all voters.[7] Government employees use a somewhat odd method of capitalizing the gains. Suppose some category of government employee is paid more than is necessary to attract an adequate number of suitably qualified personnel. There will be an excess of people who want the job. They must be rationed in some way, and the method used by the United States government (and, indeed, by many local governments) is the civil service examination. If the prices being paid are at the market level, then the civil service examination would be more or less unnecessary. The number of candidates who would turn up for the jobs would be about that which is needed, and the methods used in private industry to select suitable employees could be used.

On the other hand, if the pay is above that necessary to attract adequate labor, then the civil service exam takes the form of a rationing device. The exam is made harder than is necessary or it covers irrelevant matters such as knowledge of American history. As a result, the employees are actually over-

7. This estimate is a little shaky, but government employees do make up about 19 percent of all employed persons. They appear to vote about 50 percent more frequently than do non-government employees, and hence the computation of one-third. For investigation of the evidence on this point, see T. E. Borcherding, ed., *Budgets and Bureaucrats* (Durham, N.C.: Duke University Press, 1977). Currently, Richard L. Moss is making a much more careful investigation of the matter as part of his doctoral dissertation at Virginia Tech.

qualified for the job itself, although not for the examination. In equilibrium, individuals choosing to take a civil service job would expect about the same discounted lifetime earnings as if they had taken a job in private industry which had an inherent requirement for higher quality labor than in the civil service job.

There is a significant social cost in the sense that the jobs are held by people whose native capacity is such that they could hold better jobs equally well. For example, the private post offices that are now so successfully competing with the government Postal Service, in those areas where they are legal, normally hire much lower quality labor and pay a much lower wage than does the Postal Service. It should be emphasized that, although this is true, they also get much more work from their employees. A custom of working only part of the day has developed in the Postal Service, and many letter carriers are done with their day's work in much less than an eight-hour stint.[8]

In the particular case of the civil service employees, the initial increase in their wages is essentially a pure transfer. It is only with time, as the higher wages attract higher quality labor, that a social cost not connected with the transfer itself is generated. With respect to most of the other activities we have discussed, however, the benefit received by beneficiaries comes by way of a change in the economy which is not, in and of itself, a pure transfer. They are given monopoly privileges of some sort in most cases.

Any economist will, of course, say that pure transfers are better as a way of transferring money than the establishment of monopoly privileges. Indeed, in the case of agricultural subsidy programs, it used to be quite common for economists to demonstrate that all the beneficiaries could be given the same benefit for a small fraction of the cost to the rest of the population.

This argument is a little oversimple because it starts by assuming the total cost to the transfer is simply its tax rate. Of course, there is also an excess burden attached to each tax, and this excess burden, as in Figure 1, can be substantially identical to the excess burden of the monopoly. Nevertheless, it must be admitted that if you look over the set of government institutions which are used to generate special benefits for special groups, it is usually true that a well designed set of taxes could generate the same revenue for the beneficiaries at much lower cost to the victims.

Why, then, is the less-efficient technique adopted? So far as I know, there are only two explanations for this. The first, which is fairly old, is based on

8. "Mail Carrier Likes His Job," *Washington Post* (June 14, 1974): A-7.

the information cost.[9] Not to repeat here the full details of the argument,[10] it is simply that the pushing through of such a benefit for a special class requires that the cost of the benefit not be obvious to the very much larger collection of voters who will be injured by it. This, in turn, requires a certain degree of complexity in the subsidy and direct cash payment raised out of direct taxes would normally not meet that requirement.

In addition to this argument, Rubin has recently suggested another.[11] He points out that budgetary allocations are reconsidered every year in almost all countries. On the other hand, once an institution has been set up, it is not automatically reexamined on a regular basis, nor does its continued existence require a positive affirmative vote in the legislature. Under the circumstances, then, if a program was set in hand to give me $1 million a year out of the Treasury, I would have to face a series of annual votes on that $1 million. If, on the other hand, the laws were rearranged in such a way that I got a monopoly worth $1 million a year, this monopoly would remain in existence (and probably largely unnoticed) until such time as positive effort was made to terminate it. In the first case, I would have to have returned to the lobbying effort every year; whereas in the second case, once I get it, I keep it until something untoward happens.

Rubin points out that under these circumstances pressure groups would prefer the type of preferential benefit which does not require continuous budgetary appropriations, simply because it is cheaper. They only have to make one lobbying effort and then perhaps a defense seven or eight years later, if the issue comes up for further discussion. This is quite different from running a continual lobby to raise the issue every year as part of the budget process.

Whether one or the other (or both) of these explanations is correct, or whether there is a third which either replaces or supplements these, is not of vital importance to our present concerns. It is certainly true that this type of institution is very widely found in our society and the social cost is great. It is also true that, in general, the benefits are now long in the past. They were transitional benefits at the time the institution was first founded. As of now,

9. See G. Tullock, *Toward a Mathematics of Politics* (Ann Arbor: University of Michigan Press, 1967).

10. Ibid., 103–6.

11. See P. H. Rubin, "On the Form of Special Interest Legislation," *Public Choice* 21 (Spring 1975): 79–90.

there is no one who is positively benefiting from the organization and there is a large deadweight loss. However, there is a large number of people who would suffer large transitional costs if the institution were terminated. These transitional costs in many cases are large enough so that compensation of the losers would impose upon society an excess burden which would be of the same order of magnitude as the cost of the present institution.

6. *Summary and Conclusion*

It is hard for an economist to recommend any positive action to deal with this kind of situation. It is, as the title of this article suggests, a trap. I can recommend very strongly that we try to avoid getting into such traps in the future, but what about the ones into which we have already fallen? In those cases where there are efficiency gains from reorganizing the industry, we could presumably compensate the present beneficiaries; but the political possibilities seem to me to be very small. In those cases where the excess burden on the necessary tax for compensation would be as great as the deadweight loss, this alternative is not available even in theory. Granted the omnipresence of institutions of this sort and their very large deadweight loss, it is conceivable that simultaneously abolishing all of them would lead to a net gain for almost everyone. The individual would lose his particular privilege, but would gain from the loss of privileges of other people. It is doubtful that such a change would be truly Pareto optimal, but it might come close. As to its political practicality, I take it I do not have to explain why I think it is low.

The moral of this, on the whole, depressing tale is that we should try to avoid getting into this kind of trap in the future. Our predecessors have made bad mistakes and we are stuck with them, but we can at least make efforts to prevent our descendants from having even more such deadweight losses inflicted upon them.

EFFICIENT RENT SEEKING

Most of the papers in this volume implicitly or explicitly assume that rent-seeking activity discounts the entire rent to be derived. Unfortunately, this is not necessarily true; the reality is much more complicated. The problem here is that the average cost and marginal cost are not necessarily identical.

This is surprising because in competitive equilibrium the average cost and marginal cost are equal and rent seeking is usually a competitive industry. If marginal cost is continuously rising, then marginal and average cost will be different.[1] In the ordinary industry the average cost curve of an individual enterprise is usually U-shaped, with economies of scale in the early range and diseconomies of scale in the latter range. In equilibrium, the companies will be operating at the bottom of this cost curve, and therefore average and marginal costs will be equated.

A second and much more important reason for the equality of marginal and average cost is that if there is some resource used in production of anything produced under continuously rising costs, then the owners of that resource will charge the marginal cost. People engaged in manufacturing (or whatever activity with which we are dealing) will face a cost that incorporates these rents of the original factor owners. Thus, the assumption that the costs are constant over scale is suitable for practical use.

Unfortunately, both these reasons are of dubious validity in the case of rent seeking. First, there seem to be no particular economies of scale. As far as we can see, for example, such monster industries as big oil and the natural gas producers do not do as well in dealing with the government as do little oil or, in the gas case, householders. In general, it would appear that there is no range of increasing returns in rent seeking. However, this is admittedly an empirical problem and one for which, at the moment, we have little data. It is, in any event, dangerous to assume that the curves are all U-shaped and competition will adjust us to the minimum point of these curves. This is par-

Reprinted, with permission, from *Toward a Theory of the Rent-Seeking Society*, ed. James M. Buchanan, Robert D. Tollison, and Gordon Tullock (College Station: Texas A&M University Press, 1980), 97–112.

1. This is obviously also true if marginal cost is continuously falling.

ticularly so, since there is no obvious reason why all rent seekers should have identical efficiencies.

The second and more important reason why we can normally assume that supply curves are, in the long run, flat is that if they are continuously rising, factory owners can generally achieve the full rent by selling their factors at their marginal value; hence, the enterprises face essentially flat supply prices. Unfortunately, this has only a limited application in rent seeking. Suppose, for example, that we organize a lobby in Washington for the purpose of raising the price of milk and are unsuccessful. We cannot simply transfer our collection of contacts, influences, past bribes, and so forth to the steel manufacturers' lobby. In general, our investments are too specialized, and, in many cases, they are matters of very particular and detailed good will to a specific organization. It is true that we could sell the steel lobby our lobbyists with their connections and perhaps our mailing list. But presumably all these things have been bought by us at their proper cost. Our investment has not paid, but there is nothing left to transfer.

Similarly, the individual lobbyist spends much time cultivating congressmen and government officials and learning the ins and outs of government regulations. There is no way he can simply transfer these contacts, connections, and knowledge to a younger colleague if he wishes to change his line of business. The younger colleague must start at the bottom and work his way up. Thus, it seems likely that in most rent-seeking cases, the supply curve slants up and to the right from its very beginning. This means that rent-seeking activities are very likely to have different marginal and average costs, even if we can find an equilibrium.

It might seem that with continuously upward sloping supply curves and a competitive industry, there would be no equilibrium. This turns out not to be true, although the equilibrium is of a somewhat unusual nature. The analytical tools required to deal with it are drawn more from game theory than from classical economics.

In my article, "On the Efficient Organization of Trials,"[2] I introduced a game that I thought had much resemblance to a court trial or, indeed, to any other two-party conflict. In its simplest form, we assume two parties are participating in a lottery under somewhat unusual rules. Each is permitted to buy as many lottery tickets as he wishes at one dollar each, the lottery tickets

2. Gordon Tullock, "On the Efficient Organization of Trials," *Kyklos* 28 (1975): 745–62.

are put in a drum, one is pulled out, and whoever owns that ticket wins the prize. Thus, the probability of success for A is shown in equation (1), because the number of lottery tickets he holds is amount A and the total number in the drum is $A + B$.

$$P_A = \frac{A}{A + B} \tag{1}$$

In the previously cited article, I pointed out that this model could be generalized by making various modifications in it, and it is my purpose now to generalize it radically.[3]

Let us assume, then, that a wealthy eccentric has put up $100 as a prize for the special lottery between A and B. Note that the amount spent on lottery tickets is retained by the lottery, not added onto the prize. This makes the game equivalent to rent seeking, where resources are also wasted.

How much should each invest? It is obvious that the answer to this question, from the standpoint of each party, depends on what he thinks the other will do. Here, and throughout the rest of this paper, I am going to use a rather special assumption about individual knowledge. I am going to assume that if there is a correct solution for individual strategy, then each player will assume that the other parties can also figure out what that correct solution is. In other words, if the correct strategy in this game were to play $50, each party would assume that the other was playing $50 and would only buy fifty tickets for himself, if that were the optimal amount under those circumstances.

As a matter of fact, the optimal strategy in this game is not to buy $50 worth of tickets but to buy $25. As a very simple explanation, suppose that I have bought $25 and you have bought $50. I have a one-in-three chance of getting the $100, and you have a two-in-three chance. Thus, the present value of my investment is $33.33 and the present value of yours is $66.66, or, for this particular case, an equal percentage gain. Suppose, however, that you decided to reduce your purchases to $40 and I stayed at $25. This saves you $10 on your investment, but it lowers your present value of expectancy to only $61.53 and you are about $5 better off. Of course, I have gained from your reduction, too.

3. For a previous generalization of the model and an application to arms races, see Gordon Tullock, *The Social Dilemma: The Economics of War and Revolution* (Blacksburg, Va.: Center for Study of Public Choice, 1974), 87–125.

You could continue reducing your bet with profit until you also reached \$25. For example, if you lowered your purchase from \$26 to \$25, the present value of your investment would fall from \$50.98 to \$50, and you would save \$1 in investment. Going beyond \$25, however, would cost you money. If you lowered it to \$24, you would reduce the value of your investment by \$1.02 and only save \$1. It is assumed, of course, that I keep my purchase at \$25.

I suppose it is obvious from what I have said already that \$25 is equilibrium for both, that is, departure from it costs either one something. It is not true, however, that if the other party has made a mistake, I maximize my returns by paying \$25. For example, if the other party has put up \$50 and I pay \$24 instead of \$25, I save \$1 in my investment but reduce my expectancy by only \$0.90. My optimal investment, in fact, is \$17. However, if we assume a game in which each party knows what the other party has invested and then each adjusts his investment accordingly, the ultimate outcome must be at approximately \$25 for each party.[4] The game is clearly a profitable one to play, and, in fact, it will impress the average economist as rather improbable. However, it is a case in which inframarginal profits are made, although we are in marginal balance. At first glance, most people feel that the appropriate bet is \$50, but that is bringing the total return into equality with the total cost rather than equating the margins.

To repeat, this line of reasoning depends on the assumption that the individuals can figure out the correct strategy, if there is a correct strategy, and that they assume that the other people will be able to figure it out, also. It is similar to the problem that started John von Neumann on the invention of game theory, and I think it is not too irrational a set of assumptions if we assume the kind of problem that rent seeking raises.

But there is no reason why the odds in our game should be a simple linear function of contributions. For example, they could be an exponential function, as in equation (2):

$$P_A = \frac{A^r}{A^r + B^r} \qquad (2)$$

4. It would make no difference in the reasoning here, or in any of the following work, if there were an insurance company always willing to buy a bid at its true actuarial value. For example, if you had put in \$25, and the other party had also put in \$25, it would give you \$50 for it, and if you had put in \$26, and the other party \$25, it would give you \$50.98. But rent seeking normally involves risk, and hence I have kept the examples in the risky form.

TABLE 1. *Individual Investments (N-person, No Bias, with Exponent)*

	NUMBER OF PLAYERS			
EXPONENT	2	4	10	15
1/3	8.33	6.25	3.00	2.07
1/2	12.50	9.37	4.50 I	3.11
1	25.00	18.75	9.00	6.22
2	50.00	37.50	18.00	12.44
3	75.00	56.25	27.00	18.67
5	125.00	93.75	45.00 II	31.11
8	200.00	150.00	72.00	49.78
12	300.00	225.00 III	108.00	74.67

There are, of course, many other functions that could be substituted, but in this paper we will stick to exponentials.

It is also possible for more than two people to play, in which case we would have equation (3):

$$P_A = \frac{A^r}{A^r + B^r, \ldots, n^r} \tag{3}$$

The individuals need not receive the same return on their investment. Indeed, in many cases we would hope that the situation is biased. For example, we hope that the likelihood of passing a civil service examination is not simply a function of the amount of time spent cramming, but that other types of merit are also important. This would be shown in our equations by some kind of bias in which one party receives more lottery tickets for his money than another.

We will begin by changing the shape of the marginal cost curve and the number of people playing, and leave bias until later. Table 1 shows the individual equilibrium payments by players of the game, with varying exponents (which means varying marginal cost structures) and varying numbers of players. Table 2 shows the total amount paid by all of the players, if they all play the equilibrium strategy.

I have drawn lines dividing these two tables into zones I, II, and III. Let us temporarily confine ourselves to discussing zone I. This is the zone in which the equilibrium price summed over all players leads to a payment equal to or less than the total price. In other words, these are the games in which expectancy of the players, if they all play, would be positive. Although we

TABLE 2. ***Sum of Investments (N-Person, No Bias, with Exponent)***

	NUMBER OF PLAYERS					
EXPONENT	2	4	10	15		LIMIT
1/3	16.66	25.00	30.00	31.05		33.30
1/2	25.00	37.40	45.00	46.65	I	50.00
1	50.00	75.00	90.00	93.30		100.00
2	100.00	150.00	180.00	186.60		200.00
3	150.00	225.00	270.00	280.05		300.00
5	250.00	375.00	450.00	466.65	II	500.00
8	400.00	600.00	720.00	746.70		800.00
12	600.00	900.00	1,080.00 III	1,120.05		1,200.00

will start with these games, as we shall see below there are cases in which we may be compelled to play games in zones II and III where the expectancy is negative.

If we look at zone I, it is immediately obvious that the individual payments go down as the number of players rises, but the total amount paid rises. In a way, what is happening here is that a monopoly profit is being competed away. Note, however, when the exponent is one-third or one-half, even in the limit there is profit of $66.66 or $50.00 to the players taken as a whole. Thus, some profit remains. With the cost curve slanting steeply upward, these results are to some extent counterintuitive. One might assume that with a positive return on investment, it will always be sensible for more players to enter, thereby driving down the profits. In this case, however, each additional player lowers the payments of all the preceding players and his own, and the limit as the number of players goes to infinity turns out to be one where that infinity of players has, at least in expectancy terms, sizable profits.

Throughout the table, in zones I, II, and III, individual payments go down as we move from left to right, and total payments rise. We can deduce a policy implication from this, although it is a policy implication to which many people may object on moral grounds. It would appear that if one is going to distribute rents, nepotism is a good thing because it reduces the number of players and, therefore, the total investment. This is one of the classical arguments for hereditary monarchies. By reducing the number of candidates for an extremely rent-rich job to one, you eliminate such rent-seeking activities as civil war, assassination, and so forth. Of course, there are costs here. If we reduce the number of people who may compete for a given job, you may eliminate the best candidate or even the best two thousand candidates. This cost must be offset against the reduction in rent-seeking costs.

On the other hand, many cases of rent seeking are not ones in which we care particularly who gets the rent. In such matters as government appointments where there are large incomes from illegal sources, pressure groups obtaining special aid from the government, and so on, we would prefer that there be no rent at all, and, if there must be rent, it does not make much difference to whom it goes. In these cases, clearly measures to reduce rent seeking are unambiguous gains. Thus, if Mayor Richard Daley had confined all of the more lucrative appointments to his close relatives, the social savings might have been considerable.

If we go down the table, the numbers also steadily rise. Looking at two players, for example, from an exponent of one-third, which represents an extremely steeply rising cost curve, to an exponent of two, which is much flatter, we get a sixfold increase in the individual and total payments. This also suggests a policy conclusion. On the whole, it would be desirable to establish institutions so that the marginal cost is very steeply rising. For example, civil servants' examinations should be, as far as possible, designed so that the return on cramming is low, or, putting it another way, so that the marginal cost of improving one's grade is rapidly rising. Similarly, it is better if the political appointments of the corrupt governments are made quickly and rather arbitrarily, so that not so many resources are invested in rent seeking.

Once again, however, there is a cost. It may be hard to design civil service examinations so that they are difficult to prepare for and yet make efficient selections.[5] Here again, if we are dealing with appointments to jobs that we would rather not have exist, the achievement of profits through political manipulations and the like, there is no particular loss in moving down our table. Thus, laws that make it more expensive or more difficult to influence the government—such as the campaign contribution laws—may have considerable net gain by making the rise in marginal cost steeper. There is a considerable expense involved, however. The actual restrictions placed on campaign contributions are designed in a highly asymmetrical manner, so that they increase the cost for some potential lobbyists and not for others. Whether there is a net social gain from this process is hard to say.

5. There is another solution, which is to put the civil service salary at the same level as equivalent private salaries. Under these circumstances, there would be no rent seeking. Given the political power of civil servants, however, I doubt that this would be possible.

So much for zone I; let us now turn to zones II and III. In zone II, the sum of the payments made by the individual players is greater than the prize; in other words, it is a negative-sum game instead of a positive-sum game as in zone I. In zone III, the individual players make payments that are higher than the prize. It might seem obvious that no one would play games of this sort, but, unfortunately, this is not true.

Before von Neumann began his work on the theory of games, students of probability divided gambling situations into two categories: pure chance and games of strategy. We may take two simple examples. If Smith flips a coin and Jones calls the outcome, we have a game of pure chance, provided only that Smith does not have enough skill actually to control the coin. This is so even if the coin is not a fair one, although Jones might not properly calculate the odds under those circumstances. In this game, the properly calculated, but mathematical, odds are fifty-fifty, and there is no great problem.

Consider, however, a very similar game, in which Smith chooses which side of the coin will be up and covers it with his hand until Jones calls either heads or tails. The coin is then uncovered, and if Jones has properly called the bet, Smith pays him; if he has not, Jones pays Smith. This is a game of strategy. The early writers in this case reasoned that there was no proper solution to the game, because if there were a proper solution, both parties could figure it out. Thus, for example, if the proper thing for Smith to do was to play heads, he would know that Jones would know that this was the proper thing to do; hence, the proper thing for Smith to do would be to play tails. Of course, if the proper thing is to play tails, then Jones will also know that; therefore, the proper thing to do is to play heads. It will be seen that this is an example of the paradox of the liar.

The early students of probability argued that in circumstances like these there was no proper solution and referred to it as a game of strategy, which was roughly equivalent to throwing up their hands. In games of this sort, von Neumann discovered that there might be (not necessarily was, but might be) a solution. In the particular case of coin matching, there is no simple solution, but in many real-world situations there could be a strategy for Smith that he would still retain even though Jones could figure it out and make the best reply.

If there was such a strategy, it was called a saddle point. Von Neumann also pointed out that one should consider not only pure strategies but also mixed strategies. Further, in zero-sum games there is always some mixed strategy that has a saddle point. This proof can also be extended to differential games, which are the kind of games we are now discussing, but, unfortunately, it applies only to zero-sum games, and our games are not zero-sum.[6]

A broader concept of equilibrium was developed by Nash, but unfortunately the games in zones II and III have a very pronounced discontinuity at 0. In consequence, there is no Nash equilibrium. These games have neither dominant pure strategies, saddle points, nor dominant mixed strategies. They are games of strategy in the older sense of the word, games for which we can offer no solution.

Let us here reexamine the idea of a solution in order to make this clear. If there is such a solution, anyone can compute it. Thus, Smith must choose his strategy knowing that Jones will know what he is going to do. Similarly, Jones must choose knowing that Smith will be able to predict accurately what he will do. There is no law of nature that says all games will have solutions of this sort, and these, unfortunately, are in a category that do not.

For a simple example, consider the game shown on table 1 in which there are two players, Smith and Jones again, and assume that the exponent on the cost function is 3. The individual payment is shown as $75, and the result of the two players putting up $75 is that they will jointly pay $150 for $100. Each is paying $75 for a fifty-fifty chance on $50, which appears to be stupid.

However, let us run through the line of reasoning that may lead the two parties to a $75 investment. Suppose, for example, that we start with both parties at $50. Smith raises to $51. With the exponent of 3, the increase in the probability that he will win is worth more than $1—in fact, considerably more. If Jones counters, he also gains more than $1 by his investment. By a series of small steps of this sort, each one of which is a profitable investment, the two parties will eventually reach $75, at which point there is no motive for either one to raise or lower his bid by any small amount. They are in marginal adjustment, even though the total conditions are very obviously not satisfied.

But what of the total conditions? For example, suppose that Jones decides not to play. Obviously, his withdrawal means that Smith is guaranteed success, and, indeed, he will probably regret that he has $75 down rather than $1, but, still, he is going to make a fairly good profit on his investment.

Here we are back in the trap of the coin-matching games. If the best thing

6. Except, of course, for those games which lie along the boundary between zone I and zone II.

to do, the rational strategy, in this game is not to play, then obviously the sensible thing to do is to put in $1. On the other hand, if the rational strategy is to play, and one can anticipate the other party will figure that out, too, so that he will invest, then the rational thing to do is to stay out, because you are going to end up with parties investing at $75. There is no stable solution.

Games like this occur many times in the real world. Poker, as it is actually played, is an example, and most real-world negotiations are also examples of this sort of thing; in the case of poker, there is no social waste, because the parties are presumably deriving entertainment from the game. Negotiations, although they always involve at least some waste, may involve fairly small amounts because the waste involved in strategic maneuvering may be more than compensated by the transfer of information that may permit achievement of a superior outcome. But in our game this is not possible. In the real world there may be some such effect that partially offsets the waste of the rent seeking. In most rent-seeking cases, however, it is clear that this offset is only partial, and in many cases of rent seeking the activity from which the rent will be derived is, in and of itself, of negative social value. Under these circumstances, not only do we have the waste of rent seeking, we also have the net social waste imposed by the rent itself.

In the real world, the solution to rent seeking is rather apt to end up at $75 in our particular case instead of at zero, because normally the game does not permit bets, once placed, to be withdrawn. In other words, the sunk costs are truly sunk; you cannot withdraw your bid. For example, if I decide to cram for an examination or invest a certain amount of money in a lobby in Washington that is intended to increase the salaries of people studying public choice, once the money is spent, I cannot get it back. If it turns out that I am in this kind of competitive game, the sunk-cost aspect of the existing investment means that I will continue making further investments in competition with other people studying for the examination or in hiring lobbyists. In a way, the fact that there is an optimal amount—that even with the previous costs all sunk we will not go beyond $75 in the particular example we are now using—is encouraging. Although sunk costs are truly sunk, there is still a limit to the amount that will be invested in the game.

Note that this game has a possible precommitment strategy.[7] If one of the parties can get his $75 in first and make it clear that it will not be withdrawn,

7. Thomas C. Schelling, *The Strategy of Conflict* (Cambridge, Mass.: Harvard University Press, 1960).

the sensible policy for the second party is to play zero; hence, the party who precommits makes, on this particular game, a profit of $25.

Unfortunately, this analysis, although true, is not very helpful. It simply means that there is another precommitment game played. We would have to investigate the parameters of that game, as well as the parameters of the game shown in tables 1 and 2, and determine the sum of the resources invested in both. Offhand, it would appear that most precommitment games would be extremely expensive because it is necessary to make large investments on very little information. You must be willing to move before other people, and this means moving when you are badly informed.[8] But, in any event, this precommitment game would have some set of parameters, and, if we investigate them and then combine them with the parameters of the game that you precommit, we would obtain the total cost. I doubt that this would turn out to be a low amount of social waste.

The situation is even more bizarre in zone III. Here the equilibrium involves each of the players' investing more than the total prize offered. It is perhaps sensible to reemphasize the meaning of the payments show in table 1. They are the payments that would be reached if all parties, properly calculating what the others would do, made minor adjustments in their bids and finally reached the situation where they stopped in proper marginal adjustment. They are not in total equilibrium, of course.

Once again, the simple rule—do not play such games—is not correct, because if it were the correct rule, then anyone who violated it could make large profits. Consider a particular game invented by Geoffrey Brennan, which is the limit of table 1 as the exponent is raised to infinity. In this game, $100 is put up and will be sold to the highest bidder, but all the bids are retained; that is, when you put in a bid, you cannot reduce it. Under these circumstances, no one would put in an initial bid of more than $100, but it is not at all obvious what one *should* put in. Further, assume that the bids, once made, cannot be withdrawn but can be raised. Under these circumstances, there is no equilibrium maximum bid. In other words, it is always sensible to increase your bid above its present level if less than $100 will make you the highest

8. As an amusing sidelight on this problem, a referee of an earlier draft of this paper objected to my above paragraph on the ground that the first party should not put in $75 but some smaller number closer to $55 that would be enough to bar the other party. Note, however, that if one paused to figure out the actual optimal number, the other party would get in first with his $75.

bidder. The dangers are obvious, but it is also obvious that refusal to play the game is not an equilibrium strategy, because of the paradox of the liar mentioned above.

In games in zones II and III, formal theory can say little. Clearly, these are areas where the ability to guess what other people will do, interpret facial expressions, and so on, pays off very highly. They are also areas where it is particularly likely that very large wastes will be incurred by society as a whole. Unfortunately, it seems likely that rent seeking is apt to lead to these areas in some cases.

Obviously, as a good social policy, we should try to avoid having games that are likely to lead to this kind of waste. Again, we should try to arrange that the payoff to further investment in resources is comparatively low, or, in other words, that the cost curve points sharply upward.

One way to lower the social costs is to introduce bias into the selection process. Note that we normally refer to bias as a bad thing, but one could be biased in the direction of the correct decision. For example, a civil service exam might be so designed that it is very likely to pick out people who have the necessary natural traits and is very hard to prepare for. This would be bias in favor of the appropriate traits, but it would be a desirable thing. Similarly, we would like to have court proceedings biased in such a way that whoever is on the right side need not make very large investments in order to win, and if this is true, the people on the wrong side will not make very large investments either, because they do not pay.

On the other hand, bias can be something which, at least morally, is incorrect. We referred above to Mayor Daley's appointments of his relatives, and this would be a kind of bias. In that particular case, presumably bias would reduce total rent seeking and not lower the functional efficiency of the government of Chicago, but there are many cases where this kind of bias *would* lower efficiency.

Bias, it will be seen, is rather similar to the restriction on the number of players we have discussed above. Instead of totally cutting off some players, we differentially weigh the players. For example, assume that player *A* is given five times as many coupons for his one-dollar investment as are the other players. This would bias the game in his favor, although not to the extreme of prohibiting others from buying tickets. This kind of bias, once again, is rather similar to designing your examination to select natural traits. If player *A* can, with one hour of cramming, increase his probable score on a civil service exam as much as can player *B* with five hours of cramming, then

TABLE 3. ***Individual Investments (Two-Party, Bias, Exponent)***

	BIAS			
EXPONENT	2	4	10	15
1	22.22	16.00	8.30	5.90
2	44.44	32.00 I	16.53	11.72
3	66.67	48.00	24.79	17.58
5	111.11	80.00	41.32	29.30
8	177.78	128.00	66.12 II	46.88
12	266.67	192.00 III	99.17	70.31

the system is biased in favor of A, and we would anticipate that the total cost of rent seeking would go down.

Let us now turn to table 3. In this table, we have only two parties competing because the situation is mathematically complex and, in any event, having more than two parties would require a three-dimensional diagram. Along the top is the degree of bias toward one player, which is measured here simply in the number of tickets he gets per dollar, it being assumed that the less-advantaged player gets one ticket per dollar. We have omitted the lower exponents of table 1, because it is immediately obvious that bias very sharply reduces total rent seeking.

Table 4 is the sum over both players of all the payments shown in table 3, and, in this case, they always just double the figures in table 3.

It turns out that, using our simple mathematical apparatus, both players—the one who is favored by the bias and the one who is not—make the same investment. This is a little counterintuitive, but not very, since most of us do not have very strong intuitions on these matters. In any event, it may simply be an artifact of the particular mathematical formalism we have chosen.

It will be noted immediately that zone I is much larger in this case than in the unbiased cases of tables 1 and 2. Indeed, even with an exponent of 8—which means an extremely flat cost curve—a bias of 15 leads to the game still being in zone I. Thus, such bias does pay off heavily in reducing rent seeking.

It is also true that this kind of bias, in general, is easier to arrange by socially desirable techniques than the earlier suggestions made to reduce rent seeking. Once again, designing personnel selection procedures so that they select the best man at relatively low cost to him is an example. Another would be some kind of policy selection process that was heavily biased in favor of efficient, or "right," policies. Both these techniques, if we could design them, would have large payoffs, not only in reducing rent-seeking activity but also in increasing efficiency of government in general. Thus, it seems to me that

TABLE 4. *Sum of Investments (Two-Party, Bias, Exponent)*

	BIAS			
EXPONENT	2	4	10	15
1	44.44	32.00	16.60	11.80
2	88.88	64.00 I	30.06	23.44
3	133.34	96.00	49.58	35.16
5	222.22	160.00	82.64	58.60
8	355.56	256.00	132.24	93.76
12	533.34	384.00 III	198.34 II	140.62

introducing this rather special kind of bias into rent seeking would be desirable in many areas, even if we ignore the rent-seeking savings.

However, for many rent-seeking activities, it is admittedly very hard to find a way to introduce bias at all or to introduce bias in a way that leads to better outcomes. Once again, if we assume that Mayor Daley does not restrict his appointments to his relatives but simply gives relatives a differential advantage, depending on how close they are to him, we have a bias system that will reduce rent seeking. However, it will not lead to outcomes in any way superior. Similarly, the restrictions placed on campaign contributions and other methods of attempting to influence government policy are biased in the sense that they are heavier burdens for some people than for others, and it is not clear whether this bias will lead to policy choices superior to those obtained without it. Thus, the only gain is the possibility of reduction in total rent seeking.

Thus ends our preliminary investigation of rent seeking and ways to reduce its social cost. When I have discussed the problem with colleagues, I have found that the intellectually fascinating problem of zones II and III tends to dominate the discussion. This is, indeed, intellectually very interesting, but the real problem we face is the attempt to lower the cost of rent seeking, and this will normally move us into zone I. Thus, I hope that the result of this paper is not mathematical examination of the admittedly fascinating intellectual problems of zones II and III, but practical investigation of methods to lower the cost of rent seeking.

Mathematical Appendix, or Labor-Saving Calculation Methods

When I first began working on this paper, I discovered that the equations that would have to be solved were higher-order equations, and therefore simply assigned to my graduate assistant, William J. Hunter, the job of approximating the results by using a pocket calculator. He promptly discovered the rather astonishing regularity of column 1, which implied that it would not be all that difficult to solve the equations even if they were higher order. Before I had had time to do anything other than shudder vaguely about the problem, however, I went to lunch with my colleague, Nicolaus Tideman, told him the problem, and he solved it on a napkin. This gave us the equation for tables 1 and 2. Having discovered this simple algorithm, when we wanted to prepare tables 3 and 4, once again we asked Tideman, and he obliged with equal speed. The equations used are:

$$P_A = R\frac{N - 1}{N^2} \qquad \text{(Tables 1, 2)}$$

$$P_A = R\frac{b}{(b + 1)^2} \qquad \text{(Tables 3, 4)}$$

where

P_A = equilibrium investment,

R = exponent, or the determinant of steepness of the supply curve,

N = number of players, and

b = bias weight.

RENT SEEKING

The term "rent-seeking" was introduced by Ann O. Krueger,[1] but the relevant theory had already been developed by Gordon Tullock.[2] The basic and very simple idea is best explained by reference to Figure 1. On the horizontal axis we have as usual the quantity of some commodity sold, on the vertical axis its price. Under competitive conditions the cost would be the line labelled PP and that would also be its price. Given a demand curve, DD, quantity Q would be sold at that price. If a monopoly were organized, it would sell Q′ units at a price of P′.

The traditional theory of monopoly argued that the net loss to society is shown by the shaded triangle, which represents the consumer surplus that would have been derived from the purchase of those units between Q′ and Q, that are now neither purchased nor produced. The dotted rectangle, on the other hand, has traditionally been regarded simply as a transfer from the consumers to the monopolist. Since they are all members of the same society, there is no net social loss from this transfer.

This argument tends to annoy students of elementary economics (because they don't like monopolists), but until the development of the work on rent seeking it was nevertheless thought to be correct by most economists. Its basic problem, however, is that it assumes that the monopoly is created in a costless manner, perhaps by an act of God, whereas in fact real resources are used to create monopolies.

Most discussion of rent seeking has tended to concentrate on those monopolies that are government created or protected, probably because these are observed to be the commonest and strongest. It should be kept in mind, however, that purely private monopolies are possible—indeed, some actually exist. Concentration on government-created monopolies (or restrictions of various sorts that increase certain people's income) is probably reasonable,

Reprinted, with permission of Palgrave Macmillan, from *The New Palgrave: A Dictionary of Economics*, vol. 4, ed. John Eatwell, Murray Milgate, and Peter Newman (London: Macmillan, 1987), 147–49.

1. A. O. Krueger, "The Political Economy of the Rent-Seeking Society," *American Economic Review* 64 (1974): 291–303.

2. G. Tullock, "The Welfare Cost of Tariffs, Monopolies, and Theft," *Western Economic Journal* (now *Economic Inquiry*) 5 (1967): 224–32.

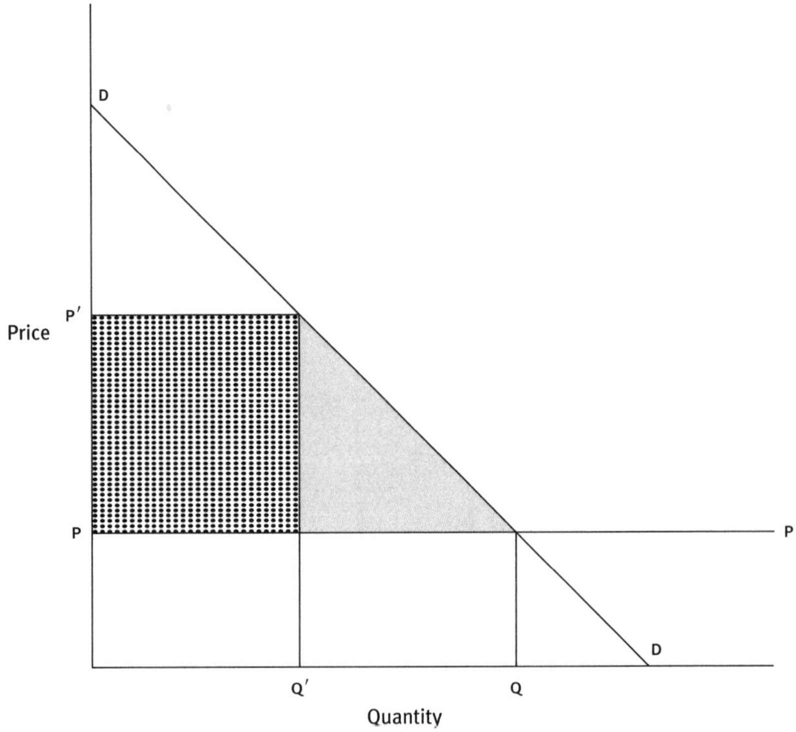

FIGURE 1

granted the contemporary frequency of such activities. Nevertheless, as we point out below there are certain significant areas where private rent seeking causes net social loss.

In the initial work both of Tullock and Krueger it was assumed that profit-seeking businessmen would be willing to use resources in an effort to obtain a monopoly, whether it was privately or government sponsored, up to the point where the last dollar so invested exactly counterbalanced the improved probability of obtaining the monopoly. From this it was deduced that the entire dotted rectangle (Figure 1) would be exhausted. Although this assumption is open to question,[3] for the time being we will continue to assume that in effect there is no transfer from purchasers to the monopolist, but simply a

3. See G. Tullock, "Efficient Rent Seeking," in J. Buchanan, R. Tollison, and G. Tullock, eds., *Toward a Theory of the Rent-Seeking Society* (College Station: Texas A&M University Press, 1980), 91–112.

social loss which comes from the fact that resources have been invested in unproductive activity, i.e. the negatively productive activity of creating a trade restriction of some sort. Theoretical reasons exist for believing that this assumption probably does not fit perfectly anywhere, but it is just as likely to overestimate as to underestimate the social cost; it will be discussed more thoroughly below.

To quote an aphorism frequently used in rent seeking: "the activity of creating monopolies is a competitive industry." For this reason it is anticipated that quite a number of people at any given time are putting at least some resources into an effort to secure a monopoly, only some of whom are successful. The situation is like a lottery, in which many people buy lottery tickets, a few win a very large amount of money and the rest lose, perhaps large or small amounts, depending on how much they have committed. In almost all existing lotteries, of course, the total investment of resources by the gamblers is considerably greater than the total payoff, whereas here it is still assumed that total resources committed to rent seeking equal the total monopoly profits.

Thus the activity of creating monopolies could both absorb very large resources, particularly those resources that take the form of exceptionally talented individuals who devote their attention to this difficult and highly rewarded activity, and lead to considerable redistribution of wealth in the community. Suppose that ten different lobbyists go to Washington representing ten different associations, and each spends one million dollars over the course of a couple of years in the hope of influencing Congress to provide them with a monopoly. Only one of the lobbyists is successful and the monopoly turns out to have a present discounted value of ten million dollars. There is a substantial redistribution of resources from the unsuccessful lobbyists to the successful.

This substantial redistribution has occurred simultaneously with a considerable waste of resources in general, both because these highly intelligent people could otherwise be doing something of higher productivity and because the economy's use of resources has been further distorted by the creation of the monopoly. Further, although so far the discussion has been primarily about monopoly, actually very many possible interventions in the market process raise the same problem. A simple maximum or minimum price may have very large redistributive effects and the people who thus benefit may put considerable resources into receiving them. Of course there are many situations in which one lobbyist is pushing for a particular restriction and another lobbyist is pushing against it. The second activity is sometimes called “rent avoidance,” but it is costly and of course would not exist if there were not also rent seeking activity.

Another area is simple direct transfers. A tax on A for the purpose of paying B will lead to lobbying activity for the tax on the part of B and against it on the part of A. The total of these two lobbying activities could very well equal the total amount transferred (or prevented from being transferred), although one or other of these entrepreneurs will of course gain if his lobby is successful. Assume that A puts in $50 for lobbying to get $100 from B, and B puts in $50 lobbying against that. Regardless of the outcome, one party will gain $50 from his lobbying. Society has lost $100.

Of course it is not true that everyone in society is in an equally good position to seek rents. Some kinds of interest are more readily organized than others and we would anticipate that they would win. There are however very many such interests and anyone who spends any time in Washington quickly realizes that there is a major industry engaged in just this kind of activity.

Actual social cost however is clearly very much greater than the mere cost of the various lobbying organizations in Washington. In particular it is normally necessary for the rent seeking group to undertake directly productive activities in a way that is markedly inefficient, because it is necessary to introduce a certain element of deception into the process. In 1937, when the US Civil Aeronautics Board was organized, it would not have been politically feasible to put a direct tax on purchasers of airline tickets and use it to pay off the stockholders of the airline companies. Regulation, which has a similar effect but at a very much higher cost to the users of airlines per dollar of profit to the owners, was, however, politically possible. The necessity of using inefficient methods of transferring funds to the potential beneficiary, because the efficient methods would be just too open and above board, is often one of the major costs of rent seeking. The rent avoidance lobbyist would have had too easy a time if the proposal had been a tax on uses of airlines for the benefit of the stockholders.

Note that in this case the argument against rent seeking turns out also to be an argument against political corruption. Suppose you are in a society which has an exchange control system and that it is possible to buy foreign currency by bribing an official in the exchange control office. This is the kind of situation dealt with by Krueger,[4] who was able to obtain a measure of the total social cost in Turkey and India where the amounts of the necessary

4. Krueger, “The Political Economy of the Rent-Seeking Society.”

bribes were well known; the cost varied from 7–15 per cent of the total volume of transactions.

Traditionally economists have tended to view this kind of bribery as in itself desirable, because it gets around an undesirable regulation. However, it leads to rent seeking. In this case the rent seeking does not come from the users of the permits but from the competition to get into the position where you can receive the bribe. Throughout the underdeveloped world, large numbers of people take fairly elaborate educational programmes which have no real practical value for their future life and engage in long periods of complicated political manoeuvring in hope that they will be appointed, let us say, a customs inspector in Bombay. Since these young men have a free career choice presumably the expected returns from this career are the same as in any other. The difference is that a doctor, say, begins earning money immediately on completing medical school whereas the young man who has studied economics and is now trying to obtain appointment as customs inspector will have a considerable period of time in which he is not appointed at all. Indeed, there will probably be enough such candidates that he has only perhaps one chance in five of being so appointed. The total cost of the rent seeking is the inappropriate education and the political manoeuvring of the five people of whom only one is appointed.

So far we have assumed that the total cost of rent seeking is the present discounted value of the income stream represented by the dotted rectangle in Figure 1. This assumes a special form for the function which "produces" the monopoly or other privilege. It must be linear, with each dollar invested having exactly the same payoff in probability of achieving the monopoly as the previous dollar.[5] Most functions do not have this form; instead they are either increasing or decreasing cost functions.

If the organizing of private monopolies, or of influencing the government into giving you public monopolies, is subject to diseconomies of scale, then total investment in rent seeking will be less than the total value of the rents derived even if we assumed a completely competitive market with completely free entry. When there are economies of scale the situation is even more unusual. Either there is no equilibrium at all or there is a pseudo-equilibrium, in which total investment to obtain the rents is greater than the rents themselves. This is called a pseudo-equilibrium because although it meets all the mathematical requirements for an equilibrium, it is obviously absurd to as-

5. Tullock, "Efficient Rent Seeking."

sume that people would, to take a single example, pay $75 for a 50-50 chance of $100.

Obviously, what is needed is empirical research and an effort to measure the production functions appropriate to rent seeking. So far, however, no one has been able to develop a very good way of making such measurements. It seems likely that it would be easier to measure the costs of generating political influence than of private monopolies, if only because many of the expenditures used to influence the government appear in accounts in various places. The costs of private monopolies, on the other hand, tend to be much more readily concealed. This does not mean that they do not exist.

The reader has no doubt been wondering what is wrong with rents and why we concern ourselves deeply with rent seeking. The answer to this is that the term itself is an unfortunate one. Obviously, we have nothing against rents when they are generated by, let us say, discovering a cure for cancer and then patenting it. Nor do we object to popular entertainers like Michael Jackson earning immense rents on a rather unusual collection of natural attributes together with a lot of effort on his part to build up his human capital. On the other hand, we do object to the manufacturer of automobiles increasing the rent on his property, and his employees increasing the rent on their union memberships, by organizing a quota against imported cars. All of these things are economic rents, but strictly speaking the term "rent seeking" applies only to the latter. Its meaning might be expanded to seeking rents from activities which are themselves detrimental. The man seeking a cure for cancer is engaged in an activity which clearly is not detrimental to society. Thus we may observe immediately that activities aimed at deriving rents cover a continuum, but that the term "rent seeking" is only used for part of that continuum.

The analysis of "rent seeking" has been one of the most stimulating fields of economic theory in recent years. The realization that the explanation of the social cost of monopoly which was contained in almost every elementary text in economics was wrong, or at the very least seriously incomplete, came as quite a surprise. Revision of a very large part of economic theory in order to take this error into account is necessary. And history also needs to be revised. That J. P. Morgan was an organizer of cartels and monopolies during most of his life is well known, as is the fact that he received very large fees for this, fees which were part of the rent seeking cost of generating these monopolies. It is possible to argue that as a stabilizing factor in the banking system, Morgan more than repaid to the United States the social cost of his monopolistic activities in industry. But that there was a very large rent seeking cost is obvious. This cost is in addition to the deadweight cost of the monopolies.

To date, research on rent seeking has to a considerable extent changed our way of looking at things. We now talk of a great deal of government activity as rent seeking on the part of somebody or other. It was known that special interest existed, but we have traditionally tended to underestimate its cost greatly because we looked only at the deadweight costs of the distortion introduced into the economy. The realization that the actual cost is much greater socially, that the large-scale lobbying industry is truthfully a major social cost, is new although presumably, at all times, anyone who thought about the matter must have realized that these highly talented people could produce more in some other activity.

PART 5

REDISTRIBUTIVE POLITICS

INHERITANCE JUSTIFIED

Although the early economists were interested in investigating the desirability of inheritance, this issue has been subject to relatively little economic discussion in recent years. I have not been able to turn up any serious effort to apply welfare economics to the problem. Nevertheless the problem of justifying inheritance of wealth is still very much with us. A great many people who do not object to other aspects of the capitalist system take exception to the inheritance of wealth. It seems likely that the relative neglect of this subject in recent years has been because those who favored private property regarded inheritance as necessarily entailed in the concept and those who objected to private property felt that inheritance was obviously wrong. As we shall see below, neither of these two positions is apodictically certain.

There have been some what we may call traditional arguments for inheritance. The principal one, of course, is the conservation of capital. This argument, however, as far as I know has never been worked out in any detail nor have modern welfare economics techniques been used to discuss it.[1] There are two other arguments which are occasionally encountered. Some have argued that the heirs of great wealth are free from social pressures. Most of them presumably use this freedom from the burden which the rest of us carry in consumption of leisure time activities. A few, however, like Robert Boyle, use their opportunities to undertake activities which are of great benefit to mankind. It is conceivable that the payoff from this small group of people might be very great. So far as I know, no one has ever examined this matter in any detail.

A final argument, which in a way is related to the argument which will be presented later in this article, is that we permit people to leave their money to

Reprinted, with permission, from *Journal of Law and Economics* 14 (October 1971): 465–74.

1. The point has not been made as strongly in the literature as one might expect. Nevertheless, it is contained in: G. E. Hoover, The Economic Effects of Inheritance Taxes, 17 *American Economic Review* 38 (1927), and Alvin H. Johnson, Public Capitalization of the Inheritance Tax, 22 *Journal of Political Economy* 160 (1914). Professor Johnson's article is interesting because he proposes to offset the reduction in capital by having the government invest in the capital market the full receipts of the inheritance tax. For this to work, of course, the elasticity of the "demand for inheritance" would have to be less than one, a point which he does not emphasize.

whom they wish, not because of interest in the legatee, but because we are interested in the testator. We are, in this view, compelled by the mere logic of private property to permit a man not only to give it away while he is alive, but also to give it away on his death. In these forms, the argument is essentially metaphysical, but as we will see it is possible to put something very similar to this in strict welfare economics terms.

It seems likely that this lack of much rigorous discussion of what is clearly an important policy issue turns, to a considerable extent, on the fact that decisions with respect to inheritance have become mixed up with certain other problems. Firstly, a great many people favor income equalization as a government policy. Secondly, there are a great many people who favor a planned, centrally-run economy as opposed to a market economy; thirdly, many people feel that the government should have, at the very least, a policy as to the amount of capital invested in the economy. Normally, people in this category favor more capital investment, but there is no logical reason why one could not favor less capital investment.[2] These issues are, in fact, independent of the desirability or undesirability of permitting inheritance, as I shall shortly demonstrate. I believe, however, that they have been mixed up with the inheritance issue by most people who have thought about it. This makes the issue appear to be an extraordinarily complex issue and has resulted in restricting discussion.

Before turning to demonstrating that these issues are not necessarily involved in the decision as to whether or not inheritance should be permitted, I should like to digress briefly to explain what I mean by permitting or not permitting inheritance. In essence, we will discuss whether inheritance should be permitted, that is, whether 100 per cent tax on inheritance of wealth is desirable. We will not discuss whether such a 100 per cent tax would be administratively feasible in the sense that it might be possible for people wishing to leave money to evade it, nor will we discuss the taxation of inheritance for revenue purposes only. As will be demonstrated, however, the arguments offered in favor of inheritance are also arguments in favor of keeping the tax on inheritance at or below that tax which brings in the largest net revenue. If, as seems likely, a 30 per cent tax level on inheritances would bring in more revenue than a 90 per cent tax, then the argument offered in this article would indicate that the 30 per cent tax should be chosen.

2. Gordon Tullock, The Social Rate of Discount and the Optimal Rate of Investment: Comment, 78 *Quarterly Journal of Economics* 331 (1964).

Returning to our main theme, however, I should like now to demonstrate that the four issues which I have described are essentially independent of each other. As an extreme case, it is possible to have a socialist state which has definite policies with respect to the amount of capital which will be accumulated and radically egalitarian objectives together with inheritance of wealth. In fact, I would argue that inheritance of wealth under these circumstances would increase the efficiency of such a state. On the other hand, it would be possible to have a completely laissez-faire market economy with no effort on the part of the government to affect the net rate of accumulation of capital or redistribute income in the direction of equality and, at the same time, prohibit inheritance. In this case, again, I would argue that prohibiting inheritance was inefficient. All of the other logical combinations of these factors are also possible and in all of these cases permitting inheritance is efficient. With four variables, each of which can take two values, we have a 16-cell matrix as shown in Figure I.[3]

The eight possible combinations of the other variables with the retention of inheritance are shown to the left of the vertical double bar and those without inheritance to the right. Each possible situation with inheritance is shown by a letter and its corresponding state without inheritance permitted is shown by the letter primed. My argument is that, by standard welfare criteria, in each case the state with inheritance is superior; A is better than A′ and H is better than H′.

Before entering into the general discussion, however, I think it would be desirable to demonstrate that these four possible variables are, indeed, independent. Further, something should be said about the efficient method of administering certain types of government control. It is widely believed, for example, that a socialist economist economic policy in which the government operates the economy must, of necessity, be combined with government control of capital accumulation. This is by no means true. There is no reason why the government could not obtain its capital solely from the voluntary sale of securities while managing the rest of the economy.[4] Under these circumstances, it would be obtaining from the individuals in society information as

3. In practice, of course, they can take many intermediate values, but for simplicity we will assume in each case there either is or is not a given institution.

4. Either a single general government bond or a series of different securities with different amounts of risk attached selling at different prices. Probably the former would be more efficient.

		Inheritance		No Inheritance	
		Market Economy	Government-Operated Economy	Market Economy	Government-Operated Economy
No Government Capital Policy	No Income Redistribution	A	B	A′	B′
	Income Redistribution	C	D	C′	D′
Government Capital Policy	No Income Redistribution	E	F	E′	F′
	Income Redistribution	G	H	G′	H′

FIGURE I

to how much they wanted to invest, granted the physical productivity of investment at that time and using these data to obtain the optimum in amount of investment. The government itself would be deciding where the investment was to be spent.

The contrary policy—government control of the rate of capital formation without government control of the economy as a whole—is equally easy. A government could institute a subsidy for capital investment if it thought capital investment was too low, or a tax upon capital investment if it thought that it was too high. Note that for this purpose it would have to have some idea of what is the "right amount" of capital accumulation, independent of the ordinary equilibrium concepts. It would be, in a sense, overriding preferences of the citizens for investment. Whether we approve of this or not, however, raises no questions as to its theoretical possibility.

Finally, income redistribution can be combined with almost any set of policies on the other variables. In general—granted that the government has some policy for income redistribution, whether from the rich to the poor or from the poor to the rich or from all of us to farmers and oilmen—this income redistribution can be most efficiently managed if it is handled through direct taxes and payments rather than by attempting to change the structure of production in such a way as to bring indirect benefits and injuries to specified groups.

Let us assume that the government has some capital policy; that is, it feels that the capital accumulation which "falls out" from the general situation, including, of course, its policies in other areas, is not optimal and wishes to change it. Let us assume for simplicity that it feels that more capital should be accumulated. There seems to be a widespread view that a policy of a government to increase capital investment must, of necessity, take the form of actual government management of all investment. This is untrue. Assume that people would, if left to their own devices, save 10 per cent of their money and the government, through divine guidance, knows that the correct amount is 20 per cent. One method of making this investment would be to tax the populace by 20 per cent of their income and use the money for direct government investments. A second technique would be to tax the populace some amount less than 20 per cent of their income and use the derived amount for subsidy upon new investment. A third possibility would be to tax the populace 10 per cent of their income and invest this directly in investments which, given prevailing rates of interest, are submarginal. If the government has infinite ability to discriminate in the size of its subsidies, it should be able to go even farther than any of these three techniques and offer discriminant subsidies on specific supermarginal investments in order to obtain its total 20 per cent investment from a tax revenue well under 10 per cent.

It is, of course, possible to combine the latter three techniques in various combinations. Clearly, any one of the last three techniques or any combination of them is better than the first. In each case, the degree to which the individual is permitted to make decisions about how his income will be spent and how it will be divided between saving and investment is greater than under a direct tax-financed investment of 20 per cent. Thus, each individual in society would be better off if the first policy involving direct government management of all investment were not resorted to simply because each individual acquires some additional freedom from this decision. The gain would be particularly great for those individuals who did not wish to invest exactly 20 per cent of their income. In general, a subsidy is the most efficient method of increasing the investment of capital, if large increases are desired and, if small increases are desired, direct investment in supermarginal areas is efficient.

Note that this would be true even if we did not believe in the market economy and had a totally government-run industrial and agricultural sector. Decisions by the government as to how much should be invested would be more efficiently implemented if the individuals voluntarily buy government securities with a suitable tax or subsidy to make certain that they bought the "right" total amount. Thus, an efficient socialist government would have (and the Soviet Union did have for many years) a market in its own bonds and would obtain the capital which is used for investment through this market. Only if the government is not concerned with providing optimal conditions for its citizens would it use its governmental powers to directly determine not only how much should be invested but who should invest it.

It might be thought, however, that an income redistribution program which was radically egalitarian requires, or at least is consistent with, confiscatory inheritance taxes. This is not true. Indeed, confiscatory inheritance taxes are a bad way of equalizing income. Any desired degree of income equalization can be obtained by suitable income taxes. Since the recipients of the inheritances will receive their inheritance by what amounts to a random time allocation, a tax which confiscates inheritances would amount to a random tax upon one particular source of income. A special tax on a single source of income combined with a general income tax is an inefficient method of equalizing income. The point can perhaps best be understood if we assume that the government of the United States not only has an income tax policy aimed at certain equalizations, but has, in addition, a $5,000 per year tax on economists on the grounds (quite correctly) that economists' incomes are above average. Clearly, this combination would be a less efficient way of achieving an income equality goal than a single tax because, in some cases, the special tax would fall on people who are already not too well off. Since any desired degree of equality can be obtained through the income tax with a negative range, the addition of a special tax for this purpose is both inefficient and undesirable.

It might be argued, however, that we want not only income equality but also a greater degree of equality in wealth. In this case, a direct equalizing wealth tax would seem to be the optimal institution. Indeed a tax on one particular form of wealth is almost of necessity an inefficient way of reducing the amount of wealth inequality in society. There has been a good deal of research in attempting to determine what tax on wealth would be equivalent to a given level of death duties. These very complicated papers derive their basic complications simply from the fact that any annual tax on wealth is vastly more efficient than the death duty as a technique of wealth equalization, and it is hard to compute the equivalent in an efficient tax for a highly inefficient tax.[5] Once again, a tax on a particular form of wealth, let us say houses, is an inefficient way of wealth equalization. Those interested in wealth equalization should approach the problem directly and use efficient tools, rather than indirectly through an inept set of methods.

The last few paragraphs have been devoted to demonstrating that the four variables shown on Figure I are in fact independent. They can be mixed in almost any combination. It now remains to demonstrate that the inheritance tax is undesirable. I do not propose to go through all of the eight possible cases, but I think that if I can demonstrate that the inheritance tax is undesirable in the two extreme cases—A, A′, the market economy with no income redistribution and no government capital policy, and H, H′, the government-run economy with income redistribution and a government capital policy—I will have made my point and may leave the filling of most of the other squares to the reader.

Let us begin with A, A′. Suppose, then, a free market government with no capital policy and no income redistribution which is considering the imposition of 100 per cent tax on all inheritances. Let us then discuss the effect of this tax first upon the situation before some given person has died and then, secondly, after he has died. The first consequence of the enactment of such a confiscatory inheritance tax would simply be that motives for accumulating capital would be much lower than otherwise. Indeed, everyone would plan to be dead broke on the day of their death. The market for annuities would become a very good one.[6]

Consider, then, some person who is now alive and realizes that he will die.

5. Cf. G. Z. Fijalkowski-Bereday, The Equalizing Effects of the Death Duties, 2 *Oxford Economic Papers* (n.s.) 176 (1950); William S. Vickrey, The Rationalization of Succession Taxation, 12 *Econometrica* 215 (1944); Nicholas Kaldor, The Income Burden of Capital Taxes, 9 *Review of Economic Studies* 138 (1942), reprinted in *Readings in the Economics of Taxation*, 393 (R. A. Musgrave and C. S. Shoup eds, 1959); A. C. Pigou, *A Study in Public Finance*, ch. 13 (3rd ed., 1949).

6. It is of some interest that probably a good deal of current savings depends on the fact that for a variety of reasons annuities are not as widely used as they theoretically could be. A law against annuities would probably be an excellent way of increasing our investment ratio.

Clearly, with the confiscatory inheritance tax, he would plan to leave no estate.[7] Clearly, this person has been made worse off by the tax because he has lost one possible degree of freedom. Before the tax was enacted, he could have saved money and left it to his heirs if he wished, and after the tax he no longer can do so. This reduction in his freedom is not offset by any gain to anyone else in society.

Indeed, as we have mentioned before, this reduction in his gains from accumulating money has been used as an argument *against* inheritance taxation. Surely with 100 per cent inheritance taxation, there will be less capital investment than there otherwise would be. But, in order to make this argument, it is necessary to believe that the amount of capital accumulated under institutions in which inheritance tax is permitted is superior to that in which it is not permitted. Granting this assumption, then the inheritance tax could, of course, be offset by a suitable subsidy on investment. This subsidy would not change the tendency of people to die penniless, but it would mean that people would save more money for the purpose of buying annuities to cover their old age than they otherwise would. The situation with inheritance taxation and such a subsidy would be inferior prior to the death of some person simply because the same capital investment would be obtained as without the inheritance tax, but there would be an additional tax imposed on the general population for the purpose of paying the subsidy. Thus, the abolition of the inheritance tax would benefit the taxpayers who otherwise would be paying for the subsidy and injure no one. But all of this, as I said before, requires the assumption that we know the ideal amount of capital investment. Those people, however, who do feel that the amount of capital which would be accumulated without inheritance tax would be too small will find this point quite convincing.

But to continue with our example, now suppose that our selected individual dies. The state obtains no funds because he has been living on an annuity, so there is no tax receipt. The people who would have inherited the money which he otherwise would have saved are worse off than they would have been under the previous set of institutions. No one benefits. Indeed, once again, the fact that there is less capital in society might well be considered a quite general loss. I think that proponents of inheritance taxation at this point would say that the abolition of inheritance, however, *did* benefit those

7. Unless, of course, he wished to make a gift to the government. Such gifts are possible without the 100 per cent inheritance tax.

people who would not have received the inheritance since they are not now confronted with a wealthier person in the society. In other words, they would normally envy a man who had received an inheritance, and this is an externality which has been eliminated by the elimination of inheritance. As I pointed out above, if this is thought of as a good social reason for an institution, the appropriate institution is a suitably graduated income tax or wealth tax, not an inheritance tax. For the moment, however, the society is assumed not to have a redistribution of income policy, and, hence, we can assume that it is not one where jealousy of those wealthier than oneself is a dominant social motive.

Thus, we have demonstrated that A is better than A′. Our proof, however, has been a proof with respect to a confiscatory inheritance tax to which the taxpayer fully adjusts by not having any money left to tax. If we assume that the annuity market is not well enough developed so that individuals can afford to put their entire wealth into such an instrument, then the proof fails but the society is not in long range equilibrium.[8]

It has not been proved, however, that a tax on inheritance is undesirable. Presumably, if inheritances are taxed at any rate less than 100 per cent, at least some people would choose to leave at least some money to their heirs, and, hence, there is a government revenue to offset the effects of the inheritance taxation.

Here, however, although we cannot prove that such taxes are unwise, we *can* prove quite readily that if the tax is larger than that tax which brings the maximum revenue it is unwise. Suppose, for example, that a 10 per cent inheritance tax would lead to a great many people choosing to leave money to their heirs with the result that the total tax collections were $100,000,000. On the other hand, assume that a 75 per cent inheritance tax would sharply reduce the number of people who wish to leave money to heirs so that the total income to the government was only, say, $75,000,000. The argument that we have offered so far would indicate that the first tax would clearly dominate the second. In other words, an inheritance tax, in order to be even dubiously Pareto optimal, would have to be either at that rate which maximizes the return from an inheritance tax (which is, of course, not the highest possible rate) or at some lower rate.

8. The role of annuities or other types of income which terminate at death is so dominant in controlling the amount of savings that such institutions as the Social Security Administration and private annuities markedly reduce total capital investment.

Note that such a tax would continue to reduce the total capital available in society and, hence, if you believe that capital generates externalities, would be a dominated policy on those grounds also.

We might temporarily move from square A to square E in our figure in order to discuss the capital problem a little more. Assume that the government uses the receipts from the inheritance tax, at least in part, to subsidize investment. It might be (although I doubt it very much) that it would turn out that there was some net profit, that is, that we could obtain the same net level of investment after the imposition of a joint inheritance tax subsidy on capital as we had before and still have some money left over for state use. As a judgment of the relative elasticities of the demand for savings under the two circumstances, I doubt that this would be true, but we may as well explore the possibility. If it were true, then, once again, one could say that the optimal institution could not involve an inheritance tax and subsidy which jointly were higher than needed to bring in the maximum amount of money which could be obtained by this combination of policies. It would not, of course, have to be that high.

The other possibility in squares E, E′, that is, that there is an inheritance tax offset by a subsidy on capital investment which turns out to cost more than the inheritance tax brings in, is clearly undesirable. If this situation occurs, square E clearly is superior to square E′. Note that these general principles will apply to all cases where the government has a pro-capital accumulation policy. In all cases, the reasoning which we have given above would indicate that not having an inheritance tax would be superior to having one, except in those cases where maximum revenue can be derived from either the inheritance tax or the combination of the inheritance tax and the subsidy; in such cases, the tax would have to be equal to or lower than the revenue maximizing level. In other words, there will be no independent reason for restricting inheritance. We would simply be choosing a tax by much the same line of reasoning as we would choose a tax on butter.

We now, however, switch to squares H, H′ where we have government which attempts to adjust capital, has an income redistribution policy (we shall assume it is an egalitarian rather than inegalitarian or horizontal income redistribution policy), and direct government control of the economy. Under these circumstances, once again, the institution of inheritance dominates the non-inheritance institution. I have previously demonstrated that it is desirable, even under these institutions, to have decisions as to who shall invest the money for capital projects left to the individual citizen by way of a government bond market (which may be selling bonds at a subsidized rate) rather than having the decisions made directly by the government on both how much should be saved and who should save it. Let us, however, temporarily disregard this proof and assume that the government we are dealing with is Maoist and does not permit its citizens to acquire any kind of capital asset except small quantities of items for personal use.

The arguments for permitting inheritance of this small amount of private property are, once again, fairly compelling. If inheritance was not permitted, individuals would be well advised to rent such goods rather than purchase them. The person who did rent them rather than purchase for this reason is injured to some extent, as is, when he dies, his potential heir, and no one gains from the institution.

If, however, we assume that the government with these policies does permit individuals to decide how much each one shall save, then the arguments for inheritance are very much like those in the free market system. It should be noted that, with a highly egalitarian policy and a government security as the only income-bearing asset, individuals would save not for the purpose of increasing their income in the future, but for the purpose of obtaining leisure either for themselves or for their heirs at future times. It might turn out that this is a weak motive for saving and, hence, the subsidy on saving might have to be quite high. Still, the argument holds. Individuals before their death would be injured if they are prohibited from passing on their estate to their heirs because it eliminates one possible alternative which they might otherwise choose. Their potential heirs would be injured after their death and, assuming state annuities are available (their absence would be inefficient), no one would gain from these two changes.

We could go through all the other pairs of squares on Figure I, but this would be tedious. The general principles still apply: by strict welfare economics methods, we can show that permitting inheritance of wealth is a desirable policy. Further, we can show that, although there is no reason why inheritance should be any more immune than gasoline from taxes for revenue purposes, any effort to raise taxes above the revenue maximizing point is always a non-optimal policy.

INHERITANCE REJUSTIFIED

The Greene, Ireland and Koller comments all raise rather technical objections to my original article. Reading them, however, has led me to a few somewhat broader reflections. First, a world in which inheritance was not permitted would be a most extraordinary world. The man with a wife and two children and a large mortgage on his house could not only not have an insurance policy which would pay off the mortgage in the event of his death, he could not even leave the house to his wife if it were in his possession free and clear. Even the most trivial property of the decedent would go to the state rather than to his family.

Under these circumstances, one would anticipate that what capital was owned in society would either be held by annuity companies or by relatively young people. Interest rates would be very sharply higher and capital accumulation would be very much lower. Indeed, we would have the opposite of our present situation in which young families spend more than they earn and older families spend substantially less than they earn, because it would be unwise for older families to save or even hold.

I doubt that this is what Greene, Ireland and Koller have in mind. Probably they are not actually in favor of abolishing all inheritance, but only large inheritances. It does seem, however, that anyone who chooses to argue for restricting inheritances should provide some set of criteria by which we can decide which inheritance should be restricted and how much. Indeed, I do not think we should take them very seriously until they do.

Turning, however, to the more technical discussion, all three base their arguments upon inspection of people's preferences. Economists have generally tried to avoid this type of analysis because anything that you care to name can be justified, providing only that an appropriate set of preferences is assumed. Nevertheless, I do not think that such arguments are illegitimate, only very difficult to deal with.

Greene has fallen into a rather special variant of the deadly sin of envy. In a way, my view of human nature is better than his. Since normally I am regarded as a cynic, this is a refreshing change. It is not obvious to me why

Reprinted, with permission, from *Journal of Law and Economics* 16 (October 1973): 425–28.

"envy may often be generated by the belief that others possess something not possessed by oneself and for which the other individual has done nothing which has not also been done by oneself" leads to the view that you should restrict inheritance of property. Surely different genetic constitutions would fall within this category, as would differential childhood environments and luck. Presumably a very large part of the difference in income which we observe in the real world is a result of genetic and/or environmental factors. The remaining part is probably largely the result of luck and that also would seem to be within the area which Greene assures us leads to envy.

I assume, however, that he is simply stating his position too broadly here and, in fact, does tend to feel that inherited physical wealth in and of itself generates more negative externality than inherited genes. I rather doubt that this is so.

If you talk to someone about people who are better off than he is, quite commonly he will tell you that the reason has to do with inherited wealth, even when this is not true. On the whole, if I am poorer than another man because he inherited his money, this reflects no discredit on me. On the other hand, if we started out equal and he won the race, then that indicates that he is not only wealthier than me but also he is superior to me. Under the circumstances, I may prefer (and many people clearly do prefer) to think that he has been the beneficiary of inherited wealth rather than inherited genes. In any event, many people clearly act as if this were part of their preference function. At the moment, if I find someone who is better off than I, I can excuse this fact to myself by claiming that he inherited his wealth. If we abolish inherited wealth, I could no longer do this and the cost in individual satisfaction might be quite great. But here I am, like Professor Greene, inspecting people's preferences and this is, indeed, a difficult field of research.

The problem, at the technical level, with the Greene argument is that he has not demonstrated that the externality is Pareto optimal. Indeed, my own personal feeling is that probably Professor Greene's feeling of benevolence toward his next-door neighbor is stronger than his feeling of envy. I suspect that if he heard that his neighbor's fire insurance had lapsed and had an absolutely safe opportunity to burn down the man's house, he would not take advantage of the opportunity. He does, indeed, resent his neighbor having this inherited wealth, but the resentment is not strong enough so that he would actually like to inflict injury on him by purely destructive means.

I may be wrong about this, however, and perhaps Professor Greene's statement of the strength of his envy in this case is correct. Note, however, that if he proposes to impose a tax which is above the revenue maximizing tax, he in essence reduces the wealth of his neighbor while at the same time reduces the wealth of some poor person who otherwise might have received the funds collected from the tax in the way of an income transfer and, ex post, the wealth of a person who left the money in trust for Greene's neighbor. The latter person, of course, is dead, but any proposal to change the law for future inheritances would involve all three of these people. Thus, even though Professor Greene might be willing to burn down his neighbor's house under the circumstances I specified above, I doubt that the pleasure he would get from this would offset the displeasure he would get from the combination of the injury to his neighbor, the injury to the poor, and the injury to potential testators imposed by a confiscatory inheritance tax. I may, of course, be wrong but in any event I doubt very much that there are many people who have this particular type of envy as there are who envy those who are better off as a result of merit. There may also be people in society who are in favor of aristocracies and, hence, are in favor of inherited wealth, per se. I should think this last group should at the very least offset Greene's.

Professor Ireland is married to a lawyer. When I referred to remainders as a way to permit people who had the particular set of motives he assumes for retaining funds to avoid estate taxation, he went to her and received a perfectly correct technical definition of the term. His argument is correct with respect to that technical definition. I had been thinking of all those methods which are available to permit a man to retain control of his wealth until his death but sell all but a life interest to someone else. There are substantially no restrictions upon such arrangements except that, under some circumstances, it may be necessary to consult with a Swiss banker. Indeed, as far as I know, it is not even a violation of the law if it becomes known.

It seems to me dubious, however, that very many people are interested in holding wealth for the reasons given by Ireland. As evidence of this, I point out the undeveloped nature of remainder law in the United States, together with the fact that the opportunities for transfers of the type I have described seem to be very little used.[1] Under the circumstances, it seems to me unlikely

1. Note that these remainders should be sharply distinguished from the inheritance-avoiding trusts, which are so common in American practice. Selling the remainder would permit a person to maximize his expenditures during life, while still retaining control of the wealth to obtain the gratifications described by Ireland. Establishing a standard tax-avoidance trust reduces the testator's control over his wealth during life, but increases the amount he can leave to his heirs.

that this particular motive would lead to very much money being held for confiscation by estate taxation.

It is, of course, possible for the state to "prevent general remainder rights" by appropriate legislation and it could, indeed, pass a law against annuities and thus undermine my whole argument. I am sure, however, that Professors Greene and Ireland would not favor such legislation which is clearly non–Pareto optimal. With some exceptions, they are in favor of letting people do as they wish with their money. I remain rather astonished at their making this particular exception.

Koller's objection to my paper depends upon the possibility that some people might be unhappy with the possibility of leaving money to their heirs, because they want to spend all of their money without their heirs realizing that this is their choice. I cannot deny that there would be people of this sort, although I doubt that they would be very common. In order to demonstrate that this causes problems for a Pareto optimal proof, however, it would be necessary to demonstrate that the total compensation required in order to leave such people as well-off after the change as before, would be greater than the benefit received by the people who would have the opposite interest. Since people who would have the opposite interest would be far more numerous and their individual interests would be considerably stronger, this seems to me unlikely.

There is a bargaining problem here. If we assume that we start with a situation in which there is a 100 per cent inheritance tax and are proposing to change to another inheritance tax which maximizes revenue potential, but as part of the change will compensate people who have what we may call Koller motives, then it would be profitable to claim to be in that position. Most of these claims, of course, would be dishonest, but they might create a very high transactions cost. Normally, in discussing Pareto optimal changes, we ignore such costs. In any event, if we start with the present status quo, in which we do not have 100 per cent inheritance taxation, and propose changing to such a level of taxation, it seems unlikely that people having the Koller-type motives would be willing to compensate all the people who would be injured.

THE CHARITY OF THE UNCHARITABLE

If I understand the common view among modern intellectuals, income redistribution is considered to be a rather simple and almost entirely ethical matter. There are, basically, two theories. The first is that those of us who are well-off use the state as a mechanism for making gifts to the poor. This is well represented by James Rodgers and Harold Hochman in their article, "Pareto Optimal Redistribution."[1] The second view, which I shall call the "Downsian," is that in a democracy the poor are able to use their votes to obtain transfers from the rest of society.[2] These two views are sometimes combined into the view that the bulk of the population takes money from the rich and gives it to the poor by use of the democratic process.

Although I have presented these two points of view very briefly, I think nevertheless that they sum up the standard justification for redistribution. Unfortunately, these essentially ethical approaches cannot explain the bulk of the redistribution in our society. It is true that they *do* explain a small amount of it, but most of it comes from other motives and achieves other ends. Since these two ideas are probably fairly firmly engrained in the mind of the reader, I should like before I begin formal analysis to briefly discuss the facts of redistribution.

Firstly, the poor vote, and the amount of redistribution that they receive, in part, is a function of the extent to which they vote.[3] Thus, to at least some extent, the money received by the poor must represent the use by the poor of

Reprinted, with permission of Oxford University Press, from *Western Economic Journal* 9 (December 1971): 379–92.

1. H. Hochman and J. Rodgers, "Pareto Optimal Redistribution," *American Economic Review* 59 (September 1969): 542–57. Hochman and Rodgers, of course, are much more sophisticated in their handling of the problem than I have indicated in this single paragraph. Nevertheless, the point of view outlined above is espoused in it. The article has attracted a large number of comments, many of which are markedly less sophisticated than the original work.

2. A. Downs, *An Economic Theory of Democracy* (New York: Harper, 1957), especially pp. 198–201.

3. B. R. Fry and R. F. Winters, "The Politics of Redistribution," *American Political Science Review* 64 (June 1970): 508–22. See also B. Frey, "Why Do High Income People Participate More in Politics?" *Public Choice* 11 (Fall 1971): 101–5, for a discussion of the reasons why the poor exert less political influence than their per capita voting strength would appear to give them.

their political power, rather than a charitable gift from the rest of society. This would seem to indicate that the first of the explanations given above cannot, at the very least, be the entire explanation.

Secondly, anybody examining the status of the poor in the modern world must realize that democracies do not make very large gifts to them. If we consider the United States, the federal government officially lists its welfare expenditures as about $100 billion a year. This would be enough to give the bottom one-fifth of our nation an income of $10,000 per family of four, even if they had no other source of income. Clearly they do not receive benefits of this sort. Another calculation carried out by the Institute for Research on Poverty at the University of Wisconsin shows the total welfare deliveries to the poor as $40 billion.[4] This would, once again, if delivered to the poor in cash, work out to about $4,000 per family of four in the bottom one-fifth of our population. Once again, it is clear they are not doing anywhere near this well.[5] U.S. Senator Abraham Ribicoff, commenting on HEW, said: "In fiscal 1972, the projected $31.1 billion for poverty programs would provide $4,800 for every poor family of four, almost $1,000 above the poverty line, if directly distributed to these families."

If we turn to actual relief and assistance payments to the poor, it turns out that they add up to much less than 1 percent of the national income. This amount could clearly be more than explained simply on the assumption that the poor make use of their votes to obtain the transfer. Indeed, the amount they receive would appear to be less than the amount that they *would* receive if the federal budget were simply divided among the taxpayers in accordance with their voting potential.

Nor is the situation greatly different in other democracies. Webb and Sieve in comparing incomes in England in 1937 with 1959 come to the conclusion "*. . . the estimate of inequality of final incomes remains constant over the period of twenty years which saw the establishment and growth to some stability of the 'welfare state.'*"[6] Granted the massive amounts of income that are transferred back

4. R. J. Lampman, "Transfer and Redistribution as Social Process," mimeographed. The figures in Lampman's study are for 1967.

5. The reasons why this particular calculation overestimates transfers to the poor will be discussed below.

6. A. L. Webb and J. E. B. Sieve, *Income Redistribution and the Welfare State* (London: Social Administration Research Trust, 1971). This comment is particularly revealing, since both Webb and Sieve are vigorous advocates of the British welfare state, and the subject matter of their book is the improvement of statistics on its effects.

and forth through the population by the British government, it is evident that the major effect and probably the major purpose of this transfer cannot be to help the poor. With well in excess of 30 percent of the average individual's received income being taxed away in one way or another and the defense burden much lower as a part of GNP than it was in 1937, it is clear there are massive resources available for aiding the poor if that was indeed the objective of the British government.

Leaving aside for the moment any further discussion of the empirical facts about redistribution, let us turn to what has been done in the way of more formal theory of redistribution in a democracy.[7] The first of these in point of time is the argument of Anthony Downs that democracy will always lead to transfer of income from the wealthy to the poor. Indeed, he regards this as a major justification of democracy. We may contrast this with Benjamin Ward's view that redistribution in democracy would be essentially indeterminate.[8] Finally, there is the view expressed in *The Calculus of Consent*[9] that the nature of the voting process in democracy is such that real resources will be transferred away from the rich, although it is not specified who will receive them. It will surprise no one that I espouse the Buchanan and Tullock view, but the Ward model will be used to supplement it by indicating that the actual output of the political process is not predetermined.[10]

The essence of the difference between the Downs model and the Ward model is simply that Downs implicitly assumes that redistribution must take place along a one-dimensional continuum in which people are arranged from the poorest to the wealthiest. At first glance, there would seem to be no obvious reason why the bottom 51 percent of the population, using their majority to take money from the wealthy, would be more likely than the top 51 percent using their majority to take money from the poor. Indeed, the

7. This paper is entirely concerned with redistribution in democracies because this is the area where our knowledge of politics is best. I should not like to leave the implication that I am convinced that redistribution operates better in despotisms.

8. B. Ward, "Majority Rule and Allocation," *Journal of Conflict Resolution* 5 (December 1961): 379–89. Note that Ward actually demonstrates that there would be cyclical majority in all such cases. Since the process must stop, however, and in observed reality *does* stop at some point, the statement that he proved indeterminancy of the process is not an unjust summary.

9. J. M. Buchanan and G. Tullock, *The Calculus of Consent: Logical Foundations of Constitutional Democracy* (Ann Arbor: University of Michigan Press, 1962), 144–45.

10. The two models may be reconciled by use of the apparatus presented by G. Tullock, "A Simple Algebraic Logrolling Model," *American Economic Review* 60 (June 1970): 419–26.

2 percent of the population lying at the middle line would be the determining factor in such a choice, and hence we might anticipate that money would come from both ends to the middle.

In practice, of course, the wealthy have more money, and hence can be subject to heavier taxes. Thus the cost of admitting a wealthy person into a coalition, which proposes to transfer money away from the 49 percent of the population not members, is higher than the cost of permitting the entry of a poor person. Following William Riker, one would therefore anticipate that voting coalitions would be made up in such a way as to minimize the number of wealthy members. This is, indeed, the element of truth in the Downs model, is part of the Buchanan-Tullock model, and must be admitted as a modification of the Ward model.

If the dominant coalition is likely to be made up of the bottom 51 percent of the population, this tells us nothing very much about how that coalition will divide the spoils. Further, it is obvious that this coalition must contain a good many persons who are not poor by any ordinary definition. If we accept the bottom 10 percent of the population as poor, then they make up only 20 percent of this coalition of the bottom 51 percent. If we are more generous and count 20 percent of the population as poor, then they make up 40 percent. Clearly, this minority cannot dominate the coalition. If they received more per head than the other members of the coalition, they would do so because the lower middle class was generous.

Turning to formal bargaining theory, it is obvious that any transfer mechanism must provide at least as much for the top portion of this bottom 51 percent coalition as for anyone else in the coalition because if it does not, the 49 percent who are not members can very readily purchase the top 2 percent for a coalition that transfers a small amount from the top income groups to this small 2 percent group and to no one else. Indeed, such a coalition might take the entire transfer out of the bottom part of the population instead of out of the top. The reasoning so far would indicate that the people toward the top of the bottom 51 percent might receive much more than the people at the lower end. The only restriction on a delivery of the bulk of the resources transferred from the wealthy to the upper end of the bottom coalition (other than charitable instincts on the part of the members of the upper end) would seem to be the possibility that the wealthy would attempt a coalition with the very poor.

If we look at the real world, we do see some signs of such coalition attempts. Among those persons who argue that all transfers should be strictly limited to the very poor by way of a stringent means test, it is likely that wealthy persons predominate. This is, of course, sensible from even a selfish standpoint. They could arrange to give to the present-day poor considerably more money than the poor are now receiving, in return for a coalition in which transfers to people in the upper part of the bottom 51 percent are terminated, and make a neat profit. This particular coalition has so far foundered largely because of miscalculations by the poor. The poor realize that the interests of the wealthy are clearly not congruent with their interests, but they do not realize that the interests of people between the twentieth and the fifty-first percentile of the income distribution are also not identical with theirs. They therefore tend to favor a coalition with the second group rather than the former.

The situation is interesting, and we may pause briefly to examine it by way of a three-person model. Suppose we have wealthy Mr. *A*, middle-class Mr. *B*, and poor Mr. *C*. Messrs. *B* and *C* form a coalition for the purpose of extracting money from Mr. *A*, and let us begin by assuming that the money is to be equally divided between them. Suppose, further, that Mr. *C*'s income is $1,000 per year before transfer, Mr. *B*'s is $2,000 per year, and Mr. *A*'s is $3,000 per year. Clearly, if the amount of transfer were somehow externally fixed at $500 but Mr. *A* were permitted to decide how it was to be allocated, he would give all of it to Mr. *C*.[11] He would reason that not until Mr. *C*'s income had risen to $2,000 per year was it sensible to supplement Mr. *B*'s income. Mr. *B* receives his payment simply because he wants it, not because there is any charitable motive involved on the part of anyone.

Under the circumstances, it is clear that Mr. *A* would be willing to enter into a coalition with Mr. *C* under which a transfer of $300 was made from *A* to *C* and none was made to *B*. This would be to the advantage of Mr. *C*, and it seems likely that only the generally bad information and low I.Q. and/or motivation which we observe among the poor prevents such coalitions. Indeed, it is possible the poor would do better if they depended entirely on the charitable motives of the wealthy. It might be that Mr. *A*, if left entirely to himself, would be willing to give Mr. *C* more than $250, although he objects to spending $500 for $250 apiece to *B* and *C*. Most persons, after all, are to some extent charitable, and it may well be that the very poor would do better than at present if they depended on the charity of the wealthy.

11. Such a decision might be made available to taxpayers by allowing them to "earmark" on their income tax returns a portion of their tax for alternative transfer programs.

For example, an organization of society in which all transfers were made by a special electorate composed of persons in the top 10 percent of the income stream who tax themselves for the purpose of benefiting other persons might lead to larger transfers to the genuinely poor than they now receive. Certainly, if we fixed the total amount of transfer away from the upper income groups at its present level but gave them complete discretion as to how it was to be spent, they would spend far more of it on the very poor.

So far, however, we have unrealistically assumed that transfers must be made between different income groups along a unidimensional continuum. If we look at the real world, we observe that the bulk of the transfers are made to groups not defined by income. Farmers, college students, owners of oil wells, owners of private aircraft, older people regardless of their income, and, in all probability, the intellectual class are the major recipients of transfers, even though the bulk of the members of these groups are by no means poor.[12]

If we accept the real world situation as being one in which transfers are made to organized groups and these organized groups receive their transfers largely in terms of their political power (which seems to be a correct statement about the real world), there is no reason why we should anticipate that the poor would do particularly well. For one thing, they are hard to organize. Thus, the very large transfers that we do observe in the world are essentially demonstrations of the Ward proof, supplemented by the Buchanan-Tullock logrolling process, which only rather accidentally benefit the bottom 10 to 15 percent of the population. For the reasons given above, we would anticipate that the top income groups would do rather badly from these transfers, and indeed they do. The Lampman study shows a transfer away from the upper income brackets of about 13 percent of their income. The beneficiaries of these transfers, however, we would anticipate would not be particularly concentrated among the poor and, indeed, granted their general political ineptness, one might expect that they would do rather badly, which is what we observe in the real world.

A somewhat cursory examination would seem to indicate that the actual percentage of income derived from wealthy people in democracies is an in-

12. The inclusion of intellectuals is essentially a subjective guess, based on general knowledge. It seems to me likely that the principal beneficiaries of those changes in our society that originated with the New Deal have been the intellectuals who, through their control of both the educational process and the media, have been able to divert very large resources into their own pockets. So far as I know, however, there is no statistical evidence for or against this point of view.

verse function of the ease with which they can migrate. Very small countries, such as Switzerland, Sweden, and Luxembourg, make no serious effort to collect taxes on the wealthy which are even as large in percentage terms as those they collect from the rest of the population. Medium-sized countries, like England, Germany, France, and Italy, are in a better position for taxing the wealthy, and the United States is able to implement substantial *effective* progression in top income brackets. In no case, so far as I know, is the actual amount of progression in the taxes collected as high as the progression in the tax tables, but it is nevertheless real in the larger countries.

When we turn to expenditures, a quite different picture emerges. Any individual's vote is worth as much as any other individual's vote in getting expenditures. Indeed the wealthy, well-informed person who is capable of making sizable campaign expenditures may well be able to receive a considerably larger portion of the total tax collections than is someone without these advantages.[13] If we subtract tax payments from receipts, we would anticipate some negative amount to turn up from a wealthy person and perhaps, although not certainly, a positive amount for the rest of the population. The reason the second sum is not necessarily positive is because of certain intrinsic inefficiencies in the transfer system. It is to be expected that expenditures that actually cost more than the net total benefit will be made.[14] Under the circumstances, it is possible that, although the rich are injured, the rest of the population make very small or negative profits.

Thus, to repeat, we would anticipate that in democracy there would be some transfer of money away from the wealthy, but there is no obvious reason that this transfer would go to the poor. If we look at the real world, we do find this pattern. This pattern is, however, a relatively minor part of the redistribution of income as seen in the modern state. Economists frequently point out that confiscation of *all* the income of the wealthy in a typical modern state would pay only a tiny part of the routine expenditures of the existing government. On the other hand, there can be no doubt whatsoever that massive redistributions of income do occur by way of the political process. These redistributions, however, are not in the main transfers of funds from the wealthy to the poor, but transfers of funds among the middle-class. The bulk of these transfers come from people who lie between the twentieth and

13. Frey, "Why Do High Income People Participate More in Politics?"

14. W. A. Niskanen, *Bureaucracy and Representative Government* (Chicago: Aldine-Atherton, 1971).

the ninetieth percentiles of income, and the bulk of them go to the same income classes. This is, of course, the area with the largest taxable capacity, and also the area where political power is concentrated in a democracy.

These transfers do not meet any egalitarian criteria. Basically they are transfers from groups of people who, for one reason or another, are not politically powerful to people who are. Always and everywhere in democracies, the farmers do very well. As a matter of practical fact, the United States probably wastes fewer resources in supporting its farm program than almost any other Western country. This may surprise Americans, accustomed to our massively inefficient method of transferring money to some people who are, on the whole, about as well-off as the people from whom the transfers come; but examination of what is done in the Common Market will convince them very quickly that Americans are fortunate in this respect.

The farm program is not the only example; the Social Security Administration transfers money from the young to the old, regardless of income. Indeed, in this particular case, the very poor are badly damaged by the institution. Due to the method in which the taxes to pay for Social Security are collected, the poor pay a very substantial part of their tiny wages to the Social Security Administration. If, however, they are very poor, i.e., require public assistance when they are old, then the local authorities will subtract their Social Security payment from the amount they receive. The result from their standpoint is that they pay taxes, but receive no net benefit. This must lead to a significant transfer of resources away from the very poor.

The urban renewal project is another obvious, even scandalous, example of the type of redistribution we observe, and another major example is, of course, the subsidized public education system. The latter is particularly obvious as a redistribution to the well-off at the university level. In general, students who can get into a university, particularly those who can get scholarships, have enough natural talent so that they enter the university with a lifetime income well above average. At the expense of the taxpayer, they are then given an even higher lifetime expected income. But even if we turn to lower-level schools, somewhat the same problem exists. To begin with, these are clearly transfers from those in society who do not have children to those who do—to say nothing, of course, of the transfer to the children themselves.

Secondly, however, it is fairly certain that the payoff to education, even at the elementary level, is greatly varying, depending on both the inherited genes and the home environment. Thus, the return in real terms to education is vastly higher to the person who both has the natural talent and the background to have a good income all his life than to the person whose natural talent and background are such that he probably will be poor. We would, if we were interested in relatively egalitarian measures, make direct payments to these two parties which could then be invested in a manner that would be most suitable in each case. By compelling the transfer to be taken in a form that is of maximum benefit to people who are going to be well-off anyway and of minimum benefit to people who are going to be poor, we make the average citizen richer and the poor poorer.

These examples are merely a small part of a wide universe. It is clear that in most democracies the poor receive relatively minor transfers—in any realistic sense—from society, although *not* zero transfers. Although very large amounts of money are redistributed by government action, the bulk of this redistribution is composed of transfers back and forth within the middle income brackets. It is obvious why these transfers occur. Obtaining such a transfer is a rational investment of resources, and people do put their resources into it. The only thing which is in any sense astonishing about this phenomenon is that it is so little noted. Almost all standard discussions of redistribution imply that it is normally from the rich to the poor. Some such redistribution does indeed go on, but it is a trivial phenomenon compared to the redistribution within the middle-class. I find the concentration of discussion of redistribution upon the very minor phenomenon of redistribution from the wealthy to the poor and the general ignoring of the major phenomenon—redistribution back and forth within the middle income groups in terms of political organization—most remarkable.

This remarkable concentration on the minor part of this activity and ignoring of the major part requires, I feel, some explanation. Unfortunately, the only explanation I can offer is basically psychological. It will be outlined below, but I should begin by apologizing to the reader for introducing a nonrigorous discussion of personal psychology, instead of something more satisfying.

We must begin by talking a little bit about a well-tested psychological phenomenon: "reduction of cognitive dissonance." It is well established that individuals' perception of the world is, to some extent, affected by a subconscious desire to reduce internal dissonance. Thus, an individual will, without any dishonesty, believe that certain activities which are in accord with motive *A* are also in accord with motive *B*, even if objectively they are not. The reason for this is that he does not wish to admit, even to himself, that he is disregarding motive *B*. Needless to say, this phenomenon occurs only when motive *A* and motive *B* would, in objective terms, lead to different actions and where the individual in fact regards motive *A* as more important than motive *B*.

Most of us have been trained in such a way that we are presented with a problem of this nature. All of us from the time we were small have been told that it is our duty to be charitable, to help the poor, and to do various other good acts. On the other hand, most of us have strong selfish drives. Clearly the injunction that if a man takes your coat, you should give him your cloak also, is not descriptive of the ordinary behavior of most human beings. It is, however, descriptive of what they say. Indeed, if we observe our colleagues in the university, we shall find that their expressed opinions are largely in accord with the ethically-given drive toward "loving thy neighbor" and "giving all you own to the poor." If we look at their actual behavior on the other hand, it turns out that they make few sacrifices for the poor.

It is clear, then, that they find these two drives—spending your own income yourself and helping the poor—in conflict, and that this should cause some internal tension. I should say, perhaps, that in my classes I commonly tell my students that if they really want to help the poor what they should do is get two jobs, work as hard as they possibly can, and then give all their income except that minimum amount that they need to stay alive to the inhabitants of India. They normally object to this pattern of behavior, but are normally not willing to admit that the reason they object is simply that they do not *really* feel that charitable.[15]

Indeed, if I ask my students or my faculty colleagues how much they personally give to the poor, it often turns out to be a small amount—in many cases zero. They very commonly explain their attitude by saying that they prefer governmental charitable activity. They seldom give any explanation as to why they should use the government channel for this activity and, in particular, never turn to the perfectly genuine externality arguments that do exist for this purpose.[16] They sometimes allege, however, that it is more ef-

15. I should say that in general the farther to the left the individual student, the more incoherent he becomes in dealing with this particular problem. It is not that the people on the right are willing to admit that they act selfishly, but simply that they are much less embarrassed by the question than the members of the New Left. Being less embarrassed, they are less likely to sputter.

16. For a statement of these reasons by a man who cannot possibly be accused of socialism, see Milton Friedman, *Capitalism and Freedom* (Chicago: University of Chicago Press, 1962).

ficient for them to vote for charity than to make a charitable contribution themselves because this brings in other people's money, too.

Suppose that it is suggested that I give $100 to the poor. Suppose further that this proposal is in the form of two options. Option 1 is that I take $100 out of my pocket and give it to some charity. Option 2 is that we vote on whether I should be taxed $100 for the purpose of making this charitable payment. The cost to me of making the direct payment is $100. The cost to me of voting for the tax, however, is $100 discounted by my estimate of the influence my vote will have on the outcome. Granted the constituency is 100,000 or more, the discounted cost to me of voting for this special tax on myself is vanishingly small. Thus, if I feel just a little bit charitable, I would not make the $100 payment but I would vote for the tax. I would make this vote in full awareness of the fact that many other persons are also voting on the same issue and that my vote will make very little difference in the outcome. Thus the cost to me of casting my vote is small. Putting it differently, the act that I am called upon to perform in voting is very low cost, even though it refers to a $100 gift; the private gift is high cost. Under the circumstances, one would predict that I would be more likely to vote for charitable activity than to undertake it myself.

Here, also, our phenomenon of reduction of cognitive dissonance comes in. If I am possessed both of selfish desires to spend my own money and a feeling that I must be charitable, I am wise to vote charitably and act selfishly. I should also tend, in discussion, to put much greater weight upon the importance of my vote than is actually justified, and to resent people who tell me that the vote makes almost no difference. At this point, the rationale for the ethical rule that private charity is bad and that all redistribution should be public becomes apparent. It provides a rationalization for "ethical" behavior in urging government redistribution while actually making almost no sacrifice. It permits one to have the best of both worlds.

Some further implications can be drawn from this phenomenon. As the size of the constituency in which I am voting increases, the likelihood that my vote will have any effect on the outcome decreases. Consider my paying $100 to charity, voting on a tax of $100 to be levied on me by my local government for charitable purposes, voting on a similar tax for similar purposes for the state government, and finally voting on a similar tax for similar purposes by the national government. Clearly, the cost to me is monotonically decreasing through this set. I would be more likely to vote for the tax by the national government than for the state government, for the tax by the state government than for the local government, and more likely to vote for the tax by the local government than to make the direct payment myself. It is quite possible that this phenomenon explains the tendency to transfer charitable activity from local governments toward the national government. Looked at from the standpoint of the voter, he can obtain the satisfaction of "behaving charitably" in a national election more cheaply than he can in the local election.

Note, however, that there is the possibility of a prisoner's dilemma here which might lead to the voting decision being the one which is binding. Suppose a proposal is made to tax everyone in the United States, who has more than $6,000 a year income, $100 for the purpose of distributing it to the poor. Each person might feel that his vote carried practically no weight and that he could gain some pleasure from voting for charitable activity, and hence vote for it. This would mean that the act would pass and everyone would in fact be charged $100. Note that there is no miscalculation here. As in the usual prisoner's dilemma, the individual would be correct in his assessment of the cost to him of voting for or against this tax. The aggregation of the votes would mean, however, that he would find himself in the lower right instead of the upper left hand corner of the prisoner's dilemma matrix, and would put out more money for charity than he really wants to. He is attempting to buy at a discount the feeling of satisfaction which comes from a "charitable act," and finds that he has to pay the full price.

Thus this line of reasoning would indicate that voting on charitable issues might lead to vast overinvestment in charity. I doubt that this is so, however. Firstly, the particular pattern of drives that leads to the type of internal cognitive dissonance reduction which I have been describing is limited pretty largely to the upper classes. We intellectuals are the primary holders of these attitudes and we, together with our colleagues among the WASPs and upper-class Jews, make up only a minority of the population. The blue-collar majority are much less prone to this type of thinking, and hence we are free to cast votes in this way without its actually costing us very much.

There is, however, another phenomenon that might conceivably put us in the prisoner's dilemma. Intellectuals, for reasons I shall explain below, may not actually vote for charity, but they certainly talk about it a great deal. In the average university community the individual who said flatly that he is opposed to charity because he likes to spend his money himself would be subject to very large private costs. On the other hand, being in favor of various charitable activities and engaging in political activity in their behalf will normally have a distinct private payoff. Thus the average intellectual who might or might not be inclined to vote in the way we have described is certainly inclined to engage in political activity in favor of government charity. Over long periods of time this might change the general opinion of society, so that the government would become more charitable, and hence the prisoner's dilemma might exist in the long run by way of the opinion-forming process. I think that it does not, but my reasons for so thinking require a little more elaboration on the structure of our electoral system.

So far the model I have been using has assumed that there are direct votes on charitable transfers. We do not observe this in the real world. The actual situation in our democracy is that we vote only periodically, and that our vote conveys relatively little information in the technical sense to the politician. The politician offers a whole collection of issues and proposals to the electorate, and is elected or not elected in terms of the whole complex. Thus the weight of his stand on any given issue in determining his election is hard to determine. In general, however, it seems fairly clear that most politicians regard transfer of funds by government process as *mainly* a way of purchasing the votes of the people *who receive the funds*, not of those people who might be charitably interested in the well-being of such people.

Thus a politician soliciting the vote of university professors will normally make a number of remarks about how we must help the poor. This is, however, merely an effort to reduce the "cognitive dissonance" in the professor's mind. What actually counts is his emphasis on how important he thinks it is that research be stimulated, that education receive larger funds, that the income tax law be provided with even more loopholes than it now has for academics, etc. The academic is normally quite capable of rationalizing all these things into a charitable activity, particularly if the candidate also makes some remarks about helping the poor. The end product is not that the prisoner's dilemma which I have been describing leads to an overinvestment in charity, but that the various pressure groups—including the pressure group of the intellectuals—get very large transfers.

This phenomenon has led me to speculate on whether the poor might not do better if they depended on pure charity, rather than on an attempt to use the weight of their votes to acquire funds. It seems to me conceivable that if *all* persons who receive a significant part of their funds from any government unit were deprived of any vote in electing that government unit, the poor would do better than they do now. However, this is mere speculation.

So far this paper has been descriptive and not normative. I fear, however, that the bulk of my readers will feel that it is essentially a denunciation of what

I have described. They probably expect me now to provide a remedy. In fact I am not at all sure the situation requires a remedy. Individuals who are obtaining a feeling of being charitable without much real cost through their use of the political process are maximizing their individual preferences and would be injured, i.e., have a lower level of satisfaction, if they were compelled to make a more objectively accurate calculation of the real effects of their behavior. It is not obvious to me that democratic government should not provide this type of satisfaction to the voters.

For those, however, who are disturbed and wish to "do something," I can suggest three possible courses of action. The first course of action—and the one which I am sure most persons who are disturbed by the paper will take—is simply to deny that it is true and go on happily reducing cognitive dissonance by the combination of being selfish in private expenditures and "generous" in politics. For most, I think, this is the utility maximizing course of action.

For those who find this impossible, there are two remaining possibilities. They can take action to bring reality into accord with what is said, i.e., they can try to make people be as charitable in their actions as they are in their language, or conversely, to make people talk as they act, i.e., change people's statements so that they are in fact descriptive of what they *do*, rather than mere expressions of loyalty to the prevailing ideals. I myself would prefer the latter and, indeed, I suspect that if we could somehow carry it out, the poor would actually get rather more money than they do now. Granted that transfer to the poor is now muddled up with truly massive transfers to other people, the voter quite rationally tries to restrict the total volume of the transfer. I think if permitted to vote on direct payments to the poor, he would probably choose to give them more. This, of course, is a guess.

Thus, if it is thought that it is desirable to do something about the situation which I describe, I suggest that it is easier to change the way we talk than to change the way we behave. Further, if we do change the way we talk, we shall be better informed about the real world (including the preferences of ourselves and our friends), and hence likely to behave in a more effective manner. The poor, along with the rest of us, would benefit from the change.

THE RHETORIC AND REALITY OF REDISTRIBUTION*

It is customary when giving a presidential address to begin by remarking on how happy you feel. I have an even stronger reason for being happy than most presidents. It will at long last permit me to break into the *Southern Economic Journal*. Up to this point, referees of that august institution have always rejected everything that I sent them. Finally, however, I am privileged to put an unrefereed paper in the *Journal* and, hence, do not have to worry about this one being rejected. The audience may feel that although it is nice for me it is hard on the *Journal*, but under the sacred traditions of the Southern Economic Association, the editors and referees can do nothing about it. The blame, if there is any, has to be laid on me and not on the management of the *Journal*.[1]

In a way, the fact that I will not face referees is important because in this paper I propose to violate a number of implicit taboos in the discussion of income redistribution. Indeed, I propose to argue that most of the current discussion of income redistribution is drastically defective. This will not only include Rawls, it will include what most members of the economic profession normally say on the subject and presumably what the potential referees of this paper would have thought.

Let me very briefly survey the existing economic, as opposed to the philosophic, literature on the redistribution of income. Firstly, a good many economists have said simply that economics can say nothing about the subject because somebody gains and somebody loses, but we can't say whether this is a good or a bad thing with our apparatus. Hochman and Rodgers[2] have started another tradition of dealing with income redistribution in which the government is seen as simply organizing what is essentially a voluntary transfer from the better off American citizens to the less well off American citizens.

Reprinted, with permission of the Southern Economic Association, from *Southern Economic Journal* 47 (April 1981): 895–907.

* Presidential Address delivered at the fiftieth annual meetings of the Southern Economic Association, Washington, D.C., November 8, 1980.

1. I have, on occasion, been permitted to review books for the *Journal*.

2. Harold M. Hochman and James D. Rodgers, "Pareto Optimal Redistribution," *American Economic Review* 59 (September 1969): 542–57.

Why the government should be used as an instrumentality for this kind of transfer was, interestingly enough, first explained by Milton Friedman.[3] Such redistribution has the interesting characteristic that it does not actually involve redistribution because the people who make the gift are maximizing their own utility and, hence, are better off. It is a case in which human preferences are so arranged that a given dollar of income benefits two people a full dollar's worth. The donor gains a dollar from expending money at its best use to him, i.e., making a gift to the poor, and the poor gain the dollar. In a somewhat metaphysical sense, it can be said here that no one is really coerced into reducing his own living standard for the benefit of others. Coercion is necessary but solely in order to avoid free riding.

To put the matter in purest terms, unanimous agreement among the donors could be obtained to use coercion to get each one of them to make a given size gift. The problem is very similar to that of hiring policemen. In practice, of course, nothing anywhere near as perfect as that exists, but I do not doubt that this particular motive is, in fact, among the reasons for income redistribution in the United States. We will argue below that it is a relatively minor motive and the major motives tend to lead to inefficiency and distortion. This particular motive, insofar as implemented, actually improves the efficiency of the economy.

The main theme of this paper, however, is not that Hochman, Rodgers, and Friedman are right, but that a great deal of the other argument for income redistribution is wrong. Let me begin my discussion of this by a brief digression on South Africa, a country which I visited recently.[4] In South Africa, the whites run a system which is quite democratic if you ignore the fact that only whites can vote. They have used this system to establish a fairly elaborate welfare state for the benefit of the white population, particularly the Afrikaners who are about half employed by the government. Significant transfers are made to "poor whites" who are defined, roughly speaking, as people whose income is lower than that of most whites and only three times as high as that of most blacks.

The blacks are also the subject of some income transfers from the whites. These transfers are not large but they are real. It is, I must admit, conceivable,

3. Milton Friedman, *Capitalism and Freedom* (Chicago: University of Chicago Press, 1962), 191–92.

4. The discussion of South Africa here is extremely oversimplified, but I think it properly presents the spirit of their institutions.

although I think not true, that those whites who administer the transfer program receive benefits that are larger than the black community nets out of the program. Nevertheless, I think that there is a real transfer of resources to the black part of the population, albeit a small one. The blacks, however, have much to complain about. They are subject to a good deal of discriminatory regulation. Most of these discriminatory rules are essentially minor annoyances, but rules which keep at least half the blacks on what used to be called reserves and are now about to be called homelands, make it impossible for most of the blacks to make the best of their human capital. It should be said, by the way, that the black human capital is very sharply lower than the white and, hence, in a completely free economy black incomes would be significantly lower than white incomes, but not nearly as much as they are under present institutions.

Once a black has permission to get a job in Johannesburg or wherever it is, he is then subject to some further controls on the type of job he has, but these in general do not seem to be very important. There are some exceptions which permit certain white employers, the Afrikaner farmers for example, to guarantee themselves adequate labor supplies at fairly low cost but that is a comparatively small phenomenon. There are, of course, in the cities also a great many illegal immigrants working hidden in the interstices of the economy. Indeed, the present government, as part of its "liberalization" procedure, has eased up on them and permitted many of the illegal immigrants to become legal. As would be expected, the result of this is that the salary of all blacks has risen but that of the blacks who formerly were legal and who now face more competition has fallen. The blacks in the city are dealt with by a special police force which has the right to arbitrarily deport them, although there is, of course, the possibility of appeal to courts.

Most people to whom I describe this system are shocked. The fact is that the system is identical to the one used by the United States and, indeed, all Western European countries. The only difference is our tradition that foreigners are not really human. What I have said about South Africa's treatment of its blacks is identical to America's treatment of Mexicans. They are kept on their "homelands" by what we call immigration control. Those who get into the United States are subject to restrictions on what they can do if they come in legally, and there are a great many of them in the country illegally who are subject to arbitrary deportation although, again, with the right of court appeal if they want it. As a result, the living standard of the Mexicans is very much lower than it would be without this rule.

The United States, in this respect, is less close to South Africa than are countries like Sweden or Switzerland. In both of these countries very large parts of the labor force are admitted into the country on a legal status which is to all intents and purposes the same as that on which a South African black gets permission to work in Johannesburg. They are confined in general to the low paying jobs and, of course, the salaries in these jobs are much lower than they would be if they were not there to keep the price down and serve as a complement rather than a substitute for the Swedish, Swiss, or white South African laborer. As a result, living standards of the Swedes, Swiss, and white South Africans are higher than they would be otherwise. The living standards of the Turks, Yugoslavs, and Zulus are also higher than they would be if they were not permitted to immigrate to these upper class areas at all, but markedly lower than they would be if they were permitted to freely immigrate.

The only distinction between the case of the United States and the Mexicans, the Swedes with the Turks, Swiss with the Yugoslavs, Italians, etc., on the one hand and the South Africans with respect to the blacks on the other is that it can be argued that the blacks of South Africa are citizens of South Africa. Legally, of course, they are not and, indeed, the South African government is in the process of setting up a whole series of "states" so that they will have other countries in which they can be citizens, but most advanced liberal thought feels that they should be citizens of South Africa.

But why should the Turks in Sweden be subject to the same kind of discrimination that the blacks are in South Africa? Why is it any worse for the South African government to prohibit more than a fixed quota from leaving one of the new Bantustans and going to Johannesburg and seeking work than it is for the government of Sweden to prohibit more than a fixed quota of Turks from working in Sweden? England now is actually changing its definition of citizenship so that they will be formal citizens of England[5] who have access to British passports and travel around the world as British citizens but who may not settle in England. But for that matter, why, when the British Labor Party took control of the British Empire in 1945, did they give India independence instead of inviting India to send delegates to the House of Commons?[6] They would, of course, immediately have taken over the House

5. Actually they are subjects of the Queen.

6. Friedrich Hayek once noted that:

If an English proletarian, for instance, is entitled to an equal share of the income now derived from his country's capital resources, and of the control of their use, because they are

of Commons since their citizenry were so much more numerous than that of the English, but why not?

These questions, I think, most people would regard as simply silly. We have built into us a very, very strong feeling that we do not want large reductions in our income. The proposals I have just made would lead to large reductions in the income of the Swedes, the Swiss, South Africa's English, and the citizens of the United States. Further, they are contrary to a particular tradition, the tradition of nationalism. We treat our fellow citizens differently than other human beings.

Now I am not arguing that we should accept any Mexican or Indian who wishes to come to the United States and take a job. Indeed, I think that would very sharply lower the living standards of most Americans, although it might in my own particular case lead to an improvement. What I am saying is that we should recognize that our motives in objecting to this are simply selfish.[7] We want to keep our living standards up and we are willing to let people die in southern India to that end. But we don't like to talk about it. This is the hypocrisy which dominates discussion of this issue.

This is an audience of economists, so I need not rehearse the numbers for you. You all know the immense difference between the incomes received by the Americans and northwest Europeans and those which are received by the majority of the human race living in places like India and Zaire. Further, the transfer of, let us say, half of our incomes to them presents no technical difficulty although of course it would take a little while to organize. Note that even if the northwest Europeans, the Americans, the Australians, the Japanese, etc. decided to transfer half of their current incomes to the poorer part of the world, they would continue to have expenditure levels which were markedly higher than those of the recipients of their charity. It we believe what is frequently referred to as the Lerner justification for income redistribution, declining marginal utility of income with wealth, the transfer should lead to a very large increase in the total world utility.

Recently, Willy Brandt was head of a commission composed of profes-

---

the result of exploitation, so on the same principle all the Indians would be entitled not only to the income from but also to the use of a proportional share of the British capital . . .

But what socialists seriously contemplate equal division of existing capital resources among the people of the world. [Friedrich A. Hayek, *The Road to Serfdom* (Chicago: Phoenix Books, 1944), 222–25.]

7. For an unselfish argument, see Charles R. Beitz, *Political Theory and International Relations* (Princeton: Princeton University Press, 1979).

sional bleeding hearts from the developed part of the world and a group of representatives of the poorer part of the world. With great fanfare, they released a report[8] pointing out how badly off the poorer parts of the world were. Despite all the strong statements about the desirability of aid, their principal actual suggestion was that a schedule of transfers from the developed to the underdeveloped world be produced such that 7/10 of 1% of the income of the developed world be transferred in 1985 and 1% in the year 2000.[9] Seldom has such a large mountain labored to produce such a small mouse. Further, there does not seem to be any real prospect of even these extremely modest recommendations being implemented. Once again I do not object to this policy. I would very much prefer continuing my present habits of life even though I am aware of the fact that if I transferred half of my income to the poorer parts of the world, I would save perhaps 30 children.

Indeed, we do not need to consider only government action here. Any one of us who wishes, by deciding to dedicate half of his income to the task and by taking a little trouble to make certain it actually is delivered, could roughly double the living standard of perhaps 20 citizens of south India. I take it no one in this audience is in fact going to take advantage of the opportunity and I also take it that the bulk of you will remove it from your memory banks as soon as possible. Indeed, some of you may devote a good deal of time to producing rational explanations as to why this is not possible. As Benjamin Franklin once said, "It is so convenient to be a rational animal because it permits us to rationalize anything we choose to do."

Note that I am not criticizing you or myself for being more interested in our own creature comforts than preventing starvation in other parts of the world. It seems to me quite normal human behavior. Nor am I criticizing you for normally avoiding thinking about this matter. After all, why should one torture one's self by thinking about something which one could do but does not intend to. What I am saying is that we should not use as an explanation for our income transfer programs a rationalization which does not fit our actual behavior. This, of necessity, will lead to a less efficient achievement of our actual goals in income redistribution than more careful and accurate thought.[10]

8. Independent Commission on International Development Issues, *North-South: A Program for Survival* (Cambridge, Mass.: MIT Press, 1980).

9. Ibid., p. 291. There are some other proposals but they are equally trifling.

10. But see my review of Guido Calabresi and Philip Bobbit, *Tragic Choice* (New York: W. W. Norton & Co., 1978), in the *New York University Law Review* [Gordon Tullock, "Avoiding Difficult Decisions," *New York University Law Review* 54 (April 1979): 267–79].

Let us take Rawls, for example. Here I am going to discuss only one aspect of his argument, which is the view that we should make decisions about income transfers as if we were behind the veil of ignorance. He specifically says that this is only for one "isolated" society.[11] In other words, behind the veil of ignorance you know that you are an American citizen. Now there are only two explanations for this. The first is that he is not talking about the real world. The immigration code, the existence of many illegal Mexicans in our cities, for that matter the existence of some 50,000,000 Mexicans right next to us all of whom would like to come in, the Cubans and the Haitians—to say nothing of the citizens of India and Egypt—all are to be ignored in deciding about income distribution.

Why? The only explanation I can think of is that it would be painful to think of them. The moment we begin talking about being behind the veil of ignorance as human beings rather than citizens of the United States, Rawls' line of reasoning indicates that American citizens' income should be reduced by an immense degree. If this had been clearly pointed out, I would predict that the book would not have been the best seller that it was nor would it have had the great public discussion, mainly approving of the book. What we actually observe in the real world is a very elaborate income transfer system which is mainly internal to individual states.

Indeed, men of good will traveling in India and observing the abominable poverty of almost the entire citizenry of that country, will complain about the government of India not engaging in enough redistribution within the coun-

11. Rawls is a bit hard to pin down on this subject. The only discussion I have been able to find is in the latter part of a paragraph, the first part of which purports to deal with international law. Here he says,

> . . . I shall be satisfied if it is possible to formulate a reasonable conception of justice for the basic structure of society conceived for the time being as a closed system isolated from other societies. The significance of this special case is obvious and needs no explanation. It is natural to conjecture that once we have a sound theory for this case, the remaining problems of justice will prove more tractable in the light of it. With suitable modifications such a theory should provide the key for some of these other questions" [John Rawls, *A Theory of Justice* (Cambridge, Mass.: The Belknap Press of Harvard University Press, 1971), p. 8)].

Note that we do have a "closed system isolated from other societies" in the form of the world. We also have other systems such that the United States which empirically is certainly not isolated from Mexico, Sweden which is certainly not isolated from Turkey, and White South Africa which is certainly not isolated from Black South Africa. If we accept the world as a closed system, Rawls is calling for immense transfers from us to the citizens of India, Africa, etc. If we take any smaller area we do not meet his conditions.

try. Apparently it never occurs to them that they themselves could, by giving away half of the difference between their own income and the income of the average Indian, actually raise the living standard of a considerable number of Indians.

They certainly never seem to show much recognition of the fact that the financial resources of the government of India are very, very small, granted the problem which they face, and the financial resources of the United States and Western Europe are large enough so that we easily could transfer to the poor in India much more than the absolute maximum that could be obtained by the government of India. It is, of course, true that visitors frequently say that the American and European aid program should be larger, and, granted the trivial size of these aid problems, this is an easy argument to make, but they never suggest that we consider all human beings as roughly equivalent and that a current transfer to an American living in Harlem who feels discriminated against because he or she does not have a color TV set could be sent to south India where they might well prevent 15 to 20 deaths a year from malnutrition.[12] However, in practice we observe that the United States and Western Europe engage in large scale transfers to their own citizens who they regard as poor but who by world standards are clearly wealthy, being normally in the top 10% of the world income distribution, rather than transferring to the very poor.

Now once again, I am not criticizing this behavior on the part of the countries concerned. It, in fact, is in accord with my own preferences. I am, however, saying that we should talk about the matter in realistic terms. We should not pretend we are doing something we are not, and we should try to clarify our own motives so that we can select institutions which fit what we want to do and not what we think it pleasant to say we want to do.

It should be pointed out that the income transfers within the wealthier states actually lower real incomes in the poorer states, albeit not by very much. Income transfers within any group will lower the total measured income of that group (albeit they might increase total utility) because it makes the marginal return on labor lower while the wealth effects tend to cancel

12. One of the rationalizations that I frequently encounter at this point is concern about the effect on population of transfers to south India. The effect on the population of the United States of the Aid for Dependent Children Program is normally ignored. In any event, however, if this is a concern, transfers could be made contingent upon suitable birth control measures. On the whole, utilities in south India will be higher if the population is kept down by birth control rather than by starvation.

out. Poor people are made wealthier and the wealthy people are made poorer. Empirical measures of this are relatively difficult but the negative income tax experiments seem to indicate that a not very aggressive income redistribution scheme would reduce production by about 10%.[13]

Since there is a world market in many things, this would mean that the surplus value generated in the poorer countries by greater production in wealthier countries is reduced because of the income transfer schemes in the wealthy countries. Put differently, the things that the poorer countries buy from the wealthy countries will be somewhat more expensive and the things that they sell to wealthy countries will be sold for somewhat lower prices than they would without this program.

It should be said by the way, that there is at least a possibility that direct large scale transfers from the wealthy countries to the poor countries would actually increase measured production. The marginal utility of labor would of course go down in both countries, but in the wealthy countries the reduced real income of each individual might partially, or on the whole, cancel that effect out with the result that the amount of work was about the same. In the poor countries, malnutrition, physical weakness, etc., caused by poverty lower the amount of work that a man can do. It might be that these transfers by getting around these physical limits would produce more work there. But this is merely a possibility. I would hate to argue strongly for its reality.

So far I have been primarily arguing that the standard rationalization of income redistribution policies does not fit. Why then do we engage in income transfers? Surely they are by any measure an extremely important function of most modern states. Further, historically, they have normally been important, albeit not as important as now.

There are, I think, a number of motives which lead to income redistribution. The first, and by all odds most important, is simply a desire on the part of the potential recipients of the redistribution to receive it. Since the donors normally do not wish to give money to people who simply want it, this leads to fairly complicated political difficulties which I will describe below. Nevertheless, I think it cannot be doubted this is the largest single explanation for income transfers in the modern state. The fact that so little of the income

13. See Michael C. Keeley, Philip K. Robins, Robert G. Spiegelman, and Richard W. West, "The Estimation of Labor Supply Models Using Experimental Data," *American Economic Review* 68 (December 1978): 873–87.

transferred goes to the poor is of course the obvious evidence for this. Once again, we are all economists here and I presume you are familiar with the innumerable demonstrations that if our income transfers were concentrated on the poor, the poor would be wealthy even by American standards whereas, as a matter of fact, in spite of all the income transfers they are still very far from that enviable state.[14]

But let me set this particular motive aside for the moment and turn to another set which, I think, undeniably does have some effect on our income redistribution policy. The first is what I would call charitable motives; Hochman and Rodgers called it interdependent utility functions, and this is—roughly speaking—our tendency to literally feel sorry for and want to do something for people who are worse off than ourselves. All human beings seem to have this particular motive to at least some extent, but it should also be said that for most human beings it does not seem to be very strong. I would suggest that the audience of this group consider how much of their income they have in fact given away to people poorer than themselves outside their immediate family.[15] If any of you exceed 5% you will be either deeply religious or a most exceptional person. The deeply religious person who tithes, and this gets up to about 16% all told with the Mormons, is not motivated by charity but by a desire not to burn in hell. It is a coerced transfer, albeit the coercion is attained not by a real threat but by a mythical threat. But if the myth is believed it is as real as a real threat.

Five per cent is, if we look at the income tax figures, actually a rather exaggerated amount for charitable transfers.[16] If we look at the other way in which charity can be organized, by the government, we normally observe that the amounts transferred to the poor are again well under 5% of GNP. Indeed, I am always astonished at how small they are because after all the poor can vote and one would presume would be willing to concentrate their political support on people who would offer them larger payments. They don't seem to do anywhere near as well out of the political process as you would think they would, granted the number of votes they have.

14. Of course they do appear wealthy from the standpoint of the citizens of India.

15. Throughout this discussion, I am talking only about extra-family transfers. Intrafamily transfers are, of course, immense.

16. The income tax figures are somewhat hard to interpret because of the inclusion of religious gifts as charitable. They apparently make up about two-thirds of all gifts and the bulk of this money, of course, does not go to help the poor but to build churches, pay salaries of ministers, etc.

Indeed, in spite of all the talk about the war on poverty, it is not clear that the poor do comparatively better than they did in 1850. Lebergott[17] has assembled some figures which seem to indicate that we've had what amounts to a floor on income, which is about 25–30% of the pay of common labor throughout most of our history. His figures are not very good, not because he is inept but because the data he worked with are very thin, but they are the best that I know. I have often wondered if the poor did not perhaps do better under the combination of local payments and private charity directed to the poor in the 19th century than they do now with programs financed mainly by the federal government, although partly by the states. This seems to me a useful doctoral dissertation project if anyone in the audience is looking for one.

It is possible that the charitable motive tends to weaken as you move away from the charitable person, both in geographical distance and in social distance. If so, this would tend to indicate that citizens of your own country should be treated better than others. It would also, however, indicate that people of your class or people who live in your town should be treated better than other citizens of your country who are not either of your class or co-citizens of the town. I do not think that the sharp difference between citizens of the country and foreigners can be explained by this motive but it does perhaps tend to reinforce other factors that point in the same direction.

The second real motive, and I do not know how strong this is, is simply envy. This is a mortal sin but it is one to which all of us are prone. It is very hard to avoid the impression that envy is an important part of the income redistribution program in most states. In most modern states, the wealthy in fact pay a more than proportional share of their income as taxes. It should be said, however, that of course some of the wealthy have gotten this large income by manipulating the government, but the cure for that is surely not to put a high tax on all upper income people. In spite of this there has been a great to-do about the loopholes for the wealthy and very little attention about loopholes which all the rest of us have. Once again, you are economists and I take it I don't have to explain these loopholes to you.

The explosion of public anger when it was revealed that there were 200 people with adjusted gross incomes of more than $100,000 a year who had not paid taxes is simply one illustration of this point. It is a particularly

17. Stanley Lebergott, *Wealth and Want* (Princeton, N.J.: Princeton University Press, 1975), 57.

good illustration because the reason they didn't pay taxes was that due to peculiar rules promulgated by the Internal Revenue Service, they were compelled to put down as adjusted gross income a figure which is very much in excess of their actual income. The tax was computed on their actual income and not on the adjusted gross income figure.[18]

It is quite widely believed by economists that the upper end of the income tax, and for that matter inheritance tax, schedules is high enough so that the actual tax revenue would be increased by lowering the rate. If this is so, then clearly envy is the only explanation, albeit this can be called negative utility interdependence.

Personal experience here may be of some minor interest. I published an article in which I argued that the inheritance tax should be lowered to the rate which maximized revenue.[19] This was severely criticized by three economists, none of whom denied that the present tax was above the revenue maximizing level but all of whom nevertheless felt that the tax should be either increased or at least retained.[20] Surely this is a clearcut example of the envy motive.

I suspect, with respect to envy, that many people will assume that merely mentioning it is criticism and that we must either conceal it or fight against it. If I were a Minister of Religion, I might agree, but I am an economist and I take utility functions as they are. I find myself periodically envying people. For example, all those people who were able to get articles in the *Southern Economic Journal* when mine were being rejected. I see no reason why we should not expect government policy to take into account real preferences.

It should, of course, be said here that envy does have the unfortunate characteristic that, from a social standpoint, it lowers total payoffs. If I earned a dollar and you were envious, the net effect on society of that dollar is less than a dollar because, although it gives me a dollar's worth of utility, it gives you negative utility. This is depressing but, aside from preaching, I can think

18. See Roger Freeman, "Tax Loopholes: A Legend and Reality," *AEI Hoover Policy Study* (May 1973): 19–26.

19. See Gordon Tullock, "Inheritance Justified," *Journal of Law and Economics* 14 (October 1971): 465–74.

20. See Kenneth Greene, "Inheritance Unjustified," *Journal of Law and Economics* 16 (October 1973): 417–19; Thomas Ireland, "Inheritance Justified: Comment," *Journal of Law and Economics* 16 (October 1973): 421–22; Rollin Koller II, "Inheritance Justified," *Journal of Law and Economics* 16 (October 1973): 423–24; and Gordon Tullock, "Inheritance Rejustified: Reply," *Journal of Law and Economics* 16 (October 1973): 425–28.

of nothing to do about it. Of course, if envy is strong enough, then taking a dollar away from me might give other people a total satisfaction which was larger than the loss of the dollar to me. Thus, plundering the Rockefeller family might be socially desirable if we had some way of measuring innate utilities.

A third argument for income redistribution is one which I seldom see in the literature.[21] I do occasionally run into it in conversation. This is the insurance motive. Risk is somewhat reduced if an institution is set up which will tax me if my income is high and supplement my income if it is low. It should be said that this particular argument also provides a direct and immediate justification for the policy of the South African and all other governments of concentrating their transfers on their own citizens. The white South African may go broke, but he will not become black. Similarly, I may be forced into bankruptcy, but I will not become a Mexican. White Englishmen will not become one of those Englishmen who are not white and whose passport does not permit them to live in England and have a share of the welfare state.

There are, of course, more subtle examples of the same thing. It is a matter of practical fact that ruling Communist parties provide arrangements under which Communists who have difficulties do not fall to the same level as individual citizens in their society.[22] There used to be a society in England for the aid of distressed gentlefolk and which saw to it that members of the upper class didn't fall to the level of the average worker. Similar institutions can be found in other areas. They are quite reasonable from the standpoint of the insurance motive, although not necessarily from other standards.

But so far we have talked about what one might call general motives. Earlier I expressed the opinion that overwhelmingly the most important reason for income transfers in our society is or was desire on the part of the recipients to receive it. The farm program, high wages of civil servants—the particular activity that almost all of us are engaged in—the development of human capital at a subsidized rate for people whose natural talent is such that they would already have a higher income than the average even without this capital, the price controls which have the purpose of transferring large

21. James M. Buchanan and Gordon Tullock, *The Calculus of Consent: Logical Foundations of Constitutional Democracy* (Ann Arbor: University of Michigan Press, 1962), is, of course, an exception; see Chapter 14.

22. Unless the difficulties are political, of course.

amounts of wealth from American owners of oil wells to Arab Sheiks (about two-thirds) and American consumers (about one-third of the transfer) are all examples.

There is one obvious characteristic of these transfers and that is that they are highly inefficient. Take, for example, the transfer from the owners of oil wells to the American consumer and the Arabs. As far as I can see, the Arabs had substantially nothing to do with the institutions which led to this transfer. They were beneficiaries of programs put in place by American politicians for the benefit of American consumers. In essence, for every dollar which was actually transferred to the consumers, $2 was, from the standpoint of the politician and the consumers, wasted. This was because the only simple, direct way of carrying out the transfer, which would not have benefitted the Arabs, would have been to put a tax on the owners of oil wells and use it to directly subsidize general expenditures of consumers. This was apparently politically impossible and so the highly inefficient scheme was adopted.

Further, it was normally discussed in highly misleading terms. I can recall being in Pittsburgh during the early part of the Arab oil embargo in 1973, and almost every day the Pittsburgh paper had two leading stories. One story would be a relatively factual discussion of the Arab program for raising American prices. The other would be a denunciation of the American oil companies for putting the price of oil up. Since the oil companies were very nearly innocent bystanders of the whole thing, the only explanation for all of this is that it was possible for the Americans without much difficulty to put penalties on the oil companies, but the only way of dealing with the Arabs would involve an invasion of the Middle East, which most people didn't want to even think about.

I mention this particular example because it is characteristic of most of the cases where transfers are made simply because the recipient wants to receive them. These transfers are characteristically extremely inefficient. In addition to the inefficiency which we would expect that comes from switching the marginal return on income away from the actual marginal product and the rent seeking inefficiency, there is normally another very large inefficiency which comes from the fact that the transfer has to be concealed as something else. A straightforward tax on the group of people who consume wheat with the receipts used to pay wheat farmers cash benefits would leave both the consumers and wheat farmers better off than they are under the present program. Further, this is well known to most economists. Indeed, when I was at the University of Chicago in the 1930s, it was frequently offered as a standard example of government ineptitude. But such a straightforward tax would never get through.

In the particular case given above of the oil well owners against the consumer and the Arab Sheiks, the consumers are immensely more numerous than the oil well owners. Most government transfers, however, are transfers to small, politically influential groups like the farmers, the civil servants, people who want to send their children to college, etc. There is no way of getting these transfers through if the simple straightforward method of cash payments is chosen. That is just a little too obvious. Deception is, in general, necessary in these cases, and the deception cannot take the form of simply lying—it has to take the form of setting up a structure which makes the transfer while purporting to do something else.[23] Relative inefficiency which is generated by this type of deception can be very much greater than either the distortion of the margin or the ordinary rent seeking cost.[24]

These inefficiencies are very large indeed. It is not clear, however, that we can do anything about this inefficiency. Economists have for a long time talked about government as a mechanism for providing public goods or dealing with externalities. It undeniably does this, but in order to do so it must have coercive powers, and the use of these coercive powers to benefit people in terms of their political influence seems an obvious thing to expect from profit maximizing individuals.

As a matter of historic fact, it would appear that the state originated out of a desire to make coerced transfer and began producing public goods and dealing with externalities as a by-product. We do not have very good data on the origin of the state, but what evidence we do have seems to indicate that it started when some individual or small group with comparative advantage in the organization of violence seized an area of land in order to compel the people living there to make transfers to them. Having the area, protecting it against other potential "governments" was an obvious necessity in order to keep up tax revenue, and preventing private crime also had advantages. The building of roads, which of course originally were primitive tracks, as a way of improving the efficiency of the military in all of these activities, and in particular in suppressing local rebellions, also occurred very early in the history of the state.

23. For a good discussion of the role of "obfuscation misdirection," see J. M. Finger, H. K. Hall, and D. R. Nelson, "Political Economy of Administered Protection" (Washington, D.C.: U.S. Treasury Department, Office of Trade Research, 1980).

24. Of course, it could be regarded as simply part of the rent seeking cost.

We should not be surprised about this, of course. As economists, we anticipate that people will produce cars not because they want to help the customers but because they want to make money. The fact that the state was set up originally because someone wanted to make money rather than because he wanted to provide public goods is also a profit maximizing explanation. It is, of course, true that throughout history most governments have had as one of their major objectives a transfer of tax money quite directly from the ordinary citizen to Kings, nobles, government officials, etc.

It seems likely that, as a matter of fact, the common citizen in most cases got a good bargain out of this, since he was better off than he would have been without the government there. It is only when we compare this kind of exploitative state with an ideal state, which exists only in imagination, that we can argue it is inferior.

Nevertheless, any economist looking at the existing democratic states in which so much money is transferred back and forth in the middle class in terms of political power and organization is normally and quite justly appalled. The inefficiencies which come from changing the marginal return on effort and investment, rent seeking costs, necessity of using deception, and the by-product of sometimes changing the whole nature of society are immense. The question is, can we do anything about it?

The first thing to be said is if we are going to provide public goods, the justification for a government which most economists use,[25] we must use coercive taxation and the purchase of various resources, including of course services of government officials. Once this state exists then, it will begin to change the incomes received by the various people in the society. Producers of goods which the government needs will find their incomes are somewhat higher, people who are burdened with taxation will find theirs lower, etc. Thus, income transfers come from the very nature of the system. This is true even if we have a society which literally followed the Pareto optimal rules of always compensating losers. There still would be some people who gained more from government activity than others and, presumably, some who gained not at all because their losses were just exactly compensated.

Real governments, of course, are not Pareto optimal, and I think the idea in the back of the minds of most economists with respect to this kind of thing is that the government should undertake the bulk of its activities with a fairly simple, straightforward cost-benefit analysis in mind. It undertakes those

25. Here I include transfer to the poor to the extent that they are in fact desired by the population in general. This is apt to be a small extent but not "0."

activities where the benefit is larger than the cost and chooses taxes which have minimum excess burdens, etc.[26] Income redistribution should then be handled by a totally separate organization which arranges some taxes on the upper income groups to pay aid to people in the lower income groups. These are indeed two of Musgrave's three functions of government.

I will not quarrel with this as a conceivably desirable system although I think we can do better through the demand revealing process, but no real government is likely to do this. There will be people with power, even very modest power, who can use that power to change the pattern of purchases and taxes to their own advantage. The best that we can hope for is to make this a relatively minor phenomenon. Further, looking at it as ourselves, mainly government officials whose salaries are paid for out of coerced taxes, perhaps we should not even be in favor of minimizing it, but simply seeing how we can maximize our own incomes.

But assuming temporarily that we do want to have a system in which the waste which comes with income transfers from one part of the population to the other simply as the outcome of the political process and pressure by the recipients which has not been adequately countered by pressure from the people who are taxed is minimized, what can we do? Unfortunately, there is not very much we can do in an immediate, direct way. If government purchases everything by the way of competitive bid, then one type of income transfer is to some extent reduced. It will still be to the best interest of various producer groups, however, to press for more purchase of their product and for individual producers to attempt to provide a lower quality than the bid actually calls for. Under modern circumstances the problem of exactly specifying the bid is so difficult that the negotiated bid, with its immense opportunities for transfer, may actually be more efficient than the competitive bid.[27] There doesn't seem to be any tax analogue of the competitive bid, and hence taxes are pretty sure to be sources of inefficiency and income transfers. The rather traditional economic recommendation of some type of very broad based tax, whether it is the income tax, expenditure tax, value-added tax, etc.,

26. Of course the calculations are often very poorly done.

27. I once worked for a company which sold a great many water wheel governors to the government. Over the years, their sales force had succeeded in gradually adjusting the government specifications for water wheel governors so that to all intents and purposes they had a monopoly. Transfers to them were probably large, although as a matter of fact they made excellent governors.

would seem to minimize the possibility of transfer in this area but it certainly does not eliminate it.

Further, these two types of recommendations more or less assume that the problem has been solved. If people can use political power to obtain transfers to themselves and other people find it necessary to use political power to attempt to avoid being the victim from such transfers, they are likely to fight over the type of taxes and the type of expenditures as well as other things. There does not seem to be any obvious reason why, if we are able to get the government to accept purchasing and tax policies which would minimize these transfers, we would not be able to minimize them almost regardless of the purchasing and tax policies we have.

There is, I think, only one bright point in this particular area. That is that the transfers, generally speaking, require deception. If they are plain and above board, they normally cannot get through a democratic process. This seems to indicate that economists could have some influence with their educational function. Of course, I don't want to exaggerate their importance here, but the fact remains that the CAB is now in the process of disappearing, the ICC is exerting its regulatory powers much less than it was, and the FCC also is moving towards reducing its transfer component and producing a more competitive market. These are very considerably examples of response by the political apparatus to a simple economic argument. It turned out that the economists were able to convince people. It was always true, with respect to all three of those agencies, that a majority of the people were injured and it was only as long as the minority who benefitted kept this a secret that they could remain in existence. Breaking through this kind of secrecy is difficult because the average person has very little motive to become more informed on the activities of, let us say, the CAB. Nevertheless, it is not necessarily impossible and we should do the best we can.

But that very minor recommendation for reform is not the main point of this paper. My main point is simply that we should stop fooling ourselves about redistribution. We have a minor desire to help the poor. This leads to certain government policies. We also have some desire for income insurance. And we also, to some extent, envy the rich. All three of these motives can lead to some income redistribution but probably to a fairly small amount. Further, they aren't necessarily particularly noble. Elaborate ethical justifications for income redistribution normally cannot be used to justify the actual policies we observe in the world. The largest single source of income redistribution is simply the desire of the recipients to receive the money.

This leads to the immense redistributions we observe to people who from any external characteristic are not particularly deserving. Perhaps because I occasionally visit Eldora, Iowa, which is right next door to Grundy County, the wealthiest county in the United States at the moment, I tend to think of the farmers as the extreme example of this kind of beneficiary of transfer, but there are many others. Many, in fact, are in this room. I shall not say whether there are any on the platform. Though we may personally benefit from these transfers, they all are negative sum games and extremely negative sum games. Society as a whole is injured and we are injured by the whole web of them. We would be better off if we could get rid of them. If that is not possible, let us at least speak the truth about them.

PART 6

BUREAUCRACY

DYNAMIC HYPOTHESIS ON BUREAUCRACY

In my review of William Niskanen's *Bureaucracy and Representative Government*,[1] I proposed a theoretical explanation for the growth of bureaucracy. Briefly, Figure 1 (reproduced from the original review) shows the cost of various sizes of bureaucracy as a horizontal line, demand by the average citizen as line C, and the demand by the bureaucrats as line B. The bureaucrats have a higher demand because they obtain not only the services, but also the salary. The politician, then, perceives some mixed demand curve, such as B,C, and purchases the appropriate amount of bureaucracy, shown as B,C on the horizontal axis. From the standpoint of the ordinary citizen, this is an oversized government as compared to C, which is what he would like. This system can lead (and that was the point of my discussion in my review) to a continuing expansion of bureaucracy since, if the Congress expands the bureaucracy in one period, that means that there are more bureaucrats in the next period, with the result that B,C shifts to the right to B′,C′.

Note that the same phenomenon would affect any provider of resources to a democratic government. This would probably be more important in the case of the bureaucracy, however, because it seems likely that $1 million in payrolls to bureaucrats purchases more votes than $1 million in payments to other factor producers who will, of course, put much of the cost into things other than hiring personnel. Still, the theory developed in the rest of this note fits all factors used in government. Fortunately, that raises no great problems for the analysis at the very general level of this note. If there is further work along these lines, no doubt it will have to be looked into carefully.

Looked at from the standpoint of the members of the existing bureaucracy, there is a superior solution. Instead of increasing the number of bureaucrats, the pay of each individual bureaucrat could be increased so that C amount of government was purchased, but at a unit cost of M, and a rent would be achieved by the bureaucrats equivalent to the rectangle above the cost line and to the left of C. This is, of course, an exploitational monopoly which ob-

Reprinted, with kind permission of Kluwer Academic Publishers, from *Public Choice* 19 (Fall 1974): 127–31.

1. (Chicago: Aldine-Atherton, 1971.) Reviewed by Gordon Tullock in *Public Choice*, 12 (Spring, 1972), 119–24. William Niskanen has very kindly looked at this note and made some useful suggestions for improvement.

tains some of the monopoly profit. Still, short of depriving the bureaucrats of their votes, it is hard to see anything much that can be done about it.

On Figure 2 I have drawn much the same diagram, but left out line B′C′ and B,C in order to simplify it. Lines D and D′ are two hypotheses about the dynamic course of employment and wages within the bureaucracy. D shows a situation in which the bureaucrats exploit their power to the utmost from what we might call a standing start. The bureaucrats would presumably not be interested in hiring new bureaucrats to replace individuals who died or retired. This would permit them to do rather better over time than is shown in Figure 1; but, on the other hand, as the number of bureaucrats declined, their political power would also decline (line B,C on Figure 1 would tend to be closer and closer to C) with the result that, although per capita incomes might continue to increase, the total expenditure on bureaucracy would tend to get closer and closer to the C line. Whether it would follow the dynamic

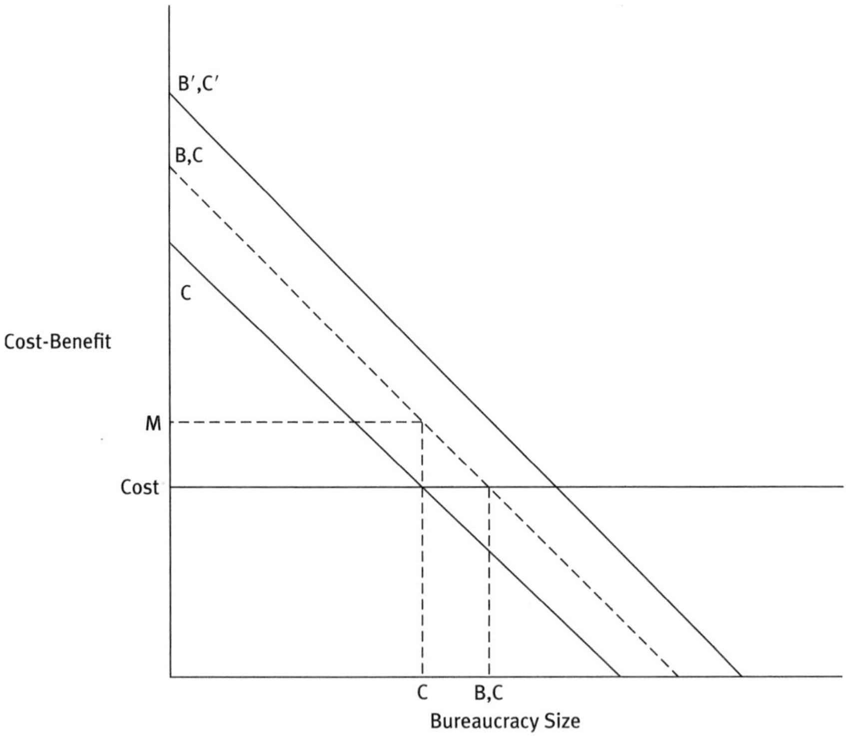

FIGURE 1

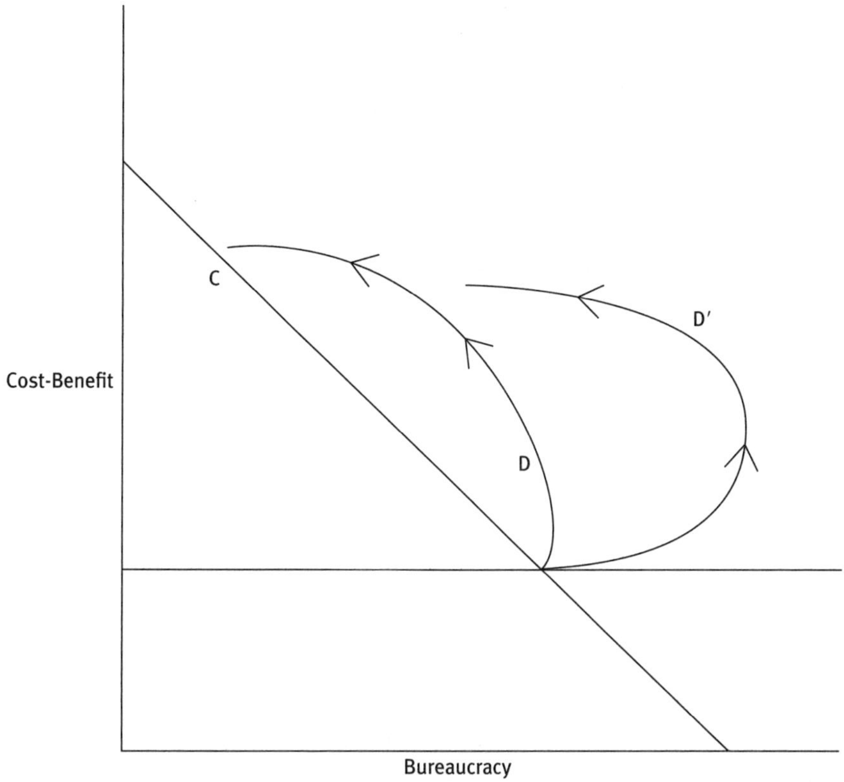

FIGURE 2

path I have drawn in as line D on Figure 2, I cannot say; but some general curve of that nature would seem to be likely.

Presumably the reason that we do not observe this kind of thing in the real world in its simple form is that the bureaucrats do not actually have enough political power to achieve it. The institutional arguments which lead Niskanen and others[2] to argue that bureaucracies tend to maximize their size have to do with restrictions on increasing income directly. The structure of most modern bureaucracies is such that large improvements in the returns to indi-

2. Including myself; see, Gordon Tullock, *The Politics of Bureaucracy* (Washington, D.C.: Public Affairs Press, 1965), pp. 134–36.

viduals are hard without considerable increase in the total number of individuals employed. In essence, the expansion of the bureaucracy increases the income of the existing bureaucrats by raising the number of supervisors that are needed.

Presumably the reason that these restrictions exist is simply that the bureaucrats' political power back at the time when the civil services were established was rather low because there were very few of them. Under the circumstances, we might anticipate that, in the early days, the bureaucrats would use their power primarily to increase the number of bureaucrats. As the number increased, however, it would become possible to use more and more of their power to directly increase wages. In a sense, the individual bureaucrat tries to increase his wages, but realizes that there are political gains from increasing the number of bureaucrats in that he will be able to have more political power to increase his wage in the next period. Expansion becomes a sort of investment.

If this is so, as the power of the bureaucracy increased, one would anticipate that more and more of the political rent would be taken in increased wages and less and less in increased size. In this case, we might anticipate that a line such as D′ would be the dynamic path of growth of a bureaucracy.

There are some signs that this in fact does represent the development of bureaucracy in the United States. Certainly at the moment the rise in wages of the bureaucracy, particularly as the result of unionization of bureaucrats, is rather more impressive than the rise in numbers. This, however, is a short-term phenomenon and I cannot think of a strong reason to believe it will continue.

Note, however, that both lines D and D′ have segments which bend back, i.e., areas in which the bureaucrats' political power is going down because the number of bureaucrats is going down. It is not clear that bureaucrats would actually be able to retain the political power to hold their high wages as their numbers decline. Thus, it may be that only the portion of line D′ lying below and to the left of the first arrow is realistic. If so, there would be a true equilibrium size of the bureaucracy.

The problem with this hypothesis is that it is extremely difficult to think of any expirical way of testing it. The exact shape of these curves is not specified, nor do I know at what point we are along the curves. Last, but not least, the D′ curve, which (as the reader will have deduced) is what I think fits our society, has two forms, in one of which it stops and the other in which it continues. Indeed, as a matter of fact it has three forms. A number of South American bureaucracies have succeeded in maintaining political support for themselves by reducing the amount of time that each individual bureaucrat must be in office. Thus, they get a very large number of bureaucrats at a relatively low cost to the taxpayer. The bureaucrat is overpaid for the time he actually puts in, but the total output is quite low. This provides a very large number of voters, and hence a great deal of political power, and shifts the line D′ sharply to the right; but, at the same time, it permits the bureaucrats to get quite high hourly payments even if they find it necessary to have other jobs.

Still, the fact that the hypothesis is hard to test does not prove that it is untrue. Unfortunately, it also does not prove it is true. Nevertheless, it is my hope that someone will think of a way to test this hypothesis, which is superficially plausible and, again superficially, appears to be in accord with the behavior of the real world.

THE EXPANDING PUBLIC SECTOR

WAGNER SQUARED

James M. Buchanan and Gordon Tullock

Government spending, as a share of total spending, has increased substantially in all democracies in the period since World War II. The common-sense inference from this record is that the real size of government has grown. Morris Beck[1] has demonstrated that this inference is invalid. Because the "price of government services rose substantially more than the price index of total output,"[2] the real size of the public sector actually declined in a majority of Western democracies, and the increase was decidedly modest in others. For the United States, to take a single case, Beck's data show that the real size of the public sector grew from 20 percent of GDP in 1950 to 24 percent in 1970, a considerably smaller growth than would be indicated by the 31 percent share of public spending in GDP. From these results Beck optimistically infers that "in real terms, the era of public-sector growth in most developed economies may have ended."[3]

Our reading of the agreed-on data is different. We infer from the record that the growth of the public sector may have, indeed, changed its form, but that predictions of long-term developments must be viewed with considerable foreboding. The data may suggest that the public sector is "out of control" in the literal sense of this term.

Not only in the United States but in a number of other democracies, rising salaries of civil servants "were a major factor in the comparatively large rise in the government price index."[4] Since the government in the United States and, for that matter, in other democracies had grown quite rapidly up to 1950, it is obvious that the wages then being paid to civil servants must have been high enough to attract not only replacements but enough employees for expansion. Thus, I think we can feel confident that the average postal

Reprinted, with kind permission of Kluwer Academic Publishers, from *Public Choice* 31 (Fall 1977): 147–50.

1. Morris Beck, "The Expanding Public Sector: Some Contrary Evidence," *National Tax Journal* 39 (March 1976): 15–21.

2. Ibid., p. 18.

3. Ibid., p. 15.

4. Ibid., p. 16.

TABLE 1. ***Pay of Government Employees as Percent of Pay of Nongovernment Employees***

CATEGORY	1952	1972
All federal employees	101	129
Civilian	128	155
Military	82	103
All state and local employees	101	110
Private service	79	80

SOURCE: *Statistical Abstract of United States*, Volumes 75 and 95 (Washington: U.S. Department of Commerce, 1954, 1974); *Historical Statistics of the United States: Colonial Times to 1970*, Parts I and II (Washington: U.S. Department of Commerce, 1975).

clerk in 1950 was not earning less than he could have earned in other employment, all perquisites properly weighted. Indeed, governmental workers at that time in the United States were earning more than service workers in general. Why, then, did governmental wages and salaries increase relative to nongovernmental stipends?

The facts are not in dispute. Table 1 indicates the comparative wage levels for various types of public-sector employees, along with service wages in general. The relative increase in the former is clear, and it is particularly impressive with respect to federal government civilian employees.[5] We confront a puzzle: Why did the salaries of civil servants rise so rapidly over this period?

The only explanation that has been offered, to our knowledge, is based on the political power of civil servants themselves. According to straightforward public-choice theory hypotheses, we could predict that the votes of bureaucrats would be partially directed toward expanding the size of their agencies and partially toward raising their own salaries.[6] So long as the bureaus or agencies remain relatively small, expansions in bureau size probably offer the most attractive payoff to employees. As agencies become larger, however, and the bureaucracy members come to make up a larger and larger share of the total voting constituency, the possibility of the usage of civil servant voting

5. The fact that the salaries of military employees have hardly moved above those for the economy-wide averages is notable, especially for the period after the abolition of conscription and when it is recognized that a high percentage of military personnel are involved in highly technical activities.

6. See Gordon Tullock, "Dynamic Hypothesis on Bureaucracy," *Public Choice* 19 (Fall 1974): 127–31.

power to expand salaries directly becomes real. Beck's data may suggest that not only the U.S. but most democracies have passed the phase of expansion in the sheer size of bureaus and have now moved into the phase of expansion of bureaucratic salaries.

It is sometimes suggested that government is inherently unprogressive because it is a labor-intensive and capital-extensive industry. So far as we know, the only empirical investigation of this subject indicates that even the civilian sector of the government is capital intensive.[7] Further, it would be hard to argue that a good deal of the military is not extremely capital intensive. Note that it seems to have obtained lower wages than the nonmilitary part of the government.

Other changes in budgetary composition parallel and reinforce those noted above. Transfers have been the most rapidly expanding component of governmental budgets in the last part of the period. The transfer budget also offers the prospect for actions by a group of voters with a direct pecuniary interest in the budgetary outcomes. So long as the recipients of transfers make up a small share of the total electorate, this group could exert relatively modest effects on the overall size of the transfer budget. Once this group becomes large, however, it can obviously exert greater political power. Until quite recently—if we take historic time—those who received transfers in a democracy were not permitted to vote.[8]

One way of looking at the disproportionate increase in the salaries of government employees is to separate the "market wage" and the "transfer" portions. This would allow us to treat a part of governmental salaries as we do

7. See William Paul Orzechowski, "Labor Intensity, Productivity, and the Growth of the Federal Sector," *Public Choice* 19 (Fall 1974): 123–26.

8. It is hard in the present day to realize what a shock the change was. As late as 1914, however, A. V. Dicey, referring to an old-age pension law which covered only a very small portion of the poor in England and which was unique at that time in permitting the recipient to vote, asked, "Surely a sensible and a benevolent man may well ask himself whether England as a whole will gain by enacting that the recipient of poor relief, in the shape of a pension, shall be consistent with the pensioner's retaining the right to join the election of a Member of Parliament?" *Lectures on the Relation Between Law and Public Opinion in England in the Nineteenth Century*, 2nd ed. (London: Macmillan and Co., 1963), p. xxxv.

There were exceptions for recipients of particular types of transfers—for example, war veterans and government pensioners. These groups have normally been (a) small in total, (b) elderly, and therefore continually shrinking, and (c) motivated not to bring additional recipients into the total transfer program.

other transfers. This leads to what we have labeled the "Wagner squared" hypothesis. The share of the population actually employed by government may be reaching its maximum in Western democracies. But this does not imply that the government budget is moving toward its own maximum share of GNP or GDP, since it may well be possible for transfer recipients (bureaucrats and others) to continue to raise their incomes. Presumably, there is some limit on this process, but it has not been determined either theoretically or empirically.

If government spending, as a share in total spending, continues to expand, but without a corresponding increase in governmental output (even if the latter is measured by inputs, itself an increasingly questionable procedure), downward pressures must be exerted on resource returns in nongovernmental employments. With stable monetary growth and downward wage rigidity, some unemployment will be generated. If, in response, the monetary authorities expand the rate of monetary growth, inflation is produced. "Stagflation," which has been called *the* economic problem of the 1970s, can at least be partially explained by the hypotheses advanced in this note, hypotheses that are fully consistent with the data now available. The public sector may indeed be "out of control" in the sense that its development is no longer related to the desires of the ultimate "purchasers" of governmental services.

PART 7

THE SOCIAL DILEMMA

THE EDGE OF THE JUNGLE

The existence of large, elaborate social structures among human beings is hard to explain on instinctive grounds. The point of this series is to look into the foundations of property rights and attempt to explain these foundations on the basis of assumptions of individual maximization. In general, we have been using the Bush model of natural distribution in which we follow "the old way, the simple plan; let him take who is able, let him keep who can." It is the purpose of this paper to add on to this model another rule of individual maximization which can, I think, be regarded as the foundation of all interhuman cooperation.

Let me begin, however, by making two modest modifications of Bush's basic model. Firstly, cooperative organizations may exist, even in a Bush state of nature. A pride of lions operates internally in terms of strength and combativeness of the individual members of the pride. Nevertheless, it is more efficient in its hunting so that a low-ranking member of the pride will normally eat more than he would if he attempted to hunt on his own. Similarly, we might expect groups organized on the Bush plan engaging in conflict, or efforts to control or enslave, other individual human beings or other groups. I take it that this is not a vital modification, but it does provide for an elementary construction of groups which gets us out of Hobbes' problem that man must sleep. A group of ten could organize among themselves according to the pure Bush-Hobbesian model; but with respect to another group of 100 slaves, they might be able to exert a great deal more control than any individual within the ruling elite can exert over the remainder of the elite.

My next modification is a bit more serious, and is an effort to deal with what I think is a weakness in the Bush model. There is no serious reason for trading to proceed between members when the stronger can seize anything he wishes. This is particularly true if one assumes an organized group exploiting a larger group of subjects. I think that we can, by a little reasoning about evolution and biology, deduce something about human beings which is observably correct and which explains the need for trade in addition to, or supplementing, straightforward, pure use of coercion.

Reprinted, with permission, from *Explorations in the Theory of Anarchy*, ed. Gordon Tullock (Blacksburg, Va.: Center for Study of Public Choice, 1972), 65–75.

Consider a pride of lions. Granted the Malthusian nature of the world, there must be periods of time in which the amount of food taken is not great enough so that the highest ranking members of the pride can completely satiate themselves, while leaving enough to keep the lower ranking members in good health. Under these circumstances, some reduction in the food consumption by the strongest members will not greatly affect their health, but will very significantly benefit the weaker members. There is, however, no way in which evolution could directly work for restraint on the part of the stronger members. Surely such restraint, if it were built in as a hereditary part of their constitution, would mean that they are less likely to survive than other, equally strong lions who do not have such restraint. The gene pool would always move toward eating food to full satiation. It would, of course, prevent the lion from eating enough food to reduce its physical efficiency by becoming fat.

If we observe lions, dogs, and human beings when they are confronted with something which they want and which is not present in large enough quantities for satiety, we see a good deal of threatening behavior among them and sometimes fighting. On one level, this would appear to be foolish from the standpoint of the weaker. Suppose that there is a quantity of meat and two lions, one larger than the other, who want it. If they fight, the larger has a very good chance of winning and the smaller, therefore, will not only get nothing to eat but will probably be quite severely injured.[1] Nevertheless, we do observe occasional fights and a great deal of behavior which can only be described as threatening of fights under such circumstances. Further, on occasion the larger lion will give way.

Granted the larger lion does occasionally give way, the behavior of the smaller lion becomes rational. In essence, the smaller lion is rationally designed to engage in irrational behavior. The smaller lion imposes upon the larger lion the prospects of physical injury, even though the prospects of physical injury for the smaller lion are much greater; hence he reduces the attractiveness of the combination of food plus fight to the larger lion below what it would be if it were simply the food with the smaller lion withdrawing. There should be some level of belligerence for the smaller lion which maximizes its evolutionary success. Note, however, that this requires that the smaller lion sometimes fight and fight hard. Since at the moment the fight be-

1. Ardrey says that the principal cause of death among lions is fights with other lions. (See, *African Genesis* [New York: Delta, 1963], pp. 41 and 103.)

gins, the odds are heavily against the smaller lion, it must again behave irrationally under these circumstances if it is to have much chance of survival.

The mechanism which makes this possible, I believe, is "loss of temper." Individuals make threatening noises about things that they want for rational calculations. The actual serious fighting by the smaller of the animals or, as we shall see in a moment, by the larger of the animals, however, requires temporarily behaving in what is an irrational way. You threaten your opponent with irrational behavior on your part and the threat is indeed rational. Therefore, a built-in, hereditary reaction pattern such that you will, on occasion, behave irrationally may be quite rational in the long run.

The existence of this type of loss of temper then automatically produces a bargaining range. Assume, once again, a large and a small lion growling at each other over a piece of meat. Assume that evolution has designed their behavior in such a way that it is basically rational. The larger lion would get some particular gain from each unit of food. Further, each unit of food he takes increases the likelihood that the smaller lion will lose his temper and there will be a fight in which the smaller lion will be killed, but the larger lion will suffer injury probably greater than the value of that unit of food. The larger lion, of course, is running down his demand curve for food as he eats. The smaller lion, on the other hand, is going up his demand curve as the larger lion eats each mouthful. Presumably there is some point at which the survival probability of the smaller lion is higher if he takes his chances in attacking the lion than if he remains without eating; but the built-in apparatus which made the smaller lion fight at an earlier stage would probably, over a large number of cases, increase the survival potential of that particular gene. In any event, if the fight occurs, the net result is a decline in life expectancy for both animals. Further, the potential of the fight is a continuously rising cost imposed on both animals. Under the circumstances, some kind of a bargain in which the danger of the fighting is reduced to zero would be desirable.

We do not observe this kind of bargaining among animals. There is a continuous threat, continuous rise of the likelihood of fighting, and occasional actual fighting. This is probably because of the limitation on what can be designed into the rather simple brains and communication systems with which animals are equipped. Human beings, having much larger computer capacity, can make conscious bargains in these cases. Note, however, that for the bargain to be rational for the large, more powerful human, the prospect of the weaker human losing his temper and attacking—even though he faces a present discounted negative value on the attack—is a necessity. The probability of losing one's temper and attacking against odds would have survival value, even though the attack itself will normally have negative payoff. This is particularly so if the larger and stronger human being hopes to continue to exploit the smaller human being over time, and hence would be most unwise to kill him. Thus, the historically observed fact that slaveowners used positive incentives very commonly to get more work out of their slaves can be explained.

This problem is, of course, very similar to what we find in game theory. The mixed strategy which is the optimal solution of many matrices will normally provide for at least some probability of an individual player being called upon to play a strategy which, taken in and of itself, is the worst on the board. Nevertheless, adopting a mixed strategy in which he sometimes engages in this apparently foolish behavior is optimal. The human being would presumably *not* adopt the dangerous strategy every fifteenth time because when the fifteenth time came, he would rationally calculate it is weaker. A built-in, automatic biological mechanism—the loss of temper—can, however, give the same results.

So much, however, for this reason why we would anticipate that the complete reliance upon coercion and physical strength would not be optimal. If we grant that it is not optimal, i.e. that sometimes there is a trading range, then the discipline of continuous dealings becomes important. Suppose, for example, that we first consider a situation in which there is a strong man and a weak man occupying the same area, but that the weak man physically is not capable of supporting both of them; hence, the strong man engages in some production himself and, in addition, preys upon the weak man to the maximum extent which he thinks is feasible. Granted the possibility of the weak man losing his temper, the strong man would be well-advised to restrict his predation to some extent. Thus, the weak man will in fact occasionally have things which the strong man would want.

It is likely that the strong man will have things that the weak man would want also, and the prospect of trade would arise. In order for this trade to be possible, the weak man must feel confident that if he produces something above and beyond his normal payments to the strong man, the strong man will not simply seize it. Thus, the strong man would, if he were sensible, have a fairly regular schedule of predation, but would be willing to make trades on things above and beyond that regular schedule. The reason is the discipline of continuous dealings. If the strong man regularly seizes three coconuts from the weak man, but on one occasion when the weak man happens to have a papaya and offers to trade it for some of the strong man's products, the strong man seizes it; then the strong man can feel confident that never again will the weak man, if he happens to have some additional papaya, offer to make the trade. The question is whether the present discounted value of the profit on a number of future trades is greater or less than the value of papaya which the weak man has at the moment. This should, of course, be added to the possibility of loss of temper on the part of the weak man when the papaya is grabbed.

Note that credit has not entered into the computations so far. Neither the strong man nor the weak man is attempting to trade something in the present for something in the future. All the contracts are contracts for simultaneous performance. The only restraint on the discipline of the continuous dealings so far is a restraint upon seizing whatever the other party has brought for the trade, instead of trading for it. There is, of course, the willingness of the stronger to give up something in return for the papaya. It is interesting that these conditions do not apparently ever occur in the animal kingdom; hence, pure trades do not seem to be observed there.[2]

Trades of this sort clearly could improve the well-being of both parties. It might be possible for the stronger to acquire for himself the bulk of the improvement, but that would simply be a statement as to where they are on the new and improved Paretian frontier, rather than a denial that they would move outward. Note, however, that this particular variant of continuous dealings will continue to exist only so long as there are no significant accumulations of property. The stronger man does not take the weaker man's property because of the present discounted value of profits in future trades. If the weaker man's property becomes a large enough quantity, then this condition would cease to be true and seizure of the property would be rational.

So far we have discussed the problem entirely in terms of the use of force and violence, but fraud, stealth, and deception are also possible. They are harder to guard against and, in fact, guarding against them normally involves fairly large resource investments. Thus the existence of these possibilities will divert a good deal of energy from the society toward protective activity and away from production, with the result that the total product will be lower.

2. There are some cases where animals or plants engage in preprogrammed behavior which has some of the characteristics of trades, if looked at from the standpoint of the entire species. Individual trades, however, appear to be unknown.

As a third problem, there has so far been no mention of credit. There will, however, be occasions in which a trade which is not simultaneous would pay; trade in which A must do something today and B reciprocate with some action or property tomorrow. The discipline of continuous dealings could permit such trades to go on, but only, again, so long as the repayment that B must make tomorrow is less in value than the present discounted value of future profits. This condition is found even today in illegal activity. Black market dealers and professional gamblers are very, very careful to keep a good reputation because it is their reputation for prompt payment which makes it possible for them to continue in business. They are, indeed, probably more careful about prompt performance than a businessman who can make a contract which will be enforced by the courts.

So far, we have seen a number of cases where trading can be organized and the reason it can be organized is simply the discipline of continuous dealings. The individuals find the present discounted value of future dealings greater than the profit they can make from seizing property or refusing to make payment today. It is clear, however, that there are many situations in which we could not depend upon this very simple variant of the discipline of continuous dealings. The obvious case, of course, is simple accumulation of property until such time as the total amount accumulated is greater than the present discounted value of a set of transactions. Surely a fairly small amount of property would normally have that characteristic, granted the fact that it must counterbalance *not* the total value of future transactions but merely the profit on them.

A credit transaction raises the same problem. Transactions in which large payments will be made in the future would be impossible if we depended solely on the discipline of continuous dealings.

Introduction of enforcement apparatus, Mr. Gunning's giant, would deal with this problem by making it possible both to accumulate and to enter into credit transactions. The enforcement apparatus could also be used to deal with the theft, stealth, and deception way of obtaining funds. In essence, the enforcement apparatus—instead of attempting to guard everything continuously—threatens the individuals with severe punishment *if* they violate some set of rules. The punishment is heavy enough so that the present discounted value of such rule violation is negative. This technique can be used to make it possible to accumulate capital, engage in extensive credit transactions, and make it unnecessary for the average citizen to put very much of his energy into guarding his property against stealthy removal. It can also be used to eliminate the advantage that the strong has over the weak, although here the arguments for doing so are not so obvious. Indeed, historically, there have been a great many societies in which the people who entered them as slaves have tended to remain slaves for long periods of time. We would anticipate that moving out of the simple Bush-type world would be highly beneficial even if the benefits were distributed in a manner which was highly unequal. The haves might gain wealth, and the have-nots might make little or no improvement in their status. Egalitarians might find the prospect painful, but it would be admitted—even by them—that it was better than the jungle.

The introduction of some kind of enforcement apparatus, then, would be desirable to all members of the society, albeit it might be more desirable to some than to others. It would be possible to distribute the profits from the establishment of such an enforcement apparatus in exactly the same ratio as the wealth held by the various denizens of the jungle before the apparatus was established. It would also be possible to adjust this distribution in several ways. The bulk of the profit could accrue to some people and not to others. It would also, we should note, be possible that the state of nature would change. It might be that certain people with relatively little wealth or income in the state of nature as it was originally set up would gain greatly by the transfer to the new system, while some individuals who had done very well under the previous system would find their income going down very sharply. In essence, we are not getting away from the state of nature, we are simply changing the technological characteristics of individual power. If we set up an enforcement apparatus, those characteristics which led to large income in a jungle may cease to lead to large income now. Diplomacy, salesmanship, and careful judgment of other people's opinions and values may make it possible for a person in the new society with an enforcement mechanism to apply force to an individual who physically is much stronger and who, in a single combat, would certainly win. This is not because we are no longer dependent upon force and violence, but because the technological conditions for using them have changed. Under the new scheme, an individual's ability to use force and violence is not so closely correlated with his personal strength and cunning.

Let us make the simplest assumption of transition conditions from the jungle to one where there is an enforcement apparatus. Assume, then, a jungle in which there are some bands—like the pride of lions—and that one of these bands succeeds in destroying or enslaving all of the others and establishes firm control. This control would, firstly, lead to a considerable change in the income distribution in the jungle in that the members of the winning band would have much larger incomes, and the losers would have lower incomes. It would be rational for the stronger members of the winning band to permit sizable improvements in the income of the weaker members at the expense of non-members of the band, simply in order to retain the support of these weak members. The cohesion of the new government would depend on suitable rewards for all members.

This new controlling group would presumably establish a system under which it "exploited" the remainder of the population to some degree which it thought was efficient. If, however, it wishes to maximize its drawings from the remainder of the population, it would be well-advised to establish a set of rules under which this subject portion of the population devotes relatively little time to fighting with each other, or guarding its own wealth against other members of the subject population, and/or attempting to get the wealth of members of the subject population. By reducing the input of the subject population in these activities, it would make it possible for the subject population to produce a larger net revenue to the new ruling group.

Under these circumstances, the discipline of continuous dealings would have relatively little to do with the relationships among and between the subject population. They would be controlled by external sanctions imposed by the rulers. It would be possible for the subjects to accumulate capital—feeling confident that other *subjects* would not be able to take it away—to enter into large contracts for future performance under the impression that they would be enforced, and in other ways take advantage of economic opportunities which would not exist if the only enforcement mechanism was the discipline of continuous dealings. It would be to the advantage of the ruling group to provide the necessary enforcement.[3]

If the collection of people now incorporated under the rule of the "upper class" is not the entire population of the world, then the possibility of clashes with external groups would exist, and it would be in the best interests of the ruling group to protect its subjects against predation from the outside.[4]

There are, however, two other possible social relations which we have not so far discussed. One of these would be the relations between the ruling

3. Of course, the degree of enforcement is subject to appropriate calculations along the lines of Becker, etc., but it will not be discussed here.

4. Once again, the resources to be put into this protection are not something we will discuss here. It would not be infinite.

group and the subjects, and the other would be the relations within the ruling group itself. Since the ruling group itself is the police force which keeps the peace among the subjects, there is no police force to control its behavior, either with regard to the subjects or with regard to other members of the ruling group. This is a problem which must, under our present model, be dealt with once again by the discipline of continuous dealings.

Looked at from the standpoint of the ruling group, the optimal policy would be to select a set of payments which members of the subject group must make to the ruling group which maximizes the return. Presumably, there are two variables. Firstly, the fees, etc., charged to the ruled people should be arranged insofar as possible to provide them with incentives for hard work. For example, if the ruling group takes all of the coconuts any individual produces above the barest subsistence for his family, the individual would have little motive for producing coconuts. On the other hand, if the ruling groups take some large quantity of coconuts from each individual and then pay little attention to whether or not his family subsists, it would provide maximum incentives for hard work on the part of the subjects, provided of course that it would be possible for most families to continue to subsist on the amount remaining.

In addition to decisions as to the appropriate type of fees to impose upon the subject group and the laws which bind the behavior of the members of the subject group with respect to each other in an efficient way, the actual decision on the total amount of transfers to the rulers must be made with some care. In general, increasing the percentage of the product produced by the subject group transferred to the ruling group will reduce the total product. At some point, the increase which is obtained from increasing the percentage of production transferred will be counterbalanced by the fall in the total product. That is the point of maximum taxable capacity and should be the area at which the ruling group aims. Note that if the ruling group is sensible, it will choose this rate at such a level that a good deal of inequality is possible among the subject people. This is in order to give the subject people incentives for hard work. If they can, indeed, improve their own status if they work hard, and starve to death if they do not, they are likely to be more productive than if they are all kept right on the brink of starvation.

Note that this last rule to some extent depends on both the possibility of loss of temper and the difficulties of information. If the ruling group were capable of exactly computing the potential productivity of each member of the subject people, it could set a tax upon such people at a rate which kept them just at the level of starvation at their maximum work-level. It is unlikely, however, that a ruling group will ever have that kind of knowledge. Further, the prospect of such behavior setting off fairly large scale loss of temper, with the losses that this would lead to on the part of both the ruled *and* ruling groups, is a consideration.

If the ruling group proposes the use of an efficient system of drawing funds from the ruled group, then it must set up some way of administering these transfers and of controlling individual members of the ruling group who might wish to exceed the standard. Suppose, for example, that the ruling group consists of 100 people and the subjects number 2,000 to 3,000. Mr. Smith, one member of the ruling group, is interested in seizing an additional coconut from Mr. Jones, one of the ruled. If he is permitted to do so, this will mean that the security, and hence the incentive, of the ruled is reduced. The gain will go entirely to Mr. Smith and not at all to the other members of the ruling group. The ruling group has, then, a motive for preventing this kind of thing from happening.

Note that the reason that the ruling group has motives for preventing this individual depredation, or depredation at a level or according to a structure which is not optimal, is the discipline of continuous dealings. They are compelled, in motivating behavior on the part of the subjects which will eventually produce a maximum income to the rulers, to give themselves a pattern of behavior on which the subjects can depend. Thus, the discipline of continuous dealings—having been eliminated for intrasubject dealings—is returned for government-subject dealings. It is subject to exactly the same requirements that we had before. If the profit from a single act of depredation is greater than the losses from the elimination of future profits on regular transactions, then the government would be well-advised to grab. The subjects, if they had an opportunity, will almost always be well-advised to attempt to throw out the rulers. The rulers must see to it that the subjects never have such an opportunity. Note, however, that the discipline of continuous dealings, in dealing between the ruling group and the ruled, is essentially a public good from the standpoint of individual members of the ruling group. Since most of the cost of reducing the security of the subjects will fall on the other members of the ruling group, while the entire profit of the particular bit of depredation will accrue to the person who does it, the individual members of the ruling group would be motivated to violate the general rules which maximize income to the ruling group. The discipline of continuous dealings would indicate that the ruling group members would have motives to, if they could, discipline each other in order to maximize the long-term value of group membership.

So far we have discussed the relations between various members of the ruled, and between the rulers and the ruled. We have not discussed the relationships between members of the ruling group. They could be in a state of nature with respect to each other, i.e. the income derived from the exploitation of the ruled would be divided among the rulers in accordance with the Bush model. This would be like the lion pride in which the lower-ranking members accept inferior status because it is still better than not being a member of the pride.

There are, however, profits available to the members of the ruling group from restricting their own internal relationships to a more orderly pattern. The ability to trade under conditions in which the discipline of continuous dealings will not afford guarantees, the accumulation of capital or other property beyond the level which would be protected by the discipline of continuous dealings,[5] and the possibility of making long-run contracts for large amounts would also be things which the ruling group would like to obtain for themselves. These are all areas where positive profits can be made by moving *out* of the Bush-type state of nature. Our subject society so far has moved the ruled out of this state of nature, but not the rulers.

A particularly important aspect of the long-term contract would be provision for the old age of members of the ruling group. The discipline of continuous dealings would never tell you not to seize the wealth of an old and feeble man, because he would never be in a position to retaliate. If you wish to assure a reasonably pleasant life in your old age, or, for that matter, to members of your family if you die,[6] or if you are badly injured, you would be interested in moving from the discipline of continuous dealings to some method of enforcing agreements, property rights, etc., which is superior to it.

The restrictions on the individual depredations of members of the ruling group upon the ruled, and upon the behavior of the rulers with respect to others, could be arranged by setting up some set of rules and arranging to have them "enforced." The problem is establishing an enforcement mechanism which will not, in and of itself, become another ruling group, thus put-

5. The ruling group might specialize in chateaux and other consumption goods.

6. It is not obvious that close relations among members of the family would be in accord with Bush's state of nature, but it is characteristic in economics to simply exempt family matters. Let us hope this custom will be terminated in the future, but it will require further research.

ting the present ruling group—or the bulk of it—into the subject category, while reviving the basic problem for the new ruling group.

The simplest way of doing this would be to use the old-fashioned posse or vigilante method. Suppose, then, whenever any member of the ruling group either engages in unauthorized depredation upon the subjects or another member of the ruling group, or fails to carry out a contract, etc., all the rest of the members of the ruling group gather in a mass and inflict some punishment upon him. The members of the ruling group are, by adopting this institution, imposing some cost upon themselves in order to enforce the rules, i.e. they must occasionally take action as members of the posse. This is, of course, the reason why Becker, etc., calculate optimal degrees of enforcement for various laws. Let us assume, as seems reasonable, that the cost will be less than the benefit. Under these circumstances, the members of the ruling group are prevented from violating contracts, etc., by the threat of retaliation, just as are the members of the subject population. The organization is only a little different. The individual members of the ruling group are impelled to join the posse, however, by the discipline of continuous dealings. They know that if they do not join the posse on one particular time, then the posse may not turn out to help them in the future. Under the circumstances, it is very unlikely that the present discounted value of failing to turn out for the posse will be higher than the costs which would be imposed by not receiving its protection later. Thus, the discipline of continuous dealings would lead to people turning out as members of the posse, and the posse would impose a "rule of law" on the whole population, including its members when they acted as individuals.

Note that there is nothing in the model so far to prevent a group of members of the ruling class, or indeed a group of members of the ruled class, from forming a counter-group and attempting to defeat the posse. Presumably there would be potential coalitions capable of doing this available at any time. It is not clear, however, that such coalitions would pay. Once again, the discipline of continuous dealings is involved. But here the discipline should be imposed by making it "illegal" to even begin the organization of such a group. If the detection apparatus is efficient, it could detect formations of such coalitions before they are far enough along to have much chance of success.

The posse, of course, is a relatively inefficient mechanism. In general, we tend to turn toward specialization and division of labor. Setting up a special organization for the purpose of policing the rules would be an improvement in efficiency, if some method could be designed which would prevent this special group of policemen from becoming themselves a ruling group. There are two basic methods for this purpose. The first is simply to have the police weak enough so that the ruling group can readily defeat them. The long-standing tradition in England that there be no standing army is an example. The general weakness of the American government, the provision that individuals may carry arms, the weakness of the king in medieval Europe before the armed nobles, and many other examples of this method may be described.

It is unlikely, however, that this method in and of itself is optimally efficient for large groups. A more efficient method is to set up the enforcement apparatus in such a way that it is not capable of organizing itself for the purpose of overthrowing the existing regime. This requires that the enforcement apparatus be composed of quite a number of different people, and that their organization be such that they could not instantaneously convert themselves into a ruling group. A conspiracy within this large organization would be necessary and there would be an effort to detect such conspiracies early, with the result that they could be disposed of before they were large enough to be dangerous. It is not obvious that this is possible; indeed, the history of coups would seem to indicate that it is quite difficult, but it is surely not utterly impossible either. In any event, this is the mechanism upon which most societies have depended.

Note, then, that although we have come a long way from Hobbes' bush, we still depend on physical power to enforce the rules. We still depend, also, upon the discipline of continuous dealings, but the discipline of continuous dealings is now used only for a small part of society. It is only those members of the police force who are expected to report potential conspiracies among their fellow officers who find it necessary to make such discipline of continuous dealings calculations. They, if they feel that the present discounted value of the conspiracy is higher than the probable rewards of continuing in their present activity, would not report it. The rest of society, however, faces the much more efficient system of rules and enforcement of those rules by a body which is enough stronger than they are individually so that they are not well-advised to resist it, and hence waste resources. As a consequence, society would be much more efficient. Indeed, the whole point of civilization may be said to be the pushing back of the jungle and the discipline of continuous dealings into a minor role. We cannot, however, completely eliminate them because they are the only motives available, in the last analysis, to motivate enforcement of the rules.

As a final *coda*, I should like to talk very briefly about cooperative states.

The state I have described so far involves a ruling group and a much larger ruled group. Normally we would like to be in states which are somewhat more egalitarian than that, unless we are fairly confident we will be in the ruling group. We can imagine the society as a whole going through the same line of reasoning we have so far described for the ruling group only. They would not, of course, be interested in the relations within the "ruled" group because this would not exist; but they would have the same motives for establishing controls within the new ruling group which is all of society, and could end up with approximately the same solution. One can imagine various other ways in which one could make the transition from the jungle to civilization, depending on the power structure at the time that the transition began.

It should be noted, however, that we are in a way still in the jungle. It is still true that our society in the last analysis depends on the combination of force and discipline of continuous dealings in order to retain its ability to enforce its rules. It may, of course, fail because the rules are bad or because it loses the desire to enforce them; but, even with good rules and a full willingness to enforce them, society will still be built on a Hobbesian foundation.

CORRUPTION AND ANARCHY

It will surprise political scientists, but a number of economists have argued for governmental corruption. The specific instances in which economists have favored corruption, however, have all been cases where the government is inept and bribery could be predicted to lead to a superior outcome. The obvious case is the official who is paid to turn his back upon black market dealing at a time when the government is attempting to simultaneously implement price controls and monetary inflation. Similarly, a number of economists were more pleased than otherwise by the discovery that some members of the FCC under Eisenhower were, in essence, selling television channels rather than allocating them according to the basically irrational criteria provided for under the existing law. We do not observe economists arguing that it would be desirable for murderers to bribe the judges.

Even in this latter case, however, economists are perhaps less opposed than political scientists because they would regard the bribe as an implicit part of the punishment. The individual who escapes execution or life imprisonment by paying a judge $50,000 is in much the same situation as he would be had he been simply fined $50,000. Indeed, if the judge took advantage of his monopoly position and extorted the maximum payment he could receive, the felon would be little (if at all) better off as a result of paying the bribe rather than accepting the punishment.[1] Only if the potential corrupt officials are in competition with each other and, hence, have their price forced down would the "corrupter" make any great gains.

Of course, if the felon is poor and has poor credit, then the bribe that he can pay may be well under whatever would be the socially appropriate punishment to impose upon him; hence, he may gain from the bribery system. Indeed, the development of a bribe system could be predicted to lead to felonies primarily being committed by poor persons.[2] There is, of course, a fur-

Reprinted, with permission, from *Further Explorations in the Theory of Anarchy*, ed. Gordon Tullock (Blacksburg, Va.: Center for Study of Public Choice, 1974), 65–70.

1. Gary Becker and George Stigler, in a paper prepared for the Friedman birthday conference, made this point with great force. Although this paper is not directly related to much of the following paper, it was, nevertheless, a great help to me.

2. Gordon Tullock, *The Logic of the Law* (New York: Basic Books, Inc., 1971), pp. 216–21.

ther problem: corrupt officials might design the laws to maximize their bribe receipts. When I was in Hong Kong, the restrictions on getting an automobile license—if you had the misfortune to be a Chinese—were such that the only way of doing so was to pay about $500 H.K. to the inspecting officer. This bribe was not collected from those Chinese who came to the inspection inadequately prepared—which might conceivably have been socially desirable—but from all Chinese. Hence, it merely effected a transfer without having any desirable social effects.

So far, however, this discussion has been discursive and not particularly precise. Let us proceed to more rigorous examination of the problem. First, we shall follow economic tradition by assuming that there are zero transactions costs. It is not at all obvious that this assumption is a sensible one outside of the traditional market area, but in this case it will produce some interesting results. I propose to introduce transactions costs at a later point.

The Coase theorem, which holds that the outcome in cases of externality is not affected by the institutions, would appear to apply to problems of corruption as well. Suppose, for example, (and, to repeat, assuming zero transactions costs) that I should like to murder some person. If we have a completely corrupt police system and no transactions costs, I would find out how much the police and courts would take to permit me to murder without punishment. My potential victim, on the other hand, would find out how much they would take to protect him. Presumably, the outcome would be that the highest bidder would prevail and, distributional problems aside,[3] the outcome is clearly Pareto optimal. It would guarantee the most efficient allocation of resources.

We could proceed to apply the same line of reasoning to any other law. Is it, however, true that complete corruption could exist for *all* laws? It would appear that if it works for each law, then it must be applicable to all; but this is not true.

In fact, a system of complete government corruption is equivalent to anarchy, i.e., of having no government at all. Surely in a situation in which there is no government it would be possible to motivate people to do anything you wish by offering them suitable compensation. In a completely corrupt government, officials could be motivated to do anything you wish by suitable payments and, hence, there would be no difference between this society and

3. It is customary in economics to deal with distributional matters separately from efficiency matters. I will follow this tradition; distributional matters will be discussed later.

that of anarchy. If, as I believe is correct, people under anarchy are every bit as selfish as they are now, we would have the Hobbesian jungle.[4] In any event, we would be unable to distinguish a fully corrupt government from no government.

To say that we are unable to distinguish fully corrupt government from no government emphatically does not mean that the Coase theorem could be applied. Under a situation in which there is no effective government, property does not truthfully exist. Individuals cannot pay bribes because they have no secure possession of things to use as a bribe. Thus, the Coase theorem cannot be completely generalized. Unless there is some secure property in the system, it is not possible to trade property for performance; hence, it is not possible to purchase your way to the Pareto optimal frontier. The system of bribes cannot be used to support a private property system, because if private property depends upon the payment of bribes, then the bribe to be extorted can be the full value of the property and, hence, the property has no value.

Note a point of some theoretical importance here. The modern justification of government turns on the joint existence of externalities and transactions costs. According to the conventional wisdom,[5] both of these conditions are necessary. We have succeeded in demonstrating that government would be necessary even in the absence of transactions costs, because without transactions costs the payments necessary to achieve Pareto optimality would be impossible unless there is some institution guaranteeing property.

So much for the situation without transactions costs. Let us now introduce them. Under these circumstances, we assume that various government policies have been selected by some process and that the people who choose them, in any event, wish to have them carried out. If it is desired to have these policies carried out rather than have them evaded, then we must attempt to insure that public officials in fact do what they are intended to do. The most primitive and simplest procedure is to give the officials the right to raise certain amounts of income by placing fines upon individuals who violate the government policies. Note that this method, however, is only available when the public policy is designed so that individual action is controlled by fines. You could not get modern roads built by this method. Under this system,

4. See, Gordon Tullock, ed., *Explorations in the Theory of Anarchy* (Blacksburg, Va.: Center for Study of Public Choice, 1972), for a working-out of the implications of the Hobbesian view.

5. See, Gordon Tullock, *Private Wants, Public Means* (New York: Basic Books, Inc., 1970), for a comprehensive statement.

you can permit police or judges to impose fines on lawbreakers and use that as part or all of their source of income.

Indeed, you can sell the job to the government official, if the total amount of fines brought in is greater than his net income and there will be some revenue to the state. In all cases, the official is motivated to seek out lawbreakers. The problem, of course, is that he is likely to over-enforce the law, i.e., to fine people who have not actually violated the rules. If we turn to other types of policy or simply hire individuals to carry out the rules, then we have the problem of preventing corruption. Indeed, the over-enforcement of rules mentioned above is simply a special case of corruption. The standard method used—always and everywhere—to prevent corruption is to attempt to make corruption have a negative payoff. Some kind of punishment is imposed so that an intelligent public official would choose not to become corrupt because the net cost of corruption is greater than the profits. Needless to say, it is necessary to take into account the likelihood that a given fine will in fact be imposed upon the corrupt official.

This is simple and straightforward, but has the disadvantage that it leads to an infinite regress. Quis custodiet ipsos custodes? If we have a special police force which watches the regular police force for corruption, then this special police force in turn can be corrupted. Eventually we must of necessity come to some person, organization, or group which enforces the rules, even if offered a large, safe bribe for violating them. Thus, eventually we must depend upon something other than avoidance of punishment as a reason for refraining from corruption. The obvious way of obtaining this ultimate enforcement without concern with bribes is to have the ultimate enforcement done by whoever has chosen the basic policy. Thus, the voters in a democracy might be thought of as the ultimate enforcers of the rules against corruption. Unfortunately, voters have essentially no motive to become well-informed about anything connected with their vote; hence, they are apt to be very bad policemen.

In a despotism, things are a little better. The despot does have good reasons for becoming well-informed and seeing to it that what profits are made in his system accrue to himself; hence, if he is wise, he will prevent corruption of the sort we have been discussing. This may not be exactly obvious with real-world despots because many despots find it desirable to pay very high incomes to some of their subordinates. Sometimes these incomes reach the subordinates by channels which would imply corruption in a democracy. I think, however, we can say that in most cases these payments are known to the despot and accepted by him as a necessary cost of obtaining services of the person who receives the payments.

There is a technique sometimes used by despots to improve their control over their subordinates which can also be used in democracies. The despot will set up not one secret police organization but a number, each of which has among its duties spying on the others. Since he rewards the leaders of these organizations for catching each other, he minimizes the amount of time and effort he must put into the problem of supervision himself. Democracies can make use of the same technique. Indeed, the division of the American government into the three coordinate branches, each with power to check the others, can be taken as a mildly modified example. By this technique, the voter may have information on corruption brought to his attention without any significant energy on his own part. Hence, the problem of the infinite regress can, at least in part, be solved and, at the very least, corruption has to be very widespread before it can be successful.

There is, however, a final phenomenon which must be discussed in any paper on corruption. It is not clear that the subject to which I will now turn fits the word "corruption," but it clearly has some relationship to it. The person (or persons) in charge of the government may make use of his powers to increase his own income above and beyond that which is necessary in order to provide the government services which justify the existence of government. A despot, for example, may choose to take for himself an income which is much larger than is the true opportunity cost for his services. Indeed, no one looking at the world would have any doubts at all that most despots have done this. They also frequently use part of this income for gifts, which amount to transfers to various favorites. There is, of course, no check on such activity because, in a despotism, the despot is the ultimate authority. The despot may, through ineptness and bad management, succeed in providing an opportunity for his overthrow; but this has relatively little to do with his consumption pattern.

Democracies raise exactly the same problem. Suppose that a group of voters, through their control of votes, chooses to transfer funds from other people to themselves. Once again, every democracy of my knowledge does in fact do this kind of thing. Perhaps the outstanding example in most modern democracies is the very large transfers made from the poor to the college students. Everybody in this room is involved in expediting this particular regressive transfer. Although there are some people who allege that higher educational procedure is justified by externalities, so far as I know nobody has ever succeeded in producing any empirical evidence that any of these externalities exist. It would seem fairly certain that the real motive for subsidized higher education is simply that a group of voters—upper-class parents—want it and that they use their political power to get it.

Since the voters are the ultimate authority in a democracy, there is nothing to prevent this kind of activity. Once again, the voters can, of course, through ineptness and incompetence, produce a situation which leads to their own overthrow. The oldest democracy in South America—Uruguay—went under not very long ago; I would predict that Chile—which is almost as old in democratic ways as Uruguay—will go under shortly. In both cases, this was a question of ineptness and incompetence; and, in both cases, very large transfers from one part of the citizenry to others who had political power were arranged. It is not, however, clear that these transfers were the cause of the overthrow.

As I remarked earlier, it is not at all obvious that this last phenomenon falls within the scope of the word "corruption." It is obvious, however, that the phenomenon is very similar to corruption and that we would like to prevent it if we could. There are, of course, some people who feel that in the case of democracy such transfers are desirable, because they believe—in the teeth of the evidence—that such transfers are normally from the wealthy to the poor. In practice, although there are some transfers to the poor and quite large transfers away from the wealthy, the bulk of the transfers do not follow a postulated course and, hence, can be argued for by no widely held normative system. Still, there seems to be nothing we can do about them and, even if the earlier types of corruption are curable, this one would appear to be intrinsic to all forms of government.

THE PARADOX OF REVOLUTION

Revolutions are a favorite subject of many modern "committed scholars." The volume of their work, in my opinion, greatly exceeds its penetration. Indeed, it is the purpose of this essay to demonstrate that the image of revolution which we find in the literature (both by the committed scholars and by more traditional scholars) is a false one. I shall also, I hope, demonstrate why this false image is so appealing to intellectuals and historians.

Let us consider, for a start, a very simple situation. Ruritania is governed by a vicious, corrupt, oppressive, and inefficient government. A group of pure-hearted revolutionaries are currently attempting to overthrow the government, and we know with absolute certainty that if they are successful they will establish a good, clean, beneficial, and efficient government. What should an individual Ruritanian do about this matter? He has three alternatives: He can join the revolutionaries, he can join the forces of repression, or he can remain inactive.[1] Let us compute the payoff to him of these three types of action. Equation (1) shows the payoff to inaction. This simply indicates that the payoff is

$$P_{In} = P_g \times L_v \tag{1}$$

the benefit which he would receive from an improved government times the likelihood that the revolution will be successful. Note that this payoff is essentially a public good. He will, of course, himself benefit from the improved government and he may well benefit from his feeling that his fellow citizens are well-off. But in this case, he will receive no special, private reward.

The payoff for participating in the revolution on the side of the revolutionaries is shown by equation (2).

$$\begin{aligned} P_r = {} & P_g(L_v + L_i) + R_i(L_v + L_i) - P_i[1 - (L_v + L_i)] \\ & - L_w \cdot I_r + E \end{aligned} \tag{2}$$

$$\begin{aligned} P_r = {} & P_gL_v + P_gL_i + R_iL_v + R_iL_i - P_i + P_iL_v + P_iL_i \\ & - L_wI_r + E \end{aligned} \tag{2a}$$

Reprinted, with kind permission of Kluwer Academic Publishers, from *Public Choice* 11 (Fall 1971): 89–99.

1. In the real world, of course, there are various shades between these clear-cut alternatives, but our simplification will cause no great damage.

This differs from equation (1) in two respects. First, the individual's participation on the side of the revolutionaries increases the likelihood of revolutionary victory to some extent, presumably to a very small extent in most cases. Second, the individual now has a chance of reward, perhaps in the form of government office, if the revolution is successful and a chance of being penalized by the government if the revolution fails. Finally, he runs an additional risk of being injured or killed.

Note, however, that generally speaking the individual's entry into the revolution will actually change the likelihood of revolutionary success very little. Indeed, the value of L_i is approximately zero. Assuming this is so, then equation (2) simplifies to the approximation (3).

$$P_r \cong P_g \cdot L_v + R_i L_v - P_i(1 - L_v) - L_w \cdot I_r + E \qquad (3)$$

Approximate equation (3), however, shows the total payoff for participation in the revolution. The individual should be interested in the net, i.e., the participation in the revolution minus the payoff he would receive if he were inactive. This is shown by equation (4).[2]

$$G_r \cong R_i \cdot L_v - P_i(1 - L_v) - L_w \cdot I_r + E \qquad (4)$$

It will be noted that the public good aspect of the revolution drops out of this equation. The reason, of course, is that we are assuming that the individual's participation in the revolution makes a very small (in fact approximately zero) difference in the likelihood of success of the revolution.

If this approximate line of reasoning seems dubious, we may go back to equation (2a), rearrange the terms a little bit, and get equation (5) which is an exact rather than an approximate expression.

$$G_r = (R_i + P_i)L_v + (P_g + R_i + P_i)\, L_i - P_i - L_w I_r + E \qquad (5)$$

Once again, it is obvious that unless L_i is large (say at least 10 percent of L_v), equation (4) is a very good approximation. What we have been saying is, once again, that the revolution itself is a public good. Individuals, we have

2. Note the rather peculiar algebraic role of P_i, the punishment the individual is likely to receive if he participates in the revolution and it fails. Due to the rules of algebra, this turns up as a minus quantity for the entire punishment with certainty, which is offset by a positive figure which is that punishment discounted by the probability of victory. It would be intuitively much simpler if our equation showed this expression in some more lucid way. It is still true, however, that increasing the weight of the punishment, something which is clearly within the control of the government, would greatly reduce G_r.

***Table of Symbols* 1**

SYMBOL	DEFINITION
D_i	Private reward to individual for participation in putting down revolt if government wins.
E	Entertainment value of participation.
G_r	Opportunity cost (benefit) to individual from participation rather than remaining neutral.
I_r	Injury suffered in action.
L_i	Change in probability of revolutionary success resulting from individual participation in revolution.
L_v	Likelihood of revolutionary victory assuming subject is neutral.
L_w	Likelihood of injury through participation in revolution (for or against).
P_d	Payoff to participation in revolt on side of existing government.
P_g	Public good generated by successful revolution.
P_i	Private penalty imposed on individual for participation in revolution if revolt fails.
P_{in}	Total payoff to inaction.
P_p	Private cost imposed on defenders of government if revolt succeeds.
P_r	Total payoff to subject if he joins revolution.
R_i	Private reward to individual for his participation in revolution if revolution succeeds.

known since Samuelson's basic article, are likely to underinvest in production of public goods.

Let us now, however, turn to the opposite possibility—entering the revolution on the side of the government. Equation (6) shows the payoff for this activity.

$$P_d = P_g(L_v - L_i) + D_i[1 - (L_v - L_i)] - P_p(L_v - L_i) - L_w \cdot I_r + E \tag{6}$$

Note that the individual's intervention by lowering the probability of revolutionary victory lowers the probability that he will receive the public good. Once again, assuming that the individual's participation has very little effect, i.e., L_i is approximately equal to zero, we find equation (7) which corresponds to equation (3), i.e., it is the net return from participating on the side of reaction.

$$P_d \cong D_i \cdot (1 - L_v) - P_p \cdot L_v - L_w \cdot I_r + E \tag{7}$$

The equivalents of equations (5) and (6) could also be produced easily.

It will be noted that the approximate result we get indicates that the individuals would ignore the public good aspects of the revolution in deciding whether to participate *and* on which side to participate. The important variables are the rewards and punishments offered by the two sides and the risk of injury during the fighting. Entertainment is probably not an important variable in serious revolutionary or counterrevolutionary activity. People are willing to take some risks for the fun of it, but not very severe ones. If, however, we consider such pseudorevolutions as the recent student problems in much of the democratic world, it is probable that entertainment is one of the more important motives. The students in general carefully avoided running any very severe risks of injury or heavy punishment, while the chance of rewards was also very slight because they directed the revolutionary activity toward such institutions as universities where little was to be gained. The fact that E is not readily measurable would raise problems in empirical testing. Fortunately it is a minor factor in serious revolutions. Thus it could be left out in testing the equation.

If we change from our approximate equation to exact equations, it makes really very little difference. Under these circumstances, the public good remains in the equation, but has very slight weight unless the individual feels that his participation or nonparticipation will have a major influence on the outcome. Since most participants in revolution should have no such illusions, it would appear that the public good aspects of a revolution are of relatively little importance in the decision to participate. They should, therefore, be of relatively little importance in determining the outcome of the revolution. The discounted value of the rewards and punishments is the crucial factor.

This is the paradoxical result which gives this essay its title. It immediately raises a number of questions in the mind of any reasonably skeptical scholar. For example, why is the bulk of the literature of revolution written in terms of the public good aspects rather than in terms of the private rewards to participants if public good aspects are, in fact, so unimportant? Second, may we not have obtained our results by oversimplifying the situation? Third, what is the empirical evidence as to the truth or falsity of what is, so far, a completely *a priori* argument? We shall take these questions up *seriatim*.

Beginning with the question of the image of revolution, we should note that this image is essentially an intellectual one. Consider an historian in his study contemplating the French Revolution. He is not going to be either penalized or benefited by participation in this revolution which happened some two hundred years ago. Under the circumstances, the only things that concern him are its public good aspects. He may have been benefited or injured by the change in society which resulted from the revolution. He surely was not benefited or injured by the system of rewards and punishments for participation in the fighting. The parts of the revolution which concern him, then, are almost entirely the public good aspects. As the potential participant disregards the value of the public good generated because its value falls to nearly zero in his personal cost-benefit calculus, the historian disregards the private payoffs to participants because their value falls to almost zero in *his* calculus. They are costs and benefits for other people, not for him.

Similarly, the reporter filing stories on a revolution and the editorial writer in New York are affected, if they are affected at all, by the public good aspects of the revolution rather than by the private rewards/punishments which might lead to direct participation in the fighting. Putting the matter more directly, each participant or observer is interested in that part of the total situation which is of maximum importance for him. That part which is important for the observer is rarely important for the participant and vice versa.

There is one class of participants who also formally emphasize the public good aspect. A great deal of our information about revolutionary overthrows comes from the memoirs of people who have participated in them, on either the winning or the losing side. These people rarely explain their own participation or nonparticipation in terms of selfish motives. Indeed, they very commonly ascribe selfish motives to rivals or to the other side, but always explain their own actions in terms of devotion to the public good.[3] Thus, they present themselves in the brightest light and their opponents in the darkest. We should not, of course, be particularly surprised by this quite human behavior on the part of these human beings, but we should also discount their evidence.

If we turn to arguments that are used during the course of a revolution to attract support—either recruits to the fighting or, perhaps, foreign aid—we will normally observe a mixture of appeals to public and private benefits. In general the approach is much like that of the army recruiting sergeant. He will undoubtedly tell his potential customers that joining the army is patriotic, etc. He will also tell them a great deal about the material benefits of military service. Indeed, this is a very common practice in all fields of life. I happened one day to be walking through the Marriott Motor Hotel in Wash-

3. It should be noted that a somewhat similar phenomenon affects the nonparticipant observers like scholars and reporters. If they have become partisans of one side, they are apt to accuse the partisans of the other side of having individualistic motives.

ington at a time when they were engaged in instructing new waitresses in their duties. As I walked by, I heard the woman who was giving the lecture explaining to them what an honor it was to operate at Marriott, that the customers at Marriott Hotels are superior customers, and that the employees there are, generally speaking, exceptionally good. This appeal to what we might call the public good aspect of employment is not uncommon in any walk of life.

Since the recruiting sergeants, the people asking for support for (or opposition to) revolutions, and the Marriott Hotels all make use of this appeal as well as more individualistic appeals, it is clear they have some effect. I would guess, however, that the effect is small. The army, in attempting to attract recruits, puts far more money into the salary of its soldiers than it does into propaganda about patriotism. Still, the joint appeal is sensible; people to some extent are motivated by ethical and charitable impulses.

We have thus explained why the intellectuals and other nonparticipant observers of revolutions normally discuss them almost exclusively in terms of public goods. We have also explained why the participants probably are more strongly motivated by direct personal rewards than by these public goods. I should like to emphasize here, however, that I am not criticizing the intellectuals for their field of concentration. Clearly, if we are evaluating the desirability or undesirability of a revolution in general terms, the public good aspect is the one which we should consider. It is only if we are attempting to study the dynamics of the revolution that we should turn to examination of the utility calculus of the participants. Generally speaking, intellectual observers have been making judgments on the desirability or undesirability of revolution, rather than explaining the revolution. It must be conceded, of course, that in many cases they have attempted to use the public good criteria to explain the dynamics, too. This is unfortunate, but we cannot blame them too much. The public good aspect, for the reason we have given above, dominates the reports of the revolution by historians and reporters. Analysts have been misled by this dominance of public good aspects of the literature. As a result they have been led to believe that it also dominates the calculus of the participants. We should avoid this error.

Thus, if we choose to evaluate revolutions in terms of their general desirability or undesirability, we would look at equation (1). If we are attempting to understand the activities of the revolutionists and their opponents, we should look at equations (4) and (7). People planning revolution or a counterrevolutionary activity should use equations (4) and (7) in their actual planning and equation (2) in their propaganda.

So much for our first problem. Let us turn to the second problem—the possibility that we have oversimplified the situation. Clearly our equations *are* very simple and it is *a priori* not obvious that we have not left out some important variable. First, we have assumed a very simple revolutionary situation in which a vicious and corrupt government is being attacked by a pure and good revolution. Obviously the real world is not this simple. If we define revolution as a violent overthrow of the government,[4] then it is clear that bad governments have been overthrown by good revolutions and good governments have been overthrown by bad revolutions; but in the overwhelming majority of cases, it is difficult to decide between the two parties. Historically, the common form of revolution has been a not-too-efficient despotism which is overthrown by another not-too-efficient despotism with little or no effect on the public good. Indeed, except for the change in the names of the ruling circles, it would be hard to distinguish one from the other.

In those cases where there is little public good aspect to the revolution, even the historians and observers discuss them in terms of the personal participant's gain. For example, most accounts of the Wars of the Roses pay little or no attention to the propaganda which was issued by both sides about good government, Christianity, ethics, etc. The only exception to this concerns the very successful propaganda by Henry Tudor about the viciousness of the man he killed at Bosworth Field.

Such revolutions are, of course, the overwhelming majority. If we turn to that more limited number of revolutions where there is a significant change in regime, I think it would be hard to argue that those cases in which the revolution was an improvement outnumbered those in which it was a detriment. In the judgment of most modern editorial critics, the military overthrows of the previous regimes in Greece, Brazil, and Argentina were all distinct reductions in the public welfare of these countries. Whether this judgment is correct or not is irrelevant for our particular purposes. Surely there are, in fact, many cases in which such overthrows are detriments. Further, it seems likely that the mere cost inflicted by the fighting and confusion is quite significant in most cases, and hence one would only favor a revolution for public goods reasons if one felt that the net benefit of the change of regime was great enough to pay this cost.

4. Some people seem to define "revolutions" as desirable violent overthrows of a government. With this definition, what we are to say below will not follow. Presumably they would be willing to accept some other word to mean violent overthrow of government, regardless of its moral evaluation, and that could be substituted for "revolution" in the rest of our discussion.

Thus our equations as they are now drawn should be modified to indicate that the public good values from the revolution may be negative. If the revolutionary party proposes to put up a less efficient system—let us say it is in favor of collective farming, and we know the historically bad results of that method of running agriculture—then, the public good term in our equations would be negative rather than positive. Again, however, this bit of realism does not detract from the conclusions which we have drawn. The individuals would participate in the revolution or in its repression in terms of the private payoffs with little attention to the public goods. Reporters, on the other hand, would talk mainly about the public good aspects.

Another aspect in which our equations might be thought to lack realism concerns their generalist approach. The public good in our equations as we have so far interpreted them is a public good for the entire society. Note that this is not a necessary characteristic of the equations. Let us suppose that some particular group within the society has some chance of gaining from the revolution and there is some other group that will probably lose. Here the public good would apply only to these two groups. This, however, would make no difference in our equations. Indeed, in this respect, our equation is very similar to Mancur Olson's analysis of pressure groups in political society.[5] Following Olson, we are in essence espousing the byproduct theory of revolutions.

Another element of possible unrealism in our equations is basic to most discussion of public goods. From the time that Samuelson began the current interest in this field, public goods have been normally analyzed in terms of their private benefits for the individual. Thus, if we regard the police force as a Samuelsonian public good and look at Samuelson's equations, I am benefited by the police force because I do not wish to be robbed, murdered, etc. I do not necessarily take into account the benefit to other people. Clearly, most human beings have at least some interest in the well-being of others and hence this is unrealistic. It is, however, an element of unrealism in almost the entirety of the formal public goods literature and is not confined to our analysis of revolutions alone.

This element of unrealism, however, is not a necessary aspect of the public goods literature. Further, individual scholars have avoided this particular simplification. My benefit from the police force is not entirely represented by

5. Mancur Olson, *The Logic of Collective Action* (Cambridge, Mass.: Harvard University Press, 1965).

the fact that I am protected against various crimes. I may also gain something from my knowledge that other people are also benefited. Clearly, most people are—to at least some extent—interested in the well-being of others.[6] Thus my evaluation of my gain from the revolution would include not only my direct personal gain, but also any pleasure or pain which I receive as a result of interdependence between my preference function and that of others. In this respect, the revolution would be much like any other charitable activity.

The issue here, however, is basically one of size. The scholars who have discussed public goods without paying any attention to this type of interdependence have been simplifying reality, but not by very much. As far as we can see, for most people marginal adjustment between benefit to themselves and the benefit to other people is achieved when something under 5 percent of the resources under their control is allocated to help "others." Thus we could anticipate that individuals might be willing to do something to aid the revolution for reasons of the benefit which this will give to other people, but probably not very much. We have here, however, a difficult empirical problem, the measurement of the degree to which individuals are willing to sacrifice for the benefit of others. The work that has been done so far is not very impressive. Still, it does not seem likely that it is wrong by an order of magnitude, and it would have to be wrong by at least that much to make this particular aspect of our equation dangerously oversimplified. Indeed, the equations would not be incorrect even if it turned out that individual evaluation of the well-being of others was very high. It would simply mean that the public good aspect of revolutions would have a larger value than it would if the individual put little weight on the well-being of other persons.

This brings us to our third problem, the empirical evidence. The first thing that should be said is that there have been no careful empirical tests aimed at disentangling the motives of revolutionaries. The literature is overwhelmingly dominated by the "public goods" hypothesis. Indeed, so far as I know, this paper is the first suggestion that it might be falsified. Under the circumstances, it is not surprising that no one has run a formal test.

Furthermore, no one has collected the type of detailed data which would be necessary to test the two hypotheses. It does not seem to me that formal statistical tests would be at all impossible, although they might be difficult. The difficulty would, of course, be particularly strong in the case of unsuc-

6. Perhaps negatively; Kenneth Boulding has done a great deal to call attention to the role of malevolence in human life.

cessful revolutions, since few records would have been kept. Still, approximating the ex ante value of the private rewards to be expected from participation in a revolution should not be impossible. It seems to me that such research would be most important and I would be delighted to see someone undertake it.

It is not, however, my intention to engage in such research here. Instead I propose to look rather superficially at the actual history of revolutions and see whether these data seem to contradict or support my byproduct theory of revolutions. First, it must be admitted that most revolutions do have some effect on government policy. The personnel at the top is changed and normally that would mean at least some change in government policy. It is hard to argue, however, that in most cases this was the major objective of the revolution. In most cases, after all, the new government is very much like the one before. Most overthrows are South American or African and simply change the higher level personnel. It is true that the new senior officials will tell everyone—and very likely believe it themselves—that they are giving better government than their predecessors. It is hard, however, to take these protestations very seriously.

One of the reasons it is hard to take these protestations seriously is that in most revolutions, the people who overthrow the existing government were high officials in that government before the revolution. If they were deeply depressed by the nature of the previous government's policies, it seems unlikely that they could have given enough cooperation in those policies to have risen to high rank. People who hold high, but not supreme, rank in a despotism are less likely to be unhappy with the policy of that despotism than are people who are outside the government. Thus, if we believed in the public good motivation of revolutions, we would anticipate that these high officials would be less likely than outsiders to attempt to overthrow the government.

From the private benefit theory of revolutions, however, the contrary deduction would be drawn. The largest profits from revolution are apt to come to those people who are (a) most likely to end up at the head of the government and (b) most likely to be successful in overthrow of the existing government. They have the highest present discounted gain from the revolution and lowest present discounted cost. Thus, from the private goods theory of revolution, we would anticipate senior officials who have a particularly good chance of success in overthrowing the government and a fair certainty of being at high rank in the new government, if they are successful, to be the most common type of revolutionaries. Superficial examination of history would seem to indicate that the private good theory is upheld by these empirical data. Needless to say, a more careful and exhaustive study of the point is needed.

Another obvious area for empirical investigation concerns the expectations of the revolutionaries. My impression is that they generally expect to have a good position in the new state which is to be established by the revolution. Further, my impression is that the leaders of revolutions continuously encourage their followers in such views. In other words, they hold out private gains to them. It is certainly true that those people that I have known who have talked in terms of revolutionary activity have always fairly obviously thought that they themselves would have a good position in the "new Jerusalem." Normally, of course, it is necessary to do a little careful questioning of them to bring out this point. They will normally begin by telling you that they favor the revolution solely because it is right, virtuous, and preordained by history.

As another piece of evidence, Lenin is famous for having developed the idea of professional revolutionaries. He felt that amateurs were not to be trusted in running a revolution and wished to have people who devoted full-time to revolutionary activity and who were supported by the revolutionary organization. Clearly, he held a byproduct theory of revolution, although I doubt that he would ever have admitted it.

Last, we may take those noisiest of "revolutionaries"—the current radical left students. It is noticeable that these students, although they talk a great deal about public goods, in fact do very little in the way of demonstrating their devotion to such goods. Indeed, the single most conspicuous characteristic of their "revolutionary" activities is the great care that they take to minimize private cost. Always and everywhere, one of the major demands is that no private cost be imposed on unsuccessful revolutionaries by way of punishment. Further, they normally carefully arrange their activities in locations—such as universities—where they feel confident that no great punishment will be imposed upon them. This is in spite of the fact that it is obvious that totally overthrowing *all* of the universities in the modern world would not significantly affect any government. The attack on a university may bring very little benefit—either private or public—but it is also accompanied by very small costs. Indeed, this may be one of the rare cases where the entertainment value of revolution is the dominant motivation.

I should not like to argue that the empirical information contained in the last few paragraphs is decisive. Clearly, however, it does prove that the evidence is not overwhelmingly against the byproduct theory of revolutions. Further, granted the fact that all previous theoretical discussions of revolutions have been based on the public goods theory, it is quite encouraging that material collected by scholars holding this point of view can be used to support the byproduct theory.

In sum, the theoretical arguments for the view that revolutions are carried out by people who hope for private gain and produce such public goods as they do produce as a byproduct seem to me very strong. As of now, no formal empirical test has been made of it, but a preliminary view of the empirical evidence would seem to support the byproduct theory. This, of course, is the paradox. Revolution is the subject of an elaborate and voluminous literature and, if I am right, all of this literature is wrong.

RATIONALITY AND REVOLUTION

In the January 1994 *Rationality and Society*, my "The Paradox of Revolution" was referred to as seminal twice[1] and classic once.[2] It was also clearly important in most of the other articles. Nevertheless, most of these authors devote their primary attention to proving that there are other factors that I did not consider. I am complimented by the attention, and don't feel particularly apologetic that my article did not solve all problems.

Interestingly the two authors who call it seminal mention only the original article in *Public Choice*, and only Muller and Weede[3] list the mildly modified version in *The Social Dilemma*. That book has four other chapters that are relevant to the problem of revolution.[4] Unfortunately, it is out of print, the second printing having been exhausted only a short time ago. I will, however, be glad to send anyone Xerox copies of these chapters together with another paper I wrote on guerrilla warfare, at cost.

I am compelled to agree that my original article is incomplete. As a matter of fact, I have changed my mind on some aspects of the article since I wrote it. I am not so strongly opposed to the modifications as might be expected. Nevertheless, I should point out that my article dealt with revolutions, not street disturbances.

An important reason for changing my mind was the earlier work by Muller and Opp,[5] of which the article in the January 1994 issue by Muller and Weede is a logical extension. There is also the laboratory experimental work, which shows that in the prisoner's dilemma you do not get 100% noncooperation. I have also become much less enamored with the perfect information assumption. It seems to be a good approximation in many areas, and greatly simplifies calculation, but no teacher with classroom experience can really believe that everyone is perfectly informed.

Reprinted, by permission of Sage Publications, Inc., from *Rationality and Society* 7 (January 1995): 116–28. Copyright 1995 by Sage Publications, Inc.

1. Pp. 9, 73.

2. P. 5.

3. Pp. 40–57.

4. Gordon Tullock, *The Social Dilemma: Economics of War and Revolution* (Blacksburg, Va.: Center for Study of Public Choice, 1974), Chaps. 4, 6, 7, and 8.

5. Edward N. Muller and Karl-Dieter Opp, "Rational Choice and Rebellious Collective Action," *American Political Science Review* 80 (1986): 471–89.

It can be said that there are various difficulties with the experimental work. Lack of perfect information is obvious from the fact that behavior changes as the subjects gain experience. As a general rule, the more the people being experimented upon understand the problem, that is, the more experience they have with it, the larger the amount at issue, and the larger the number of individuals playing, the less cooperation you get. Still, you always get some. Indeed as the experiments are improved it looks as if they are approaching a limit somewhere about 5% cooperation.

Some time ago, in other work,[6] I came to the conclusion that people are, on the average, about 5% altruistic. That is, most people are willing to give away about 5% of their wealth to help those who are worse off than they. This is an average figure with some individuals giving much more, and some much less.

Thus I am not particularly surprised to find at least a few people who are willing to go a long way in doing things that will benefit themselves very little but may help other people. There are a few that are willing to go far enough so that they risk their lives. Sixty percent of Medals of Honor are awarded posthumously.

In most demonstrations, the participants are, in fact, making rather minor contributions. They are appearing at a demonstration under circumstances where it is very unlikely that the police will machine-gun them. Within any large group there are probably a few people who are willing to make the last sacrifice. This is particularly true if they are religiously motivated because death from their standpoint is merely a quick way of getting to heaven. The people who died with Koresh, I would say, were very badly informed examples of this phenomenon.

The Muller, Dietz, and Finkel study[7] of Peru in which there appears to have been a considerable badly informed (I would say) support for the shining path[8] seems to show a group of people who were discontented with the existing government, and who had a lot of contact with each other, and

6. Gordon Tullock, *The Economics of Income Redistribution* (Dordrecht: Kluwer, [1983] 1984).

7. Edward N. Muller, Henry A. Dietz, and Steven E. Finkel, "Discontent and the Expected Utility of Revolution: The Case of Peru," *American Political Science Review* 85 (1991): 1261–82.

8. The shining path is, like the Mafia, a good example of the use of coercion to get cooperation.

thought they would be successful. They seemed to have thought that their personal activity would have considerable effect on their success. They appear to be a set of people who had close connections and who reinforced each other's delusions. They were behaving rationally on the "information" they had, but had adopted a poor strategy in information collection.

The reports as to their opinions were to some extent corrupted by the fact that the shining path is an extremely violent organization and was willing to kill people who the members thought either opposed it or had insufficient enthusiasm.

In my original equations, I had a letter E for the entertainment value of the disturbance. This was intended to take care of the students who, at the time when I wrote the article, were causing disturbances on the campuses of most universities. These disturbances quieted down very sharply at my campus when the president suspended 104 students. The remaining students suddenly became law abiding, although needless to say, they fully exercised their rights of free speech.

I would now prefer to follow Silver[9] and use V to stand for "Psychic Income." In other words, I now think that this factor should be sharply expanded to take in the effect of various things that increase people's satisfaction out of the act of rioting, actually revolting, or taking risks in military operations. So far as I know, there are no measures of the effect.

With regard to action for the public good, I would like to stick to my 5%. This is, of course, an average. A small minority are willing to run great risks; most will make only trivial sacrifices, but the total averages out with a considerable number willing to make at least some sacrifice for the poor or the public good. It is likely that people trying to obtain this psychic value are less careful in collecting information than they would be if they were buying a more material advantage.

The basic importance of the prisoner's dilemma is that it indicates that in many cases we must "coerce ourselves" in order to get things done. A 5% cooperation ratio doesn't change that particularly, although it does mean that the line of reasoning is a bit more complicated. It's not that no one will cooperate at all, but that the cooperation is severely limited. Coercion remains necessary to get such things as bridges, roads, or armies.

There is a more general point. Various theorems of economics have been

9. Morris Silver, "Political Revolution and Repression: An Economic Approach," *Public Choice* (Spring 1974): 89–199.

tested by statistical means. This means we have never tested whether they actually apply strictly speaking to individuals, but to the central tendency of a group.[10] For most purposes, that is adequate. Even if there are some wealthy people in the United States who would contribute their "fair share" of taxes even without the Internal Revenue Service, this does not mean we do not need the Internal Revenue Service.[11]

Still, when we turn to successful revolutions, in all of the cases with which I am familiar, there is a split inside the government. The officials do not have the option of remaining neutral, and hence the equations of "The Paradox of Revolution" do not apply to them.[12] Thus we would expect the officials would almost always participate in any attempt to overthrow the government, either as defenders of the government or attackers, and there would be few, if any, who were neutral. This explains the absence of what I call "romantic revolutions."

Finally, I would like to talk a bit about Eastern Europe, which I think some people have simply misunderstood. The Communists set up a firm, highly centralized, highly repressive regime that as far as we can tell was widely disliked and, certainly in Eastern Europe, detested by almost everybody. It was strong enough so that the people hired to engage in coercion were easily able to keep the people down.

They got a man at the head, Gorbachev, who didn't like the system, and who, particularly, didn't like the use of violence. We owe Gorbachev a major debt. This is not because he had carefully laid out plans; indeed, apparently he simply stumbled from one expedient to another. Nevertheless, in essence, by removing the threat of force and violence he doomed the system. Even the most ironclad dictatorship has no defense against its own dictator.

This situation was extreme in places like East Germany where it is likely that, with the exception of a few high officials, no one really liked the regime. It depended on the highly realistic threat of the Russian army of occupation. Once it was clear that the Russians would not use force, and might actually prevent the German employees of the regime from doing so, the system was doomed.

The specific downfall occurred after some street demonstrations in which

10. The work of Muller and Opp is a partial exception.

11. There are other wealthy people in the United States on the other hand who succeed in not paying their taxes in spite of the Internal Revenue Service.

12. See Tullock, *The Social Dilemma*, pp. 60, 87.

people found that small demonstrations were, if not completely safe, at least not particularly dangerous. This led to larger demonstrations, and finally the police vanished. The early participants in these operations no doubt ran some risk, but not very much. Their children's education might be interfered with, but the whole family would not be sent to the Gulag.[13]

It is notable that Gorbachev did not have complete control over the Secret Police in all communist countries. There were five with their own repressive structure: Romania, China, North Korea, Vietnam, and Cuba. Romania collapsed apparently through simple ineptitude on the part of the dictator, but the other four are still with us. China and Vietnam have apparently decided to abandon their religion and become capitalist, and the other two are fighting hard to continue impoverishing their citizens.

With the exception of these five, in all cases the collapse of communism was a collapse from within when it became obvious that the Russian organs of repression were immobilized. A few brave people were willing to run minor risks, and when it became clear that there weren't even minor risks, the governments fell. In a number of cases, the leaders of the governments saw the writing on the wall[14] and demolished it themselves.

It seems to me that the part of economic reasoning based on "the prisoner's dilemma" and "the paradox of revolution" requires modification, but the modification is not radical. We have to accept a number of deviant cases around the main trend. In some cases, the number will be sizable, but in all cases it at least modifies our reasoning. The Buddhist Bonzes who caused the death of Diem by publicly burning themselves to death[15] were sacrificing themselves for what they thought was the good of their religion. In this case, they had a major effect through the perverse functioning of the American press. Obviously, this kind of behavior is just a certain amount of static surrounding the main message.

13. Well before Gorbachev, Tibor Machan asked some indiscreet questions in class. As a result, his mother had some unpleasant interviews with the police and he was transferred to a trade school that taught brick making.

14. Mene Tekel Uphsarin.

15. Apparently they were well opiated first.

PART 8

THE PROBLEM OF SOCIAL COST

PUBLIC AND PRIVATE INTERACTION UNDER RECIPROCAL EXTERNALITY

James M. Buchanan and Gordon Tullock

Market organization fails to produce results that satisfy the necessary conditions for Pareto optimality when Pareto-relevant externalities remain in equilibrium. This statement is tautological, but it accurately reflects the content of significant portions of theoretical welfare economics. From this statement, a second, and quasi-tautological one emerges. Given the presence of Pareto-relevant externalities in market equilibrium, collectivization *could* modify the results so as to guarantee the attainment of the Pareto welfare surface. There are no grounds for disagreement here, although, of course, the following less familiar statement is also indisputable. Given the presence of Pareto-relevant externalities in political equilibrium, marketization *could* modify the results so as to guarantee that the welfare surface is reached.

We propose to extend the analysis of both market organization and collective organization in the presence of a specific sort of externality relationship. We shall demonstrate that this extension introduces complications that are not normally considered, despite their importance for any comparative evaluation of the two organizational alternatives.

We limit the analysis to those activities which involve reciprocal externalities. That is to say, the behavior of a single unit in a group exerts external effects on remaining members of the group, while, at the same time, the behavior of any other single unit in the group exerts external effects on the first unit.[1]

Reprinted, with permission, from *The Public Economy of Urban Communities*, ed. Julius Margolis (Washington, D.C.: Resources for the Future, 1965), 52–73.

1. For a definition of an externality, and for a careful distinction between a Pareto-relevant and a Pareto-irrelevant externality, see James M. Buchanan and William C. Stubblebine, "Externality," *Economica* 29 (November 1962): 371–84. For an important paper that introduces some of the complications of the reciprocal externality case, and for an unpublished paper further developing some ideas related to those treated here, see Otto Davis and Andrew Whinston, "Externalities, Welfare, and the Theory of Games," *Journal of Political Economy* 70 (June 1962): 241–62; and Davis and Whinston, "Some Foundations of Public Expenditure Theory," unpublished manuscript. Ralph Turvey, "On Divergencies Between Social Cost and Private Cost," *Economica* 30 (August 1963): 309–13, summarizes the recent developments.

Since the argument for collectivization rests largely on the presence of significant external economies, we shall consider only this case, neglecting external diseconomies. Given any activity that is characterized by relevant reciprocal external economies, private or market organization will result in the simultaneous undertaking of the activity by many persons. If a municipal government does not exist for the performance of such functions, private citizens will, independently, hire guards and night watchmen, vaccinate their dogs against rabies, install fire protection devices, plant flowers in the spring, keep boulevards clear of snow in winter, send their children to school, paint their own houses, feed the birds. The list could be lengthened readily. It is clear that, in many such activities, the private behavior of each person may exert relevant external economies on some or all of the other persons in the community.

There may or may not exist a determinate equilibrium as a result of the interaction of individuals responding independently in activities of this sort. This equilibrium, if it exists, may involve a greater or smaller resource outlay than that which is necessary to satisfy the necessary conditions for Pareto optimality.[2] The mutual adjustment process under independent behavior must be carefully examined before the efficacy of market organization can be compared with that of collectivization.

Private and Collective Adjustments

MARKET ADJUSTMENT

Consider a simple example. Immunization against communicable disease protects the individual who takes the shots, but, at the same time, it reduces the likelihood that others in the community catch the disease. If all persons other than one in a community are protected, the remaining member is unlikely to get the disease for the simple reason that there is no one from whom he may catch it. A situation of this sort under a world-of-equals model is represented diagrammatically in Figure 1.

First, consider a discrete case in which it is assumed that one shot provides complete protection to the person who takes it over some relevant time period. If an individual does not get a shot, his chances of contracting the dis-

2. For a demonstration of the point that private adjustment may generate a greater than optimal outlay, see James M. Buchanan and M. Z. Kafoglis, "A Note on Public Goods Supply," *American Economic Review* 52 (June 1963): 403–14.

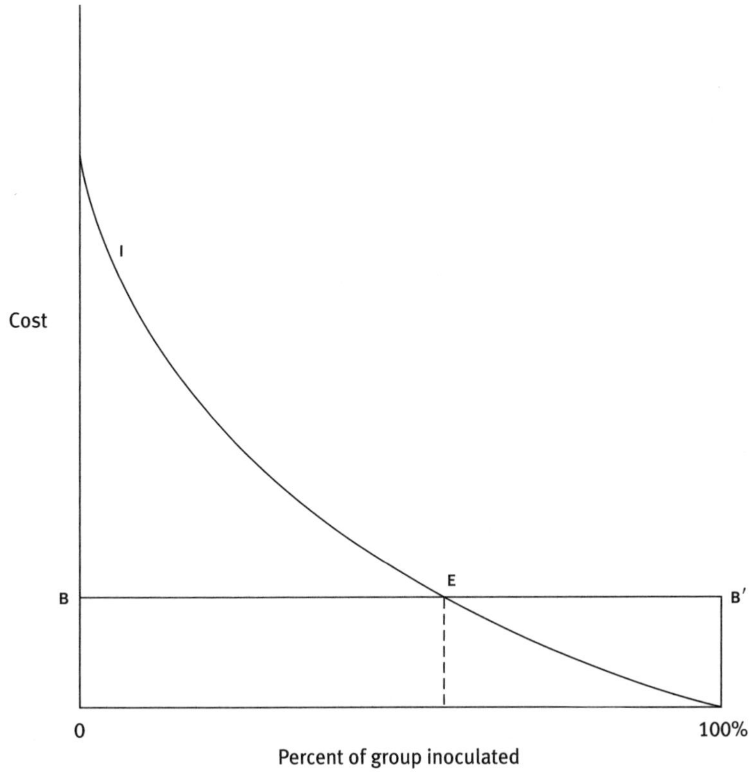

FIGURE 1

ease decrease as the numbers of others in the community who are inoculated increase. The disease is assumed to be painful; it "costs" something, but it is not fatal. Also, assume that being inoculated costs something. On the vertical axis of Figure 1, measure costs, in dollars, either of being inoculated or the properly computed expected dollar equivalent of the pain and inconvenience of getting sick. Conceptually, one can think of the latter as the current insurance premium on a policy providing complete indemnification of illness from the disease.[3] On the horizontal axis is measured the percentage of the population in the group that is inoculated; the group is assumed to be closed. The

3. If the world-of-equals assumption should be relaxed, there would, of course, be a different external economies curve for each person. This complicating factor would not change the basic conclusions of the analysis.

cost, to an individual, of getting a shot is shown by 0B. The expected cost of the disease, to the individual, is indicated by the curve, I, which may be labeled the "curve of external economies."

If all private decisions are to be made simultaneously, no position of stable equilibrium is present in this simple system. Initially, given the costs as depicted in Figure 1, all members of the group purchase inoculations. And, once having done so, all members seek to change their decisions. If it is assumed that immunity lasts for one period only, the simultaneous adjustment model would produce a cyclical swing between full inoculation and no inoculation. The model produces quite different results if the reasonable assumption is made that individuals make decisions in some temporal sequence, even though they may remain, for relevant purposes, essentially identical. In other words, one need assume only that "someone acts first." Under these conditions, individuals will continue to purchase inoculations so long as the discounted or expected costs of getting the disease exceed the costs of the shot. Equilibrium is reached at point E in Figure 1. Note that, in this position, persons who are inoculated and those who are not are in roughly equivalent situations. Those who purchase insurance policies pay premiums equal to the costs of the inoculations.

Point E represents a position of group equilibrium, when each individual acts independently. Note that, although individuals act independent of each other, they do take into account the presence of external economies in their behavior. The location of the individual along curve I depends, not on his own behavior, but on that of all others in the group. This location becomes the basis for his own decision. There is, of course, no means of identifying which individuals will become immunized and which will not.

COLLECTIVE ADJUSTMENT

The position of group equilibrium attained under private adjustment must be compared with that which would be attained under collectivization, provided the underlying conditions of the model are not changed. Assume, as before, that all members of the group are identical for relevant purposes. How will collectivization of the activity affect the two cost functions confronted by the single individual, as drawn in Figure 1? Since individuals are assumed equal in this model, tax financing will impose on each person an equal charge. Hence, one can derive a tax-cost function, T, which runs from 0 to B′ in Figure 2. Only if each person in the whole group is inoculated will the tax-cost per person equal the cost of purchasing one shot privately.

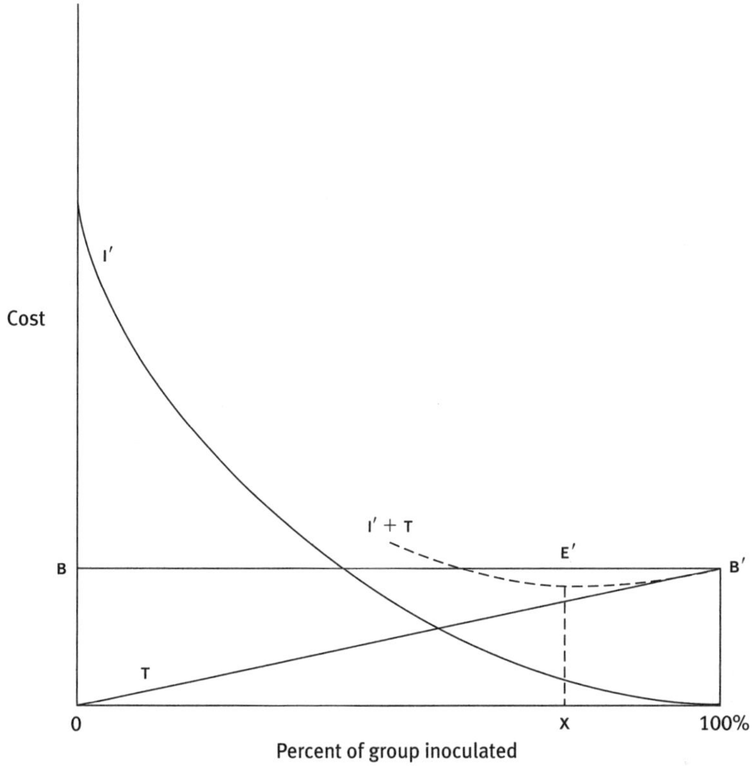

FIGURE 2

Under collectivization, it is assumed that the group, as a group, decides upon the percentage of the total number to be inoculated and that, once this decision is made, individuals to be immunized are chosen in some random fashion. Thus, regardless of the collective decision, an individual stands some chance of being in the immunized group. This fact must be taken into account in deriving the external economies curve under collectivization. For each level of inoculation for the group, it will be possible to compute the expected costs of the disease, costs that will become relevant to the individual as he participates in the collective decision process.[4] Because of some positive

4. Note that this "external economies" curve is analogous to that derived in the private adjustment model, but that it is not identical. For each level of collective immunization it would be possible to derive a whole curve that would be identical in construction to that in Figure 1. In this context, the curve in Figure 1 is drawn on the basis of zero collective immunization.

probability that he will be in the immunized group, at any percentage level, the external economies curve under collectivization, drawn as I′ in Figure 2, will lie below the analogous curve, I, in Figure 1 throughout its range, assuming that the basic parameters of the model remain unchanged.

By utilizing the two cost functions in Figure 2, I′ and T, it becomes possible to depict the position of group equilibrium under collective organization. This position is *not* indicated by the intersection of these two curves. These are total cost curves, and, in the collectivization model, as different from the private adjustment model, the individual is able, through some political voting procedure, to choose the position for the "group." The optimal position, for the individual, is indicated by the low point in the curve of total cost, I′ + T, which is derived by the vertical summation of the two components.[5] This "solution" is to the right of and below the position of equilibrium attained under private provision. In other words, collectivization produces both a greater degree of immunization and a lower cost per person than that which would be present under independent or market adjustment.

There is, of course, nothing at all startling about this result, which is strictly orthodox. The construction introduced does, however, allow attention to be focused on one or two features of the model that are not usually taken into account. Note that, even in ideal collective equilibrium, marginal external economies remain. What are eliminated are the Pareto-relevant externalities, not all externalities. Secondly, the model draws attention to the question as to why the ideal or optimal solution is not achieved under independent adjustment. Return to the insurance premium version. Why does the rational insurance firm not subsidize some of its own clients, encouraging them to be inoculated? If there is only one firm, it could clearly increase profits by carrying out such subsidization to the point where the same amount of immunization that is present under collectivization would be achieved. One firm might, of course, go further and exploit its monopoly position. However, even if there should be a number of insurance firms, each would find it profitable to subsidize inoculation to some extent. One need

---

The composite "external economies" curve in Figure 2, I′, traces out a locus of points on a whole family of such curves, drawn for each level of collective immunization.

5. The constructions here are similar to those that have been employed by James M. Buchanan and Gordon Tullock, *The Calculus of Consent: Logical Foundations of Constitutional Democracy* (Ann Arbor: University of Michigan Press, 1962), in their analysis of political voting rules.

not, however, rely on the insurance version of the model. Without insurance against the disease, it remains rational for individuals to "bribe" others in the group, each other, to secure inoculation, so long as Pareto-relevant externalities remain. It is, of course, the costs of organizing such bribes or compensations among large groups, and not the presence of externalities, *per se*, that provide the legitimate basis for collectivization.

MARKET FOR EXTERNALITIES

Such cost barriers to the organization of interpersonal markets point up a rather curious development in the theory of markets. Economists have often assumed that markets work perfectly for the exchange of goods and services, but that markets do not work at all for the exchange of those activities generating external effects. If, in fact, markets should work "perfectly" in a more inclusive sense, all gains from trade would be eliminated, including those that exist, by definition, when Pareto-relevant externalities are present. "Optimal" results are guaranteed by "perfect" markets in this broader model of trade. In the real world, of course, markets work, more or less, for the exchange of goods and services and for the exchange of externalities. The difference is one of degree, not of kind. Side payments for externalities do exist, and institutions are continually emerging to internalize these. Cost barriers to the organization of such interpersonal markets are more severe than those present for ordinary commodity and service markets, but these costs are not necessarily insurmountable.[6]

DISTRIBUTIONAL EQUITY

The model suggests yet another important point that often tends to be overlooked. As the cost functions are drawn in Figure 2, collectivization, if ideally operative, will involve only some share of the total population securing inoculation. In the real world, this result may not be forthcoming. Generally accepted standards of equity may, in such instances, require that all persons be inoculated, or that inoculations be made free to all who choose voluntarily to take them. Under the assumptions made, these alternatives would produce the same results; everyone would be inoculated. Note that this solution will not represent any improvement over private provision. All

6. The fundamental paper by Ronald H. Coase, "The Problem of Social Cost," *Journal of Law and Economics* 3 (October 1960): 1–44, should be noted in addition to those previously cited.

persons will be inoculated; more resources will be devoted to vaccine and clinics; insurance costs will be zero; taxes will be high. Given any bias toward individual freedom of choice, this solution will be less satisfactory than private market adjustment. As compared with "ideal" immunization, this equity solution involves a relative overextension whereas the private adjustment process involves a relative underextension. The cost equivalence between these two inefficient results stems, of course, from the assumption that shots are available at constant costs. If increasing costs should characterize this service, the equity solution would be inefficient, even for the totalitarian. With decreasing costs, the equity solution would always be the efficient one.

The practical implication of this point is that it may be necessary, in order to achieve tolerable efficiency under collective organization, to devise some means of choosing those members of the total population who are to be directly benefited. This means must not appear to violate generally accepted standards of nondiscrimination. The desired results may be broadly attained by certain class distinctions, such as, for example, that only children or the aged shall be immunized. Alternatively, direct-user pricing could be introduced; inoculations could be made freely available to all who choose to pay a direct-user charge. This charge would be set at a level that would generate approximately the optimal outcome. In any case, either administrative rules or direct-user pricing must, if introduced, be substantially "correct." If not, there may arise particular institutional diseconomies that would have to be taken into account in any comparative evaluation of public and private organization.

COLLECTIVIZATION WITHOUT RELEVANT EXTERNALITY

One useful benchmark case that is not normally considered, but which will be helpful, involves the collectivization of an activity that is not characterized by relevant externality in market organization. Suppose, for example, that through some error, inoculation against the communicable disease is not collectivized but that, instead, the medical treatment of the disease is. (The current practice of the National Health Service in Great Britain, which provides free hospital care but charges small fees for drugs, may be a partially applicable real-world example.) The situation is depicted in Figure 3, where the underlying conditions are assumed the same as before. The expected cost of the disease is reduced for the individual, since treatment is provided "free"; the external economies curve becomes I″, which is clearly lower than I in Figure 1 (drawn as dotted in Figure 3), and may be, although it will not neces-

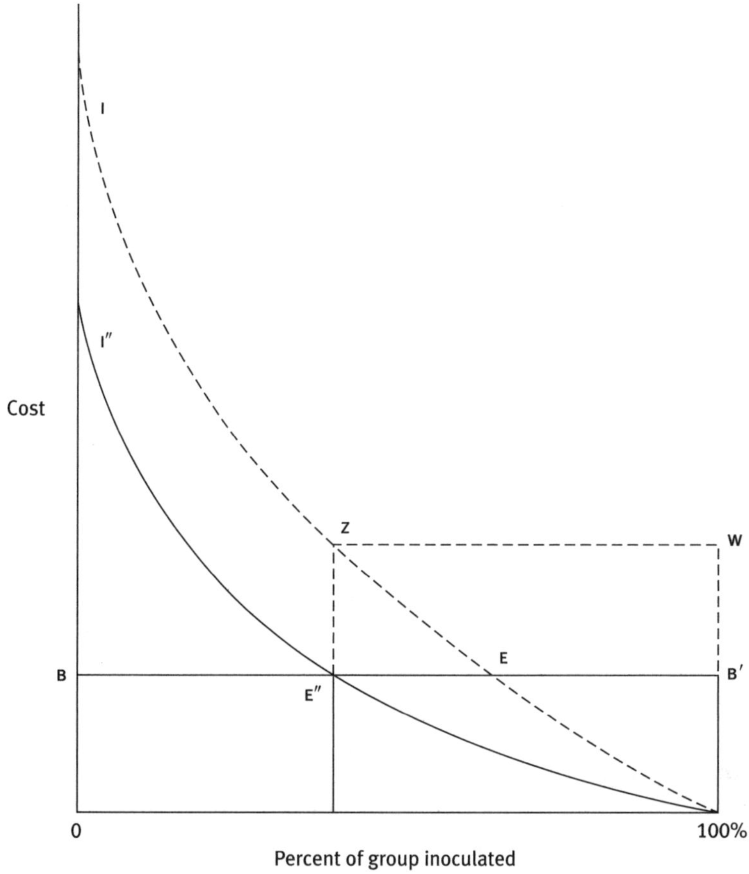

FIGURE 3

sarily be, lower than I′ in Figure 2. The cost of inoculation is not changed. Hence, independent adjustment will produce group equilibrium at E″. Note that, under this scheme, there will be fewer inoculations and more disease than under wholly private organization. Each individual will, however, bear the same direct cost as under wholly private provision. The tax-costs of treatment are wholly excess. The amount of these costs, for the group, is shown by the rectangle, E″ZWB′. This result need not be surprising. Treatment of disease is "free," and the individual adjusts his behavior to this fact. Since there are, by assumption, no relevant external economies involved in treatment, *per se*, only full-cost user pricing could eliminate the inefficiency under these arrangements. But, of course, such pricing would undermine the rationale for the collectivization.

The particular details of the example are not important. It should be noted, however, that when an activity that generates no significant external effects is collectivized, some distortion in resource use will necessarily result, unless goods and services are distributed through a system of voluntary purchases at market prices. This point is a familiar and obvious one, but it does represent one side of the whole externality-collectivization discussion that tends to be sidetracked. Arguments for decollectivization based on government failure in such cases are on all fours with arguments for demarketization based on market failure.

EXCESS BURDEN OF TAXATION

To this point, as is normal with economists who discuss topics such as these, we have assumed that tax-supported collective activities are financed with zero excess burden. If one is to complete the catalogue of externalities that must be relevant to any decision among alternative organizational forms, this element must be incorporated in the model. It is widely accepted that any tax, other than a purely hypothetical lump-sum construction, modifies the conditions for choice of the individual and, therefore, distorts his behavior to some extent. This possibility can be introduced into the simple geometrical model without difficulty. In Figure 4, Figure 2 is reproduced, only here allowance is made for some excess burden of taxation. The tax curve, T, is shifted upward to, say, T′. This, in turn, shifts the total cost curve, I′ + T′, upward, and, with the configuration as drawn, this shifts the "optimal" position to the left. If the excess burden involved with raising tax revenues is sufficiently large, the final results achieved under collectivization may actually be less "efficient" than those achieved under market adjustment, despite the admitted presence of noninternalized and relevant reciprocal external economies in the latter. The implication is clear that the size of the excess burden of taxation should, in fact, be considered along with the other externalities in any choice of organization.

This point, like the others, is an obvious one. However, it seems rarely to have been made explicit in the discussion. Cost-benefit analysis, which is now becoming a popular pastime, has developed with very little attention being paid to the excess burden that might be involved in raising given revenue sums through taxation.

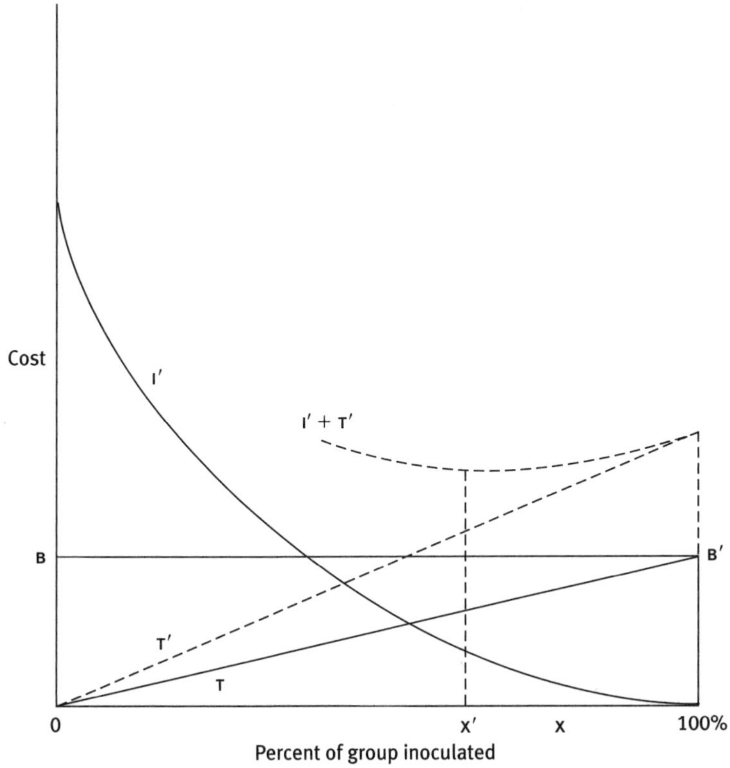

FIGURE 4

Multiple Alternatives

MARKET ADJUSTMENT WITH MULTIPLE ALTERNATIVES: THE UNEQUAL DISTRIBUTION CASE

In the simple model introduced in the first section, it has been assumed that each individual confronts only two alternatives of choice. He either gets inoculated or he does not. In the more general case, many alternatives will be open to him. Staying within the immunization model for the sake of expositional continuity, one can think of the individual either doing nothing, getting one shot, two shots, three shots, etc. Each additional shot will provide him with additional protection against disease and also generate external benefits for his fellows, but never reduce his risk to zero. Infantile paraly-

b_4	30	70	12	62	4	64	2	72	0	80
	0	30	10	22	20	24	30	32	40	40
b_3	50	86	22	67.5	8	63	4	68	0	72
	0	50	10	35.5	20	28	30	34	40	40
b_2	62	96	27	70	12	64	5	63	0	64
	0	62	10	37	20	32	30	35	40	40
b_1	70	110	29	78	13	70	5.5	67.5	0	62
	0	70	10	39	20	33	30	35.5	40	40
b_0	75	150	30	110	14	96	6	86	0	70
	0	75	10	40	20	34	30	36	40	40
B / A	a_0		a_1		a_2		a_3		a_4	

FIGURE 5

sis vaccinations provide a partially applicable real-world example here. The reciprocal externality relationship is assumed to extend over the whole range of possible action open to each member of the group.

One means of illustrating this model is provided in the matrix of Figure 5. Here for consideration is a two-person group only, consisting of individuals A and B. Each person can either get no shots or any number of shots up to a maximum of four per time period, producing a twenty-five cell matrix. For convenience, payoffs are measured negatively in terms of costs; hence, each "player" will attempt to minimize his relevant payout. In each matrix cell several entries are included. These are to be read as follows: In the upper left-hand corner of each cell is the expected cost of the disease computed from the probability of contracting it and the cost of suffering it once contracted. For simplicity, this may again be considered as the cost of an insurance premium per period. In the lower left-hand corner of each square is the cost of inoculations, assumed to be \$10 per shot. These two costs are summed in the lower right-hand corner of each cell, giving the total cost to the individual, who is A in the payout matrix shown. Individual A will attempt to minimize the figure in the lower right-hand corner. Again for simplicity in exposition, it is assumed that A and B are identical in relevant respects. This makes the matrix confronting B the transpose of that confronting A. Thus, for example, the figure in the lower right-hand corner of the cell, A_3B_1, gives a total cost to A of \$35.50. This must be the same as the total cost to B in the cell B_3A_1.

One can in this way compute the costs to B in each cell. Adding these to those for A, one obtains a total social cost figure, which is entered in the upper right-hand corner of each cell.

Consider now the adjustment process under private organization. Assume that no elements of strategic behavior are present, an assumption that will be justified later in the paper. Under these conditions, each person will purchase two shots per period. If, for any reason, some cell other than (A_2B_2) is found to exist, one or both of the individuals will find it advantageous to shift his own behavior. Note, however, that the social optimum is located at (A_4B_1) or (A_1B_4). In this case, total costs can be minimized (total benefits maximized) by a significantly unequal distribution of services between the two persons. It is, of course, obvious that this particular result stems from the values assigned in the matrix illustration. The result is interesting, nevertheless, for it suggests one possibly important basis for collectivization that is seldom discussed. It is possible that the reciprocal external economies are such that only through collective organization can a sufficiently *unequal* distribution of services be implemented, so as to achieve efficiency. In this instance, collectivization allows a specific technological improvement in distribution to be made that is not possible under private provision. This seems reasonably common with some real-world public services. Police do not patrol every street with the same intensity. The national defense establishment concentrates its services at strategic points.

MARKET ADJUSTMENT WITH MULTIPLE ALTERNATIVES: THE EQUAL DISTRIBUTION CASE

Despite the importance of the unequal distribution of services in securing overall efficiency in particular situations, it will be profitable to return to the equal-distribution model since it is slightly more amenable to analysis. Continue to assume that individuals in the group are substantially identical. A matrix similar to that of Figure 5, but with different payoffs, is shown in Figure 6. Note that here each person would be motivated to take one shot, but neither would take a second, since he could not expect the other person to do likewise. However, if the two parties could make an agreement, each would be better off with both parties taking two shots. This is, of course, the traditional reciprocal external economies case, presented here as a version of the prisoners' dilemma game. Note, however, that if inoculation should be collectivized, with services being made free to individuals, that is, with the receipt of services wholly divorced from tax payments, both A and B would

b_4	13 58 X 0 13	8 61 10 18	2 63 20 22	0 70 30 30	0 80 Z 40 40
b_3	15 52 X 0 15	10 55 10 20	3 56 20 23	2 64 30 32	0 70 40 40
b_2	21 50 X 0 21	12 49 O 10 22	4 48 O′ 20 24	3 56 30 33	1 63 40 41
b_1	26 56.5 0 26	15 50 X 10 25	7 49 O 20 27	5 55 30 35	3 61 40 43
b_0	30 60 0 30	19.5 56.5 10 29.5	9 50 X 20 29	7 52 30 37	5 58 40 45
B / A	a_0	a_1	a_2	a_3	a_4

FIGURE 6

take four shots. This position is less desirable than that reached under private adjustment, given the payoffs of the matrix. Such free provision of partially divisible services leads individuals to extend consumption to the point where marginal evaluation is zero, resulting in excessive utilization.[7]

Five cells in the matrix of Figure 6 are marked with X's. These represent simply the best situations for A, given each possible choice on the part of B. Note that the configuration of these "A optima" cells has specific characteristics. Its general direction is north-northwest, with the total costs for A becoming lower and lower as movement is made in this general direction. Call this locus of low points for A "the river," or "A's river," since one can think of these X cells as the locus of the lowest points on the third-dimensional cost surface of the matrix.

Three other cells on the matrix are marked with O's. These make up the set of positions that show lower social costs than A_1B_1, the position of independent adjustment equilibrium. The cell A_2B_2, marked O′, is the single

7. The leaders of the Soviet Union, presumably on ideological grounds, distribute bread at prices far below costs, and they often discuss making bread "free." This practice has led to weird, but predictable, results, including the feeding of cattle on bread rather than grain. Even the secret police have not been able to force consumers to behave in a Marxian manner toward bread.

"optimum," but for both individuals in the group, either of the O cells would be preferable to the private equilibrium position. This whole set may be called the "social provision area."

CONTINUOUS VARIATION

It is relatively easy to shift from the matrix illustration that incorporates discrete and discontinuous alternatives to the more familiar case of continuous variation. Figure 7 simply converts relationships similar to those in Figure 6 to the continuous case. The "river" now becomes a smooth curve. Private equilibrium is shown by the intersection of the river, labeled R, with a 45-degree line drawn from the origin. The 45-degree line is, of course, the result of the assumption of identical persons and equal distribution of the activity. For B, it would be possible also to draw in a river curve, which would be the transpose of that drawn in for A under the stated restrictions. The two rivers would, of course, both cut the 45-degree line in the same point, labeled E, in Figure 7.

This construction has the advantage of facilitating the shift from the two-

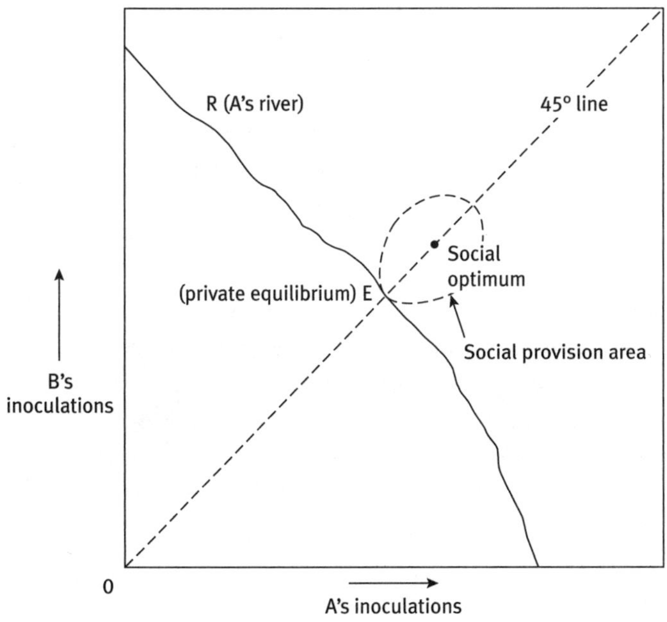

FIGURE 7

person case to the n-person case without difficulty. So long as one retains the assumption that all persons are identical in relevant respects, the analysis is not modified. On the one axis we simply measure the activity of "all others than A." Given appropriately defined scales, one can still utilize the 45-degree line construction. Any point along this line represents equal consumption of the service by all members of the n-person group.

In the two-person model, we have assumed, arbitrarily, that individuals did not engage in strategic bargaining behavior. The basis for this assumption can now be clarified, and with this assumption, two-person models may be used to attain results applicable to n-person groups. In an n-person group, a single individual, say A, will realize that the behavior of the $n - 1$ others in the group will influence his own utility. Recognizing this externality, he will adjust his own behavior to it. He will not, however, consider his own action to be sufficiently important as to influence the aggregate behavior of others. Hence, rational behavior consists in his adjusting or adapting his own activity to the situation in which he finds himself. This is, of course, fully analogous to the standard assumption concerning behavior of the individual buyer or seller in competitive markets.

Figure 8 illustrates the n-person model. This is identical with Figure 7 except for the fact that "all others than A" are substituted for B. A's river may be drawn in, as before, and the position of group equilibrium under wholly private adjustment, E, remains determined by the intersection of the river and the 45-degree line. This position will not be optimal. If joint action is possible, there must be points to the northeast of E that are preferable to E, for A and also for all others in the group. Topologically, the "river" represents the locus of low points on the third-dimensional cost surface, as this is confronted by A, acting independently. Remaining members in the group will confront similar cost surfaces, upon which similar "rivers" can be traced. The final position will be determined by the independent action of each person. Joint action is required to shift into the preferred area, which we have called the area of "social provision." Each point in this set is lower on the cost surface than E, for A, and for everyone else in the group. But each point is dominated, for A and for everyone else, by points along the river, if independent adjustment is allowed.

EXCESS-BURDEN QUALIFICATION

The excess-burden qualification must be incorporated into the geometrical model. If collectivization necessarily involves the imposition of taxes that

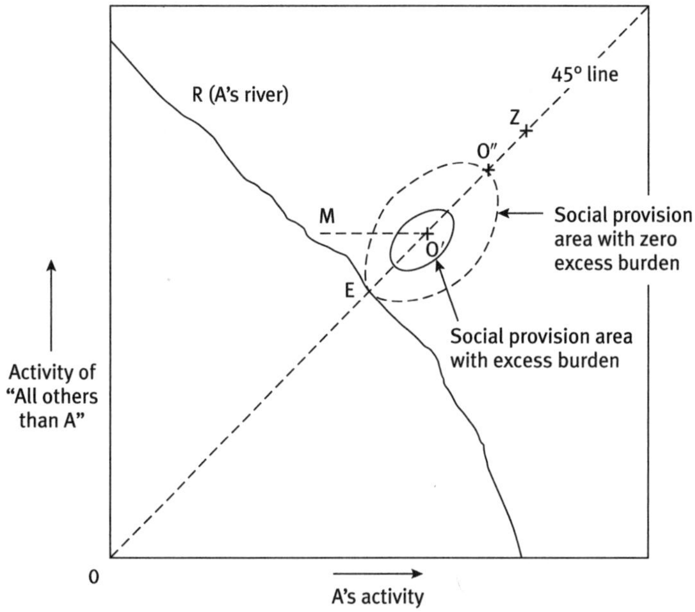

FIGURE 8

have allocative-incentive effects, the "social provision" area is smaller in size than that which is indicated under the assumption of zero excess burden (shown by the dashed-circular area in Figure 8). It is possible, of course, that the external costs imposed by tax collection would eliminate altogether any net advantages of collectivization. However, the illustration is deliberately drawn to suggest that, even with some positive excess burden of taxation, a social provision area remains, as shown by the area enclosed by the solid line in Figure 8. Any position within this area represents some improvement, for A and all other members of the group, over E. A single optimal position, within this area, is shown at O′. This position will be located along the 45-degree line, from our assumption of equal distribution of the activity or service.

RATIONING DIFFICULTIES

Again we emphasize that there is nothing particularly new in this construction. It does help to point to some of the complicating features that must be taken into account. Refer to the area of social provision shown in Figure 8. The shift from private organization, which would attain position E, to collective or political organization, is efficient only if the group can insure a final location within the preferred area. There are, however, two separate problems that must be surmounted before such insurance is present. First of all, as previously suggested for the discrete case, unless either administrative controls or price rationing is introduced, collectivization may result in an excessive utilization of available facilities. Suppose, for example, that government finances the activity in question from general tax revenues, and, to stay with the example, then makes immunization shots free to all who want them in whatever quantity desired. The adoption of this "needs" approach to budgeting, which is not at all uncommon in real-world fiscal experience, would surely lead to some position such as that shown by Z in Figure 8, a position that may clearly be less desirable than E.

This problem becomes serious only insofar as individuals are able, by their utilization of a collectively provided service, to reduce the quantity available for others. Hence, for a purely collective good, defined in the strict Samuelson sense, this problem need not arise. It is known, however, that few goods or services are wholly indivisible. Most collective services embody both divisible and indivisible elements. To remain within the social provision area, therefore, something other than the mere collectivization of an activity must be introduced. The various administrative schemes for carrying out the necessary rationing are familiar. Police protection is provided generally, but a policeman cannot be asked to stand in front of every house. Firemen will respond to calls if fire breaks out, but only on occasion will they take pet cats out of trees, and severe fines are imposed for false alarms. Normally, only certain types of rubbish are picked up by municipal garbage collectors.

This first problem of keeping government efficient has been traditionally recognized in the theory of public finance. A time-honored principle states that governments cannot, efficiently, give away services for which the demand is price elastic over some range between cost price and zero. The treatment of the problem here is couched in different terms, but remains basically within the orthodox tradition.

CHISELING UNDER COLLECTIVIZATION

The second problem of government efficiency also brings up a familiar issue in price theory, which, to our knowledge, has not been developed with respect to the provision of public goods or services. The price theory analogue here is the enforcement of cartel agreements. Each partner to an agreement has an opportunity to "chisel," and, thereby, to secure differential profits for himself, although he recognizes that, if all parties to the agreement do the same, everyone will be damaged.[8] Competitive pressures are usually held to be sufficiently strong to guarantee that chiseling will take place in large-number groups until and unless severe sanctions are in some fashion imposed against all potential price-cutters.

The same analysis is clearly applicable to the problem of remaining within the area of efficient social provision under collectivization of an activity. Refer to Figure 8. Note that, by the construction of the river, A will be motivated, always, to move in an east-west direction (the only way that he can move) so as to reach the lowest point on his cost surface. Assume now that the activity has been collectivized, and that the optimal position, O′, has been reached. Individual A finds himself located at O′, on the 45-degree line. Clearly, if he retains any freedom of private action he would find it preferable to shift to point M, the lowest point in the plane cut horizontally through O′. If he should succeed in reaching M, he will be better off than at O′. But, since we assume that all individuals act similarly, the group will eventually end up again at E, where all will be worse off than at O′. In fact, they will be worse off than they were initially since they will be bearing the excess burden of providing part of the activity in question by taxation.

WAGNER'S LAW OF INCREASING GOVERNMENT ACTIVITY

The point made in the previous paragraph is worth developing in some detail since it provides one explanation of Wagner's law of ever-increasing government activity. The question that arises is how and why will the individual shift from the social provision area? If the activity is collectivized, the individual will, presumably, be subjected to some coercive levy of taxes. Hence, he will not be able, by his own independent action, to reduce his own share of the cost of providing services for the group. If he were allowed purely private adjustment, he could shift to point M and reduce costs. Since he cannot do so, he will have no incentive to shift from O′ to M. No problem of chiseling arises.

If the activity in question should be wholly independent of other activities

8. G. Warren Nutter, "Duopoly, Oligopoly, and Emerging Competition" (unpublished manuscript), has recently developed a generalized "theory of chiseling" that does much to clarify the standard economic-theory treatment.

within the adjustment possibilities of the individual, no process analogous to chiseling will take place. There would be no incentive for the individual to break the implicit agreement that collectivization enforces. It is known, however, that many separate activities, whether these are publicly or privately organized, are interdependent for the individual's decision calculus. Remaining within the immunization example, at E, the position of private equilibrium, assume that the individual is fully adjusted to the external actions of other persons. He will secure the indicated number of shots; he will also take certain other actions that may be closely related to direct immunization. Assume these include the maintenance of certain standards of sanitation in the treatment of garbage. Now assume that the immunization program in the community is collectivized, and the individual shifts to position O′. While he will have no incentive to modify his consumption of the service, assuming coercive tax payments along with ideal rationing schemes, he will not be in equilibrium with respect to those privately purchased services that are related to immunization. If, as has been assumed, individual A is in full equilibrium at E, then at O′ he will find that he has an unnecessarily high level of sanitation. He will be able to, and he will have an incentive to, reduce his private spending on sanitation. As a result of this adjustment process, all individuals will find that position O′, with respect to immunization from the disease, is no longer optimal. The effect of the private adjustment process is to increase the value of the external economies from direct immunization. Hence, position O′, assumed to be optimal in relation to a determinate level of closely related activities, assumes non-optimal properties. The group, despite the fact that it has collectivized inoculations, remains in an external economies dilemma. Thus, there is an incentive to expand the immunization further, to, say, O″. The whole area of social provision shifts to the northeast, but this is not drawn in Figure 8. Once again a private adjustment process will take place, and, for the same reason, rational individual behavior in collective choice will further increase the level of the activity. The spiral-like process will continue, with public expenditures rising and private expenditures falling until some position is reached where the interdependence between immunization and other activities under the private control of the individual becomes insignificantly small.

If the excess burden resulting from public provision is taken into account, the possibility that the ultimate outcome may be undesirable is increased. Returning to Figure 8, suppose that the society has previously moved from E to O′, and then that private adjustment has taken place in other activities making an extension of government provision desirable. For the move to O″ to be taken, it is only necessary that the *additional* excess burden be less than the gain expected. The process of adjustment may, through this effect, remove the net benefit from public provision. In order to avoid this result, the following steps would have to be taken: Before making each adjustment, not only the excess burden would have to be taken into account, but also the predicted private adjustment to each new arrangement of services.

Practical illustrations of the relationship noted here are surely abundant in emerging municipalities. Without collective fire protection devices, home owners buy fire extinguishers and introduce private sprinkler systems. Once collective fire departments are installed, these individual devices are not replaced. Rational home owners, and potential owners, depend upon municipally supplied protection, once it is provided, and, because they do so, investment in further expansion of municipal protection becomes necessary. In established municipalities it can be predicted that increased efficiency could be achieved by some substitution of individual or private fire protection devices for collective protection, provided that the institutional means could be found through which such a substitution would be possible. There would probably be a greater return, at the margin, from investment in more and better locks than in an addition to the police force.

In these illustrations, collectively supplied services stand in some substitute relationship to privately supplied services. This seems the most realistic case, although complementarity could also be present. The provision of a public park may, for example, encourage people to expand their private purchases of picnic supplies and equipment. This, in turn, makes them desire more picnics, for which some greater investment in public parks may be necessary. The outcome is the same; a spiral-like expansion of public expenditures until all of the secondary adjustments in private behavior produce some overall equilibrium.

INTERGOVERNMENTAL APPLICATIONS

The mechanism of adjustment analyzed here can be applied without difficulty to intergovernmental fiscal relationships. It is commonly observed that when the federal government begins to supplement state expenditures for particular functions, there seems an inexorable tendency for state-local expenditures to be totally replaced by federal. This is, of course, readily explained by the fact that states and localities adjust to their own optimal levels, creating as they do still further need for expansion in federal outlay. Viewed in this light, matching provisions on the various conditional grants-in-aid may be seen as one device aimed at keeping state-local behavior restricted so as to guarantee that some position in the social provision area is maintained for the particular function. The matching grant would be analogous to an administrative requirement that all warehouses provide private sprinkler systems, even after the organization of a municipal fire department.

Collectivization and Growth

To be sophisticated in the mid-1960's, any discussion on matters remotely economic must, at some point, introduce the effects of the model on growth or the effects of growth on the model. Does the fact of growth affect the decision as to whether particular activities should, on efficiency grounds, be publicly or privately organized? There seems to be agreement on the fact that growth does modify the conditions of the problem, but there is also widespread disagreement as to the direction that the influence takes. It will be instructive to apply the models developed in this paper to this issue.

Return to the matrix illustration contained in Figure 6. Assume that, as growth takes place, personal incomes rise. With higher personal income levels, the money values for the opportunity costs of getting the disease increase. If, for purposes of this example, one can assume that these costs consist solely in time lost from the earning of salaries, a doubling of personal incomes will tend to double opportunity costs of illness. The number in the upper left-hand corner in each matrix cell of Figure 6 can then be doubled. Let it also be assumed that the costs of inoculations do not increase, but remain at $10 per shot. Figure 9 incorporates the necessary changes from Figure 6, changes that are due to growth in the manner postulated.

The rather dramatic change in results can best be noted by examining the cells marked with the X's in the two matrices. Figure 9 exhibits column dominance; regardless of what action B takes, A will find it advantageous to take two shots. Since the matrix confronted by B is merely the transpose of that facing A, he will also take two shots. Private adjustment will, therefore, attain the social optimum. There exists no position that is socially superior to the cell marked X′, the position of private equilibrium. There is no social provision area.

Note that the external economies are not eliminated by the fact of income growth; these continue to exist as before. What the change has accomplished

b_4	26	76	16	72	4	X	66	0	70	0	80
	0	26	10	26	20		24	30	30	40	40
b_3	30	74	20	70	6	X	62	4	68	0	70
	0	30	10	30	20		26	30	34	40	40
b_2	42	80	24	68	8	X′	56	6	62	2	66
	0	42	10	34	20		28	30	36	40	42
b_1	52	102	30	80	14	X	68	10	70	6	72
	0	52	10	40	20		34	30	40	40	46
b_0	60	120	40	102	18	X	80	14	74	10	76
	0	60	10	50	20		38	30	44	40	50
B / A	a_0		a_1		a_2			a_3		a_4	

FIGURE 9

is the conversion of external economies that were Pareto-relevant, at the private equilibrium solution of Figure 6, into external economies that are not Pareto-relevant, at the private equilibrium solution of Figure 9. Individual A's situation continues to be affected by B's level of immunization; the more shots B takes, the better off A finds himself. Total costs for A fall as he moves north along any column of the matrix. The same holds for B, of course, in the transpose matrix; "rivers still run downhill." In the equilibrium position, X′, in Figure 9, however, A and B cannot, by mutual agreement, attain any other position that is preferred to X′. Each person would be willing to contribute up to $2 for either his own or his fellow's securing an additional shot. But this leaves a $6 deficit when benefits are compared with the $10 cost.

The matrix of Figure 9 represents, of course, only one simple numerical example that is deliberately constructed to make the point desired. The result derived can be made generally applicable if it is carefully applied. So long as the process of economic growth and development serves to increase the opportunity costs arising from failure of individuals to act privately more than it serves to increase the private cost of the activity itself, there will surely be some tendency for the independent or private adjustment equilibrium to shift toward the social optimum in the process, "optimum" being defined by the standard Paretian criteria. The external economies become less relevant as the society becomes more affluent. At some point in the process of development, these may become irrelevant, and, if they do, the activity should be returned to private organization providing it has been previously collectivized.

Practical examples are available to illustrate these general results. It is probably correct to say that the external or spillover benefits argument for governmental or collective support for elementary schooling becomes less and less relevant as the average level of income in a community rises. The case for socialized medicine is not so strong in 1964 as it would have been in 1938, on pure efficiency grounds, other elements of the problem remaining unchanged.

For completeness, it should be noted that the process of economic growth could make the external economies more significant in certain cases. If, for example, as personal incomes double, and opportunity costs of disease double (as between the situation in Figure 6 and Figure 9), the costs of inoculations should also double, the external economies remaining relevant. What is important here is the relationship between the opportunity costs (the benefits) of the action generating reciprocal external effects and the direct costs of carrying out the activity. With economic progress, it seems reasonable to suppose that the former should increase more rapidly than the latter, although peculiar circumstances may alter this relationship.

The analysis is not intended to suggest that, considered overall, the aggregate collectivization of the economy need decrease as economic development proceeds. Other elements of change surely introduce different, and to an extent, offsetting factors. It seems safe to say that the external economies argument for expansion in the public sector will diminish over time, as this argument suggests. However, there will probably arise other interrelationships among persons, for the most part external diseconomies, which will require additional collective action in order for tolerable efficiency to be achieved. This may be summarized by saying that, as people get richer, they need to rely less and less on their neighbors to co-operate in securing the indivisible benefits of possible joint activities, but they may need to rely more and more on some collective mechanism to prevent themselves, and their neighbors, from imposing mutually undesirable costs on each other. In its broadest sense, "congestion" replaces "co-operation" as the underlying motive force behind collective action.

Analytically, external diseconomies and external economies are basically equivalent. There are important implications for the trend of public expenditure totals over time, however, if the thesis here is accepted. The collective action required in the case of Pareto-relevant external diseconomies can often be carried out by the introduction of simple administrative rules. Municipalities can simply prohibit transistor radios on public beaches, for example. By contrast, if the same municipality desires to see that all its school children get hot school lunches, it will normally expend funds to provide such lunches. It could, of course, simply require that all children purchase hot lunches. But distributional considerations prevent the extension of administrative rules to the external economies side comparative with their application on the diseconomies side.

Non-symmetrical Reciprocity

A WORLD OF UNEQUALS

There remains the task of extending the models so as to make them apply to a social group that contains persons who are *unequal* in respects relevant to the reciprocal externality relationships under consideration. As before, it is useful to begin with a two-person matrix illustration. Figure 10 duplicates Figure 6 in payouts confronting Individual A. Let us now assume that, instead of being equal with A, Individual B is, relatively, poor. The monetary value of benefits (opportunity costs) to B is, therefore, lower for B than for A. For simplicity, assume these to be one-half those for A. The matrix confronted by B is, in this case, no longer the simple transpose of that confronted by A, but instead is the transpose with the figures in the upper left-hand corner of each cell reduced by one-half. The payouts actually confronting B are shown in Figure 10 in the bracketed figures. Assume that the price of getting the shots remains the same as before.

The optimum values for A remain unchanged, as is shown by the cells marked by X's. Note, however, that the behavior of B will be substantially different. As the figures are computed for the example, B finds himself in a position of row dominance. Regardless of what A does or might do, B will not find it advantageous to get any immunization on his own. The cells marked with the B's trace the optimum values for B over all possible actions of A. In this case, cell A_2B_0 becomes the private adjustment equilibrium. Note, also, that this is the collective or social optimum under the revised set of payoffs. This result need not, of course, be a general one. It does indicate, however, that private adjustment may, in fact, generate the socially optimum solution, even in the presence of reciprocal external economies.

b_4	13 55.5 (2.5) X 0 13 (40) (42.5)	8 59.5 (1.5) 10 18 (40) (41.5)	2 62.5 (.5) 20 22 (40) (40.5)	0 70 (0) 30 30 (40) (40)	0 80 (0) 40 40 (40) (40)
b_3	15 48.5 (3.5) X 0 15 (30) (33.5)	10 52.5 (2.5) 10 20 (30) (32.5)	3 53.5 (1.5) 20 23 (30) (31.5)	2 63 (1) 30 32 (30) (31)	0 70 (0) 40 40 (30) (30)
b_2	21 45.5 (4.5) X 0 21 (20) (24.5)	12 45.5 (3.5) 10 22 (20) (23.5)	4 46 (2) 20 24 (20) (22)	3 54.5 (1.5) 30 33 (20) (21.5)	1 62 (1) 40 41 (20) (21)
b_1	26 46 (10) 0 26 (10) (20)	15 42.5 (7.5) X 10 25 (10) (17.5)	7 43 (6) 20 27 (10) (16)	5 50 (5) 30 35 (10) (15)	3 57 (4) 40 43 (10) (14)
b_0	30 45 (15) B 0 30 (0) (15)	20 43 (13) B 10 30 (0) (13)	9 39.5 (10.5) XB 20 29 (0) (10.5)	7 44.5 (7.5) B 30 37 (0) (7.5)	5 51 (6.5) B 40 45 (0) (6.5)
B / A	a_0	a_1	a_2	a_3	a_4

FIGURE 10

DISCRIMINATORY PRICING

When the world of unequals is introduced, and especially when the collectivization alternative is examined, the assumption that individuals will be confronted with uniform prices for the services in question becomes highly unreal. The poor may be allowed to purchase services at lower prices than the rich. One could, somewhat realistically in the particular example of medical care, assume that the private suppliers of inoculations made shots available to the poor at lower prices than to the rich. This would, of course, modify the private adjustment solution. This pricing change may or may not shift the solution closer to that which satisfied the necessary conditions for Pareto optimality. The relationship of the change to the Pareto frontier would depend upon the precise nature of the reciprocal externality in reference to the particular form of discrimination introduced.

DISCRIMINATION IN TAX-PRICES

A more interesting, and applicable, model, for the purposes of this discussion, is that which assumes the service to be collectivized, with the financing of the combination of services provided carried out on the basis of some familiar pattern of taxation. Suppose, for example, that the payout situation confronting A and B is that shown in Figure 10. However, the activity will now be under collective organization, and the direct outlay for inoculations is to be financed by the levy of a proportional income tax. Assume that A has an income that is double that for B. Hence, out of each aggregate outlay, A will pay two-thirds, and B only one-third. The results of this change are shown in Figure 11.

The figures in the upper left-hand corner of each cell are the same as shown in Figure 10, since the opportunity costs of the disease have not changed. Similarly, the figures in the upper right-hand corner of each cell are not changed. Neither opportunity costs nor direct costs have been modified, for the group as a whole. For each cell, however, the distribution of direct costs has been modified. Note, for example, cell A_0B_1; under the private adjustment situation, B pays $10 for one shot; A pays nothing since he gets no shots. However, in the proportional income tax model, for this same physical activity, B will pay only one-third of the total cost of $10, while A will pay two-thirds. The figures in the lower right-hand corner of each cell, indicating individual cost totals, are changed appropriately to reflect this modification in the allocation of direct costs.

It is clear that the individually desired positions will be modified by this imposed change in the allocation of costs. Individual adjustment is not, of course, possible since it is assumed that the activity is now collectivized. It is useful in evaluating the collective result that may emerge, however, to trace through the positions of individual optima under these modified conditions. The cells marked by X's trace out the positions that A would choose, given each level of B's activity. Similarly, the B cells trace out the same thing for B.

Now assume that both persons must agree on any collective solution, but that some constitutional rule requires proportional taxation. The position of

b_4	13 55.4 (2.5) X 26.6 39.6 (13.3) (15.8)	8 59.4 (1.5) 33.3 41.3 (16.6) (18.1)	2 62.5 (.5) 40 42 (20) (20.5)	0 69.9 (0) 46.6 46.6 (23.3) (23.3)	0 79.9 (0) 53.3 53.3 (26.6) (26.6)
b_3	15 48.5 (3.5) X 20 35 (10) (13.5)	10 52.4 (2.5) 26.6 36.6 (13.3) (15.8)	3 54.4 (1.5) 33.3 36.3 (16.6) (18.1)	2 63 (1) 40 42 (20) (21)	0 69.9 (0) 46.6 46.6 (23.3) (23.3)
b_2	21 45.4 (4.5) B 13.3 34.3 (6.6) (11.1)	12 45.5 (3.5) B 20 32 (10) (13.5)	4 45.9 (2) BX 26.6 30.6 (13.3) (15.3)	3 54.4 (1.5) 33.3 36.3 (16.6) (18.1)	1 62 (1) 40 41 (20) (21)
b_1	26 45.9 (10) 6.6 32.6 (3.3) (13.3)	15 42.4 (7.5) C 13.3 28.3 (6.6) (14.1)	7 43 (6) X 20 27 (10) (16)	5 49.9 (5) 26.6 31.6 (13.3) (18.3)	3 56.9 (4) 33.3 36.3 (16.6) (20.6)
b_0	30 45 (15) 0 30 (0) (15)	20 42.9 (13) 6.6 26.6 (3.3) (16.3)	9 39.4 (10.5) XO′ 13.3 22.3 (6.6) (17.1)	7 44.5 (7.5) B 20 27 (10) (17.5)	5 51.4 (6.5) B 26.6 31.6 (13.3) (19.8)
B / A	a_0	a_1	a_2	a_3	a_4

FIGURE 11

political equilibrium in this case is that indicated by cell A_1B_1, marked as C. This may be shown by examining the process through which agreement is reached. Clearly, both persons would agree to move from A_0B_0, the no-activity cell, to A_1B_1. However, at least one person would object to any moves beyond this, in any direction. Note, however, that the political equilibrium solution is not the social optimum under the revised payoffs. This is shown, as in Figure 10, in the cell, B_0A_2, marked O′ in Figure 11.

There is nothing especially new in this conclusion. Collective organization should not be expected to produce optimal results unless the structure of tax-prices should be such as to guarantee that the Pareto conditions are satisfied. And it should be evident that it would be, indeed, highly unlikely that the distribution of total taxes on the basis of any of the familiar institutions of taxation would produce optimal results. The model is helpful in that it does indicate the necessary correspondence between the structure of tax-prices and the political solution that might emerge.

In a more realistic setting, larger groups would have to be considered, along with different political rules for reaching collective decisions. The two-man model can be applied to a limited, but helpful, extent in this connection. Suppose, for example, that the poor were in the majority, and that majority rule prevailed, although the constitutional requirement of proportional taxation remained in force. In this case, a solution approximating that shown at A_0B_2 would be predicted. On the other hand, should the rich be in the majority under similar circumstances, cell A_2B_0 could be predicted as the result. It is, of course, pure circumstance that the latter would be, in the configuration of the numerical example, the socially most desirable result.

Conclusion

In this paper we have attempted to examine, with the aid of some very simple examples and some very elementary models, the adjustment process in the presence of reciprocal external economies. Several points have been developed which have not, possibly, been adequately recognized in the more hurried discussions of external economies and diseconomies. The importance of the social decision concerning the basic organizational structure of activities generating reciprocal external economies cannot be underestimated. Perhaps the major single point to be gained from this paper is that there are many more complications relevant to this social decision than might appear upon cursory examination. The results have been primarily negative; it is far easier to indicate that certain solutions fail to produce the ideally desired results than it is to indicate alternative institutional arrangements that will do so. Perhaps the greatest single need for improved analysis in theoretical political economy is for somewhat more careful recognition and analysis of the institutional processes through which people, publicly or privately, carry on economic activities.

SOCIAL COST AND GOVERNMENT ACTION

In Illinois where I was born—and indeed in most of the two American continents—the common mosquito is a major pest. With the development of DDT during World War II, a cheap way of reducing the mosquito population became available, and a very large number of communities in the years after World War II hired aircraft to fly low over the city and spray it with DDT. Recently this has become much less common. The reduction in the amount of such spraying is partially the result of a realization that the DDT spray has other effects on the natural environment than the reduction of the mosquitoes, and that some of these other effects may be quite undesirable, and partially the result of home air conditioning. A person living in an air-conditioned home is unlikely to spend as much time outside as a person living in a non-air-conditioned house. Although the amount of aerial spraying of mosquitoes has been considerably reduced in recent years, a number of other techniques which are both less effective in dealing with mosquitoes and more expensive have been adopted in some areas. They are not as widespread as aerial spraying was, let us say, ten or fifteen years ago.

The reader may wonder why a discussion of social cost should begin with this technological discussion of a rather unusual local problem. The reason is simple. Almost all of the problems involved in decisions as to what types of activity should be undertaken by the government will be found in this simple example. Further, there is absolutely nothing in the way of a traditional solution to this problem. One of the greatest problems in talking about the new discoveries in the field of social cost, externalities, and what we might call the economics of the government sector is that most people have learned, normally very early in life, the existing tradition. Those who have not accepted the existing tradition normally learn some particular attack on it which is in many ways just another tradition. Thus discussion of government activities runs instantaneously into a barrier of very strongly held ideas. If we discuss mosquito abatement, however, we normally find a complete absence of these traditions or antitraditions and hence can deal with the problem with less emotional difficulty.

Reprinted, with permission of the American Economic Association, from *American Economic Review* 59 (May 1969): 189–97.

To return, then, to the mosquitoes, let us assume that we are in 1952 and that we are living in a small town in Iowa where our mosquito problem is bad. We could undertake a spraying campaign in our own backyard. We could buy in a local supermarket a suitable insect spray and spray our backyard and perhaps spray a little into the neighbor's yard. This spray would in general reduce the number of mosquitoes in the area, partly by killing the ones who were there at the time we sprayed and partly because the spray left some residium on the vegetation and mosquitoes landing on the residium might be killed. Nevertheless, this would be a very expensive and not tremendously efficient way of reducing the number of mosquitoes.

Another method of mosquito abatement was available, however; for $50.00 we could hire an airplane and this would spray the entire town with a density to give me or any other citizen considerable mosquito abatement. This method, like the use of handsprays, could be intensified with additional deaths of mosquitoes. The situation is shown on Figure 1. For some individual the demand for mosquito abatement is shown by the usual slanting line. If he chooses to use the handspray method, then the line marked $1.00 will indicate the cost of killing "one unit" of mosquitoes. The individual will choose to purchase *A* units, and the total cost he will run for this will be represented by the rectangle to the left of *A*. The individual will not be interested in hiring an airplane which, from the standpoint of the individual, is completely dominated by handspraying. He can obtain any amount of mosquito abatement in his own yard that he desires more cheaply by handspraying than from the air.

The situation changes radically, however, if the individual clubs together with the other citizens of the town to hire the airplane. Suppose there are 1,000 citizens in the town and they get together to hire the plane. The cost to each of them for mosquito abatement in his backyard falls to five cents a unit and the total amount consumed would rise to *C*. Under these circumstances the entire mosquito abatement demand would be taken up by air spraying rather than handspraying because, once again, there is strict dominance of this particular technological method.

Clearly, the individual if given a choice would prefer *C* mosquito abatement by air spraying to consuming *A* units by handspray. Thus there would be a good argument for collective provision of mosquito abatement. Suppose, however, that instead of having some government instrumentality undertake mosquito abatement, an effort is made to have various individuals privately contribute money to hire an airplane. Under these circumstances

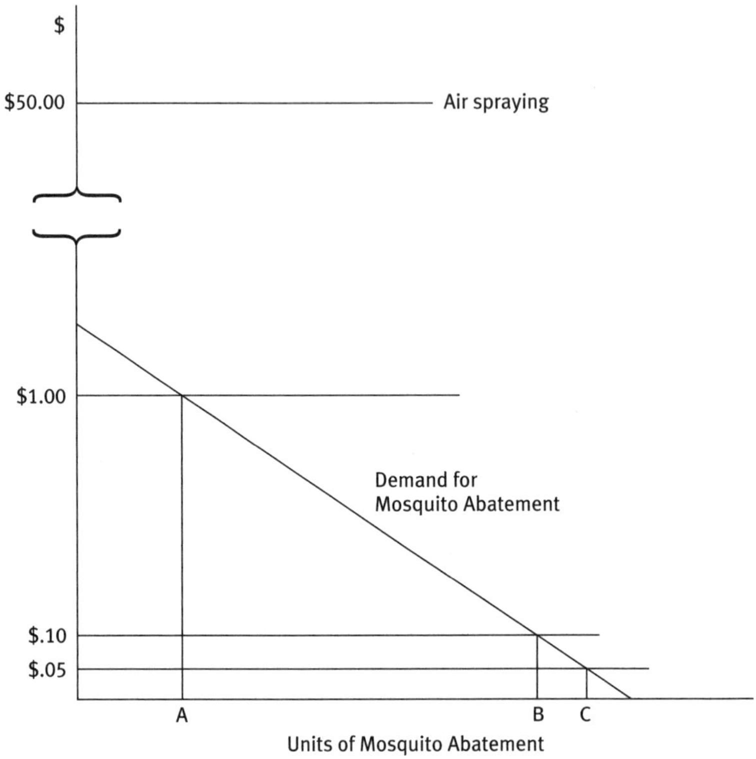

FIGURE 1

the cost of hiring an airplane depends on the number of people who have contributed. If only 500 people are willing to contribute, then the cost of mosquito abatement by air (per unit) would be ten cents and they will choose to purchase the amount *B*.

Assuming that this voluntary method of purchasing mosquito abatement is adopted, the individual would be rational not to make his ten cent payment. If he is not a member of the group making the payment, he receives the mosquito abatement free. If, on the other hand, he decides to make his payment and we assume that the amount of money he puts in is then invested in purchasing additional aircraft time for the whole city, then he faces a price for purchasing mosquito abatement in his yard of $50.00 a unit. This price is clearly way above the amount that he wishes to pay. It is extremely unlikely that individuals would be willing to make voluntary contributions. Normally only a government could provide the airplane spraying.[1]

We thus have what appears to be a fairly unambiguous argument for a governmental agency compelling the citizens of this small town to make the five cent payments for the hire of an airplane. The citizens themselves would be better off under this arrangement and would presumably favor it. There has, however, been an implicit assumption in the discussion so far—which is that each of the citizens has exactly the same demand for mosquito abatement. Presumably, this is not true. This means that a decision must be made as to how much mosquito abatement should be purchased. In order to consider this decision, let us shift to Figure 2 in which we show the demand curves for mosquito abatement of three citizens (Mr. A, Mr. B, and Mr. C). Note that if there is no decision to hire an airplane, the three individuals will simply purchase different numbers of units of mosquito abatement through the use of the handspray: Mr. A purchasing a' units, Mr. B purchasing b' units, and Mr. C purchasing c' units.

If, however, it is decided to hire an airplane and engage in collective provision of mosquito abatement, then some kind of decision must be made as to how much mosquito abatement should be purchased. It will be noted that the three individuals have different ideas as to how much this should be—represented by *a*, *b*, and *c* on the diagram. I have carefully constructed this example so that their preferences on this particular point would be what is known as "single peaked."[2] If we consider ourselves as dealing with only a three-man community and they make decisions by majority voting, and in this particular type of situation there are arguments for doing this, then we would predict that they would purchase the amount *b* of mosquito abatement. This means that Mr. A and Mr. C have failed to obtain their optimum amount of mosquito abatement.

It does not, of course, follow from the fact that the individuals could make a perfect adjustment of how much mosquito abatement they wish to purchase if we use handsprays and must anticipate in most cases that they will not obtain their exact optimum amount of mosquito abatement if we use airplanes to spray, that handspraying is superior. It merely follows that there is

1. Sometimes informal pressures can function very much like a government. As a general rule, however, human experience seems to indicate that informal pressure is not sufficient and we normally use governmental pressure in such cases.

2. Cf. Duncan Black, *The Theory of Committees and Elections* (Cambridge, 1958).

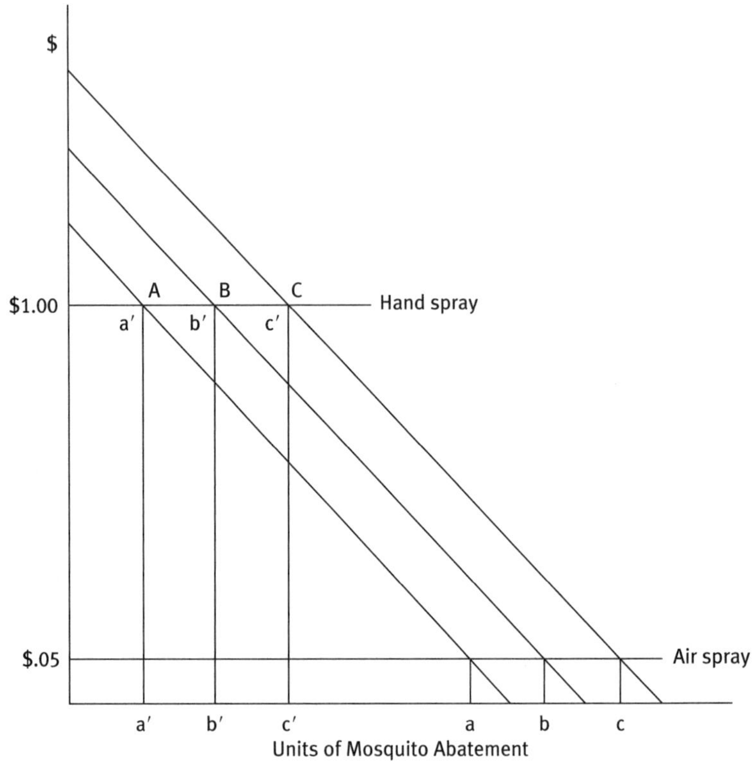

FIGURE 2

a cost involved in the air spraying which should be taken into account. Assuming again that we have our society of 1,000, I would compare my desire for handsprays (that is, how much I would purchase in the way of mosquito abatement by hand) with what I thought was the likely outcome of the voting process in terms of the amount which would be obtained by collective provision. I would anticipate that the collective provision would not turn out to be exactly the amount that I wanted at that price. It would not follow from this that I would favor exact adjustment under what we might call market provision to imperfect adjustment under collective arrangements. Indeed, I presume most people in areas where mosquitoes are bad if confronted with the particular problem that I have outlined would choose the collective provision. Note, however, that this means that they are choosing a less than optimal arrangement of the resources by their own preference ordering. There is, in a sense, an externality imposed upon them by the choice of the collective decision process. They will no longer be able to make an ideal adjustment.

Let us now inquire what is the ideal size of the government unit which deals with mosquito abatement. First, we should note the limits that are placed upon this by the technology of aircraft spraying. In order to be efficient, the aircraft should spray the entire town and certain nearby mosquito breeding areas. An effort to spray half of the town would give much less than half the protection. In other words, it would be a very bad bargain. Therefore, the minimum size of government units which decide to hire the airplane would be our small town in the Middle West.

By rather similar methods we can determine the maximum size of government units for mosquito abatement. In general, every increase in the size of the unit reduces the likelihood that the final provision will be very close to the desires of a given citizen. This is particularly true in something like mosquito abatement where different communities presumably have different levels of mosquito infestation. In general, as the size of government units is increased the number of externalities internalized is increased but the adjustment of the government activity to the desires of any individual voter is decreased. In our particular case, mosquito abatement, the laying off of these two factors leads pretty unambiguously to the view that the small Iowa community should provide its own mosquito abatement. With other problems, of course, other solutions should be expected.

So far, we have been talking about the problem of mosquito abatement about ten years ago. There has been considerable technological change since that time. Let us confine ourselves to considering only those discoveries which indicate that simple airplane spraying of DDT is not a desirable way of dealing with the problem. It has been realized that there are a large number of secondary costs from this operation and that these secondary costs may well be much in excess of the benefit to the spraying process. As a result, the technology of mosquito abatement no longer mainly depends on this very cheap method of killing mosquitoes. We need not go into the more complicated and more expensive methods that are now in general use. It is perfectly possible that tomorrow someone will invent another method of getting rid of mosquitoes that is as cheap as aerial spraying of DDT was thought to be when it was widely used, but we can simply note that present methods are expensive and inquire what effect this would have on the reasoning so far.

The first possible effect of the increase in expense of mosquito abatement by collective measures might be that the unit cost of a given amount of mosquito abatement by collective measures would be equal or higher than if one restricts mosquito abatement to the private use of sprays in one's own backyard. In this case, which is an easy one, the proper decision of course would be to abandon completely all collective efforts to reduce mosquitoes. The second possibility (also very easy) is that mosquito abatement either by public or by private means might become so expensive that it would be no longer desired by individuals. Here, again, the proper solution is to have no public program for mosquito abatement, and we would also anticipate that there would be no private abatement either. Both of these are easy problems and in both cases we need go no further with our analysis.

The interesting question, however, is what would we do if the use of various public means for reducing the mosquito population (let us say, specialized treatment of breeding areas of mosquitoes) is still a less expensive method of obtaining a certain amount of mosquito abatement than is private spraying, but that the difference becomes small. On Figure 3, I have drawn in this problem.

We assume here that methods of mosquito abatement by collective means exist and these are efficient enough so that if all members of the community are compelled to contribute the cost of purchasing one unit of mosquito abatement it will be \$.95 per head, whereas private purchase of one unit of mosquito abatement would remain at \$1.00. If we consider only Mr. B, clearly collective provisions would be desirable. He would be better off purchasing *x* units of mosquito abatement at \$.95 instead of purchasing *b* units at \$1.00 which is his market economy alternative. His net benefit is measured by the areas shaded horizontally and slanting to the left in Figure 3.

If, however, we consider a community consisting of three members (Mr. A, Mr. B, and Mr. C), the situation is more complicated. Mr. A, for example, benefits from the establishment of the new level of mosquito abatement to the extent of the horizontally shaded trapezoid in the upper left. He is injured through the necessity of buying more mosquito abatement than he wants even at the new price to the extent of the vertically shaded triangle. Clearly, he is much worse off with collective provision than he would be with individual provision. Mr. C is affected in a somewhat more ambiguous way. His gross gain is the gross gain of Mr. B plus the little dotted triangle. He, however, suffers a loss to the extent of the shaded triangle from not being able to purchase the additional mosquito abatement privately. This loss will only be suffered if it is not possible for him (for technological or for legal reasons) to supplement the public provision at the same cost as he could have

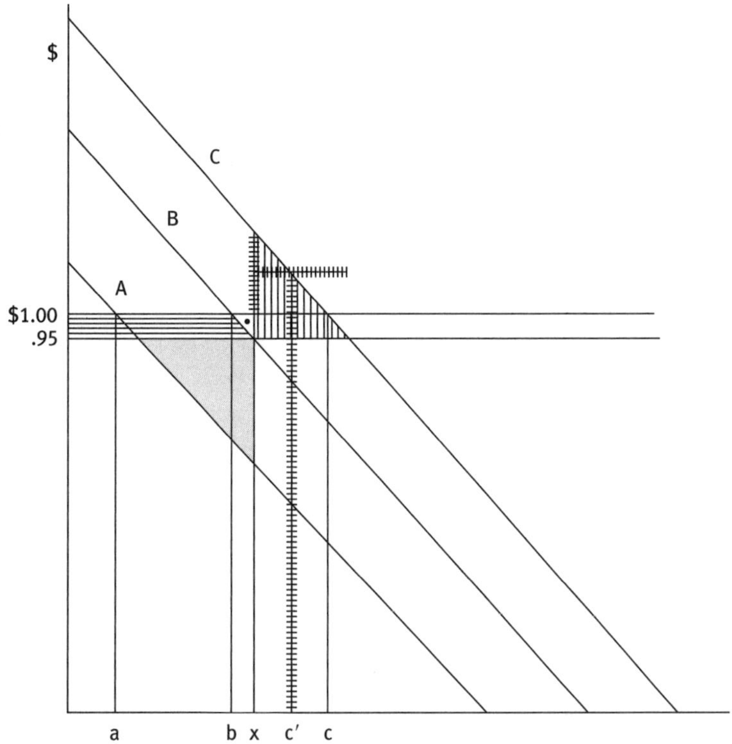

FIGURE 3

bought mosquito abatement privately before. If the public provision of mosquito abatement actually reduced the cost of additional mosquito abatement (which is conceivable), he might gain. If the public provision did not completely bar private but simply made private supplement rather inefficient (which I imagine is the common case), then Mr. C would face a supply curve somewhat like the horizontal dashed line and would purchase $c' - x$ amount of private mosquito abatement. The gross cost to him of the new arrangement then would be the trapezoid lying between this horizontal dashed line and the $1.00 line. If this were a smaller area than the rectangle to the left of the new supply quantity, he would gain in net terms.

Now the question arises naturally whether it would be desirable to undertake public provision of the mosquito abatement granted that we have this small three-person community. If the provision of public mosquito abatement injures both Messrs. A and C and benefits Mr. B, then the ordinary welfare economist can inquire whether Mr. B is able to compensate Messrs. A and C for this injury. If (and this is also quite possible) the provision benefits both B and C but injures Mr. A, then, of course, it will be more likely that compensation can be undertaken. Unfortunately, when we are talking about public goods and where the quantity of public good consumed is set by voting or any other collective process, compensation becomes almost impossible in the real world.

The problem is that we will be unable to find out the amount of the compensation. Mr. A probably has not given much thought to how much he would require to compensate him for a combination of *x* provision collectively and the appropriate taxes. If asked to give thought to this rather strange problem, he has absolutely no motive to correctly interpret his own feelings. This would be particularly true if we were dealing not with our small three-man community. Mr. A might be concerned with the prospect that too large a claim for damages on his part might make the whole project impossible. Thus, there will be some limit to the degree to which he would exaggerate the loss which he would suffer. Similarly, Messrs. B and C even if they are benefited probably would be hard pressed to put a monetary value on their benefit if we asked them and have substantially no motive to do so accurately.

As a general principle, attempting to get voters voting on some issue to compensate each other out of their individual surpluses for their individual losses is not a feasible political proposition. Thus, we cannot use the traditional welfare economics method of making a direct payment from the people who gain to the people who were injured. There is, however, another and rather debatable tool in the welfare economist's tool kit. Some (but not by any means all) welfare economists would argue that if we could compute that the payment would be possible, then it is not necessary to make it. Under this line of reasoning if there is a net social benefit, we don't need to concern ourselves with the way in which it is distributed. This method of applying the Paretian criterion is controversial and I do not wish to endorse it here. There is, however, a variant on it which is clearly a respectable rule and one which we will use.

According to this variant, if we anticipate making a large number of decisions in the future and if we cannot tell who will be benefited and who will be injured by each of these collective decisions but anticipate that most members of the society will find themselves benefited sometimes and injured sometimes, then the rule of simply computing whether there is a net benefit or not and using that for all of these decisions would probably give to each individual in society a positive discounted future income stream. It could be said under this argument that if we found a "net gain" we could undertake the collective provision of mosquito abatement without worrying about the fact that some people (particularly Mr. A) are injured. It will be noted that the use of this argument involves an income transfer. Mr. A is injured, Mr. B is benefited, and depending on the particular parameters of the problem Mr. C may be either benefited or injured. This transfer is clearly not something we would positively favor. That is particularly true since as a general rule most members of society who are interested in restricting the consumption of any particular good are apt to be poorer members. Thus transfers of the sort we are now talking about are apt to be transfers from the poorer to the better-off members of the community. Poor Mr. A is made worse off, middle-class Mr. B is benefited, and upper-class Mr. C may gain.

It will be noted that the basic parameters which have led us to choose either collective or private provision of mosquito abatement have been essentially technological. It is, therefore, sensible to pause briefly and inquire exactly what the nature of technological superiority of collective provision is. At first glance, one might think that it was simply an example of an ordinary scale economy, but this is clearly not so. General Motors has surely exhausted all the scale economies that are available in the manufacture of Chevrolets, yet we find no need for collective provision here. General Motors can sell its cars to people scattered all over the United States without worrying very much about whether the next-door neighbor of any given purchaser of Chevrolet has a Ford.

The special characteristic of aerial spraying of mosquitoes is that it is generally impossible to do it economically on one city lot at a time. In order to get any economy into the operation at all it is necessary to spray a fairly broad area. This is partly because the plane must fly from its airport to the place where it releases the spray anyway and partly that the characteristics of the spray are such that it is apt to cover several surrounding house lots anyway. If only one of them is paying for it, the others will receive a free ride. The problem, then, is geographical contiguity. Geographical contiguity is a basic characteristic of almost all such areas where we would choose collective provision. The distinction between any economy of scale which can be obtained only if the customers are located next door to each other and an economy of scale which can be obtained without this type of contiguity is fundamental.

PUBLIC DECISIONS AS PUBLIC GOODS

It is now orthodox in economics to explain the desirability of government by pointing to the existence of public goods and the difficulties which the private market would have in dealing with them.[1] It is the theme of this article that the operations of the government itself raise a new and extremely difficult public-goods problem. Consider a federal judge who is making a decision on some case. The decision is a direct generation of externalities by him —the externalities falling on the participants in the case. In addition to these rather restricted externalities, he is participating in the production of a public good: law enforcement. If he should, for example, decide to bring in a decision which is not in accord with the law, he not only changes the situation in this particular case, but he also, in a sense, changes the law for the future.

This latter phenomenon is most important in those cases in which judges are actually making law; their decisions generate a pure public good (or public bad). Note, however, the judge himself has almost no private incentive to reach the "right" decision. Suppose that he reaches a decision which leads to an increase in the crime rate; the rise in the crime rate might have a significant effect on the country as a whole, but the likelihood that this particular judge or his immediate family would be victims is very low compared with the damage inflicted on others. The same principle would apply if the judge extended the definition of some crime to include acts which had previously not been regarded as within the statute.

Once again, it would be extremely unlikely that he himself would suffer any damage from the act; hence, he has created a public good (or bad) without significant private gain (or loss). He cannot be removed from office, nor

Reprinted, with permission of the University of Chicago Press, from *Journal of Political Economy* 79 (July/August 1971): 913–18.

1. The tradition dates from Paul Samuelson, "The Pure Theory of Public Expenditure," *Review of Economics and Statistics* 36 (November 1954): 87–89; for further examples of this, see Richard A. Musgrave, *The Theory of Public Finance* (New York: McGraw-Hill, 1959), James M. Buchanan and Gordon Tullock, *The Calculus of Consent: Logical Foundations of Constitutional Democracy* (Ann Arbor: University of Michigan Press, 1962), and many others. The simple slogan "public goods" conceals a large collection of difficulties. I would like to skip over these problems for the purposes of this article because, as we shall see, the public good discussed herein is particularly simple and straightforward.

can his salary be reduced. In practice it is also impossible to even deny him pay raises which are given to other members of the judiciary. It is true that in some cases the judge's decision will not be final; there may be an appeal. A reversal, however, may be a little hard on his self-esteem, but it does not really injure the judge. Supreme court judges are immune from even this control. Thus, the judge is in a position where his behavior generates public goods or public bads and where he gets almost no private costs or benefits as a result of these decisions.

If the judge has no private motives that influence him on any particular decision, then the very feeble effect on himself of the public good would be enough to lead him to the correct decision. He could not be a free rider because there would be no gain from bringing in a "wrong" decision. This is presumably the reason that we are so concerned with possible conflicts of interest in the case of government officials. But it is always better to have someone strongly interested in a correct outcome than merely feebly interested. Further, the judge has reasonably strong private motives which may lead him to reach a decision contrary to that which would maximize his production of public goods. He can be (and very likely is) a free rider.

In the first place, the judge may well have preferences with respect to the issue under consideration, even if he has no conflicting interest. In particular, his personal ethical system may not be that of the legislators. Under these circumstances, he would bear a certain private cost if he followed the legislators' views rather than his own. He may, of course, have an ethical system which not only provides, for example, that execution of murderers is wicked but also that judges should follow the will of the legislature. In this case, he would have an ethical conflict if the law provides for capital punishment. Still, there would be some personal cost involved in carrying out the law in this case. This private cost would be offset against the public good.[2]

I do not know how important this particular private cost is. When I was a law student, there was a good deal of talk about the "fireside equities," lawyer's language for common, ordinary ideas of morality instead of the law. The problem is particularly severe because different judges may have different private ethical systems, with the result that the "law" can vary considerably from

2. Many people who are opposed to capital punishment believe that it also does not generate public goods because it has no effect on the murder rate. In this case, the judge would, at best, be generating the public good of developing respect for the laws that existed if he carried it out, rather than carrying out his own personal preferences.

judge to judge. To offer a guess, I would think that judges are, to a considerable extent, affected by their personal preferences; and when their personal preferences are contrary to the law for any one of a number of reasons, the public-goods aspect of the law is likely to receive relatively short shrift.

Another and more important aspect of the problem, however, concerns the energy and thought which the judge puts into making the decision. This is, for him, a purely private cost. Suppose a particularly difficult question is presented to him. He can produce a quick solution to the problem without much thought. If, however, he wants to be sure that he makes the "correct" decision, he must devote a great deal of time and thought to it. This is a private cost, and the decision will primarily produce public goods.[3] Ordinary public-goods reasoning would imply that he would underinvest in this private expenditure to obtain the public good of a superior decision.

So far, I have talked about judges because they are an almost perfect illustration. Most other government officials are also examples. Indeed, many have policy-making responsibilities which lead to even more severe conflicts between their private costs and the public good or bad that they are producing. Consider the average civil servant. Although it is not true that he cannot be discharged for inefficiency, it is extremely difficult to fire him. Under the circumstances, if he makes a decision, there is no strong reason why he should go against his own preferences if these happen to conflict with the preferences of the majority. In addition, he has no strong reason to work overly hard.

This last factor is particularly likely to be important if he has a very strongly ingrained opinion with respect to some subject. He will be extremely reluctant to take the trouble to study the problem for the specific purpose of finding out whether his judgment is good or bad. There is very little cost to him if his judgment is bad, and the cost of the work together with the change of mind is considerable. Further, discovery that his judgment is bad on some subjects may imply that he has made a number of erroneous decisions in the past and thus has worked considerable harm. The desire to avoid admission of such mistakes is readily understandable. Thus, there are a number of private costs which can be set against the public good of a careful and accurate decision. Needless to say, the same general principles apply to bureaucrats who wear military uniforms.

3. It is quite possible that judges sometimes get pleasure out of thinking about the problems which come before them, but surely the amount of energy put into these problems for entertainment of the judge is not the social optimum.

So far, we have been talking about government officials who are essentially free from the possibility of being fired. In a democracy, the officials who hold the most important positions are not immune from discharge. Politicians can be fired by the voters, and they obviously do have some control over civil servants, if not over the judges. Politicians, then, are motivated to consider the effects of their decisions on their own personal future, and, hence, do have a significant private benefit as well as a private cost attached to the intellectual effort of producing a desirable decision. In this respect they are similar to an employee of a firm producing goods for the market, but unfortunately there is also a major difference between the elected politician and the official of a private company.

Consider, for example, General Motors. They have an employee who is engaged in designing bumpers for Chevrolets. Presumably, the benefit that he is likely to receive from a superior bumper is, in direct terms, very small. He may or may not buy a Chevrolet, but if he does, the effect upon him of a good bumper design is vastly smaller than the effect on the nation as a whole. Further, his production of this bumper is the generation of a "public good" for the company, that is, it will affect the company's profits. Once again, however, injury to the individual designer from shrinkage of General Motors sales because he has designed a poor bumper will be vastly less than the effect on General Motors. General Motors deals with the problem by imposing upon him a private cost in order to motivate him to produce this "public good"—a good bumper design—for his own private reasons.

To return to our governmental example, the politician is subject to somewhat the same kind of sanction as the General Motors employee. He can be easily fired by the voters if he displeases them. Further, he does have some influence on the future careers of the civil servants and even (in terms of getting salaries) of the federal judges. This influence is much milder than the influence we normally anticipate in the market part of the economy, but it is not zero. Here, we encounter another very important public-goods problem. The individual citizen, in choosing what car he will purchase, is making a private decision, the full cost of which will fall upon himself. Thus, he is motivated to put an optimal amount of energy into finding out what is the best car for him. In addition, if he makes a mistake, no one pays for it but himself. If, on the other hand, he is considering voting, then, as Kenneth Arrow[4] points out, "since the effect of any individual vote is so very small, it does not

4. Kenneth Arrow, "Tullock and an Existence Theorem," *Public Choice* 6 (Spring 1969): 105–11.

pay a voter to acquire information unless his stake in the initial issue is enormously greater than the cost of information." The individual voter is producing a public good when he casts his vote, and he has very little, if any, reason for acquiring information to see to it that his vote is properly cast. The probable cost to him of miscasting his vote is trivial.[5]

Under the circumstances, we would not anticipate that the voter would bother to become very well informed. Data on information held by voters seem to confirm this hypothesis. People who do not know the names of their congressmen are common. Misjudgments of political issues and, for that matter, belief that the parties are making promises which are directly opposite to the promises that they are actually offering are normal. Granted the public-goods theorem, all of this is what we should expect and what we do observe. Thus, there is a fundamental difference between the market and politics in that the ultimate customer is engaged in producing a private good for himself when he makes a decision to purchase in the private market. When he casts his vote in the "public market," he is producing a public good. Since there are private-information costs associated both with purchase and with voting, we would anticipate that these private costs would be incurred up to the point where their marginal utility balances that of an improved decision to the individual. This is near zero in the case of the vote.

In the private market, the ultimate prosperity or failure of the entrepreneurs depends on their sale of goods or services to persons who are purchasing private goods for their own benefit. In the public market, the political entrepreneurs succeed or fail in terms of selling public goods to individuals whose misjudgments will redound mainly on others rather than on themselves. The information conditions are quite different in these two markets, and we would expect a far lower degree of consumer satisfaction in the public market than in the private market, simply because the consumer sensibly invests very much less energy in making his decision in the public market. Here again, the public-goods theorem indicates that rational individuals will make choices which are socially nonoptimum.

To return to the theme of this article, democratic governments, which are now normally explained in economics courses as efforts to deal with public goods, generate an extremely difficult public-goods problem themselves. The

5. See Anthony Downs, *An Economic Theory of Democracy* (New York: Harper, 1957), and Gordon Tullock, *Toward a Mathematics of Politics* (Ann Arbor: University of Michigan Press, 1967).

public decision-making process is a procedure for generating a public good; and the persons involved in it, whether they are the voters, judges, legislators, or civil servants, all can be expected to treat it as any other public good. Hence, we can anticipate that they will invest less in the "private costs" of considering that public decision than is optimal.

Having pointed out a major problem, it is the custom to suggest a solution. Unfortunately, in this case, I cannot do so, although in one situation there is a possible solution. Local governments in the area around major cities frequently are in competition with each other for residents. The individual deciding where to live will take into account the private effects upon him of the bundle of government services and taxes in each suburb. In this case, the decision is a private decision, the bulk of the cost of which falls upon the person making it. Even in this case, however, we do not have a purely private good similar to a car, because the government of the community will be appointed, not by profit-seeking persons attempting to maximize the number of their customers, but by the majority of the customers themselves working through the voting market. Although the individual has a strong motive to consider carefully in which suburb he will live, he has only weak motives to exercise his vote intelligently once he gets there. Since the various alternatives which he faces are all managed in this public-good-dependent way, it is likely that the tendency to "adjust to the demand" is very much weaker than it would be if the suburbs were profit-making firms. There would be very great difficulties in applying this solution to major government units, but the idea is worth further study.

The end product of this investigation is rather depressing. The private market can provide an adequate solution for only those externalities which can be fully internalized privately. The public market which can fully internalize many more "public goods" generates an extreme public-goods problem in its decision process. Thus, we have a choice between a private market which will systematically produce biased decisions and governments which will equally systematically produce ill-considered decisions.

INFORMATION WITHOUT PROFIT

Charitable activities are a significant part of our economy, but they have received surprisingly little attention from economists.[1] The usual method of organizing large scale charity is the non-profit corporation, and it has received even less attention from the economists. This is particularly surprising when it is remembered that most economists are employed by non-profit organizations, and hence would seem to have exceptional opportunities to use their analytical tools on that form of organization. This article will be a foray into the relatively unexplored area of the economics of charity. Its basic tool will be a cost-benefit analysis of information in the manner of Anthony Downs.[2] Analysis, however, is not the sole purpose of the article; it will end with suggestions for institutional reform.

Most human beings have charitable feelings, and most make at least some allocation of resources to charitable objects. Sometimes these charitable feelings lead to direct gifts to individuals, but more normally some non-profit organization is used as an intermediary. This non-profit instrumentality may be the government, in which case the charitable individual votes for or exerts pressure in favor of spending tax money in ways that will benefit some person or group whom he wishes to help. In the case of private charities, the individual normally makes a gift to, say, Harvard University or the Cancer Foundation.[3] Although these institutional forms are different, the problems examined in this article are not much affected by the difference. It will, therefore, mainly deal with gifts to private charities with only occasional references

Reprinted, with kind permission of Kluwer Academic Publishers, from *Papers on Non-Market Decision Making* 1 (1966): 141–59.

1. There has, of course, been some investigation of the charitable field. See: *Philanthropy and Public Policy*, Frank G. Dickinson, ed. (New York: National Bureau of Economic Research, 1962), and the panel on "Economic Theory and Non-Profit Enterprise," *American Economic Review* (May 1965), pp. 472–509.

2. Anthony Downs, *An Economic Theory of Democracy* (New York: Harper & Bros., 1957), pp. 207–60.

3. The charitable motives may be rather indirect, as in the case of both Harvard and the Cancer Foundation. Instead of directly helping the poor and downtrodden, the donor makes a contribution intended to improve the situation by increasing our knowledge. He may also be interested in improving culture by a gift to a symphony orchestra.

to the use of governmental instrumentalities and tax money for charitable purposes.

Economics courses usually will include, somewhere, a statement to the effect that a decision to make a charitable contribution is no more economically irrational than a decision to buy a car. Both are ways of using income to "purchase" satisfaction; both increase utility. It is not the purpose of this article to contradict this traditional view of the individual rationality of charitable activity, but to suggest that there is, nevertheless, a substantial element of something very like irrationality in the charitable use of resources. The donors of the charitable gift, whether they are private individuals making a contribution to the Heart Fund or voters disposing of tax funds, are apt to be exceptionally ill informed about the effects of their gift.[4] As a result of the poor information conditions, charitable activity is likely to be badly designed and ineptly carried out. Once this problem is recognized, it becomes possible to discuss possible improvements.

A recent discussion concluded: "In a distressing number of cases . . . donors wish simply to discharge their moral obligations by a gift of suitable size, and do not care whether the donation ever bears fruit. In fact, through such devices as the United Fund, they both escape from having to choose carefully among alternative organizations and excuse the recipient organization from accounting to them for an efficient use of funds."[5] That this describes much charitable activity, few would doubt. The author, however, offers no explanation for the sharp difference he perceives between the behavior of people expending resources on charity and on private goods. In this he is typical. The relative lack of interest in the charity itself by its donors has been widely noted,[6] but even attempts at explanation are rare.

4. A general, and widely noted, information problem in charity turns on the fact that the donor can hardly have good information on the utility schedule of the beneficiaries. Thus his gift, unless it is a straight money donation, will probably not exactly fit the desires of the beneficiaries. I do not wish to deny the importance of this problem, but the information difficulty discussed in this article is a different one.

5. Charles Lindblom, "Private—But Not for Profit," *Challenge* (March-April, 1966): pp. 20–23, quotation on page 22. Richard Cornuelle's *Reclaiming the American Dream* (New York: Random House, 1965) is basically a plea for the expansion of the charitable sector, yet it is replete with examples of extreme inefficiency in that area.

6. ". . . the exhilaration which results from 'doing good,' that is, from intending to do good, for the average heart does not require assurance of the result." Lilian Brandy, *How Much Shall I Give?* (New York: The Frontier Press, 1921), p. 20.

As we shall see, the explanation is not difficult when consideration is given to the information costs involved. Before attempting to develop a rigorous model, however, let us consider a parable of vice and virtue: Benefactor organizes an enterprise called "Aid for the Sick and Starving Children of Gwondonaland," and solicits voluntary gifts for its support. This enterprise does not, however, waste any of its money in Gwondonaland. All of the contributions that it receives (except Benefactor's entrepreneurial profit) are devoted solely to raising the utility of the donors. It publishes a newsletter (on what appears to be cheap paper) full of affecting stories of suffering and its alleviation. These stories, produced by the best writers money can hire, are illustrated by touching before and after pictures produced by skilled photographers using all the resources of the New York modeling agencies. Any donor who gives more than $10.00 receives a "personal letter" in a childish scrawl expressing gratitude and suggesting further contributions. Donors of more than $100.00 receive "native handicraft" allegedly produced by the children of Gwondonaland. Extensive promotional activity with the objective of attracting new contributors is also carried on. As a result of Benefactor's activities, many contributors have the satisfaction of thinking that they are alleviating suffering. As a result of his investment of almost the total value of their gifts into providing "information" flows to them which indicate that their charity is both needed and successful, they are happier about this charity than they would be if money were put into actually helping the children and the flow of newsletters, etc., were less well financed.

This project, which is likely to arouse considerable indignation among non-economists, meets the welfare criteria of Paretian economics. It produces a warm glow in the hearts of the donors, provides employment for many writers, models, photographers, printers, etc., in New York, and sizeable profits for Benefactor. Its creation raised the state of satisfaction of many people and reduced the satisfaction of no one. There is no change which can be suggested which would "benefit at least one person while injuring no one." In particular it should be noted that the starving children of Gwondonaland are in no way injured by the organization. They would, of course, be better off if the AFTSASCOG were to divert some of its resources from directly serving its customers, the donors, to help in Gwondonaland, but they would also be better off if U.S. Steel similarly made contributions to their welfare. The fact that the managements of U.S. Steel and AFTSASCOG are primarily interested in serving their customers and do not make charitable contributions to the children of Gwondonaland is no doubt unfortunate, but it does not actually injure the children.

So much for virtue. Now enters vice in the form of Meddler, a man totally untrained in economics who has never even heard of Pareto Optimality. Meddler investigates AFTSASCOG and releases the results of his inquiries to the newspapers. As a result of his failure to give Benefactor an opportunity to make suitable side payments to prevent publication, the donors lose their warm feeling of righteousness and are made very unhappy. The models, photographers, etc., employed by AFTSASCOG are forced to seek other employment, and Benefactor goes to prison which means that the taxpayers must support him for several years. Meddler's uneconomic intervention is almost the exact contrary to a Paretian change. There are some people who get pleasure out of reading sensational news of this sort in the newspaper, and they are benefitted by his activities. With the exception of these newspaper readers, no one is made better off by Meddler's action, and a great number of people are injured.

Let us suppose, now, that Benefactor comes out of prison sadder but wiser. He accordingly organizes "Aid for the Sick and Starving Children of Beuchanaland" which is designed to avoid the sad end of AFTSASCOG. It does not spend all of its income on promotional activities, but actually uses some of it to feed starving Beuchanaland children. As a result it is unable to distribute to its donors as much in the way of newsletters, native handicrafts, etc., as had AFTSASCOG. Further, on advice of his lawyers, Benefactor now makes certain that all accounts of suffering and its alleviation in his literature are genuine, and that they are illustrated by pictures of actual Beuchana children taken in Beuchanaland. Since truth is seldom as interesting as fiction, and since the Beuchanas are not as good models as the professionals in New York, nor are there first class photographers in Beuchanaland, the product is considerably less effective than the pure fakes he has used before. As a result he is able to attract fewer donations and the donors, on the average, are less satisfied than were the donors to AFTSASCOG before the revelation. In a sense, the expenditures in Beuchanaland are insurance against another disaster. They protect both Benefactor and his donors against the type of exposure which ended AFTSASCOG.

The situation may be clarified by consideration of a somewhat similar situation which faced manufacturers before the development of fire insurance. The manufacturer in the early 19th century, like Benefactor, faced the possibility of a disaster, but in the form of fire rather than exposure.[7] Any resources

7. Also like Benefactor, the disaster might be total or partial. An exposure might affect only a few potential donors just as a fire might destroy only part of a plant.

he put into precautions against fire, for example storing all flammable raw materials at a distance from the factory with concomitant increases in manufacturing costs, would either increase the cost he must charge or make it necessary for him to produce a poorer product. The customers would make their choices solely in terms of the product and price, and would not be interested in the relative likelihood that his plant would burn down tomorrow. The manufacturer, on the other hand, is interested in both selling his product and keeping his factory safe. Every dollar put into fire precautions reduces his ability to sell his product profitably, but increases the probability that he will still have a factory next year. Similarly, every dollar that Benefactor puts into actual aid for the children reduces the resources he can put into improving the satisfaction of his customers, the donors.

The analogy is not, of course, perfect. The customers of the manufacturer are completely indifferent to his future well being, and consequently completely uninterested in whether he does have fire insurance. The donors, on the other hand, will also suffer, by being made to look like fools, if Benefactor is exposed as a fraud. They therefore have some interest in information about the likelihood of such exposure, and the question of whether or not he actually is a fraud would therefore interest them. Note, however, that this applies only to the possibility that the charity is actually fraudulent. If the charity is simply extremely inefficient, or devotes an undue percentage of its collections to soliciting more gifts, it is highly unlikely that this will damage the donor. Thus the potential donor would be interested in information indicating that the charity actually did carry on charitable activities, but not in the efficiency with which it operates. This is in fact the pattern of the "information" that charities put into their fund solicitations.

The Peace Corps, for example, in its early days put out a very attractive recruiting poster showing a volunteer doing something in the foreground and with a large legend; "What in the World Are You Doing?" I wrote in to inquire what he was doing. This set off a long correspondence in which it became plain that they did not know or care what he was doing.[8] He was clearly a very attractive young man, and he surely had only the best of intentions. This, they implied, should be enough. Inquiries as to what he was doing, or whether whatever it was, was a sensible way to help the inhabitants of the suburb of Bogota in which he was living, were not really important enough

8. The theories proposed ran the gamut from building a rail fence to constructing some rabbit hutches.

to deserve a careful answer. The issue of efficiency was too vague to make the likelihood of "exposure" a real risk.

These results clearly are paradoxical, yet they appear also to be logical. The problem, of course, is the peculiar nature of the product sold by the "welfare industry." If I buy a car I then receive the car, and will necessarily become aware of any defects that it possesses. Similarly, if I vote for a candidate for Congress because he promises more money for research in the social sciences, I will (if enough other special interest groups also vote for him and the other members of his party) find it easier to get research grants for myself. Both of these activities involve an expenditure of resources to obtain an end which will directly affect me. Since I know that any defect in the product that I am "buying" will work directly to my disadvantage, I am well advised to invest resources in finding out exactly what I will get before I make any commitment.

With charitable expenditures, on the other hand, I am not inevitably going to have any defects in the product brought to my attention, and defects will, in any case, not directly affect me. If I make a contribution to the starving children of Gwondonaland, or vote for a congressman who promises to use public funds for that end, I will not be in any way injured by a *successful* fraud or by inefficiency. As long as I continue to think that the children have been helped by my contribution, the fact that they have not been will not reduce my state of satisfaction. The situation is radically different if I am purchasing some object or service for my own use, since I will automatically find out if the product or service does not come up to expectations.

The basic problem arises from the radically different nature of the satisfactions arising from a charitable expenditure and from the purchase of something to be directly consumed. These different satisfactions lead to a different set of costs and benefits attaching to the investment of resources in obtaining information. Naturally this leads to different attitudes toward information, and a difference in the effort put into getting it. The incentives for becoming well informed are extremely weak in charitable expenditures, and we should accordingly expect that a high degree of information would be rare. Similarly, the managers of charitable organizations, whether private or governmental, will find that they get more funds if they take this fact into account. They are "selling" a feeling of satisfaction derived from sacrifice; whether the sacrifice does or does not improve the well being of someone else is not of direct interest to the donor. He is interested not in what actually happens, but in his image of it. The entrepreneurs, accordingly, should polish the image.

In order to consider the matter more carefully, let us use a little simple algebra. To simplify matters we will confine ourselves to private transactions, leaving aside the political mechanism which the individual can use for both private gain and charity. The farmer voting for a candidate who has promised an increase in subsidies is clearly using his vote to purchase a private gain. If, on the other hand, he votes for a man who proposes to cut farm subsidies and let the price of bread fall, he is engaging in charity through the government. But we shall generally ignore this complication and assume that we are talking about the private purchase of private goods or private charitable contributions. In the problems raised here, the basic difference is between private or charitable ends, and the choice of private or public means for reaching those ends will not be of much importance.

Consider, then, a person who has purchased a car or made a contribution to a foreign mission fund. His satisfaction (S) will equal the sum of a number of different factors as shown in equation 1.

$$S = P + U + R_p + R_u + P_s - C \tag{1}$$

In this equation P is the actual pleasure he gets from the act of purchase, U the pleasure he gets from consumption of the good or service (if it is a private purchase), R_p is his evaluation of the effect on his reputation of making the purchase, R_u his evaluation of the effect on his reputation of being seen to possess or consume the good or service, P_s is the increase of his satisfaction from the post-sale activities of the seller. Mostly we don't think of this particular source of satisfaction, but most merchants will do at least a little to convince the purchaser of their goods that he has obtained a good bargain. The salesman who tells you that a suit you have just bought looks well on you is perhaps the best example. In private purchases this is a small factor, but in the case of charities it may be a major one. Lastly, there is C, the cost of the purchase or gift, the other possible uses of the resources committed to this particular transaction. See table 1.

If we consider the ordinary private purchase of goods or services, it is obvious that the satisfaction derived from P, R_p, and P_s is very small and R_u will usually be quite small. Equation 2 would be regarded as a satisfactory approximation for most cases.

$$S = U - C \tag{2}$$

For a charitable contribution, on the other hand, the individual will not make use of or consume the goods or services which his contribution provides. Equation 3 is a correct statement of his situation.

$$S = P + R_p + P_s - C \qquad (3)$$

But equations 2 and 3 have quite different effects if it is assumed that information is not free. An individual considering purchasing a private good would be impelled to begin by acquiring information about the good even at the sacrifice of real resources because he is going to get most of his satisfaction out of consuming it, and if it is defective he will be the one who suffers. Given his choice between devoting a certain quantity of resources to the purchase of a car or devoting part of that quantity to investigating the market situation for cars and then purchasing a car with the remainder, he will normally choose the latter. This gives him less money to spend on the car, but also makes it less likely that he will regret his decision. He is purchasing a stream of future services to himself and will wish to ascertain as accurately as possible the value of that stream before he buys it.

The man contemplating a charitable gift, on the other hand, is essentially purchasing a present good. Both P and R_p depend entirely on his act in making the gift. He need not make any inquiries about the efficiency of the charity to get the feeling of satisfaction derived from making a sacrifice since he is clearly making the sacrifice. The gain to his reputation, R_p, depends upon the opinion of others, and he should find out what they think, but what he needs to know is what they think now, which means that he need invest no resources in finding out what the charity actually does with its money, only

TABLE 1. ***Table of Symbols***

C = Cost, price paid.
C_p = Cost of production, money spent on ostensible object of charity.
I = Gross receipts, total contributions.
P = Pleasure derived by individual from making contribution to charity directly or through some collective body such as the state; or the pleasure derived by the individual from the act of purchasing a private good.
P_r = Profit earned when organization is, either legally or in fact, profit oriented.
P_s = Pleasure derived from post-sale activity of seller.
P_{sc} = Cost of post-sales activity undertaken to increase satisfaction of contributor or purchaser.
R_p = Individual evaluation of the effect on his reputation of making a purchase or contribution.
R_u = Individual's evaluation of the effect on his reputation of possessing good or service.
S = Total satisfaction from transaction.
S_c = Sales or promotional costs.
U = Pleasure from consumption, or use, of good or service.

with its reputation.[9] Further, he need not learn its general reputation, but only its reputation with people with whom he normally comes in contact. His gift will improve his reputation with the people who count to him if *they* think the charity is a good one. The existence of a group of sophisticates who disapprove of the Red Cross need not concern the average contributor.

If we return to equation 3, however, we will find one factor contributing to the satisfaction of the potential donor which does refer to the future, the P_s, standing for the contribution of his well-being by the post-sales activity of the seller. If the charitable organization conducts itself so that it becomes publicly known as a complete fraud after the donor has made his gift, clearly P_s would assume a substantial negative value. Leaving this matter aside for the moment, however, surely charities devote more resources to post-sales activities than do sellers of private goods and services. The donor to any well-organized charity can expect to be deluged with publications of the charity telling him what a good job it is doing and how great the need for further expenditures. This is rational since this is the only direct service the charity can give to its donors. By raising *their* satisfaction in this way, it makes future gifts more likely.

In most cases the material distributed by the charity itself, or stories planted by its public relations counsel, are the only source of "information" on its activities available to its donors. This is because most charities are simply not large enough to attract the attention of the mass media with any regularity. Pure fraud by a purported charity might, however, be an exception. The exposure of hypocrites is always popular, and Benefactor of our story no doubt would make the headlines. Simple inefficiency,[10] on the other hand,

9. During the course of composing this article I have been collecting direct mail solicitations for charitable contributions. The sample is small, but it includes such large, well-managed charities as the Heart Fund. They are notable for their lack of figures from which one could deduce how they actually spend their money and their obvious dependence upon emotional appeals. Apparently the advertising agencies who design these campaigns (not infrequently as a "public service") are trying to increase the satisfaction that comes from giving as an act in itself, not to convince the potential donor that the charity is well managed and efficient.

10. Note that "inefficiency" is used as it is by the layman in ordinary speech. If we use the words "efficiency" and "inefficiency" to mean what they mean in most economic discussions, then an organization which maximized the satisfaction of its donors would be efficient, regardless of what happened to the ostensible objects of the charity. In this article, then, "efficiency" will mean "efficiency in terms of the presumed objectives of the organization" rather than its technical meaning.

would seldom rate a newspaper story. In the first place it is hard to judge efficiency of a charity, so accusations of inefficiency might be complex and uninteresting to the casual reader. Secondly, there would be little interest in a story which merely said that a group of well-intentioned people were not meeting some ideal standard. Allegations of wickedness are normally necessary to spice up an exposure.[11]

Thus the donor is unlikely to have his satisfaction in his gift reduced if the charity is simply inefficient. He has, of course, no motive to investigate himself after he has made the gift. Any derogatory information which he might dig up would just reduce his satisfaction. Indeed, at the subconscious level, he probably will avoid information which might hurt his self-esteem by indicating that his gift had been ill-advised. With the newspapers uninterested in inefficiency, and all of the donors having a positive aversion to evidence indicating that they had been suckers, it is unlikely that the donor will have any inefficiency of the organization brought to his notice. Under the circumstances, P_s will consist almost entirely of the flow of "information" furnished to the donor by the charity itself. There will be a small probability that he will be annoyed by the discovery that it is a fraud, but the likelihood that poor performance on the part of the charity will reduce his satisfaction is small. If there is deception it will probably be successful. Since the donor gets the same satisfaction from contributing to a fraudulent charity which successfully conceals its frauds, as from a contribution to an honest charity,[12] he is not injured by a successful fraud.

But, as we have noted, fraud is not terribly easy to conceal. The newspapers will be interested in it, allegations of fraud are likely to bring on formal investigations by the police, and various employees of the organization may be motivated to "expose" direct fraud. The donor, therefore, should be willing to devote at least some resources to making sure that a charity to which he is thinking of making a contribution is not a pure fraud. Inefficiency is another matter. Inefficient operation of a charity is not a crime so the po-

11. The possibility of "exposure" probably reduces the efficiency of many charities. The large charities are sizeable enough so that their efficient management would require high quality personnel. A charity paying its principal executive officer $150,000 would, however, almost certainly face a major scandal. Consequently most charities get by with the less competent management which can be purchased for moderate salaries.

12. Indeed the fraud, as in the case of Benefactor, may give its donors more satisfaction. It can put more resources into giving them favorable information.

lice and other law enforcement agencies will not be interested in it. Rarely would it make a good enough story to interest the newspapers. Under the circumstances it is unlikely that the donor will be embarrassed by an "exposure" of the inefficiency of the charity to which he makes gifts. He would, therefore, be irrational to invest significant resources in attempting to determine the efficiency of the charity before he makes his gift. His satisfaction from the gift will be little affected if it is actually badly run.

One particular form of inefficiency for a charity would be the investment of "too much" resources in promotional activity. This would, however, not reduce the satisfaction of the donor; indeed it should increase it unless it is forcefully brought to his attention that too much is being spent on this aspect of the organization's activities. Since "too much" is a vague concept, this is unlikely under present circumstances. Most of the remainder of this article will be devoted to this particular kind of inefficiency.

The concentration on over-expenditure on promotional expenditures is not intended to imply that this is the only, or principal type of inefficiency in charitable organizations. Very commonly inefficiency results from the fact that charities hire people to engage in services of various sorts which are intended to help the beneficiaries of the charity. It is easy for the charity to slip into the habit of making administrative decisions in terms of the welfare of the employees of the charity rather than in terms of the well-being of the beneficiaries. Another important source of inefficiency is simply mistake. The federal government's Aid to Dependent Children program, for example, pays mothers of dependent children according to a schedule of payments which provides a sizeable incentive for the mother of one or two children to produce more. Since raising the birth rate surely was not the intention of Congress, this is highly inefficient.[13] We will not discuss these types of inefficiency, but only because they would require more advanced tools than the ones used in this article.

But to return to our main subject, an ideal charity would try to maximize its total charitable payments. Putting C_p, the cost of production of its services, on the left, it would try to maximize equation 4.

$$C_p = I - S_c - P_{sc} \tag{4}$$

13. It is possible that this is not the result of miscalculation. The bureaucrats gain by expansion of their funds when additional children are born into the program. It would be interesting to look into the advice given Congress by the professional administrators of the bureau.

Where I equals total receipts or income, S_c is the cost of sales, and P_{sc} is the cost of post-sales activity undertaken to raise the satisfaction of the contributor. Note that this equation would be misleading if used for any other purpose than an analysis of expenditures on promotional activities. Efficiency in the expenditure of funds on the actual charitable output is simply ignored. A profit maximizing firm would try to maximize profit, P_r, under the conditions of equation 5.

$$P_r = I - C_p - S_c - P_{sc} \tag{5}$$

Note that this equation fits a profit making organization manufacturing automobiles as well as one engaged in some charitable activity for profit. It is probable that profit maximizing charities exist only in a quasifraudulent underworld. There are companies which engage in the business of managing charities, but they normally do not take their return in the form of a residual. Usually either they are paid a fixed fee or their compensation varies with the total size of the organization which would give them the same maximization objectives as the bureaucratic organizations to be discussed below. One can readily imagine, however, someone like Benefactor after his stay with the government, who calculates how much he must put into the actual charity as a cost, and takes the remainder for his own use.

Most charities, whether private or governmental, are managed by professional bureaucrats. These people do not draw their compensation as a residual, but as part of the cost of running the charity. In general their prestige, compensation, and power will vary roughly with the total size of the charitable organization. Like Baumol's sales maximizing executives they are motivated to maximize total receipts, I, as in equation 6.

$$I = C_p + S_p + P_{sc} \tag{6}$$

The larger the charity or bureau, the better off they are. Note that this equation is identical to (5) if P_r is set equal to zero. The only difference between the entrepreneur and the bureaucrat is that the entrepreneur is permitted to take resources from the organization for a trip to Jamaica while the bureaucrat can only increase his income by expanding the organization. Both the bureaucrat and the profit seeking owner are interested in expansion, but the private owner would stop investing resources in expansion when their return in that use fell below their value to him in his private life. The bureaucrat is prohibited from spending the resources himself, and hence will carry the expansion further.

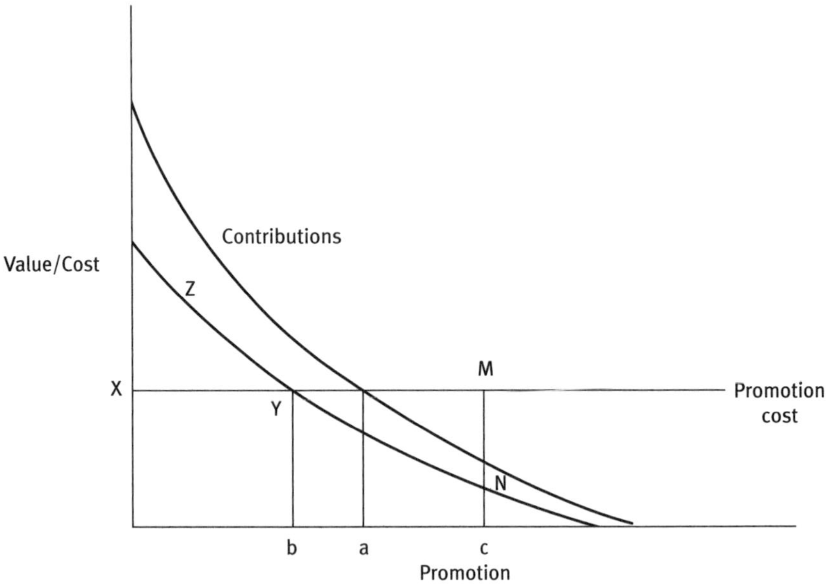

FIGURE 1

The situation is presented graphically in Figure 1.

On the vertical axis is shown the value or cost of each increment of income or expenditure. Each dollar spent on promotion ($S_c + P_{sc}$) costs a dollar, hence promotion costs are a horizontal line. The return on each dollar of promotional expenditure in gifts is shown by the "contributions" line which exhibits the usual declining returns. An ideal charity would expand its promotional activity until the marginal return on a dollar of additional promotion was a dollar, or to point *a*. This would leave the triangular area bounded by the promotion cost line, the contribution line, and the vertical axis as the amount available for charitable expenditure.

The profit making entrepreneur, however, would realize that he had to put at least something into the charity itself, which means that his profit would be total collections less the promotional cost and the cost of whatever he decided to spend on the charity. It seems reasonable that he would feel that his charitable expenditures should increase when his donations increase, so that there would be at least some charitable expenditure for each additional dollar of income. For simplicity I assume that he feels that he must put roughly a third of the contributions he receives into actual charitable activities. Line ZN shows the amount left over after this necessary "cost" has been taken care of.[14] The private entrepreneur, thus, will curtail his promotional campaign at point *b* and build a smaller organization.

The bureaucrat, whose pay and prestige vary with the size of the charity, is interested in using the resources of the organization for promotional purposes, with the objective of maximizing its size. He will be like the profit seeking businessman, however, in realizing that he must put at least some resources into the production of the charity. Once again we assume for simplicity that he puts a constant share of the gifts received into charitable uses, retaining the rest for promotional expenses. He should expand the organization until the total expenditure on promotion and on the production of charity equals total receipts. In other words, until total cost equals total receipts. On Figure 1, triangle XZY will be equal in area to the triangle YMN. Unlike the private owner, the bureaucrat is willing to spend, say, $1.20 on soliciting $1.00 because this increases the total size of the organization and because the $.20 does not come out of the bureaucrat's pocket while the expansion will improve his position.[15]

From our model we can draw certain simple conclusions about the magnitude of various factors under the three different types of management.[16] The bureaucratic charity will be the largest in overall size, with the ideal charity and the private enterprise following in that order. The absolute size of the promotional budget of the bureaucratic enterprise will be the largest, with the ideal charity and the private enterprise following in that order. The same will apply to the percentage of receipts spent on promotional activity. In absolute terms the ideal charity will spend the most on the assumed objects of the organization, while the bureaucratic organization and the private enterprise will spend successively less. In percentage terms the ideal charity will put the highest proportion of its funds into the actual charity, but it cannot be said for certain which of the other two would be second in this regard.

14. The general conclusions are not affected by the exact shape of this line. As long as he increases his charitable "production" when his contributions go up the results follow.

15. The ideal charity would also be unwilling to spend a dollar on soliciting unless prospective returns were above a dollar because it would have to take the difference out of its charitable expenditures which it wishes to maximize.

16. The reasoning here closely resembles that of Armen Alchian's work on the role of profits.

From all of this it would appear that the ideal charity is, indeed, the ideal. Unfortunately it is probably rather rare. Small, essentially local, charities may operate in this way, but the larger charities almost always come under the control of their professional employees. Charitable activity by the government is, almost by definition, run by bureaucrats. Granting this, and the inefficiency which results, we now turn to a discussion of possible remedies. The first thing to be admitted is that I have no real cure for the disease, only palliatives. Perhaps the reader may be able to find solutions which have escaped me. If so, I urge that he publish them as soon as possible. Charity is an important part of our economy, and it is desirable that its efficiency be improved.

The basic problem is simply that the man thinking of making a charitable contribution has much less motive for obtaining information about the likely performance of the charity than the man contemplating the purchase of an automobile has for finding out about the car. It is not true, however, that the potential charitable donor has no interest in accurate information; it is just that his motivation is weak. If information were readily available at low cost he might be interested in looking at it. Thus the arguments for compelling the provision of information would seem to be strong. Individuals purchasing consumption goods, stocks, or borrowing money, have strong motives for searching out information on the subject, yet we legally require the purveyors to provide them with a good deal of information. Given the weakness of the motivation for search in the case of charity, making information cheap by requiring the charitable organizations to provide it would seem much more desirable.

The fact that we have numerous laws requiring private businesses to provide information to potential purchasers by, for example, printing the contents of a can on the label, while there is a complete absence of such legislation with respect to charity probably reflects mainly the fact that people really don't think much about their charitable contributions. They vaguely think that charities are, by definition, doing good, and hence that they do not need to be supervised like profit seeking businessmen. This would appear to both reflect and contribute to the poor information that people have about the charitable organizations. Compelling charities to make information readily available to potential donors could hardly help but improve the efficiency of the "Third Sector."[17]

17. Richard Cornuelle, *Reclaiming the American Dream*.

Unfortunately governmental action to compel charities to provide information is unlikely to have very much effect on those large and important charities which are operated by the government itself. Still, even here something could be done by requiring that all records be open. Sweden does this on the largest possible scale[18] and a modest beginning has been made in the poverty program here.[19] Requiring all governmental and private charities to put their records at the disposal of any interested inquirer[20] would be a sensible first step.

As a second reform, and unfortunately this would apply only to private charities, an equivalent of the labeling laws might be passed. Each piece of literature used by the charity for the direct or indirect solicitation of funds could be required to carry a functional account of how its resources are used.[21] This budget should, in particular, emphasize the size of the administrative and promotional activities of the charity. Since many charities use a great deal of voluntary labor, such labor should also be included. It is hard to evaluate such matters as the time of a housewife soliciting contributions for the Heart Fund; voluntary labor, therefore, could be entered in hours rather than dollar amounts. The additional printing costs for the charity would be as insignificant as the cost of printing details on the label of a can of soup, and granting the difference in information conditions, far more likely to affect the "consumer's" decision.

The detailed budget, however, could easily be very misleading if simply left to the public relations counsel of the charity. Here we need something like the Securities and Exchange Commission to set standards. It would seem

18. See Donald C. Rowat, "How Much Administrative Secrecy?" *Canadian Journal of Economics and Political Science* (November, 1965). A bill providing much the same set of institutions has died in committee in three successive sessions of the U.S. Congress.

19. "Local antipoverty agencies across the nation were ordered today to open all their books for public inspection upon demand. The directive covers all financial records, applications for federal money, minutes of public meetings and details of contracts signed," *New York Times*, March 24, 1966, p. 1. Note that the director of the antipoverty campaign required such publicity only for *local* agencies and did not offer to open up his own records. Even this modest step immediately aroused objections from Senator Javits who apparently feared that full knowledge of the activities of the antipoverty organization might retard its growth.

20. A modest fee might be charged to keep frivolous inquirers out.

21. In order to reduce temptation, the expenditures in the past year, rather than plans for the year ahead, should be listed. If the charity wished to include a prospective budget also, there would be no objection, but this would be regarded as a binding promise.

reasonable to require every charity engaging in soliciting sizeable amounts of money to file a statement modeled on the prospectus required for the issuance of securities. The governmental commission could set standards for this prospectus, developing criteria which would make it possible for the potential donor to get an accurate idea of the actual functioning of the charity from simply reading this document. The development of criteria for measuring the actual amounts of resources devoted to promotion and administration, as opposed to those directly expended upon the beneficiaries of the charity, would be both especially important and especially difficult. These criteria would also apply to the budgets printed on each piece of literature used in soliciting funds, and the commission would also require that these budgets be accurate.

Under the Securities and Exchange Act, copies of the prospectus must be given to any potential purchaser of the security. This would put too much of a burden on the charities, and is, in any case, unnecessary.[22] Making such prospectuses readily available, both by mail and on display in every office or installation of the charity, would be sufficient. All these steps would, by making information very readily available, make it somewhat more likely that potential donors would acquire knowledge about a charity in spite of the extremely weak motives to do so. The purchasers of stocks and bonds have the strongest possible motives to inform themselves about the securities before purchase. Further, a large part of these securities are purchased by highly expert investment bankers or investors. Under the circumstances, improving the availability of information would be predicted to have only a marginal effect.[23] The "purchasers" of charity, however, have weak incentives to acquire information about the objects of their self-sacrifices, and few of them are professional experts in the field.[24] Under the circumstances reducing their information cost should have considerably larger effect.

Improving information, however, is merely a palliative, and more drastic institutional changes seem called for. The main aim of this article has not been to urge one particular reform, desirable as I think it would be, but to

22. These prospectuses are in most cases thrown away unread.

23. Recent investigations seem to indicate that the effect was, in fact, either non-existent or small.

24. There are professional experts in the giving of charitable gifts, in the foundations for example, but they tend to put their money into quite different organizations than those which solicit public contributions. Perhaps this reflects their expertise.

attract attention to a generally neglected field. Clearly the charitable sector of our economy should receive much more study than it has so far. We can hope that this further research will lead to further suggestions for reform. Economists normally have made suggestions for institutions which are intended to guide "as by an invisible hand" selfish men into serving the best interests of others. In charitable activities, the basic motive is a desire to help others, and this has apparently convinced students that the institutional structure is irrelevant. The good intentions of the donors, in a sense, substitute for the careful design of the institutions. The road to hell, of course, is paved with good intentions. Fortunately our present organization of charity will not lead to disaster, but it does cause serious waste. We must add careful thought and sensible design of institutions to the existing good intentions if we want the "Third Sector" to be not only "good," but also efficient.

POLLUTERS' PROFITS AND POLITICAL RESPONSE

DIRECT CONTROLS VERSUS TAXES

James M. Buchanan and Gordon Tullock

Economists of divergent political persuasions agree on the superior efficacy of penalty taxes as instruments for controlling significant external diseconomies which involve the interaction of many parties. However, political leaders and bureaucratic administrators, charged with doing something about these problems, appear to favor direct controls. Our purpose in this paper is to present a positive theory of externality control that explains the observed frequency of direct regulation as opposed to penalty taxes or charges. In the public-choice theory of policy,[1] the interests of those who are subjected to the control instruments must be taken into account as well as the interests of those affected by the external diseconomies. As we develop this theory of policy, we shall also emphasize an elementary efficiency basis for preferring taxes and charges which heretofore has been neglected by economists.

I

Consider a competitive industry in long-run equilibrium, one that is composed of a large number of *n* identical producing firms. There are no productive inputs specific to this industry, which itself is sufficiently small relative to the economy to insure that the long-run supply curve is horizontal. Expansions and contractions in demand for the product invoke changes in the number of firms, each one of which returns to the same least-cost position after adjustment. Assume that, from this initial position, knowledge is

Reprinted, with permission of the American Economic Association, from *American Economic Review* 65 (March 1975): 139–47.

We wish to thank the National Science Foundation for research support. Needless to say, the opinions expressed are our own.

1. Charles Goetz imposes a public-choice framework on externality control, but his analysis is limited to the determination of quantity under the penalty-tax alternative. C. J. Goetz, "Political Equilibrium vs. Economic Efficiency in Effluent Pricing," in J. R. Conner and E. Loehman, eds., *Economic Decisionmaking for Environmental Control* (Gainesville, 1973).

discovered which indicates that the industry's product creates an undesirable environmental side effect. This external diseconomy is directly related to output, and we assume there is no technology available that will allow alternative means of producing the private good without the accompanying public bad. We further assume that the external damage function is linear with respect to industry output; the same quantity of public bad per unit of private good is generated regardless of quantity.[2] We assume that this damage can be measured and monitored with accuracy.

This setting has been deliberately idealized for the application of a penalty tax or surcharge. By assessing a tax (which can be computed with accuracy) per unit of output on all firms in the industry, the government can insure that profit-maximizing decisions lead to a new and lower industry output that is Pareto optimal. In the short run, firms will undergo losses. In the long run, firms will leave the industry and a new equilibrium will be reached when remaining firms are again making normal returns on investment. The price of the product to consumers will have gone up by the full amount of the penalty tax.

No one could dispute the efficacy of the tax in attaining the efficient solution, but we should note that in this setting, the same result would seem to be equally well insured by direct regulation. Policy makers with knowledge of individual demand functions, the production functions for firms and for the industry, and external damage functions could readily compute and specify the Pareto-efficient quantity of industry output.[3] Since all firms are identical in the extreme model considered here, the policy makers could simply assign to each firm a determinate share in the targeted industry output. This would then require that each firm reduce its own rate of output by X percent, that indicated by the difference between its initial equilibrium output and that output which is allocated under the socially efficient industry regulation.[4]

Few of the standard arguments for the penalty tax apply in this setting.

2. This assumption simplifies the means of imposing a corrective tax. For some of the complexities, see Otto Davis and Andrew Whinston, "Externalities, Welfare, and the Theory of Games," *Journal of Political Economy* 70 (June 1962): 241–62; and Stanislaw Wellisz, "On External Diseconomies and the Government-Assisted Invisible Hand," *Economica* 31 (November 1964): 345–62.

3. See Allen V. Kneese and Blair T. Bower, *Managing Water Quality: Economics, Technology, Institutions* (Baltimore: Johns Hopkins Press, 1968), p. 135.

4. No problems are created by dropping the assumption that firms are identical so long as we retain the assumption that production functions are known to the regulator.

These arguments have been concentrated on the difficulties in defining an efficient industry output in addition to measuring external damages and on the difficulty in securing data about firm and industry production and cost functions. With accurately measured damage, an appropriate tax will insure an efficient solution without requiring that this solution itself be independently computed. Or, under a target or standards approach, a total quantity may be computed, and a tax may be chosen as the device to achieve this in the absence of knowledge about the production functions of firms.[5]

In the full information model, none of these arguments is applicable. There is, however, an important economic basis for favoring the penalty tax over the direct control instrument, one that has been neglected by economists. The penalty tax remains the preferred instrument on strict efficiency grounds, but, perhaps more significantly, it will also facilitate the enforcement of results once they are computed.[6] Under the appropriately chosen penalty tax, firms attain equilibrium only at the efficient quantity of industry output. Each firm that remains in the industry after the imposition of the tax attains long-run adjustment at the lowest point on its average cost curve only after a sufficient number of firms have left the industry. At this equilibrium, there is no incentive for any firm to modify its rate of output in the short run by varying the rate of use of plant or to vary output in the long run by changing firm size. There is no incentive for resources to enter or to exit from the industry. So long as the tax is collected, there is relatively little policing required.

This orthodox price theory paradigm enables the differences between the penalty-tax instrument and direct regulation to be seen clearly. Suppose that, instead of levying the ideal penalty tax, the fully informed policy makers choose to direct all firms in the initial competitive equilibrium to reduce output to the assigned levels required to attain the targeted efficiency goal for the industry. No tax is levied. Consider Figure 1, which depicts the situation for the individual firm. The initial competitive equilibrium is attained when each firm produces an output, q_i. Under regulation it is directed to produce only

5. This is the approach taken by William Baumol, who proposes that a target level of output be selected and a tax used to insure the attainment of this target in an efficient manner. W. J. Baumol, "On Taxation and the Control of Externalities," *American Economic Review* 62 (June 1972): 307–22.

6. See George A. Hay, "Import Controls on Foreign Oil: Tariff or Quota?" *American Economic Review* 61 (September 1971): 688–91. His discussion of the comparison of import quotas and tariffs on oil raises several issues that are closely related to those treated in this paper.

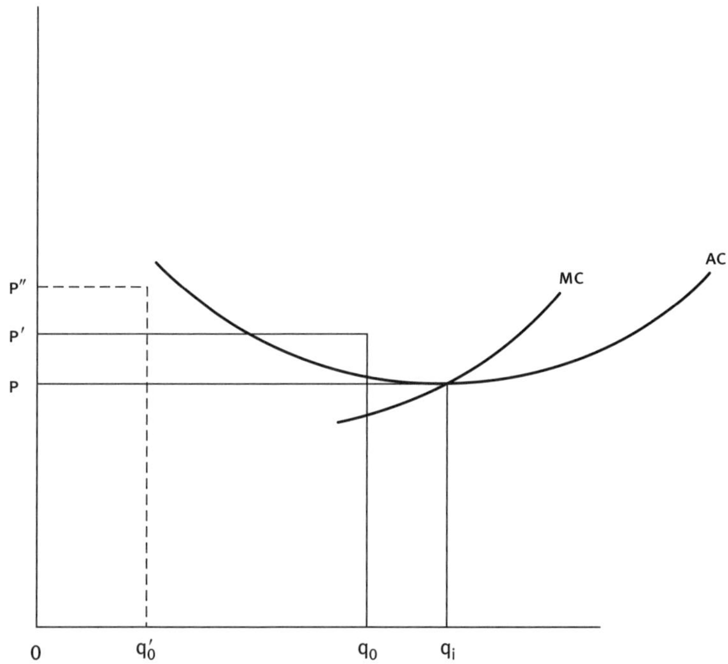

FIGURE 1

q_0, but no tax is levied. At output q_0, with an unchanged number of firms, price is above marginal cost (for example price is at P'). Therefore, the firm is not in short-run equilibrium and would if it could expand output within the confines of its existing plant. More importantly, although each firm will be producing the output quota assigned to it at a somewhat higher cost than required for efficiency reasons, there may still be an incentive for resources to enter the industry. The administrator faces a policing task that is dimensionally different from that under the tax. He must insure that individual firms do not violate the quotas assigned, and he must somehow prevent new entrants. To the extent that the administrator fails in either of these tasks, the results aimed for will not be obtained. Output quotas will be exceeded, and the targeted level of industry production overreached.

If the administrator assigns enforceable quotas to existing firms and successfully prevents entrants, the targeted industry results may be attained, but there may remain efficiency loss since the industry output will be produced at higher average cost than necessary if firms face U-shaped long-run average cost curves. Ideally, regulation may have to be accompanied by the assignment of full production quotas to a selected number of the initial firms in the industry. This policy will keep these favored firms in marginal adjustment with no incentives for in-firm adjustments that might defeat the purpose of the regulation. But even more than under general quota assignment there will be strong incentives for firms to enter the industry and to secure at least some share of the rents that the restriction of industry output generates. If the response to this pressure should be that of reassigning quota shares within the unchanging and targeted industry output so as to allow all potential entrants some share, while keeping all firms, actual and potential, on an equal quota basis, the final result may be equivalent to the familiar cartel equilibrium. No firm will be earning more than normal returns, but the industry will be characterized by too many firms, each of which produces its assigned output inefficiently.

II

When we examine the behavioral adjustments to the policy instruments in the manner sketched out above, a theory of policy emerges. Regulation is less desirable on efficiency grounds even in the presence of full information, but this instrument will be preferred by those whose behavior is to be subjected to either one or the other of the two policy instruments. Consider the position of the single firm in the fully competitive industry, depicted in Figure 1. Under the imposition of the tax, short-run losses are necessarily incurred, and the firm reattains normal returns only after a sufficient number of its competitors have shifted resources to other industries. The tax reduces the present value of the firm's potential earnings stream, whether the particular firm remains in the industry after adjustment or withdraws its investment and shifts to alternative employment. In terms of their own private interests, owners of firms in the industry along with employees will oppose the tax. By contrast, under regulation firms may well secure pecuniary gains from the imposition of direct controls that reduce total industry output. To the extent that the restriction is achieved by the assignment of production quotas to existing firms, net profits may be present even for the short term and are more likely to arise after adjustments in plant. In effect, regulation in this sense is the directional equivalent of cartel formation provided that the individual firm's assigned quota falls within the limited range over which average cost falls below price. Such a range must, of course, exist, but regulatory constraints may possibly be severe enough to shift firms into positions where short-term, and even possibly long-term, losses are present, despite increased output price. Such a result is depicted by a restriction to q'_0 in Figure 1, with price at P''.

Despite the motivation which each firm has to violate assigned quotas under regulation, it remains in the interest of firms to seek regulatory policy that will enforce the quotas. If existing firms foresee the difficulty of restricting entry, and if they predict that governmental policy makers will be required to accommodate all entrants, the incentive to support restriction by regulation remains even if its force is somewhat lower. In final cartel equilibrium, all the firms will be making no more than normal returns. But during the adjustment to this equilibrium, above-normal returns may well be available to all firms that hold production quotas. Even if severe restriction forces short-term losses on firms, these losses will be less than those under the tax. Rents over this period may well be positive, and even if negative, they will be less negative than those suffered under the tax alternative. Therefore, producing firms will always oppose any imposition of a penalty tax. However, they may well favor direct regulation restricting industry output, even if no consideration at all is given to the imposition of a tax. And, when faced with an either/or choice, they will always prefer regulation to the tax.

III

There is a difference between the two idealized solutions that has not yet been discussed, and when this is recognized, the basis of a positive hypothesis about policy choice may appear to vanish. Allocationally, direct regulation can produce results equivalent to the penalty tax, providing that we neglect enforcement cost differentials. *Distributionally*, however, the results differ. The imposition of tax means that government collects revenues (save in the case where tax rates are prohibitive) and these must be spent. Those who anticipate benefits from the utilization of tax revenues, whether from the provision of publicly supplied goods or from the reduction in other tax levies, should prefer the tax alternative, and they should make this preference known in the political process. To the extent that the beneficiaries include all or substantially all members of the community, the penalty tax should carry the day. Politicians, in responding to citizenry pressures, should heed the larger number of beneficiaries and not the disgruntled members of one particular industry. This political choice setting is, however, the familiar one in which a small, concentrated, identifiable, and intensely interested pressure group may exert more influence on political choice making than the much larger majority of persons, each of whom might expect to secure benefits in the second order of smalls.

There is an additional reason for predicting this result with respect to an innovatory policy of externality control. The penalty tax amounts to a legislated change in property rights, and as such it will be viewed as confiscatory by owners and employees in the affected industry. Legislative bodies, even if they operate formally on majoritarian principles, may be reluctant to impose what seems to be punitive taxation. When, therefore, the regulation alternative to the penalty tax is known to exist, and when representatives of the affected industry are observed strongly to prefer this alternative, the temptation placed on the legislator to choose the direct control policy may be overwhelming, even if he is an economic theorist and a good one. Widely accepted ethical norms may support this stance; imposed destruction of property values may suggest the justice of compensation.[7]

If policy alternatives should be conceived in a genuine Wicksellian framework, the political economist might still expect that the superior penalty tax should command support. If the economist ties his recommendation for the penalty tax to an accompanying return of tax revenues to those in the industry who suffer potential capital losses, he might be more successful than he has been in proposing unilateral or one-sided application of policy norms. If revenues are used to subsidize those in the industry subjected to capital losses from the tax, and if these subsidies are unrelated to rates of output, a two-sided tax subsidy arrangement can remove the industry source of opposition while still insuring efficient results. In this respect, however, economists themselves have failed to pass muster. Relatively few modern economists who have engaged in policy advocacy have been willing to accept the Wicksellian methodological framework which does, of course, require that some putative legitimacy be assigned to rights existent in the status quo.[8]

7. For a comprehensive discussion of just compensation, see Frank I. Michelman, "Property, Utility, and Fairness: Comments on the Ethical Foundations of 'Just Compensation' Law," *Harvard Law Review* 80 (April 1967): 1165–1257.

8. For a specific discussion of the Wicksellian approach, see J. M. Buchanan, "Positive Economics, Welfare Economics, and Political Economy," *Journal of Law and Economics* 2 (October 1959): 124–38.

IV

To this point we have developed a theory of policy for product-generated external diseconomies, the setting which potentially counterposes the interest of members of a single producing industry against substantially all persons in the community. External diseconomies may, however, arise in consumption rather than in production, and these may be general. For purposes of analysis, we may assume that all persons find themselves in a situation of reciprocal external diseconomies. Traffic congestion may be a familiar case in point.

The question is one of determining whether or not persons in this sort of interaction, acting through the political processes of the community, will impose on *themselves* either a penalty tax or direct regulation. We retain the full information assumption introduced in the production externality model. For simplicity here, consider a two-person model in which each person consumes the same quantity of good or carries out the same quantity of activity in the precontrol equilibrium, but in which demand elasticities differ. Figure 2 depicts the initial equilibrium at E with each person consuming quantity Q. The existence of the reciprocal external diseconomy is discovered. The community may impose an accurately measured penalty tax in the amount T, in which case A will reduce consumption to Q_a and B will reduce consumption to Q_b. Total consumption is reduced from $2Q$ to $(Q_a + Q_b)$, but both A and B remain in equilibrium. At the new price P', which includes tax, neither person desires to consume more or less than the indicated quantities. The government collects tax revenues in the amount $[2(PP'JH) + HJLK]$. Alternatively, the community may simply assign a restricted quantity quota to each person. If the government possesses full information about demand functions it can reduce A's quota to Q_a, and B's quota to Q_b, securing results that are allocatively identical to those secured by the tax. However, under the quota, both A and B will find themselves out of equilibrium; both will, if allowed quantity adjustment, prefer to expand their rate of consumption.

It will be useful to examine the ideal tax against the quota scheme outlined above, which we may call the idealized quota scheme. If individuals expect no returns at all from tax revenues in the form of cash subsidies, public goods benefits, or reductions in other taxes, both A and B will clearly prefer the direct regulation. The loss in consumers' surplus under this alternative is small relative to that which would be lost under the penalty tax. Each person will-

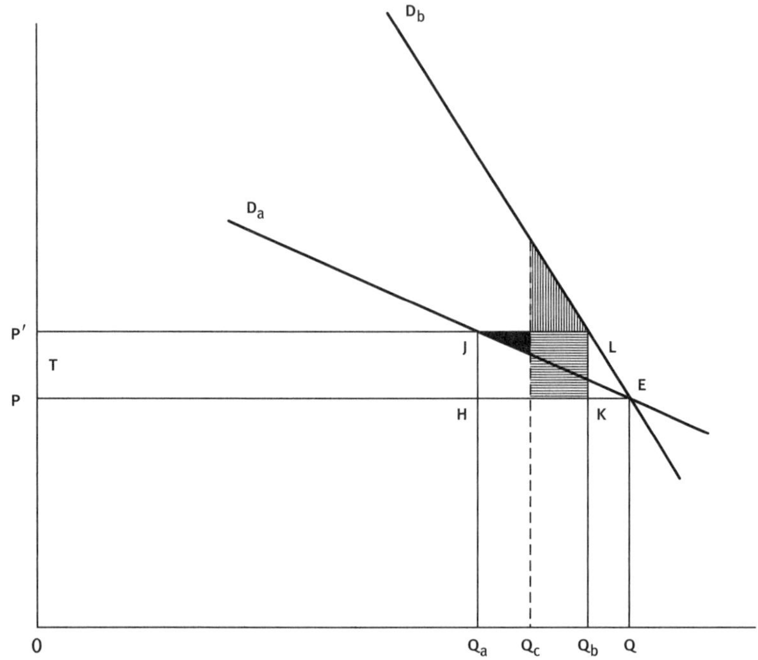

FIGURE 2

ingly trades off marginal quantity adjustment for the more favorable inframarginal terms offered under direct regulation, given our assumptions that both instruments achieve the same overall externality control objective.

Under extreme fiscal illusion, individuals may ignore benefits from tax revenues, but consistent methodological precept requires that we allow persons to recognize the benefit side of the fiscal account, at least to some degree. Let us allow all revenues under the penalty tax to be returned in equal shares to all taxpayers. Under this arrangement, each person expects to get back one-half of the amount measured as indicated above for Figure 2. Simplifying, each expects to get back the amount *PP′JH*, which he personally pays in, plus one-half of the amount measured by the rectangle *JHKL*, all of which is paid in by *B*. From an examination of Figure 2, it is clear that individual *A* will favor the penalty tax under these assumptions. The situation for individual *B* is different; he will prefer direct regulation. He will secure a differential gain measured by the horizontally shaded area in Figure 2, which is equal to the differential loss that individual A will suffer under this alternative. The policy result, insofar as it is influenced by the two parties, is a standoff under this idealized tax and idealized quota system comparison.

For constitutional and other reasons, control institutions operating within a democratic order could scarcely embody disproportionate quota assignments. A more plausible regulation alternative would assign quotas proportionate to initial rates of consumption, designed to reduce overall consumption to the level indicated by target criteria. The comparison of this alternative with the ideal tax arrangement is facilitated by the construction of Figure 2 where the initial rates of consumption are equal. In this new scheme, each person is assigned a quota Q_c, which he is allowed to purchase at the initial price P. We want to compare this arrangement with the ideal tax, again under the assumption that revenues are fully returned in equal per head subsidies. As in the first scheme, both persons are in disequilibrium at quantity Q_c and price P. The difference between this model and the idealized quota scheme lies in the fact that at Q_c the marginal evaluations differ as between the two persons. There are unexploited gains-from-trade, even under the determined overall quantity restriction.

It will be mutually advantageous for the two persons to exchange quotas and money, but, at this point, we assume that such exchanges do not take place, either because they are prohibited or because transactions costs are too high. Individual A will continue to favor the tax alternative but his differential gains will be smaller than under the idealized quota scheme. In the model now considered, A's differential gains under the ideal tax are measured by the blacked-in triangle in Figure 2. Individual B may or may not favor the quota, as in the earlier model. His choice as between the two alternatives, the ideal tax on the one hand and the restriction to Q_c at price P on the other, will depend on the comparative sizes of the two areas shown as horizontally and vertically shaded in Figure 2. As drawn, he will tend to favor the quota scheme, but it is clearly possible that the triangular area could exceed the rectangular one if B's demand curve is sufficiently steep in slope. In any case, the choice alternatives for both persons are less different in the net than those represented by the ideal tax and the idealized quota.

While holding all of the remaining assumptions of the model, we now drop the assumption that no exchange of quotas takes place between A and B. To facilitate the geometrical illustration, Figure 3 essentially blows up the relevant part of Figure 2. With each party initially assigned a consumption quota of Q_c, individual A will be willing to sell units to individual B for any

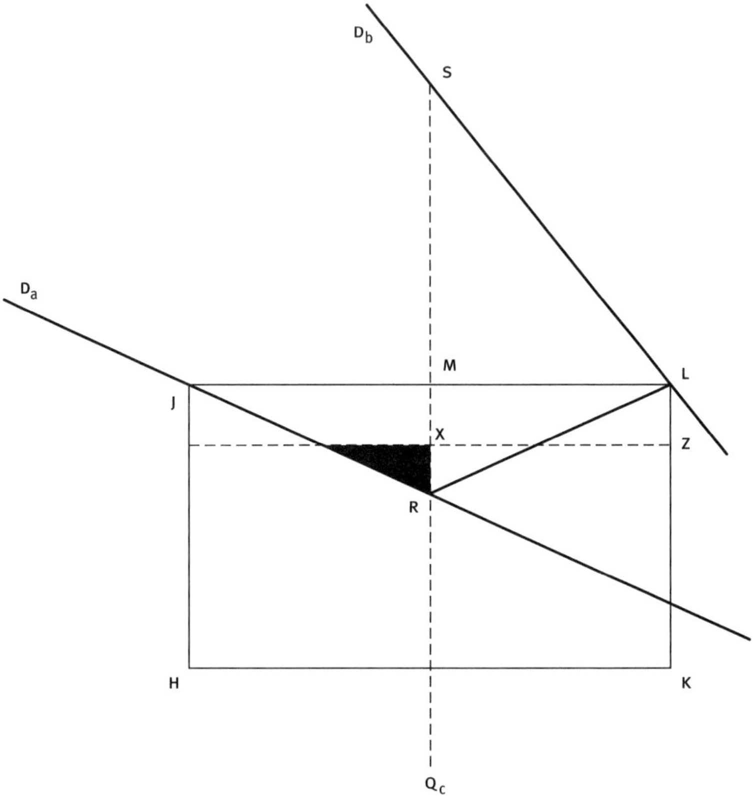

FIGURE 3

price above his marginal evaluation. Hence, the lowest possible supply price schedule that individual *B* confronts is that shown by the line *RL* in Figure 3. The maximum price that individual *B* is willing to pay for additional units of quota is his marginal evaluation, shown by *SL*. The gains-from-trade are measured by the triangular area *RLS*. The distribution of these gains will, of course, be settled in the strict two-man setting by relative bargaining skills, but let us assume that individual *B*, the buyer, wants to purchase consumption quota units from *A*, but also to do so in such a way that individual *A* will come to prefer this system over the tax. To accomplish this, he must insure that *A* gets a share of the net gains at least equal to the area *RML* on Figure 3. Individual *B*, the buyer, retains gains of *MSL* under this division of the spoils. But in this arrangement, both persons are indifferent as between the policy alternatives. The system is on the Pareto frontier, and the quota scheme plus the exchange process produces allocative and distributive results identical to those generated under the ideal tax. This becomes the analogue of the Coase theorem in the context that we are examining.[9]

V

These somewhat inconclusive results may seem to provide anything but a positive theory of policy akin to that presented with respect to production externalities. The comparisons are, however, a necessary stage in developing such a theory. Recall that we have made these comparisons under the most favorable possible assumption concerning anticipated return of revenues under the penalty tax. In the real world, individuals will not anticipate that these will be returned dollar-for-dollar, and they will tend to place at least some discount on the value of benefits that they expect.

Let us say that each person expects an aggregate benefit value of only 80 cents on the dollar from tax revenues collected under the penalty tax. Consider what this single change does to the results of the last comparison made, that which involves proportionate quota assignments along with a free market in quotas. In this case, individual *B*, the buyer, can offer individual *A*, the seller, more than the amount required to make him prefer the quota alternative, while he himself continues to secure differential benefit under this alternative. Individual *A*'s differential gains from the ideal penalty tax are reduced to the shaded area in Figure 3. By paying individual *A* the amount measured by *RML*, he has improved *A*'s position relative to the penalty tax. And, in the process, he has retained for himself a differential gain measured by the area *MXZL*. Both persons in full knowledge of the alternatives will prefer the quota system, and political leaders will presumably respond by opting for regulation.

The same reasoning can readily be extended to apply to any quota system. In the idealized quota assignment first considered, we demonstrated that one person would favor the penalty tax and the other the quota. Individual *A*, who favors the penalty tax, loses no consumer's surplus, and he does expect

9. See Ronald H. Coase, "The Problem of Social Cost," *Journal of Law and Economics* 3 (October 1960): 1–44. For a related extension of the Coase theorem, see J. M. Buchanan, "The Coase Theorem and the Theory of the State," *Natural Resources Journal* 13 (October 1973): 579–94.

to secure an income transfer through the return of tax revenues. When we modify the assumptions concerning expectations of the value of returned revenues or benefits, however, this conclusion need not hold. Individual *A* will, of course, expect to get back in benefits some part of the tax revenues paid in by *B* that is in excess of that contributed by *A* himself. If, however, individual *A* applies the same discount factor to all revenues collected, the deadweight loss may more than offset the income transfer effect. Examination of Figure 2 indicates that under the 80 percent assumption, one-fifth of the area measured by *PP′JH* will represent deadweight loss to *A* from the revenues that he pays in. This deadweight loss may well be larger than the measure of the income transfer that he expects, which amounts to 80 percent of the horizontally shaded area in Figure 2. Once we introduce any plausible discount factor into the expectation of individuals concerning the return of tax revenues, it is relatively easy to demonstrate situations under which both persons may be led by private self-interest to favor the direct regulation alternative.

VI

We have developed a positive theory of externality control policy for both the production and consumption interactions under highly abstract and simplified models which allow us to isolate influences on policy formation which have been neglected. Decisions on the alternative policy instruments in democratic governments are surely influenced by the preferences of those who are subjected to them. The public-choice approach, which concentrates attention on the individual's choice as between policy instruments, allows us to construct hypotheses that explain the prevalence of direct regulation.[10] For economists who continue to support the penalty-tax alternative, the analysis suggests that they had best become good Wicksellians and begin to search out and invent institutional arrangements that will make the penalty tax acceptable to those who are primarily affected.

10. Much of the analysis developed in this paper can be applied more or less directly to policy alternatives proposed in the energy crisis of late 1973 and early 1974. For such application, see J. M. Buchanan and Nicolaus Tideman, "Gasoline Rationing and Market Pricing: Public Choice in Political Democracy," Research Paper No. 808231-1-12 (Center for Study of Public Choice, Virginia Polytechnic Institute and State University, January 1974).

POLLUTERS' PROFITS AND POLITICAL RESPONSE

DIRECT CONTROL VERSUS TAXES: REPLY

James M. Buchanan and Gordon Tullock

Basically the three comments published above are improvements or extensions on our basic paper. We have only rather minor objections to them. The note by Robert Main and Charles Baird points out an error in our original exposition. We regret the error (which was first pointed out to us in private correspondence by Yew-Kwang Ng of Monash University, Australia) and are happy that it has no disastrous consequences for our basic argument. The other two comments, by Philip Coelho and by Gary Yohe, introduce institutional structures different from the ones which we discussed. This is no criticism; it is clearly desirable that many different institutional structures be examined. The Coelho comment considers a situation where once production quotas have been issued, they are freely purchased and sold. In a framework of analysis wholly consistent with Coelho's, the outcome derived from his process seems to represent transitional rather than a final equilibrium. With full divisibility of quotas, and with no transactions costs, smaller firms operating at their minimum average cost levels of production could purchase quotas at a higher price than oversize firms. The real problem here, however, is the degree to which such quotas are salable and the administrative restrictions put upon transfer by the government agency administering the quota scheme. We return to this question below.[1]

The Yohe note seems technically correct. However, it is not germane to

Reprinted, with permission of the American Economic Society, from *American Economic Review* 66 (December 1976): 983–84.

1. J. M. Buchanan and G. Tullock, "Polluters' Profits and Political Response: Direct Controls versus Taxes," *American Economic Review* 65 (March 1975): 139–47; R. S. Main and C. W. Baird, "Polluters' Profits and Political Response: Direct Controls versus Taxes: Comment," *American Economic Review* 66 (December 1976): 979–80; P. R. P. Coelho, "Polluters' Profits and Political Response: Direct Controls versus Taxes: Comment," *American Economic Review* 66 (December 1976): 976–78; G. W. Yohe, "Polluters' Profits and Political Response: Direct Controls versus Taxes: Comment," *American Economic Review* 66 (December 1976): 981–82.

our argument. The original producers would surely prefer quotas that are administratively assessed to the Dales-like licenses to pollute that Yohe discusses. His licenses are, in one sense, a different and highly efficient set of taxes.[2]

Both the Coelho and Yohe notes raise questions of methodology that transcend the discussion of pollution control alternatives. These questions involve the analyst's choice among models. What institutional constraints are to be imposed? What is to be allowed to vary? In a world where transactions costs are literally zero, efficiency always exists, and there is very little that the economist can offer. But we observe allocative results that seem to us to be inefficient. We try to "explain" these by applying our standard tools. Success or failure in such application depends on the plausibility of the constraints that are implicitly or explicitly introduced into the analytics. In our original paper, we sought to explain the widespread resort to quotas despite economists' preferences for taxes. We made no claim that the results observed describe a genuine "institutional equilibrium." In this, as in so much else, the ultimate choice and judgment must remain basically aesthetic.

None of the comments refers to the normative argument for quotas, an argument that was admittedly secondary in our analysis. Positively, observed quotas reflect the political power of regulatees, but this policy also has normative advantages in its own right, even if on other than efficiency criteria. The imposition of any pollution control scheme involves the taking of property from existing producers, presumably for the furtherance of the "public good." Arguments for compensation in this case seem on all fours with those involved when a person's house is destroyed for the construction of an interstate highway. We need not argue that a quota scheme is necessarily an efficient manner of making such compensations to producers. But, institutionally, it may represent a politically viable way-station between confiscation of values and a Wicksellian approach of efficient compensation. When and where possible, we should, of course, recommend the latter as a means of enhancing the efficiency of both our political and our economic process.

2. J. H. Dates, *Pollution, Property, and Prices* (Toronto, 1968).

HAWKS, DOVES, AND FREE RIDERS

Many economists are now familiar with John Maynard Smith's Hawk/Dove equilibrium. There may be some who are not, however, and since Smith's work is going to be the foundation of this paper, I will begin with a very simple outline.[1] Assume some species of birds—we'll call them pigeons from now on—in which at least part of the behavior is inherited and there are two possible behaviors. Those pigeons with "hawk" genes, when they approach food and there's another bird there, attack it, and if they're eating food and another bird approaches, they attack also.

The pigeons with "dove" genes, on the other hand, if there's another bird present, may go up and begin eating, but they will flee if the occupying bird attacks. If they are eating when another bird appears, they will continue unless the other bird shows signs of aggression, in which event they'll fly away.

It's obvious that a "hawk" in a population composed solely of "doves"[2] would have a great advantage, since it could always drive them away from the food. If there are other hawks in the population, however, this advantage is to at least some extent counterbalanced by the fact that he will get into fights with other hawks and be injured, or perhaps killed. As the percentage of hawks in a society increases, the advantage of being a hawk falls off and eventually we may reach a situation in which the danger of being injured by fight-

Reprinted, with permission of Blackwell Publishing, from *Kyklos* 45, fasc. 1 (1982): 25–36.

1. For those who are interested in more about "Evolutionary Stable Strategies," a good start is John Maynard Smith's *Evolution and the Theory of Games* (Cambridge: Cambridge University Press, 1982). Note that he goes far beyond what I am presenting. Further, there has been a great deal of additional work done in this since 1982 by both Maynard Smith himself and by a variety of other scholars. *The Theory of Sex Allocation* by Eric L. Charnov (Princeton: Princeton University Press, 1982) is a good example. All of this additional work is quite complicated and involves a lot of extensions of the initial model and a good deal of empirical testing in the biological area. Further, any economist could gain by reading a good deal of the material since the methods have human applications, too. For my purposes, however, the very simple model herein is adequate.

2. From now on I will omit the quotation marks. The reader should remember that we are talking about pigeons, but they have different genetic patterns. The process of natural selection works on these genes.

ing with another hawk is as likely a cause of evolutionary failure as malnutrition caused by being driven off by hawks.

It is not, of course, obvious that there would be a mixed equilibrium in this case, but with not unlikely parameters there is. If hawks were rare, their numbers would increase, generation by generation, until the danger of being injured in fighting another hawk equalled the danger of malnutrition for the doves.[3]

All of this is highly simplified. There might be more than two types, and individual pigeons might play mixed strategies with quite complex outcomes. These problems have been dealt with at length by the biologists, but can be skipped here.

We now turn to free riding. The doves, although they lose from the mere existence of hawks, gain from the fights between the hawks. When one hawk kills or badly injures another, he increases the life expectancy of the doves although the doves have done nothing to bring this result about. This is closely analogous to free riding among humans. A highly belligerent hawk who kills many other hawks would be conferring a significant gain on the doves without the doves investing anything. Economists would expect that when there are free riders, the resulting equilibrium is not efficient.

Efficiency in a biological system is not easily defined. Biologists normally pay little attention to what a welfare economist calls "efficiency" and when they do they use a rather crude measure, weight of biomass.[4] It is, however, clear that each time a hawk is injured or killed, the population of doves will increase.

Optimality might, however, require other controls. If the environment in which they operate is one in which the equivalent of "over-grazing" can reduce total food resources, then permitting the doves to multiply without the check of the hawks may lead to deterioration in the environment. As a result, the total number of doves could be lower than they would be even when competing with hawks.

This kind of problem has caused a good deal of trouble for the managers

3. An all-hawk equilibrium might be possible with appropriate parameters. It would not be invadable by doves. An all-dove system, on the other hand, would be easily invaded by hawks.

4. Biologists make a great deal of use of another form of efficiency. There are many articles in which some characteristics of one sort or another for a particular plant or animal are examined. The biologists assume that evolution will select an efficient design. This is testable, and many such tests are run.

of our national park system because the elimination of a predator, the wolf, together with the unwillingness to permit that most efficient of all predators, the human being, to cull the flock has led to over-grazing and various serious difficulties in the western mountains.

A more direct example of the same thing is the pigeons who are a nuisance in many of our larger cities, but could be easily disposed of by poisoning or similar methods. Environmentalists feel these "unnatural" causes should not be permitted and hence have quite literally introduced "hawks" in the form of falcons into our major cities. The falcons are flourishing and the pigeons are not. Apparently, the environmentalists feel that pigeons prefer to be killed by a falcon than by poison. The artificially introduced falcons are regarded as a natural method for some reason.

It turns out that the falcons are absolutely delighted by the artificial environment of a major city—putting nests on skyscrapers, etc. They are messy eaters, however, and litter the city with pigeon parts. An ecology in which pigeons and falcons come into some kind of equilibrium in the highly artificial environment of Manhattan is hardly a good example of a natural method. And particularly so since the falcons had to be artificially introduced.[5]

To return to our two forms of pigeons, if we assumed that maximizing the number of pigeons a city can support is a measure of efficiency, then eliminating the hawk would be a good first step. Granted that the pigeons are fed largely on human waste products, supplemented by food deliberately thrown to them by small children, etc., it is dubious that the large number of pigeons would damage the environment so there would be a need for population control. They would expand to the limits of the food supply and then malnutrition would prevent further growth.

I am not going to claim that this is in fact efficient. It obviously involves various value assumptions and few people have any value assumptions at all about how many pigeons there should be. The point is simply that the natural equilibrium in our case involves free riding. The doves would be better off without hawks, and the tendency of the hawks to kill each other benefits the doves.

Basically, my argument in this article will be that human society frequently also has an analogical equilibrium problem. Different humans follow different behavior patterns. These different behavior patterns may be an equilib-

5. The situation may not reach equilibrium since it seems almost perfect for a Lotka-Voltera cycle.

rium in the sense that there is nothing to be gained by any individual from shifting his behavior pattern. Of course, in this case the selection of behavior patterns is mainly a conscious decision rather than an evolutionary matter. Evolution is only involved in that unsuccessful businesses go under.

Even though the system is in equilibrium and everybody is making a voluntary choice about their behavior pattern, there may be free riding. In the cases below, it's easy to prove theoretical inefficiency, but it's hard to suggest any way of changing society to eliminate the inefficiency. Free riding in these situations, although technically inefficient, may nevertheless be optimal.

But let us go to examples. The first of them deals with the ordinary retail market that we observe in so many places in the United States. Many people almost never engage in any comparison shopping. They look at things, and if they seem to be worth their prices and are needed, they buy. They don't try to find out whether this is the cheapest place in the neighborhood for this particular product. This is one possible behavior pattern, and one which a good many people follow for most of their purchases.

There is another possible behavior pattern, also very widely followed. There are people who engage in very careful price comparison, looking at the thick advertising supplements that come with the Sunday paper, checking several stores, etc. The careless shoppers depend on such people to make sure that merchants do not charge widely varying prices. Clearly, they are free riding on the people who do the comparison shopping. The outcome, therefore, must be theoretically inefficient. Not enough resources are invested in comparison shopping.

Of course, the population does not break neatly into these two categories. Everyone at least occasionally compares prices in two different stores, but the amount of comparison shopping that is done varies greatly from individual to individual, from object being purchased to object being purchased,[6] and from time to time. There's probably a good deal less of it now that so many women work than there was when a large number of women were plain housewives.

But let us stick to our binary behavior pattern. In the case of pigeons, there are also many different behavior patterns but the model, counting only two, is very helpful in understanding the more complex real world.

Consider a careful shopper who does engage in comparison shopping.

6. Marshall Jevons based the solution to one of his mysteries (*Murder on the Margin*) on this point.

She acquires a single observation of a price and then goes to another store and finds out what their price is.[7] There is a 50-50 chance that the new price is lower than the first one. If she continues, there is a 1/3 chance that the third is lower than the lower of 2, etc. The more observations she makes the lower the lowest price observed.

But the improvement she gets from additional observations declines and eventually she reaches the situation where the probable improvement for one more observation is less than the cost to her making that observation, and she stops.

The fact that there are some shoppers who do make a considerable number of observations puts pressure on all of the merchants to keep their prices at least level with their competitors'. But let's not exaggerate here. Apparently, the secret of successful retailing is to charge careful shoppers less than careless shoppers and, hence, various techniques like sales or loss leaders are used to attract the careful shoppers. Careless shoppers may buy things between sales when prices are up, or at a store that is not using that particular item as a loss leader. Nevertheless, there is no doubt that the careful consumers do generate a benefit for careless consumers. If all careless shoppers could somehow be organized into making payments to the careful shoppers to be just a trifle more careful, there would be a mutual benefit.

This potential Paretian move, however, is organizationally impossible. The necessary policing would be extremely difficult and determining what is the right amount is impossible. Still, these things are at least theoretically possible.

In the real world, of course, different people engage in radically different amounts of comparison shopping and there are no simple ways to break them into two categories. It is still true, however, that those who do little or no comparison shopping free ride on those who do a lot. The people who do some comparison shopping, but not a lot, both provide a benefit to others and to some extent free ride on the people who do a lot of comparison shopping.

The situation is fully analogous to the hawk/dove situation. It is stable in the sense that no one has any motive to change it. A careless consumer changing to one who did a good deal of checking would improve the situation of the careless shoppers by providing more supervision over the prices charged

7. Or, alternatively, she flips through the different stores' advertisements in the Sunday paper.

by the merchant. At the same time, it would mean that this additional supervision should lead one of the careful shoppers to drop at least one of his observations because someone else is, in essence, taking care of the matter. Further, it involves free riding, hence in the human situation we can say that theoretically it is inefficient. On the other hand, it does seem to be the best we can do.

I feel confident that at least some of the proponents of the new economics of information will argue that the merchants, particularly those who are interested in large volume and low unit profit, will do their best to overcome these problems by advertising or other techniques. This is obviously true. As long as there are a large number of people who don't bother to look at department store or supermarket ads, they won't overcome it perfectly. Indeed, we always observe some difference in prices. The true "one price" is extremely rare in real world retail markets.

We can readily think of many other cases where this kind of situation exists. Different people may use different strategies, all of which are individually optimal, but some of which free ride on the existence of the others. This leads to underinvestment and free riding. Hence, the situation is socially inefficient in the normal technical usage of that term.

A good example of this will be found in organized markets such as the stock market. Let us consider only two basic strategies for stock purchase. One of them is to select stocks more or less at random. The other pattern, followed by banks and professional investors, is very careful investigation in an effort to predict future prices and then make a profit by anticipating them. I shall call the people who do the careful study "scholars" and the people who make deliberately random choices the "random investors." A third category, the "unwashed," will be explained below. Clearly, but unfortunately only to a limited extent, this is a description of how the market actually functions. There are lots of people who engage in random purchases and there are others who invest a good deal of time in studying the market and receive a return for that activity. It should be said that apparently the people who do best in the market are those who have special access to information.

When someone uses such private information to trade, I accept the arguments that insider trading should not be illegal. Whether it is legal or not, information will not be instantaneously known to everyone in the market, including the random purchasers.

It seems likely that the basic pressure behind the laws against insider trading comes from the one group of people who would benefit from banning it—professional brokers and investors. If no one may trade on any information until it appears in the stock ticker or the *Wall Street Journal*, those people who have the fastest access to the stock ticker and the fastest potential for purchasing or selling stock, *i.e.*, professional brokers, will have a time advantage over the rest of the market. They also have much lower transaction costs. If insiders trade first and then make the knowledge public, this time advantage for brokers, although it still exists, is of very much less value.

The average investor is going to get access to the information and take action on it after either the insider or the professionals have made their plays. The laws against insider trading say it shall be the professionals rather than the senior executives of businesses. This means that a corporation which wishes to pay its senior executives low salaries and let them make profits in the stock markets cannot do so because the profits which they would have made in the stock market will be made by a professional speculator.

But, leaving that aside, the situation here is a free riding one, just like the one we dealt with before. In fact, individual scholars who engage in careful investigation will only carry that investigation far enough so that their own investment gains will pay for the work. This means that they will not carry as far as would be optimal if the entire market were taken into account. This market will predict the future less well than it would if we could somehow make this kind of investigation more widespread. Of course, imposing the duty of investigation on individuals is not a good way of making it more widespread.

But here we have a real problem. Professional investors who sell their information to the public, whether by way of mutual funds or by selling advisory newsletters, don't seem to do any better than random investors. The old AT&T, before divestiture, had local boards scattered all over the country composed of prominent local businessmen, primarily as a public relations activity. They had to have something for them to do, however, and hence they had them manage AT&T's quite considerable financial portfolio. While these were undeniably highly qualified people, a statistical investigation indicated that the random purchase and sale would get as good results and would certainly be cheaper.[8]

Part of this problem can be explained by the selection process for the speculators. Assume a group of young men come down from Harvard Business School to Wall Street and all of them immediately begin giving advice on in-

8. Personal conversation with Dr. Edward Zajac, a former executive.

vestments, either to the public or to their immediate employers, and investing on their own account. After a while, some of them stop providing advice and simply live on their own speculative talents. These are the ones who have done well. The ones who have done badly on their own portfolio continue selling advice.

This would explain why advice is not terribly good, but not why people buy it. There are two sets of potential purchasers, the first of which is the big investment houses who actually buy for their own accounts. This is a smaller business than you might think. Still, it is big from the standpoint of a professor of economics in Arizona. These large speculators probably depend, to a very large extent, on getting information very early.

It is not clear that they violate the insider trading laws, but it is clear that they would know what is going on and be able to act on it before the average trader and, hence, new information entering the market would be acted on by them first. Indeed, various demonstrations that you can't beat the market normally depend on daily data. It may be that new information on a given company is integrated into the market fully in the first half hour. Of course, it is the existence of these well-informed large scale traders which makes the market adjust to information. Somebody has to know the new information and take action based on it. This action is buying or selling quickly.

People who sell information, of which there are many, don't predict very well and the issue is why people bother to buy it. I am going to defer discussing Robert Shiller's "Noise Trader"[9] for a few paragraphs and consider some other problems.

It seems likely that many investors in the market invest, to some extent, because they get entertainment out of it. It should be pointed out that if you believe, as one of the stock market advisors who had a minor newsletter did believe, that the country is run by a small conspiracy of wealthy people and they communicate to each other by coded messages hidden in the comic strips and that you could decode the messages, then the play of your readers would closely approximate true randomness.

In Las Vegas most of the gamblers normally act as if they thought there was some type of intelligent play. This intelligent play does not, in general, involve knowing the odds and hence minimizing the rate at which you lose your money. In fact, of course, there's very little gambling at Las Vegas. As Jack Hirshleifer has pointed out, the outcome of several days of playing the

9. Robert Shiller, *Market Volatility* (Cambridge, Mass.: MIT Press, 1989).

slot machines, roulette, or whatever is really quite highly predictable. Presumably, the players in fact know this but play the game anyway.

Several of the casinos offer free schools in "How to Win at Roulette." From the fact that they advertise them, it may be they get at least some of the people to attend them. Surely, the people who attend these schools don't really think that the management is teaching them how to take money away from it. Anyway, they get fun out of the activity.

It is likely that many people in the stock market behave in the same way. I shall call these investors the "unwashed." Investing money in the stock market is a good way to save money if you're in an inflationary economy. Putting so much a month, or directly investing randomly is dull. Engaging in a little calculation as to what you should buy and what you should sell is more fun, and it doesn't cost very much. Granted the lack of information that most people who speculate have, it's very close to random purchase and sale, which is for an uninformed person the ideal procedure.

Presumably, they don't do quite as well as they would with random purchase and sale. But this kind of speculation has an advantage over true gambling since that has a negative social connotation whereas stock market speculation does not.

We assume that scholars, who actually study the world carefully and make decisions as to what is going to happen next, have a better than random choice of being right. But normally they do not have access to infinite funds. Further, some of the scholars reach their decisions before others. It is likely that the market will begin moving up or moving down as the result of these studies gradually coming on line.

But if this is so, it is not irrational for our unwashed speculators to take movements in the stock market as information as to what is going to happen next. If they observe a rise it may be a random fluctuation, it may be an instantaneous adjustment to new information, or it may be a gradual adjustment to improving conditions in some particular industry which have been observed through careful study by scholars. Buying when the prices are rising, which makes them rise further, is thus not irrational.

It should be kept in mind here that every time someone buys a share of stock somebody else sells, thus there must be a difference of opinion. Unwashed behavior would tend to exaggerate the effect of the initial investments of the scholars. Further, some of these rather careless unwashed speculators may not notice the original rise but may notice the later rise which comes from some of the unwashed having noticed the first ones. As a result, the market would regularly overreact, which is what Shiller's studies [10] show that it does.

If the unwashed behave in this way then small fluctuations in the market price are apt to grow into large fluctuations. This is a result of the immense degree to which the unwashed outnumber the scholars. It is likely that once the price begins going up and the scholars decide it's now too high, the mass of unwashed, who have just today heard that the price of U.S. Steel began going up two weeks ago, will more than counterbalance the rather limited financial resources of the scholars. This is, of course, simply a somewhat different approach to Shiller's "Noise Traders" phenomenon.

Unfortunately, it gets even more complicated. One of the ways in which a scholar could make money in the stock market, and, indeed, probably the one which provides the highest return on the lowest investment, is to become not an expert on the fundamentals with respect to stocks but an expert on the current rumors wandering around in the stock market.

To somewhat bowdlerize Lord Keynes, the rumors that have just popped up are going to be heard, if they're going to be heard at all, by the bulk of the stockholders after they are heard by the specialist. Professionals develop skill in guessing which of these particular fads will catch on, how fast and how long they will last, etc. This is, of course, Keynes' contest in which the problem is not to select the most beautiful girl but the girl who will be thought most beautiful by other people.

Keynes, of course, pointed out that there are further stages in this process. Granted the large number of ill-informed people, large scale movements in prices which have no foundation in the fundamentals are to be expected. Shiller has demonstrated that they do in fact exist.

But note that there is nothing which we can criticize if we consider only individual traders. The trader who chooses not to become well-informed is undoubtedly making a good decision as to how his or her time should be invested. He could engage in random investment because he thinks the return from careful study would be less than the cost of the time. The scholars also are making rational decisions, and we have another example of the kind of hawk/dove equilibrium which we saw in the retail market.

In this case, however, it is a little ironic that if the unwashed did no studying at all the market would work better. If there was a clear-cut division between the scholars who studied the market fundamentals and the random in-

10. Ibid.

vestors, the price would stay fairly close to the price predicted by the scholars. There would be no motive for anyone to become an expert in guessing what the unwashed are going to do. In this case, a little knowledge, if not dangerous, is at least inconvenient.

Nor can we criticize the unwashed for following a tactic which gives them at least a little entertainment and doesn't cost them very much. It would be nice if they stopped from the standpoint of efficient functioning of the security market, but the average investor would be irrational to abandon the small amount of entertainment he gets out of his present investment tactics in order to make his tiny contribution to a more efficient market for society as a whole.

Once again, we have here a hawk/dove equilibrium. The scholars are not motivated to put enough resources into research to reduce the amount of random variance to the socially optimal amount. Note here that the limitation is the limitation on their funds, as well as the amount of time they put in. They put in less time than they would if they had more funds.[11] But even if there was no limit on the funds they can invest, they would not take the convenience of other investors into account.

Again, we find a situation in which the market reaches an equilibrium in which each person is doing as well as he can, but in which some of them are clearly free riding on the work of others. Once again, I can think of no change which would improve this situation. The market is full of such free riding.

Unfortunately, the principal alternative method, hierarchical structure,[12] has the same phenomenon in somewhat different form. Lower ranking officials if they are sensible will devote less attention to working out good solutions for the future than determining what their superiors want.

Niskanen was fired as Director of Economics at Ford Motor Company because he refused to endorse a restriction on the import of Japanese cars as being good for the United States as a whole. As a matter of fact, he didn't even think it was good for Ford Motor Company. The man who fired him, Caldwell, was one of the more successful presidents of a large automobile com-

11. I cannot leave this subject without pointing out that making insider trading freely possible improves the quality of the market for the unwashed by getting faster adjustment and making it possible for corporations to pay their higher executives less.

12. There is quite a large collection of books on the subject, but my own *The Politics of Bureaucracy* (Washington, D.C.: Public Affairs Press, 1962, and American Academic University Press) will do, as a first source.

pany in modern history. In their final conversation he said, "Bill, I've noticed that the people who rise in Ford Motor Company wait for their superiors to make a decision and then say something constructive." This is an almost perfect description of free riding in a hierarchical structure.

Free riding is endemic in our society. We should, of course, do our best to reduce it and there are many cases where it is possible to reduce or eliminate it. Moderation of our ambitions along these lines is, however, necessary. Whenever we see an example of free riding we should consider what could be done to eliminate it, but we should not be terribly surprised if the answer is "nothing."

PART 9

LAW AND ECONOMICS

AN ECONOMIC APPROACH TO CRIME

Among the various approaches to the study of crime, the economic perspective has been one of the least developed and utilized.[1] The purposes of this article are to demonstrate the utility of the economic perspective and to present some simple computational tools in two areas of the law with which the reader is likely to have fairly extensive personal experience—motor vehicle code violations and tax evasion. In the case of the former, we are not only fully experienced, but we also have a very good and clear idea in our own minds of the consequences of the violation. While our knowledge and experience in regard to tax evasion are rather less than those concerning violations of the traffic code, most of us have at least contemplated padding our expenses on the income tax form, and we find very little difficulty in understanding why other people actually do it fairly regularly.

In addition to reader knowledge based on experience, there is a further advantage to discussing motor vehicle offenses and tax evasion. The customary element in such laws is extremely small. Most of our laws on crime came down from great antiquity and hence contain all sorts of quaint nooks and corners. The motor vehicle law is almost entirely a creation of the 20th century and is periodically changed quite drastically. Similarly, the income tax code is largely a recent development, and in this case is being continuously changed by both legislative enactment and the actions of various administrative bodies. Thus, we do not have to deal with the weight of immemorial tradition when we turn to these problems.

Reprinted, with permission of Blackwell Publishing, from *Social Science Quarterly* 50 (June 1969): 59–71.

This article is part of a larger project in which efforts are made to apply economic reasoning to many aspects of law including more serious crimes than are discussed herein.

1. The approach is new only in terms of the 20th century. Bentham, Mill, and a number of other 19th-century scholars took a rather similar approach to crime. Unfortunately, the modern apparatus of welfare economics or cost-benefit analysis was not available to the 19th-century scholars and hence they were not able to make as strong a case for their position as can now be made. For a recent example of much the same approach see Gary Becker, "Crime and Punishment: An Economic Approach," *Journal of Political Economy*, 74 (March-April, 1968), pp. 169–217.

Illegal Parking

To begin, let us consider the most common and simplest of all violations of the law, illegal parking. This is a new problem. In the days of yore, there were not enough idle vehicles to require special parking laws; when, however, common men began to buy automobiles, the number of vehicles was such that simply permitting people to park where they wished along the side of the street led to very serious congestion. The number of spaces was limited, and rationing on a first come, first served basis seems to have been felt to be unsatisfactory.[2] In any event, the proper governmental bodies decided that there should be a "fairer" distribution of parking space, and it was decided that individuals should vacate spaces at some specified time, frequently an hour, after they occupied them.

The question then arose as to how to assure compliance. The method chosen was to fine noncompliance. The police were instructed to "ticket" cars which parked beyond the time limit, and the owners of the ticketed cars were then fined a small sum, say ten dollars. Thus, the individual could choose between removing his car within the prescribed period or leaving it and running some chance of being forced to pay ten dollars. Obviously, the size of the fine and the likelihood that any given car owner would be caught would largely determine how much overparking was done. The individual would, in effect, be confronted with a "price list" to overpark, and would normally do so only if the inconvenience of moving his car was greater than the properly discounted cost of the fine.[3]

Not all overparking is the result of a deliberate decision, however. Clearly a good deal of it comes from absentmindedness, and part is the result of factors not very thoroughly under control of the car owner. Nevertheless, we do not in general feel that the fine should be remitted. The absence of a criminal intent, or indeed of any intent at all, is not regarded as an excuse. When I was working in the Department of State in Washington, I served under a man who got several parking tickets a week. I think that I knew him well enough to be sure that all of these violations occurred without any conscious intent

2. We are now discussing the early development of parking regulations. The relatively recent invention of the parking meter has changed the situation drastically and will be discussed later.

3. I am indebted to Professor Alexandre Kafka for the "price list" analogy. He insists, following his own professor, that the entire criminal code is simply a price list of various acts.

on his part. He would get involved in some project and forget that he was supposed to move his car. The District of Columbia was levying what amounted to a tax on him for being absentminded.

As far as I could tell, the police force of Washington, D.C., was not particularly annoyed with my superior. Apparently, they thought the revenue derived paid for the inconvenience of issuing tickets and occasionally towing his car away. Suppose, however, they had wanted to make him stop violating the parking laws. It seems highly probable that a drastic increase in the fines would have been sufficient. Absentmindedness about ten dollars does not necessarily imply absentmindedness about 100 or even 1,000 dollars. With higher fines he would have felt more pressure to train himself to remember, to avoid parking on the public streets as much as possible, and to arrange for his secretary to remind him. Thus, the fact that he was not engaging in any calculations at all when he committed these "crimes" does not indicate that he would not respond to higher penalties by ceasing to commit them.

So far, however, we have simply assumed that the objective is to enforce a particular law against parking. The question of whether this law is sensible, or how much effort should be put into enforcing it, has not been discussed. In order to deal with this problem, let us turn to a more modern technology and discuss a metered parking area. In such areas the government in essence is simply renting out space to people who want to use it. It may not be using a market-clearing price because it may have some objectives other than simply providing the service at a profit, but this does not seriously alter the problem. For simplicity, let us assume that it is charging market-clearing prices. It would then attempt to maximize total revenue, including the revenue from fines and the revenue from the coins inserted in the parking meters minus the cost of the enforcement system. We need not here produce an equation or attempt to solve this problem, but clearly it is a perfectly ordinary problem in operations research, and there is no reason why we should anticipate any great difficulty with it.

Other Motor Vehicle Laws

However, parking is clearly a very minor problem; in fact, it was chosen for discussion simply because it is so easy. In essence, there is very little here except calculation of exactly the same sort that is undertaken every day by businessmen. For a slightly more complicated problem, let us consider another traffic offense—speeding. Presumably, the number of deaths from auto accidents, the extent of personal injuries, and the material damage are all functions of the speed at which cars travel.[4] By enforcing a legal maximum on such speed, we can reduce all of them. On the other hand, a legal maximum speed will surely inconvenience at least some people, and may inconvenience a great many. The strictly material cost of lowering speeds is easily approximated by computing the additional time spent in traveling and multiplying this by the hourly earning power of an average member of the population. This is, of course, only an approximation, leaving out of account such factors as the pleasure some people get out of speed and the diversion of economic activity which would result from the slowing of traffic. Nevertheless, we could use this approximation[5] and the costs of deaths, injuries, and material damage from auto accidents to work out the optimal speed limit, which would be simply the limit which minimized total costs in all of these categories. The computation would be made in "social" terms because the data would be collected for the whole population. Individuals, however, could regard these figures as actuarial approximations for their personal optima.

To the best of my knowledge, no one has ever performed these calculations in a reasonably direct and precise way. Presumably the reason for the omission is an unwillingness to consciously and openly put a value on deaths and injuries which can then be compared with the strictly material costs of delay. When I point out to people that the death toll from highway accidents could be reduced by simply lowering the speed limit (and improving enforcement), they normally show great reluctance to give any consideration to the subject. They sometimes try to convince themselves that the reduction would not have the predicted effect, but more commonly they simply shift quickly to another subject. They are unwilling, for reasons of convenience, to approve a substantial lowering of the speed limit, but they do not like to consciously balance their convenience against deaths. Nevertheless, this is the real reasoning behind the speed limits. We count the costs of being forced to

4. Recently this relationship has been somewhat obscured by the publication of Ralph Nader's *Unsafe at any Speed*. It is undoubtedly true that cars can be designed to reduce fatalities in accidents and, for that matter, that highways can be designed to reduce accidents. Recent discoveries of methods of reducing skidding by improved highway surfaces probably indicate that there is more potential in highway improvement than in car redesign. Nevertheless, for a given car and highway, speed kills.

5. For those who object to approximation, more elaborate research, taking into account much more of the costs of slowing down traffic, could be undertaken.

drive slowly and the costs of accidents, and choose the speed limit which gives us the best outcome. Since we are unwilling to do this consciously, we probably do a bad job of computing. If we were willing to look at the matter in the open, consciously to put a value on human life, we could no doubt get better results.

As an example of this reluctance to think about the valuation we are willing to put upon deaths and injury in terms of our own convenience, a colleague of mine undertook a study of the methods used by the Virginia Highway Commission in deciding how to improve the roads. He found that they were under orders to consider speed, beauty, and safety in presenting projects for future work. The beauty was taken care of by simply earmarking a fixed part of the appropriations for roadside parks, etc. For speed they engaged in elaborate research on highway use and had statistical techniques for predicting the net savings in time from various possible changes. It was the possibility of improving these techniques which led them to invite my colleague to make his study. For safety, on the other hand, they had no system at all.

It was clear that they did take safety into account in designing roads, and spent quite a bit of money on various methods of reducing the likelihood of accidents. They did not, however, have any formula or rule for deciding either how much should be spent on safety or in what specific projects it should be invested. They must have had some trade-off rule which they applied. This rule, however, remained buried in their subconscious even though they used fairly elaborate and advanced techniques for other problems. This is particularly remarkable when it is remembered that, given any exchange value, the computations of the amount to be spent on safety would be fairly easy.

If, for example, it is decided that we will count one fatal accident as "worth" $500,000 in inconvenience to drivers (measured in increased travel time), then, with statistics on accidents and volume of traffic, it would be possible to work out how much should be spent on safety and how much on speed. Since the Highway Commission did not spend all of its money on safety, some such "price" for accidents must have taken some part of its reasoning, but rather sophisticated engineers were unwilling to admit, probably even to themselves, that this was so. Perhaps more surprising, my colleague fully approved of their attitude. Basically a "scientific" type, with a great interest in statistical decision theory, he felt that here was one place where careful reasoning was undesirable. He did not want to consider ratios between deaths and convenience himself, did not want the people who designed the

TABLE 1. *Effects of Speed Limits*

SPEED LIMIT (MPH)	DEATHS PER 100,000,000 MILES	COSTS OF DELAY
10	1	$50,000,000,000.00
20	2	35,000,000,000.00
30	4	22,500,000,000.00
40	8	15,500,000,000.00
50	16	5,000,000,000.00
60	32	2,000,000,000.00
70	64	500,000,000.00

highways on which he drove to consciously consider them, and did not want to discuss the subject with me.

But even if we do not like to critically examine our decision process, clearly the decision as to the speed limit is made by balancing the inconveniences of a low limit against the deaths and injuries to be expected from a high one. The fact that we are not willing to engage in conscious thought on the problem is doubly unfortunate, because it is difficult enough so that it is unlikely that we can reach optimal decisions by any but the most careful and scientific procedures. The problem is stochastic on both sides since driving at a given speed does not certainly cause an accident; it only creates a probability of an accident. Similarly, our convenience is not always best served by exceeding the speed limit, so we have only a stochastic probability of being inconvenienced. There will also be some problems of gathering data which we do not now have (mainly because we have not thought clearly about the problem) and making reasonable estimates of certain parameters. In order to solve the problem we need a table of probabilities rather like Table 1. Obviously, with this table, and one more thing, a conversion factor for deaths and delay, we could readily calculate the speed limit which would minimize the "cost" of using the road.[6]

Equally obviously, no direct calculation of this sort is now undertaken, but our speed limits are set by a sort of weighing of accident prevention against inconvenience. The only difference between our present methods and the ones I have outlined is that we are frightened of having to admit that we

6. Note that I am ignoring all consequences of accidents except deaths and that it is assumed that the speed limit is the only variable. These are, of course, simplifying assumptions introduced in order to make my table simple and the explanation easy. If any attempt were made to explicitly utilize the methods I suggest, much more complex data would be needed. The figures are, of course, assumed for illustrative purposes only.

use a conversion ratio in which lives are counted as worth only some finite amount of inconvenience, and we refuse to make the computations at a conscious level and hence are denied the use of modern statistical methods.

Having set a speed limit, we now turn to its enforcement. If, for example, the limit is 50 MPH, then it does not follow that people who drive over that speed will automatically have accidents. Nor does it follow that driving at 51 MPH is very much more likely to lead to an accident than driving at 50 MPH. The use of a simple limit law is dictated by the problems of enforcement rather than the nature of the control problem itself. If we had some way of simply charging people for the use of the streets, with the amount per mile varying with the speed,[7] this would permit a better adjustment than a simple speed limit. In practice, the police and courts do something rather like this by charging much higher fines for people who greatly exceed the speed limit. Let us, however, confine ourselves to the simple case where we have a single speed limit, with no higher fines for exceeding it by a sizable amount.

Our method of enforcing this law is in some ways most peculiar. In the first place, if a citizen sees someone violating this law and reports it, the police will refuse to do anything about it. With one specific exception, which we will footnote in a moment, you cannot be penalized for speeding unless a police officer sees you do it. Think what burglars would give for a similar police practice in their field of endeavor.

A second peculiarity is that the penalty assessed is unconnected with the attitude of mind of the person who violates the speed limit.[8] Driving at 70 MPH may get you a fine of 100 dollars or a ten-year sentence, depending upon the occurrence of events over which you have no control. Suppose, for example, two drivers each take a curve in the highway at 70. The first finds a police car on the other side, gets a ticket, and pays a fine. The second encounters a tractor driving down his side of the road and a column of cars on the other side. In the resulting crash, the tractor driver is killed, and the outcome may be a ten-year sentence for the driver of the car.[9] We can assume

7. Needless to say, the cost of driving 50 MPH in a built-up area would be higher than in the open countryside.

8. There is a partial and imperfect exception to this for certain special cases. The man who speeds to get his wife to the hospital before the birth of their child is perhaps the one who gets the most newspaper attention.

9. Note that the rule that a traffic offense is prosecuted only if seen by a police officer is not followed in the event of a serious accident. A third driver may be imagined who took the curve

both men exceeded the speed limit, for the same motives, but the second had bad luck. Normally we like to have penalties depend upon what the defendant did, not on external circumstances beyond his control. (The only other situation in which this kind of thing is done involves the rule which makes a death caused while committing a felony murder regardless of the intent.)

The peculiarity of this procedure is emphasized when it is remembered that the man who risks being sent up for ten years for killing someone in an accident almost certainly had no intent to do so. He was driving at high speed in order to get somewhere in a hurry, an act which normally leads to a moderate fine when detected. The heavy sentence comes not from the wickedness of his act, but from the fact that he drew an unlucky number in a lottery. The case is even clearer in those not terribly rare cases where the accident arises not from conscious violation of the law but from incompetence or emotional stress (losing one's head). In ordinary driving we frequently encounter situations where a small error in judgment can cause deaths. A man who has no intent to drive carelessly may simply be a bad judge of distance and try to pass a truck where there is insufficient room. An excitable person may "freeze" when some emergency arises, with the result that there is an accident which could easily have been prevented. Both of these cases might well lead to prison terms in spite of the complete lack of "criminal intent" on the part of the defendant. "If a driver, in fact, adopts a manner of driving which the jury thinks dangerous to other road users . . . then on the issue of guilt, it matters not whether he was deliberately reckless, careless, momentarily inattentive, or doing his incompetent best."[10]

As anybody who has studied game theory knows, a mixed strategy may pay off better than a pure strategy. It may be, therefore, that the combination of three different treatments is better than a simpler rule providing a single and fairly heavy penalty for speeding, regardless of whether you hit anyone or happen to encounter a policeman while engaged in the criminal act. But, although we must admit this possibility, it seems more likely that a single penalty based on the intent of the individual would work better in preventing speeding. The probable reason for the rather peculiar set of rules I have outlined is simply the functioning of the court system. If someone who disliked me alleged that he had seen me speeding and I denied it, the court

at the same speed and met neither the police nor the tractor. He would, of course, go off scot-free even if his offense were reported to the police.

10. Hill v Baxter, 1 *QB* (1958), p. 277.

would have to decide who was lying without much to go on except the expressions on our faces. Since "dishonesty can lie honesty out of countenance any day of the week if there is anything to be gained by it," this is clearly an uncertain guide. Thus, under our current court system, permitting people to initiate prosecutions for speeding by stating that they had seen someone doing so would almost certainly mean that innumerable spite cases would be brought before the courts, and that the courts would make many, many mistakes in dealing with them.

Similarly, the use of two sets of penalties for speeding, depending on factors not under the defendant's control, is probably the result of judicial performance. Charging a very heavy fine or relatively brief imprisonment for every speeding conviction would very likely be resisted by judges who do not really think speeding is very serious unless it kills somebody. That this is the restriction cannot strictly be proven but at least some evidence can be provided for it. In Virginia, as in many states, multiple convictions for traffic offenses can result in removal of the driving license. The state has encountered real difficulty in getting its judges to carry out this provision. Under the conditions of modern life the deprivation of a driver's license is a real hardship, and judges apparently do not like to impose it for a speeding offense simply because the offender has been convicted twice before. Similarly, if a license is suspended, the courts are unlikely to inflict a very heavy penalty on the man who drives anyhow, provided he avoids killing someone.[11]

It is probable that problems of judicial efficiency account for another peculiarity of the motor traffic code; i.e., it is almost impossible for an individual to defend himself against the accusation. Normally the police officer's testimony is accepted regardless of other evidence. Further, in general, the penalty exacted for the average minor violation of the code is small if the defendant pleads guilty, but high if he does not. Parking offenses, for example, may very commonly be settled for one or two dollars on a guilty plea, but cost ten to twenty if you choose to plead not guilty. This amounts to paying the defendant to plead guilty. As almost anyone who has had any experience

11. Possibly, given the difficulties of enforcement, a restriction of the license rather than a removal might be wise. Restricting the license of a multiple offender to a limited area, including his home, a couple of shopping centers, and his place of employment, together with a low speed limit, say 30 MPH, might appeal to judges who would be unwilling to remove the license totally. Judges might also be more inclined to give heavy sentences to people who violate such restrictions than to people who continue to drive to work in spite of the lack of a license.

with a traffic court is aware, most of the people who get tickets are indeed guilty, but those who are not guilty normally plead guilty anyway because of this system of enforcement.

Obviously we could apply the same line of reasoning to deal with all other parts of the traffic code. The problem is essentially a technological one. By the use of some type of exchange value and evidence obtained from statistical and other sources, we could compute a complete traffic code which would optimize some objective function. In practice we do not do this because of our reluctance to specify an exchange value for life. Nevertheless, we get much the same result, albeit with less accuracy and precision, by our present methods.

Tax Evasion

Turning now to the income tax law, we must begin by noting that apparently almost anybody can get special treatment. The present laws and regulations are a solid mass of special rules for special groups of people. There are innumerable cases where some particularly wealthy man or large corporation has succeeded in obtaining special tax treatment. Nevertheless, we can consider how the existing tax code should be enforced.

Unfortunately, even the enforcement is full of loopholes. In the first place, there are a great many people (special classes that readily come to mind are doctors, waitresses, and farmers) who have special facilities for evading the income tax. It is also widely believed that certain groups (the farmers in particular) have been able to make use of their political power to see to it that the Internal Revenue Service does not pay as much attention to detecting evasion by them as by other groups. Nevertheless, we can assume that the tax code contains within it both a set of special privileges for individuals and instructions for evasion which apply only to certain classes, and hence that the true tax law is residual after we have knocked all these holes in what was originally a rather simple piece of legislation.

There are further difficulties. The individual presumably is interested in the taxes being collected from other people because he wants the government services which will be purchased by them. He would prefer to be left free of tax himself, but this is unfortunately not possible. He, in a sense, trades the tax on his own income for the benefit which he obtains from the purchase of government services by the entire community. It is by no means clear that for everyone the present amount of government services is optimal. If I felt that the total amount of government services being purchased today was excessive (i.e., that lower tax rates and lower levels of service were desirable), presumably I would feel relatively happy about systematic evasion of a tax law on the part of everyone. On the other hand, if I felt that the present level of government services was too low and the taxes should be higher, I might conceivably feel that "overenforcement" is desirable.

Even if I am happy with the present level of government expenditures, it is by no means obvious that I should be terribly much in favor of efficient enforcement of the revenue code. I might favor a revenue code which sets rates relatively high and an enforcement procedure which permits a great deal of evasion to lower rates and better enforcement procedures which brought in the same revenue. Surely I would prefer the former if I had some reason to believe that I would be particularly able to evade the taxes. But even if I assume that everyone will have about the same ability to evade, I might still prefer the higher rates and higher level of evasion. Nevertheless, it seems to me that most people would prefer the lowest possible level of tax for a given net return. I have been unable to prove that this is optimal,[12] but it does seem to me to be reasonable that this would be the appropriate social goal. In any event, that is the assumption upon which our further calculations are built. It would be relatively easy to adjust these calculations to any other assumption on this particular matter.

Under these circumstances and on these assumptions, the return in taxation to the government from various levels of enforcement can be seen by Equation 1, which is fairly lengthy but really simple. (See Table 2 for definitions of symbols.)

$$T_R = L_C \cdot R \times I + (1 - L_C) \cdot I' \times L_D \cdot P - C_R \qquad (1)$$

The first term on the right of the equal sign is the likelihood that individuals will fully comply with tax laws, multiplied by the tax rate and income. Note that this is deliberately somewhat ambiguous. It can be taken as any individual's tax payments or the payments for the economy as a whole, depending on which definition we choose for income. We add to this the probability that an individual will attempt to evade payment of taxes on all or part of his income, times the probability of detection of his evasion, times the penalty he will be compelled to pay on the evasion. This gives us the total return

12. I sincerely hope that some of my readers may be able to repair this admission.

TABLE 2. *Definitions of Symbols*

C_P = Private cost of enforcement (includes cost of incorrect tax penalties)
C_R = Cost of revenue protection service
I = Income
I' = Some part of income
L_C = Likelihood of compliance
L_D = Likelihood of detection of evasion
N = Social return on tax (excess burden not subtracted)
P = Penal rate for detected noncompliance
R = Tax rate
T_R = Tax revenue (net of direct enforcement costs)

which the community will receive. There is, of course, the cost of maintaining the inspection and revenue collection system, which is subtracted from this output in the final term, C_R.

Ignoring, for the moment, the taxpayer's propensity toward accepting risks, the condition for a favorable decision to attempt *to evade* the tax legally payable on some particular portion of his income is

$$L_D \cdot P \cdot I' < R \cdot I' \qquad (2)$$

That is to say, if the likelihood of detection times the penalty he must pay on detection is less than the rate that he would legally pay, he would appropriately attempt to evade. It will be noted that both in this inequality and in the previous equation there is an implicit assumption that the individual will be able to pay a fine if he is found to have evaded the tax law. The reason that the individual is normally able to pay a fine is simply that in general those who get into income tax difficulties are well off.

Nevertheless, although this is a very good approximation, it is not entirely accurate. The income tax authorities do sometimes attempt to put people in prison for tax evasion. In general, the Internal Revenue Service has a dual system. If you make a "tax saving" which is relatively easy for them to detect, they will normally adjust your return and charge you a relatively modest interest payment. If, on the other hand, you do something which is quite hard to detect, which normally means a directly dishonest statement, they assess a much heavier penalty. From their standpoint no doubt this is sensible as a way of minimizing enforcement costs.

There is another peculiarity of the income tax policing process. Usually the policeman himself (i.e., the Internal Revenue man) simply assesses a deficiency on the face of the form if he does not suspect what is technically called evasion. This is usually the complete legal proceeding. In small cases the individual normally pays, although he may complain to the person making the assessment. It is highly probable that in this matter, as in other small claims litigation, there is a great deal of inaccuracy on both sides. Since these are small matters, the use of a cheap but relatively inaccurate procedure is optimal. For major matters, however, very elaborate legal proceedings may be undertaken. These proceed at first through the administrative channels of the Internal Revenue Service and turn to the regular courts only if all administrative methods are exhausted. Here one would anticipate a great deal more care and far fewer errors, and there is no doubt that this is the case.

Returning, however, to our basic equations, it will be noted that the likelihood of quiet compliance (i.e., the likelihood of the income-tax payer's making no effort to evade) is a function of the likelihood of detection of evasion as shown in Equation 3:

$$L_C = g(L_D) \tag{3}$$

The likelihood of detection of evasion in turn is a function of two things, as shown in Equation 4:

$$L_D = h_1(C_R) + h_2(C_P) \tag{4}$$

One of these, of course, is simply the amount of resources that we put into the revenue service. The second, however, is the resources that we force the private taxpayer to put into keeping records and filing returns and doing other things which make it easier to enforce the tax revenue code. Thus, Equation 1 was incomplete. Equation 5 shows the net social benefit or loss from the tax, including the factor C:

$$N = L_C \cdot R \cdot I + (1 - L_C) \cdot I' \cdot L_D \cdot P - C_R - C_P \tag{5}$$

It will be noted that I have, for these computations, ignored problems of excess burden.

The term C_P is interesting and very comprehensive. It not only includes the troubles involved in filling out the income tax forms, which we all know may be considerable, but also the necessity of keeping our accounts in such form that the Internal Revenue Service may survey them. It includes the possibility that we will be audited even if we have not violated the law. It does not include any penalty which we might incur if we have violated the law, because that is included under P. It includes a number of other things which are somewhat less obvious, however. It includes the inconvenience we might suffer occasionally when the Internal Revenue Service is investigating a potential violation of the internal revenue code by someone other than ourselves; we might, for some reason, have some evidence which the Internal Revenue Service wants and be compelled to furnish it. It also includes the possibility that the Internal Revenue Service will wrongly suspect us and will then assess an incorrect fine upon us. Lastly, of course, it includes legal expenses involved in all of the above. Thus, it is by no means a small figure.

Still, the problem is relatively easy. We should simply maximize N.[13] Examination of this equation indicates some superficially not terribly probable consequences. We could, for example, be in favor of increasing enforcement even though we know it is likely to raise our own payments. It will be noted that there is nowhere in the equation the assumption that we will obey the law and others will not. If we really believe that the government money is being spent for something worthwhile, then we make a net gain of some nature from increasing N. It is true that the N in our equation represents this net gain very crudely, since it takes a total figure rather than a marginal figure, but we need not worry about this.

As noted above, we might feel it desirable to include some kind of risk aversion factor. If the penalty for evasion of the tax code is quite large, let us say 25 times the tax that is evaded, and if we feel that there is a fair probability of the Internal Revenue Service going wrong in assessing such penalties, then our term C_P could be large. This might still maximize the value of N, but if we are risk avoiders, we might prefer a lower value of N in order to avoid the risk of being assessed such a very large penalty.

But these are refinements. Basically we could calculate an optimum tax enforcement policy from a set of equations such as those here. I think that if the reader considers his own reactions he will realize that his own attitude toward the income tax authorities is based upon something like this form of reasoning. He does, of course, hope that the income tax authorities will give him special treatment and does his best to obtain it. But insofar as this special treatment has already been taken into account, his behavior would be appropriately described by Equation 2. His behavior with respect to general social

13. J. Randolph Norsworthy has studied present-day Internal Revenue procedures on the assumption that they behave somewhat in accord with the instruction of maximizing T_R. His methods are quite different from ours, but his doctoral dissertation is well worth studying: *Tax Evasion*, University of Virginia, 1965.

policy in this period would then be described more or less by a desire to maximize N in Equation 5. There may be some people who have strong moral feelings about their own payments under the income tax, but I have never run into them. Most of my friends will talk about the desirability of the income tax, but I also find them discussing in detail what they can get away with. In fact, I suspect that moral considerations are less important in tax enforcement than any other single part of the law.

THE COSTS OF A LEGAL SYSTEM

Warren F. Schwartz and Gordon Tullock

Introduction

In the absence of a legal system, a person performing an act that increased the total social product would be obliged, in order to capture the benefits created by the act, to detect and ward off the efforts of others to appropriate those benefits. Such an arrangement would impose heavy costs on a person contemplating a productive act both in uncertainty as to his ability to retain the benefits he had created and in the commitment of resources to detection and prevention of harmful activity by others. The legal system can reduce these costs by defining the rights of individuals in the social product, providing a means for resolving disputes about facts relevant under the prescribed definitions, and marshalling, in support of the determinations of the institutions authorized to resolve disputes, enforcement resources sufficient to overcome the efforts of private individuals to violate the law.

The efficiency of the legal system is thus a function both of the definition of rights and of the means employed to invoke governmental force in support of them. A great deal of scholarly attention has been paid recently to the efficiency of various assignments of rights. Some beginnings have also been made in assessing the efficiency of different types of legal proceedings. What has not been done, however, is to view the system as a whole.[1] Thus, discussions of the efficient distribution of rights customarily put enforcement costs aside. Similarly, appraisals of enforcement mechanisms omit any precise for-

Reprinted, with permission, from *Journal of Legal Studies* 4 (January 1975): 75–82. We wish to thank Jerry Mashaw and John Moore for valuable suggestions. They are not, of course, responsible for any errors that may remain.

1. A considerable body of work examines both procedural and substantive aspects of the legal regimes studied. See, *e.g.*, Guido Calabresi, *The Costs of Accidents* 28 (1970); Richard A. Posner, "An Economic Approach to Legal Procedure and Judicial Administration," 2 *Journal of Legal Studies* 399, 402 (1973); Gordon Tullock, *The Logic of the Law* 133 (1971). As far as we know, however, no theory has been advanced for evaluating the overall efficiency of a legal system.

mulation of how the "output" of legal proceedings contributes to the social gain realizable through the assignment of "efficient" rights.

In the present paper we will try to identify the costs of a legal system designed to enhance efficiency and develop a model for minimizing these costs. Our approach provides a means for incorporating systematically what have been traditionally regarded as "substantive" and "procedural" considerations.

Of course, in deciding whether a legal regime should be adopted, it is necessary to identify and quantify benefits as well as costs. The present paper does not, however, deal at length with the question of determining the benefits provided by a particular legal arrangement. Instead we make two weak assumptions that we believe are true with respect to most if not all legal arrangements designed to enhance efficiency. The first is that the arrangement, if adhered to, would enhance efficiency by increasing the correspondence between cost and benefit as they in fact exist and as they are brought to bear on the relevant decision makers. This notion is often referred to as "internalizing" social cost or benefit. Our second assumption is that the regime creates incentives for violations if they can be committed without cost.

These assumptions would hold for both private and public regimes. For example, someone knowing that he will want to occupy a house in six months can either wait and choose among the houses available at that time or enter into a contract to have a house constructed for him. Similarly, the residents of a particular neighborhood can either leave to the choice of the owner such matters as how far from the street houses will be set back or whether for-sale signs can be displayed, or the governmental unit having jurisdiction can promulgate rules regulating the conduct. With respect both to voluntary arrangements and to rules promulgated by governments, if they are indeed efficiency-enhancing, it must be because the increased social product realizable by taking account of the additional opportunities exceeds the costs imposed by the regime. An inevitable consequence of these arrangements, however, is that parties subject to them are obliged to act contrary to their self-interest (sanctions aside for the moment). For their efficiency enhancement depends crucially on persons acting in terms of consequences to others —consequences which by definition would not be brought to bear through private bargaining. Thus efficiency-enhancing regimes create incentives for violation and are therefore dependent for their success on the imposition of sanctions which internalize for the relevant decision makers the external costs and benefits of their actions.

On these assumptions every legal regime has three types of cost (all viewed *ex ante*). First, each party must calculate as a cost the harm that will flow from anticipated violations by other parties ("the costs of breach"). Secondly, all parties must consider the costs of enforcing the arrangement ("the costs of enforcement"). Thirdly, if the enforcement mechanism does not assure perfect accuracy, each party is subject to the risk of a sanction's being wrongfully imposed even if he does not violate the governing rules ("the costs of error").

The costs of breach and the costs of error will be incurred in either of two ways, depending upon transaction costs at the time the choice whether to breach is made. If, in view of the calculation we later explain, it is to be anticipated that a violation will occur, bargaining may lead to an additional payment by a person benefitting from performance to the person contemplating breach which induces him instead to perform. Similarly a person who would be deterred from performing an act by the possibility of having a sanction imposed can purchase a release from liability. If, however, these payments *ex post* are not desired *ex ante* they must be calculated as a cost of the arrangement. And if transaction costs, *ex post*, are too high then the costs of actual breaches or failures to engage in conduct which the parties desire to permit will have to be incurred.[2]

Parties contemplating a contract or a legislature contemplating the enactment of a statute (if acting rationally) would seek to minimize the sum of these costs for any given substantive prescription.[3] For each alternative regime under consideration[4] the costs thus minimized would be compared with the benefits in efficiency enhancement and the regime offering the greatest net benefits chosen.

The Costs of Enforcement

At the time a person chooses between compliance and violation he is affected, first, by the expected value of the applicable sanction if he does vio-

2. This analysis is, of course, based on Professor Coase's classic exposition of efficient adaptation in the face of different rules of law. See Ronald H. Coase, "The Problem of Social Cost," 3 *Journal of Law and Economics* 1 (1960).

3. If the sanction imposed is paid to the person harmed by the violation the calculation would have to include the value of recovering both on true and on false claims of violation.

4. We have also assumed that the substantive objectives of the regime are perfectly understood and expressed in the governing rules. Consequently there are no uncertainty costs and as a result no benefits in the form of reduced uncertainty generated by an enforcement proceeding.

late—that is, the magnitude of the prescribed sanction multipled by the probability of its being imposed (we shall call this "the effective sanction" and the amount fixed as a penalty "the nominal sanction")—and, secondly, by the costs to him of the proceeding in which the issue of violation is determined.[5] The probability of a sanction's being imposed if a breach occurs is a function of the costs incurred in detecting violations, providing data to the tribunal having jurisdiction, and staffing the tribunal. In minimizing the total costs of the arrangement (that is, costs other than of the inputs required for performance) the parties thus have to make two basic calculations. First they have to determine the total costs of achieving a given effective sanction. Secondly, they must ascertain the costs that result if an effective sanction deviates from the one intended.

The initial issue that must be addressed in making these calculations is the determination of the effective sanction which the parties desire to control the conduct of a person contemplating breach. Traditionally in contracts this is taken to be the value of performance to the promisee. More generally it may be said to be equal to the value of the benefits to others resulting from compliance with the rules of the governing regime. We will not here consider the determination of an appropriate effective sanction but merely assume that agreement has been reached on the effective sanction that is desired.

Since the effective sanction is the product of the nominal sanction and the probability of its imposition, it is the factors affecting either of these basic determinants that can be manipulated so as to minimize total costs. We assume that the probability of a sanction being imposed can be increased either by providing more information to the person or persons authorized to decide the dispute or by employing more skilled persons as decision makers. In determining the most efficient way to increase the probability of a sanction being imposed, it is, of course, necessary to know what impact various expenditures on information or for better judges will have. Little of a quantitative nature, however, is really known about this, and we shall merely assume a production function in which increased expenditures enhance the probability of a sanction's being imposed.

Under this general assumption a number of issues must be resolved in or-

5. In every relevant calculation the amount of enforcement costs which would have to be borne in various eventualities by the person making the calculation would have to be taken into account. Since we do not in this article address the question of how efficiently to distribute enforcement costs we will simply assume that the impact of the relative share borne by each of the parties on their calculations is not material. We also assume risk neutrality.

der to minimize the costs of efficiently producing a desired effective sanction. There are three types of enforcement costs which affect the probability of a sanction being imposed. These are interdependent but incurred pursuant to choices made at different times and under radically different constraints.

First there are what we will call the "fixed costs of enforcement." It is necessary to have in place a tribunal capable of deciding cases with the postulated degree of accuracy on certain assumptions as to the supply of information about the controversy available to the tribunal. This is a cost of all beneficiaries of all legal regimes over whose enforcement the tribunal has jurisdiction. The ability of the tribunal to reach a correct result in a particular percentage of cases affects private decision making in all situations where violations would occur if they could be committed costlessly. Thus the capacity of the tribunal is a public good of all beneficiaries of legal regimes it is empowered to enforce.

The second type of cost is that of determining whether other parties have performed in accordance with the governing rules. We shall call these "monitoring costs." These must be incurred whether or not actual litigation occurs. For if a person benefitting from performance knows that a violation has occurred, or has instituted a monitoring system that would detect violations if they did occur, the person obliged to perform, taking into account the decision which the tribunal would make if evidence of violation were presented, may voluntarily cure the violation or decide in the first instance to comply. The expenditures for monitoring and the response of the actual or potential violator are, however, influenced by the assumptions made about the cost and outcome of an enforcement proceeding.

The third type of cost is that of communicating data with respect to a claim of violation to the person or persons authorized to decide the case. We shall call these "variable enforcement costs." These costs have aspects of "jointness" with the preceding category. Information cannot be used to persuade a judge unless it has first been gathered. Thus a person incurring monitoring costs will consider the value of the information both in inducing voluntary compliance and in prevailing in litigation. The parties, however, share an interest in avoiding the costs attendant upon communicating information to the decision maker. If they can agree on the outcome of the litigation there is no reason to have it.

Deciding upon an efficient mix of these costs and devising a system which will induce efficient expenditures are obviously questions of great complexity. In the present paper we will not pursue these problems further and simply assume that they have been resolved. In other words, we postulate that each dollar is efficiently expended, be it for fixed enforcement costs, monitoring costs, or variable enforcement costs, and that the resulting increase in the probability of the nominal sanction's being imposed is known.

On this assumption the question remains—how great a probability do we wish to purchase? The initial response, in efficiency terms, is as little as possible. For since it is costly to increase the probability that a sanction will be imposed and the effective sanction can be set at the desired level simply by increasing the nominal sanction why not adopt a solution that combines a high nominal sanction with a low probability that the sanction will be imposed?[6]

The answer is that if the reduction in resources committed to enforcement which leads to a lower probability that a sanction will be imposed for an actual violation also results in a higher probability that a false claim of violation will succeed, then the costs of error are increased.[7] This effect is, moreover, increased by the high nominal sanction adopted in a solution of this kind. For the higher probability of a false claim's succeeding is applicable to the large nominal sanction necessarily employed when it is assumed that a sanction will be infrequently imposed in cases where a violation has in fact occurred.

We are not able fully to elaborate the relationship between the decreased probability that a true claim will be successfully lodged and enforced and the increased probability that a false claim will succeed that obtains as reductions in the various types of enforcement costs are introduced. We are, however, able to identify one important respect in which a reduction in resources committed to enforcement should greatly increase the likelihood that a false claim will succeed. To the extent that the reduction in expenditures takes the form of a decrease in fixed enforcement costs the result is diminished accuracy in deciding cases—holding monitoring and variable enforcement costs constant. Since this reduction in accuracy goes hand in hand with a nominal sanction greatly in excess of the desired effective sanction, the result is a greatly enhanced value for a false claim. The value of a false claim, starting theoretically at zero with perfect accuracy and increasing as accuracy declines and the nom-

6. See Gary S. Becker, "Crime and Punishment: An Economic Approach," 76 *Journal of Political Economy* 169, 180–84 (1968); William Breit and Kenneth G. Elzinga, "Antitrust Penalties and Attitudes Toward Risk: An Economic Analysis," 86 *Harvard Law Review* 693 (1973).

7. A system which readjusted the array of costs after deciding that a claim was false could in principle be created. It would, of course, add to total enforcement costs. We put this possibility aside.

inal sanction increases, is a cost which must be taken into account when the choice of a mix of nominal sanction and probability necessary to yield the desired effective sanction is made.

In sum, then, the efficient way to achieve a desired effective sanction is to select that combination of probability of imposition and nominal sanction where the marginal enforcement cost is equal to the marginal cost of error resulting from the assertion of false claims.

One further class of costs must be considered. We have been assuming that it is possible to classify cases in advance as yielding a certain probability of having a sanction imposed if a certain commitment of resources is made to enforcement. We have also been assuming that it is desirable to strive for the effective sanction and minimize the costs of achieving it. It would seem, however, that in many instances the probability generated will vary from the one desired. The parties, who will have access to many of the facts relating to the dispute, will be at least partially aware of this disparity. If this occurs the effective sanction will also diverge—unless there is some way to compensate by an *ex post* modification of the nominal sanction. Also, it may be substantially less costly to achieve an effective sanction that varies somewhat from the postulated one than to produce the exact effective sanction. If the effective sanction diverges, either deliberately or inadvertently, from the desired one, costs result. In the case of an effective sanction that is "too low," conduct that is intended to be deterred will occur. If the effective sanction is too high, conduct that is intended to be permitted will instead be deterred. As indicated above, if the costs of *ex post* bargaining are not too great the actual deviation in conduct may not occur but rather, in the case of too low a sanction, payment will be made by the obligee to induce performance by the obligor and, in the case of an effective sanction that is too high, an additional payment will be made by the obligor in order to induce the obligee to grant permission for the obligor's nonperformance. In any event since these payments represent unwanted wealth transfers they must be calculated as costs when the efficiency of the legal arrangement is being appraised *ex ante*.

Conclusion

Our analysis has a number of implications for public policy. First, the notion that the costs of enforcement can be economized upon efficiently by raising the nominal sanction to offset the attendant decrease in the probability that a sanction will be imposed is subject to serious qualification. A solution of this kind may entail high costs of error particularly if the saving is effected by a reduction in fixed enforcement costs that leads to a decrease in the accuracy of decision making.

Secondly, given the fact that the effective sanction is a product of the nominal sanction and the probability of its imposition, and that the latter of these is difficult to predict *ex ante*, efficiency might be enhanced if a method could be devised to increase or decrease either of the variables at some point after a dispute arose in order to produce the desired effective sanction. Conceivably, for example, discretion in fixing the magnitude of a sanction could be utilized as a means of achieving the desired effective sanction in view of the probability of imposition at the time of violation as the judge, after hearing the case, perceives it to have been. Enforcement expenditures might be similarly "fine tuned." For example, prosecutors and police might allocate enforcement resources among all violations of a particular statute subject to the same nominal sanction so that the same probability of imposition is achieved in all cases, for presumably the same effective sanction is intended for all of these offenses.

The third policy issue upon which our analysis has bearing is the distribution of litigation costs between the parties (putting aside the appropriate share of each of them) and the state. If indeed the capacity for correct decision making purchased with fixed enforcement costs is a public good of all people benefitting from compliance with the laws then it would be inefficient to finance these exclusively through user charges—if by user is meant parties to litigation. This notion provides justification for the present practice of not charging the litigants for the full opportunity cost of judges and physical facilities utilized in litigation.

The distinction we have drawn between fixed and variable enforcement costs has another implication. The litigants' choices in incurring variable costs, which they largely bear, that arise when a good deal is known about the dispute and that can be avoided by compromise appear to have aspects of efficiency lacking in the choice of fixed enforcement costs. It may therefore be wise, in devising a mix of fixed and variable costs, to rely heavily on the latter. Our present system in civil litigation, with its great emphasis on pretrial discovery (in which the judge plays a relatively small role) to facilitate compromise and lessen the resources utilized in actual trials, appears consonant with a rationale emphasizing variable enforcement costs.

The final implication of our analysis is how complex theoretically and empirically it is to determine the costs attendant upon the establishment of a legal regime. It does not, however, seem to us that this conclusion leads to the answer that since having laws appears to impose large but as yet unmeasurable costs we ought to have fewer of them. For, as we tried to make clear at the outset, any notion of efficiency presupposes a controlling system of property rights. Nothing we have said provides an easy answer to the question of what that system should be.

ON THE EFFICIENT ORGANIZATION OF TRIALS

Since Aristotle, economists have realized that efficient functioning of the economy requires the existence of firm property rights. This is even true of socialists, although the property they have in mind is somewhat different. The theft of state property is, after all, one of the more severe (and, apparently, also one of the commoner) offenses in Russia. The fulfillment of a contract and the enforcement of various rules which prevent people from inflicting negative externalities on each other are also part of orthodox economics. All of this assumes, usually implicitly rather than explicitly, that there is some kind of enforcement mechanism which will see to it that the rules are carried out.

This enforcement mechanism can be analyzed in two parts: first, a mechanism that decides who has broken the rule, contract, and/or trespassed on other people's property; second, the actual apparatus of force which compels the person violating the rule to stop violating it or which imposes some kind of sanction upon him if the violation has occurred in the past. This article is concerned with the first of these mechanisms, *i.e.*, the actual court process. In spite of the very general title, I will actually confine myself to a comparison of only two different procedures and will, in fact, assume a rather simplified model even of those two.[1]

Among Western countries there are two basic court methods. One, which descends from the Roman law, is used by most Continental countries; and the other, which descends from medieval precedents, is used in the Anglo-Saxon countries. There are a number of differences between these two methods, but only one will be discussed in this article. The Anglo-Saxon procedure is called the adversary system, because the proceeding is dominated by the two parties to the litigation with, in some cases, one of the parties being the state in the form of a prosecuting attorney. It descends from trial by battle in which the government official present at the trial simply refereed the contest. Under modern circumstances, the evidence and arguments are pre-

Reprinted, with permission of Blackwell Publishing, from *Kyklos* 28, fasc. 4 (1975): 745–62.

1. A more general discussion of the problem will, eventually, be presented in a book on which I am now working.

sented by the two sides and a government official, board of officials, or a group of conscripted private citizens (called jurors) decides which one has won.

The other system, used on the Continent, is usually called the inquisitorial system. In this system, the judges or judge in essence are carrying on an independent investigation of the case, and the parties play a much more minor role. It is the thesis of this article that the Roman jurists were right and the medieval feudal lords, who established the adversary system, were wrong in their choice of trial procedure. But that is simply to warn the reader. The line of reasoning used in this article will not rigorously prove this proposition.[2] Further empirical research will be necessary in order to prove that the inquisitorial system is superior to the adversary system. In this article, I shall merely establish a theoretical structure for the analysis of the two systems and present a fairly strong argument that the inquisitorial system is better.

In practice, of course, the inquisitorial system of necessity has some adversary elements, since the parties are given some role in court; and the adversary system has some inquisitorial elements, because the judge (and, in some rare cases, the jury) also engage in some direct investigation of the case. The judge, for example, may ask questions of the witnesses on occasion.

Consider the situation of a party in the adversary-type proceedings. He can invest various amounts of resources in hiring lawyers, investigating the facts, testifying himself—either truthfully or falsely, *etc*. Since he knows a good deal about the facts of the case and can make an estimate of the resources the other party will invest in his case, he should have an idea of the likely probability of success for various investments of resources. On Figure 1, line P_1 shows for one party, Mr. Right, the probability of success for various resource commitments in a particular litigation.

We assume, as we shall throughout this article, that there are two parties, Mr. Right and Mr. Wrong, and that, as their names suggest, Mr. Right in fact is the one who (if we had divine justice) would win. Line P_1 then shows the probability of success that he can purchase by each investment of resources in his case. The investment exhibits declining marginal productivity, as we would anticipate. *R*'s tastes are depicted by a set of indifference curves and his bliss point is in the upper left-hand corner, with a certainty of success and a zero resource investment. He chooses the resource commitment where his highest possible indifference curve is tangent to the production function line,

2. See, Gordon Tullock, *The Logic of the Law*, New York, Basic Books, Inc., 1971, for a "commonsense" argument for the European system as opposed to the Anglo-Saxon system.

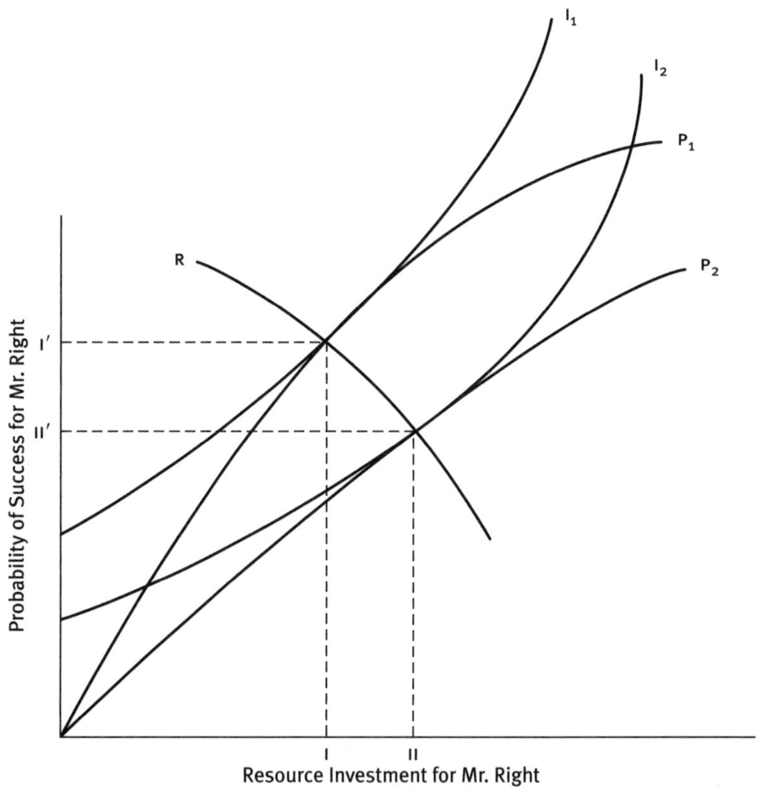

FIGURE 1

with the result that he invests *I* resources and obtains a probability of success of *I*′, as shown on the diagram.

The evidence available for the case is more or less unchanging, but the resources the other party may put in are subject to adjustment. Suppose that Mr. Right, instead of assuming that Mr. Wrong would put in the number of resources which generated curve P_1, thought Mr. Wrong would put in more resources, and hence that there was a lower probability of success with each investment by Mr. Right. This would produce curve P_2. Mr. Right is forced to be satisfied with the lower indifference curve I_2. Under these circumstances, he would invest *II* resources and obtain *II*′ possibility of success.

Note that, although in this case an increase in resources invested by Mr. Wrong leads Mr. Right to both increase his resources *and* reduce his likelihood of success, this is not general. In cases in which the resource commitment or evidence is very one-sided, an increase in resources by the party in the stronger position may change the situation so that the other side will reduce his resource commitments and take the corresponding increased probability of losing the suit (see Figure 3 below). It depends on the payoff to the marginal dollar of resources invested and, where it is less than $1, there is a motive for reducing instead of increasing resources.

If we consider all possible resource commitments by Mr. Wrong, each would be accompanied by a risk-production function, like P_1 or P_2, for Mr. Right, and Mr. Right would have an indifference curve tangent to it at some point. A line could be drawn connecting all such points. A segment of such a line is shown as R in *Figure 1*. It is the reaction curve of Mr. Right to possible investments of resources by Mr. Wrong. In *Figure 2*, reaction curves for both of the parties are shown. On the vertical axis are the resources invested by R and on the horizontal are those invested by W. Granting declining marginal returns and that the evidence is reasonably close to equal, the two curves will have the shape shown and will intersect as shown in the figure. The point of intersection is the equilibrium of the model, which would occur with Mr. Right investing R resources and Mr. Wrong investing W.

In Figure 3, I have shown by line P the situation in which the evidence happens to be very strong for Mr. Right, and hence that he can purchase a high probability of success with a relatively modest investment of resources. Line P_1 goes up very steeply and is, of course, tangent to a very high indifference curve with a relatively low resource investment and a high probability of success. It might be, however, that the evidence is positively misleading, and hence that Mr. Right would have a great deal of difficulty in raising his probability. Line P_2 shows these circumstances, and the indifference curve tangent to it, II_2, which is a low one, shows the best that Mr. Right could do under these circumstances. It will be observed that Mr. Right would choose to put fewer resources into his suit in the unfavorable case than in the very favorable case; but this is simply an artifact of the particular lines I have drawn. The reaction curves for the latter case are shown on Figure 4, and the equilibrium point is, of course, very near to the horizontal axis.

Looked at from the economic point of view, it is immediately obvious from Figure 2 that the outcome is not apt to be optimal. I have drawn a line from the equilibrium point to the origin and put a point O on it. Point O has the same probability of success for the two parties, but with a much lower investment of resources. Clearly, it dominates the equilibrium solution. This is

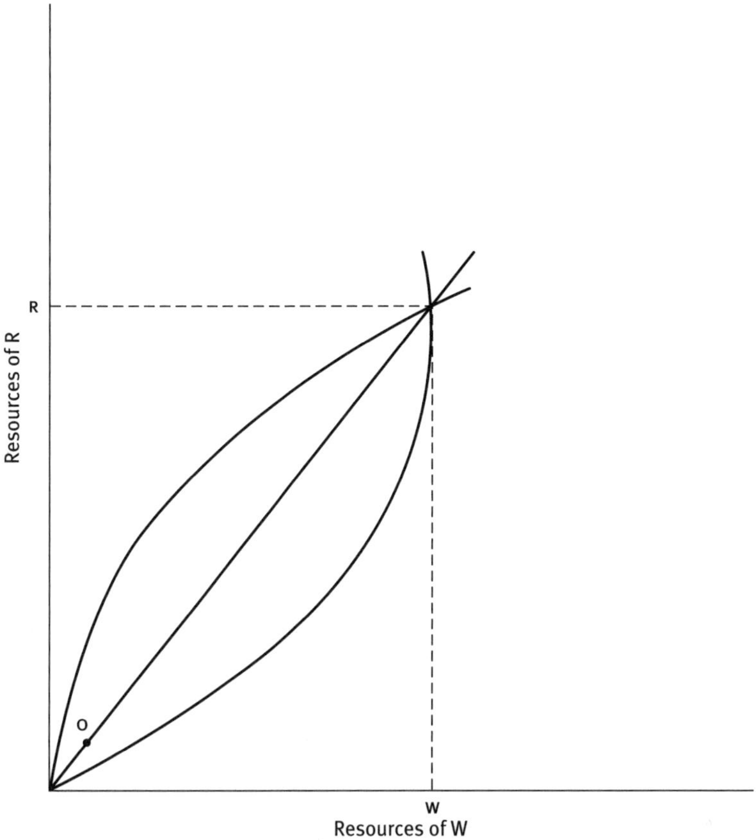

FIGURE 2

also true of point *O* on Figure 4. The only question is whether *O* is possible. As a brief digression, our diagram can also be used to deal with the international problem of arms races. The equilibrium would be the point reached in an arms race *without* agreement, and point *O* the result of an arms agreement, if there were no cheating anticipated.[3]

I should now like to introduce a game I have invented and which is helpful in analyzing court proceedings. Suppose that a sum of money is put up for a prize for a particular form of lottery. The lottery has only two con-

3. This analysis was originally developed using other techniques; but in my book, *The Social Dilemma: The Economics of War and Revolution*, Blacksburg, Va., Center for Study of Public Choice, 1974, I use diagrams almost identical to those in this article to deal with the problem.

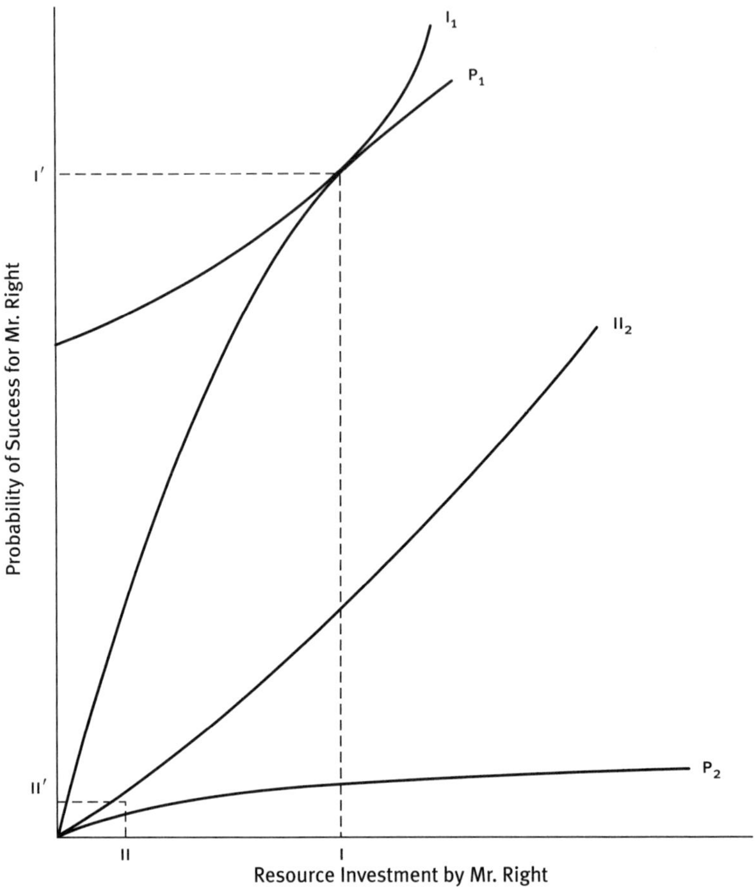

FIGURE 3

testants and each of them may buy as many tickets for the lottery as he wishes for $1 each. One ticket is drawn at random, and the owner of that ticket receives the prize. Note that the payments for the tickets are not added on to the prize. The payoff to this game for our two parties is shown in the set of equations (1).

$$V_R = D \cdot \frac{R}{R + W} - R$$
$$V_W = D \cdot \frac{W}{R + W} - W \tag{1}$$

The *ex ante* value for Mr. Right, for example, is the prize (D) times the probability that the ticket purchased by Mr. Right will be drawn [$R/(R+W)$], minus the amount of money put in by Mr. Right (R). Mr. Wrong's value is symmetric. It is obvious that we could solve this equation set, although in the real world we would want to add in risk aversion.

This set of equations, of course, would generate a set of lines of the same nature as those drawn on Figure 1 and a set of reaction functions similar to those shown on Figure 2. The probability of success is a function of resources, depends also on the resources put in by the other party, and exhibits declining marginal returns. The indifference curves would also be of the same shape as in our normal trial.

This game can be changed so that it maps many different types of trial institutions. For example, in England the defeated party pays the winning party's attorney fees. It is easy to alter the above equations to take that into

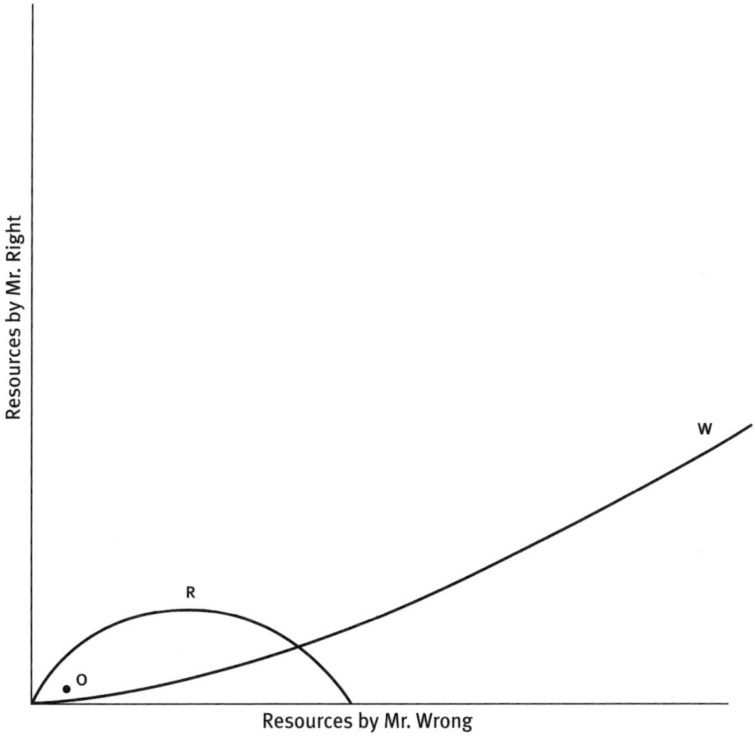

FIGURE 4

account. However, we are interested only in one particular type of alteration here. The equations as given are egalitarian, *i.e.*, they indicate that two parties, in the nature of things, have the same inherent likelihood of winning. In the real world, the physical evidence available in a case means that it is rare that two parties have exactly the same probability of winning. This can be very easily dealt with by adjusting the equation in a variety of ways.

For example, we might alter the rules of the game so that Mr. Right can purchase two lottery tickets for \$1, whereas Mr. Wrong must still pay \$1 for each one. This would increase the value for Mr. Right. Indeed, there are many complications of this sort that can easily be put into the game; but since we do not know a great deal about the real world parameters of trials, it seems that there is no great reason for us to be extremely complex in our discussion of the matter. No doubt the payoff to various conditions which may make the trial less than completely equal—such as evidence in favor of one side—is quite complex; but, for the moment, let us use a very simple function. A variant of the game, in which the number of tickets Mr. Right can buy for \$1 is R times some function of the evidence (E), is shown in equation set (2).

$$V_R = D \cdot \frac{f(E)R}{f(E)R + W} - R$$
$$V_W = D \cdot \frac{W}{f(E)R + W} - W \tag{2}$$

In order to make it easier to deal with some matters to which we will turn shortly, I should like to further simplify these equations and change them from statements as to the payoff of the game to the probability of success. This permits us to drop part of the equation, as in equation set (3).

$$P_R = \frac{f(E)R}{f(E)R + W}$$
$$P_W = \frac{W}{f(E)R + W} \tag{3}$$

Note that the reason I have attached the evidence function to R instead of to both R and W is simply that they would be different functions, and, without any knowledge of their exact shape, it seems a waste of time to make the matter more complicated than is necessary.

In this form, the equation shows in a particularly pure form the externality associated with adversary proceedings. It will be noted that in each case the investment of resources by one party generates damage to the other party of exactly the same size as the benefit to himself. We have perfect 100 percent externality here. If I increase the likelihood that I will win by 1 percent, I automatically reduce the likelihood that you will win by 1 percent. Under the circumstances, the likelihood that I will choose the resource investment which is socially optimal is, to put the matter mildly, slight.

In this connection, I have collected a little empirical information, unfortunately, by the crudest of all possible methods, *i.e.*, asking practicing lawyers. For what it may be worth, practicing attorneys with whom I have discussed the matter agree that in a law suit between two private parties, each party will normally pay in legal expenses about one-third of the amount at issue. This means, as the reader can readily observe, that if there is \$1,000 at issue, \$666 will be expended in the decision process; there are also court costs. Clearly, this is a highly expensive proceeding, although the fact that it is very expensive does not, in and of itself, prove that it is not efficient.

So far, we have discussed almost exclusively the adversary proceeding rather than the inquisitorial, and hence I have not fulfilled my promise that the two will be compared. In order to make a comparison, I would like to introduce another set of equations, set (4).

$$
\begin{aligned}
P_R &= \frac{f(E)R}{f(E)R + W} + g(E, J) \\
P_W &= \frac{W}{f(E)R + W} - g(E, J)
\end{aligned}
\tag{4}
$$

This is, of course, the same as set (3), except that another term has been added on at the right. This term shows the investment of resources in the actual judging process, something which, up to now, we have not considered. This function is assumed to improve Mr. Right's chances as the evidence (E) becomes better and as the resources invested in judging (J) are increased.

With this modification, we can now deal somewhat more generally with the problem. It is clear that increasing the skill or diligence of the decision-makers will increase the likelihood of accuracy. However, this particular change is not subject to the kind of externality we were discussing earlier. The difference can perhaps best be seen from considering a rather unusual way of investing resources in a trial. Suppose that instead of permitting the parties to decide how much they were going to invest in legal fees for their own attorneys, we let them decide how much they would like to put in to hire a judge. Each one could put in whatever he wished, and then the authorities would purchase for this trial the best judge that could be obtained for the sum of the two contributions. Of course, they would not tell the judge which of the two parties had put up the most money.

Unless we assume that in making selection of judges we are random or, perhaps, systematically perverse, surely a better judge would be hired if there were more resources available.[4] If, then, with larger amounts of money we get a decisionmaker who is better qualified and more likely to reach the *right* conclusion, it will be contrary to the interests of Mr. Wrong to have a very good judge and he would tend to put no money at all into the pot. Mr. Right, on the other hand, would want the best judge available and would be willing to make a suitable payment. Presumably the amount he would be willing to pay would be less if the case looked to him to be an easy one, and hence suitable for a rather poorly qualified judge, than if the case looked to him to be a difficult one.

The interesting feature of this little *Gedankenexperiment*, however, is not Mr. Right's investment but Mr. Wrong's. Mr. Wrong would have no motive to try to improve the quality of the judiciary, because the better the judiciary, the worse off he is going to be. Whereas he might have very strong motives to hire excellent attorneys and put a lot of money into his legal defense under the adversary system, under this system he would have no motive for investment at all.

Peter Bernholz, when this paper was given orally in Basel, suggested that a good judge in essence changes the production function of the initial parties, as shown on *Figure 1*, in the sense that he raises the production function for Mr. Right and lowers the production function for Mr. Wrong. Thus, each improvement in the quality of the judge tends to move cases in the proper direction.

The point of this article has been to compare the European-type procedure (inquisitorial) with that used in Anglo-Saxon countries (adversarial). It can be seen that the basic difference between these two is the amount of resources put on the two parts of our set of equations. The adversary proceeding puts almost all of its resources on R and W in (4); and the inquisitorial proceeding puts almost all of them on J. We have, so far, been simplifying the situation when we talk about the adversary proceedings by assuming that $g(E, J)$ is zero, and we could take the complementary simplification and assume that, in Europe, R and W are zero.

4. Needless to say, it might be wiser to hire a board of judges rather than an individual, a technical specialist rather than a legal specialist, *etc.*

In practice, of course, there is at least some resource investment in the judicial process in the adversary proceedings, and the parties do have some things they can do that will affect the outcome in inquisitorial proceedings, so it is a matter of emphasis rather than a matter of absolute exclusion of one of the two factors. Nevertheless, in general the conclusions we draw from our simplified model will not be much wrong.

The basic difference between the two, as will be seen, is the *W* which appears in all of the equations. In essence, a great deal of the resources in the adversary proceedings are put in by someone who is deliberately attempting to mislead. Assume, for example, that in the average American court case 45 percent of the total resources are invested by each side and 10 percent by the government in providing the actual decisionmaking apparatus. This would mean that 55 percent of the resources used in the court are *aimed* at achieving the correct result, and 45 percent at reaching an incorrect result. Under the inquisitorial system, assume that 90 percent of the resources are put up by the government which hires a competent board of judges (who then carry on an essentially independent investigation) and only 5 percent by each of the parties. Under these circumstances, 95 percent of the resources are contributed by people who are attempting to reach the correct conclusion, and only 5 percent by the saboteur. Normally, we would anticipate a higher degree of accuracy with the second type than with the first. Surely, the same degree of accuracy could be obtained with less resources, also.

This line of reasoning is so simple that I always find it difficult to understand why the Anglo-Saxon court system has persisted. Its origins, from trial by battle, are obvious enough and, at a time when the law quite literally was the will of the stronger, it was indeed quite rational. Its persistence can perhaps be explained in terms of the inertia of established custom, but customs do change.

There is, of course, an immensely powerful interest group dependent upon the preservation of the present situation in Anglo-Saxon courts. The number of lawyers per capita in Anglo-Saxon countries (and, in particular, the United States) is a high multiple of the number needed in the systems using the inquisitorial system. We also probably have more judges per capita than such countries as Switzerland or Sweden in spite of the greater emphasis put on judicial decisionmaking in those countries. The higher inherent accuracy of their court systems means that there are fewer cases brought before the courts; and, once a case is brought before the court, the judge makes the decision as to how much time will be spent on it, rather than the parties, with the result that cases are frequently disposed of quite quickly with good accuracy.

It is likely that a change from our system to the Continental system would, quite literally, eliminate about 90 percent of the demand for lawyers. This statement is not, of course, made under the assumption that our lawyers spend all of their time in court; indeed, they spend relatively little of their time in court. The advice they give, however, is very heavily affected by the type of judicial proceeding they anticipate if a court case does arise. Further, they spend much time negotiating cases and preparing for cases. All of this is immensely less expensive in Europe.

A fall of 90 percent in the demand for lawyers, of course, quite literally would impoverish the present profession. Immense numbers of lawyers would be fighting for a very limited amount of business, many of them becoming vacuum cleaner salesmen, law schools would be compelled to close, immense bodies of accumulated personal capital would cease to be of any relevance, and, altogether, the legal profession would suffer a major disaster.[5] Under the circumstances, the opposition of the lawyers to the type of legal system used on the Continent is understandable. Nevertheless, although I have started with two reasons why one might anticipate that there would be opposition to changes which are not intellectually respectable, the lawyers defending our current system do offer some arguments for it. The first I usually encounter in talking to the average American lawyer is an expression of incredulity that any other system exists. They will also (and consistently) normally tell me a few myths about European procedure, such as, that the defendant is compelled to prove his innocence rather than the prosecution being compelled to prove his guilt; but, once one has penetrated through this smoke screen, there is an intellectually possible defense of our system.

The point of this defense is that the judge may be undermotivated, and hence will not work hard enough. The two sides, whatever else may be said about them, are strongly motivated; hence, they can be expected to put a great deal of resources into reaching the decision. The judge has nothing personal riding on it and may not put in many resources, and hence may not reach a good decision according to this argument.[6]

5. It is my personal opinion that the social benefits would be large enough so that a Pareto optimal move is available, *i.e.*, we could fully compensate them for this loss and still make a gain.

6. For a discussion of the general problem of the undermotivation of government officials, see, Gordon Tullock, "Public Decisions as Public Goods," *Journal of Political Economy*, Vol. 79 (1971), July/August, pp. 913–18.

To deal with this situation, we should begin by talking a little bit about the factual problem of accuracy. Legal research has almost completely and totally shunned the question of how often the courts go wrong. However, I have been able to put together some evidence on accuracy, mainly by taking data generated for other purposes and interpreting them in terms of accuracy. For example, a research group in Oxford arranged, in 28 cases, to have a regular jury impaneled and then a jury of 12 men drawn from the regular jury list sit in the front of the spectators' row and listen to the cases; afterwards, they went off to deliberate and voted on them.[7] This was done, as I said, for 28 cases; in 21 of the cases, the two juries agreed, in 7 they disagreed. It is surely true that one of the two juries was wrong in the 7 cases on which they disagreed, and this provides for a minimum of one-eighth of the decisions of juries being in error.[8]

Obviously this research design is far from perfect, in particular, the jury which is not going to have its decision count presumably puts less effort into it than the one that will have its decision count. Nevertheless, it is some evidence.

The University of Chicago Jury Project made an experiment which can be regarded as a test of the accuracy of courts in general, in which a questionnaire was circulated to judges, and they were asked to mark down their decision and the decision of the jury in cases they had heard.[9] Once again, if the judge and jury disagree, one of them must be wrong; and rough calculations indicate an error term for these two decisionmaking bodies of about the same order of magnitude.[10] As a third test, the University of Chicago Jury Project made up tapes of two law cases and then played them for a number of experimental "juries."[11] In this case, the difference between the juries was very

7. See, Peter Evans, "'Shadow' jurors disagreed with one court verdict in four, penal research report says," *The (London) Times*, 18 December 1974, p. 4. This is a resume of the following book: Sarah McCabe and Robert Purves, *The Shadow Jury at Work*, Oxford, Basil Blackwell, 1974.

8. Actually, the percent of error necessary to provide for the difference of opinion in one-quarter of the cases is slightly higher than one-eighth, because there should be at least some cases in which both juries are wrong.

9. See, Harry Kalven, Jr., and Hans Zeisel, *The American Jury*, Boston, Little, Brown & Company, 1966, pp. 12–193.

10. The data are published in a form that makes it impossible to do anything more than very rough calculations.

11. For examples, see: Rita James Simon, "Status and Competence of Jurors," *American Journal of Sociology*, Vol. 64 (1959), pp. 563–70; "Trial by Jury: A Critical Assessment," in:

much larger than can be explained by a one-eighth error term, but I believe the two cases used for this were harder than normal.

All of this does not indicate, of course, that the inquisitorial system would be better than the adversary system. An error term of one-eighth is high; but it might conceivably be true that the inquisitorial system has an even higher one. Still, it is surely true that we can do a good deal to improve. Unfortunately, I know of absolutely no empirical evidence on the accuracy of European courts.

One of the problems in research of this type, of course, is that the courts have the power to prevent themselves from being investigated, and they do not want to be investigated. In general, we take the view that people who try to avoid investigation do so because the investigation would turn up things that are not to their credit; but it must be admitted that courts may have a valid reason for not wanting to be investigated. It is possible to argue that the judicial system works better if it is surrounded by myths and magic than if everyone concerned knows that the court regularly makes mistakes.

Regardless of this, we now turn to a second issue, which is how hard judges work. Once again, the judges have prevented serious investigation of this matter, but there are a few scattered bits of evidence.[12] It seems fairly certain that judges and juries are not particularly highly motivated in law cases, and hence there is something to be said for the view that leaving everything

---

Applied Sociology: Opportunities and Problems, ed. by A. W. Gouldner and S. M. Miller, New York, The Free Press, 1965, pp. 294–307; and "Jurors' Evaluation of Expert Psychiatric Testimony," in: *The Sociology of Law: Interdisciplinary Readings*, ed. by Rita James Simon, San Francisco, Chandler Publishing Co., 1968, pp. 314–28.

12. For example, Robert Gillespie cites an official study of "all 336 U.S. District Judges, who were asked to keep time diaries of their judicial activities over the approximately 95 working days from October 1969 through February 1970." Only about two-thirds of the judges actually filled out the form, presumably the most energetic two-thirds. There is, I think, no possibility that they underestimated their workload. It works out to an average of 4.2 hours per day for "judicial activities." See, Robert W. Gillespie, "Measuring the Demand for Court Services: A Critique of the Federal District Courts Case Weight," *Journal of the American Statistical Association*, Vol. 69 (1974), March, pp. 38–53. Other studies with which I am familiar produce about the same picture. It should, of course, be noted that all of the more detailed studies have turned up individual judges who work very hard, apparently because they treat their job as a hobby. The situation is rather similar to academic life, where the bulk of the faculty do not work very hard; but a certain number of people, who are deeply interested in their subject matter, do.

to them would be undesirable. It should be pointed out that there are various methods used in Europe to provide stronger motives for judges than are provided under the Anglo-Saxon system. The judicial career is organized with promotion, regular transfers, *etc*. This would normally motivate judges under this system more than the judge under the Anglo-Saxon system. Certainly the jurors, who are conscripted amateurs, have practically no motives to work hard and, indeed, do not.

In fact, there is no reason to believe that judges and juries under either system are motivated to the optimal extent, and further research should be undertaken for the purpose of developing institutions which will give them a better motivation. For the moment, however, it should be pointed out that the undermotivation is more extreme with respect to the jury and the Anglo-Saxon judge than with respect to the European judge. It is true that in Anglo-Saxon adversary proceedings the parties have every motive to put great resources into presenting their case; but this case is to be presented before a group of people who, in the case of the jury, are amateurs and of only average intelligence; in any event, they are not motivated particularly to hard intellectual labor to understand the case. As a result, the parties' arguments are unlikely to be designed in such a way as to put great strain on the minds of the listeners, even if the situation is such that truth can only be obtained *with* a great strain.

Still, the lack of motivation for the public officials concerned is a defect in both court systems. It is not obvious that it is less of a defect for the Anglo-Saxon than for the European system, but it is clear that public officials play a larger role in the European system. Thus, it is at least conceivable that the undermotivation of the judges more than counterbalances the overinvestment of resources by the parties, with which this article has been mainly concerned.

It will not have escaped the reader of this article that, personally, I favor the European system. It seems to me the theoretical arguments in its favor are much stronger than those against it. But I cannot be sure. The whole field of legal research has been dominated by essentially unscientific techniques. This has been particularly true of the comparison of these methods of reaching decisions in law suits. This article has been an effort to set the matter on a sound theoretical basis. Without further research, particularly empirical research, it is not possible to be certain that the Continental system is better than the Anglo-Saxon, but the presumption is surely in that direction.

ON THE EFFICIENT ORGANIZATION OF TRIALS

REPLY TO MCCHESNEY, AND ORDOVER AND WEITZMAN

The two critical papers contain a very, very large number of arguments against my position. Mainly, the arguments are presented in very brief form, but reasonable replies can hardly be made in such short form. Thus, if I attempted to reply to every single point they raise, I would produce a reply which is considerably longer than the sum of the two papers. In view of the shortage of journal space, I have decided to confine myself to a few of the main themes. This is not because I agree with the minor criticisms but because they are just too numerous to be dealt with in reasonable space.

Turning, then, to the major thrust of these articles, one of the intriguing features of both of them is that they regard the fact that the parties frequently try to avoid going through adversary trials as an indication of superiority of this trial system. The normal assumption would be that the parties are apt to turn to either arbitration or pretrial settlement if they face an inefficient legal system. If we assume, on the other hand, a divinely efficient legal system which always reaches the right conclusion at zero cost, it is clear that both of these institutions would disappear.

McChesney appears to believe that arbitration is available only in Anglo-Saxon jurisdictions, which is not true. Ordover and Weitzman, on the other hand, emphasize the pretrial settlement as apparently a special feature of Anglo-Saxon law. Arbitration tribunals are available everywhere; admittedly one would expect them to be less used in areas where the basic court system is highly efficient than where it is less efficient. Therefore, one would anticipate that they would be commoner in adversary jurisdictions than in jurisdictions using the inquisitorial procedure; and, as far as I can see, this is indeed correct. Indeed, this has led to certain scale economics, with the result that the collection of arbitral tribunals existing in London attracts cases from all over the world, as McChesney points out. Thus, although I agree with McChesney that it is desirable to let parties experiment with the tribunals

Reprinted, with permission of Blackwell Publishing, from *Kyklos* 30, fasc. 3 (1977): 517–19.

they favor, it is certainly not true that this indicates that adversary procedures are better than inquisitorial.[1]

The existence of pretrial settlements is a characteristic of any legal system, not just the adversary system. Further, the greater volume of litigation in the United States would seem to indicate that our pretrial settlements are rarer than on the continent of Europe, where the number of actual law suits is much smaller. But, whether that argument is accepted or not, it is clear that the efficiency of the tribunal would change the nature of pretrial settlements.

If the court which will decide a contract case is highly efficient, then the parties are apt to be careful in carrying out the contract. However, if there is a genuine difference of opinion between the parties as to the meaning of the contract, they are likely to take the matter to court, since this is a relatively low-cost and accurate activity. Where the courts are inefficient, on the other hand, deliberate breaches of contract by a party who feels that he can get away with it—or, in any event, that the costs of litigation are high enough so that the other party will be willing to accept a favorable settlement—are much more likely. On the other hand, genuine differences of opinion would have a higher tendency to be compromised rather than litigated, because of the parties' distrust of the efficiency of the courts.[2] Note that the court inefficiency here could be either a tendency to "bad" decisions and/or great expense. But, in any event, the existence of pretrial settlements is no argument for either adversary or inquisitorial procedure.

Another argument of my critics concerns the role of court procedures in common-law jurisdictions in actually making the law. Note that this does not require adversary proceedings rather than inquisitorial. Traditional Roman law and traditional Muhammadan law were both developed by "common-law" methods. The court systems in both cases, however, were inquisitorial rather than adversary. Therefore, strictly speaking this is a red herring.

1. One of the problems in legal research is that the lawyers who dominate the field have done almost nothing in the way of empirical work in their own procedures. Thus, it is not certain whether arbitral tribunals are basically inquisitorial, basically adversary, or some mix. It is my impression that they are basically inquisitorial but that, in Anglo-Saxon countries, they have a sort of veneer of "due process" built on top of the basic procedure, with the intent of insuring that the regular courts will enforce their decisions.

2. "Undoubtedly, the prospect of costly and protracted litigations creates incentives to settle the case early in the pretrial stages," Ordover and Weitzman, "On the Efficient Organization of Trials: A Comment," *Kyklos*, Vol. 30 (1977), 3.

It happens, however, that I am opposed to this particular way of making law. My objections have been chronicled elsewhere.[3] Under the circumstances, I will not go into them here; however, two points perhaps should be made. First, the courts are apparently beginning to realize that there are difficulties with this kind of law. The Supreme Court has just upheld[4] a lower court decision in which a Chicago court refused to permit a case to be cited as precedent on the grounds that the law was already too complicated. Further, the volume of administrative law in the United States is now getting so gigantic that it is fairly clear we are moving toward having administrative interpretation rather than court interpretation as our basic method of "interstitial" law making.[5]

One of the disadvantages of the Anglo-Saxon system, in which the parties, by their arguments before the judge, may create new law, is the penalty imposed on the parties themselves. If the law with respect to some particular point is in fact unclear, then when the judge makes a decision the parties will be subject to an *ex post facto* law. In general, we do not like this, although it happens to be true that no legal code can ever be designed with sufficient precision so that such cases may be reduced to zero. Nevertheless, it seems likely that in Anglo-Saxon law, particularly in the U.S., the degree of uncertainty of the law is very much higher than is necessary. My critics point out that it is not necessarily obvious to the parties to much litigation who is in the right and who is in the wrong. I think they exaggerate this point; I think that parties frequently *do* quite consciously know what they are doing.[6] But insofar as they are right, surely nothing more strenuous could be said in criticism of our law than that people may not be able to figure out their rights under it by any method except an expensive law suit. There are cases in Anglo-Saxon law where no one in court knows who is right or wrong until the judge has spoken. The fact that such cases are numerous enough so that my critics can regard them as normal is a strong condemnation of that legal system.

3. Gordon Tullock, "Courts as Legislatures," paper presented at Law and Liberty conference, San Francisco, Calif., January 1976.

4. Without opinion.

5. Here, as in many other areas, I prefer the European method of producing administrative law to the American method, but that is not relevant to this comment.

6. Chapin, just before being sentenced in one of the Watergate cases, said, "There's only one person in the courtroom who knows for certain whether I am guilty or innocent, and that is me." He was right, although there is no strong reason to believe that he would honestly communicate that knowledge to the court. This is, I think, the normal situation.

That the traditional system would have its defenders was something to be expected. Notably, the defenders have not sought out empirical evidence nor really tried to deal with my theoretical structure. I hope that this first round of critics will be succeeded by others who put greater weight on these two techniques of analysis.

JUDICIAL ERRORS AND A PROPOSAL FOR REFORM

I. J. Good and Gordon Tullock

Before discussing technical aspects of this paper, we argue that it is possible for a judge or court, specifically the Supreme Court of the United States, to be wrong. It is extraordinary that any human institution should be assumed always to be right, but many people do assume that the Supreme Court can do no wrong. A professor of political science who overheard a conversation between us regarding the frequency of judicial errors said that in this context "error" had no meaning. In phrases that recall the contention of the legal realists that the law is what the judges say it is, he concluded simply and categorically that the "Court makes its decision and that is the law."

This is an especially pertinent remark because the same professor would never say Congress passes a law and that is the law and therefore you cannot refer to it as being wrong. He certainly would not have said that Presidential decisions, many of which are subject to no appeal, cannot be wrong, or that the House of Lords, or the Pope speaking ex cathedra, cannot be wrong. In each of these cases the decision, once made, is not subject to appeal and binds as law some group of people. One can give further examples. The House of Commons in England, Stalin while he was alive, and Idi Amin while he was still in power all made decisions that were not subject to appeal, but could clearly be wrong.

Further, our colleague quite regularly criticizes specific Supreme Court decisions in language that appears to indicate he thinks they are after all erroneous. Since he is an ardent Democrat, the decisions he criticizes are the Burger cases, and he may well point out that when Warren was chief justice, "this kind of thing" did not happen. We have other colleagues who would simply reverse the personalities and feel equally convinced that other Supreme Court decisions are erroneous.

What has happened here is that the question whether a decision can be appealed has been confused with the question whether it can be in error. There is no doubt that the Supreme Court decides a given case, in the sense that

Reprinted, with permission, from *Journal of Legal Studies* 13 (June 1984): 289–98.

there is nearly always no appeal.[1] It is necessary that lawsuits stop somewhere. Under Islamic law, itself a very sophisticated and venerable legal system, cases stopped in the court of first instance. We doubt if any Islamic scholar ever alleged that that fact proved that all the decisions were right. Today, in the United States, England, and other common-law countries, most cases stop in the court of first instance. Again, we do not think anyone claims that such decisions are consequently always right. Further, if we accept the idea behind traditional American judicial theory, any decision by a jury on a question of fact is largely free of review by a trial judge and virtually immune from appellate review. We do not think anyone would say that this proves juries are always right.

Any decision maker (or decision-making body) must use some implicit or explicit criteria. These implicit criteria may be ones of which we would heartily disapprove, but they must exist. We all hope that courts use desirable rather than undesirable criteria, and indeed the higher courts always write long justificatory opinions explaining why they have reached a specific decision. They presumably do so in an effort to convince people that the decision is indeed the right one.

So far, we have talked of "right" and "wrong" as if they had clear meanings. If they did, the philosophers of ethics would not have needed to write so much since the days of Socrates. In modern terms one could perhaps define an "ethically right" decision as one that maximizes expected social utility, but such a welfare definition is difficult to apply. It seems preferable to use a different definition for our purposes.

People frequently say, incorrectly, that there is no way of telling how often a court is wrong unless one has some outside knowledge of the correct conclusion. Whenever there is a difference between a judge and jury, two judges, or two courts, one of them must be wrong whatever the precise meaning of "wrong," provided only that we assume, by two-valued logic, that a court's decision is either right or wrong in accordance with that meaning. It is, of course, possible that the judge and jury (and so forth) are both wrong, but one can compute the minimum number of erroneous decisions necessary to generate the amount of difference of opinion that *is* generated. This procedure was used in two books by Tullock, who simply calculated the

1. The Court can reconsider the case and on occasion other branches of the government have reversed Supreme Court decisions. The Dred Scott case, to take a very famous example, was reversed at Gettysburg. Dred Scott v. Sandford, 60 U.S. 393 (1856).

likelihood that courts of first instance would be wrong in criminal cases, using essentially the difference of opinions between judges and juries or between different juries.[2] Here we are going to deal with judges in the Supreme Court of the United States, and we shall use a much better statistical technique.

We shall use a reasonable criterion to estimate what percentage of judicial decisions are wrong, given the voting of the court. We shall then turn to possible reforms suggested by our results.

The Proposed Interpretation of Right and Wrong and Its Implications

To make the idea of judicial error clear without producing any detailed criteria, we introduce a sort of judicial equivalent of the statistician's urn. Let us consider all the people who would be regarded as suitable for the Supreme Court. Presumably this is a large collection of outstanding lawyers, some of whom of course are law professors, some judges of inferior courts, and some practicing attorneys.[3] Only nine members of this universe are, in fact, members of the Supreme Court, and they are not truly a random sample; but if we consider the characteristics that lead people to be selected as members of the Court, it is clear that essentially accidental factors having to do with connections and personal preferences are highly important. Assuming that the Court is a reasonably good representative sample of this larger universe, then, would appear to be legitimate.

Note that operationally we have no way of defining this larger universe. Since we are going to use it for purely theoretical reasons only, that is not important; but if the reader wishes, he can confine himself to that collection of people who have been seriously considered for appointment to the Court at the time that the present Justices were actually selected. This would give a number of potential members of the Court much larger than the Court itself.

Having this large idealized population,[4] for our purposes the right deci-

2. Gordon Tullock, *The Logic of the Law* (1971), and *Trials on Trial: The Pure Theory of Legal Procedure* (1980).

3. Some, like Warren, are practicing politicians, but they have almost all started out as lawyers.

4. As a matter of fact, for mathematical purposes we converted it into an infinite population rather than a finite population of ten thousand or so, but the difference in outcome is very slight and the simplification in the mathematics very great. The assumption of idealized infinite populations has been familiar in statistical practice at least since the early days of R. A. Fisher.

sion will be the one that would be reached by the majority within this enlarged population. Note that this is the definition of "right" maximizing the estimated probability that the Supreme Court will be right. If we had some external standard of right or wrong, then either (i) this standard is accepted by the judges and their conferees whom we use in our population, in which event our decision rule would give the correct estimates for the probabilities of the decisions' being right; or (ii) this "right" principle would not be accepted by the members of the Court nor by the population from which it is selected, with the result that our system would overestimate the probabilities. Our real reason for not using an extrinsic rule, however, is that so far as we know there is no such rule generally agreed upon.[5]

The assumption that the Supreme Court has been selected at random from this ideal population is not strictly correct because "political appointments" are made, but it would be too complicated to take this biased selection into account.[6] It is intuitively reasonable to assume that the estimated probability of an incorrect decision, as derived from the "random selection" model, given an (r, s) split in the vote,[7] will be an underestimate of the true probability, because bias in selection is likely to decrease the reliability of the Court.

If $r > s$, then the "yes" decision, which is the majority decision, is more likely to be "right" than "wrong." As Mr. Justice Stevens said, "For the most significant work of the court, it is assumed that the collective judgment of its majority is more reliable than the views of the minority."[8]

If $r > s$ and $r + s = 9$ (or any other fixed value, 12 being one interesting value), then the larger $r - s$ is, the more "reliable" will be the decision. Our model satisfies this modest requirement.

Let the fraction of the infinite population of judges that would have voted "yes" on a specific occasion be p. This can be thought of as a "physical probability." Evidence for its value is available from the knowledge that the court

5. Each of us is willing to express his opinion whether given court decisions are right or wrong, using extrinsic criteria. We presume most of the readers will also be so willing.

6. We could, of course, change our universe to include not only wisdom and information but also political bias. Thus the assumption would be that there are many people who are as wise and well informed as, and politically rather similar to, the current members of the Court. This would, we think, be a truthful assumption.

7. An (r, s) split means r votes for "yes" and s for "no." We are going to be concerned only with "yes-no" or dichotomous decisions.

8. A speech delivered by Justice Stevens at New York University Law School (Oct. 27, 1982). This report is from the *Washington Post*, October 29, 1982, at A-3.

has voted (r, s). We do not know the value of p; in fact it must vary according to the nature of the case being judged and especially according to its difficulty. Instead of assuming a constant value of p, we adopt a Bayesian approach, that is, we assume a prior distribution for p. The simplest and most natural assumption is the Bayes postulate of a uniform prior. Then we can derive the subjective, logical, or epistemic probability $p_{r,s}$ that an exceedingly large court drawn at random from the infinite population will agree with the decision of the original court, that is, that the majority of the very large court will vote "yes" if $r > s$. The details of the mathematics are given in the Appendix. The result is

$$p_{r,s} = 1 - \frac{1}{2^{r+s+1}}\left[1 + \binom{r+s+1}{1} + \binom{r+s+1}{2} + \cdots + \binom{r+s+1}{s}\right]$$

In particular $p_{9,0} = .99902, p_{8,1} = .98925, p_{7,2} = .94531, p_{6,3} = .82812$, and $p_{5,4} = .62304$. It may be noted that the formula also gives, for example, $p_{4,5} = .37696$, as it should, because $p_{5,4} + p_{4,5} = 1$. When $(r, s) = (5, 4)$ the probability that the court's decision is wrong is at least 37 percent.

It is surprising that the theory implies that $p_{r,s}$ is equal to the probability of obtaining at least $s + 1$ heads when a fair coin is tossed $r + s + 1$ times. This fact can be used for the easy recovery of the numerical value of $p_{r,s}$.

If two independent courts have "splits" (a, b) and (c, d), it might be sensible in some circumstances to combine these votings to give $r = a + c$ and $s = b + d$, instead of thinking of one court as overruling the other.

The Supreme Court of the United States has nine members and at various times in the past has had fewer, and the President at one time recommended raising it to fifteen. As a result we present in Table 1 the probability of correct decisions for all court sizes from 1 to 19. In any case, we do not wish to confine our study to a single institution. Values for a court of nine are included in Table 1. The values of $p_{r,s}$ for $19 \geq r \geq s \geq 0$ are shown in Table 1. A statistician will note that this probability is well approximated by the tail-area probability of a normal deviate equal to

$$\frac{r - s}{(r + s + 1)^{1/2}}$$

These normal approximations to $p_{9,0}, \ldots, p_{5,4}$ are, respectively, .9978, .9866, .9431, .8296, and .6241, which may be compared with the exact values just given. The errors of the normal approximation are presumably smaller than

TABLE 1. ***Values of*** $p_{r,s}$

	s									
r	0	1	2	3	4	5	6	7	8	9
1	.7500	.5000								
2	.8750	.6875	.5000							
3	.9375	.8125	.6562	.5000						
4	.9688	.8906	.7734	.6367	.5000					
5	.9844	.9375	.8555	.7461	.6230	.5000				
6	.9922	.9648	.9102	.8281	.7256	.6123	.5000			
7	.9961	.9805	.9453	.8867	.8062	.7095	.6047	.5000		
8	.9980	.9893	.9673	.9270	.8666	.7880	.6964	.5982	.5000	
9	.9990	.9941	.9807	.9539	.9102	.8491	.7228	.6855	.5927	.5000
10	.9995	.9968	.9888	.9713	.9408	.8949	.8338	.7597	.6762	.5881
11	.9998	.9983	.9935	.9824	.9616	.9283	.8811	.8204	.7483	
12	.9999	.9991	.9963	.9894	.9755	.9519	.9165	.8654		
13	.9999	.9995	.9979	.9936	.9846	.9682	.9423			
14	1.0000	.9997	.9988	.9962	.9904	.9793				
15	1.0000	.9999	.9993	.9978	.9941					
16	1.0000	.9999	.9996	.9987						
17	1.0000	1.0000	.9998							
18	1.0000	1.0000								
19	1.0000									

NOTE.—When the voting of a court is $(r, s)(r \geq s)$, the probability that it is "wrong" is at least $1 - p_{r,s}$. For $r > 19$ the tail-area probability of the normal deviate $(r - s)/(r + s + 1)^{1/2}$ differs from $p_{r,s}$ by less than .0001. r = number of judges in majority, s = number of judges in minority.

the errors implicit in our basic assumptions. We claim for our theory only that it is the best one so far proposed.

A Proposed Reform

Let us now turn to our proposed reform. It is simply that in those cases where the probability is low that the court is correct, that is, in the Supreme Court the five to four and six to three cases, the decision should not be regarded as a precedent. The Court would await another case dealing with the same point of law, but with different parties and somewhat different facts. The procedure will be very similar to what we now have in those rare cases in which the Court ties. A striking case occurred while we were preparing this article. A $1,000 limit for "independent expenditures" in presidential campaigns was struck down by an appellate court and the appellate case was appealed to the Supreme Court, where, because Justice O'Connor abstained, a four to four tie resulted. The Federal Election Commission (FEC) decided that it would ignore the decision of the appellate court and enforce the law in spite of its apparent conflict with free speech. This will lead to another lawsuit and another hearing before the Court, in which, presumably, there will be a decision that will be binding. We are proposing that this procedure be used much more widely.[9]

More precisely, a threshold should be set on the value of $p_{r,s}$ before a precedent is set. The determination of the threshold could be made by means of a Constitutional amendment, an act of Congress, or possibly by a Supreme Court decision, preferably unanimous.

But this is just for the Supreme Court, and there are many other courts in the United States. For simplicity, we will talk only about the inferior federal courts, but the principles can be applied elsewhere. The federal appellate court normally hears cases in panels of three drawn from a larger total bench. It can be seen from the table that a two to one majority of a group has not a very high probability of being correct.[10] We therefore suggest that such decisions not be regarded as a precedent. This would mean that the courts of first incidence in this particular circuit could go on making decisions in accordance with their view as to what the law should be. These cases could be appealed to the appellate court, but there should be rules that the appellate court must give them full hearing if they are appealed. Preferably, the panel for the rehearing would be, to the extent practicable, composed of different judges from those who heard the first case. This would continue until a unanimous decision was reached in this particular circuit.

It could be argued that even a unanimous decision by the three judges should not be authoritative if it was different from the previous decision. For example, suppose that in the first trial there is a two to one majority for A and in the second appeal a three to zero majority for $\overline{A}$. Six judges have

9. *Washington Post*, Friday, May 13, 1983, at A-34. Common Cause v. Schmitt, 455 U.S. 129 (1982). See 9 FEC Record 8–9 (Aug. 1983).

10. We suppose here that a purist would say we have to use a different universe, that is, those who are thought eligible for appellate court rather than those who are thought eligible for the Supreme Court. Fortunately, this makes no difference in our calculations.

looked at the case; four decided one way and two the other; and if we look back at our table we observe that with six judges, a majority of four to two does not give a very high probability of accuracy. Nevertheless, we believe that the later court has been able to make the decision after a longer period of consideration with a good deal more litigation. Consequently, the rule has been applied to a larger collection of real-world facts, and it is more authoritative. In any event this decision can, of course, be reversed by the Supreme Court.

The appellate court, itself, would not regard a decision by a five to four majority of the Supreme Court as a valid precedent. Thus, there would be no pressure for the circuits to reach uniform decisions in such cases. Appeals of cases to the Supreme Court could go through the usual certiorari process. If the Supreme Court asked our advice, and we doubt that it will, we would recommend that it normally grant certiorari only after a reasonable period of time for more cases to have been argued in the lower courts. The objective of this process is to give difficult points in law longer and more careful consideration, and the Supreme Court should therefore wait until the law has been applied in a number of different cases before making what will turn out to be the ultimate decision.[11] Note that it would be necessary to provide specifically that the Supreme Court could not issue certiorari and then give a summary opinion. It would be compelled to give a full hearing to any case of this sort once it had issued its certiorari.

All of this is quite different from our current practice. It would mean that we were deliberately imposing a delay in the hope of getting improved law. Note, however, that our present practice imposes immense delays because of the time it takes to get to the Supreme Court, and the only argument we know for this slow process, in which a case wanders gradually up to the Supreme Court, is that we get better law by that method than by others. We are suggesting a somewhat longer delay to get still better results. Obviously, the easy cases would be determined with large majorities and then the problem would not arise; only in the cases in which the best law is unclear would this problem arise. Note that the individual litigants would receive certainty under this system in the sense that their cases were determined. We would have far fewer official reversals of the court's previous decisions, because the cases

11. Of course, it might turn out that the Supreme Court, even after a three-year wait, still had only five to four. This would be further evidence that this is a really difficult point of law and hence, that further delay before a final decision was sensible.

that are difficult and doubtful would not become precedents until they had been thoroughly explored by several cases.

Although this procedure appears radical, it is really the current one that should be regarded as radical. Something like our suggestion has not been very uncommon in common law in the world as a whole. Roman law, for example, developed out of the writings of the jurisconsults, but they normally did not consider a single decision as a binding precedent. Similarly, British common law was until quite recent times organized in a set of courts, each jealous of its prerogatives, with the result that a precedent was not considered entirely binding until the same decision on the subject had been given several times.[12] Similarly, a number of decisions were required before precedent was established both in the law developed out of the Koran, which is essentially a common law for Islamic countries, and in the common law developed all over Europe as essentially Continental common law, which Napoleon abolished.

The view that we should make a definite final decision every time a matter comes up is, of course, widely held. The Supreme Court has a positive policy of refusing to accept certiorari until a case is "ripe." We suggest that the Court take cases that are not ripe and then make nonbinding decisions on them. From the standpoint of the individual litigants this will mean that they get a Supreme Court decision instead of being forced to stop at the appellate level; and from the standpoint of the nation as a whole it will mean that, in those cases where the legal decision is difficult or obscure, great care is taken by the ultimate decision maker. Easy cases, those in which there is a large majority on one side or the other, will be determined quickly. In our opinion this is superior to the more traditional practice of requiring *all* cases to be heard several times before they become precedent.

Both the reform we suggest, and our initial calculation of the probable percentage of errors by the Court, are apt to be regarded as very radical by conventional minds. The view that the Court cannot make mistakes has been widely held, although, given the number of times it has reversed itself, it is hard to see why. The view is also widely held that once the Court has taken a case it must either send it back on the grounds that certiorari has been imprudently given or must make a decision that is a binding precedent. We see no justification for this widely held view, and we claim that the reform we

12. See Bruno Leoni, *Freedom and the Law* (1961), at 87, 184–85.

propose should improve the quality of the judicial precedents at the cost of making some of them a little slower to attain.

Appendix

PROOF OF THE FORMULA FOR $p_{r,s}$

If p were known, the probability that a count of $M = 2N + 1$ judges (taken as an odd number for convenience) would come to the "yes" decision would be

$$x = \sum_{v=N+1}^{2N+1} \binom{M}{v} p^v q^{M-v}$$

(where $q = 1-p$).

Denote the probability that the Supreme Court will reach an (r, s) split, conditional on the values of p and of $r + s$ (the size of the court, usually nine), by

$$P[(r, s)|p, r + s]$$

Then

$$P[(r, s)|p, r + s] = \binom{r + s}{s} p^r q^s$$

and this, or just $p^r q^s$, is the *likelihood* of p when (r, s) occurs. Assuming a uniform prior for p from 0 to 1, then its posterior density is proportional to $p^r q^s$. Therefore

$$E[p^v q^{M-v}|(r, s)] = \frac{\int_0^1 p^{v+r} q^{M-v+s}\, dp}{\int_0^1 p^r q^s\, dp}$$

$$= \frac{(v + r)!(M - v + s)!(r + s + 1)!}{(M + r + s + 1)!r!s!}$$

Therefore

$$p_{r,s} = E[x|(r, s)]$$

$$= \sum_{v=N+1}^{2N+1} \frac{M!(v + r)!(M - v + s)!(r + s + 1)!}{v!(M - v)!(M + r + s + 1)!r!s!}$$

$$= \sum_{v=(M+1)/2}^{M} \binom{v + r}{r}\binom{M + s - v}{s} \Big/ \binom{M + r + s + 1}{M}$$

$$\sim \sum_{v=(M+1)/2}^{M} \left[\frac{v^r}{r!}\frac{(M - v)^s}{s!} \Big/ \frac{M^{r+s+1}}{(r + s + 1)!}\right]$$

(for large M),

$$= \frac{(r + s + 1)!}{r!s!M^{r+s+1}} \sum_{v=(M+1)/2}^{M} v^r(M - v)^s$$

$$= \frac{(r + s + 1)!}{r!s!} \frac{1}{M} \sum_{v=(M+1)/2}^{M} \left(\frac{v}{M}\right)^r\left(1 - \frac{v}{M}\right)^s$$

$$\rightarrow \frac{(r + s + 1)!}{r!s!} \int_{1/2}^{1} u^r(1 - u)^s \, du$$

when $M \rightarrow \infty$. The integral is an incomplete beta function. By partial integration we can obtain a recurrence relation for $p_{r,s}$, namely,

$$p_{r,s} = p_{r+1,s-1} - \binom{r + s + 1}{s}\frac{1}{2^{r+s+1}}$$

from which we derive

$$p_{r,s} = 1 - \frac{1}{2^{r+s+1}}\left[1 + \binom{r+s+1}{1} + \binom{r+s+1}{2} + \cdots + \binom{r+s+1}{s}\right]$$

as asserted in the main text.

COURT ERRORS

That the courts make errors is not doubted by anyone, but there has been very little study of those errors. This is partly because empirically such a study is difficult, although I discuss some empirical work toward the end of this paper, and partly because I think most people don't like to think about courts doing such things as putting people in prison through error. Still, it is an important subject, and this paper is an effort to begin the development of a theory of such errors and to suggest further empirical work.

Errors can occur either in interpreting the law or in matters of fact. This paper addresses primarily errors of fact because in the Anglo-Saxon tradition courts' decisions actually make a good deal of the law and hence the meaning of error is somewhat ambiguous here.[1]

Let us assume, as in so many murder mysteries, a baronet is found dead in his library with a knife of oriental design sticking out of his back. Scotland Yard is called in and comes to the conclusion that the butler did it because he was mentioned in the baronet's will for 1,000 pounds. Will the butler be convicted? The answer depends primarily on the strength of the evidence against him.

Anyone who has talked to police officers knows they frequently maintain that they know who committed some particular crime but that the evidence is too weak for a conviction.[2] Whether the police are right about this is a matter of some speculation, but many crimes are committed for which the evidence against the perpetrator is weak. Indeed, in many cases the perpetrator is totally unknown.

Figure 1 is an effort to analyze the situation using some simple assumptions about the distribution of evidence. The horizontal axis shows the strength of evidence against a large number of different butlers who have

Reprinted, with kind permission of Kluwer Academic Publishers, from *European Journal of Law and Economics* 1 (1994): 9–21. A version of this paper was published in *Journal of Legal Economics* 2 (July 1992): 57–70.

1. But see R. J. Good and Gordon Tullock, "Judicial Errors and a Proposal for Reform," *Journal of Legal Studies* 13(2) (1984): 289–98.

2. "Capt. Michael R. Ulichny, supervisor of detectives at the Tucson Police Department, said while detectives believe they know who killed Mills (two years ago), he's not confident an arrest will ever be made." *Tucson Citizen* (September 24, 1990): B-1.

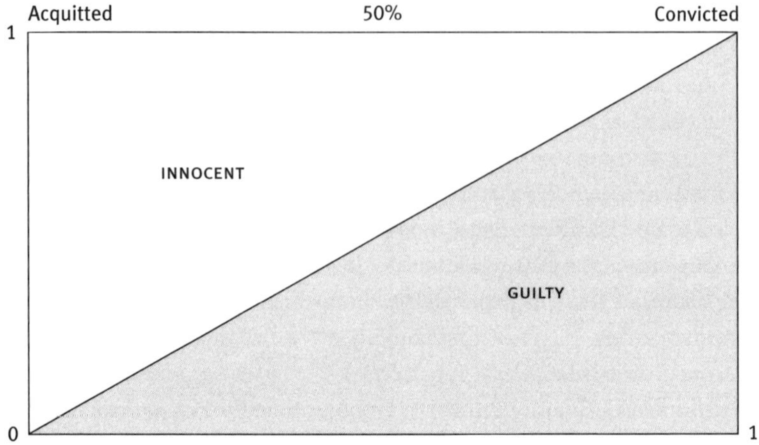

FIGURE 1

been implicated in various murders. The vertical axis shows the percentage of those butlers who in fact are guilty with each volume of evidence against them. Those in the shaded area are in fact guilty and the rest innocent. The court, however, does not know who is guilty. It simply knows how much evidence there is against each person. Thus, each person is known to be somewhere in a vertical column above, let us say, point 17 on the horizontal axis, which means that of all the people with that amount of evidence against them, 17 percent are in fact guilty.

The court must then decide on the basis of the evidence, and inevitably it will sometimes be wrong. There are various rules it can use, and I will canvass a number of them, starting with the rule now used in civil suits rather than criminal—take whichever is the most probable result. All butlers to the right of the 50 percent line on the horizontal axis would be convicted and to the left, acquitted. This minimizes total errors, type 1 and type 2. The guilty butler has a three-out-of-four chance of being convicted and a one-out-of-four chance of being acquitted. The innocent butler has a three-out-of-four chance of being discharged and a one-out-of-four chance of being convicted.

The actual penalty that would deter the crime depends on the gain from the crime and the likelihood that people committing it will be detected. It should be noted that throughout I use the rule that the penalty should be the minimum required to deter the crime. This by no means is noncontroversial. My basic reasons for using it are that it happens to be my personal preference and that it maps other rules in general. Most legal systems have the severity of the penalty affected by both the seriousness of the crime and the likelihood of conviction. In this case it will be exactly proportionate.

For the purposes of this example, assume that no butlers are in any way not connected with a murder; hence the likelihood of being convicted is shown by the 45 percent line. The other possibility—the existence of many crimes for which there are no suspects—is dealt with later.

If we wanted to deter this crime and if the butler's motive for committing the murder is that he was to receive a legacy of 1,000 pounds, it would be necessary to fine him 1,000+ pounds if he knew in advance for certain that he would be caught and then convicted. With the present rule he has only a three-out-of-four chance of being caught and convicted, and the minimum fine which would deter him from committing the crime, assuming he is risk neutral, is 1,334 pounds. This means, however, that the innocent person who runs a one-in-four chance of being convicted has a present discounted fine of, once again assuming risk neutrality, 333 pounds odd.

The normal rule in criminal law is that the defendant will be convicted only if the evidence is fairly strong against him. Assume, then, that the weight of the evidence required for conviction gives a probability of 80 percent or better of guilt.

As a result of the switch to requiring a higher likelihood of guilt in order to convict, it is necessary to increase the penalty.[3] In this case, in order to deter the murderer, who was motivated by desire for 1,000 pounds, it is necessary to charge a fine of 2,777.78 pounds.

The innocent person, whose probability of acquittal under these conditions is less than 80 percent, faces a 4 percent chance of conviction. If he is convicted, he will be fined 2,777.78 pounds also. The present discounted value of this for him, assuming risk neutrality, is 111.11 pounds.

A number of values computed in this way are shown on Table 1. It appears that the advantage to an innocent person of increasing the amount of evi-

3. As far as I know, this particular problem has been discussed only in Gordon Tullock, *The Logic of the Law* (New York: University Press of America, 1988 [originally published by Basic Books, 1971]), 175–92, and Tullock, *Trials on Trial: The Pure Theory of Legal Procedure* (New York: Columbia University Press, 1980), 182–83. Still, the point is obvious.

TABLE 1

DECISION RULE	PROBABILITY OF BEING CONVICTED AND GUILTY	DISCOUNTED VALUE	PROBABILITY OF BEING CONVICTED IF INNOCENT	DISCOUNTED VALUE
40%	.85	$1,190.48	.36	$428.57
50%	.75	$1,333.33	.25	$333.33
60%	.64	$1,562.50	.16	$250.00
70%	.51	$1,960.78	.09	$176.47
80%	.36	$2,777.78	.04	$111.11
90%	.19	$5,263.16	.01	$52.63
99%	.019	$52,631.58	.0001	$5.26

dence needed to convict is not as great as one might think if the necessity of increasing the size of the fine is not included. Indeed, from the innocent person's standpoint, if he is risk averse, it might actually be perverse.

A man who buys fire insurance on his house knowing that the premiums he is paying over his lifetime are worth much more than the probable expected value of the disaster, but wanting to avoid a sharp negative risk, might actually prefer a lower level of probability, which gives him a much higher chance of paying a low fine.

In a small, unscientific poll conducted among my colleagues, a two-thirds majority preferred the 25 percent chance of being fined $1,333 to a one in 5,000 chance of being fined $50,251.26. In the poll, I did not say that I was talking about court proceedings or the rule that people should be found guilty beyond reasonable doubt. The poll was unscientific, and the numbers were obtained on the basis of a totally arbitrary calculation. It should be pointed out, however, that although these numbers are the result of an arbitrary calculation, a somewhat similar structure must exist in the real world.

But there is substantially no evidence of a statistical nature on the shape of the function shown by the straight line in Figure 1. Further, the only ways that I can think of to develop such evidence are extremely costly, and I don't have the resources necessary to do so. Thus, the relation between amount of evidence and guilt might be different. Figure 2 shows a simple curve in which a sine function is substituted. Intuitively, this seems to me to be more reasonable than the straight line, but I don't think my intuition is of much value here.

In any event, Table 2 is the same as Table 1 except that the numbers are

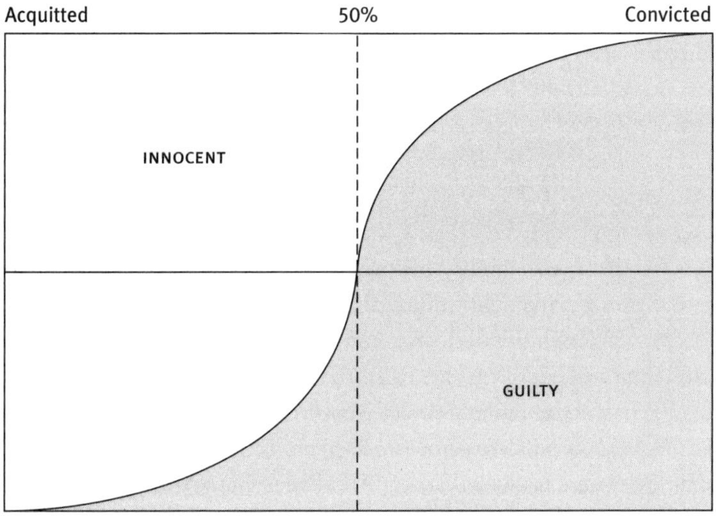

FIGURE 2

computed using the function of Figure 2 instead of Figure 1. Once again, note that for the innocent person the increase for the burden of proof on the prosecution is by no means an unmitigated gain. If he is risk averse, he might prefer some moderate assumption as to the amount of evidence needed to convict with its lower fine even though he knows that will increase the likelihood he himself will be convicted.

In addition to the probability of conviction at a trial, there is also the prospect of out-of-court settlement, which is more common than a trial, as well

TABLE 2

DECISION RULE	PROBABILITY OF BEING FOUND GUILTY IF GUILTY	DISCOUNTED VALUE	PROBABILITY OF BEING FOUND GUILTY IF INNOCENT	DISCOUNTED VALUE
40%	.9027	$1,107.79	.2973	$329.35
50%	.8183	$1,222.05	.1817	$222.05
60%	.7027	$1,423.08	.0973	$138.47
70%	.5575	$1,793.72	.0425	$76.23
80%	.3871	$2,583.31	.0129	$33.32
90%	.1984	$5,040.32	.0016	$8.06
99%	.0200	$50,000.00	1.65×10^{-6}	$.08

as the issue of legal costs. Consider the prospect of an out-of-court settlement aside from the issue of the costs of the trail. In this case, people will settle out of court almost exclusively as a result of risk aversion.

One popular theory of the likelihood of settlement,[4] which I believe to be erroneous, argues that people normally settle if the two parties anticipate differing outcomes. The defendant might think he is more likely to be convicted than the prosecutor does, and hence both he and the prosecutor would regard some figure between their expectation as desirable. Where they are in agreement on the probability of conviction, they might also settle. A settlement is unlikely when they differ in the sense that the defendant thinks his probability of conviction is lower than the prosecutor does.

This theory depends on the assumption that the actual trial is always the result of a particular kind of error. Economists, particularly from Chicago, tend to feel that errors are not terribly likely. I am not going to quarrel with them on this point. Clearly, judgments about who is going to win a case are difficult to make. The general attractiveness of this argument is shown in the following quotation from Eisenberg.[5]

> By the time the case is well into the litigation process and reaches trial, cases in which parties agree about the outcome will settle. The parties' different expectations about prevailing in light of the decision standard generates trials. In a simple model, intuitively, the distribution of plaintiffs' errors to overestimate success is the same as the distribution of defendants' errors to underestimate plaintiffs' success (that is, approximately half of those disputes litigated will be attributable to plaintiffs' overestimates and half attributable to defendants' underestimates).[6] Similarly distributed error terms lead, in the limiting case, to 50 percent victories for plaintiffs.

The problem with this line of reasoning is the assumption that the attorneys and parties are attempting to determine who will win the case rather than the probabilities of victory. If the odds are about fifty-fifty neither party is going to feel highly confident that he will win. However, one party might

4. For a clear statement see George L. Priest and Benjamin Klein, "The Selection of Disputes for Litigation," *Journal of Legal Studies* 13 (1984): 1. This article and most of its successors are discussed, tested, and rejected in Theodore Eisenberg, "Testing the Selection Effect: A New Theoretical Framework with Empirical Tests," *Journal of Legal Studies* 19(2): 337–58.

5. Eisenberg, "Testing the Selection Effect," p. 340.

6. [Priest and Klein, "The Selection of Disputes for Litigation," n. 42.]

feel he has 60 percent odds on his side, while the other party might feel that it is an even contest. The same difficulty can arise even if the evidence is quite one-sided.

Some years ago a case received a great deal of publicity when a man convicted of rape was sentenced to one day in prison as a result of a pretrial bargaining. Everyone involved with the case thought the evidence against the accused was extremely weak, but he didn't want to run the risk of a trial. This led to a big upsurge of public indignation. The plea of guilty was withdrawn, he was tried and found innocent, thus indicating that the judgment of probability made by the two parties in the original trial had been accurate.

If we consider that people are making judgments not of who will win or lose but of the odds for winning or losing—which is, after all, what determines the size of a cash settlement in a civil suit or the length of imprisonment in a criminal case—it's generally as hard to make the judgment when the case appears to be one-sided as when it appears to be even. The 50 to 60 percent case given above can be matched by a 90 to 95 percent case in one-sided situations of the evidence.

In any event, here we have some empirical evidence: the overwhelming majority of those criminal cases that actually go to trial result in convictions. This is not at the 50 percent level. Civil cases, of course, are to some extent different.

Data on the decision to settle out of court is difficult to collect because in many cases settlement out of court takes the form of one party deciding to accept the position of the other without any significant negotiations. In the case of crime, for example, the police decide that they can't prove a crime and hence don't do anything, and in other cases the proceeding goes from the police to the prosecuting attorney, perhaps even with an indictment, but the prosecuting attorney decides simply to drop it.

In many civil cases one party or the other thinks about doing something that might lead to a lawsuit and then decides that he won't, with the result that this out-of-court settlement never appears in the record anywhere.

In the criminal field, this is particularly conspicuous. The vast majority of all crimes committed in the United States never lead to any legal proceeding because no trial is attempted. In some of these cases the failure is a failure at the police level, and these guilty persons get away because they simply are not caught. In other cases, release is a decision on the part of the prosecutor.

Prosecutors in general desire to have fairly good success records, and they can obtain such a good success record by the simple expedient of refusing to prosecute cases where the odds are not heavily on their side. This is the reason for the high level of success that prosecutors have in cases they try. It's not that they are particularly effective but that they select strong cases for prosecution.

Legal costs, the attorneys themselves, and their personal desires change all of this. I've already mentioned that the prosecuting attorney makes decisions to keep his record clean. I have no idea about the motives of the public defenders who defend most criminal cases. They usually lose and also normally recommend that their clients cop a plea. It would be interesting to find out why.

Turning to private attorneys, however, they have some similar motives. It doesn't do a lawyer any good to lose, although losing half of his cases will not ruin his reputation. Nevertheless, private attorneys do not like to go to court with a very weak case and hence would put considerable pressure on their clients not to undertake it.

But clients make the ultimate determination here, since they can always get another lawyer. Lawyers are the suppliers, and clients the customers.

There is, however, a fairly strong relationship between the strength of the case and the amount that a client would be willing to spend to defend it. It is reasonably certain that the marginal value of another dollar's worth of attorney services is higher at the 50 percent level than it is at either the 5 percent or the 95 percent level. This being so, one would expect that the amount that clients would be willing to spend on hiring attorneys at either end of the spectrum would be less than they would be willing to spend near the middle.

I practiced law as a junior lawyer for five months in Chicago, and in two cases in which the probability of success was low I was sent out more or less without instructions to handle them on my own. In one case I not only lost but was reproved by the court. In the other case, however, I won, and my employer was more distressed by this win than by my loss. He apparently thought that I might have done something improper because he didn't see how the case could possibly have been won.[7]

Although one anticipates that fewer resources are available in one-sided cases, this doesn't tell us anything about the frequency of settlements. The defendant would be as annoyed at paying a settlement of 90 percent when the

7. The client called to thank my employer and tell him that he had been wrong in telling her she shouldn't press the case. He was a highly temperamental person and responded to this call negatively.

odds, in his opinion, are only 80 percent for his opponent, as he would be for paying a settlement of 60 percent when he thinks the odds are fifty-fifty. The usual risk aversion in the very one-sided cases is stronger for the person who is on the weak side than for the person who is on the strong side and has less real risk than the fifty-fifty case. After all, the settlement in which I pay 90 percent is not all that much of an improvement over having to pay the whole 100 percent after litigation. Of course, all of this costs money. But litigation costs are likely to be less in the one-sided cases because of lower return to investment in litigation, which simply reinforces this line of reasoning.

It seems that the client most likely to win would be willing to put up more money for attorneys' fees than the one most likely to lose, but as I said above, intuition here is not very well informed. This tendency to spend more money on attorneys if the case is more or less evenly balanced than if it's one-sided, I think, does tend to produce more litigation in more or less evenly balanced cases.

The mechanism through which this occurs is quite different from that of Priest and Klein.[8] Consider a civil case where the 50 percent rule is, at least in theory, used.[9] Assume that the plaintiff sues the defendant for $30,000 and that both parties at the time the suit is first seriously contemplated assume that they will pay one-third the amount at issue or $10,000 in legal fees. They both think that there is a fifty-fifty chance of success.

The plaintiff, then, has a discounted value of $5,000 on the case and the defendant has a present discounted value of −$25,000. There is a very large bargaining range, and trying to obtain the bulk of that bargaining range would seem to be a logical objective of the attorneys. Thus, the plaintiff would offer to settle for $24,500, and the defendant would counteroffer by suggesting $5,500 as a reasonable settlement.

The bulk of the legal maneuvering, then, would take the form of attempting not to eliminate the risk, although there is risk, but to get this bargaining range for one of the parties. This legal maneuvering, although it partly takes

8. "The Selection of Disputes for Litigation." The following is largely drawn from G. Tullock, "Negotiated Settlements," in G. Skogh and M. Schulenberg, eds., *Law and Economics and the Economics of Legal Regulation* (Boston: Kluwer, 1987), 39–50.

9. For example, in criminal law if 90 percent is the amount of evidence necessary to convict, you would anticipate the 90 percent level to function much like the 50 percent level in civil cases. Granted, however, that most criminals are defended by public defenders, it is not at all obvious that this is true.

the form of writing nasty letters, primarily consists in spending resources in preparing a strong case.

As time goes by, more and more of the bargaining range of $20,000 becomes sunk cost, and the likelihood of a settlement goes steadily up. Eventually, we see settlements just before the trial, during the trial, and occasionally after the jury has retired. It should be pointed out that after the jury has retired, the only issue is the risk. There is no bargaining range left unless the two parties differ on their estimate of the outcome.

This is not to deny that the parties might differ and that if, for example, the plaintiff gives his possibility of success a lower likelihood than the defendant does, it might make it more likely that there would be an agreement. But even if the defendant thinks his probability of success is quite high and the plaintiff disagrees, there will normally still be a bargaining range.

Let us suppose the defendant feels he has a two-out-of-three chance of winning and the plaintiff gives himself also a two-out-of-three chance of winning. This gives a considerable bargaining range. The plaintiff feels that his present expectancy is $10,000, and the defendant feels his present expectancy is −$20,000. Settlement for both sides would be sensible.[10] Thus, we might find the two parties eventually going to trial, although once again as they come closer to trial, the bargaining range tends to shrink.

In sum, one would anticipate that when the case is evenly divided, the parties have strong motives to settle but strong motives to be difficult in their negotiations with the other party. The one who is most unpleasant and holds out longest will make a large profit, and the one who is reasonable and willing to negotiate will lose.

I should not like to argue, however, that things are always symmetrical. For one thing, in a large number of cases plaintiffs are represented by a lawyer on a contingency fee. In a largely overlapping set of cases the defendants are in fact insurance companies. Insurance companies are presumably risk neutral but would like to establish a reputation for toughness and success. Thus they might settle on a fifty-fifty case and make an inadequate offer when they think the odds are in their favor.

The actual plaintiff would prefer to go ahead almost regardless since it doesn't cost anything. The basic decision on that side will probably be made by the contingency fee lawyer, and it's not obvious exactly what decision he

10. It's almost impossible granted the height of American legal fees for the two parties' expectancies to be so radically different that there is no bargaining range.

would make. Thus, we should not be particularly surprised at a considerable variance in the negotiating strategies of the parties.

Consider the situation on one of the edges of the probability distribution. Let us suppose both parties think that the plaintiff has a 95 percent chance of winning. Under these circumstances, it is fairly certain that they're not both going to invest one-third of the amount at issue in legal costs. When the evidence in the case makes the odds high for the plaintiff, there is relatively little that lawyers can do. There won't be a great deal of legal investment. The marginal return on a dollar invested in legal resources is relatively low.

Assume that—once again using our $30,000 case—both parties think that the plaintiff has a 95 percent chance of winning and hence the plaintiff regards his expectancy (not counting legal costs) as $28,500 and the defendant's −$28,500. Each is prepared to spend $1,000 on legal expenses if there is no settlement. The plaintiff has an expectancy of $27,500, and the defendant, −$29,500. The bargaining range is small.

Like the situation late in the trial of a fifty-fifty case, there isn't much to be gained by being unpleasant in the negotiating process. We therefore assume that negotiated settlements would be more common than in a fifty-fifty case. The reason, however, is not that the parties are ill-informed in either case but simply that bargaining and holdouts are less profitable in the ninety-five–five case than in the fifty-fifty case.

Thus, I come close to accepting the Priest and Klein result but not their way of reaching it. It may indeed be true that lawyers are frequently bad at guessing outcomes, and this is certainly true in individual cases because of the extremely high randomness in jury decisions. But that doesn't mean there are systematic errors. It is likely that experienced attorneys looking over cases will come up with pretty similar figures as to the probability of success for the plaintiff.

This would be true both of the fifty-fifty cases and the ninety-five–five ones. The gains from hard bargaining are less for the ninety-five–five cases, however. Of course, in cases in which a professional plaintiff's attorney faces an insurance company, motives are not exactly offsetting, so the outcome is uncertain.

Now let us turn to evidence on errors, again looking at facts rather than law because under Anglo-Saxon procedure it's ambiguous to say that a court makes an error of law. An error of fact is much simpler.

There is also a definitional problem. Suppose that Mr. Smith, a smooth-talking con man, sells Mr. Jones, a rather stupid fellow who is also physically unprepossessing and tends to confuse easily but who inherited a lot of money, a gold mine that turns out not to have any gold in it. Mr. Jones now sues Mr. Smith.

All the attorneys connected with the case may agree that Mr. Smith defrauded Mr. Jones and should be compelled to pay. They all also may agree that Mr. Smith, a glib type, will do very well on the stand and Mr. Jones is likely to collapse under cross-examination. Under the circumstances, they predict success for Mr. Smith with at least a 90 percent probability.

Under these circumstances is it an error if the court decides for Mr. Jones or, alternatively, for Mr. Smith? This is close to a metaphysical problem, and although I've raised it here, I regret to say that I will not be able to solve it. The test for accuracy we will use depends on the actual decisions made by the court. We will look only at the outcome, not the evidence.

Empirical information on the accuracy of courts is hard to get. In Europe, where an appeal is routinely available in fact as well as law,[11] simply counting reversals would almost certainly give an exaggerated number of errors.

A somewhat similar situation has arisen in the United States due to the changes in tort law. Some large corporations are being sued repeatedly on essentially the same facts having to do with alleged product defects. In some of these cases the juries are in radical disagreement. Statistics on the frequency in which this happens would be interesting, but once again this is not a random sample of the total universe.

We are thus driven to other methods. One procedure would be to compare different decision-making groups on the same case. The simplest procedure is to consider cases where a jury decision has been reached and then ask someone else who is present and who had good reason to think about the matter whether he or she agrees with the decision. Kalven and Zeisel in their book *The American Jury*[12] and Baldwin and McConville in their *Jury Trials*[13] use this method. In addition, both books discuss the previous work in this area and so are useful bibliographic sources. Baldwin and McConville, getting into the business after Kalven and Zeisel, do a more thorough job, although their sample was the smaller. Because their work was done in En-

11. In the United States, in theory, the seventh amendment makes it impossible to appeal the fact. In practice there's a good deal of cheating on this provision. Still, normally the original decision on the facts stands.

12. H. Kalven and H. Zeisel, eds., *The American Jury* (Boston: Little, Brown, 1966).

13. J. Baldwin and M. McConville, eds., *Jury Trials* (Oxford: Clarendon Press, 1979).

gland, and Kalven and Zeisel's was done in the United States, there are presumably some differences.

When the judge and jury disagree, it is not at all obvious who is right. It is also obvious that one of them must be wrong. When they agree, they both might be wrong. It is, however, a fairly simple bit of algebra to determine the minimum error likely for one or the other or a mix. Since in the United States a great many criminal trials are in fact conducted by judges and hence U.S. judges are at least as important as juries, judicial error is important. Using algebra, the minimum error that is possible is about one in eight.[14]

Another method is to arrange to have several juries for the same case and then compare their results. This has been done several times with the comparison juries actually sitting in the courtroom. I believe the best published example was conducted by McCabe and Purves, *The Jury at Work*.[15] There have been some cases in the United States, but in general the samples are too small to draw any reliable result. In the English study we again get about one in eight as the minimum error term.[16]

A number of other people have arranged to have court trials recorded or photographed, usually substituting actors for some of the participants, and then have shown these recordings to large numbers of experimental juries. The best and most recent example of this is Hastie, Penrod, and Pennington.[17]

In their example the juries considered a murder charge. Since there was no doubt that the victim was dead and that the cause of his death was a knife stuck into him by the defendant, the only issue was what kind of murder—such as manslaughter, or first degree—should be brought in by the jury. In about two-thirds of the cases the jury reached the decision that the legal advisors of Hastie, Penrod, and Pennington said was correct. Note that accuracy here isn't much greater than 50 percent. But at least none of the juries found the defendant not guilty.

A number of other experiments have run somewhat similar methods,

14. For discussion of the methods together with some bibliography, see Tullock, *Trials on Trial*, pp. 13–48.

15. Sara McCabe and Robert Purves, eds., *The Jury at Work* (Oxford: Basil Blackwell, 1974).

16. Note that this is the minimum. It requires the assumption that juries and courts are more likely to make the correct decisions than errors. The reverse assumption would mean error of seven in eight.

17. R. Hastie, S. Penrod, and N. Pennington, *Inside the Jury* (Cambridge, Mass.: Harvard University Press, 1983).

mainly by the University of Chicago jury project, and they generally show an even higher error rate than this. It does seem that Hastie, Penrod, and Pennington and earlier studies selected more difficult than normal cases to be considered. The technical difference between different levels of murder is a complex issue, and a jury probably would be less adept at determining whether one particular set of acts falls under each level than it would be in determining whether the set of acts occurred. Some of the early University of Chicago studies depended on the unusual claim of not guilty by reason of insanity.

It appears that the criminal court system has an error rate of at least one in eight.[18] Existing experimental and empirical work, however, has been based on the almost complete absence of theoretical considerations of the issues at hand. Researchers have in general shown a great tenderness in their handling of the issue, perhaps because they feel that this area of research might get them into difficulty in their careers or perhaps because they find it painful to consider the likelihood of convicting innocent persons.

This latter issue may be the reason that most experiments involve situations in which the defendant committed a crime so that a decision of guilty is less stressful than it would be if the experiment involved a possibly innocent defendant. Classifying a killing into the right category or deciding whether a man who committed a murder did so while he was insane may be less stressful for participants.

But we need more and better empirical work. Experimental methods have been improving steadily, but researchers need to devote more attention to theory. Further, legal students in general need to pay more attention to the prospect of simple error in the decisions of the courts.

18. This rate is for those cases that are tried. It is difficult to say what the error term is in the ones where the prosecution is dropped or the defendant plea bargains. The tendency on the part of prosecutors to give substantial discounts for a plea, however, is evidence that error is substantial.

LEGAL HERESY

PRESIDENTIAL ADDRESS TO THE WESTERN ECONOMIC ASSOCIATION ANNUAL MEETING—1995

It is always sensible to start a lecture with a joke. As it happens, I know a very good one about presidential addresses. Unfortunately, it is not original with me, it was produced many years ago by a president of the Economic History Society, but the younger of you presumably have not heard it.

A president of a learned society is much like an insect. He lives one year, lays an egg, and dies. You are about to hear my egg.

I started out as a lawyer long ago, and wrote the first book on Economics of the Law,[1] but in essence I have been cast into the outer darkness where there is wailing and gnashing of teeth by the law and economics movement in the United States. The reason for this is simple and straightforward—I am a heretic. I propose to use this opportunity to do a little proselytizing in favor of my heresies.

I should say that the basic characteristic of my heresy is that I am not a great admirer of the Anglo-Saxon common law. Note, I say I am not a great admirer, not that I am a thoroughgoing opponent. I dislike the procedural methods of our legal system, but the substantive law is not markedly worse than that of any other country. Indeed, comparisons usually indicate that on important matters of substance legal systems are much alike, and on the unimportant matters it doesn't make much difference.

I want to concentrate on important laws. For example, my first book explained why we should have laws against theft, robbery, etc. instead of simply accepting that we do. Most work on law in law and economics deals with less important parts of the law, and demonstrates that the courts have it right, which frequently they do, or, particularly in antitrust law, that they have it wrong. There is little on murder, or robbery, not even explanations as to why they should be illegal. Apparently this is thought to be a purely moral matter.

Let us look at the matter a little more formally. In essence, the law consists of three different stages. Firstly, there is some mechanism which detects the violator of the law. If it is the criminal law we normally depend on the police

Reprinted, with permission of Oxford University Press, from *Economic Inquiry* 34 (January 1996): 1–9.

1. *The Logic of the Law*. New York: Basic Books, 1971.

for this, for civil law the person injured is expected to bring the matter to the attention of the court. The court exists essentially to make certain there are no errors in the first stage. In other words the court does not seek out murderers. What it does is try to make sure that the police have actually got the murderer and not some innocent person. We call this the trial. There may be appeals at this stage.

The next stage is the application or threat of coercion to carry out the court's decision. If it turns out that the accused should go to prison for a certain period of time or that the person who loses the civil suit should pay a significant amount of money to the winner, normally it will require force or the threat of force to make certain that the decision is carried out.

The organizational distinction between these three functions is not necessarily the one which we use in the United States. In the European countries, for example, the investigation is supervised or in some cases actually carried out by a legally trained official or magistrate, although he has different titles in different countries. In the investigation this legal official formally decides that the person under investigation is guilty or innocent, and if he decides that he is guilty it goes to a trial, normally before a bench of three.

Thus, the first and second stages of our procedure are to some extent intermingled and the "court" in many ways is sort of half way between our court of first instance and an appellate court. Appeal procedures in Europe differ from ours in one radical way. At least in theory, in the United States the appeals court considers only possible errors of law and not errors of fact. I know that the appeals courts frequently cheat on this issue, but nevertheless normally they follow that rule. In Europe, the appeal is for both law and fact.

Why do we assume that the police will be less accurate than the courts? Stalin made the opposite assumption, and one of the problems of present day Russia is the weak structure of their courts. Vishinsky said that the appearance of the prosecuting attorney in court is the ultimate proof of the guilt of the accused. In general, under the old regime in Russia, the police department was depended upon to decide whether people were innocent or guilty, and the courts had minor functions. Perhaps in some cases like divorce they might actually make a decision, but in crimes they simply ratified the decision of the police.

I take it no one here would regard that as a good system, but why is it that obvious? In most criminal cases in the United States there is no trial. The police and prosecuting attorney decide that they don't really know for certain who committed the crime, and drop further investigation or the accused pleads guilty in return for a lower sentence. Trials occur in only a tiny fraction of the crimes and even a small fraction of all those cases in which a defendant is formally charged. Civil legal disputes also rarely go to trial.

I am going to continue here to talk about the United States system, rather than other arrangements. The question automatically arises of how accurate are our courts and the police. If the courts were perfectly accurate then we would not have to worry about police errors, but on the other hand if the police were perfectly accurate we could refrain from having a court system. Police inaccuracy is obvious from the fact that the overwhelming majority of all crimes go unsolved. With the courts there is a somewhat more difficult problem, but fortunately there is empirical work which makes it possible to put minimum levels of error on the court activity.

To begin with, the empirical data I am going to use have all been gathered by other people. As you probably know I am rather lazy and rarely collect data myself. The people who have done the data collecting in this area normally don't use it to determine the accuracy of the courts. They sometimes argue that it is impossible to determine how many errors are made as you have to know what the correct decision is in order to determine if the court is in error.

This is not strictly true. If a given case has been examined by more than one judge or jury, and they disagree, one must be wrong. When they agree it is possible that both are wrong, but from a given amount of disagreement the minimum level of error which is consistent with that level of agreement can be determined by the application of simple high school algebra.

The University of Chicago jury project circulated a questionnaire to judges covering about 3,000 cases.[2] Among the questions the judges were asked was whether they agreed with the jury decision in a given case. It turned out that they disagreed about one time in four. The minimum percentage of error that is consistent with this, assuming that the error could be either by the judge or by the jury, is one in eight. The data collection was duplicated in somewhat improved form in England with roughly the same conclusions.[3] The English scholars criticized the Chicago jury project heavily for various methodological lapses.

There is another method of dealing with the problem, and that is to arrange to have a number of juries hear the same case and compare their re-

2. H. Kalven and H. Zeisel. *The American Jury*. Boston: Little, Brown, 1966.

3. John Baldwin and Michael McConville. *Jury Trials*. Oxford: Clarendon Press, 1979.

sults.[4] In one case the University of Chicago actually arranged to have three juries, empaneled by somewhat different methods, seated in the court room. One of them was the genuine jury, and the other two were experimental juries. This experiment was stopped after only a few cases had been heard.[5]

I should say there is a minor but non-zero literature by people who have served on juries and who later write up their experience in spite of being told not to. The fact that juries were told not to discuss the case and until recently normally carried out those instructions indicates that proponents of the jury system were deeply suspicious of what would be found if we knew what was going on in the jury room.

It is possible to set up experiments in which people are organized in experimental juries, presented with a case, and record what happened.[6] The University of Chicago jury project began very early doing this, using rather crude recordings of a couple of cases and giving them to a rather large number of groups of people who were told to pretend that they were on the jury. In many cases they did not agree, but instead of dealing with those I am going to turn to a much better study recently carried out by Reid Hastie, Steven Penrod, and Nancy Pennington.[7]

In this experiment, they empaneled a grand total of sixty-nine juries. This was done with the cooperation of a court which was interested, and the jurymen or -women simply were drawn from the usual panel. They did not have to participate in the experiment if they did not want to, and could simply remain in the panel and be called for regular cases, but none of them took advantage of this opportunity.

When the experiment was carried out the juries were divided into three different groups, with twenty-three juries in each group. Each group had a different decision rule. This was the main interest of the authors, but from our standpoint can be ignored. The actual experiment was well done and a genuine case was reenacted with the judge and the two attorneys playing the

4. For some reason duplicate judges have never been used by the experimenters here.

5. The reason for stopping, according to Hans Zeisel who was supervising the experiment, was simply that the results from the non-trial jury were radically different from those of the trial jury. Experimental juries found all defendants guilty, including two cases where the judge had dismissed the charges.

6. Part of the jury project was actually to tape the proceedings of discussion of a real jury. Unfortunately, these records were all destroyed, and presumably the court ordering them destroyed felt that they would bring the institution of the jury into discredit, but it never said that.

7. *Inside the Jury*. Cambridge, Mass.: Harvard University Press, 1983.

roles that they had played in court. Professional actors played the parts of all witnesses. It took about two hours and the trial had taken much longer. Presumably the difference was the time taken up by lawyers in squabbling out of the hearing of the jury.

The result of all this showed an error rate much higher than what we have seen thus far, but in my opinion, the case was more difficult than the ordinary criminal case, although not more difficult than the ordinary civil case.

Specifically, a man had been stabbed and the person who had killed him was on trial. The issue was not whether he had killed the man, but what the charge should be, first- or second-degree murder or manslaughter. The two attorneys and the judge agreed that the correct decision in this particular case was second-degree murder, and thirty-nine out of the sixty-nine juries decided on second-degree murder. You will note this, the obvious compromise decision, is decidedly better than the twenty-three juries who would have chosen this charge if the decisions had been random. Still, it is hard to regard it as a distinguished performance. The error term is much higher than the previous studies. It would appear that our courts are far from perfectly accurate in determining the facts.

In our courts, at least in theory, the judge makes the legal decisions and if he makes an error it can be appealed to a higher court. There is a sort of public myth that judges do not make any mistakes about the law. As far as I know there is no one involved in the legal business who doesn't agree that the judges frequently make mistakes of law. If you talk to a lawyer over a drink he can very easily be pushed into a discussion of the ghastly errors that judges he has dealt with have made and will tell you that some judges are positively stupid. Lawyers are unlikely to say this in public.

There is another bit of evidence. The law in the United States is taught from a case book, although the cases are being reduced in importance. The class consists largely of discussion of these cases and the students are encouraged to criticize the judges' statements about the law. Most students must come to the conclusion that at least one-third of the cases in the case book are wrong.[8] How the students come out with an admiration for the accuracy of the law I don't know, but the fact remains they do. Indeed, I did.

Jack Goode and I worked out a method which makes it possible to determine the minimum number of errors made by the higher level courts.[9] It only applies in cases where there are more than one judge and where dissents are

8. The case books are designed to stimulate controversy by presenting discordant cases.

9. "Judicial Errors and a Proposal for Reform." *Journal of Legal Studies*, June 1984, 67–72.

recorded. If there is a dissent, someone must be wrong. Of course, if there is no dissent, the decision could still be wrong, but it is possible to figure out the minimum error consistent with these disagreements. For the United States this means we can get a minimum error for the appeal and supreme courts. In cases where the Supreme Court splits five to four, the likelihood that the majority is wrong is about 45 percent.

A great many lawyers will take the view that the Supreme Court can't be wrong. Once again, if you change the subject and begin talking about specific cases you will rapidly find that they think a number of the court's decisions were in fact wrong, but this does not prevent them from repeating that the court is infallible. Since the court's decisions become law once made, in a way this is correct. Nevertheless, if any law decided upon by the Supreme Court is by definition right regardless of any other consideration, we could save a great deal of money by simply flipping coins.

Incidentally many legal systems did something very similar to that by making the decisions depend upon various random natural phenomena. Almost as nearly random, in Rome the emperor was frequently a military man who was engaged in campaigns which took up almost all of his mental energy, and who had no legal training. He was nevertheless the ultimate Court of Appeal, and his decisions had the same effect as our Supreme Court decisions do. No one would argue that they were always right.

Proceedings in a given case must at some point come to a halt, and there must be an ultimate decision. This is true whether it is ended by the Supreme Court of the United States, a successful Roman soldier who is temporarily emperor and hearing cases between battles on the borders, or the ordeals which terminated cases in most of Western Europe for a long time.

The fact that we must have some way of ending a case does not indicate that way of ending it is either right with respect to that case or a good way of setting law for the future. It seems more likely that our Supreme Court is right in a given case or with respect to future law than an ill-informed outsider, but to say that is not strong praise.

In talking about the law here I want to point out that many of our cases are decided by juries who in theory decide only the facts and leave the law to the judge. Among people who actually deal with juries, there is no one who believes this theory accurately describes reality. As a matter of fact juries don't know most of the law and in any event they may disapprove of the law and decide to ignore it.

Hastie, Penrod, and Pennington gave all of their jurors a questionnaire after their deliberations in which they asked them about the judge's instructions on the law. The result was so depressing they simply gave up. Apparently, the jurors were only very slightly better than random in their recall of the judge's instructions. Further, this is a case in which the jury would not have very much in the way of personal feelings which might conflict with the law.

Anyone who attends an American court proceeding will be impressed by the degree to which the law is debated by the lawyers. If it is a jury trial the jury is normally excused for this debate, and it may well take up more time than the actual presentation of evidence and argument to the jury. If the law were well known and certain, this kind of debate would be a fairly minor part of our trials, and it is not.

The other evidence of the vagueness of the law is that the courts frequently disagree. For example, the Supreme Court every now and then reverses an earlier decision, frequently with remarks about how bad the previous decision was. Appeal exists to permit the higher courts to reverse the lower courts, although they only do so in a minority of cases. That a great many judges make errors in the law is clear from simply reading the appellate cases. If judges didn't make errors there wouldn't be these differences between the two sets of courts. Granted the extraordinary complexity and vagueness of Anglo-Saxon law, this is no surprise.

I think that many standard law and economics students have by this time in my address begun wondering what it has to do with law and economics. Strictly speaking, very little, because law and economics professors and researchers normally assume implicitly, not explicitly, but implicitly, that the courts will reach the correct decision on the facts and apply the law.

Law and economics specialists mainly devote their efforts to refinements in the law. The characteristic law and economics article will either be a demonstration that a given legal rule in our common law is the most efficient rule of the law for that purpose or, in the minority of cases, a suggestion that it be changed. All of this you will observe assumes that the courts get it right.

It is not true that if the courts have a random error term we should be totally uninterested in the law which they are enforcing. If the courts get the thing right two out of three times, and my guess is they are much better than that, it probably would be desirable that the law to be applied be the most efficient law even though it would only be applied two out of three times. Still the effort which is worth devoting to make certain that the law is perfect would obviously be much lower if it is only going to be correctly applied two out of three times.

When I was in high school computers were not even a dream, and we used slide rules. In using standard slide rules you were taught not to write down more than 3 digits as a solution to any given problem. The reason was that the slide rule lost accuracy beyond that point and the additional digits would be misleading.

It seems to me that we have somewhat the same kind of problem in the economics of the law. The desire to make the actual law perfect implicitly assumes that the slide rule can present as many digits as a mainframe computer. It seems to me that law and economics scholars should devote the bulk of their attention not to refining the details, but to what we might call the main points of the law. The rules against murder, robbery, etc. are basically correct. For this purpose we should be interested in improving the efficiency of the courts.

I was on a committee called together by the attorney general to consider legal reforms. The man sitting next to me was professor of law at Yale, and before the meeting began I remarked to him that the Anglo-Saxon legal procedures were very unusual and out of the scope with the type of legal procedures used in most of the world. He looked at me disapprovingly and said: "You are wrong, our methods are used everywhere." He paused briefly and then said "except in Europe where they don't have civil liberties."

He was implying that Russia, still communist at that time, and Communist China, to say nothing of various African tribal governments, all were using our system, and it was only in barbaric places like Switzerland and Sweden that they were not.

I can see him in my mind's eye shuddering as he encounters a Swiss policeman on the Bahnhofstrasse. When I first visited Sweden the police were still carrying swords, which would surely have convinced him that his life was in danger. I have just said the methods used in most of the rest of the world are drastically different from ours, but my own guess is that you are much safer before a Swiss or Swedish court if you are innocent, and in much more danger before those courts if you are guilty, than with American courts.

Unfortunately, the empirical data to test the accuracy of courts on the continent of Europe are not available, therefore, I can only offer that as an opinion. This opinion is based simply on the view that their method of investigating crimes is more sensible than ours. It is certainly a great deal cheaper.

Obviously, it would be desirable to reduce both the cost and the number of errors made by our courts. Of course, there should be some trade off between cost and error. The cost could be minimized by flipping a coin, and that certainly would not minimize the number of errors.

There are ways of cutting costs and reducing the number of errors, but I must first pause to deal with a problem which I am sure will interest most people in the audience, and that is the general proposition that we want the proceedings to be biased in favor of the accused in criminal cases. We do not seem to think that it should be biased in favor of the defendant in civil cases.

If we bias the proceedings in favor of the defendant, convictions of both innocent and guilty will be less common.[10] It means that in order to acquire the same deterrent effect from the punishment, it is necessary to increase it because guilty people will face a lower probability of receiving it at all. Thus, the innocent person faces a lower probability of receiving a more severe punishment.

I have no empirical knowledge on the degree to which changing the Rules of Evidence to bias a proceeding in favor of a defendant lowers the likelihood of conviction of either guilty or innocent. My article "Court Errors" makes two rather arbitrary calculations on this. I asked some colleagues whether they would prefer a lower penalty with the higher chance of conviction shown by these calculations to a higher penalty with a lower chance of conviction.

In general, buying fire insurance shows considerable risk aversion. My colleagues showed similar risk aversion in my little poll and mostly chose the higher chance of conviction with a lower penalty. I don't think we can put much dependence upon this in view of the arbitrary nature of the calculations. Nevertheless, it is not obvious that biasing the proceedings in favor of the accused is a good idea. It may or may not be. We need further research.

I would now like to turn to certain aspects of the use of the jury. I take it there is no one here who, facing a problem which you think is difficult, and which is important, would suggest going out and collecting twelve people off the street and letting them listen to a contest between two skilled lawyers.

Our courts also distrust juries. *Evidence in a Nutshell* by Paul F. Rothstein says at the beginning of the discussion of evidence "Many (if not most) of the exclusionary rules of evidence exclude evidence because judges have felt that juries would be inclined to give the evidence more effect than they ought. That is, juries could not be trusted to give the evidence its logical, rational weight, or to perceive that it had none, but instead would, perhaps because of the emotional impact of the evidence, allow it to be more persuasive or influential than they should. This can happen where the evidence has some warranted weight as well as where it has none, so long as there is the danger

10. Lenin, characteristically, thought they should be biased against the defendant.

that the jury will not evaluate it properly, but will overinflate its role to an extent that renders the trial better off without the evidence."[11]

Odd as it may seem this distrust is the basis of most of the laws of evidence, although not all. As a comic side-effect here, judges themselves actually conduct many trials. In these cases, the judge is bound by the same laws of evidence and must also avoid evidence which is relevant and material but might prejudice the jury. If you attend courts you will sometimes hear a judge listening to some particular bit of evidence in order to find out whether it violates the laws on evidence, deciding that it does, and then announcing that he will not pay attention to it later in the proceedings. Not many judges actually have the kind of mental discipline necessary to carry out that promise.

One would rather suspect that as the result of many of the laws of evidence (not all of them), the court is automatically somewhat erroneous as it simply ignores certain parts of the valid evidence.

Let us turn to one particular example of this, the hearsay rule. We are perfectly willing in making decisions to consider statements made by A about what was said by B. We wouldn't give it as much weight as we would a direct statement by B, but we would normally give it some weight. Most of the courts in the world follow this rule. We don't, we ban hearsay.

This is not necessarily a protection to the accused. Turning once more to Rothstein: "Suppose D was the only eye-witness and he is now dead; and there is no other evidence either way on the issue. It would seem that the jury is more likely to reach a correct result if the evidence (given by D in a previous trial) is admitted than if it is excluded. This becomes highlighted if we further suppose that his statement is the only thing that can clear Mr. Q of a charge of murder. Remember that all that is needed to acquit is a reasonable doubt. But considerations such as these seem to have no part in the official doctrine, except to the formalistic extent that need and reliability are recognized in the exceptions to the hearsay rule, infra. If it is hearsay, and it does not come within one of the recognized exceptions (which this probably would not), it is inadmissible. And yet, citizens, in making important decisions in their daily lives, commonly rely on their ability to correctly evaluate hearsay."[12]

As a final item of procedural rules where I think we could improve, there is the Fifth Amendment. This is a unique characteristic of Anglo-Saxon law,

11. St. Paul, Minn.: West Publishing Co., 1970, 4–5.

12. *Evidence in a Nutshell*, 119–20.

and until fairly recently it was not even true in Canada. Most people would regard the refusal of a person who is accused of some crime to respond to questions on it as fairly good evidence that he is guilty. It would not be conclusive as there are special circumstances in which he might refuse to respond even though he was not guilty of the crime, but normally we would regard this as evidence of his guilt.

Apparently juries normally behave this way. If the defendant does not take the stand in his own defense they are likely, not certain, but likely to regard this as evidence that he is guilty, even though the judge tells them they shouldn't. There is a somewhat interesting problem here. A number of scholars think that the judge telling them they should ignore the fact that the defendant has not taken the stand is likely to call it to their attention and make them more likely to take it into consideration. Thus, whether the judge should or should not instruct them to ignore it is a somewhat controversial question.

If suspected of a crime in "barbaric" Switzerland or Sweden one of the first things that will happen is that the examining magistrate will ask you about the facts. In France, there is almost a ceremony of taking you off to the scene of crime and questioning you there. Needless to say, you are not tortured for not talking, and it is not a crime to refuse to answer such questions any more than it is a crime in the United States to say you are not guilty when you are guilty. The only known reason for not taking the refusal as evidence in the United States is a long-standing tradition.

There are, then, a number of fairly obvious ways of improving the accuracy of our courts at no significant cost. Another approach would be simply to compare carefully our proceedings and those in other countries. Following the implicit view of my former neighbor from Yale, we could study Iran and Communist China as well as places "where they don't have civil liberties" like Switzerland and Sweden, in order to determine whether our procedure can be improved.

Even better would be to set up formal experiments. We could use rather simple experiments in which we specify a problem where there is a correct answer and see how well different possible court procedures reach it. The early experiments would no doubt be very primitive, not very helpful, but not terribly expensive. It is likely that after we have had experience we would be in a position to set up much more complicated experiments which would, no doubt, be very expensive. Still, given the number of trials we have, and the cost socially of going wrong, spending money would seem reasonable.

As a matter of fact there is something a little bit like this already in existence. It is called arbitration and is actually a private trial which the two parties have agreed to. Presumably, they are interested in low cost and high accuracy before the incident which leads to the arbitration has occurred. After the occurrence of the cause of the action, it may be that one of the two parties is not interested in high accuracy if he thinks the other party is right. Agreements to arbitrate are easiest to negotiate before the incident occurs.

This method is not as helpful as it might be as these arbitration tribunals depend upon the regular courts to enforce their decisions eventually. The regular courts insist upon at least some pretense of following standard legal procedure before they will enforce an arbitrator's decision. Thus arbitrators are not completely free to experiment with any possible procedure. Still, from what I know of what they actually do they seem to a large extent to behave much like a European Continental court dealing with a civil case. They never call juries. Interestingly, in general there is no appeal.

What we need here obviously is careful review not of the minutiae of the law, but of methods we use to enforce it. This will lead to a great deal of conflict with an awful lot of the mythology which most people have been trained in. Our current system was not the result of conscious design but of ad hoc decisions made by judges, kings, bishops, etc. in the past. The Continental system which is radically different from ours is equally the product of such a long series of ad hoc decisions.

In both of these cases after that long period of decisions without central planning, codes were enacted, on the Continent primarily by Napoleon, and in our case by a very large number of special legislative actions. These codes followed the procedure which was already customary in their particular area. This procedure has little to recommend it except tradition. We should try to do better in the future and for this we need a good deal of research which the economists are better fitted to carry out than the lawyers.

JURIES

The jury is a very old institution, but it is not the normal human way of dealing with crimes or disputes. If we look at the world as a whole it has not been used a great deal. The more normal ways are a professional judge or judges or, in many cases, simply an executive officer who has judicial decisions as one of his duties. The district commissioner of the old British Empire, the magistrate in the old Chinese Empire, and the Roman Emperor are all examples.

As an introduction to the study of the jury, let us begin by inquiring why anyone might want a jury to make decisions as opposed to the other two methods that I have just mentioned. Let us begin with a little investigation of relatively pure theory.

Athenian Juries

Consider, for example, Athens. I should here emphasize that the origin of the American or English jury was not the Athenian jury. Indeed the Norman jury from which our system started was quite radically different. It seems unlikely, granted the fact that this was before the full revival of classical learning, that any of the people involved actually even knew about the Athenian jury. Nevertheless, our present jury oddly enough resembles the Athenian jury more closely than it does its actual historical antecedents.

The Athenian jury is not only to some extent similar to ours but also permits a more sensible theoretical investigation than do the early juries which were in fact the ancestors of ours. The voting population, which was a large part of the total population, assembled on the Pynx to vote on various governmental matters.

We can divide the things that they dealt with into two rough classes, depending on the importance of the issue. Clearly, deciding individual legal cases would tend to be less important than: "Shall we go to war?" Going to the Pynx and voting was a tedious activity, so tedious that many of the citi-

Reprinted, with permission of Palgrave Macmillan, from *The New Palgrave Dictionary of Economics and the Law*, vol. 2, ed. Peter Newman (London: Macmillan, 1998), 395–400.

zens only went there occasionally. A way of factoring out the less important cases would seem sensible, and hence the delegating of law cases to a smaller group.

One way of doing this would be to draw a random sample of the potential voters and let them hear the evidence and make up their minds on the less important decisions. This was the method chosen by Athens. There could be two possible justifications for this. The most important one is simply that it would produce, with some random variance, the same solution as would the meeting of the entire citizen body on the Pynx dealing with the same case.

Obviously this random variance could be easily calculated by modern statistical methods to which the Athenians had no access. Nevertheless, they were presumably aware of the fact that on occasion juries would bring in a different result than would the entire people if it had been presented to them. In a way it was a low cost method of approximating a meeting of the entire body politic.

Insofar as juries are drawn randomly this is still true, although our present juries are small enough that the random variance would presumably be quite high. Note that the random variance here would depend on what one might call the strength of the evidence on both sides. In conclusive cases, the citizen body voting as a whole would presumably be close to unanimous and hence random samples drawn from it would tend to come close to unanimity too. In more difficult cases the citizen body might split, so one would expect that the juries would have a good deal of variance in their outcome. This would account for the failure to use juries for such things as declarations of war.

Rationale for Juries, I

There are two possible explanations for this desire to get a decision similar to what the populace as a whole have produced. One of these is simply a democratic feeling that what everybody wants is what should be done. The majority, in other words, is its own justification.

Even if one doesn't feel that the majority should control such things as criminal cases one might still feel that domestic peace would be best maintained if decisions were always those which the majority would probably approve. Thus, the jury would produce a result which could be depended on not to set off riots or other difficulties.

This argument would apply not just to democracies but to despotisms.

Napoleon was a great proponent of the use of jury. Probably he was less interested in whether John Smith did indeed murder Jane Smith than in preventing popular discontent over the outcome of the case. If the case is decided by a random sample of the population, disturbances are on the whole unlikely because the population will probably approve of the decision and will, in any event, not blame the despot. Whether this is important or not, I do not know.

Rationale for Juries, II

We return later to the question of getting the same decision by the jury method as the populace as a whole would reach. Let us turn now to the second possible reason for regarding the jury as desirable: that it is a good way of getting at the truth. Mr. Simpson either did or did not murder his wife. Is the jury, or in this case, two juries, a good way of reaching this decision?

I have difficulty in believing that anyone would think that it is a good way to reach the truth. Insofar as I know there is no place in our entire governmental or private decision making processes where we call in a group of twelve people who know nothing about the subject, have advocates on both sides present arguments, require unanimity in most cases, and then accept their decision. The U.S. Constitution, Article seven, says "No fact tried by a jury shall be otherwise re-examined in any court of the United States than according to the rules of common Law."

In any event, bias is by no means absent from the jury. Today, in 1997, we are in the process of recovering from the two jury trials of Mr. Simpson for murder. In the first trial a jury which consisted of ten African-Americans, one Mexican-American, and one white woman found him innocent.

The civil suit was decided by a non-African-American jury. This jury found him guilty. Thus, as can be seen, there was a complete racial break on the decision in this matter. These were exceptional cases, however. Normally the juries do not have this degree of ethnic purity. Racially mixed juries do not show such apparent extreme racial determinism.

In practice, the higher courts sometimes find ways of avoiding the decision of a jury, but it is certainly true that this group of citizens, who know very little about the case when they come in, and frequently know very little about it at the end of trial (a matter which we will discuss below), usually makes the final decision. This is true even if the subject matter is the execution of an individual or a civil suit in which perhaps hundreds of millions of dollars are involved. The famous *Texaco v. Pennzoil* case[1] involved more than half a billion dollars.

It should perhaps be mentioned that although the jury is probably a pretty good measure of what the average citizen would do, in the United States most non-federal judges are subject in one way or another to an election process and hence are probably apt to respond to the average person's preferences also. The judicial selection process tends to be complicated and perhaps heavily biased, but is still subject to popular control.

Judges in most state courts are probably not as close to the average citizen as would be a randomly selected jury, but they are not wildly different. In the 1980s a man who believed in the Law of Moses, i.e. the Bible as the ultimate law code, was *elected* to the Texas Supreme Court. This was apparently because he had the same name as a recently deceased, highly popular Senator.

Accuracy of Jury

Consider the jury procedure as a way of determining the truth. The author of this essay has published several books containing measurements of the likely error in jury cases. I also used it as a theme in my presidential address to the Western Economic Association Annual Meeting in 1995.[2] I have also dealt with it in a number of unpublished lectures. None of these computations has aroused comment. This is quite notable, because the empirical data that I used to calculate these error measures have always been collected by others, who have themselves never used them to calculate the probable accuracy of the courts.

I rather suspect that jury accuracy or inaccuracy is a taboo subject. After all, any person is subject to the prospect of being falsely accused of a crime and finding that he has to convince a group of twelve people that he is innocent. Thinking about the likelihood that the twelve people will go wrong is painful and apparently most scholars refrain from doing so.

Possibility of Corruption

Another possibility is the feeling that the majority is more likely to be factually right than is the decision of some specialist or a high-ranking executive

1. *Texaco, Inc. v. Pennzoil*, 729 SW2d 768 (Tex. 1987).

2. G. Tullock, "Legal Heresy," *Economic Inquiry* 34(1) (1996): 1–9.

official. When I talk to people about this they normally present bias and bribery as arguments for the jury. I see no reason to believe that the specialist is more likely to be biased than the people as a whole. Aristides was, after all, exiled, Socrates put to death, and Aristotle found it necessary to flee Athens. Jury bias, of course, would be in the direction of current public opinion.

The bribery argument is to some extent true since directly bribing a large number of people would be difficult. Still, historically popular assemblies have been strongly influenced by combining the decision on one proposal with another, the second proposal being to give everybody or some powerful bloc some advantage. American Justices of the Peace were for a long time compensated by keeping half of any fine they levied. It is frequently alleged that this led them to be particularly likely to convict. Juries would probably respond to a similar fee system much like the Justices of the Peace. Fortunately, this is not our practice. It should be pointed out that popular assemblies and for that matter elected assemblies do behave that way. The farm programme of practically any democratic government may be used as an example. There is a better example in Athens itself. The Athenian government developed the habit, voted on by the citizens, of paying a fee to every citizen who turned up to vote. This had much to do with the decline of Athenian power since it led to fiscal stringency and a decline in appropriations for the navy.

Nevertheless, preventing bribery of judges should be fairly easy if the government in fact wants to do it. In order for the judge to be bribed he must let the litigants know that he is in the market. In other words, he must discreetly advertise. A police that really wanted to prevent corruption on the part of judges (or juries) could presumably look out for such advertisements and make the arrest.

Anglo-Saxon Origins

So much for a basically theoretical discussion of juries. We will return to factual measures of how they perform in a moment, but let us first consider actual historic origins of the jury in England and Normandy about the time of the Conquest. As we will see, the early juries were almost the exact opposite of present juries. Instead of selecting a group of people who did not know the case and presenting evidence to them, the jury was expected to make the decision on its own without evidence because the people selected were thought to know the truth.

It should be realized that in a small isolated village such as most of the English population lived in around 1100, that its leading citizens would know who had committed crimes recently is not a terribly unlikely hypothesis. In any event there was to some extent in the previous Anglo-Saxon government and in the Norman government in France a system of obtaining information for government use by conscripting a small collection of normally prominent and trustworthy local citizens, and asking them to make statements under oath. The Domesday Book, for example, seems to have been compiled largely by this method.

This procedure was carried out with respect to crimes and civil suits, insofar as there were civil suits in those days, as well as for collecting data for taxes and the like. In the beginning a person that was found guilty of a crime by some of his more prominent neighbours, who had heard no evidence, could ask for a trial by ordeal or abjure the realm. If he were a noble he could, of course, choose trial by battle.

Historical Development

The gradual shift of the jury from a collection of people who were expected to know whether the defendant was guilty or innocent to a system where they were expected to make their decision on the evidence is not well documented.

In 1219 the Lateran Council prohibited priests from participating in trials by ordeal, and since the priest's presence was necessary in such trials, England suddenly found itself without any real trial procedure at all. Although the history here is rather vague, the English courts seem then to have fallen back on the jury.

The original jury clearly was assumed to know the truth, with the consequence that it was not necessary to present evidence; but, with time, evidence began to be presented. Even though defendants were legally prohibited from having a lawyer, producing evidence which might be helpful was something which the defendants could still do, and of course the crown would produce evidence on the other side.

There is once again some difficulty here, but it would appear that with time the jury which decided that somebody should be tried and the jury which actually conducted the trial (if the defendant was not simply "known" to be guilty by public knowledge) became separate. The juries, however, still depended very strongly on their own local knowledge. Indeed as late as the reign of Edward VI it was formally decided that the evidence could not overbalance the prior knowledge of the jury.

It should be emphasized that the juries, even when they began to be primarily people who listened to evidence and made a decision on that, were not random selections from the population. They tended to be substantial upper-class citizens.

To the present day a member of the peerage has the right to be tried by the House of Lords, although it has been quite a while since any of them has availed him- or herself of the right. It seems likely that if one did, the right would rapidly disappear.

In the United States, on the other hand, from the beginning we had a much wider part of the population eligible for juries. In recent years England has followed in the same path. Of course the introduction of the arrangement under which lawyers can play a considerable role in selecting who actually sits on the jury is also a relatively recent innovation.

Continental Procedure

If we leave the English-speaking countries, there are still various remnants of Napoleon's desire to impose the jury all over Europe. Indeed it is even being expanded: Spain has just adopted the jury as its basic trial method, and the jury has been adopted in some parts of Russia since the reform. Considering the nature of the Russian judiciary, that was probably an improvement. In most places where the Napoleonic juries have left behind some remnants, only very special cases are tried by jury.

There is a good deal of difference in jury procedures. Some of the Swiss cantons until recently used a jury of fifteen, which convicted on two-thirds majority and acquitted on a simple majority. In the American and English jury, unanimity is generally required, so hung juries are quite possible. In recent years a number of states in the United States have adopted ten out of twelve for at least civil juries and in some cases juries may be set at numbers other than the sacred twelve. The author of this essay was called as an expert witness in a case where there were only six jurors.

Recently in a number of European countries there has been another effort to get laymen into court proceedings. The bench in a trial will consist of one professional judge and two laymen. The way the laymen are selected varies from country to country, but they normally hold office for only very short periods of time. The actual trial is largely conducted by the professional judge, although the laymen are of course free to ask questions, and the three of them then retire and make their decision.

The argument for this, and it is also sometimes offered as an argument for the jury, is that they do not want the procedure to be too legalistic. To be frank I have never understood this. If you don't like the laws, the sensible thing to do is to change or repeal them, not keep them on the statute books but then deliberately fail to enforce them.

Empirical Studies

But to return to the issue of jury accuracy and the facts, we find scattered through judicial opinions and legal commentaries remarks about "the great practical knowledge" of the jury and nearly no research to indicate that this is indeed "great." There is, however, some research which makes it possible to make calculations on the accuracy of our courts.

Kalven and Zeisel at the University of Chicago sent letters to judges in about three thousand cases in which they asked them various questions about individual cases. These were all jury cases although somewhat more than half of American trials are conducted by the judge alone.

One of the questions was whether they agreed with the jury. In one-quarter of the cases they did not. Kalven and Zeisel[3] say you cannot tell how accurate the jury is because you do not know what the actual truth is, but if the judge and jury disagree, at least one of them must be wrong. When they agree it is possible that they are both wrong. This is an elementary problem in high school algebra. The minimum number of errors which will generate the numbers reported by Kalven and Zeisel is about one case in eight.

Baldwin and McConville[4] repeated more or less the same experiment in Britain, with considerably more methodological sophistication. Their sample was somewhat smaller, but the numbers permit calculating the accuracy of the courts with about the same results as Kalven and Zeisel. Note that they, like Kalven and Zeisel, did not calculate the accuracy themselves.

There is another obvious way of measuring the accuracy of juries, which

3. H. Kalven and H. Zeisel, *The American Jury* (Boston: Little-Brown, 1966).

4. J. Baldwin and M. McConville, *Jury Trials* (Oxford: Clarendon Press, 1979).

is to let a number of juries watch the same trial. There is only one case in which this was even experimented with. It was in Chicago and was given up before any significant results had been developed.

Experiments

It is possible, however, to produce a film strip of a case and then show that to a number of juries. Presumably the juries would not be quite so conscientious in making their decisions as if something really turned on them, but it is still a good research design. Hastie, Penrod, and Pennington[5] used this method. They took a perfectly genuine murder case and with the assistance of a trial judge impanelled, one after another, sixty-nine juries.

These were ordinary juries conscripted in the usual way and then asked if they wished to participate in an experiment, or go back into the regular pool. About 75% chose to participate, so these juries were relatively normal, except that they had passed only an abnormally brief *voir dire* procedure, which is a part of a normal trial that permits the attorneys to do some things to make the jurymen more likely to be biased on their side.

The experimental case was presided over by the judge who presided over the original case and the prosecuting and defence attorneys were those who participated in the original case. In general, the original case was duplicated as closely as was practicable.

There were four possible outcomes here. The defendant made a rather feeble effort to convince people that he acted in self defence. This was largely ignored. This left the choice of one of three outcomes, first-degree murder, second-degree murder, or manslaughter, for the jury to decide. The jury verdicts were split: 6 first-degree murder, 39 second, and 20 for manslaughter. Four juries were hung. The judge and the two attorneys thought that second-degree murder was the correct decision, and the jury in the actual trial had reached the same conclusion.

This performance is better than random, but far from distinguished. It is likely that juries have more difficulty with essentially legal questions than with matters of fact. Since the distinctions between the various types of illegal killing are less than perfectly clear, the variance here may have been greater

5. R. Hastie, S. Penrod, and N. Pennington, *Inside the Jury* (Cambridge, Mass.: Harvard University Press, 1983).

than in cases where only factual matters must be decided. Advocates of the jury, however, never suggest that they should not decide cases where they must judge legal problems as well as factual.

Hastie et al. made no effort to compute the accuracy of the juries. Their experiment had been designed to test which of various jury voting rules was best. The results cast no light on this question. Their failure to calculate accuracy from their data, however, does suggest the existence of some sort of taboo on that subject.

After the trial was over a test was administered to the juries to test their recall of the evidence and the judge's instructions on the law. The jurymen answered the questions right 60% of the time for facts and 30% in matters of law.

Legal Comments on the Jury

It is not only the more or less scientific studies I have been discussing thus far that show inaccuracy of the jury. The courts themselves seem to distrust them. There are a large number of rules requiring the exclusion of various types of evidence. The *Nutshell* series is a set of reference books for law students. Paul F. Rothstein in the *Evidence* volume[6] summarizes the standard view:

> Many (if not most) of the exclusionary rules of evidence exclude evidence because judges have felt that juries would be inclined to give the evidence more effect than they ought. That is, juries could not be trusted to give the evidence its logical, rational weight, or to perceive that it had none, but instead would, perhaps because of the emotional impact of the evidence, allow it to be more persuasive or influential than they should. This can happen where the evidence has some warranted weight as well as where it has none, so long as there is the danger that the jury will not evaluate it properly, but will over-inflate its role to an extent that renders the trial better off without the evidence, but clearly the courts do not have much confidence in juries.

6. P. F. Rothstein, *Evidence in a Nutshell*, 5th ed. (St. Paul, Minn.: West Publishing Company, 1974).

Further on the Rationale of the Jury

So far I have talked about the reasons for believing that the jury is not a wonderful technique, if what one is trying to do is to find out the truth. If what one is trying to do is to produce the democratic outcome, i.e., the outcome which the people as a whole would vote for if they were given a chance, the jury is an excellent technique. If that is our purpose, however, we could make large economies by throwing away most of the existing law libraries and shortening legal training.

If the jury is as bad as I think it is, why do we continue to use it? It could be that I am mistaken, but it is also possible that there are good reasons why even an inept scheme will be continued. For several centuries doctors regularly bled people for whatever ailed them, although bleeding (with a dirty knife) is bad for almost every disease.

The most obvious explanation is simply inertia. That was no doubt one of the reasons that bleeding was continued for such a long time, and in political matters inertia is certainly a very strong factor.

Although inertia is an obvious explanation, it is usual for Public Choice scholars like myself to try to seek out some special group or power which has either the ability to create some institution or to retain it. In this case the obvious group is the trial lawyers. Historically, lawyers have earned a good deal of money by arguing before jurors and there is no doubt that the length of time and skill needed to present a case to jurors is a good deal higher than that needed to present a case to three judges, as in the Continental procedure.

This doesn't seem a terribly strong argument over the long period of history, but American legislatures have been dominated by lawyers throughout most of our history.

Today in the United States there is a very obvious set of very powerful interests that want to retain the jury. These are the tort lawyers, who are very organized, very wealthy, and who give very large gifts to the candidates for various government offices. There are also experts who testify before the jury for high fees. Their major expertise is looking sincere, and that would probably not impress judges. The strength of this combination is illustrated by the long series of lawsuits which forced Dow-Corning into bankruptcy in spite of the weak, indeed almost non-existent, scientific evidence.

Further, the tort lawyers are experts at convincing the average citizen.

They have beaten a number of referendums aimed at weakening their power by the use of basically the same persuasive strategy as in influencing a jury.

Once again, it seems that the pressure that the organized lawyers can exert would have been less in the past. In England, where the barrister and solicitor appear to have less power, the jury seems to be in a process of gradual abandonment. It's pretty much gone in civil litigation and there are signs that it will be sharply restricted in criminal matters also.

The present discussion of the reasons for retaining the jury are not very conclusive. Indeed, some of my colleagues believe that inertia is the obvious and total explanation and I am far from certain that they are wrong. It may be that inertia is simply reinforced by the pressure groups I have listed above.

Jury Selection

Rules differ a good deal from place to place, but in much of the United States, particularly in state courts, attorneys are permitted to question the potential jurors and throw some of them out either because they can convince the judge that the candidate would be biased, or arbitrarily since they usually have a certain number of arbitrary challenges.

In recent years the Supreme Court has been taking an interest in this matter and ruling that the use of arbitrary challenges to get rid of blacks or women may be improper. In the first Simpson trial the defence seems to have used its powers to get rid of as many whites as possible, but the courts have not held that improper.

The federal courts have a great deal of freedom in choosing their jurors. My own recent experience was in a case of considerable importance where they had called 114 jurors to be sure that they would have enough for the case after the attorneys had objected to some.

The Chief Judge of the federal court in Tucson went around the 114 candidates and asked each one of them three or four questions. Then we were removed and the lawyers who had been sitting quietly while this was going on flocked to the bench. We were then called back and 14 (12 members and two alternates) were announced as the jury by the judge, and the rest of us dismissed.

This is a federal court where the judges have a good deal of discretion, and apparently the Chief Judge thought that this was a suitable system. In the state court, in general, the matter would have taken a great deal more time and the attorneys would have questioned the candidates in the hope of selecting people who, if not biased in favour of their side, at least were not biased against it.

I should perhaps say that if you are called for jury and don't want to serve, simply exhibiting bias or incoherence during this question period will get you out; say: "I am completely impartial, I just want to know if he was drunk at the time."

Further Research

It used to be that juries were instructed not to speak to anyone about the deliberations after they were over, and it was contempt of court to question them. This is no longer so and the jurymen are routinely questioned after the trial by the attorneys who want to find out what they did right or wrong and reporters who hope for a story. Insofar as I know, academics have not devoted serious research time to this kind of questioning of jurors.

Here in Tucson we are about to have a new experiment. Several trials are going to be carried out with television cameras not only in the court room but actually in the jury room. The results are to be broadcast over cable. The number of cases is very small and I doubt that the jurors will behave under these circumstances as they would in a closeted jury. I am not sure that the information will be valuable, but students probably should look at it.

Summing Up

The jury is not a good technique and personally I would prefer to be tried by a professional judge if I were falsely accused. Nevertheless, it is not true that juries do not take the matter seriously. The evidence we have indicates that they think the matter over and discuss it. The problem is they may not fully understand the case or they may be seriously biased. Further, as a general rule they do not know the law, and the judges' instructions are normally confusing. If they did know the law they would still be likely to follow their own ethical principles even if they conflicted with the law.

The statement that the United States is a country ruled by law and not by men is false when juries make the final decision.

PART 10

BIOECONOMICS

THE COAL TIT AS A CAREFUL SHOPPER

The interrelation between economics and biological sciences has perhaps been less obvious in recent years than it was in the days of Malthus, Darwin, and Wallace. Still, structural similarities between the two fields do exist, and the recent interest in ecology has led a great many economists to become concerned with biological problems and biologists to become concerned with economic problems.[1] The particular interrelation between economics and biology discussed in this article is not a direct result of concern about pollution, but it may be that I — an economist — read Lack[2] as an indirect consequence of concern with the problems of pollution and population.

Regardless of the reasons, it is true that I was reading Lack's book, and in it I came across a summary of the work of J. Gibb on the consumption of the eucosmid moth *Ernarmonia conicolana* by coal tits which contains a figure (reproduced here) which looks surprisingly like a standard economic demand and supply diagram.[3] A little examination indicated that it was not a true demand and supply curve, but nevertheless that economic principles do apply quite readily. Indeed, it can be said that the coal tits are maximizing the return to their labor in searching out food supplies. We need not, of course, argue that the coal tits have thought the matter out in the same way that human beings would. Presumably, they have inherited an efficient pattern of behavior resulting from natural selection which would eliminate inefficient heritable behavior patterns.

Before discussing this matter, however, it would be best to explain very briefly the data assembled by Gibb.[4] In the winter, the coal tit eats the larvae

Reprinted, with permission of the University of Chicago Press, from *American Naturalist* 105 (January–February 1971): 77–80.

1. Garrett Hardin, "The Tragedy of the Commons," *Science* 162 (1968): 1243–48; Gordon Tullock, "Switching in General Predators: Comment," *Bulletin of the Ecological Society of America* 51 (1970): 21–23.

2. David Lack, *Population Studies of Birds* (London: Clarendon Press, 1966). 94 p.

3. Ibid., p. 396.

4. J. Gibb, "Predation by Tits and Squirrels on the Eucosmid *Ernarmonia conicolana (Heyl.)*," *Journal of Animal Ecology* 27 (1958): 375–96, and "Tits and Their Food Supply in English Pine Woods: A Problem in Applied Ornithology," in *Festschrift der Vogelschutzwarte f. Hessen, Rheinland-Pfalz und Saarland* (1962), 58–66.

of *E. conicolana* dormant in small cavities just under the surface of pine cones. The coal tit finds them by tapping the outside of the cone. Fortunately, from the standpoint of the ecologist, it is possible to tell by looking at the pine cone in the spring whether any individual larva was eaten by the coal tit, destroyed by some other cause, or survived and became a moth. By examining the pine cones in various portions of the forest, Gibb first determined how many larvae had been in the pine cones the preceding fall. The result, arranged in order of density from left to right, is shown as the upper line in figure 1. The gently curving lines—*A*, *B*, and *C*— drawn in on the figure are my contribution, and were not on Gibb's original diagram.

The shaded area shows the number of *E. conicolana* larvae who survived predation by coal tits in each area. The space between the shaded area and the upper line is the number of grubs of *E. conicolana* consumed by the coal tits. The pattern of consumption is said by Lack to be "density dependent," and Gibb offers as an explanation a concept called "hunting by expectation." It seems to me, however, that a much simpler explanation exists. The birds are behaving much like a careful housewife; that is, they are shopping in the cheapest market. This human analogy may seem bizarre, but I hope to prove it is not misleading. The amount of energy put into seeking out each *E. conicolana* larva is, in a way, a "price" which the bird must pay to consume the larva. It is clear that any animal, in order to remain alive, must be economical in its use of energy to obtain food. An inherited behavior pattern which led to such economy would have survival value, not only in consumption of *E. conicolana* but in many other types of food as well.

This presents us with a rather simple economic problem. First, note that the amount of pine cone tapping which would be necessary to find an unconsumed larva would be inversely proportional to the density of these larvae in any given area. In other words, the "price" which the coal tit must pay for each larva it consumes is the reciprocal of the density at any given time. Just as a careful housewife will buy at a cheaper shop, one should anticipate that the coal tit would seek its grubs in those areas where the energy cost would be lowest.

There is, however, an important difference between the housewife and the bird, in that the housewife can discover the prices in different shops without affecting the stock-in-trade held by the shops; she notes the price, but does not buy if it is high. The bird, however, would fly from place to place and explore the density of grubs by tapping a number of pine cones. Even in low-density areas (such as those at the right of the distribution in the figure), this would lead to some consumption of grubs. Hence, one would anticipate that there would be at least some reduction in the number of larvae by coal tit

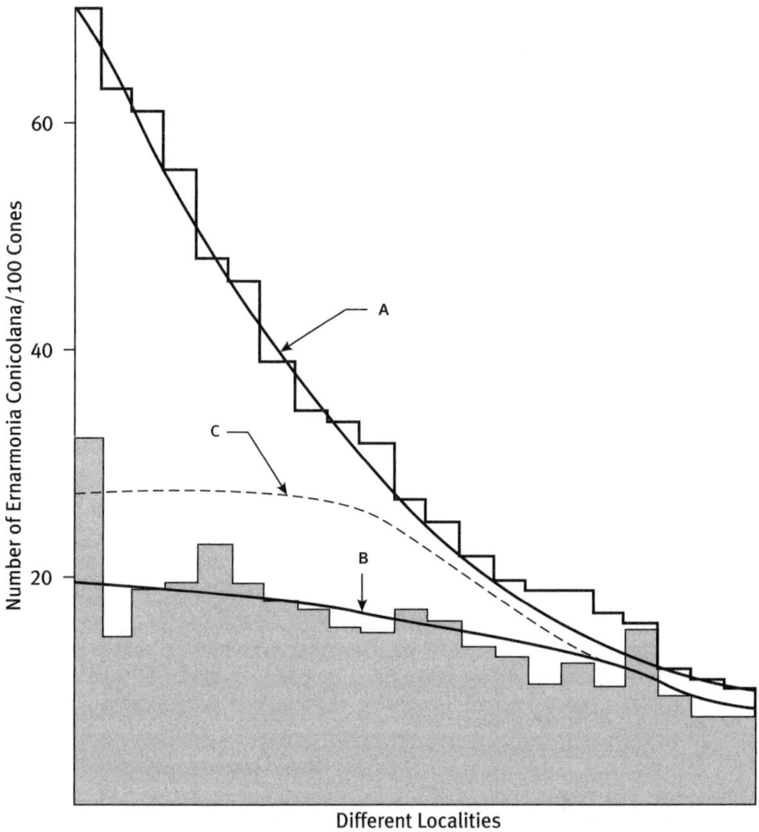

FIGURE 1

Numbers of *Ernarmonia conicolana* larvae per 100 cones in 21 localities, arranged in descending order of initial intensity of larvae. Upper (hollow) "skyline" graph gives initial number of larvae, lower (shaded) graph the number after predation by tits in the winter of 1955–56. The two curves *A* and *B*, are eyefit curves approximating the two skyline graphs. Curve *C* is a hypothesized intermediate stage during the predation season.[5]

predation in all areas. This is the coal tit equivalent of comparison shopping. Basically, however, the bulk of the predation would occur in those areas in which the grubs were commonest.

Note that as the winter went on, and grubs were eaten in the areas where they were densest, the density there would fall, and a switch of effort to other

5. Modified from figure 3 in Gibb, "Predation by Tits and Squirrels."

areas would become desirable. We would anticipate that at any time during the winter the general structure of the surviving larvae population would follow roughly the conformation of the dotted line. There would be an approximately flat plateau on the left and, on the right, a line which more or less followed the original density but was lower. The search process would probably lead to the plateau actually slanting somewhat to the right, and that portion of the line to the right of the inflection point gradually approaching the original density to the right. By spring, a line similar to that which was found in Gibb's empirical investigation would be expected. Note that this hypothesis is empirically testable. It predicts that the distribution of surviving larvae in pine plantations from month to month during the winter should follow a series of progressively lower lines, each characterized by a plateau on the left and a curving structure on the right. If this does not turn up empirically, the theory would be falsified.

So far, however, I have simply argued by analogy to the housewife's behavior. It is not immediately obvious that bird behavior patterns would duplicate human behavior. If we assume, however, that the bird has inherited reasonably efficient patterns of behavior, then we can obtain the same result. Assume that the bird, like any other food-consuming animal, explores a number of different food sources, and then settles on the one which provides the most food with the least energy expended. Since it would tend to exhaust the food supplies in that particular area, it should be "programmed" in such a way that it periodically investigates different areas. If I may put it in anthropomorphic terms, the animal should be hungry, lazy, and curious. We need not assume that the bird has feelings which are close to these human emotions, but a behavior pattern which leads to a similar output would be relatively easy to conceive of. Its survival value is, I take it, obvious. A bird that did not inherit behavior patterns which led it to economize on the energy investment in obtaining its food would presumably not survive very long.

It may surprise biologists and certainly will surprise economists to learn that it is possible to use segments of economic theory to explain biological phenomena. Nevertheless, it seems to me that the problems of biologists are difficult enough so that they should seek help wherever it seems to them that their particular competence may be of value. This essay is, then, an effort to establish a minor link between two fields which at one time were very closely connected, but have grown apart. The fact that the link is not one of major importance is unfortunate, but such interconnections seem worthwhile even if they are on a small scale.

BIOLOGICAL EXTERNALITIES

The recent rise of interest in problems of pollution and similar matters has led to considerable contact between those biologists interested in ecology and economists interested in the special economic field of "externalities."[1] It is the point of this essay to indicate that there are certain interrelations between the economics of externality and the problems of ecology, which are different from those ordinarily studied. Specifically, I propose to use the economics of externality as an analytical tool in dealing with natural ecological systems. Plants and animals have effects on other plants and animals, and the effects of these externalities are very much the same as the externalities which human beings impose on each other or upon the natural environment.

The results of this investigation will be, I think, somewhat startling to the biologist. I think I can demonstrate that the climax state of any ecological system is inferior. That, substantially, regardless of what value one puts upon the individual species within the ecological system and/or their usefulness to man, it is nevertheless possible always to improve upon the system produced by "nature." In order to make such a judgment which will fit any one of a vast number of different sets of values, I will be compelled to make use of an economic concept known as Pareto optimality, albeit in a radically reformed manner. Pareto optimality was first suggested as a way of avoiding making certain types of value judgments, and it can be used in evaluating biological systems in a similar way.[2]

Reprinted from *Journal of Theoretical Biology* 33 (December 1971): 565–76, with permission from Elsevier.

1. Otherwise referred to as neighborhood effects or public goods and bads. At this point, I shall not include a technical definition of externalities since the meaning of the term will become clear to the reader as he goes along. I should perhaps warn economists that the word, although within the normal scope, will have somewhat different application than the one to which he is accustomed. For some recent literature showing the contact between biologists and economists, see G. Hardin, "The Tragedy of the Commons," *Science* 162 (1968): 1243–48; G. Tullock, "Switching in General Predators: Comment," *Bulletin of the Ecological Society of America* 51 (1970): 21–24; and Tullock, "The Coal Tit as a Careful Shopper," *American Naturalist* 105 (1971): 77–80.

2. V. Pareto, *Cours d'Economie Politique, Rougé, Lausanne*, 2 vols. (Geneva: Droz, 1964). For modern developments in this area, see J. Buchanan, *Journal of Conflict Resolution* 6 (1962): 341, 354.

For the purpose of this article, I propose to use a very simple system. This simple system will not exist anywhere in the real world—it is too simple for that—but it closely approximates a situation which one does find very commonly in the real world.[3] The system is composed of two species: grass and some herbivore. One may consider it to be an approximation of the situation in the Old West in which cattle grazed upon grasslands.[4] For the time being, I shall assume that these are the only two species. This simplification is introduced in order to make the line of reasoning easier; it can be demonstrated that the same principles apply even if one has many species and the ecology is quite a complex one. This demonstration, however, will not be included in this article, since it *is* quite complicated and the outcome seems intuitively obvious.

Under these circumstances, one may feel fairly confident that what is known as "over-grazing" would occur. The cattle would multiply until such time as there were enough cattle exactly to consume the maximum amount of grass produced by the plot. This grass, however, in part would be produced by mature plants; in other words, it would be possible for the number of cattle temporarily to rise to a larger number than could be permanently maintained by the process of eating the existing plants back down to the point where they no longer are fully efficient. In a sense, this is consumption of capital in the form of grass to support additional cattle.

In order to make the matter clear, consider Fig. 1. On the horizontal axis, I have shown varying amounts of grass that could be on the plot of land. The vertical axis then shows the increment that one could expect in a short period of time, say one day, granted that one has that amount of grass shown on the horizontal axis at the beginning of the time period. If one has very little grass already in existence and, hence, is on the left-hand end of the horizontal axis, there will be relatively little growth in any given short period. Similarly, if the grass is already up to the maximum that the land can hold, there will be no increment; hence the line once again hits the horizontal axis.

3. This situation has been considered a great deal by economists, particularly those concerned with the undeveloped areas, because of its relationship to meat production by pastoral activities. Economists, of course, have considered it solely in terms of its long-run effect on the human beings who engage in pastoral activities in the areas concerned. I shall be considering it without this ethnocentric bias.

4. Although I have chosen to illustrate this example with cattle and grass, the same system exists in many natural situations. One example is presented by J. P. Dempster, in T. R. E. Southwood, ed., *Insect Abundance* (Oxford: Blackwell Scientific Publications for the Royal Entomological Society, 1968), 8–17.

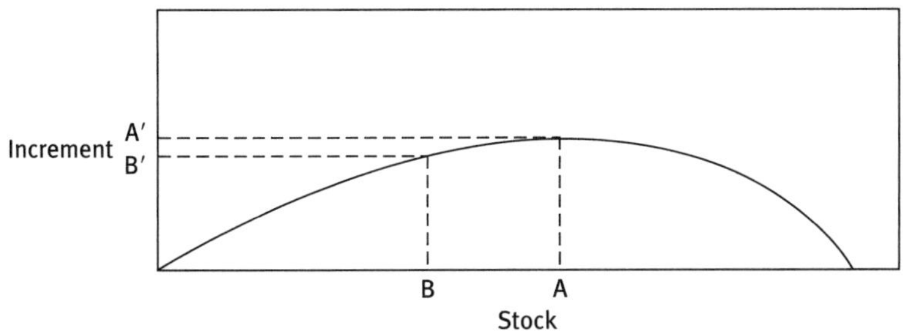

FIGURE 1

Between these two points, the increment rises as the amount of grass increases, and eventually falls off. If one proposes to harvest the maximum amount of grass that one can from this plot, then one should choose to maintain the stock of grass at amount A and harvest, during this period, A' of grass. Assume that the method of harvesting the grass is to let cattle graze upon it. One should also assume that the line drawn represents the amount of grass which the cattle can take in each day, although in practice this line would probably be somewhat below the physical increment in the diagram, because the cattle are not perfectly efficient in removing grass in such a way as to inflict the least possible damage on the remaining grass.

Suppose, then, that one attempts to graze more cattle on the land than can be supported by eating the grass A'. Under these circumstances, they would eat not only the increment in any given period, but some additional grass, let us say the amount $A - B$ on the horizontal axis. As a result, in the next period the total amount of grass available to produce *more* grass would be smaller, hence only B' amount of grass would be produced. Under these circumstances, the cattle would once again cut into the existing stock and move one farther to the left. Eventually, one would reach a situation in which grass was scarce, and the few scrawny cattle which grazed upon it would find the energy involved in chasing down their grass enough so that they could not increase in population. Under these circumstances, a new equilibrium would be reached somewhere to the left of A.

Hereditary selection of the "fit" makes this outcome inevitable. If some of the cattle had a relatively low rate of reproduction and others a rather high rate of reproduction, and the cattle with the low rate of reproduction had a rate of reproduction such that they remain in exact balance with the grass supply, the only effect of this would be that in each generation there would be more cattle of the high reproduction strain and a lower percentage of cattle in the low reproduction types. The death rate from over-grazing would be spread across both types, independent of these reproductive capacities; hence the end product would be the gradual disappearance of the low reproduction strain.

Note the following situation, however. By artificially restricting the number of cattle, one can increase the amount of grass produced each year and, thus, in the long run produce more cattle. It is possible by intelligent management to produce a situation in which both more grass and more cattle (or both elements of our simple ecology) exist than would exist under natural climax conditions. Suppose that point *B* in Fig. 1 is the natural climax with the amount of cattle which consume exactly B' grass. Under these circumstances, by reducing the number of cattle temporarily, one could increase the amount of grass and make it possible to maintain a larger number of cattle on the same land in the future.

Intelligent range managers do exactly this. A well-functioning cattle ranch supports more poundage of beef animals than it could support if the manager did not balance the grass and the beef artificially. This balance is essentially an artificial structure which could not occur in a state of nature, and the natural balance would involve less of both grass and cattle. The movement from the cattleman's organized ecology to natural balance ecology would involve a natural (and temporary) increase in the number of cattle, which would then graze back the grass supply. Similarly, a movement from the natural ecological balance to the cattleman's superior ecology would involve a temporary restriction of the number of cattle in order to permit the grass to grow up to a higher level of productive efficiency.

Ranch managers, in dealing with this kind of problem, have a fairly simple and straightforward objective: they want to maximize the production of beef or whatever else it is they are raising. The present system, however, has no such obvious maximum. Consider Fig. 2. On the vertical axis, I have put the total amount of grass on some particular plot of land, and on the horizontal axis, the total number of cattle. Since there is some minimum amount of grass necessary to sustain each head of cattle, I have drawn in a line representing this minimum, starting at the origin. In actual fact, the line would probably be slightly concave downward and not quite hit the origin, due to the fact that the cattle must use more energy to seek out grass when it is scarce, but one can ignore this minor correction. All of the points in the area

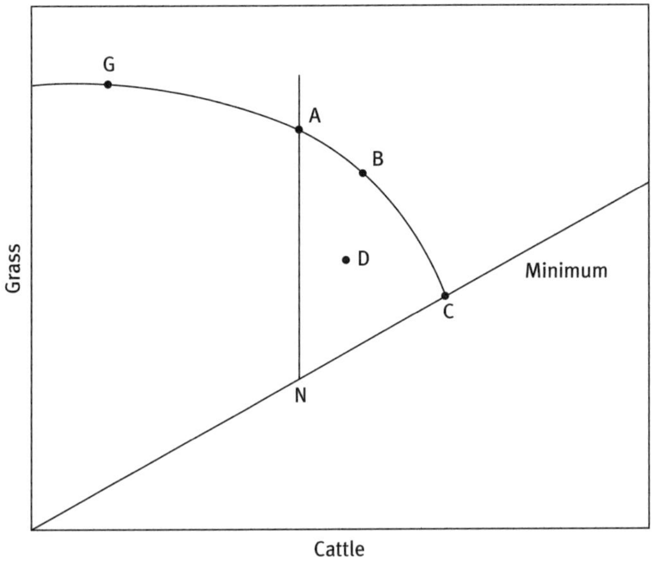

FIGURE 2

above the minimum line and below the curving line, *GABC*, are feasible, i.e. it is possible to reach any combination of grass and cattle shown in this area.

The line, *GABC*, is the maximum amount of the two species which can be supported by the land in varying combinations. It corresponds to the production frontier of standard economic theory. The maximum amount of cattle which can be raised or the cattleman's maximum is shown at *C*. Similarly, the maximum amount of grass which can be raised is shown at *G*. Note that *G* is not drawn at the vertical axis, because I assume that the fertilizer produced by the cattle has at least some effect in stimulating grass production. This might not be so in some circumstances, in which event the maximum grass production would be obtained without any cattle at all. The other points on the line *GABC* represent other combinations of production of cattle and grass, and in each case they are maxima, i.e. one cannot produce more with the same ratio. The area within the production frontier and above the minimum, which after all is simply part of the production frontier, represents those combinations of cattle and grass which are achievable, but are less productive than the areas on the frontier.

Let us suppose that *N* is the natural equilibrium of the system. It is the point to which the system will proceed if there is not regulation on the number of cattle. Any point in the triangle—bounded on the bottom by the minimum line, on the left by the vertical line drawn through *N*, and on the upper right by the curved line *ABC*—is superior to *N* in production of grass and cattle. Any point in this area will be better from the standpoint of both increasing grass production and increasing cattle production than is *N*.[5]

Note, however, that there is a good portion of the production frontier—that running between the vertical axis and the vertical line running through *A*—which one cannot say is clearly dominant over the natural climax. In order to make any judgment here, one would have to have some way of evaluating grass against cattle. If one did feel that grass was much more important than cattle, one would probably aim at point *G*, even though this would reduce the number of cattle. But this requires a value judgment; movement up and to the right from *N* requires no judgment as to the relative merits of grass or cattle, it merely requires a feeling it is desirable to have more. Hence, if movement into this triangle is movement into a permanently suitable system, it seems hard to argue against the view that one would have as much of the natural product as possible. Certainly, the ecology buffs cannot complain about it.

It is very hard, however, to decide what specific movement from *N* would be optimal without some kind of value system putting cattle against grass. Movement out to point *D* and then on, say, to point *B* clearly involves two improvements from the standpoint of both cattle and grass. From the standpoint of the grass, however, *A* would be better and from the standpoint of the cattle, *C* would be better. Here one is confronted with a situation which frequently confronts economists, and I shall follow the economist in refusing to solve the problem. With an external value system, one could decide which point was the best. Without such an external value system, however, all one can say is that the diagram shows a number of points which are superior to the natural equilibrium point, but gives no way of choosing among these points. Since any one of them is superior to the natural equilibrium, on the

5. This is, of course, the standard Pareto criterion and it should be noted that movement along the vertical line through *N* would increase grass production, but not cattle production. Thus, we would be increasing one and holding the other constant. This is what leads to the Paretian slogan: improve the welfare of one unit while injuring no one. In practice, of course, we seldom are able to move along the boundaries and, therefore, benefit both or all of the factors.

whole, movement to any one of them would be desirable. The decision as to which point on the frontier is optimal is equivalent to the distribution problem in economics, and, as in economics, can only be solved by bringing in external value judgments. I have no objection to the reader bringing in such a value judgment, but I suspect that the readers have different judgments. It can be agreed, however, that movement up and to the right would be desirable, even though there might be disagreement as to which of the various directions within the pie-shaped space would be optimal.

So much for the simple two-species ecology. I shall now engage in a somewhat more rigorous investigation of the tools which have been used in this example, and then indicate how a more general version of these tools can be applied to a more realistic ecology. First, note that I have had only two species on Fig. 1. Economists have discovered that a simple two-item diagram like this can be a great help in analyzing many-dimensional situations. The real ecology could be placed in a multidimensional space with each species, or indeed each subspecies, on a separate dimension. This hyperdimensional diagram would then have a hypersurface, its equivalent of the curved line, and there would again be an area inside this which was achievable but not fully efficient.

A simple two-dimensional diagram which can, after all, be drawn on a piece of paper can be thought of as a cross-section of that much more complex diagram. Alternatively, it can be considered to be a special two-dimensional space in which one of the axes is a particular species and the other is a composite bundle of all the other species. By this method, each species can be taken out by and of itself and its interrelation with the *whole* ecology (minus itself) analyzed. This latter technique is perhaps less convenient for ecological problems than it is in economics, because in economics one has a rather simple measure of the purchasing power. One can consider the baskets of goods which are being contrasted to the single good as having whatever their monetary value is. The most elegant way of dealing with a many-dimensional space with many species, each represented by one dimension, would of course make use of the Cartesian algebra in its many-dimensional version. Although this is the most elegant method, it is generally speaking much too tedious and, in any event, we seldom have enough empirical knowledge to make it sensible to move to such a complicated representation.

A second special problem has to do with values. It is good Catholic doctrine that the natural world exists solely for the benefit of man, and that man, therefore, is the measure of the ecology. This would, needless to say, raise the question of *which* man; hence, one would be back to the distribution problem of economics. There is, however, an even more fundamental difficulty here. A great many people are now saying that they do not think that man should be the measure of all ecological problems, and that one should take into account the well-being of other species. In part, these people are simply expressing themselves badly. Many of them do in fact hold the well-being of mankind as their major goal, but feel that long term calculations of the well-being of mankind require some temporary sacrifices of human well-being in the aid of the well-being of certain other species.

In this sense, there is no particular problem with our diagrams. The point on the efficiency frontier would be the long-run sustainable output; hence one could still retain the desire to maximize the return for human beings. In Fig. 2, since human beings do not eat grass and do eat cattle, one would choose point *C*. Some of the members of the Sierra Club, however, apparently actually *do* believe that it is worth sacrificing some long-run human goals for long-run growth of other species. For them, the value system is not quite so straightforward.

Fortunately, the Paretian apparatus makes it possible for us to deal with this matter without much difficulty.[6] The Paretian apparatus was first designed for the specific purpose of dealing with some change which might injure one person and benefit another. It was pointed out by Pareto that there was no positive reason for believing that the injury and the benefit were commensurable. It might well be that what one thought was a rather minor injury to Mr. *A* actually hurt him more than the benefit received by what to us appeared to be a very significant improvement for Mr. *B*. Pareto, therefore, suggested that a very modest criterion be accepted: any change which benefits at least one person and injures no one must be an improvement. It is clear that this rule gives guidance only in a general way. Returning to Fig. 2, it indicates that one should move up and to the right from point *N*, but does not tell us the exact location. It is an astonishing fact that this very simple rule has permitted a very large amount of calculation on improvement in the eco-

6. Note that in strict terms, there is no way in which we can avoid maximizing the utility functions of human beings. The members of the Sierra Club are human beings; if they feel that it is better to have a smaller population of human beings and a larger population of redwoods, they are maximizing their own utility functions when they aim at or achieve this goal. Redwoods cannot vote. Thus, in a sense, any policy carried out by human beings will aim at the maximization of at least one human being's utility function, rather than at some other goal. The well-being of non-human species comes in only insofar as some or all human beings may have the well-being of such non-human species as arguments in their utility function.

nomic system. I hope to demonstrate that it will be of almost equal use in the biological system.

For people who have strong personal feelings on the evaluation of different species, the rule will not be ideal. They might feel very strongly that some particular point on the frontier shown in Fig. 2 is superior to all others. There is no reason why they should not feel this way and they can, of course, make calculations very similar to the ones I have made; thus, they get results which are in essence a specialization of the very general results I get. The advantage of the very general results, however, is that they are not dependent upon the particular value system of the investigator. One does not have to choose between grass and cattle to accept a movement up and to the right from point *N*. If I am interested in the well-being of either human beings or of these particular species or any one of them, such a move is an improvement, even though it may not be a movement toward the point which exactly maximizes my particular goal. If, for example, I was pro-grass, I would regard movement from *N* to *D* to be an improvement; but I would regard any point between *A* and *C* as inferior to *G*. Such a move, however, would be a marked improvement over *N*.

The system, thus, is relatively value-neutral simply because it is consistent with a tremendous range of possible values, not because it imposes any value system of its own. Individuals are likely to regard their own personal value system as better than this criterion which, instead of aiming wholeheartedly at fulfilling their value, aims at giving at least some benefit under a very large range of values. The principal argument for the Paretian rule is that it does avoid most of the controversies which any more specific rule would entail. Actual decision in any specific case must involve putting in more in the way of a preference function than the Paretian rule. The Paretian rule demonstrates in Fig. 2 that improvements are in fact possible; it does not specify which of the many improvements should be undertaken.

Let us now discuss the concept of externality. Externalities were originally developed in economics to analyze certain areas where the market economy worked badly. They are probably more familiar to biologists than most other tools of economics simply because the problems of pollution are very good examples of externalities in the pure economic sense. I, however, am not talking about externalities generated by human beings, but externalities generated by plants and animals.

Externalities are rather easily understood. Any given species will have some effects upon the development of some other species. The grass, for example, provided a food for the herbivores, and the cattle reduced the total amount of grass by eating it. In the first case, one has a positive externality, that is, a species providing something of benefit to other species; and in the second case, one has a negative externality, that is, a species doing something to injure another species.

One need not, however, confine oneself to these very direct relationships of eating and being eaten. Most plants release into the soil and into the atmosphere various chemicals. The obvious case, of course, is free oxygen into atmosphere, but there are many others. Confining oneself to chemicals found in the soil, one finds that these chemicals have an effect upon the soil which makes it more or less suitable for the growth of other plants. This is an example of an externality. There are innumerable other similar examples. Indeed, in a real sense, the whole science of ecology is devoted solely to the study of such externalities. The existence of one plant or animal has significant effects on many other parts of the ecological community, and the study of this chain of effects from each plant or animal to all the other plants and animals is the subject matter of ecology. I will not, however, make an effort to develop the collection of interactions in any existing ecology, but to discuss the theoretical consequences of the mere existence of such interaction.

I shall begin this discussion with a very simple example. Assume two plants which customarily live in close proximity and assume, further, that each produces, as a by-product to its life processes, a chemical which is of benefit to the other. Thus, each plant will grow somewhat better in the presence of the other.[7] Here there is an externality. Naturally the plants, having no minds, do not take this externality into account; but evolution will select the plants for efficiency in generation of these by-products as well as for efficiency in other matters. One can, therefore, discuss what is the most efficient rate of generation of the by-product for the plants and, as will be seen, the rate of generation of the by-product which would be selected by natural selection is inferior to another rate. The details of this argument are quite complex, but one may begin by simply assuming that each of the plants is available in two strains, as shown on Fig. 3. Species A is available in variant A_1 and A_2. A_2 produces the by-product only insofar as that by-product is essential for the maximization of the growth of the strain in and of itself. In other words, it has no energy "opportunity cost" in producing additional amounts of that by-product. A_1, on the other hand, sacrifices some of its own growth in or-

7. In many cases, the chemical persists in the soil so that the history of the area may be more important than its current use. This would, however, merely strengthen the relationships discussed.

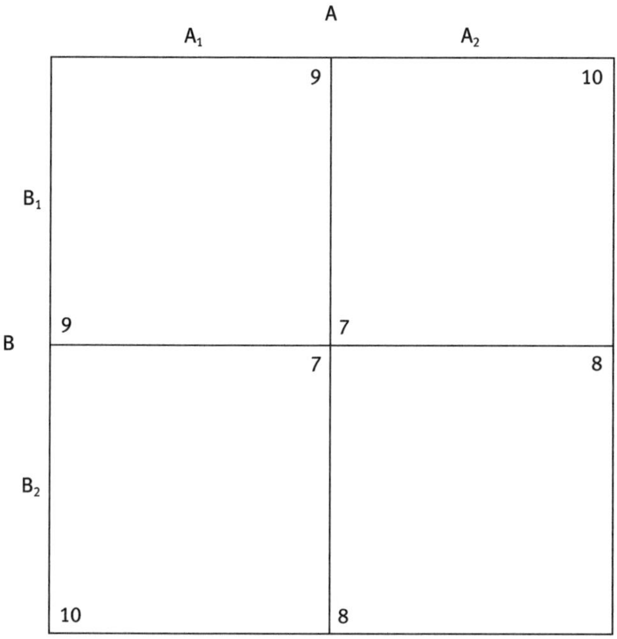

FIGURE 3

der to produce more of the by-product. With species *B*, the same situation obtains, with B_2 being the strain which produces only enough of the by-product as is consistent with maximum growth of itself, and B_1 being the one which produces more of the by-product and which tends to get somewhat less growth itself.

In the Figure, the weight each of these plants mixed in a given space of land can be expected to support is shown with *A* in the upper right-hand corner and *B* in the lower left of each cell. Since each species' by-product benefits the other species and since, in this case, the benefit is "Pareto relevant,"[8] the weight of each plant is higher in the upper left-hand corner where each of the plants is using some of its energy to provide "fertilizer" for the other than in

8. The concept of "Pareto relevance" is rather complex, but in this case it can be interpreted very simply. As long as the numbers in the upper left-hand corner are larger than those in the lower right, the externality will be Pareto relevant. This is *not*, of course, a necessary condition in the real world. I would anticipate that sometimes one would find it and sometimes one would not.

the lower right, where each of the plants is composed of the "2" strain, which simply attempts to maximize its own development while ignoring the development of the other. Both types of plant have a higher net weight in this upper left square than in the lower right; hence, the upper left can be regarded as being superior from the standpoint of either plant.

Note, however, that the structure of this diagram is that of the prisoner's dilemma. It is clear that the strains which would be selected by natural selection are not A_1 and B_1, but A_2 and B_2. One can see this very easily by observing that if a mixture of A_1 and A_2 were placed in a field with either B_1 or B_2 (or a mixture of them), the A_2 would grow more rapidly than A_1, as shown by the matrix. Over a number of generations, A_2 would completely replace A_1. For example, if the strain of B which happened to be in the field was B_1, then a given amount of plant seed for A_2 would produce ten-ninths as much as the same amount of plant seed would for A_1. Similarly, if the field was planted in B_2, the ratio would be 8/7. Since the diagram is symmetric, the same line of reasoning applies to B. Thus, natural selection would select strains which produce a lower quantity of these plants than other strains. With selective breeding, it would be possible to produce strains which produced more of both of the two plants.

Needless to say, positive externalities of the sort shown in Fig. 3 are not the only ones found in nature. Plants may also cause great injury to or exterminate other plants, and the same is, of course, true of animals. One could make up an example similar to Fig. 3 to deal with such cases, and one would find once again that the natural selection optima would not be that which maximizes the output of the two strains. Further, the use of two strains is dictated only by a desire for simplicity. One could have a very large number of strains and, for that matter, mixtures of different strains. The end product would be the same. Further, the use of two species instead of the many species of the average ecology is dictated solely by the fact that I am using a two-dimensional piece of paper. The argument is, in fact, much stronger if there are many species than if there are only two.

BIOLOGICAL APPLICATIONS OF ECONOMICS

Both Darwin and Wallace, the two independent discoverers of biological evolution, specifically said that the idea came to them while reading Malthus's work on population. Since Malthus was history's first professor of Economics, this was clearly the most important influence of economics on biology. It is particularly interesting because Malthus's book on population has turned out to have relatively little predictive value in dealing with the human race in the roughly 150 years since it was written, but does fit non-human species rather well. In a way he was a better biologist than an economist.

Surprisingly, after this promising start, to a large extent, economics and biology developed independently. Herbert Spencer made some use of evolution in his economic work, and other economists—Armen Alchian is the name that comes immediately to mind—have also made use of evolutionary ideas in economics. But until very recently there was almost no evidence of any biological concern with economics. There would be occasional articles in each of these disciplines which would show some minor contact with the other, but the phenomenon was of the second or third order of smalls.

This comparative lack of cross-stimulation was quite surprising granted the fact that both disciplines involve essentially the same intellectual construct, maximization subject to constraint. If one looks at present-day articles, in the *American Naturalist* and the *American Economic Review*, their superficial resemblance is quite high and their basic structure is also rather similar. In both cases, the standard article consists of application of optimizing methods to predict phenomena in the real world, and then statistical testing. Interestingly, in both cases, these articles normally perform their statistical tests on data which have been collected by other people. In both cases of course, a certain amount of direct data collection either by observation or experiment is present, but basically the dependence is on data provided by others.

In fact, the structural similarity between biology and economics is extremely strong. The evolutionary hypothesis in biology implies quite strongly that individual plants and animals "act" as if they were attempting to maxi-

Reprinted, with permission of Palgrave Macmillan, from *The New Palgrave: A Dictionary of Economics*, vol. 1, ed. John Eatwell, Murray Milgate, and Peter Newman (London: Macmillan, 1987), 246–47.

mize the frequency of their genes in the future. Of course, there is no genuine "acting." The dandelion, for example, doesn't do anything much. Nevertheless, the selection process, together with random changes in the genes, makes the dandelion more and more efficiently adapted to its environment. Of course the other species are also changing so that the environment is continuously changing. It is equivalent to firing at a randomly moving target.

Biologists regularly use language which might imply to the careless reader that animals and plants do consciously make plans and attempt to maximize. This is of course not what the biologist means. The process of actual selection itself functions as a mapping of what in human beings would be a set of conscious if not (as Michael Ghiselin emphasizes) terribly intelligent decisions.[1]

But although there has been some recent biological interest in economics, the present rather economic appearance of the biological journals is I think an independent development. One can find clear-cut examples of economic cross-stimulation. For a single example, a four-page note by the present author in the *American Naturalist* collected a grand total of 53 footnote citations in other parts of the biological literature.[2] This was a simple economic explanation for the observed feeding habits of an English bird. Nevertheless, although there are other examples of the same kind of thing, most of the development was independent.

Evidence of this independence was the simple fact that although the general structure of articles in the two journals is very similar, there is an important stylistic difference. Economic articles usually take the form of a theoretical exposition which is entirely deterministic. Statistical theory is then brought in when it is tested with real world data. The biologist usually begins with probabilistic equations. The biological method is clearly more elegant, but also much harder. It is not obvious which is the most efficient research tool, but it is obvious that the biologists have not copied the economists in this area.

That there was a long period in which the two disciplines were operating with rather similar theoretical structures but with almost no cross-stimulation requires an explanation. The most likely explanation seems to be that from, let us say, 1860 until quite recently, most biologists were engaged in cataloguing and understanding the immensely diverse body of species in the world.

1. M. T. Ghiselin, *The Economy of Nature and the Evolution of Sex* (Berkeley: University of California Press, 1974).

2. Gordon Tullock, "The Coal Tit as a Careful Shopper," *American Naturalist* 15 (January–February 1971): 77–80.

No one knows exactly how many species there are; the number certainly exceeds ten million and biologists have devoted most of their attention to simply trying to find out what is out there. Darwin's book on barnacles[3] was more typical of 19th- and early 20th-century biological research than his book on evolution.

The diversity of the biological world is almost unbelievable to the nonbiologist. Even after a species has been studied and described and entered into his reference books, the total number of such species is so immense that some may remain totally unknown even to experts in that field. E. O. Wilson, for example, is a very prominent biologist and would be so even if he had never written *Sociobiology*.[4] His special field is non-human societies. The mole rat, a mammal with a life pattern rather similar to that of social insects, and the social spiders have been catalogued in the formal literature for over fifty years now. In *Sociobiology*, Wilson showed no signs of knowing they even existed. This is not in any sense a criticism of Wilson, but an indication of the real problem posed by the extraordinary diversity of the biological world. Had he decided to go through the entire literature and look for all social species, it would have taken many hundreds of lifetimes.

Be that as it may, there was relatively little contact between the two disciplines until recently, and although there is now more intellectual contact, it tends to be in certain rather applied fields, particularly environmental concerns. Garrett Hardin for example, a prominent biologist concerned with certain environmental problems, reinvented the economics of overgrazing, which he called "The Tragedy of the Commons"; when it was called to his attention that this was essentially economic, he began a serious study of that aspect of economics. Since then he has worked with economists to produce joint projects in this general area.[5]

This is merely the most significant example of what is now quite a large body of cooperative research on such problems as pollution and environmental degradation. To a considerable extent the economic contribution to this joint research has amounted simply to pointing out that there are costs

3. C. Darwin, *A Monograph of the Fossil Lepadidae: or, Pedunculated Carripedes of Great Britain and A Monograph of the Fossil Balanidae and Verrucidae of Great Britain*, 2 vols. (London: Palaeontographical Society, 1851 and 1854), and Darwin, *A Monograph of the Sub-Class Cirripedia*, with Figures of All the Species, 2 vols. (London: Ray Society, 1851 and 1854).

4. E. O. Wilson, *Sociobiology* (Cambridge, Mass.: Belknap, 1975).

5. G. Hardin and J. Baden, *Managing the Commons* (San Francisco: W. H. Freeman and Company, 1977).

involved in preserving natural ecologies. Biologists tend to be extremely conservative in their approach to technology. The economist's role is frequently confined to pointing out that human welfare is also involved and suggesting trade-offs.

Another area where economists have for a long time been involved in biology is the specialized subdiscipline of agricultural economics. It should be said, however, that in this case cross-fertilization has been rather minor. The basic objective of the professors of agricultural economics in our schools of agriculture has been to improve the returns of the farmers. For this purpose, they have engaged in applied economic research in a number of fields. In general, however, they do not seem to have had any particular influence on the biological research which goes on in the same schools of agriculture. It should also perhaps be said here, that a great many of the agriculture economists devote their time to rationalizing economic subsidy programmes which, although they certainly benefit farmers, injure everyone else.

The only other area of application is of course in the field of sociobiology. This has attracted a great deal of attention from economists and other social scientists and hence it is perhaps wise to emphasize here that it is currently only a minor field within the biological disciplines themselves. Nevertheless, it seems an obvious area for application of economics and such applications have been made.

The first problem here is that of territoriality which is frequently confused with the property relations which we find in human society. In fact, the biological species have no guarantee of ownership and must one way or another defend their territory. The situation, thus, is rather similar not to property ownership, but to competing retail establishments in a geographical area. The work of Losch[6] is obviously relevant here and biologists have made good use of it. Indeed, the author of this note has contributed a couple of minor communications to the development of this area.[7] The curious reader can find on page 272 of Wilson's *Sociobiology* a photograph of the Losch hexagons produced by a territorial species of fish.[8]

6. A. Losch, "Population Cycles as a Cause of Business Cycles," *Quarterly Journal of Economics* 51 (August 1937): 649–62, and A. Losch, "The Nature of Economic Regions," *Southern Economic Journal* 5 (July 1938): 71–78.

7. G. Tullock, "Sociobiology and Economics," *Atlantic Economic Journal* 18 (September 1979): 1–10; "Territorial Boundaries: An Economic View," *American Naturalist* 121 (March 1983): 440–42.

8. A. Losch, *The Economics of Location*, translated by William H. Woglom (New Haven: Yale University Press, 1964).

As we move to more complex social structures it is more difficult to apply economics. Once again, Wilson used linear programming to study the distribution of Castes in the social insects. But an examination of the bibliography of his book will indicate that he was much more influenced by sociology than by economics in his general approach.

The dominance order, another important organizational structure found in the animal kingdom, does not seem to have any direct analogies in economic reasoning. It is of course possible to apply economic analysis to the dominance order, but so far little progress has been made along these lines. There is no reason to believe that economics has any comparative advantage here.

The complex societies of the social insects, the mole rats, possibly the social spiders, and certainly the sponges clearly are subject to economic analysis. All of them engage in complex cooperative activity which should be readily amenable to economic analysis. So far the opportunity has appealed to only one economist, the author of this item. Since his manuscript was never published, the field is open to any ambitious pioneer.

Michael Ghiselin has undertaken a serious project to create an organization which will bridge the gap. So far he has been able to stimulate little interest in either discipline. This is not because of conscious opposition, but because most scholars find themselves too involved in their own discipline to take on the extra work. It is a particularly clear case of the narrow specialization which, unfortunately, dogs the learned professions.

Altogether, the amount of cooperation between economists and biologists is surprisingly small. In spite of similar roots and similar methods, the two disciplines have gone their own ways. In a few areas practical problems have brought them together, and there are occasional cases of the use of tools from one field in the other. This item covers economic applications in biology, but there are examples of reverse influence, the evolutionarily stable strategy, for example. Basically these influences are minor. I would like to say that the situation is changing and that there are signs of greater inter-disciplinary cooperation developing. Unfortunately, this would be to mislead the reader. I hope such developments will occur but the present signs are unfavourable. Economic analysis probably has a greater future in dealing with the communities of the social insects, but so far, little has been done in this area.

THE ECONOMICS OF (VERY) PRIMITIVE SOCIETIES

Law students are introduced to the judicial opinion of a judge who said that he could not define pornography but he could recognize it when he saw it. I am in somewhat the same situation in that I cannot define "societies" but I can recognize them when I see them. This raises some problems for this essay, because some of the things that I am going to refer to as societies may not appear to be societies to others. That problem also, of course, arises with pornography. Nevertheless, I think that my readers will agree that various things that I am going to call societies do have some resemblance to societies even if they are not all normally referred to under that rubric.

In any event, most people will agree that the word "society" is of wide scope and includes many non-human as well as human societies. The obvious case is the social insects. The economic efficiency of these social organizations is well-known and older explanations of societies depended primarily upon that economic efficiency. More recently, Hamiltonian altruism, probably better referred to as "nepotism," has been used as an explanation. The theme of this essay, other than to point out the existence of a vast number of societies that normally are not discussed, is to urge that the older explanation is better than the newer one, although there is no doubt that the newer one does have importance in some areas.

Let us begin our collection of societies with the group in which the new explanation is best applied. The highest members of the wasp family have an unusual reproductive technique, with the result that the degree of gene overlap among sisters may be three-quarters instead of the one-half which one finds among humans and most other sexual species. In practice, it is frequently less than that, but let us temporarily set that question aside.

The system reaches its pure form in an ant nest or bee hive in which there is only one queen and in which that single queen has been fertilized by only one male. Using the arguments of Hamiltonian altruism, or again, nepotism, it is obvious why individual bees, ants, and so on would be selected by evolution to sacrifice themselves for the well-being of sisters to a much greater

Reprinted from *Journal of Social and Biological Structures* 13 (1990): 151–62, with permission from Elsevier.

degree than in a more normal situation where brothers and sisters have an overlap of genes of only one-half. An extreme example is the situation for most honeybees in which stinging, although it defends the hive, is suicidal for the bee. On the other hand, no one has ever alleged that the Japanese kamikaze pilots were motivated by this kind of genetic drive.

There is in this behavior pattern a rather special problem regarding the mole rat, which does seem to have a social order very similar to that of the members of the wasp family. (Although known about since the latter part of the nineteenth century, mole rats have only recently begun to be seriously studied.) There is a queen, some males that apparently do nothing except fertilize her, and a group of non-functional females that work. These animals are, of course, diploid.

There is another not very closely related species which in the past was called "white ants," i.e., termites. They have both a king and a queen and the king has a full set of chromosomes; hence, the three-quarter overlap of genes does not occur. Indeed, termite nests, if for some reason the royal pair is eliminated, will generate a sort of collective breeding pool with a number of males and females, none of which are as bloated in size or as productive of eggs as the female termite queen, but which are nevertheless among them able to produce an adequate number of new termites.

Here we must pause briefly and outline the two possible explanations or theories.[1] It will be immediately noticed that they are not truthfully inconsistent with each other. Both could exist simultaneously, so the question is: which is the dominant explanation?

Hamiltonian altruism, in essence, is based on the proposition, very familiar to biologists, that genes are selected by evolution in order to maximize the number of their duplicate genes in society. Thus, to take a famous statement by Haldane: "I would take a fifty-fifty chance of being killed in order to protect a brother, a quarter to protect a cousin, etc." Each degree of "altruism" maximizes the numbers of the particular gene which imposes its behavior patterns in the population. Thus, that gene would tend to be selected by evolution and one would therefore anticipate that this amount of what I shall from now on call "nepotism" would be expected.

In the case of members of a bee family, this gene overlap ratio can be three-

1. Actually there is a third, Triver's reciprocal altruism. Perhaps because I spend most of my time on economics and political science, I have never been able to take it seriously as an explanation of eusocial societies. In any event, it is not truthfully inconsistent with the two others.

quarters instead of one-half. Hence, one might expect bee females to be more likely to sacrifice themselves—or, in particular, to give up the right to breed to perpetuate the descendants of a sister—than would species with less peculiarly designed hereditary patterns.

Note that although they would be more likely to sacrifice themselves, there is a further requirement that the system be more efficient. In other words, for the nepotism theory to work, it is necessary that the worker bee committing suicide in defense of the hive increase the number of her genes in the next generation. This is true because if the hive is destroyed, her genes will not have any posterity anyway—her sacrifice would have been worthless. Her sacrifice makes evolutionary sense only if the hive is efficient, which, of course, it is.

In the case of the *Vespidae*, both of these conditions—individual sacrifice and nest efficiency—exist. The special reproduction method does not fit the termites, however. As far as we know, it does not fit the mole rats either, and these other societies are not radically different from the *Vespidae*. Thus, the special reproductive method of the bees, wasps, and ants is not necessary to produce very similar societies. Further, of course, there are a great many solitary wasps, bees, ants, and so on, that do not live in large societies in spite of this particular advantage. Haploidy is neither necessary nor sufficient for eusociality.

It is true, however, that this kind of social organization seems to be more common among the *Vespidae* than among the cockroaches—which are, of course, what the termites are[2] — and it is certainly much less common among the mammals where the mole rat is the sole true example.

There are, however, many other social species. Let us begin with the colonial coelenterates, which develop into large societies of comparatively small multi-celled animals whose social integration is so complete that the name "superorganism" is sometimes used. This latter is a theme to which we will return later. Each of these little polyps has a specialized function, and they share what amounts to a common digestive tract, a common circulatory system, and a common nervous system. Note that when I say these things are common, I am not alleging that there is a separate organization. It is organized by cooperation among the individual polyps.

In this case, the degree of gene overlap is even greater than it is in an ant nest because the individual polyps are produced by cloning. Thus, the fact

2. E. O. Wilson, "Termites Are Almost Literally Social Cockroaches," in *Sociobiology* (Cambridge, Mass.: Belknap, 1975).

that sexual reproduction of daughter jellyfish is handled by only a few specialized polyps, with the bulk not having direct descendants,[3] is not in any way contrary to the genes attempting to maximize the number of their duplicates in the sense of the number or frequency of their particular gene in the total population.

But mutations can occur in clonal reproduction too. Suppose one of the polyps in a jellyfish is struck by a cosmic ray and clones another viable polyp which is different from the rest. If this polyp is indeed viable, then it probably reduces the efficiency of the whole jellyfish.[4] If it produces by cloning very many duplicates, it will have no viable posterity because jellyfish with such mutated polyps are less efficient than those without. By cloning, the new polyp may become a bigger and bigger part of the jellyfish and even may attempt direct reproduction of other jellyfish, but its inefficiency dooms it by dooming the jellyfish.

Here we have something which looks very much like old-fashioned group selection. A mutation in which one of the polyps was made more efficient as a polyp while reducing the efficiency of the whole jellyfish would be selected out by the failure of the jellyfish. The mutated polyp might have numerous clones in the individual jellyfish, but if this lowers the efficiency of the jellyfish, they will die. In this case, Hamiltonian nepotism would lead to the same result.

Cloning of this sort is not by any means confined to jellyfish. Indeed, one finds it among certain plant species. Here I am going to deviate from the normal discussion by talking about plant societies. An aspen grove, for example, normally will consist of a number of aspens which have cloned from the initial individual or perhaps small group. They have a certain amount of connection underground as, indeed, is characteristic of many other trees. Exactly why this is an efficient arrangement is not obvious. Possibly the gain that the aspen grove attains is generated through some type of collective defense against insect predators.[5]

The raspberry patch is an even more extreme example—there being one

3. This is so except for the polyps' clones within the individual jellyfish.

4. There is always the possibility that the mutation will be favorable. Since it would only be one of the polyps in the jellyfish, and probably not one of the reproductive polyps, the results would be extremely complex, but it could lead to a new species.

5. Michael Ghiselin suggests in private correspondence that these aspens may lack the opportunity to reproduce by seeds, and thus the clones are necessary for survival.

raspberry patch which covers 2,000 acres and is believed to be at least 12,000 years old, i.e., the first raspberry bush (or vine or whatever you want to call it) started back at that point in time. In this case, the raspberry patch, of course, is designed as a defense against a considerable number of predators who are much larger than insects. It is notable, however, that the raspberries are also rather well protected against predatory insects, or at least it is my experience that you rarely find things like Japanese beetles destroying raspberries. Again, this is done by cloning, and there is an underground interconnection. I do not see how these two sets of plant communities can be called anything other than societies. They meet all of the characteristics we accept in a society except that they are plants rather than animals.

In essence, the entire animal kingdom is parasitic upon the vegetable kingdom. There are, of course, also vegetable parasites, most of which are parasites upon vegetation—mushrooms, for example, parasitic on dead vegetation; and the beautiful flame vine in Florida which kills its tree hosts, parasitic on trees—but basically, the plants are the real base of life on earth and the animals are a luxury fringe. In the case of such things as the venus flycatcher, the plants have partially turned the tables on the animal kingdom. But the "carnivorous" plants use their animal prey for only a small, if vital, part of their growth.

But this is not very relevant to the issue of society. In this particular case, very close relatives engage in cooperative behavior: it is obviously a society.

It is also possible that we could call other plants with some kind of stinging defense, like nettles, social if they tended to live together even if they were not closely related. They would be offering protection to each other. If it is, indeed, true as some researchers have recently argued that a particular parasite on one tree leads neighboring trees to develop defenses against it before it infests them, then that act might indicate that forests are generally, at least to some extent, social.

This automatically raises another issue. As I mentioned, the aspen and the raspberries are produced by cloning. The rather elaborate literature which argues that the peculiar reproduction methods of the wasp are a cause of sociability rarely discusses cloning. There are many insects—aphids, for example—which reproduce by cloning or some similar mechanism for quite a number of generations and they do not seem to be social.[6] There are even some lizards and fish that produce offspring by parthenogenesis.

6. Soldiers have been observed in some aphid species. This would seem to indicate at least some social aphids.

If the normal explanation for the wasp being highly social is true, surely these would be examples of even a better base for social ordering. As far as I know, there are no higher animal societies that use this method of reproduction, although as I have said, there may be plant societies. In the case of the plant societies, the only problem here is the reluctance to refer to plants as having societies.

We now turn, however, to two rather complex societies at an even lower level than the coelenterates: the slime molds and the sponges. At its simplest, a sponge consists of a living cup with arrangements so that water is driven into it through pores in the wall and then out through the mouth of the cup. Some of the surface cells of the cup pump the water and others remove pieces of food from the water. Most sponges are more complex, but they are elaborations on the same theme.

In fact, the sponge itself, even if it is only a single cup as some of the more primitive specimens are, is a complex society of single-celled animals of which many are imbedded somewhere in the structure—like, for example, the individual polyps of the colonial coelenterates—but others of which are free-moving amoeba-like entities that move through the jelly, combining with silicon or calcareous spicules[7] to make up the interior of what appears to the outsider to be a solid cup.

But before we return to the sponges, let us look at slime molds. I want to devote myself only to one category because it raises the problem in a particularly pure way. This type of slime mold has a complex life cycle; let us begin our investigation of it at a time when the slime mold consists of a large number of amoeba-like entities wandering over the floor of a forest. Like amoebas, in general, they ingest food and, hopefully, grow. At some point in time, however, a large number of these amoeba-like organisms will collect into a much larger entity, an entity which usually is plainly visible to the human eye. In fact, it may be several inches long.

In any event, once they have accumulated into this entity, they form a shape roughly like a cigar. Unlike almost all other animals or plants, however, in this case there are no cell-walls within. The various nuclei of the cells which joined to make up this larger entity simply all exist within what, in essence, is a very large cell which is the entire cigar-shape, and which, again, may be two or three inches long.

This entity now begins moving across the forest floor by a method rather

7. This is the case for most sponges. Some have no spicules; hence, the motile cells are the only occupants of the jelly.

like a Caterpillar tractor. The bottom of it, including all of the nuclei which happen to be there, remains stationary. The nuclei and other protoplasm at the back move upward and forward and then come down with the result that the whole thing moves forward. Each individual nucleus spends some time at the bottom and some time rising up and over to reach the front.

The interesting feature of this, however, is that eventually the slime mold stops, shoots up a stalk, and produces spores which are dispersed to reproduce the next generation of amoebas. Not all of the nuclei produce spores, so some of the nuclei will reproduce the entire next generation and others will have no descendants. Given the method of spore dispersal and re-agglomeration, the nuclei in a given cigar must come from many different "parents." Hence, nepotism can hardly explain the sacrifice of some for the others.

Clearly what we have here is a society of nuclei. Equally clear is that the question of which particular nucleus or which set of nuclei will make up the reproductive mechanism and produce the next generation is one of great importance to the nucleus. This reproductive process appears to be more or less random since nuclei which somehow could gain an advantage in sporulation would, in a few generations, completely replace the others, and a high degree of specialization in spore production could lower the efficiency of the mold—hence, be terminal. What we would expect would therefore be a strategy which attempted to get an advantage in sporulation but did not invest enough in that goal to make the whole organism non-viable.

It is not that the nuclei are sacrificing themselves for their close relatives; their only way of continuing alive and getting a chance to reproduce is to be part of this cooperative organization. They cannot reproduce by any other method, so if they do not reproduce by this method, they suffer no loss. Note, of course, that for this to be so, the slime mold must in some way have a competitive advantage in its niche over free living amoebas.

I remarked that I was proposing to discuss the older, rather than the newer, explanation of animal societies, and this is a clear-cut example. The individual nuclei need have no Hamiltonian nepotism for other nuclei. It is simply that their own survival is only possible within this kind of society. If they mutate in such a way as to give themselves an advantage, they make the whole society less viable. Thus, they select themselves out—as well, of course, as selecting out a very large number of other nuclei which do not carry that particular mutation. Presumably such mutations have occurred in the past and have left no descendants.

In this view, the reason for non-human societies is not only that individuals in the societies gain by having their genes passed on by other members of the society: it is that the society itself cannot exist in a tough competitive environment unless all of the members of it have a suitable genetic composition. But let us temporarily leave the theory until we have dealt with the sponges.

The sponges are an even more clear-cut case. We shall consider for our purposes a very small freshwater sponge which consists of only one cup, and which lives in the northern part of the world and therefore lives only through the summer, and then uses gemmulation to insure another generation next year.

What happens in this case towards fall is that the large number of the amoeboid cells that normally wander around the inside of the sponge and which engage there in all sorts of constructive and productive activities collect into small spheres of maybe ten thousand such cells each. These spheres also collect considerable energy in the form of some cells which have ingested large quantities of fat, and so on, so that they can not only live through the winter, but also reproduce a new tiny sponge the following year.

These spheres are expelled at the end of summer from the interior of the sponge. The "parent" sponge then dies and these spheres go through the winter and start new sponges the following year. The point, again, is that not all of the cells in the sponge make this transition. Those that do are able to make it in a collection of several thousand, so that if one of these cells had some special mutation, the new sponge would have some of its descendants, but far more of the other kind of descendant.

Sponges, like some plants, can "mate" if two of the same species happen to be close together. The two will join into a larger complex sponge. This means that not all of the amoeboid cells which form the gemmulation body are necessarily of the same parent strain even many cell divisions back. Hence, nepotism could not explain self-sacrificing behavior.

Even if the cells all come from the same parent stock, a mutation might give one some advantage in the contest to be a member of the gemmulation body rather than a performer of normal duties within the sponge. Why do we not observe mutations which give individual cells an improved chance of entering this reproductive set? The answer is, again, that if they did, the total entity would fail. It is not that the individual cells have any altruism of the nepotistic Hamiltonian type so that they are interested in preserving the genes of the other cells from the same sponge, but that specialization in competition with the other amoeba-like cells for reproduction would, with time, lead to non-survival through the inefficiency of the whole sponge.

	C	PC	NC
C	5, 5	3, 7	1, 9
PC	7, 3	4, 4	2, 6
NC	9, 1	6, 2	3, 3

FIGURE 1

	C	PC
C	5, 5	3, 7
PC	7, 3	4, 4

	PC	NC
PC	4, 4	2, 6
NC	6, 2	3, 3

FIGURE 2

But let us turn to more formal theory. Figure 1 is a rather complicated prisoner's dilemma matrix. It has three columns and rows because I want to include partial cooperation (PC) as well as cooperation (C) and non-cooperation (NC). In the real world frequently there are levels of cooperation rather than a simple dichotomy between cooperation and conflict. This large matrix contains within it two more conventional prisoner's dilemma matrices as shown in Figure 2.

Let us assume a species which has an obligate pairing arrangement—that is, it must pair up with another member of its species for life. We have a very small society here. Any member of the species can have C, PC, or NC genes and will transmit them to its descendants. This matrix shows the outcome for one generation with the offspring then pairing up randomly for the next round. Without more, the long-run outcome is the lower right corner of the matrix.

But let us assume that the environment is a tough one, and that with values of 3 or less the individuals cannot produce enough descendants to replace themselves. Perhaps with 1 only 1/4 of the entities will produce a child; with 2, 1/2; and with 3, 3/4. With 4 there is exact replacement, and 5, 6, 7, and 9 lead to multiplication in the next generation. The immediate conclusion would be that the species is not viable in the long run.

Suppose, however, that the animals live in a number of small sub-environments with only a few in each.[8] Some environments would, by accident, have only C and PC, and in those environments the species would flourish with PC outcompeting C. In the other sub-environments, NC would outcompete C and PC. Since NC is not viable if there are no C and PC around, the species would vanish in those environments.

If by mutation or immigration an NC entered one of the C, PC environments, the population would shrink and eventually disappear. Once a population has been wiped out, however, immigration from a C, PC sub-environment to the vacant pocket would be possible. Most of the time only C, PC communities would be observable. Occasionally, a mutation would produce an NC in one of the sub-environments. It would temporarily flourish and lead to the extinction of the species in that particular sub-environment. The sub-environment could eventually be replenished by migration from C, PC communities.

I have chosen this system in order to emphasize that various degrees of cooperation are possible. If the environment were less favorable so that a value of 5 or better was necessary for survival, only Cs would be observed.

The social groups we have been studying are all obligate members of many-entity societies. My usual method of dealing with a many-party prisoner's dilemma is to use a table of strategies for each individual like the one

8. The social spiders might be a good example with each collection of webs being one sub-environment. The individual nests of bees would also have some aspects of such a sub-environment.

	C	NC
(N − 1) C	10	11
(N − 2) C	9	10
(N − 3) C	8	9
(N − 4) C	7	8
(N − 5) C	6	7
(N − 6) C	5	6
(N − 7) C	4	5
(N − 8) C	3	4
(N − 9) C	2	3
(N − 10) C	1	2
(N − 11) C	0	1
(N − 12) C	−1	0
(N − 13) C	−2	−1

FIGURE 3

in Figure 3. The individual is assumed to be the column player and its payoff to C and NC depends on how many of the other members of the group are cooperators. The individual is always better off playing NC, but as more and more of its colleagues play NC, its return shrinks and eventually goes negative.

Suppose that one of the nuclei in a slime mold undergoes a mutation which leads it to compete strongly to produce spores in the next generation.

That nucleus gains and in the next generation there will be numerous descendants of it. These will push the society down the table with the result that while the descendants will still have a differential advantage, the whole slime mold is less efficient. Eventually the slime mold will be non-viable.

Obviously it would be likely that slime molds which survive would have some protection against this kind of NC, perhaps in the form of police nuclei. There would also have to be some mechanism to prevent the police from selecting themselves out. Perhaps there would be an equilibrium between the police and the non-cooperators analogous to the hawk/dove equilibrium.

One of the points in using the large matrix of Figure 1 is to emphasize that there may be degrees of cooperation. The mechanism of Figure 3 becomes complicated and multi-dimensional with more than two strategies.[9] What we need is a differential game, and equation 1 shows a single member's strategy payoffs in such a game.

$$P_i = (EC_j, \ldots, EC_n) + C_i \qquad (1)$$

P_i is the payoff to i from the outcome of the game. C_i is the effect on i from cooperating. Since the individual is sacrificing to help others, the payoff is a negative number proportional to the degree of the individual's cooperation. EC_j is the external effect on i of cooperation by j, once again proportional to the degree of cooperation. The effects on i of other members of the society are also in the bracket.

Evolution will select a gene not for its own survival, but for that of its descendants. That nucleus will be selected to maximize the survival of the gene's whole posterity. Thus if non-cooperation meant that the gene's descendants would tend to multiply until they made the host slime mold non-viable, this line would be cut off. It might well be that total cooperation, which would amount to avoiding strategic maneuvers to produce spores and simply taking the luck of the draw, would maximize the number of descendants 100 generations in the future. Less perfect cooperation might be better, but the maximum must take the well-being of the community of nuclei, i.e., the slime mold, into account.

Thus, in a real sense, the nucleus, or the cell in the case of the sponge, is preserving genes directly of itself and its descendants if it does not badly damage the efficiency of the larger general entity in which it operates. The selection which has led to and has perpetuated these societies does not take the

9. The mechanism requires even more dimensions if mixed strategies are included.

form of individual entities being designed solely to do something which protects the genes of their relatives in the Hamiltonian nepotistic way. The whole society must be protected for its survival.

Of course, this is not to rule out the prospect that if an individual's design could also benefit its relatives, this would be helpful. Thus, I am not denying that the wasp family because of its peculiar reproductive method is particularly likely to develop a society. I am somewhat surprised, though, that most biologists do not seem to have carried this line of reasoning into the clone societies like the colonial coelenterates, corals, the aspens, and the raspberries. It is, indeed, true that there are many cloning species.

I have already mentioned that certain lizards and fish clone, but do not develop this kind of society. I suppose, from the standpoint of the traditional Hamiltonian approach to society, this must be a puzzle. From my standpoint, of course, it raises no difficulties. They just happen to have an evolutionary niche where large-scale social organization does not pay.[10]

Let me turn to another case of a society, a case which is not all that often dealt with. In an unpublished manuscript,[11] I concluded that the organic view of society should be replaced by the social view of organism. Any multicellular animal can be thought of as a society of cells and these cells have the same hereditary pattern; but because of the environment, they adapt to different tasks. In this case, the environment, of course, is the internal environment of the organism, but it is not radically different from the situation which leads particular polyps of a colonial coelenterate to specialize in one particular activity.

In this case, only a few of the cells are engaged in reproduction. The other cells, which are, of course, clones, find that this reproduction is the only conceivable way in which their genes can be duplicated in the next generation. Note also that the only conceivable way that the cell can stay alive is to keep the large society—say, a person—functioning appropriately. It pays to invest in survival of one's neighbors.

We have, in this case, quite a large body of experience with what happens when there is a mutation in one of the non-reproducing cells. If the matter is

10. A number of aphids of the type that do reproduce by cloning are actually part of a larger society because they are herded by ants. Systems in which a society consists of more than one species (frequently called "commensal") will be dealt with subsequently in this article.

11. G. Tullock, "Coordination without Command: The Organization of Insect Societies" (1960). Unpublished manuscript.

seriously negative, we call it cancer. The end product is that it kills itself because the person dies and in so doing kills all the other cells. There is no reproduction in this case, and, indeed, if the mutation happened to occur in some of the cells which do engage in reproduction, it would produce nonviable offspring in most cases. If it turned out to be one of those rare cases in which the mutation is favorable, of course, we might have a species change.

But for most of the cells of the human body, such a mutation is simply a way of committing suicide since a mutated cell will kill the main organism if it is able to survive within the human body.

Let me finally turn to rather more complex societies—societies with more than one species. It is usual to refer to the less important species in the group as "commensals," but this would complicate my discussion without providing a countervailing benefit. Most complex animals probably are examples of this because we no doubt have within us a great many things that are sometimes called parasites. Most of these are harmless. It is even conceivable that in some cases they benefit us some way or another.[12]

Occasionally, one or some of these parasites are seriously dangerous. But it should be pointed out that the parasite that kills its host is, in essence, a failure. It is far better from the parasite's standpoint to keep the host alive while using some method to spread to other hosts.[13] Indeed, it seems likely that most of the dangerous diseases to which human beings are susceptible are rather accidents in which a parasite which lives without killing some other animal is transmitted to the human being where it is dangerous.

I would like to talk about another type of society with mixed species. Now I realize here that I am expanding the word "society," but it does seem to me that in ordinary usage something like a relationship between termites and those protozoa which live in their digestive tract and which are necessary to the digestion of the wood which is the primary constituent of a termite's diet forms a society in which both the protozoa and the termite are members. Of course, the termite is then normally a member of another larger society.

This particular arrangement is quite common. In fact, common enough so that the problem of how it evolved should have attracted more biological

12. The nano-technology movement has as one of its aims the insertion into human beings of artificially created entities much smaller than cellular size, which will benefit us by making repairs to improve our health.

13. If the parasite is able to spread to one or more other hosts before the original host dies, then the parasite is only a partial failure.

attention than it has. Some ants, for example, cultivate a particular kind of mushroom for food, the mushroom being found only in those ant nests.[14] The mushroom forms the only item of diet for the ants and the mushrooms themselves subsist on dead vegetable matter which has been specially prepared for them by the ants.[15] This appears to me to be not just an ant society but a society in which both ants and mushrooms are involved.

I mentioned the ants who herd aphids and one can find other examples, but the one that I would like particularly to talk about again are the termites. When a termite "eats" wood, protozoa in the termite's digestive tract convert the cellulose into something which can be digested by the termite.

Now I regard this as a society of the termite and the protozoa. But consider the situation if one of the protozoan suffered a mutation which led it to begin hoarding energy rather than transmitting part of its energy as a by-product to the termite. The mutant protozoan would have a larger access to energy than the other protozoa. This should make it possible for it to divide more frequently; hence, produce more offspring than the others. Given that the period between divisions is short compared to the life span of the termite, one would anticipate that the mutant protozoa's descendants would eventually crowd the others out. The effect, of course, would be the death of the termite; hence, the death of all these new protozoa. Further, if these protozoa were transmitted to the other termites,[16] the whole nest would die.

How many termites have died from this cause in their long history I cannot guess. But note, the protozoan is selected by evolution to avoid this kind of behavior, not because it is attempting to protect in the Hamiltonian nepotistic way its close relatives, but because it is attempting to protect another entity, the termite, certainly about as distantly unrelated to it as one can get in the animal kingdom.

Now I have described the "society" as consisting of both the protozoa and the termites. The same line of reasoning would apply, however, if we think of the society as consisting of the protozoa in a given termite's gut, or, for that matter, the guts of all the termites in a given nest. It is still necessary for the individual protozoa to avoid actions which will kill the termite.

The theme of this essay has been that Hamiltonian nepotism is not a par-

14. Different types of mushrooms apparently correlate to different species of ants.

15. Some of these ants in Tucson apparently think that I am also part of this society. I have done my best to disillusion them.

16. There is a good deal of protozoa exchange among termites.

ticularly overwhelming foundation for the social insects. Even if we turn to ants, we frequently find more than one queen in the nest. With bees and ants, the female has probably been fertilized by a number of males with the result that the relationship among the workers is not three-quarters, but much less. If there is more than one queen and they have been separately fertilized, two workers might not even be related at all.

In other words, biology has been led down a wrong track. Hamiltonian altruism would, indeed, make societies somewhat more probable, particularly in the *Vespidae*. But it is quite unnecessary. What is needed, simply, is that the society be a markedly more efficient way of operating in some particular niche than an individual. If that is so, then the society may develop. This can happen whether other members of the society have copies of your gene or not.

Acknowledgments

I should like to thank Michael Ghiselin and Jack Hirshleifer for helpful comments. I also have gained by reading several books by Ghiselin and articles by Hirshleifer. Leo Buss's recent book *The Evolution of Individuality* was also important in stimulating this work.

PART II

IN THE PUBLIC INTEREST

A (PARTIAL) REHABILITATION OF THE PUBLIC INTEREST THEORY

From the earliest work in Public Choice, scholars have tended to assume that the public interest is not a major theme in the operation of government, certainly in democratic government. In a way, this was a sensible and desirable reaction to the dominance of public interest type thinking in traditional political science. Further, public interest defined as abstract devotion to the public good is probably of little importance in politics. There is, however, another more restricted meaning of public interest in which it is of considerable importance and it is this restricted meaning that I intend to discuss.

If we look at active governments, we see that they engage in a large number of activities whose benefit is not narrowly focused on certain small groups or individuals. Military establishments are an obvious example. There are no doubt manufacturers of military equipment who gain from increased military appropriations and the soldiers themselves, of course, gain from raising of wages, but the bulk of the population vote for or against such military machines, without any direct special interest in them. There are, then, at least some cases of public interest voting. Further, if we consider even the special interest groups, let us say farmers who want higher prices for wheat, we can easily demonstrate that any individual farmer would be better off if he did nothing and let his fellow farmers take on the expense of influencing the government. We do observe individual farmers doing just that, but we also observe a fair amount of pressure being brought to bear on congressmen in such areas. This, from most of our standpoints, is regarded as a public bad, but from the standpoint of the small group that will benefit, it is a public good. Here again, I think that we must include some explanation of this kind of public interest activity in a complete theory of politics.

I do not want, of course, to quarrel with the existing literature here. Indeed, the problems involved in generating public goods, which were so powerfully outlined in Olson's pioneering book, are fully accepted. I do want to explain, however, why the voters we describe in public choice theory will vote for such public interest matters as national defense, government farm programs, and a police force.

Reprinted, with kind permission of Kluwer Academic Publishers, from *Public Choice* 42 (1984): 89–99.

A very clear-cut (and traditional) reason why voters might be motivated to put the public interest into their decision process is simply that most people are, to some extent, charitable and interested in helping others. This affects their voting behavior as well as their private behavior. An individual who is trying to help others may do so, in part, by voting for some public good, even though he doesn't expect to benefit from it himself. He may also choose to make charitable gifts through the government.

It should not be necessary to point out that although this is a genuine motive it is not a very strong one. In private life people are willing to give away perhaps five percent of their incomes to help the poor or other worthy causes. There is no reason to believe that in politics they are any more charitable. In fact, if we look at the modern welfare state and observe how much of the national income is, in fact, given to the poor, it normally turns out to be markedly less than five percent.

But here two problems, the tendency of the particular expenditure to be diverted by selfish interest and poor information, are important. The special self-interest of particular groups of people who would like to be subjects of charity and, more importantly, of those civil servants and others who are engaged in the process of distributing the charity or producing the public interest activities is always important here. I suspect that for a great many people the Kennedy Center, in Washington, is thought of as a sacrifice which we are willing to make for the public good. There is no doubt, however, that for the people directly involved in it, it is a selfish interest and that they devoted a good deal of time and energy to making certain that it was bent in their direction.

As a more topical example, the National Fund for the Humanities is intended to generate higher culture for the United States, an objective which we know, from history of such things as symphony orchestras, opera companies, and museums, that individuals are willing to endow out of essentially charitable motives. It has, however, developed a group of people who are dependent on it and recent proposals to cut it have been opposed by fairly straightforward client groups. In this case, it should be said that bad information is very important in continuing the support of the Fund. If the average voter knew the kind of "art" that is in fact supported, he would most assuredly vote against it. This may, of course, indicate that the average voter is not as artistic as the civil servants who run the program, but in any event that is his attitude. So much for what you might call pure public-good reasoning. There is another, and I think very large area where the voter may vote in terms of the "public interest" because, in essence, that is the only thing he can do. He has no selfish interest in the matter. In order to discuss it, let me take a brief digression away from preference aggregation to an area where we are attempting to determine what is, rather than what people like. Specifically, let us consider judicial administration.

We make every effort to see to it that judges and juries have no material interest in the matters they try. The idea is that they should be completely unbiased. Granted that they have no interest, one might inquire how they make up their minds. The answer must, of necessity, be that they do what they think is right because they have no countervailing motive. This system can be criticized. Surely if they had a motive to reach the right decision, they would put more energy and thought into their decisions than if we simply deprive them of all motive to go wrong. But to say that this can be criticized is not to offer any constructive suggestions for improvements. We do use this technique.

The point of this digression has been that this same technique is through accident, not through planning, an important aspect of democratic politics. The average voter making up his mind as to how he shall vote in any given election has absorbed, by way of TV and the newspapers, some information. The knowledge that he has about the current issues in the campaign is apt to be rather sporadic and inaccurate, but one characteristic that is fairly certain to be true most of the time is that most of the issues that seem to divide the candidates will be issues in which he either has no selfish motive himself or, alternatively, ones in which although he might have a selfish motive if he thought about the matter carefully, he has not thought about the matter carefully and doesn't intend to. At the conscious level he has no selfish motive.

To take a particularly clear-cut example,[1] one of the Western states recently had a referendum on a bill which would permit individuals selling their houses to, if they wished, refuse to sell the house to practicing homosexuals. It seems to have gotten a good deal of newspaper publicity and was, in fact, voted down in the referendum. Surely there were very few people in the district who voted on this particular issue because they had any selfish motives. Presumably, some homosexuals want to make it easier to purchase homes, but this must have been a very, very small minority of those who voted on the bill. The bulk of the people voting on this particular issue must have been primarily concerned with what they vaguely thought was the public interest.

1. This is also an example of the lack of careful research and thought in this area. I have not bothered to go back and find the details of an article I read rather casually in a newspaper.

This is, of course, an extreme example. But anyone reading the newspapers about any election, or for that matter almost any referendum, must quickly realize that the bulk of the people voting on any given issue have no particular selfish motive to be concerned with many issues. They will vote in terms of the public interest.

We do not here, however, want to be naive. In the average election, although most of the issues which are given great emphasis in the press and hence come to the attention of the average voter, are issues that do not affect him particularly in any direct selfish way, i.e., not measures in which he can be regarded as himself a member of a special interest bloc, there are some such cases in almost every election. Further, it seems likely that most voters are apt to pay more attention to these special issues than to the more general issues in which they have no direct interest. Thus the concentration of interest on special interest legislation is, I think, perfectly sensible. But we should not deduce from it that general interest or public interest considerations are totally without weight in politics.

The individual who simply absorbs information through the newspapers and then makes his decision on voting is not likely to be very well informed about any aspect of politics, but is apt to have heard more about those issues which don't affect him particularly than the issues which specially affect him. Thus he may end up voting, to some extent, on what he thinks is public interest rather than his own selfish interests.

This factor is to a considerable extent counterbalanced if we consider the situation of a congressman who is considering how to vote, with careful attention as to how that will affect the next election by the fact that there are specialized channels of information for those people who are members of interested minorities, and these specialized channels of information are likely to produce information to the small group of voters who are particularly interested in it. Nevertheless, the congressman must, of necessity, look at both sides of the ledger. We observe this fairly directly from the fact that there are no straightforward open transfers of funds to special interest minorities. We do not see a general and small tax used to pay cash sums to small minorities. This would be too blatant. We do see governments engaging in activities which are intended to generate public goods but which, in fact, do not. It is highly probable that the average citizen of almost any democracy thinks that a firm price control would be a good idea in order to end inflation. We periodically observe governments responding to this kind of pressure by enacting such price controls. Why they do so is not hard to understand. Indeed, granted the motives of a politician, the difficult question is why they ever repeal price controls. This is a case in which individuals badly informed are under the mistaken impression that a particular type of government policy is in the public interest when, as a matter of fact, it is not.[2]

Before leaving these cases in which the voter votes pretty consciously in the public interest, I perhaps should say a little about the information conditions. When he is deliberately acting charitably in his vote, he probably has at least some motive to become well informed about the specific charitable act. This does not mean he will be well informed but he won't be hopelessly badly informed. In those cases in which he is driven to vote in the public interest simply because he has no selfish interest, he has even weaker motives to become well informed. This is the area where casual fads, fancies, and fashions are particularly important in democratic politics. Thus, the "public interest" vote is very apt to be very badly informed.

So much for genuine public interest. We now turn to two areas where individuals vote in a way which to the outside observer might appear to represent the public interest, but where their actual motives are selfish. We should, of course, not oversimplify. The person who is genuinely interested in doing good may also vote in the same way that the selfish person in these areas does, and it is likely that for most people the two motives are, at least to some extent, intermingled.

We shall begin with technological public goods. Consider the Army, for example. It is, on the whole, impossible for an individual to vote for his own interest without voting for that of others at the same time. Thus, if I thought that the Vietnamese war was important to defend me,[3] the only way I could vote for it would tend to produce the same "good" for all other people, too.

This is, in general, true with respect to military activities. The economies of scale are so immense that individuals are unable to do much on their own and, hence, any decision that they make has to be collective. Under the circumstances, my completely selfish desire to have strong military protection has the by-product that I will protect other people. In other words, I will vote

2. It should be said here that the price control legislation may be a misunderstood private good legislation rather than misunderstood public good legislation. It is sometimes suggested that the average individual thinks that the rise in the price of the things that he purchases is caused by inflation, while the rise in the price of whatever he sells is caused by his own virtue. Thus he may think that a fair price control system would permit his income to continue rising while stopping the prices he pays from rising. Thus he has a selfish rather than a public good motive here. I doubt that this is, in fact, the explanation, but it might be.

3. Or for that matter thought that it endangered me. The arguments are opposite but have the same relevance for this paper.

in such a way as to generate a public good. There are a number of activities of this sort—the police, the highway net, the weather bureau, or a patent system are all examples.

We immediately notice that in all of these cases, in addition to these very general drives for the "public interest," there are narrow interests also involved. I do not believe, however, these narrow interests can be regarded as dominating the political process here. They bend the political process in various ways, but without the overwhelming "public interest" vote, these various goods would not be provided.

There is another collection of government services which are not technologically public, but where from the voter's standpoint it is much like the Army, etc. They are goods or services that are technologically private but where the government can be used to provide them if large numbers of voters vote for them. Suppose, for an example, a special tax on a group of people used to pay pensions to another group of people. From all of these people's standpoint these are private goods or bads. Nevertheless, no individual could anticipate that he would receive his pension unless other people voted for it, too, and hence there would be no point in his voting for a pension for himself alone. He is apt to treat this large collection of private goods as if they were a public good. In practice, I suspect that this kind of thing is much commoner in modern political structure than true technological public goods. Of course, many, many cases are intermediate between the two.

Here again, one must expect that individuals, although basically voting for or against such programs with full awareness of the fact it affects many other people, would do their best to bend it in their own direction. In this respect it is like the public goods. Just as the arms manufacturer hopes that the defense appropriation will largely be spent on buying his particular product, so the old age pensioner feels that, let us say, a special adjustment in the old age pension for the exceptionally high cost of living in his section of the country would be desirable.

To anticipate later discussion, the individual who votes in the way we are describing here has little motive to become well informed. He may cast a vote intending to increase his pension which will actually reduce it because he doesn't understand the complex actuarial calculations necessary to fully predict the outcome of his vote. Further, in general, it will not be worth his time to learn to understand such calculations, with the result that such ignorance is apt to be permanent. This, again, will be discussed further after we have dealt with some other reasons why people might vote in the public interest.

Nevertheless, such programs as social security politically have all of the standard characteristics of a public good. Of course, we can readily find cases in which a public good is considered good or bad by large numbers of people, for example, the defense appropriation. We can also find cases where a private good is primarily pushed by a small group of people. The standard pork barrel project is obviously such a case.

There is, of course, an intermediate situation in which individuals face a public good for a small group. Suppose, for example, the farmers, as they have in the United States, approach the government and suggest the government raise the price of their products. This is, for the individual farmer, a public good although a public good that surely does not extend to the entire population. Its cost, on the other hand, does extend to practically the entire population and so is a public bad, although apparently most of the population doesn't know that it exists.

Looking at the matter entirely from the standpoint of the voter, the special interest is really no different from general interest. Mr. Smith has preferences A through M for various subjects. Two of them are matters of very special interest to him and the others are of things which are, or at least he thinks are, matters of public interest. From Smith's standpoint his vote for a candidate will have as much effect on any one of these subjects as on any other. It is only if he personally evaluates one more strongly than others that he will give it additional weight.

It is often thought that the individuals in a pressure group can, somehow or other, get more out of their vote by voting for the special interest than for the public interest. This is not true. A vote is a vote is a vote. There is something to be gained for members of a pressure group by developing a reputation of being highly reliable and always selling their vote to the highest bidder on one particular subject and ignoring all others. An individual who chooses not to do so, however, will normally not have any significant effect on the prospect of this group's promise being believed next time. Our data on elections are far too imprecise to be able to detect an individual switch and, in any event, the individual would be of little interest to the congressmen.

It should be said here that from the congressmen's standpoint a special interest would be simply something that interests a concentrated group of voters rather than substantially everybody. It would not necessarily conform to the view of public goods held by economists. Let us return to the legislation permitting individual discrimination against homosexuals in selling houses. Presumably, this was pushed by a small intense group. From the politician's standpoint they are just as much a special interest group as people who want the harbor of their city dredged.

It is likely that, on the whole, if we look at those public goods that the government does generate, a great many of them are thought of by the politicians as concessions to various special groups. For a very long period of time the veterans' organizations in the United States pushed hard for increased military appropriations.[4] They were, I am sure, thought of by politicians as a special interest that had to be conciliated by large appropriations. In this case, of course, they were pushing for something which had much wider public support than would, for example, making Tulsa a deep water port, but the fact remains that from the politicians' standpoint they were a special interest.

Looking at the voters from the standpoint of the politician, there are a large number of people who have interests in various issues and these interests are of varying degrees of intensity. He attempts to choose a location in the multi-dimensional issue continuum which maximizes the probability of his being elected, granted that he has an opponent who will be trying to do the same thing. This means he must take into account the intensity of preference as well as the actual direction of preference on all issues.

It also means he must take into account the information conditions facing the voters. This leads to various tradeoffs in which he may take a position which is generally but not very strongly opposed and strongly favored by a special group, more often than not, small.

It is not by any means obvious, however, that only small groups have strong preferences. The Swiss government, for example, has never proposed simply abolishing its military machine which, on a per capita basis, is probably the most powerful in the world. If it did, I suspect they would find that substantially the entire population of Switzerland was intensely and vigorously opposed. Because of the widespread use of the referendum technique in Switzerland, intense minorities have less power and importance than they do in purely representative democracies. Still, intense minorities which are small enough so as not to attract the attention of the country as a whole regularly get all sorts of special privileges out of the Swiss government by virtue of, in essence, threatening contrary votes at the next election.[5]

4. Not quite so hard as they did for improved pensions, of course.

5. The particular method of proportional representation used in Switzerland means that many, many members of the legislature can be unseated by really quite small changes in the preferential vote.

In the more normal type of democracy in which referendum is not as important as in Switzerland, it is likely that intense minorities do much better, simply because they are more likely to affect an elected politician thinking about the next election two years from now than they are to affect public opinion in general.

Looking at the matter in general terms, it is clear that from the voter's standpoint the distinction between public goods and private goods is not particularly relevant. Consider the social security administration. This is simply a very large collection of private goods and bads with individuals who anticipate their taxes to be greater than their receipts getting a private bad and individuals who have the opposite expectation getting a private good. In this respect it is like most transfers.[6] This is, however, a case in which we would anticipate very large numbers of people holding preferences of varying degrees of intensity one way or the other. For an alternative which is on quite the other extreme, suppose a proposal to censor some local pornography source. The groups favoring and opposing this would probably be rather small in spite of its "publicness."

These subtle distinctions are of little or no interest to the voter who simply makes up a list of things he favors and opposes, determines which candidate favors each one, and then weighs them according to his intensity. They are also of no great importance to the politician who is simply interested in the effect of his decision on any given issue on the vote he will receive in the next election. He doesn't care whether the reason people favor or oppose a particular vote is the existence of public good or private good. He is, of course, interested in the number of people who are on each side of any issue and how strongly they feel. In particular, how likely they are to remember the whole thing at the next election and either reward or penalize him.

The way this works in politics is that the political entrepreneur who, let us assume, is somebody running for Congress who makes up a platform of various proposals which he will push and, of course, emphasizes his previous record if he has one, as evidence of what he is likely to do. He attempts to design this in such a way that it will get him at least a majority of votes against his opponent. This means that he engages in what we called implicit log-rolling, i.e., he balances a special provision for voter A which he knows voter A wants a great deal against two or three things which he knows voter A opposes, but

6. In some cases, of course, the transfer involves an essentially voluntary present from the well off to the poor and, in this case, there are public good aspects.

which voter A doesn't feel very strongly about. The result of this mechanism is that he is apt to make up a platform which consists of certain issues which he believes are widely supported, together with a large collection of other issues each of which is distinguished by an intense minority on the side which he favors and a relatively moderate majority on the other side. If he has done his job well, he will be elected.

Once the congressman gets into Congress he is in a position where he should attempt more or less the same pattern, but in this case he is trying to create not a set of promises for the future but a pattern of behavior which will lead people to reelect him. For this purpose it is important for him to be able to say that he has gained things for his constituency. It is also important for him to be able to say that he has voted with the majority of his constituents on these issues where the majority is likely to know what has happened, and to be interested in the matter. Thus his pattern of behavior will, in this case, tend to follow not the implicit log-rolling pattern described above but an explicit log-rolling pattern in which he actually makes trades with other congressmen on various issues.

The result of this pattern is likely to be something like the American defense appropriation process. Most congressmen will be in favor of that amount of defense which is favored by the majority of their constituents. There is also a very strong desire on their part to see to it that defense expenditures are made in such a way as to benefit each individual constituency. For the first, it is not terribly difficult to get a general majority position in Congress. For the second, an elaborate procedure of log-rolling is put in train with the result that we have the pattern of military bases that we now observe.[7]

Let us consider the information conditions confronting the average voter. Firstly, he has very little motive to become informed unless, for one of a variety of reasons, he actually likes to know something about politics. Information that he picks up casually from the press and the TV is not likely to be

7. This, by the way, is not in any sense a new phenomenon. When Jefferson first became president he found himself with the combination of a fairly large military machine and a rather difficult foreign policy situation. He decided to cut sharply on the military in spite of the difficult foreign policy situation; a decision which imposed on his successor and friend, President Madison, the disastrous war of 1812. The intriguing feature of his budget cuts on defense, however, is that although he cut back very, very sharply on the actual fighting part of the army and navy, he did not close down naval bases or arsenals. The combat part of the military was cut back but the log-rolling part was not. In this, as in so many other areas, Jefferson was the founder of modern American Politics.

very profound and will, to a large extent, depend on current fashions and fads. If he does have some specific subject in which he is interested as sort of a hobby, he may be very well informed on this but the number of such voters is small enough so that they probably have no effect on politics.

The very well worked out proofs that the average voter has no instrumental motive to become informed about things of public interest will not in any way be denied here. He may have the motive to become, at least to some extent, well informed on matters which will affect some small group of which he is a member. There his vote has a greater impact. Still, the motive is not likely to be high.

Thus, his information situation tends to exaggerate the effects we have discussed above. There is one particular area, the special interest legislation area, where his information lack is apt to be particularly appalling. Those special interest acts now being pushed politically, which inflict a very small cost on him in order to provide a large benefit to some concentrated minority, are probably totally unknown to him. If he does learn about them, he is apt to pick up some deceptive cover story circulated by the special interest group. Here we intellectuals could make a real contribution. If we simply educate the populace on the actual costs of these things, we would find that the bulk of them would not go through. Unfortunately, historically intellectuals have tended to favor large collections of special interest legislation, with the result that, if anything, they have contributed to the deception.

It should, of course, be pointed out when talking about special interest legislation that the individual is probably totally uninformed about the very large number of opportunities for special benefit to himself. The number of special interest groups that actually exist is probably but a tiny fraction of the potential total for such groups. The problems so well outlined by Mancur Olson mean that in most cases a special interest group is never organized. The initial investment of capital in informing the members of the group that they have common interests, inventing a cover story which will permit it to be passed through Congress, and then getting the bill passed depend on individuals within the pressure group behaving in a way which is, from the standpoint of that pressure group, publicly interested. We do not expect that they will and, hence, only a very small portion of potential public interests in fact become politically viable. This is a very fortunate fact.

To sum up, the purpose of this paper has been to argue that public choice should not totally ignore public interest or public interest voting. It should certainly not ignore issues where there are very large numbers of people, all of whom have a private interest that points in the same direction. It is likely that the extremely forceful article by Samuelson, in which he presented the argument for public provision of public goods, has misled the students in this field.[8] The government does provide public goods but it also provides many other things. Basically, it provides things in a democracy for which a majority of the people will vote. This does not mean they will vote for each individual item but that the whole package is attractive to them.

This package includes a certain number of things that we readily recognize as public good. It also includes a large number of matters in which a small minority is interested, but interested very intensely, such as the standard logrolling issues. Last but by no means least, it includes private goods which are provided for by the government because their provision requires the use of coercion. Transfers are the most obvious example. This last category of private goods can be those that benefit fairly small but intense minorities or programs that benefit very large groups of people, like the various "welfare" programs first introduced by Bismarck in Imperial Germany. The tendency to completely overlook the public interest legislation and public interest motive, and even more completely to overlook large scale transfers as a motive for government activity should, I think, be changed. I do not, of course, want to argue that public interest is the dominant motive in politics but it is a motive.

8. "The Pure Theory of Public Expenditures," *Review of Economics and Statistics* 36 (Nov. 1954), 387–89.

HOW TO DO WELL WHILE DOING GOOD!

Economic research always has the potential of contributing to public welfare since improved knowledge can have an effect on the world that is desirable and is unlikely to have an effect that is undesirable. Nevertheless, I would estimate that the average article in economic journals these days has very little prospect of contributing to the well-being of the world. Most economists know this and worry more about publication and tenure than about the contribution their research will make to public welfare. The argument of this chapter is that virtue does not have to be its own reward. The average economist can benefit his career while simultaneously making a contribution to the public welfare.

Consider, for example, the case of the dissolution of the Civil Aeronautics Board (C.A.B.). In 1937, Congress cartelized the U.S. air transport industry, establishing a government agency, the C.A.B., to supervise and control the cartel. As a result, in the United States air transportation prices were held well above their equilibrium, even though they were lower than the prices charged internationally and in Europe.[1]

In 1984, the C.A.B. was abolished, and it is clear that economists played a major part in its destruction. A group of economists (Jim Miller is the one that I know best) devoted a great deal of time and effort to economic research in connection with the airline industry and to what we may call public relations activities in connection with it. They formed an improbable political alliance between the American Enterprise Institute and Senator Kennedy for the purpose of bringing the control device to an early grave. Further, they were able to convince some of the airlines that they would gain from the elimination of the C.A.B.

As far as I can see, when these economists began their campaign there was substantially no public interest in the matter at all; most people and politi-

Reprinted, with permission, from *Neoclassical Political Economy: The Analysis of Rent-Seeking and DUP Activities*, ed. David C. Colander (Cambridge, Mass.: Ballinger, 1984), 229–40.

1. The apparent reason that American airlines' prices were lower than those in Europe was not that our airlines were any less monopolistic but that they were more efficient, with the result that the optimum monopoly price for them was lower than the optimum monopoly price for such monsters of inefficiency as Air France or Japan Airlines.

cians would have argued that the C.A.B. was necessary in order to prevent the airlines from exploiting the passengers. It is also true that most of the economists who looked at the problem had approved the regulation. It should be said that a good many of the economists that looked at it were members of that small subset of the profession who were professional public utility economists and whose own personal income depended very heavily on the continued existence of these boards for which they could give expert testimony. Miller could have joined this small group but chose the other side, and in view of his subsequent career, it is hard to argue that he was not right, both from the standpoint of the public interest and his own career.

I do not want to, indeed am not competent to, go into the detailed history of this successful campaign, but I should like to point out two important factors: the first is that the average citizen, if he or she had known the truth about the C.A.B., would always has been opposed to it. This is one of the reasons why you can argue that it was in the public interest. The second is that it was not too hard to get the actual story out. The problem was mainly that of explaining the matter to the politician and the media. This is not necessarily easy since neither of these groups has any particular motive to think hard about the true public interest. They are both much more interested in the image of public interest currently in the minds of the citizenry. But to say that it is not easy, is not to say that it is impossible, and here we have a clear-cut case where it was accomplished. The theme of this sermon is "Go Thou and Do Likewise."

The C.A.B. is not by any means the only example. Banking regulation has to a large extent collapsed in recent years. This was to a considerable extent the result of technological developments, but the existence of a vigorous group of economic critics of the regulations was no doubt important. After all, the regulators could have just changed their regulations to take in the new technology. The fact that they did not was certainly, to some extent, the result of the work of the antiregulation economists in this area. The partial deregulation of the trucking industry is almost entirely the result of economic activity and, indeed, during the latter part of the Carter administration an economist was acting chairman of the ICC.[2]

In all of the cases originally the majority of the economic profession was on the wrong side, *favoring* regulation. This is one of the problems we face

2. Unfortunately, this partial deregulation seems to have stopped. (I hope temporarily.) Once again, it is encouraging that most economists were opposed to this regulation.

when we talk about economists having a good effect on policy. We must admit that in the past economists have frequently had a bad effect. Good economists have always had a good effect, however, and those who had a bad effect were bad economists. This is not just an ad hoc argument; I believe that one can look into the matter and discover that the people who favored such agencies as the ICC at the time they were set up were markedly poorer economists than the ones who objected to it.

There are other striking examples. In 1929 the United States was probably the world's highest tariff nation. It is true that during the intervening years we have developed a habit of setting up quotas and voluntary agreements, but even if you add those on, we still are a very low trade barrier nation. This change seems to be almost entirely an outcome of steady economic criticism. Certainly, it is very hard to put your finger on any other reason for the change.

Once again however, the history is not clear. The protective tariff, of course, has long been a bête noire of the economists, but a review of the advanced theoretical literature over the last years shows far more discussion of optimal tariffs than of the desirability of getting rid of tariffs. This is particularly surprising because the articles dealing with optimal tariffs rarely, if ever, point out that their optimality is a rather special one and that, in any event, it would be impossible to calculate an optimal tariff in the real world.[3] Still, the majority of economic opinion was always against protective tariffs even if this point of view did not get much attention in the technical journals. In a way the success of the tariff-lowering movement depended a great deal on the fact that the secretary of state for some twelve years was a former southern congressman who had learned free trade in his youth and stuck with it. Cordell Hull, of course, has been dead for many years, but the trend that he started continued. Certainly, the general favorable economic climate for such cuts was important there.

What can we do now and, more specifically, what can readers do that is good but will also help them in their careers? My argument is that there are numerous instances that almost all economists can agree are rent-seeking and detract from general welfare. In such cases virtue need not be its own reward.

3. It is not that the optimal tariff literature is wrong. It is that it can be misused and that economists are more likely to have a positive effect on public policy because rent-seeking forces will be pushing for a tariff that is far beyond any optimal tariff.

An Example of an Anti-Rent-Seeking Argument

Let me begin with an example on which almost all economists would agree. There are about 300 British Columbian egg producers, and some time ago it occurred to them that they were not as wealthy as they would like to be. They pressed the British Columbia government into setting up the British Columbia Egg Control Board, a cartel in which the government not only fixed prices but actually engaged in civil service employing operations. Specifically, the Egg Control Board purchased the eggs from the owners of egg factories and then sold them to the public.

The original arguments for this program (other than that it would make the egg producers wealthy) were that they would stabilize prices and protect the "family farm." They have stabilized prices. If you compare prices in British Columbia to those in Washington State, which has roughly the same conditions, it is clear they fluctuate more in Washington State. However, they have stabilized prices primarily by preventing the falls in price that periodically cause so much distress for producers of eggs in Washington. Whether this particular kind of stability is admired by the housewife, as opposed to the egg producer, is not pellucidly clear. As for protecting the "family farmer," I doubt that these enterprises really should be referred to as family farms, but it is true that there is some evidence that the average size is possibly slightly suboptimal in British Columbia.

In order to charge a monopoly price it is, of course, necessary to prevent entry into the business. This is done by the traditional grandfather clause, so that those who were producing eggs in British Columbia when the scheme started are the only ones who are permitted to do so. As a result, the wealth of the farmers has increased very greatly because the permits to produce eggs are now valuable. Indeed, for the average egg producer, the permit is more than half his total capitalization.

It should be pointed out, however, that in addition to the egg producers there is one other beneficiary of this scheme. The egg producers produce more eggs than can be sold in British Columbia at what the British Columbia Egg Marketing Board thinks is a stable price. The additional eggs are sold on the international market for conversion to things like dried eggs at whatever the market will bring.

How do I know all of this about the British Columbia Egg Marketing Board? The answer is simple. Two economists decided that it would be a worthwhile study and the Fraser Institute published it in the form of a small booklet.[4] Borcherding and Dorosh thus acquired a reasonably good publication, probably quite easily. It is no criticism of the pamphlet to say that it involves no particular economic sophistication or advanced techniques. It may have been a little difficult, because I presume the Egg Board was not exactly enthusiastic about cooperating with them. Nevertheless, I would imagine that the cost/benefit analysis of this pamphlet, in terms of getting a publication and the effort put into it, was very exceptionally favorable. Further, the pamphlet itself certainly will make the survival of the Egg Board, at least, a little less certain, a result most economists believe would be beneficial.

Of course I hope that more is done here. The pamphlet was published by the Fraser Institute, which exists essentially for the purpose of doing this kind of thing and attempting to influence public policy by its research. The head of the Fraser Institute frequently appears on television. I would think that the prospects for the Egg Board are clearly worse than they were before all of this started. I hope that Borcherding and Dorosh follow up on this, not so much by further research although that of course probably can be done, as by trying to get other publications in the local media.

Here, I am going to suggest that they do something unprofessional; I believe economists should make an active effort to interest the local newspaper and other media in such issues. Stories of a small entrenched interest robbing the general public are the kind of story that does go well once you sell a reporter. Further, they are not particularly complicated.

Such activities are not the ones economists normally engage in; moreover, it will be a little difficult to interest newspaper reporters. Newspaper reporters tend simply to say what other newspaper reporters have said.[5] Granted that reporters behave this way, they are nonetheless normally looking for a scandal which they can make headlines about, and there are innumerable examples. The licensing of private yacht salesmen in California is my favorite case of the public being protected against low commission rates, but I am sure most economists can think of a half dozen more. But let us defer further discussion of general publicity for now.

4. The booklet is *The Egg Marketing Board, A Case Study of Monopoly and Its Social Costs*, by Thomas Borcherding and Gary W. Dorosh (Vancouver: The Fraser Institute, 1981).

5. The "deregulation" that has been so successful in recent years in the United States is an example. It has become more or less a fad with most of the correspondents for the *Washington Post* who were in favor of it without having any clear idea why.

We can roughly divide into three categories various rent-seeking activities for which there is likely a consensus among economists that they are indeed rent-seeking: those that involve spending money in a way that in the standpoint of the average taxpayer is foolish but that benefits a particular group, those that involve fixing prices above equilibrium, and those that involve obtaining cartel profits by restricting entry into a business.[6]

Economists have not been very successful in their efforts to stop federal government expenditures resulting from rent-seeking. Jack Hirshleifer, for example, devoted a good deal of time and energy, together with a number of experts in the field, in attempting to prevent the Feather River Project from being built in California. It has not been completed yet, but, on the whole, their efforts cannot be said to have made a major impact. I do not know why it is harder to stop government expenditures of this sort than the other kinds of government activity, but I suspect the problem is simply that from the standpoint of the citizens of California, the project is in fact a good one.[7] Their efforts were very largely concentrated in California. The cost, on the other hand, was very largely borne outside of California. There has been relatively little in the way of efforts on the part of economists to stop locally financed expenditures where I think they could have more impact. In making attacks on local expenditures, I think it is wise to keep in mind that in many cases the money actually is federal. It is not unwise of the local government to accept a gift from the national government even if the gift is not in optimal form. The conclusion that can be drawn is that rent-seeking can most often be stopped if the groups that are bearing the cost can be informed.

Turning to the other two categories, entry restriction and price control, most of these are state and local regulations, although there are, of course, federal examples. At these lower levels of government the beneficiaries and the injured groups are somewhat closer together and informing the injured group is somewhat easier. Further, an individual's activities are more likely to have effect in such a restricted area, and last but not least, most of these projects are fairly simple. Thus, it seems better to concentrate anti-rent-seeking activities in these areas.

Let us begin with the cases in which the prices are fixed by some govern-

6. I leave aside here those cases in which if we look only at the short run, as unfortunately the voter does, the beneficiaries outnumber the people who pay. Price controls on gas are a current example.

7. Ignoring, of course, those particular farmers who will be damaged by the canal across the delta.

ment board, with a maximum and minimum price. This is essentially the British Columbia Egg Board, and there is a simple argument to be used against it, which is that there should be no minimum price. Consumers can hardly be protected by a minimum price. If you can get the minimum price out, the pressure group that set the thing up in the first place will probably see to it that the maximum price is eliminated.

At this point, I should perhaps mention the standard rationalization[8] that advocates of the minimum price will almost certainly use. They will allege that if the minimum price is not imposed then some company with a lot of money will cut prices, drive the competition out of business, and then exploit its monopoly. This argument is eliminated by not arguing against the maximum price, and instead leaving that to the regular political process. The lesson here is a simple one: the best economic reasoning is not always (indeed, it is generally not) the best politics. Policy economists must formulate arguments that are most liable to lead to the desired outcome, not that are most elegant.

Restrictions on entry are subject to a variety of forms of arguments. The formal rationalization—that is, that they make certain that the service provided is on a certain level of quality—can be countered by Milton Friedman's "certification," which is that the state or local government could provide certificates of competence to anyone who passed their regulations, but not prohibit people who do not have such certificates from practicing provided that there was no fraud. In other words, the person without a certificate would not tell people who solicited his services that he had one. This procedure would probably eliminate most of the monopoly gains and convert the present arrangements into something that might even be socially desirable.

The usual argument against this, of course, is that people are not bright enough even to look at the certificate. (Why people who argue this way think that people are bright enough to vote, I don't know, but they do.) To counter this argument one can move to a second line of defense, by pointing out that these regulations are not and, in fact, make very little effort to pretend to be, efforts to raise the quality of services.

Uniformly, when such restrictions are put on, everyone now in the trade is grandfathered in. Indeed, that is the reason they are put on—the current people in the trade want to have their lifetime income raised by reducing competition. Clearly, if everybody now in the trade is competent without in-

8. I encountered it in high school.

vestigation of any sort, it is unlikely that an investigation is of any use. Thus, all new proposals of this sort can be opposed quite readily.

If we turn to the older trades, there may well be an examination, usually an irrelevant examination, but the examination is given only to new entrants. The appropriate argument here is simply that it is possible for a person practicing, whether as a doctor or as a plumber, to fail to keep up with new developments, forget old developments, or, for that matter, become a dipsomaniac. It would be desirable, therefore, that everyone in the trade not only be examined when he enters but be reexamined from time to time. It is hard to think of any argument against this, but it clearly would eliminate the political pressure for the restriction if the restriction had to take the form of continuing examinations.

Finally, there is a constitutional argument. The Supreme Court has held that requiring a waiting period for a new entrant into a state before he can go on relief violates his constitutional rights to travel freely. Prohibiting him from practicing his trade as a carpenter would also do so. Of course, if the restriction were literally evenhanded—that is, if the New York restriction on carpentry is the same for New Yorkers as for Californians who want to migrate to New York, then this constitutional argument would not exist. Such a restriction, however, would imply that if all people who are practicing carpentry in New York at the time the law was passed are admitted without examination, people who are practicing carpentry in other states at that time should also be admitted without examination. If we could get the Supreme Court to hold that this is what the Constitution said, we could feel confident that there would be absolutely no political effort to establish new restrictions on entry in the states and local governments throughout the United States.

If an examination for carpenters has been in existence for a long time so that there are not very many carpenters from other states who were carpenters at the time that the original carpenters were grandfathered in, there is a somewhat more difficult constitutional problem. Here, however, an argument would be needed that the examination is not really intended to certify people's ability as carpenters but to prevent migration from other states. It seems to me that the simple fact that the examination is not given regularly to people who are already practicing in order to make certain that they are retaining their skills, and not becoming dipsomaniacs, would be adequate here. Such constitutional arguments may or may not be successful in the courts. I recommend its use in economic arguments, even though it is not strictly relevant, simply because I think it will have a persuasive effect on the average voter.

In making any anti-rent-seeking argument, one should always point out that the data are inadequate (one can also imply in a tactful manner, that the reason that the data are inadequate is that the guilty are concealing or keeping secret evidence of their guilt). More data are always needed and generally the pressure group is to some extent unwilling to provide data because it fears strengthening your argument. Mainly, however, this argument places you in a very good position for rebuttal. Almost certainly, the pressure group representatives will argue that you are simply ignorant in their field. A response in which you say that your ignorance is partly because they are keeping secrets and then ask them to provide further information generally would be helpful. In the unlikely event that they do provide additional information, of course, you have opportunity for further and better research.

A second argument that inevitably can be made is that the pressure group has something material to gain from its activities. Although we, as economists, do not regard this as in any way discreditable, the average person does. In fact, the pressure group will normally be arguing that its existence benefits people it in fact injures, but they will normally not deny that its own members are gaining, too. You will thus merely be giving strong emphasis to something the pressure group tends to pass over lightly.

If individual economists would select some blatantly undesirable activity, preferably of a state or local government, and become a modest expert on it, it is my contention that the economy would improve. Doing so does not involve a major investment. In general, these programs are not complicated, but nevertheless becoming an expert will involve some work. After becoming an expert, the economist should attempt to get media publicity for the position with the result first, of certainly attracting the attention of the pressure group, which may or may not be useful, and, second, if the economist pushes hard enough and is persistent, he probably will have at least some effect on the activity of the pressure group.

Here, I should emphasize that though I am suggesting this as an individual effort, there is no reason why small collectives of economists should not be involved, and there is certainly no reason why you should not seek out the support of other groups. The League of Women Voters, for example, tends to go about looking for good causes and you may be able to improve their taste. There are also various business groups, Rotary Clubs, and so on that are always on the lookout for a lecturer and that would give you an opportunity to provide some influence.

Persistence will, however, be necessary. The pressure group will continue and a mere couple of months' noise about it is helpful but unlikely to accomplish a great deal. Persistence is not difficult, however. Once you have passed the threshold of knowing enough about the organization so that you can regard yourself as a modest expert, it is very easy to keep up with further developments and incorporate additional data into your analyses. Further, your contacts with the media are apt to be self-reinforcing. After you have convinced people that you know a great deal about, let us say, controls on egg production, you are likely to find television program directors asking you questions about all economic matters. You should answer them, of course, to the best of your ability, and this will not only, we hope, contribute to the economic information of the public but also give media representatives an idea of your expertise so that when you bring up the subject of eggs or whatever it is, they are likely to pay attention.

Most economists only occasionally give lectures to something like the Rotary Club. I am suggesting that this aspect of professional life be sharply increased. Furthermore, I am suggesting that you become an expert on some rather obscure topic instead of giving your lecture to the Rotary Club on what is right or what is wrong with Reaganomics. This is indeed a change from the normal academic life but not a gigantic one. I am not suggesting that you devote immense amounts of time to these joint projects, merely that you do indeed devote some time to them. In a way it may be a pleasant change from the more profound and difficult work that I am sure mainly occupies your time.

So far I have been telling you how you can do good and have not explained why I think you can also do well. The first thing to be said is that of course the kind of research I am proposing does have some potential for publication in the regular economic literature. The *Journal of Law and Economics*, the *Journal of Political Economy, Public Policy*, and others all are interested in such articles. I would also suggest that the political science journals would be interested, although it would be necessary to make a few changes in your approach if you submitted articles to them.

But while all of these people would be interested and, I think, the prospects for publication are quite good, it has to be said that if a great many economists began working in this area it would rapidly exhaust the desire for such articles in these journals. After a while, only the very best of such articles could be published there. Further, in this case "best" would not refer entirely to the quality of the work but also to the importance of the subject matter. A new twist in cartel economics would, for example, probably be publishable when hundreds of studies of specific cartels would not.

So far, of course, the tolerance of these journals for this kind of article has by no means been exhausted and those of you who get in first could no doubt take advantage of that tolerance. Once we turn from this kind of journal publication, however, there are a number of other places with gradually decreasing prestige where you can get published. There is now a chain of economic institutes who are in general interested in studies of this kind of cartel.[9] The Borcherding and Dorosh pamphlet is a good example. Clearly this is a perfectly suitable publication to put on your vita even if it does not carry quite so much weight as publication in the *Journal of Political Economy*. I, as a matter of fact, have three such things on my own vita. Indeed, I would imagine that in cost/benefit terms these things are considerably more highly paying than *JPE* articles because although the payoff is not as high, the cost of producing them is also low.

Below that level there is the possibility of fairly widespread publication in such things as articles in local newspapers, letters to the editor, and so on. These are not great publications and you might want to indicate on your bibliography that you think they are not. For example, you could have a separate section for newspaper articles and letters to the editor. You might even mention your appearances on TV in this separate section.

With respect to these less important articles, speeches, and the like, the payoff in academic life is, of course, quite low per unit. Most universities, however, regard activity in the public arena as meritorious and pay it off in higher wages. It also carries with it the advertising value that an article in the *Journal of Political Economy* carries, although, once again, at a lower level.

But although these are less important publications, their cost is also quite low. Once you have become an expert in this area you could grind them out practically at will, producing a letter to the editor, for example, in a half hour. Thus, once again, the cost/benefit analysis from a pure career standpoint seems to be positive.

But this may immediately raise a question in your mind. How do I know that better information is likely to cause the end of these special-interest arrangements? After all, they have been in existence a long time and most economists know about them in general even if the public does not. They do not seem to be very secretive. I believe that they depend on either ignorance or misinformation on the part of the public. My reasons for believing so are two: first, if you discuss any of them with average voters it will turn out that

9. The bulk of them owe their origin to the energies of Antony Fisher.

they have never heard of them, or if they have heard of them, they are badly misinformed about them. In the case of the British Columbia Egg Board, the average voter probably does not know that there is such an organization. The voter who does probably has bought the argument that the organization stabilizes prices and protects the family farm.

But in addition to this informal public opinion poll, there is another and, in my opinion, more important reason. If we think of the British Columbia Egg Board, any economist could quickly arrange a set of taxes on eggs together with direct subsidies to the people who were in the business of producing eggs[10] that would make both the customers and the producers of the eggs better off. We do not see this direct subsidy being used. Why do pressure groups not simply aim at a low tax on the entire population that is used to pay a direct sum of money to them rather than these clearly non-Pareto-optimal arrangements that we in fact observe? I think the only available explanation for this is that they know that a certain amount of confusion and misdirection is necessary. A direct cash transfer, a tax of $10 per family in British Columbia for the purpose of paying a pension to the 300 people who happened to own egg factories at the time the program was put into effect, would never go through because it is too blatant and obvious. It is necessary that these things be covered by some kind of deception. Granted that I am right about this—that these programs require that the people be misinformed—informing them is likely to terminate the program. No politician is going to tax all of his constituents a small sum of money in order to give a large sum of money to a small group no matter how well organized that small group is if everyone knows that is what he is doing. Economists can see to it that they do know.

Note here, also, that the nature of the mass media is on your side. The mass media all aim at large audiences. The small pressure group does not have much chance of getting the attention of the mass media except, possibly, unfavorable attention. The small pressure group very likely has its own journal, which it uses for internal communication, but the owner of a TV station or a newspaper will tend to come down for his customers en masse, not a tiny minority of his customers. Thus, not only is secrecy and deception necessary here but the nature of the mass media means that unmasking of these villains is likely to be popular with those who want to make money in the media business.

10. Some of these might, of course, decide to stop producing eggs and move to Hawaii on the subsidy.

I am sure all of this sounds rather wild to most of you. I gave an earlier version of this paper at my own university, and a young ABD, who had been listening and apparently could not believe his ears, came up afterward and asked me whether it was really true that I was suggesting that he not only study up on some local government-managed cartel but seek publication in places other than the *JPE*. I assured him that was my objective. He went away looking astounded, not, I think, at the brilliance of my ideas, but at the eccentricity.

This particular young man will, I think, have great difficulty getting any publications ever in the *JPE*. Competition is stiff (even to this day I have about half of my submissions turned down[11]), and most economists will never get a single article published in a leading journal. Still, I assume all of you are members of that small minority who do occasionally break into print in such places as the *JPE*, the *AER*, and the *QJE*.

Turning to the problem of the man who does have great difficulty getting anything published, something on his vita is better than nothing, and the proposal that I am making is a way in which he can pretty much guarantee he will have at least something on his vita. For the more productive economist, who does currently produce articles for the leading journals, it is still helpful to add additional items even if these additional items are not of Nobel prize quality. Once again, the cost of producing these things is comparatively low, so you make a good deal per unit of effort.

Even if there were no beneficial impact on your career, nevertheless, I would urge it on you. All of us are, to some minor extent, charitable and this is a particularly convenient way for economists to work out their charitable feelings. Getting rid of the British Columbia Egg Board might not impress you as a major accomplishment, but individuals can expect to have only small impacts on the massive structure that we call modern society. It is likely that you will do more good for the world by concentrating on abolishing some such organization in your locality than the average person does—indeed, very much more. It is an unusual form of charity, but a form in which the payoff would be high. But although such work falls squarely in the path of virtue, it also has positive payoffs. You can, to repeat my title, do well while you are doing good.

11. I have a large collection of unpublished articles.

APPENDIXES

GORDON TULLOCK

BIOGRAPHICAL NOTE

Gordon Tullock was born in Rockford, Illinois, on February 16, 1922. His father, George, was a hardy midwesterner of Scottish ancestry; his mother, Helen, was of equally hardy Pennsylvania Dutch stock. He obtained his basic education in the public schools of Rockford, displaying from early childhood a superior intellectual ability that clearly distinguished him from his peers. In 1940 Tullock left for the University of Chicago Law School to combine a two-year program of undergraduate courses with a four-year formal law program. In fact, he completed the initial two-year program in a single year.

His law school program was interrupted when he was drafted into military service as an infantry rifleman in 1943, but not before he had all but completed a one-semester course in economics taught by Henry Simons. This course was to be Tullock's only formal exposure to economics—a fact that no doubt enhanced rather than hindered his future success in contributing highly original ideas in that discipline.

Tullock served in the U.S. military until shortly after the end of hostilities, returning to civilian life in December 1945. He took part in the Normandy landings on D-Day +7 as a member of the Ninth Infantry. His life almost certainly was spared by the good fortune of being left behind at division headquarters to defend three antitank guns. The original members of the Ninth Infantry were decimated on their hard-fought route across France and into Germany.

Following behind, Tullock eventually would cross the Rhine, he claims while still asleep. Ultimately, he would end up in the Russian sector. Although Tullock modestly dismisses his wartime service as uneventful, this can be only with the advantage of hindsight. Participation in a major land war as part of the poor, bloody infantry is never without the gravest of risks.

Following this three-year wartime interruption, Tullock returned to Chicago and obtained a Juris Doctor degree from the law school in 1947. He failed to remit the five-dollar payment required by the university and thus never received a baccalaureate degree.

His initial career, as an attorney with a small but prestigious downtown Chicago law firm, was controversial and, perhaps, mercifully brief. During his five-month tenure, Tullock handled only two cases. In the first case, one of the partners in the firm had advised a client not to pursue his case. Tullock took it and won. The second case he should have won, but lost. He was admonished by the court for his poor performance.[1] Fortunately for the world of ideas, these events persuaded him to seek out an alternative career.

Prior to graduation Tullock had passed the foreign-service examination and was admitted to the extremely exclusive ranks of the foreign service in fall 1947, receiving an assignment as vice consul in Tientsin, China. This two-year assignment included the Communist takeover in 1948. Following Tullock's return to the United States, the Department of State dispatched him to Yale University (1949–51) and then to Cornell University (1951–52) for advanced study of the Chinese language.

In late 1952 he joined the mainland China section of the Consulate General in Hong Kong. Some nine months later he was reassigned to the political section of the U.S. Embassy in Korea. Tullock returned to the United States in January 1955, where he was assigned to the State Department's Office of Intelligence and Research in Washington. He resigned from the foreign service in fall 1956.

Over the next two years Tullock held several positions, including, most notably, that of research director of the Princeton Panel, a small subsidiary of the Gallup organization in Princeton. Essentially he was in a state of transition, marking time until he was ready to make a bid for entry into academia.

Unusually, Tullock had already published in leading economics journals, even during his diplomatic service, articles on hyperinflation and monetary cycles in China and on the Korean monetary and fiscal system. Thus, he whetted his own appetite for an academic career and signaled an extraordinary facility for creative thinking through the observation of his own environment. Furthermore, he had read and had been intellectually excited by the writings of such scholars as Joseph Schumpeter, Duncan Black, Anthony Downs, and Karl Popper,[2] scholarship that provided the basis for reintegrating economics and political science within a strictly rational choice frame-

1. Gordon L. Brady and Robert D. Tollison, "Gordon Tullock: Creative Maverick of Public Choice," *Public Choice* 71 (September 1991): 141–48.

2. Joseph A. Schumpeter, *Capitalism and Democracy* (New York: Harper and Row, 1942); Duncan Black, "On the Rationale of Group Decision-Making," *Journal of Political Economy* 56 (1948): 23–34; Anthony Downs, *An Economic Theory of Democracy* (New York: Harper and Row, 1957); Karl Popper, *The Logic of Scientific Discovery* (New York: Basic Books, 1959).

work. In short, Tullock was ready to play a significant role in extending the empire of economics into the territory of contiguous disciplines.

Encouraged by Warren Nutter, in fall 1958, at age thirty-six, Tullock accepted a one-year postdoctoral fellowship at the Thomas Jefferson Center for Political Economy at the University of Virginia. Still a relatively unknown quantity at that time, Tullock nevertheless brought with him to the center two indispensable assests—namely a brilliant and inquiring, if still unfocused, intellect and an unbounded enthusiasm for his adopted discipline of political economy. Quickly he forged a bond with the director of the center, James M. Buchanan—a bond that would result in some of the most original and important political-economic scholarship of the mid-twentieth century.

Tullock's fellowship year at the center was productive, resulting in an important publication on the problem of majority voting.[3] In fall 1959, Tullock was appointed as assistant professor in the Department of International Studies at the University of South Carolina. Publications continued to flow,[4] while Tullock crafted a seminal draft paper entitled "An Economic Theory of Constitutions" that would become the fulcrum for *The Calculus of Consent*.[5] On this basis, Tullock quickly advanced to the rank of associate professor before returning to the University of Virginia and renewing his relationship with Buchanan in February 1962, just as the University of Michigan Press was publishing their seminal book, *The Calculus of Consent*.

In 1966 Tullock edited and published the first issue of *Papers on Non-Market Decision Making*, the precursor to *Public Choice*. Between 1962 and 1967, Tullock published innovative books on bureaucracy, on method, and on public choice, as well as a rising volume of scholarly papers that earned him international recognition as a major scholar.[6]

Despite this distinguished resume, Tullock would be denied promotion to

3. Gordon Tullock, "Problems of Majority Voting," *Journal of Political Economy* 67 (1959): 571–79.

4. Gordon Tullock, "An Economic Analysis of Political Choice," *Il Politico* 16 (1961): 234–40; "Utility, Strategy and Social Decision Rules: Comment," *Quarterly Journal of Economics* 75 (1961): 493–97; "An Economic Theory of Constitutions," University of South Carolina, 1959, manuscript.

5. James M. Buchanan and Gordon Tullock, *The Calculus of Consent: Logical Foundations of Constitutional Democracy* (Ann Arbor: University of Michigan Press, 1962).

6. Gordon Tullock, *The Politics of Bureaucracy* (Washington, D.C.: Public Affairs Press, 1965); *The Organization of Inquiry* (Durham: Duke University Press, 1966); *Toward a Mathematics of Politics* (Ann Arbor: University of Michigan Press, 1967).

full professor of economics on three consecutive occasions by a politically hostile and fundamentally unscholarly university administration. In fall 1967, Buchanan protested these negative decisions by resigning to take up a position at the University of California at Los Angeles. Tullock also resigned to become a professor of economics and political science at Rice University. With Ronald Coase having resigned for similar reasons in 1964 to take up a position at the University of Chicago, it appeared that the nascent Virginia School of Political Economy might have been deliberately nipped in the bud by the left-leaning administration of the University of Virginia.

As a result of a successful initiative by Charles J. Goetz, the University of Virginia plot failed. Goetz succeeded in attracting Tullock to join the Virginia Polytechnic Institute and State University in Blacksburg as a professor of economics and public choice in fall 1968. Goetz and Tullock immediately established the Center for Studies in Public Choice as the basis for promoting scholarship in the field and as a means of attracting Buchanan to join them at Virginia Tech. This initiative bore fruit in 1969, when Buchanan joined the faculty and assumed the general directorship of the center, which was immediately renamed the Center for Study of Public Choice. Simultaneously, Tullock's journal, *Papers in Non-Market Decision Making*, became *Public Choice*, and the new subdiscipline set down fruitful roots in the foothills of the Appalachian Mountains.

Henceforth, Tullock would never look back. Over the next thirty-odd years, he forged for himself a reputation as a brilliant entrepreneurial scholar and a formidable debater. To this day he refuses to rest on well-earned laurels as a founding father and as an entrepreneurial pioneer of three important subdisciplines of economics, namely public choice, law and economics, and bioeconomics.

PROFESSIONAL POSITIONS

1947	Attorney
1947–56	Foreign service officer, U.S. Department of State
1956–58	Research director, Princeton Panel
1958–59	Postdoctoral fellow, University of Virginia
1959–62	Assistant and associate professor, University of South Carolina
1962–67	Associate professor of economics, University of Virginia
1966–69	Editor, *Papers on Non-Market Decision Making*
1967–68	Professor of economics and political science, Rice University
1968–72	Professor of economics and public choice, Virginia Polytechnic Institute and State University

1969–90 Editor, *Public Choice*
1972–83 University Distinguished Professor, Virginia Polytechnic Institute and State University
1983–87 Holbert L. Harris University Professor, George Mason University
1987 Philip Morris Visiting Distinguished Scholar, Baruch University
1987–99 Karl Eller Professor of Economics and Political Science, University of Arizona
1999– Professor of law and economics, George Mason University

HONORS

1982 Recipient of the Leslie T. Wilkins Award for outstanding book in the field of criminology and criminal justice, Criminal Justice Research Center, Albany, New York
1985 Honorary Doctorate of Letters, Basel University
1992 Honorary Doctor of Law, University of Chicago
1993 Adam Smith Award, Association of Private Enterprise Education
1996 Award for outstanding contributions in the field of law and economics, George Mason University School of Law
1998 Distinguished Fellow, American Economic Association

OFFICES HELD

President, Public Choice Society
President, Southern Economic Association
President, Western Economic Association
President, Atlantic Economic Society
President, Association of Private Enterprise
President, Henry Simons Society
Honorary Chairman, Bionomics Society

CONTENTS OF THE SELECTED WORKS OF GORDON TULLOCK

Volume 1 *Virginia Political Economy*

Volume 2 *The Calculus of Consent: Logical Foundations of Constitutional Democracy* (with James M. Buchanan)

Volume 3 *The Organization of Inquiry*

Volume 4 *The Economics of Politics*

Part 1. The Nature of Public Choice

"An Economic Analysis of Political Choice," *Il Politico* 16 (1961): 234–40.

"Origins of Public Choice," in *The Makers of Modern Economics*, vol. 3, ed. Arnold Heertje (Aldershot, U.K., and Brookfield, Vt.: Edward Elgar, 1997), 122–39.

"People Are People: The Elements of Public Choice," in *Government: Whose Obedient Servant? A Primer in Pubic Choice*, ed. Gordon Tullock, Arthur Seldon, and Gordon L. Brady (London: Institute of Economic Affairs, 2000), 3–18.

Part 2. What Should Government Do?

"Mosquito Abatement," in *Private Wants, Public Means: An Economic Analysis of the Desirable Scope of Government* (New York and London: Basic Books, 1970), 3–28.

"Property, Contract, and the State," in *Private Wants, Public Means: An Economic Analysis of the Desirable Scope of Government* (New York and London: Basic Books, 1970), 29–54.

"Bargaining," in *Private Wants, Public Means: An Economic Analysis of the Desirable Scope of Government* (New York and London: Basic Books, 1970), 55–70.

"Externalities and All That," in *Private Wants, Public Means: An Economic Analysis of the Desirable Scope of Government* (New York and London: Basic Books, 1970), 71–95.

"The Costs of Government," in *Private Wants, Public Means: An Economic Analysis of the Desirable Scope of Government* (New York and London: Basic Books, 1970), 96–128.

"Remedies," in *Private Wants, Public Means: An Economic Analysis of the Desirable Scope of Government* (New York and London: Basic Books, 1970), 129–57.

"The Social Costs of Reducing Social Cost," in *Managing the Commons*, ed. Garrett Hardin and John Baden (San Francisco: W. H. Freeman, 1976), 147–56.

Part 3. The Vote Motive

The Vote Motive: An Essay in the Economics of Politics, Hobart paperback no. 9 (London: Institute of Economic Affairs, 1976), 1–58.

Part 4. Rational Ignorance and Its Implications

"Political Ignorance," in *Toward a Mathematics of Politics* (Ann Arbor: University of Michigan Press, 1967), 100–114.

"The Politics of Persuasion," in *Toward a Mathematics of Politics* (Ann Arbor: University of Michigan Press, 1967), 115–32.

"The Economics of Lying," in *Toward a Mathematics of Politics* (Ann Arbor: University of Michigan Press, 1967), 133–43.

"Some Further Thoughts on Voting," *Public Choice* 104 (July 2000): 181–82.

Part 5. Voting Paradoxes

"A Measure of the Importance of Cyclical Majorities" (Colin D. Campbell and Gordon Tullock), *Economic Journal* 75 (December 1965): 853–75.

"The Paradox of Voting—A Possible Method of Calculation," *American Political Science Review* 60 (September 1966): 684–85.

"Computer Simulation of a Small Voting System" (Gordon Tullock and Colin D. Campbell), *Economic Journal* 80 (March 1970): 97–104.

"The Paradox of Not Voting for Oneself," *American Political Science Review* 69 (September 1975): 1295–97.

"Avoiding the Voter's Paradox Democratically: Comment," *Theory and Decision* 6 (November 1975): 485–86.

"An Approach to Empirical Measures of Voting Paradoxes" (John L. Dobra and Gordon Tullock), *Public Choice* 36 (1981): 193–94.

Part 6. The Median Voter Theorem

"Duncan Black: The Founding Father, 23 May 1908–14 January 1991," *Public Choice* 71 (September 1991): 125–28.

"Hotelling and Downs in Two Dimensions," in *Toward a Mathematics of Politics* (Ann Arbor: University of Michigan Press, 1967), 50–61.

Part 7. Vote Trading and Logrolling as Mechanisms of Political Exchange

"A Simple Algebraic Logrolling Model," *American Economic Review* 60 (June 1970): 419–26.

"More Complicated Log-rolling," in *On Voting: A Public Choice Approach* (Cheltenham, U.K., and Brookfield, Vt.: Edward Elgar Publishing, 1998), 105–24.

"Efficiency in Log-rolling," in *On Voting: A Public Choice Approach* (Cheltenham, U.K., and Brookfield, Vt.: Edward Elgar Publishing, 1998), 125–41.

Part 8. More on Demand Revealing

"Some Limitations of Demand-Revealing Processes: Comment" (T. Nicolaus Tideman and Gordon Tullock), *Public Choice* 29 (Spring 1977): 125–28.

"Coalitions under Demand Revealing" (T. Nicolaus Tideman and Gordon Tullock), *Public Choice* 36 (1981): 323–28.

"More Thought about Demand Revealing," *Public Choice* 38 (1982): 167–70.

Part 9. Voting Methods and Political Market Behavior

"Proportional Representation," in *Toward a Mathematics of Politics* (Ann Arbor: University of Michigan Press, 1967), 144–57.

"Democracy as It Really Is," in *The New Federalist* (Vancouver: Fraser Institute, 1994), 53–60.

"A Bouquet of Governments," in *The New Federalist* (Vancouver: Fraser Institute, 1994), 61–76.

"Thoughts about Representative Government," *European Journal of Political Economy* 10 (May 1994): 27–39.

"Voting, Different Methods and General Considerations," in *On Voting: A Public Choice Approach* (Cheltenham, U.K., and Brookfield, Vt.: Edward Elgar Publishing, 1998), 157–69.

"A Bouquet of Voting Methods," in *On Voting: A Public Choice Approach* (Cheltenham, U.K., and Brookfield, Vt.: Edward Elgar Publishing, 1998), 170–84.

Volume 5 *The Rent-Seeking Society*

Part 1. Rent Seeking: An Overview

"Rent Seeking: The Problem of Definition," in *The Economics of Special Privilege and Rent Seeking* (Boston: Kluwer Academic Publishers, 1989), 49–58.

Rent Seeking, The Shaftesbury Papers, vol. 2 (Aldershot, U.K., and Brookfield, Vt.: Edward Elgar, 1993), v–vi, 1–98.

Part 2. More on Efficient Rent Seeking

"Efficient Rent-Seeking Revisited," in *The Political Economy of Rent-Seeking*, ed. Charles K. Rowley, Robert D. Tollison, and Gordon Tullock (Boston: Kluwer Academic Publishers, 1988), 91–94.

"Back to the Bog," *Public Choice* 46 (1985): 259–64.

"Another Part of the Swamp," *Public Choice* 54 (1987): 83–84.

"Still Somewhat Muddy: A Comment," *Public Choice* 76 (1993): 365–70.

Part 3. The Environments of Rent Seeking

"Rent Seeking as a Negative-Sum Game," in *Toward a Theory of the Rent-Seeking Society*, ed. James M. Buchanan, Robert D. Tollison, and Gordon Tullock (College Station: Texas A&M University Press, 1980), 16–36.

"Industrial Organization and Rent Seeking in Dictatorships," *Journal of Institutional and Theoretical Economics* 142 (March 1986): 4–16.

"Transitional Gains and Transfers," *Cato Journal* 6 (Spring–Summer 1986): 143–54.

"Rents and Rent-Seeking," in *The Political Economy of Rent-Seeking*, ed. Charles K. Rowley, Robert D. Tollison, and Gordon Tullock (Boston: Kluwer Academic Publishers, 1988), 51–62.

"Why Did the Industrial Revolution Occur in England?" in *The Political Economy of Rent-Seeking*, ed. Charles K. Rowley, Robert D. Tollison, and Gordon Tullock (Boston: Kluwer Academic Publishers, 1988), 409–19.

"Rent Seeking and Tax Reform," *Contemporary Policy Issues* 6 (October 1988): 37–47.

"Rent-Seeking and the Law," in *Current Issues in Public Choice*, ed. José Casas Pardo and Friedrich Schneider (Cheltenham, U.K.: Edward Elgar, 1995): 179–88.

"Excise Taxation in the Rent-Seeking Society," in *Taxing Choice: The Predatory Politics of Fiscal Discrimination*, ed. William F. Shughart II (New Brunswick and London: Transaction Publishers, 1997), 369–73.

Part 4. The Cost of Rent Seeking

"The Costs of Rent Seeking: A Metaphysical Problem," *Public Choice* 57 (1988): 14–24.

"Rents, Ignorance, and Ideology," in *The Economics of Special Privilege* (Boston: Kluwer Academic Publishers, 1989), 11–28.

"Efficient Rent Seeking, Diseconomies of Scale, Public Goods, and Morality," in *The Economics of Special Privilege* (Boston: Kluwer Academic Publishers, 1989), 41–48.

"Are Rents Fully Dissipated?" *Public Choice* 82 (January 1995): 181–84.

"Where Is the Rectangle?" *Public Choice* 91 (1997): 149–59.

"Which Rectangle?" *Public Choice* 96 (1998): 405–10.

Part 5. Exchanges and Contracts

Exchanges and Contracts, no. 3, *The Blackstone Commentaries*, ed. Amanda J. Owens (Fairfax, Va.: Locke Institute, 2000), 1–54.

Part 6. Future Directions for Rent-Seeking Research

"Future Directions for Rent-Seeking Research," in *The Political Economy of Rent-Seeking*, ed. Charles K. Rowley, Robert D. Tollison, and Gordon Tullock (Boston: Kluwer Academic Publishers, 1988), 465–80.

Volume 6 *Bureaucracy*

The Politics of Bureaucracy (Washington, D.C.: Public Affairs Press, 1965).

Economic Hierarchies, Organization, and the Structure of Production (Boston: Kluwer Academic Publishers, 1992).

Volume 7 *The Economics and Politics of Wealth Distribution*

Part 1. Why Redistribute Wealth?

"Income Redistribution," in *Private Wants, Public Means: An Economic Analysis of the Desirable Scope of Government* (New York and London: Basic Books, 1970), 247–57.

"Helping the Poor," in *Welfare for the Well-to-Do* (Dallas: Fisher Institute, 1983), 15–29.

"Reasons for Redistribution," in *Economics of Income Redistribution*, Kluwer-Nijhoff Studies in Human Issues: An International Series in the Social Sciences (Boston: Kluwer-Nijhoff, 1983), 1–15.

"Reasons for Redistribution," in *The Economics of Wealth and Poverty* (New York: New York University Press, 1986), 15–41.

"Objectives of Income Redistribution," in *The Economics of Wealth and Poverty* (New York: New York University Press, 1986), 42–56.

Part 2. Private and Semiprivate Redistribution Mechanisms

"Charitable Gifts," in *Kluwer-Nijhoff Studies in Human Issues, Economics of Income Redistribution* (Boston: Kluwer-Nijhoff, 1983), 49–72.

"Local Redistribution," in *The Economics of Wealth and Poverty* (New York: New York University Press, 1986), 113–27.

"Aid in Kind," in *The Economics of Wealth and Poverty* (New York: New York University Press, 1986), 128–35.

"Demand Revealing, Transfers, and Rent Seeking," in *The Economics of Wealth and Poverty* (New York: New York University Press, 1986), 136–42.

"Epilogue—The Grating People," in *The Economics of Wealth and Poverty* (New York: New York University Press, 1986), 205–6.

Part 3. Redistributive Politics

"The Machiavellians and the Well-Intentioned," in *Welfare for the Well-to-Do* (Dallas: Fisher Institute, 1983), 31–50.

"Helping the Poor vs. Helping the Well-Organized," in *Welfare for the Well-to-Do* (Dallas: Fisher Institute, 1983), 63–72.

"Horizontal Transfers," in *Kluwer-Nijhoff Studies in Human Issues, Economics of Income Redistribution* (Boston: Kluwer-Nijhoff, 1983), 17–31.

"Information and Logrolling," in *Kluwer-Nijhoff Studies in Human Issues, Economics of Income Redistribution* (Boston: Kluwer-Nijhoff, 1983), 33–48.

"The Mixed Case," in *Kluwer-Nijhoff Studies in Human Issues, Economics of Income Redistribution* (Boston: Kluwer-Nijhoff, 1983), 73–96.

"General Welfare or Welfare for the Poor Only," in *Kluwer-Nijhoff Studies in Human Issues, Economics of Income Redistribution* (Boston: Kluwer-Nijhoff, 1983), 97–110.

Part 4. The Expanding Frontiers of Wealth Redistribution

"Old Age Pensions," in *Kluwer-Nijhoff Studies in Human Issues, Economics of Income Redistribution* (Boston: Kluwer-Nijhoff, 1983), 111–22.

"Risk, Charity, and Miscellaneous Aspects of Social Security," in *Kluwer-Nijhoff Studies in Human Issues, Economics of Income Redistribution* (Boston: Kluwer-Nijhoff, 1983), 123–35.

"Education and Medicine," in *Kluwer-Nijhoff Studies in Human Issues, Economics of Income Redistribution* (Boston: Kluwer-Nijhoff, 1983), 137–56.

"Administrative Transfers," in *Kluwer-Nijhoff Studies in Human Issues, Economics of Income Redistribution* (Boston: Kluwer-Nijhoff, 1983), 157–73.

"Giving Life," in *The Economics of Wealth and Poverty* (New York: New York University Press, 1986), 158–69.

Part 5. What to Do—What to Do

"What to Do—What to Do," in *Kluwer-Nijhoff Studies in Human Issues, Economics of Income Redistribution* (Boston: Kluwer-Nijhoff, 1983), 175–87.

Volume 8 *The Social Dilemma: Of Autocracy, Revolution, Coup d'Etat, and War*

Part 1. The Roots of the Social Dilemma

"The Roots of Conflict," in *The Social Dilemma: The Economics of War and Revolution* (Blacksburg, Va.: Center for Study of Public Choice, 1974), 1–8.

"The Cooperative State," in *The Social Dilemma: The Economics of War and Revolution* (Blacksburg, Va.: Center for Study of Public Choice, 1974), 9–16.

"The Exploitative State," in *The Social Dilemma: The Economics of War and Revolution* (Blacksburg, Va.: Center for Study of Public Choice, 1974), 17–25.

Part 2. The Goals and Organizational Forms of Autocracies

Introduction to *Autocracy* (Dordrecht and Boston: Kluwer Academic Publishers, 1987), 11–15.

"The Uses of Dictatorship," in *Autocracy* (Dordrecht and Boston: Kluwer Academic Publishers, 1987), 115–30.

"Becoming a Dictator," in *Autocracy* (Dordrecht and Boston: Kluwer Academic Publishers, 1987), 131–50.

"The Problem of Succession," in *Autocracy* (Dordrecht and Boston: Kluwer Academic Publishers, 1987), 151–74.

"Democracy and Despotism," in *Autocracy* (Dordrecht and Boston: Kluwer Academic Publishers, 1987), 175–207.

"Monarchies, Hereditary and Nonhereditary," in *The Elgar Companion to Public Choice*, ed. William F. Shughart II and Laura Razzolini (Cheltenham, U.K., and Northampton, Mass.: Edward Elgar, 2001), 140–56.

Part 3. Revolution and Its Suppression

"Revolution and Welfare Economics," in *The Social Dilemma: The Economics of War and Revolution* (Blacksburg, Va.: Center for Study of Public Choice, 1974), 26–35.

"The Paradox of Revolution," in *The Social Dilemma: The Economics of War and Revolution* (Blacksburg, Va.: Center for Study of Public Choice, 1974), 36–46.

"The Economics of Repression," in *The Social Dilemma: The Economics of War and Revolution* (Blacksburg, Va.: Center for Study of Public Choice, 1974), 47–59.

"'Popular' Risings," in *Autocracy* (Dordrecht and Boston: Kluwer Academic Publishers, 1987), 53–78.

"Legitimacy and Ethics," in *Autocracy* (Dordrecht and Boston: Kluwer Academic Publishers, 1987), 79–114.

Part 4. The Coup d'Etat and Its Suppression

"Coup d'Etat: Structural Factors," in *The Social Dilemma: The Economics of War and Revolution* (Blacksburg, Va.: Center for Study of Public Choice, 1974), 60–70.

"The Theory of the Coup," in *The Social Dilemma: The Economics of War and Revolution* (Blacksburg, Va.: Center for Study of Public Choice, 1974), 71–86.

"Coups and Their Prevention," in *Autocracy* (Dordrecht and Boston: Kluwer Academic Publishers, 1987), 17–34.

Part 5. The Economics of War

"International Conflict: Two Parties," in *The Social Dilemma: The Economics of War and Revolution* (Blacksburg, Va.: Center for Study of Public Choice, 1974), 87–106.

"Agreement and Cheating," in *The Social Dilemma: The Economics of War and Revolution* (Blacksburg, Va.: Center for Study of Public Choice, 1974), 107–25.

"Three or More Countries and the Balance of Power," in *The Social Dilemma: The Economics of War and Revolution* (Blacksburg, Va.: Center for Study of Public Choice, 1974), 126–38.

Epilogue to *The Social Dilemma: The Economics of War and Revolution* (Blacksburg, Va.: Center for Study of Public Choice, 1974), 139–40.

Volume 9 *Law and Economics*

The Logic of the Law (New York and London: Basic Books, 1971).

"The 'Dead' Hand of Monopoly" (James M. Buchanan and Gordon Tullock), *Antitrust Law and Economics Review* 1 (Summer 1968): 85–96.

"Does Punishment Deter Crime?" *The Public Interest* 36 (Summer 1974): 103–11.

"Two Kinds of Legal Efficiency," *Hofstra Law Review* 8 (Spring 1980): 659–69.

"Optimal Procedure," in *Trials on Trial* (New York: Columbia University Press, 1980), 70–86.

"Technology: The Anglo-Saxons versus the Rest of the World," in *Trials on Trial* (New York: Columbia University Press, 1980), 87–104.

"Various Ways of Dealing with the Cost of Litigation," in *Trials on Trial* (New York: Columbia University Press, 1980), 105–18.

"The Motivation of Judges," in *Trials on Trial* (New York: Columbia University Press, 1980), 119–34.

"Defending the Napoleonic Code over the Common Law," in *Research in Law and Policy Studies*, ed. S. S. Nagel (Greenwich, Conn.: JAI Press, 1988), 2–27.

"Negligence Again," *International Review of Law and Economics* 1 (June 1981): 51–62.

"Welfare and the Law," *International Review of Law and Economics* 2 (December 1982): 151–64.

The Case Against the Common Law, vol. 1, *The Blackstone Commentaries*, ed. Amanda J. Owens (Fairfax, Va.: Locke Institute, 1997), 1–65.

Volume 10 *Economics without Frontiers*

Part 1. The Economic Approach to Human Behavior

"The Economic Approach to Human Behavior" (Richard B. McKenzie and Gordon Tullock), in *The New World of Economics: Explorations into the Human Experience* (Homewood, Ill.: Richard D. Irwin, 1975), 3–22.

Part 2. The New World of Economics

"Marriage, Divorce, and the Family" (Richard B. McKenzie and Gordon Tullock), in *The New World of Economics: Explorations into the Human Experience* (Homewood, Ill.: Richard D. Irwin, 1975), 95–107.

"Child Production" (Richard B. McKenzie and Gordon Tullock), in *The New World of Economics: Explorations into the Human Experience* (Homewood, Ill.: Richard D. Irwin, 1975), 108–23.

"The Economic Aspects of Crime" (Richard B. McKenzie and Gordon Tullock), in *The New World of Economics: Exploration into the Human Experience* Homewood, Ill.: Richard D. Irwin, 1975), 129–45.

"The Economic versus the Sociological Views of Crime" (Richard B. McKenzie and Gordon Tullock), in *The New World of Economics: Explorations into the Human Experience* (Homewood, Ill.: Richard D. Irwin, 1975), 146–56.

"Why Government" (Gordon Tullock and Richard B. McKenzie), in *The New World of Economics: Explorations into the Human Experience*, 4th ed. (Homewood, Ill.: Richard D. Irwin, 1975), 191–200.

"Rationality in Human and Nonhuman Societies" (Gordon Tullock and Richard B. McKenzie), in *The New World of Economics: Explorations into the Human Experience* (Homewood, Ill.: Richard D. Irwin, 1975), 263–78.

"Universities Should Discriminate against Assistant Professors," *Journal of Political Economy* 81 (September–October 1973): 1256–57.

Part 3. Bioeconomics

"Sociobiology" (Gordon Tullock and Richard B. McKenzie), in *The New World of Economics: Explorations into the Human Experience* (Homewood, Ill.: Richard D. Irwin, 1975), 279–96.

"Economics and Sociobiology: A Comment," *Journal of Economic Literature* (June 1977): 502–6.

"Sociobiology and Economics," *Atlantic Economic Journal* 8 (September 1979): 1–10.

"Territorial Boundaries: An Economic View," *American Naturalist* 121 (March 1983): 440–42.

"Evolution and Human Behavior," *Journal of Bioeconomics* 4, no. 2 (2002): 99–107.

The Economics of Nonhuman Societies (Tucson: Pallas Press), 1–87.

Part 4. Public Finance

"Science Fiction and the Debt," in *Deficits*, ed. James M. Buchanan, Charles K. Rowley, and Robert D. Tollison (Oxford: Basil Blackwell, 1987), 75–78.

"Subsidized Housing in a Competitive Market: Comment," *American Economic Review* 61 (March 1971): 218–19.

"Optimal Poll Taxes," *Atlantic Economic Journal* 3 (April 1975): 1–6.

"Optimal Poll Taxes: Further Aspects," *Atlantic Economic Journal* 4 (Fall 1976): 7–9.

"Bismarckism," in *Taxation and the Deficit Economy: Fiscal Policy and Capital Formation in the United States*, ed. Dwight R. Lee (Pacific Research Institute for Public Policy, 1986), 225–40.

Part 5. Monetary Economics

"Hyperinflation in China, 1937–49" (Colin D. Campbell and Gordon Tullock), *Journal of Political Economy* 62 (June 1954): 237–45.

"Paper Money—A Cycle in Cathay," *Economic History Review* 9 (June 1957): 393–407.

"Some Little Understood Aspects of Korea's Monetary and Fiscal Systems" (Colin D. Campbell and Gordon Tullock), *American Economic Review* 47 (June 1957): 336–49.

"Competing Monies," *Journal of Money, Credit and Banking* 7 (November 1975): 491–97.

"Competing Monies: A Reply," *Journal of Money, Credit and Banking* 8 (November 1976): 521–25.

"When Is Inflation Not Inflation?" *Journal of Money, Credit and Banking* 11 (May 1979): 219–21.

Part 6. Size and Growth of Government

"An Empirical Analysis of Cross-National Economic Growth, 1951–80" (Kevin B. Grier and Gordon Tullock), *Journal of Monetary Economics* 24 (September 1989): 259–76.

"Provision of Public Goods through Privatization," *Kyklos* 49 (1996): 221–24.

Part 7. The Theory of Games

"An Economic Theory of Military Tactics: Methodological Individualism at War"(Geoffrey Brennan and Gordon Tullock), *Journal of Economic Behavior and Organization* 3 (1982): 225–42.

"Jackson and the Prisoner's Dilemma," *Journal of Economic Behavior and Organization* 8 (December 1987): 637–40.

"Adam Smith and the Prisoners' Dilemma," *Quarterly Journal of Economics* 100 (1985): 1073–81.

"Games and Preference," *Rationality and Society* 41 (January 1992): 24–32.

INDEX

References to bibliographic information appear in italics.

academic disciplines: framework for promoting cooperation among, 7–10; overlapping of economics and biology, 555–57; spread of economics among, 3–7. *See also* economics; political science; public choice theory; social sciences

academic journals: economics journals, 589; edited by Tullock, 36, 42; printed comments on papers in, 41–42; publication in, 598–601; refereeing of papers for, 39–41

academic research: cooperative interdisciplinary, 555–56; effect of government funding on, 208; money allocation for, 37–38

adversary system of law, 465–66; compared with inquisitorial system, 473–79, 510; disadvantage, 482; judges and juries in, 477–78; relative inefficiency, 475

aggregate preferences: Arrow's impossibility theorem, 90, 104; optima, 101–4; problems of aggregating, 73

agreement equilibrium, 199

agreements. *See* bargaining

agricultural economics, 556

agricultural subsidies, 218, 269, 583

airline industry cartel, 589–90

Alchian, Armen, 553

altruism, 337, 342, 345. *See also* nepotism

anarchy, 324–25

anger, rationality of, 310–11

Anglo-Saxon system of law. *See* adversary system of law

animals: dominance behavior, 309, 310–11, 313, 557; social activities, 557; welfare of, 428–29, 548. *See also* societies, primitive

annuities, 253 n. 6, 255 n. 8

antitrust policies, 178

ant societies, 558, 560, 571

apartheid, 278

appropriations. *See* funding

arbitration of litigation, 480–81, 520

Ardrey, Robert, *310 n. 1*

aristocratic coalitions, 111

Armey, Richard, *125 n. 2*

arms races, 469

Armstrong, W. E., *66 n. 11*

Arrow, Kenneth, 102 n. 18, *391 n. 4*; *Social Choice and Individual Values*, 90, 91, 103, 104, 124–25; on voting, 391–92. *See also* impossibility theorem

assumption of transitivity. *See* transitivity

Athenian juries, 521–22

attorneys. *See* lawyers

Auster, R. D., *213 n. 4*

automobile accident costs, 444–47

Baden, J., *555 n. 5*

Bain, Joe S., *71 n. 2*

Baird, Charles W., 425, *425 n. 1*

Balageur, G., *23 n. 8*

balance of power in U.S. government, 32

Baldwin, John, *511 n. 3*, *528 n. 4*

banking industry regulation, 590
bargaining: costs, 152–53; loss of temper while, 311–12; as negative sum game, 184; in pretrial settlements, 503–4; welfare costs, 180–85. *See also* logrolling
bartering, 308–13
Baumol, William, *414n. 5*
Beck, Morris, 302–4
Becker, Gary, *174n. 10*, *323n. 1*, *441n. 1*, *461n. 6*
bee societies, 558–59, 560
begging, 186
Beitz, Charles R., *280n. 7*
Bennett, J. T., *23n. 9*, *23n. 10*, *113n. 19*
bias as desirable, 233–34
biological applications of economics, 553–57. *See also* societies, primitive
biological externalities, 541–52
Black, Duncan, 16, *95n. 12*, *101n. 16*, 606; "majority motion," 98; single-peaked preference curves, 90–91; *Theory of Committees and Elections*, *16n. 1*, *51n. 2*, *51n. 3*, *90n. 5*, 105, *381n. 2*
blue laws, 215–16
Borcherding, Thomas E., *218n. 7*, *593n. 4*
Borda voting method, 126–27
Boulding, Kenneth, *3n. 1*, 337n. 6
Bowen, H. R., *134n. 6*
Bower, Blair T., *413n. 3*
Brams, S. J., *115n. 26*
Brandt, Willy, 280–81
Brandy, Lillian, *395n. 6*
Breit, William, *461n. 6*
Brennan, Geoffrey, 232
bribery: of government officials, 240–41, 323–24; relation to collectivization, 355
Britain: government transfers to poor, 263–64; immigrants in, 279–80; National Health Service, 356; parliamentary system, 76–77; voting peculiarities, 32
British Columbia Egg Control Board, 592–93
Browning, Edgar K., *194n. 1*, *195n. 5*
Brunner, Elizabeth, *71n. 2*
brute force. *See* coercion
Buchanan, James, *66n. 12*, *541n. 2*, 607, 608; "A Note on Public Goods Supply," *350n. 2; Calculus of Consent*, 25, 108–12, 264; *Calculus of Consent*, cited, *125n. 3*, *129n. 6*, *288n. 21*, *354n. 5*, *388n. 1;* "Externality," *349n. 1;* "Gasoline Rationing and Market Pricing," *424n. 10;* "Polluters' Profits and Political Response," *425n. 1;* "Positive Economics, Welfare Economics, and Political Economy," *418n. 8;* "Public and Private Interaction under Reciprocal Externality," *177n. 13;* "The Coase Theorem and the Theory of the State," *423n. 9;* "The 'Dead Hand' of Monopoly," *212n. 2;* "The Political Economy of Franchise in the Welfare State," *160n. 9*
bureaucracies: continuing expansion of, 297, 305; cost, 84; equilibrium size, 300; need for research on, 28; South American, 300–301. *See also* theory of bureaucracy
bureaucrats: compared to entrepreneurs, 406, 407; growth of wages, 298–300, 303–4; lobbying by, 194–95; motives, 16, 23; voting by, 23–24, 218. *See also* civil servants; government officials; political appointees
Bush model of natural distribution, 309; advantages to moving out of, 319
Butler, H., *113n. 18*, *118n. 28*

C.A.B. (Civil Aeronautics Board), 589–90
Calabresi, Guido, *456n. 1*
Calculus of Consent, The (Buchanan and Tullock), 25, 108–12, 264
California, 31
campaign contribution restrictions, 228, 235
Campbell, C. D., *90n. 2*
campus protests. *See* student protests
capital accumulation: inheritance tax to promote, 256–57; preconditions for, 314, 316
cartels, 212, 594, 595–96; British Columbia Egg Control Board, 592–93; publishing about, 599; as result of government regulation, 416; taxi medallion, 213–15; U.S. airline industry, 589–90
case law, 513
cattle grazing example, 543–46
cement factory in small country example, 71–75
Center for Study of Public Choice, 608
certification examinations, 595, 596; civil service, 228. *See also* licenses
charitable donors: difference from consumers, 399, 400–402; lack of incentive to be well-informed, 403
charitable giving: actions that can be taken, 274–75; cognitive dissonance about, 270–71, 273; through government, 262, 285–86, 407–8, 409; through government at federal level, 272–73; political activism as a form of, 601; to the poor, 270–72, 273; similarity with revolution, 337; welfare costs of, 182, 185–87. *See also* charities
charitable motives, 285–86, 394–95; are not enough, 411
charities: advertising, 399, 402n. 9, 404; fraud, 397–98, 403; fundraising, 396; inefficiency, 402–4; management, 403n. 11, 406, 407; marketing, 402, 404–7; maximization of payments to, 405–6; suggested reforms, 408–11
Charnov, Eric L., *427n. 1*
choice: real world, 12–14; science of, 10. *See also* preferences
Civil Aeronautics Board (C.A.B), 589–90
civil servants: examinations, 228; higher-than-competitive wages, 218–19, 303–5; power over political appointees, 23–24. *See also* bureaucrats; government officials
civil service system, 74. *See also* theory of bureaucracy
Clarke, Edward, 134, 141
Clarke tax, 135–36; formula for, 145
cloning, 560–62, 570
coalitions of voters: bargaining problems in establishing, 165–66; in demand-revealing process, 146–47; examples, 53–57; and income redistribution, 265–66. *See also* formal logrolling coalitions
coal tits, "shopping" by, 537–40
Coase, Ronald, 37–38, 607; "The Problem of Social Cost," *355n. 6*, *423n. 9*, *458n. 2*
Coase theorem: applied to corruption, 324–25; consumption externality control analogue, 423
cockroach societies, 560
Coelho, Philip, 425
coercion: drawbacks, 308–12; effect of removal, 343–45
collections costs of tariffs, 171
collectivization: adjustment under, 352–55; arguments for, 361, 379; and chiseling, 366–67; effect on individual, 367–69; externalities imposed by, 383–84; geographical

collectivization (*continued*)
contiguity as basis, 387; and growth, 370–73; impact of equitable solutions on, 355–56; optimal, 376–77; rationing under, 366; without relevant externality, 356–58; tax collection effects on, 364–65
colonial coelenterate societies, 560
commensals, 570–71
common law, 481–82
communism, collapse, 344–45
comparison shopping, 430–32, 538–39
compensation mechanism: in bargaining, 180; for collective actions by government, 386–87; quotas as, 426
compensation mechanism in voting, 134; compensating voters who lose, 137–38; in demand-revealing process voting, 159–60, 161; per unit, 142
competition: government need of, 25, 75–77; for government transfers, 204, 206, 208–11; for territory, 556; that leads to lower welfare, 206
confiscatory actions of government: inheritance taxes, 252; seizure of property, 426
conflict, welfare costs, 192–93
congressmen. *See* elected officials; politicians
constitutions, 34
constraint, problem of moving to, 150–52
consumers: coal tit as careful shopper, 537–40; comparison shopping, 430–32; cost-saving vs. convenience, 216; difference from charitable donors, 399, 400–402
Continental system of law. *See* inquisitorial system of law
contingency cases, 504
cooperative behavior of animals, 557; and survival of societies, 566–69
cooperative organizations, 369
Cornuelle, Richard, *395 n. 5*, *408 n. 17*
corporate take-overs, 166
corruption. *See* government corruption
cost-benefit analyses, 358
costs: bargaining, 152–53; bureaucracy, 84; individual recordkeeping, 453–54; legal system, 456–64; lobbying, 174, 188–91; logrolling, 119; in lowering vehicle speeds, 444–47; pork-barreling, 194; from possibility of transfers, 191–93; protective tariff, 172; road repair or nonrepair, 201; transfers, 173–79. *See also* social costs; welfare costs
countries: logrolling by, 117–18; peacetime deficits, 29–30; taxation of the wealthy, 268
court decisions: "correct," 484–89, 511–12; errors of fact, 495–508; probability of "correct," 488, 493–94; role in making law, 481–82, 491–92
courts: disagreements between, 515; distrust of juries, 530; European, 516; function, 309–10; proposed reforms, 489–93, 516–20. *See also* court decisions; judges; juries; trials; U.S. Supreme Court
credit, 314
crime control. *See* enforcement of legal activities
criminal justice system, 177. *See also* defendants; evidence of crime; illegal activities
curve of external economies. *See* external economies curve
cyclical majority, 91, 92–93
cycling: and assumption of transitivity, 62–63; Black's expectation of, 105; detecting, in real world, 98–100;

among discrete groups, 102–3; in voting, 19–20, 95–98; when using demand-revealing process, 140–41

Darwin, Charles, 555
Dates, J. H., *426n. 2*
Davis, Otto, *349n. 1*, *413n. 2*
death duty, 253
debt repayment, 314
deception, 313, 314; by charities, 402; exposing, 600; about transfers, 289–90, 293
decision-making: changes of mind, 64, 67–68; about charitable giving, 394–95; consumers compared with voters, 72–73; of courts, 484–93, 511–14, 518; demand-revealing process, 135–38; in democracies, 104; erroneous, 484–85; games of strategy, 229–30; information costs, 401; in inquisitorial proceedings, 473–75; involving bundles of alternatives, 83–84; of juries, 514–15; of legislatures, 25; private vs. public sector, 388–92; when voters are self-interested, 162. *See also* choice; preferences
defendants: falsely charged, 461–62, 517; odds of losing cases, 501; relation between guilt and evidence, 497–99. *See also* trials
deficits. *See* national deficits
de la Vallee Poisson, D., *135n. 8*
demand-revealing process: advantages, 153–54; and coalitions, 146–47, 164–66; compensation mechanism for, 133–34; confiscatory characteristics, 138; costs, 152–53; difference from other voting processes, 134–35, 153; equilibrium, 145–46; examples, 135–48, 164–65; limitations, 154–57, 159–60; similarity with market process, 158; Tullock's preference for, 110; uses, 156, 157–58; wealth and income distribution problem, 160–63; wealth effect in, 140–41; as a welfare criterion, 158–59
democracies: comparing to dictatorships, 33; control of corruption in, 325–26, 327; government spending, 302, 305; as illusion or fraud, 19–20; income redistribution in, 264–65; representative, 52; stability, 105; stability vs. efficiency, 120; successful functioning, 104; theory of economic externalities, 78; variations of, 31. *See also* nondemocratic systems
demonstrations, 342. *See also* revolutions; student protests
Dempster, J. P., *542n. 4*
Demsetz, Harold, *174n. 10*
density dependent consumption, 538
dependence on irrelevant alternatives, 139–40
deregulation of industries, 590
despotism, 326–27; juries under, 522–23
Dicey, Albert V., *304n. 8*
dictatorships, 29, 32–33, 46; demand-revealing process in, 157
Dietz, Henry A., *342n. 7*
direct regulation: of consumption, 419–24; of output, 412, 413, 414–17. *See also* quotas on consumption; rationing
direct transfers. *See* taxes
discipline of continuous dealings, 314, 317, 318, 320; role in civilization, 321
disciplines of study. *See* academic disciplines
discovery (legal), 463
discrimination in tax-prices, 375–77
discriminatory pricing, 374–75

disease treatment vs. immunization example, 356–58
distribution problem applied to ecology, 547, 548
Dorosh, Gary W., *593n. 4*
Downs, Anthony, 606; *An Economic Theory of Democracy*, 5–6, *17n. 2*, *51n. 2*, *137n. 10*, *262n. 2*, *392n. 5*, *394n. 2;* income redistribution in democracies, 262, 264–65; rule of ill-informed voters, 137
Downs paradox, 145
Dreze, J. H., *135n. 8*
driver's licenses: revocation vs. restriction, 449

Eastern Europe, 344–45
ecology, 541, 550
economics: assumptions of, 14; common basis with biology, 553; development of the field, 4–5; effect on policy, 589–91; link with political science, 5–6, 7–8, 16; methodological differences from biology, 554–55; publication in, 36–47, 589, 593, 598–99; relation to public choice theory, 9, 16–17; relation with other social sciences, 10–11; role of reason and the passions in, 8; scarcity in, 13–14; study of preferences, 9–10; of theft, 174–77, 178; Tullock's role in, 606–8. *See also* economists
economics imperialism, 3–7; definition, 4n. 1
Economic Theory of Democracy, An (Downs), 5–6
economists: educational influence, 293; efforts to stop rent seeking, 594; as experts for the public, 597–601. *See also* academic research; publication in economics
efficiency: in biological systems, 428; of charities, 398–99; effect on survival of societies, 564–65, 572–73; as explanation for society, 558; in government, 75, 291–92, 366–67; of legal systems, 462–64; quantity of public good needed for, 141; required for nepotism to work, 560
egalitarian coalitions, 111
egalitarian governments, 321–22
egalitarian systems of voting, 157–58
Eisenberg, Theodore, *500nn. 4, 5*
elected officials: compensation, 76; difference from others, 391–92; fixed fee system for, 73–74; logrolling by, 112–16, 119–20, 585–86; losers as auditors of winners, 88–89; selling out by, 111–12; timesaving devices, 119–20; voting by, 580. *See also* legislatures; politicians
election procedures. *See* voting process
Ellsberg, Daniel, *56n. 6*
Elzinga, Kenneth G., *461n. 6*
eminent domain, 426
enforcement of legal activities, 314–16; applied to ruling class, 319–20; costs, 458–62, 463; speed limits, 447–49; and transition from the jungle, 315; two parts to, 465. *See also* fines upon individuals; penalties; police force; sanctions; trials
England. *See* Britain
Enlightenment, The, 8
entertainment value: investing, 434–35, 437; revolutions, 332, 339
entry barriers, 71; and economics of monopolies, 74–75; and efficiency of government services, 75–76
environmentalists, 429, 547–48
envy, and income redistribution, 286–88
equality in wealth, 252–53
equilibrium: agreement vs. independent adjustment, 199; Lindahl,

145–46; Nash, 230; natural vs. man-made, 542–46; political, 376; pseudo, 241–42; rent seeking, 222–23. *See also* hawk/dove equilibrium
European dominance of the world, 30
European system of law. *See* inquisitorial system of law
European vs. United States legislatures, 118
Evans, Peter, *477n. 2*
evidence of crime, 495; effect on litigation, 503; exclusionary rules of, 517–18, 530; as recent methodology, 525–26
evolutionary theory, 427–28, 553–54. *See also* natural selection
expenditures. *See* funding
expertise: of economists, 597–601; stock market, 436–37
explicit logrolling, 119, 120–22, 586
external diseconomies: in consumption, 419–24; in production, 413–18; ways of controlling, 412
external economies curve, 352, 353n. 4; under collectivization, 354
external economies equilibrium solutions, 371
externalities: alternative ways of internalizing, 204; associated with adversary proceedings, 472–73; from choice of collectivization, 383; definition, 349n. 1; and ecology, 541, 550; generated by plants and animals, 549–50; and government grants, 211; and inheritance of wealth, 258–60; market for, 355; and optimal government size, 78, 80–81; positive and negative, 550–52. *See also* public goods; reciprocal externalities
extinction of species, 566–69
falcons and pigeons, 429
farmers. *See* agricultural subsidies
FCC (Federal Communications Commission), 293
federal appellate courts, 490–91
federalism, problems of scale, 78–89
Ferejohn, J. A., *114n. 23*
fields of study. *See* academic disciplines
Fifth Amendment protection, 518–19
Fijalkowski-Bereday, G. Z., *253n. 5*
financial standards for charities, 409–10
fines upon individuals, 325–26; parking, 442–43
Finger, J. M., *290n. 23*
Finkel, Steven E., *342n. 7*
force. *See* coercion
foreigners, attitudes toward, 278–80
formal logrolling coalitions, 109, 110–11; absence in real world, 112–13, 115; building, 115–16; instability, 116–18; with stable outcomes, 120; two types, 111
Fraser Institute, 593
fraud, 313, 314; by charities, 397–98, 399, 402, 403; gold mine example, 505–6. *See also* deception
Freeman, Roger, *287n. 18*
free riding, 428, 430, 437–38
free trade, 178
Frey, Bruno S., *24n. 11*, *262n. 3*, *268n. 13*
Friedman, Milton, *271n. 16*, *277n. 3*, 595
Friedman's Second Law, 212n. 1
Frontiers in Economics, 36
Fry, B. R., *262n. 3*
funding: effect of annual renewal, 220; favoring limited group of people, 195–96; formula allocation, 119–20; government aid to localities, 202–3, 204–5, 207–11; of highways, 203–4; intergovernmental

funding (*continued*)
fiscal relationships, 369–70; of judicial system, 463; with strings attached, 210–11; among two alternatives, 127–28. *See also* subsidies; transfers
fundraising by nonprofits, 396

gambling, 229; on stocks, 434–35
games of strategy, 229; degrees of cooperation, 569; differential weighting of players, 233–34; precommitment games, 231–32; rent seeking as, 230–31
game theory mixed strategies, 229, 312, 448–49
General Impossibility Theorem. *See* impossibility theorem
"General Irrelevance of the General Impossibility Theorem" (Tullock), 106
geographical contiguity and collectivization, 387
geometrical model of voting, 93
Ghiselin, Michael T., *554n. 1*, 557, *561n. 5*
Gibb, J., *537n. 4*, *539n. 5*
Gillespie, Robert, *478n. 12*
Goetz, Charles J., *412n. 1*, 608
Good, R. J., *495n. 1*
Gorbachev, Mikhail, 344–45
government agencies: capital intensive nature, 304; costs of expansion, 81–84; determining maximum size, 383; economies of scale, 78–79, 80; external effects of one on another, 85
government aid programs, 212
government corruption, 323–28; bribery of government officials, 240–41, 323
government income transfers. *See* transfers
government monopolies, 213–15
government officials: bribery of, 240–41; imperfect knowledge, 22; public choice theory view of, 16; public-goods problem created by, 390; during revolutions, 338, 344. *See also* bureaucrats; politicians
government reform. *See* theory of constitutions
governments: activities of, 291–92; aid to localities, 202–3, 204–5; capital accumulation policies, 251–52; charitable giving through, 262, 271–73, 285–86, 407–8, 409; contracting out of services, 25, 71–74, 292; dealings with citizens/subjects, 318; degree of federalization, 88; efficiency vs. orderliness, 89; egalitarian, 321–22; hereditary monarchies, 227–28; highly centralized, 89; and inheritance of wealth, 249–50, 253–57; international comparisons, 33–34; minimizing influence on, 228, 235; natural monopolies of, 69–70, 74–75; necessary conditions for, 325; need for competition, 25, 75–77; optimal size, 78, 80–81; organizational alternatives within, 365–66; origin, 290–91; size of, relative to GNP, 28–29; three branches, 327; use for transfers, 277; Wagner's law of increasing activity, 367–69. *See also* bureaucracies; democracies; funding; legislatures; nondemocratic systems; public choice theory
government services: collective action vs., 379–81; free, 361–62, 365–68; how voters choose, 85–86; optimal scale, 78–80, 86–88; rental of parking spaces, 443; roughly equal to private, 384–87
Great Britain. *See* Britain
Greene, Kenneth V., 258–60, *287n. 18*
group selection, 561
Groves, Theodore, 134, *148n. 15*

growth and collectivization, 370–73
growth paradox, 28
growth rate of grass, 542–43

Hall, H. K., *290n. 23*
Hamiltonian altruism, 558, 559. *See also* nepotism
Harberger, A. C., *169n. 4*
Hardin, Garrett, *537n. 1*, *541n. 1*, *555n. 5*
Harsanyi, John, *12*
Hastie, R., *507n. 17*, *512*, *529n 5*
hawk/dove equilibrium, 427; investing as, 437
Hay, George, *414n. 6*
Hayek, Friedrich, *279n. 6*
hearsay rule, 518
higher education subsidies, 327–28
highway funding, 203, 204; costs for safety, 445–47. *See also* road repair examples
Hobbes, Thomas, 309, 322
Hochman, Harold M., *262n. 1*, *276n. 2*
Hoover, G. E., *247n. 1*
human/bird analogy, 540
Hume, David: interdisciplinary approach, 7; on reason and the passions, 8

ICC (Interstate Commerce Commission), 293
illegal activities, 174n. 10, 314; deterrence, 496–97; economic approach to, 441–55; relation between evidence and guilt, 497–98. *See also* bribery; fraud; theft
illegal parking, 442–43
immigrants, 278–79, 282
immunization example, 352–55, 359–64
implicit logrolling, 52, 120–22; definition, 585
import quota and tariffs, 414n. 6
impossibility theorem, 90, 104; and demand-revealing process, 140, 148; hidden assumption in, 124–25, 129
improvement, Pareto definition, 548–49
incentives for being well-informed, 399, 402
income: estimation in demand-revealing process, 143; psychic, 343; relation to need for collectivization, 370–73. *See also* wealth equalization
income inequalities and reciprocal externality, 373–77
income redistribution: and confiscatory inheritance taxes, 252; in democracies, 262, 264–65, 291; economic literature on, 276–77; Lerner justification for, 280; through lobbying for monopolies, 239; motives for, 284–89; need for honesty about, 293–94; as reason for government, 291; relation to other government policies, 250–51; through voting, 160–63. *See also* transfers
income tax in United States, 195–96; evasion, 450–55
independent adjustment equilibrium, 199. *See also* bargaining
India, 282–83
indifference in transitive nature of preference orderings, 64n. 8, 65–67
individual bargain logrolling, 109–10; persistence of, 114–18; small groups left out, 113–14
individual preferences. *See* preferences
inefficiency: in charities, 399, 402–4; definition, 402n. 10
inegalitarian societies, 315–19
information: access to, 432–33; assumption of more or less perfect,

information (*continued*)
112; assumption of perfect, 341–42; about charities, 398–99, 408–10; costs, 401; effect on public interest, 578; about special interests, 597
"Information without Profit" (Tullock), 36
inheritance of wealth: absence of, 258; arguments against, 258–64; arguments for, 247–48; permitting or not permitting, 248
inheritance taxes, 252, 253–57; argument against, 254; avoidance of, 260–61; Pareto optimal, 255
inquisitorial system of law, 466; advantages, 516; appeals under, 506; arguments against, 476–77; compared with adversary system, 473–79, 510; history, 527–28
insider trading, 432–33, 437n. 11
insurance premiums, 498
intellectual capital as disputed turf of scholars, 6, 7
intellectuals, 267n. 12, 273–74
interdisciplinarity: of early economics, 7–8; in modern economics, 3–7
Internal Revenue Service (IRS), 452
intransitivity: experimental errors that cause, 63; May's hypothesis, 63, 64–65, 67
"Intransitivity, utility, and aggregation in preference patterns" (May), 63, 64–65, 67
investment advice, 433–34
investors in stocks, 432–37
involuntary transactions, 187
Iran, 32
Ireland, Thomas R., *185n. 1*, 258–60, *287n. 20*
IRS (Internal Revenue Service), 452

Jefferson, Thomas, 586n. 7
jellyfish societies, 561
Jevons, Marshall, *430n. 6*
Johnson, Alvin H., *247n. 1*
Johnson, David B., *185n. 1*
Journal of Economic Criticism, The, 36
judges: amount of work done by, 478–79; attempt to select unbiased, 579; disagreement with juries, 507; economic consequence of good, 474; effect on adversarial system, 475; errors, 484–94, 513, 515, 518; motivations, 479; public-goods problems created by, 388–90; relation to average citizen, 524; research about, 477–78; sample population of, 486–87; traffic court, 449–50. *See also* courts; sanctions
juries: accuracy of, 524, 528–29; attempt to select unbiased, 579; court distrust of, 517–18, 530; decision-making, 514–15; historical development, 526–27; motivation, 479; numbers serving on, 527; origin, 521–22, 525–26; rationales for, 522–24, 524–25, 531; research about, 477–78, 507–8, 511–13, 529–30; research needed, 533; selection, 532–33

Kafka, Alexandre, *442n. 3*
Kafoglis, M. Z., *350n. 2*
Kaldor, Nicholas, *253n. 5*
Kalven, Harry, Jr., *477n. 9*, *511n. 2*, *528n. 3*
"Kantian" median voting, 54–55, 59
Keeley, Michael C., *284n. 13*
Kennedy Center (Washington, D.C.), 578
Keynes, John Maynard, 436
Keynesianism as cause of government growth, 29
Klein, Benjamin, *500nn. 4, 6*
Klingaman, David., *114n. 22*
Kneese, Allen V., *413n. 3*

Koller, Roland H., II, 258–60, *287n. 20*
Krueger, A. O., *237n. 1*, *240n. 4*

labor, maximizing return to, 537–40
Lack, David, *537nn. 2, 3*
Lampman, R. J., *263n. 4*
law. *See* enforcement of legal activities; legal system
lawyers: motives of trial attorneys, 502; special interest groups of, 475–76, 531–32
Lebergott, Stanley, *286n. 17*
Ledyard, J., *148n. 15*
legal activities. *See* enforcement of legal activities; illegal activities
legal system: case law, 513; common law, 481–82; costs, 457–58; economic value of, 456; efficiency, 456; imperfection, 516; suggested reforms, 462–64, 516–20; three stages, 509–10. *See also* adversary system of law; courts; criminal justice system; inquisitorial system of law
legislatures: decision-making procedures, 25; European vs. American, 118; influence of lawyers on, 531–32; logrolling, 107–8; opposition parties in, 76–77; proportional representation, 31, 34; single-member constituency voting, 31–32; two-chamber, 31, 32; unicameral, 32; widespread benefit-sharing within, 113–14
Leibenstein, Harvey, *169nn. 1, 3*
Lenin, Vladimir, 339
Leoni, Bruno, *492n. 12*
licenses: driver's, 449; to pollute, 426. *See also* certification examinations
Lindahl equilibrium in demand-revealing process, 145–46
Lindahl taxes, 159, 161
Lindblom, Charles, *395n. 5*
lion societies, 309, 310–11
litigation, 463; arbitration, 520; contingency cases, 504–5; effect of evidence on, 503; probability of success in, 466; resource commitments in adversarial proceedings, 466–68, 473. *See also* pretrial settlements
lobbying: by bureaucrats, 194–95; decision to engage in, 197; gains to individuals not involved in, 197–98; as major social cost, 243; Wagner-type, 194. *See also* rent seeking
lobbying costs, 188–91; of special interest groups, 220
local politics, 75–76. *See also* road repair examples
Loeb, M., *134n. 5*
logrolling, 51; Arrow's omission of, 125; concerning funding, 119–20; costs, 119; with cycling, 105; implicit vs. explicit, 52, 120–22, 585–86; individual vs. coalition, 108–10; non-Pareto optimal outcomes, 112; and optimum distribution of resources, 59; simple model, 53–54; simple model results, generalized, 59–61. *See also* bargaining; formal logrolling coalitions; individual bargain logrolling
Losch, A., 556
lose-lose outcomes, 183–84
lottery example, 469–73
lying, 184–85. *See also* deception; fraud

Main, Robert S., 425
"majority motion" (Black), 98
majority voting: difference from demand-revealing process, 134, 138–39; explanations of stable outcomes from, 105; imperfect outcomes, 91; involving large numbers,

majority voting (*continued*) 103–4; juries as representative of, 522–24; with and without log-rolling, 106–12; Pennock's argument for, 81; problems of, 51–61; above simple majority, 31, 59; tendency toward cycling, 94–98; by U.S. Supreme Court, 487–89. *See also* coalitions of voters; demand-revealing process
Malthus, Thomas, 553
Margolis, Julius, *51n. 1*, *52n. 4*
market economies: adjustment under, 350–52; and inheritance of wealth, 250, 253; three different cases of, 359–64
markets: assumption of perfect, 355; cheapest, 538; comparing to collectivization, 350
Martin, William H., *71n. 2*
Martinus Nijhoff, 45
mass media, working with, 597, 600
mathematical models of voting, 16, 19–21
maximization: of beef production, 545; in biology and economics, 553
"maximizers," 55
May, Kenneth O., "Intransitivity, Utility, and Aggregation in Preference Patterns," 63, 64–65, 67
Mayberry, E. R., *113n. 19*
McCabe, Sarah, *477n. 2*
McChesney, Fred S., 480–83
McConville, Michael, *511n. 3*, *528n. 4*
McKelvey, R., 106
median line, 95
Michelman, Frank I., *418n. 7*
middle class, transfers among, 268–71
Migué, Jean-Luc, *23n. 8*
military expenditures, 577, 581–82
Mitchell, William C. (Bill), 46
Modigliani, Franco, *71n. 2*
mole rat societies, 559
monarchies, 227–28
monopolies: costs, 242; costs to create, 237–39; welfare costs, 169, 174–79. *See also* natural monopolies
Moon, J. W., *140n. 11*
Morgan, J. P., 242
Morgenstern, O., *111n. 13*
Morrison, Clarence, article on second best, 47
mosquito abatement example, 378–86
Moss, Richard L., *218n. 7*
motor vehicle code violations, 441–49
Muller, Edward N., *341n. 5*, *342n. 7*, *344n. 10*
multi-peaked distributions, 102–3
Mundell, R. A., *169n. 2*
murder: example, 495–97; Pareto optimal, 324
Musgrave, Peggy B., *195nn. 6, 7*
Musgrave, Richard A., *195nn. 6, 7*, *388n. 1*
mutations: effect on nonreproductive cells, 570–71; effect on reproduction of societies, 564–69

Nader, Ralph, *444n. 4*
Nash equilibrium, 230
national deficits, 29–30
National Fund for the Humanities, 578
nations. *See* countries
natural monopolies: of the majority, 70–71; techniques for dealing with, 69–70
natural selection, 543, 550–52, 569–70. *See also* evolutionary theory
nature, improvability of, 541–46
negotiation. *See* bargaining
Nelson, D. R., *290n. 23*
nepotism, 559, 565, 572–73
Newing, R. A., *90–91*, *95n. 12*
newspaper articles, 593
Ng, Yew-Kwang, 425
90-per-cent-selfish hypothesis, 14

Niskanen, William A., *21n. 7*, 179n. 15, *268n. 14;* Tullock's review of book by, *297n. 1*
nondemocratic systems, 27. *See also* despotism; dictatorships
nonprofit organizations, 394; fundraising, 396
Norsworthy, J. Randolph, *174n. 10*, *454n. 13*
Nutter, G. Warren, *367n. 8*

old age, 319. *See also* pensions
Olson, Mancur, *336n. 5*
Opp, Karl-Dieter, *341n. 5*, *344n. 10*
opposition groups in government, 76–77
optimal amount of public good, 142
optimal outcome, 468
optimal resource allocation and majority voting, 61
optimal speed limits, 444–47
Ordover, Janusz A., 480–83, *481n. 2*
Organization of Inquiry, The (Tullock), 37, *41n. 2*
Orzechowski, William Paul, *23n. 9*, *23n. 10*, *304n. 7*
over-grazing, 428–29; example, 542–46

Papers on Non-Market Decision Making, 36, 37; funding, 38, 39; pricing, 38; printed comments about papers in, 41–42; production, 38; refereeing, 39–41. See also *Public Choice*
"Paradox of Revolution, The" (Tullock), 341, 344
paradox of the liar, 229
paradox of voting, 91, 124–29
parasites, 562, 571, 572
Pareto, V., *541n. 2*
Pareto criteria, 546n. 5, 548
Pareto improvement, 149
Pareto optimality, 163, 541
Pareto-relevant externalities, 551n. 8; and collectivization, 349
parking meters, 443
parliamentary governments, 75–77
passions, 8. *See also* preferences
Peltzman, S., *213n. 3*
penalties: to deter crime, 496–97; for income tax evasion, 452; not based on intent, 448; traffic court, 447–49. *See also* fines upon individuals; sanctions
penalty taxes: on consumers, 419–24; on industries, 412–18
Pennington, N., *507n. 17*, *512*, *529n. 5*
Pennock, James, *81*
Penrod, S., *507n. 17*, *512*, *529n. 5*
pensions, 582
Peru, shining path, 342–43
pigeons and falcons, 429
Pigou, A. C., *253n. 5*
plants: externalities, 549, 550; natural selection problem, 550–52; societies, 561–62
Plott, C. R., *113n. 20*
police force: accuracy, 510–11; cost, 177; curtailing power of, 320–21. *See also* enforcement of legal activities; illegal activities; secret police
political activism by economists, 597–98
political appointees, 23, 25
political corruption, 240–41
political costs of transfer mechanism, 194–98
political economy, 8; modern use of title, 37
political equilibrium vs. social optimum, 376
political parties: coalitions of, 77; difference from department stores, 69; incumbent party advantage, 74–75; logrolling by, 117–18; as successful coalitions, 165–66

political science: differences with economics, 10–11; link with economics, 5–6, 7–8; relation to public choice theory, 16–17
politicians, 18–19; local, 75–76; logrolling by, 585–86; view of transfers, 274. *See also* elected officials
politics: entry barriers, 69–77; importance of public interest, 577
pollution control, 412–14, 425–26, 549
Pommerehne, Werner W., *24n. 11*
poor people in democracies: coalitions with other classes, 265–66; government transfers to, 262–64, 267, 285–86
poor people in other countries, 278–81; transfers to, 280–81, 282–83, 284
Popper, Karl, 606
pork-barreling, 194
positive correlation fallacy, 12–14
positive externalities, 550–52
Posner, Richard A., *456n. 1*
precommitment games, 231–32
preference ordering, 138–39, 381–82
preferences: behavioralist research about, 12, 13; costs of aggregating, 152–53; difficulty of ascertaining, 10; economists' approach to, 9–10; within groups, 13; and inheritance of wealth, 258–60; interdependence of, 101–2, 161–63; motivating voters to state, 135–36; roots in human passions, 8; science of, 10; sociologists' approach to, 9–10; voting for one's own, 124–27. *See also* aggregate preferences; choice; passions; tastes; transitivity
preference weighting. *See* logrolling
Presidential election example, 164–65
Presidential logrolling, 586n. 7
pressure groups. *See* special interest groups
pretrial settlements, 480–81, 499–502; bargaining, 503–4; frequency, 502–3
price controls, 580–81, 594–95
prices: comparison shopping, 430–32; energy expenditures as, 538; real world, 432
Priest, George L., *500n. 4*, *500n. 6*
prisoner's dilemma: bargaining as, 184–85; degrees of cooperation in, 341–42; of government transfers to the poor, 272; of how species become nonviable, 566–69; importance, 343; of mutually beneficial plants, 552
private property. *See* property rights
private rent seeking, 238
private vs. public sector decisions, 388–92
privatization: effect on economies of scale in government, 80; of government services, 25
progress, defining, 183–84, 548–49
progressive tax systems, 196
property accumulation, 314
property rights, 309; difference from territoriality, 556; effect on trade, 313; relation to efficiency, 464; using bribery to support, 325
proportional income tax, 375–77
proportional representation, 31, 34, 88–89
protective tariffs. *See* tariffs
psychic income value, 343
publication in economics, 589, 594, 598–99. *See also* academic journals; academic research
Public Choice, 42; binding, 44–45; editorial policies, 46–47; funding, 42–43, 44; related products, 47. See

also *Papers on Non-Market Decision Making*
Public Choice Society, 42
public choice theory: four areas of study, 17; goal, 17; origin, 16, 37; problems in need of study, 28–35; promise of, 26; and public interest theory, 587–88; relation to economics, 9, 16–17; relation with social choice theory, 42; research methods, 105
public education subsidies, 269–70
public finance, 9
public goods: argument for public provision of, 588; aspects of revolution, 332, 334, 336, 338; definition, 336–37; government-created problem with, 388–93; multidimensional or multiple, 147–48; for small groups of people, 583; technological, 581–82. *See also* externalities
public interest, 577
public interest groups, 18
public vs. private sector decisions, 388–92
Pullman, N. J., *140n. 11*
Purves, Robert, *477n. 2*

quotas on consumption, 419–24, 425–26. *See also* rationing

race, 277–78
raspberry patch societies, 561–62
rationality: of irrational behavior, 310–11; irrational outcomes from, 57; and revolution, 341–45; role of reason in economics, 8; social scientists' view of, 10–11
rationing, 365–66. *See also* quotas on consumption
Rawls, John, 282
Ray, B. A., *113n. 21*
reason, role in economics, 8. *See also* rationality
reciprocal externalities, 349; non-symmetrical, 373–77
refereeing of academic journals, 39–41
referendum on government policies, 31, 584–85; relation to logrolling, 51–52; with two alternatives, 127–28
regulation. *See* direct regulation
remainders, 260–61
rent avoidance, 239–40
rent seeking: from bribery of public officials, 241; categories, 594; connotations, 242; costs, 240–42; definition, 237; economists' efforts to stop, 594, 597–601; equations, 235–36; equilibrium, 222–23, 230; as game of strategy, 230–33; games, 223–25, 226–27; and hereditary monarchies, 227–28; measuring, 242; minimizing, 228; minimizing, with selection bias, 233–34; pseudo-equilibrium, 241–42
representative democracy, 52
reproductive rate variations, 543–44; within animal societies, 558–62
reputation effect of purchases, 400, 401–2
restaurant menu choice example, 81–83
revolutionaries, 338–39; motives, 333
revolutions: arguments for, 333–34; bias in study of, 332–33; criteria for evaluating, 329–32, 334–35; definition, 335; entertainment value, 332, 339, 343; factors of participation, 332; public good aspects, 332; and rationality, 341–45; similarity with charitable activity, 337; theories of, 336, 338–40; three reactions to, 329–32; welfare costs, 192–93

Ricardo, David, 8
Riker, William H., *98n. 14*, *115n. 26*
risk reduction: in court cases, 500, 503, 517; as motive for transfers, 288; and tax evasion penalties, 454–55
road repair examples, 53–54, 55–57, 199–203. *See also* highway funding
Robins, Philip K., *284n. 13*
Rodgers, James D., *262n. 1*, *276n. 2*
Rose, Arnold M., *62n. 3*, *63nn. 6*, *7*
Rothenberg, Jerome, 62
Rothstein, Paul F., *517–18*, *530n. 6*
Rowat, Donald C., *409n. 18*
Rubin, P. H., *220n. 11*
ruling class, role in society, 315–19

Samuelson, Paul, *388n. 1*, *588*
sanctions: discretion in fixing magnitude, 463; effective vs. nominal, 459; enforcement probability, 459; enforcement probability relation to cost, 461–62; most efficient way to achieve, 462; why needed, 457. *See also* fines upon individuals; penalties
Schelling, Thomas C., *231n. 7*
scholarly journals. *See* academic journals
Schumpeter, Joseph A., 606
sciences of choice and sciences of preference, 10
Scitovsky, Tibor, *171n. 7*
secret police, 327; in communist countries, 345
selection bias as desirable, 233–34
seniority systems, 217
settlements. *See* pretrial settlements
Shapiro, David L., *195n. 4*
Shepsle, K. A., *115n. 24*
Shiller, Robert, *434n. 9*
shoppers. *See* consumers
Sierra Club, 548
Sieve, Jack E. B., *196n. 9*, *263n. 6*
Silver, Morris, *343n. 9*
Simon, Rita James, *477n. 11*
simple income transfers, 206–7
Simpson trial, 523, 532
single-peak assumption about voting, 20
single-peaked preference curves, 90; for two dimensions, 90–91
slavery, 309, 312, 315
slime mold societies, 563–64; example, 566–69
Smith, Adam: interdisciplinary approach, 7; views on reason and the passions, 8
Smith, John Maynard, *427n. 1*
Social Choice and Individual Values (Arrow), 90, 103, 104, 124–25
social choice theory: propositions of, 20–21; relation to public choice theory, 42; weaknesses, 133
social costs: charity, 185–87; conflicts and wars, 192–93; income transfers, 177; monopoly, 242; tariffs, 171; theft, 175–76. *See also* welfare costs
Social Dilemma, The (Tullock), 341
social inequality, 315
socialism and control of capital accumulation, 249–50, 252
social provision area, 363
social sciences: coordinating research among, 7–10, 14–15; debates among fields within, 10–11; general theory underlying, 12–14
social security. *See* pensions; U.S. Social Security Administration
social waste: from grants-in-aid, 205–6, 211; from unionization, 217–18
societies, primitive: based on mutual defense, 562, 572; based on reproduction, 558–62; of commensals (paired species), 570–73; effect of mutation on, 564–69; explanations

of, 558; of nuclei, 564; of plants, 561–63; of slime molds and sponges, 563–65
sociobiology, 556–57
Sociobiology (Wilson), 555
sociology, 9–11
solutions: in games of strategy, 230–31; inefficient but optimal, 430–32
South Africa, 277–78
South American bureaucracies, 300–301
South Vietnam, 345
Soviet system of voting, 88
Soviet Union, 344–45
special interest groups: cartels as, 212; effect on public interest, 578, 583–85; and government officials, 580–81; how they arise, 212–15; impact on voters, 18; of lawyers, 475–76, 531–32; methods of opposing, 597–98; transfers by, 327–28; why they persist, 219–21
speculation in stocks, 435–36
speeding violations, 443–47
speed limit enforcement, 447–49
Spencer, Herbert, 553
Spiegelman, Robert G., *284n. 13*
sponge societies, 563, 565
stagflation, 304
standing armies, 321
states. *See* countries; governments
Stigler, George J., *212n. 2*, *323n. 1*
stock market example, 432–37
stock market fluctuations, 435–36
stock options for executives, 433
Stubblebine, William C., *349n. 1*
student protests, 332, 339, 343. *See also* demonstrations; revolutions
subsidies: agricultural, 218, 269, 583; higher education, 327–28; to increase capital accumulation, 251–52; in private markets, 354–55; public education, 269–70. *See also* cartels
Supreme Court. *See* U.S. Supreme Court
survival of the "fit." *See* natural selection
survival probability, 311
Sweden, 279, 409
Switzerland, 31, 279, 584–85
synergetics, 70

take-over bids, 166
tariffs: combined with excise tax, 172–73; economists' position on, 591; welfare costs, 169–72
tastes, 12, 14; effect of communication on satisfaction of, 83. *See also* preferences
taxation as part of voting, 137, 141–45; Clarke tax, 135–36; composite tax, 143; excess revenues from, 143, 145; Lindahl taxes, 159, 161
taxes: beneficiaries of, 268; and collectivization, 375–77; excess burden from, 358, 364–65; and lobbying, 240; social benefits/losses to payers, 453; as sources of inefficiency, 292–93; vs. special interest subsidies, 219–20; on wealth, 253–54, 286–87. *See also* inheritance taxes; penalty taxes; tax evasion; tax reform
tax evasion, 441, 450–55
taxi medallions example, 213–15
tax reform, 195–96
temper loss, rationality of, 310–11
termites, 559; and protozoa, 571, 572
territoriality, 556
theft, 174–77, 178; as involuntary transfer, 187; welfare costs, 182, 192–93
theory of bureaucracy, 21–24
Theory of Committees and Elections, The (Black), 105
theory of constitutions, 17; suggested reforms, 24–26

Theory of Moral Sentiments, The (Smith), 8
Thompson, E., *135n. 7*
Tideman, T. Nicolaus, *110n. 12*, *135n. 9*, *153n. 2*, 236, *424n. 10*
toll highways, 203, 204
trading, 308–13
trading of votes. *See* logrolling
traffic congestion example, 419
transfers: by competitive vs. negotiated bids, 292; costs, 173; costs from possibility of, 191–93; from developed to poorer nations, 280–81, 282–83, 284; effect of competition for, 204, 206, 208–11; effect on government, 304–5; effect on income within groups, 283–84; governmental budgets for, 304; highly inefficient, 289–90; involuntary, 187–88; methods of, 206–7; among the middle class, 268–71; vs. monopoly privileges, 219; need for deception about, 289–90; political costs, 194–98; politician's view of, 274; from poor to better-off, 386–87; from rich to poor, 197, 263–64; social costs, 177; by special interests, 327–28; of technologically private goods, 582; among U.S. taxpayer groups, 197–98, 267; welfare costs, 180–91; willfully ignorant decisions about, 282. *See also* income redistribution; taxes
transitional gains trap, 213–14; examples, 217–19; reasons for, 219–20; recommendations, 221
transitive nature of preference orderings. *See* transitivity
transitivity, 62; without indifference, 64–65; indifference and, 64n. 8, 65–67; proof of, 64
trials, 310; falsely charged defendants, 461–62, 517; hearsay rule, 518–19; one-sided, 500–501, 502–3, 505; outcomes of, 500–502; Simpson trial, 523, 532; votes needed for conviction, 527. *See also* courts; evidence of crime; illegal activities
Triver's reciprocal altruism, 559n. 1
trusts for avoiding inheritance taxes, 260n. 1
truth-telling, 184–85; juries as arbitrar of, 523. *See also* deception
Tullock, Gordon, 605–9; editorial experiences, 36–47; Luddite attack on, 6n. 3; Malthusian aspiration of, 4
Tullock, Gordon, writings: "A Measure of the Importance of Cyclical Majorities," *90n. 2;* "A New and Superior Process for Making Social Choices," *110n. 12*, *153n. 2;* "A Simple Algebraic Logrolling Model," *107n. 8*, *264n. 10;* "A Theory of Government Punishments and Rewards," *174n. 10;* "Avoiding Difficult Decisions," *281n. 10; Calculus of Consent*, 25, 108–12, 264; *Calculus of Consent*, cited, *125n. 3*, *129n. 6*, *288n. 21*, *354n. 5*, *388n. 1;* contents of selected works, 611–21; "Coordination without Command," *570n. 11;* "Courts as Legislatures," *482n. 3;* "Dynamic Hypothesis on Bureaucracy," *303n. 6; Economics of Income Redistribution*, *342n. 6;* "Efficient Rent Seeking," *238n. 3*, *241n. 5; Entrepreneurial Politics*, *108n. 11; Explorations in the Theory of Anarchy*, *325n. 4;* "General Irrelevance of the General Impossibility Theorem," *20n. 4*, *106n. 2;* "Information without Profit," 36; "Inheritance Justified," *287n. 18;* "Inheritance Rejustified: Reply," *287n. 20;* "Judicial Errors and a Proposal for Reform," *495n. 1*, *513n. 9; Law and*

Morals, *174n. 10;* "Legal Heresy," *524n. 2; Logic of the Law*, *323n. 2*, *456n. 1*, *466n. 2*, *486n. 2*, 497n. 3, *509n. 1;* "On the Efficient Organization of Trials," *223n. 2; Organization of Inquiry*, *37n.1*, *41n. 2; Politics of Bureaucracy*, *21n. 5*, *299n. 2*, *437n. 12;* "Polluters' Profits and Political Response," *425n. 1; Private Wants, Public Means*, *325n. 5;* "Public and Private Interaction under Reciprocal Externality," *177n. 13;* "Public Decisions as Public Goods," *476n. 6;* "Revealing the Demand for Transfers," *154n. 4*, *155n. 5*, *160n. 10; Social Dilemma*, *224n. 3*, 341, *344n. 11*, *469n. 3;* "Sociobiology and Economics," *556n. 7;* "Switching in General Predators: Comment," *537n. 1*, *541n. 1;* "The Coal Tit as a Careful Shopper," *541n. 1*, *554n. 2;* "The Cost of Transfers," *149n. 1;* "The 'Dead Hand' of Monopoly," *212n. 2;* "The Paradox of Revolution," *341*, 344; "The Social Rate of Discount and the Optimal Rate of Investment: Comment," *248n. 2;* "The Welfare Cost of Tariffs, Monopolies, and Theft," *237n. 2; Toward a Mathematics of Politics*, *17n. 3*, *106n. 4*, *112n. 17*, *220nn. 9, 10*, *392n. 5; Trials on Trial*, 497n. 3 *507n. 14;* "What's Wrong with Editing," *41n. 2*
Turkish immigrants, 279
Turvey, Ralph, *349n. 1*
two-species ecology example, 542–47

unicameral legislatures, 32
unionization, 217–18
United States government: income tax, 195–96, 450–55; opening of records, 409; treatment of Mexicans, 278
United States law. *See* adversary system of law
universal adult suffrage, 33
University of Chicago Jury Project, 477, 511
urban renewal projects, 269
U.S. Civil Aeronautics Board (CAB), 212, 293
U.S. Congress. *See* elected officials
U.S. Constitution, 35
U.S. Department of State, 23
U.S. Federal Communications Commission (FCC), 293
U.S. Interstate Commerce Commission (ICC), 293
U.S. Social Security Administration, 255n. 8, 269, 583, 585. *See also* pensions
U.S. Supreme Court: assumption of infallibility of, 484; effect on the Constitution, 35; errors, 514; sample selection example, 486–89; suggested reforms, 489–90, 491–93
utility: negative utility interdependence, 287; Paretian taboo on comparison of, 183

values and value judgments, 547–48
Vickrey, William S., *253n. 5*
Vickrey's incomplete compensation mechanism, 133–34
Virginia School of Political Economy, 608
voluntary charity. *See* charitable giving
voluntary labor, 409
voluntary transactions, 187
von Neumann, John, *111n. 13*, 229
vote-buying. *See* logrolling
voters, 19–21; aggregate demand by, 141; decision-making, 72–73; desire to receive transfers, 288–89; differ-

voters (*continued*)
ence from consumers, 391–92; ill-informed, 17, 137, 392, 586–87; increasing the well-being of, 52–53; influences on, 18; lack of selfish motives among, 579–80; "maximizer," 55; motivating honesty in, 134, 137, 143, 144–45; motivating public interest by, 578; motivating to vote, 137; poor, 262–63; restrictions on, 33, 162. *See also* voting; voting process
voting: among alternatives, 127–29; Arrow's hidden assumption about, 124–25; on choice of government services, 84–86; discontinuities in, 93–94; effect of logrolling on, 53; effect of population size on, 32; geometrical model, 93; by government officials, 23–24, 218, 303–4, 580; by juries, 527; "Kantian" median preference, 54–55, 59; "maximizing equilibrium," 55–57, 58; vs. private charitable giving, 271–72; probability of "correct," 486–89, 493–94. *See also* decision-making; logrolling; majority voting; voting process
voting process: agenda control, 20, 21, 95n. 11, 106–7; Borda method, 126–27; campaign contribution restrictions, 228; changes in, before elections, 32; effect of bureaucracy on, 23–24; efficient, 88–89; importance of, 129; probability of cycling in, 95–96; suggestions for improving, 24–25; two-party, 107; worldwide variations in, 31–32. *See also* demand-revealing process; referendum on government policies

Wagner, Richard E., *194n. 2*
Wagner's law of increasing government activity, 367–69
"Wagner squared" hypothesis, 305
Wagner-type lobbying, 194
war: as involuntary transfer, 187; Wars of the Roses, 335; welfare costs, 182, 192–93. *See also* demonstrations; revolutions
Ward, Benjamin, *95n. 11*, 264
wasp societies, 558, 559–60
wealth. *See* income
wealth equalization, 252–53
Wealth of Nations, The (Smith), 7, 8
wealthy people in democracies: coalitions with the poor, 265–66; taxes on, 286–87; transfers from, 267–68
Webb, Adrian L., *196n. 9*, *263n. 6*
Weingast, B. R., *115n. 24*
Weitzman, Martin L., 480–83, *481n. 2*
welfare costs: monopolies, 169, 174–79; tariffs, 169–74; theft, 175–77; transfers, 180–98. *See also* social costs
welfare economics, 149
welfare programs, 404
welfare transfers to poor, 263–64
Wellisz, Stanislaw, *413n. 2*
Wemelsfelder, J., *173n. 9*
West, Richard W., *284n. 13*
Whinston, Andrew, *349n. 1*, *413n. 2*
Wicksellian approach, 418, 426
Williamson, Oliver E., *84n. 4*
Wilson, E. O., 555, 557, *560n. 2*
Winters, R. F., *262n. 3*
women, effect of their vote, 33

Yohe, Gary W., 425, *425n. 1*
Yugoslavian immigrants, 279

Zajac, Edward, *433n. 8*
Zeisel, Hans, *477n. 9*, *511n. 2*, *528n. 3*
Zulu South Africans, 279

The typeface used for the text of this book is Galliard, an old-style face designed by Matthew Carter in 1978, in the spirit of a sixteenth-century French typeface of Robert Granjon.
The display type is Meta Book, a variant of Meta, designed by Erik Spiekermann in the 1990s.

This book is printed on paper that is acid-free and meets the requirements of the American National Standard for Permanence of Paper for Printed Library Materials, Z39.48-1992. ♾

Book design by Richard Hendel, Chapel Hill, North Carolina
Typography by G&S Typesetters, Inc., Austin, Texas
Printed and bound by Sheridan Books Inc., Chelsea, Michigan